Lecture Notes in Computer Science 8531

Commenced Publication in 1973
Founding and Former Series Editors:
Gerhard Goos, Juris Hartmanis, and Jan van Leeuwen

Gabriele Meiselwitz (Ed.)

Social Computing and Social Media

6th International Conference, SCSM 2014
Held as Part of HCI International 2014
Heraklion, Crete, Greece, June 22-27, 2014
Proceedings

 Springer

Volume Editor

Gabriele Meiselwitz
Towson University
Department of Computer and Information Sciences
Towson, MD, 21252, USA
E-mail: gmeiselwitz@towson.edu

ISSN 0302-9743   e-ISSN 1611-3349
ISBN 978-3-319-07631-7   e-ISBN 978-3-319-07632-4
DOI 10.1007/978-3-319-07632-4
Springer Cham Heidelberg New York Dordrecht London

Library of Congress Control Number: 2014939635

LNCS Sublibrary: SL 3 – Information Systems and Application, incl. Internet/Web
and HCI

Typesetting: Camera-ready by author, data conversion by Scientific Publishing Services, Chennai, India

Printed on acid-free paper

Springer is part of Springer Science+Business Media (www.springer.com)

Foreword

The 16th International Conference on Human–Computer Interaction, HCI International 2014, was held in Heraklion, Crete, Greece, during June 22–27, 2014, incorporating 14 conferences/thematic areas:

Thematic areas:

- Human–Computer Interaction
- Human Interface and the Management of Information

Affiliated conferences:

- 11th International Conference on Engineering Psychology and Cognitive Ergonomics
- 8th International Conference on Universal Access in Human–Computer Interaction
- 6th International Conference on Virtual, Augmented and Mixed Reality
- 6th International Conference on Cross-Cultural Design
- 6th International Conference on Social Computing and Social Media
- 8th International Conference on Augmented Cognition
- 5th International Conference on Digital Human Modeling and Applications in Health, Safety, Ergonomics and Risk Management
- Third International Conference on Design, User Experience and Usability
- Second International Conference on Distributed, Ambient and Pervasive Interactions
- Second International Conference on Human Aspects of Information Security, Privacy and Trust
- First International Conference on HCI in Business
- First International Conference on Learning and Collaboration Technologies

A total of 4,766 individuals from academia, research institutes, industry, and governmental agencies from 78 countries submitted contributions, and 1,476 papers and 225 posters were included in the proceedings. These papers address the latest research and development efforts and highlight the human aspects of design and use of computing systems. The papers thoroughly cover the entire field of human–computer interaction, addressing major advances in knowledge and effective use of computers in a variety of application areas.

This volume, edited by Gabriele Meiselwitz, contains papers focusing on the thematic area of Social Computing and Social Media, addressing the following major topics:

- Designing and evaluating social computing and social media
- Analysing, visualising, and modelling social networks

- Online communities and engagement
- Identity and presence in social media
- Games, gamification, and entertainment in social media

The remaining volumes of the HCI International 2014 proceedings are:

- Volume 1, LNCS 8510, Human–Computer Interaction: HCI Theories, Methods and Tools (Part I), edited by Masaaki Kurosu
- Volume 2, LNCS 8511, Human–Computer Interaction: Advanced Interaction Modalities and Techniques (Part II), edited by Masaaki Kurosu
- Volume 3, LNCS 8512, Human–Computer Interaction: Applications and Services (Part III), edited by Masaaki Kurosu
- Volume 4, LNCS 8513, Universal Access in Human–Computer Interaction: Design and Development Methods for Universal Access (Part I), edited by Constantine Stephanidis and Margherita Antona
- Volume 5, LNCS 8514, Universal Access in Human–Computer Interaction: Universal Access to Information and Knowledge (Part II), edited by Constantine Stephanidis and Margherita Antona
- Volume 6, LNCS 8515, Universal Access in Human–Computer Interaction: Aging and Assistive Environments (Part III), edited by Constantine Stephanidis and Margherita Antona
- Volume 7, LNCS 8516, Universal Access in Human–Computer Interaction: Design for All and Accessibility Practice (Part IV), edited by Constantine Stephanidis and Margherita Antona
- Volume 8, LNCS 8517, Design, User Experience, and Usability: Theories, Methods and Tools for Designing the User Experience (Part I), edited by Aaron Marcus
- Volume 9, LNCS 8518, Design, User Experience, and Usability: User Experience Design for Diverse Interaction Platforms and Environments (Part II), edited by Aaron Marcus
- Volume 10, LNCS 8519, Design, User Experience, and Usability: User Experience Design for Everyday Life Applications and Services (Part III), edited by Aaron Marcus
- Volume 11, LNCS 8520, Design, User Experience, and Usability: User Experience Design Practice (Part IV), edited by Aaron Marcus
- Volume 12, LNCS 8521,Human Interface and the Management of Information: Information and Knowledge Design and Evaluation (Part I), edited by Sakae Yamamoto
- Volume 13, LNCS 8522, Human Interface and the Management of Information: Information and Knowledge in Applications and Services (Part II), edited by Sakae Yamamoto
- Volume 14, LNCS 8523, Learning and Collaboration Technologies: Designing and Developing Novel Learning Experiences (Part I), edited by Panayiotis Zaphiris and Andri Ioannou
- Volume 15, LNCS 8524, Learning and Collaboration Technologies: Technology-richEnvironments for Learning and Collaboration (Part II), edited by Panayiotis Zaphiris and Andri Ioannou

- Volume 16, LNCS 8525, Virtual, Augmented and Mixed Reality: Designing and Developing Virtual and Augmented Environments (Part I), edited by Randall Shumaker and Stephanie Lackey
- Volume 17, LNCS 8526, Virtual, Augmented and Mixed Reality: Applications of Virtual and Augmented Reality (Part II), edited by Randall Shumaker and Stephanie Lackey
- Volume 18, LNCS 8527, HCI in Business, edited by Fiona Fui-Hoon Nah
- Volume 19, LNCS 8528, Cross-Cultural Design, edited by P.L. Patrick Rau
- Volume 20, LNCS 8529, Digital Human Modeling and Applications in Health, Safety, Ergonomics and Risk Management, edited by Vincent G. Duffy
- Volume 21, LNCS 8530, Distributed, Ambient, and Pervasive Interactions, edited by Norbert Streitz and Panos Markopoulos
- Volume 23, LNAI 8532, Engineering Psychology and Cognitive Ergonomics, edited by Don Harris
- Volume 24, LNCS 8533, Human Aspects of Information Security, Privacy and Trust, edited by Theo Tryfonas and Ioannis Askoxylakis
- Volume 25, LNAI 8534, Foundations of Augmented Cognition, edited by Dylan D. Schmorrow and Cali M. Fidopiastis
- Volume 26, CCIS 434, HCI International 2014 Posters Proceedings (Part I), edited by Constantine Stephanidis
- Volume 27, CCIS 435, HCI International 2014 Posters Proceedings (Part II), edited by Constantine Stephanidis

I would like to thank the Program Chairs and the members of the Program Boards of all affiliated conferences and thematic areas, listed below, for their contribution to the highest scientific quality and the overall success of the HCI International 2014 Conference.

This conference could not have been possible without the continuous support and advice of the founding chair and conference scientific advisor, Prof. Gavriel Salvendy, as well as the dedicated work and outstanding efforts of the communications chair and editor of *HCI International News*, Dr. Abbas Moallem.

I would also like to thank for their contribution towards the smooth organization of the HCI International 2014 Conference the members of the Human–Computer Interaction Laboratory of ICS-FORTH, and in particular George Paparoulis, Maria Pitsoulaki, Maria Bouhli, and George Kapnas.

April 2014
Constantine Stephanidis
General Chair, HCI International 2014

Organization

Human–Computer Interaction

Program Chair: Masaaki Kurosu, Japan

Jose Abdelnour-Nocera, UK
Sebastiano Bagnara, Italy
Simone Barbosa, Brazil
Adriana Betiol, Brazil
Simone Borsci, UK
Henry Duh, Australia
Xiaowen Fang, USA
Vicki Hanson, UK
Wonil Hwang, Korea
Minna Isomursu, Finland
Yong Gu Ji, Korea
Anirudha Joshi, India
Esther Jun, USA
Kyungdoh Kim, Korea

Heidi Krömker, Germany
Chen Ling, USA
Chang S. Nam, USA
Naoko Okuizumi, Japan
Philippe Palanque, France
Ling Rothrock, USA
Naoki Sakakibara, Japan
Dominique Scapin, France
Guangfeng Song, USA
Sanjay Tripathi, India
Chui Yin Wong, Malaysia
Toshiki Yamaoka, Japan
Kazuhiko Yamazaki, Japan
Ryoji Yoshitake, Japan

Human Interface and the Management of Information

Program Chair: Sakae Yamamoto, Japan

Alan Chan, Hong Kong
Denis A. Coelho, Portugal
Linda Elliott, USA
Shin'ichi Fukuzumi, Japan
Michitaka Hirose, Japan
Makoto Itoh, Japan
Yen-Yu Kang, Taiwan
Koji Kimita, Japan
Daiji Kobayashi, Japan

Hiroyuki Miki, Japan
Shogo Nishida, Japan
Robert Proctor, USA
Youngho Rhee, Korea
Ryosuke Saga, Japan
Katsunori Shimohara, Japan
Kim-Phuong Vu, USA
Tomio Watanabe, Japan

Engineering Psychology and Cognitive Ergonomics

Program Chair: Don Harris, UK

Guy Andre Boy, USA
Shan Fu, P.R. China
Hung-Sying Jing, Taiwan
Wen-Chin Li, Taiwan
Mark Neerincx, The Netherlands
Jan Noyes, UK
Paul Salmon, Australia

Axel Schulte, Germany
Siraj Shaikh, UK
Sarah Sharples, UK
Anthony Smoker, UK
Neville Stanton, UK
Alex Stedmon, UK
Andrew Thatcher, South Africa

Universal Access in Human–Computer Interaction

**Program Chairs: Constantine Stephanidis, Greece,
and Margherita Antona, Greece**

Julio Abascal, Spain
Gisela Susanne Bahr, USA
João Barroso, Portugal
Margrit Betke, USA
Anthony Brooks, Denmark
Christian Bühler, Germany
Stefan Carmien, Spain
Hua Dong, P.R. China
Carlos Duarte, Portugal
Pier Luigi Emiliani, Italy
Qin Gao, P.R. China
Andrina Granić, Croatia
Andreas Holzinger, Austria
Josette Jones, USA
Simeon Keates, UK

Georgios Kouroupetroglou, Greece
Patrick Langdon, UK
Barbara Leporini, Italy
Eugene Loos, The Netherlands
Ana Isabel Paraguay, Brazil
Helen Petrie, UK
Michael Pieper, Germany
Enrico Pontelli, USA
Jaime Sanchez, Chile
Alberto Sanna, Italy
Anthony Savidis, Greece
Christian Stary, Austria
Hirotada Ueda, Japan
Gerhard Weber, Germany
Harald Weber, Germany

Virtual, Augmented and Mixed Reality

**Program Chairs: Randall Shumaker, USA,
and Stephanie Lackey, USA**

Roland Blach, Germany
Sheryl Brahnam, USA
Juan Cendan, USA
Jessie Chen, USA
Panagiotis D. Kaklis, UK

Hirokazu Kato, Japan
Denis Laurendeau, Canada
Fotis Liarokapis, UK
Michael Macedonia, USA
Gordon Mair, UK

Digital Human Modeling and Applications in Health, Safety, Ergonomics and Risk Management

Program Chair: Vincent G. Duffy, USA

Design, User Experience, and Usability

Program Chair: Aaron Marcus, USA

Distributed, Ambient and Pervasive Interactions

**Program Chairs: Norbert Streitz, Germany,
and Panos Markopoulos, The Netherlands**

Juan Carlos Augusto, UK
Jose Bravo, Spain
Adrian Cheok, UK
Boris de Ruyter, The Netherlands
Anind Dey, USA
Dimitris Grammenos, Greece
Nuno Guimaraes, Portugal
Achilles Kameas, Greece
Javed Vassilis Khan, The Netherlands
Shin'ichi Konomi, Japan
Carsten Magerkurth, Switzerland

Ingrid Mulder, The Netherlands
Anton Nijholt, The Netherlands
Fabio Paternó, Italy
Carsten Röcker, Germany
Teresa Romao, Portugal
Albert Ali Salah, Turkey
Manfred Tscheligi, Austria
Reiner Wichert, Germany
Woontack Woo, Korea
Xenophon Zabulis, Greece

Human Aspects of Information Security, Privacy and Trust

**Program Chairs: Theo Tryfonas, UK,
and Ioannis Askoxylakis, Greece**

Claudio Agostino Ardagna, Italy
Zinaida Benenson, Germany
Daniele Catteddu, Italy
Raoul Chiesa, Italy
Bryan Cline, USA
Sadie Creese, UK
Jorge Cuellar, Germany
Marc Dacier, USA
Dieter Gollmann, Germany
Kirstie Hawkey, Canada
Jaap-Henk Hoepman, The Netherlands
Cagatay Karabat, Turkey
Angelos Keromytis, USA
Ayako Komatsu, Japan
Ronald Leenes, The Netherlands
Javier Lopez, Spain
Steve Marsh, Canada

Gregorio Martinez, Spain
Emilio Mordini, Italy
Yuko Murayama, Japan
Masakatsu Nishigaki, Japan
Aljosa Pasic, Spain
Milan Petković, The Netherlands
Joachim Posegga, Germany
Jean-Jacques Quisquater, Belgium
Damien Sauveron, France
George Spanoudakis, UK
Kerry-Lynn Thomson, South Africa
Julien Touzeau, France
Theo Tryfonas, UK
João Vilela, Portugal
Claire Vishik, UK
Melanie Volkamer, Germany

HCI in Business

Program Chair: Fiona Fui-Hoon Nah, USA

Andreas Auinger, Austria
Michel Avital, Denmark
Traci Carte, USA
Hock Chuan Chan, Singapore
Constantinos Coursaris, USA
Soussan Djamasbi, USA
Brenda Eschenbrenner, USA
Nobuyuki Fukawa, USA
Khaled Hassanein, Canada
Milena Head, Canada
Susanna (Shuk Ying) Ho, Australia
Jack Zhenhui Jiang, Singapore
Jinwoo Kim, Korea
Zoonky Lee, Korea
Honglei Li, UK
Nicholas Lockwood, USA
Eleanor T. Loiacono, USA
Mei Lu, USA

Scott McCoy, USA
Brian Mennecke, USA
Robin Poston, USA
Lingyun Qiu, P.R. China
Rene Riedl, Austria
Matti Rossi, Finland
April Savoy, USA
Shu Schiller, USA
Hong Sheng, USA
Choon Ling Sia, Hong Kong
Chee-Wee Tan, Denmark
Chuan Hoo Tan, Hong Kong
Noam Tractinsky, Israel
Horst Treiblmaier, Austria
Virpi Tuunainen, Finland
Dezhi Wu, USA
I-Chin Wu, Taiwan

Learning and Collaboration Technologies

Program Chairs: Panayiotis Zaphiris, Cyprus, and Andri Ioannou, Cyprus

Ruthi Aladjem, Israel
Abdulaziz Aldaej, UK
John M. Carroll, USA
Maka Eradze, Estonia
Mikhail Fominykh, Norway
Denis Gillet, Switzerland
Mustafa Murat Inceoglu, Turkey
Pernilla Josefsson, Sweden
Marie Joubert, UK
Sauli Kiviranta, Finland
Tomaž Klobučar, Slovenia
Elena Kyza, Cyprus
Maarten de Laat, The Netherlands
David Lamas, Estonia

Edmund Laugasson, Estonia
Ana Loureiro, Portugal
Katherine Maillet, France
Nadia Pantidi, UK
Antigoni Parmaxi, Cyprus
Borzoo Pourabdollahian, Italy
Janet C. Read, UK
Christophe Reffay, France
Nicos Souleles, Cyprus
Ana Luísa Torres, Portugal
Stefan Trausan-Matu, Romania
Aimilia Tzanavari, Cyprus
Johnny Yuen, Hong Kong
Carmen Zahn, Switzerland

External Reviewers

Ilia Adami, Greece
Iosif Klironomos, Greece
Maria Korozi, Greece
Vassilis Kouroumalis, Greece

Asterios Leonidis, Greece
George Margetis, Greece
Stavroula Ntoa, Greece
Nikolaos Partarakis, Greece

HCI International 2015

The 15th International Conference on Human–Computer Interaction, HCI International 2015, will be held jointly with the affiliated conferences in Los Angeles, CA, USA, in the Westin Bonaventure Hotel, August 2–7, 2015. It will cover a broad spectrum of themes related to HCI, including theoretical issues, methods, tools, processes, and case studies in HCI design, as well as novel interaction techniques, interfaces, and applications. The proceedings will be published by Springer. More information will be available on the conference website: http://www.hcii2015.org/

General Chair
Professor Constantine Stephanidis
University of Crete and ICS-FORTH
Heraklion, Crete, Greece
E-mail: cs@ics.forth.gr

Table of Contents

Analysing, Visualising, and Modelling Social Networks

Online Communities and Engagement

Identity and Presence in Social Media

Games, Gamification, and Entertainment in Social Media

Designing and Evaluating Social Computing and Social Media

A Review of Using Online Social Networks for Investigative Activities

Adnan Abdalla and Sule Yildirim Yayilgan

Gjovik University College
Po. Box. 191, 2802 Gjøvik, Norway
adnanbodo@gmail.com, suley@hig.no

Abstract. In this paper, we will describe the use of online social networks (OSNs) for law enforcement. With the increased growth of use of OSNs, the use of OSNs for law enforcement has also shown a parallel growth. Such a trend can easily be seen in the increase of reported number of criminal cases being solved by police officers of various countries. It is of interest to find out how OSNs are actually used by law enforcers to anticipate a crime, how they are being used by law enforcers to solve a crime committed, how they are used by criminals to commit a crime and what possible further needs law enforces have in using OSNs for predicting and solving crimes.

In order to be able to answer these questions, we have done an extensive review of the literature and existing available crimes. This led us to understand the nature of using OSNs for law enforcement. Further, we have contacted a questionnaire with the top level law enforcers in Turkey in order to find answers to the given questions above.

Keywords: Online Social Networks, Law Enforcement, Framework, Investigation, Digital Forensics, Evidence, Analysis, Tool, Digital Crimes, Activity.

1   Introduction

During the last few years, the activity of online social networks (OSNs) has increased excessively throughout all layers of society and nations. According Alexa traffic data, Facebook has now a total of 1.155 billion monthly active users. In Africa and Latin America, Facebook has 346 million users, Asia 339 million, Europe 272 million, and US and Canada 198 million users [1]. The excessive use of OSNs activities makes them an attractive arena to perform digital crimes (e.g. harassment, grooming, and child pornography) and classical crimes (e.g. Burglary, Kidnap, sex trafficking) [2] [3].

In contrast, widespread use of OSNs and their applications on diversity of digital devices (e.g. PC, pad, smartphone, etc.) attracted law enforcement agencies (LEAs) for help to solve and prevent any crimes linked and non-linked to OSNs, from evidence collection, to criminal identification and location [4][5].

G. Meiselwitz (Ed.): SCSM 2014, LNCS 8531, pp. 3–12, 2014.
© Springer International Publishing Switzerland 2014

Examining the activities of users on OSNs will provide a useful source for law enforcement investigators (LEIs) to find any missing information about particular person during digital investigation process. Nevertheless the law enforcement professionals (LEPs) are facing significant problems since there is no consistent, systematic, and legal framework built specifically for investigation on OSNs [6].

Based on reviewed existing literature of digital forensics investigation models for OSNs, most of these models have similar approaches which are focusing on internet investigations, but none of these have the nuance related to the investigatory process on OSNs.

In this paper we outline the current use of OSNs for investigative activities which describe the current system and framework for conducting investigation. In addition to that, the outline also categorizes crimes been employed by criminals which are involved directly and indirectly with OSNs.

Based on recent developed models of digital forensics investigation for OSNs, we propose an improvement for existing frameworks which describes the integration of analysis of user's behaviors in OSNs. Finally we will present a result of online study conducted among LEPs of various ages, geographies and experience levels in Turkey to understand the use of OSNs in law enforcement and current resources and processes used when utilizing OSNs in investigations.

2   Crimes Involving OSNs

OSN is a resource of information that can be employed by criminals to commit different types of crimes [7] [8]. The propagation of criminal activity on social networking sites is hard to define. This excessive use of social network activities makes them an attractive arena for different types of cybercrimes (e.g. malware distribution, fraud, harassment, grooming etc.). In addition to cybercrime as a specific activity, the social networks also serve as an informational valuable source for criminals in more traditional crimes (Assault, burglary, domestic violence, kidnapping). Because of this aggressive pattern of usage of social networking platform, we are being exposed to some bigger issues such as terrorism and organized crimes. We have divided crimes that involved OSNs into classical and digital crimes. These crimes are described in the following sections.

2.1   Classical Crimes

OSN is a place for criminals to perform their classical crimes. For instance, Facebook users can update their status by posting their current location, for how long they are away from home and what are they doing, which gives potential thieves enough time to take their chance to burgle into their property. There are numerous cases like this that appeared in the media [8].

A survey was conducted by Friedland UK's Home Security Week on 2011 among fifty convicted burglars. According to the survey, 78% of burglars stated that they believed OSNs like Facebook, Twitter, and FourSquare are fruitful tools for burglars targeting specific assets, while 74% stated that Google Street View was an important role in home burglaries [9].

2.2   Digital Crimes

OSN involves numerous illegal activities including; unauthorized or illegal access, interception by technical means of transmissions of digital devices to, from, or within digital devices. Types of digital crimes where digital evidence has been located: Social engineering, Cyber-Identity Theft, Cyber-Threats, Scams, Cyber-stalking, Online credit card fraud, Cyber-Harassment and more [10]. The majority of digital crimes on OSNs are cyber based, and social engineering can be used as one of technique for these crimes [11]. From statistics and real cases studied, we divided the crimes into digital and classical as shown in figure 1. All types of crimes which have been discussed above are widespread crimes in OSNs such as, Facebook and Twitter that provide a powerful communication tool for potential criminals to initiate their communication and to connect them to others anywhere at any time. While criminals are finding ways to cover and shield their posts from people, in the same way the criminal investigator works hard to discover any evidence related to criminals.

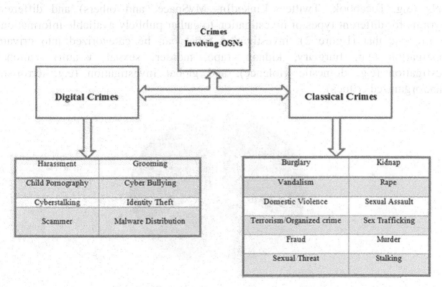

Fig. 1. Current crimes been involved by OSNs

3   Analysis of Online Social Networks

Social network analysis as a method is not something new, but a method that has emerged from social science, used by researchers to examine group structures and communication flows within a chart network by focusing on the relationships between entities. This type of analysis approach can provide efficient filtering of network information, quick identification of potential key individuals or groups for better prioritization of (often limited) resources and the ability to look beyond the network structure into its dynamics to identify characteristics that may not be immediately apparent. This type of monitoring and analysis of groups and individuals of particular interest, which are generated from social networking data, can help forensics examiners to answer possible questions in their investigation.

3.1   Existing Digital Forensics Tools for OSNs Analysis

The confidential nature of work by LEAs and companies of OSNs was one of obstacles and barriers for our research to have structured interview with officers from National criminal investigation service. There is need to know how law enforcement officers deal with incidents that involved OSNs, and whether there are any standard instruments or computer programs utilized for extracting and analysis of public and private information of OSNs users.

We observed that LEIs have used different software or tools for different types of social networks to collect and analyze "publicly available" information. Based on our research we found that LEIs have been using different tools for different types of OSNs (e.g. Facebook, Twitter, LinkedIn, MySpace, and others) and different programs for different types of investigation to gather publicly available information. We propose that (figure 2), investigation types can be categorized into private investigation (e.g. burglary, kidnap, rape, murder, sexual assault), national investigation (e.g. domestic violence), and global investigation (e.g. terrorism attack/organized crimes).

Fig. 2. Types of investigations in OSNs

One of the major challenges for LEIs is how to gather and analyze public information from OSNs by utilizing different tools with different features within short period of time. LEIs stated that there are more valuable information that can be collected from OSNs than traditional investigation process such as interview with family members and acquaintances of the person of interest.

Examining the activities of OSNs users can help the investigators to extract direct feeling of person whenever he/she shares it in OSNs. For instance a person's post photos of holiday trip in somewhere with someone, can give a direct impression of happiness that he/she is having in specific time of posting the photo, or post comments about incident happened expressing the sadness that he/she feeling it. Visualization and geographically presenting user's activities over time were dominant feature in most of tools been utilized. To enhance validity and accuracy of data collection of these tools, we have a need for a framework that visualizes the emotions of people based on their activities on OSNs by analyzing activities such as comments, tweet posts and other. A framework can correlate detected user's behavior on OSNs and compare it to Real-time incident. The framework must geographically estimate the expressions of feelings in ordinary and slang language. Mapping the mood over time can help the investigators to analyze the reactions of people for any incident can help in guiding national and private policy on the best way to counter major incidents.

3.2 Proposed Framework for the Forensic Analysis of User Interaction with OSN

We propose our improvement based on existing literature on framework for forensic analysis of user interaction with OSN as shown in figure 3. The investigation is initiated by acquiring data in two different approaches. Gathering evidence from public domains which are created by individuals where they made their pieces of information publicly available to anyone with internet access. In the second approach law enforcement has to legally request OSNs provider to obtain restricted data of user's information which they made their data private and not accessible for anyone with internet access.

Continuing the investigation process the forensic investigators have to run a search through large amount of different types of users' activities where data that can be collected and utilized as evidence (e.g., photos, comments, videos, link, posts in news, tagged photos and others). Nonetheless due to time consuming and huge amount of data that have to be examined, filtering the data is applied to identify temporal and geographical analysis of user activities, such as what, when, and where the user posted or commented, uploaded, tagged photos, or any updated statutes over time. Identifying the temporal analysis by highlighting peaks of activities (e.g., posting photos of visited places) over time and at particular point of time with geographical changes can help the forensics examiners to answer the needs by comparing temporal and spatial changes of users activities with real-time incidents. Analyzing accurate expression of user feelings in real time (e.g. just fine, bored, bored, tired, happy, hungry, confused, embarrassed, guilty, smart, hurt, annoyed, mad, sad, upset, angry, scared, disgust, surprise, and shame) and geographically and tracking how they develop these feelings over time, will give great advantage to forensics examiners to see real-time record of how and what people were feeling and if there is a relation between these expressions with real-time incidents that happened in a criminal case. Analyzing individuals' emotions can be achieved by developing a program with visualization features applied which help forensics investigators to determine the direction of investigation of mass amount that represents someone's virtual community.

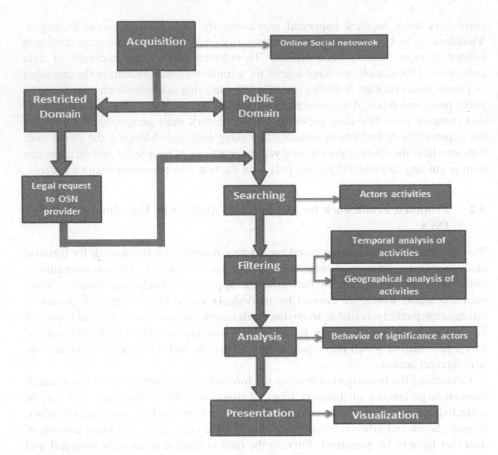

Fig. 3. Proposed framework for the forensic analysis of user interaction with OSN

4   Questionnaire

We designed the questionnaire in a way that lead us to answer to the main objectives for discovering related facts to highlight and understand the use of OSN for law enforcement, specifically with regards to criminal intelligence and investigative process.

We distributed questionnaire among law enforcement agencies in Turkey. Fortunately we received response from some law enforcement with different designation and possessing high experience ranging between 10 to 19 years. The participants were having various positions from deputy chief of police, leadership, special police units (SPU) officer, war crimes investigator and police officer. Majority of their ages were in the range of 40-49 and 30-39 years. In addition, the participants were representing from different provinces and highly populated areas such as Istanbul, Antalya and Bursa. Therefore, we believe the numbers of participants from these law enforcement agencies are sufficient to allow us in drawing statistical analysis.

Questionnaire contains fifteenth questions which focus on the scope of research work. Questionnaire starts with brief explanation about the purpose of the study and informing that the identity of participants will be kept hidden. The participants will be asked to provide (if they feel it comfortable) information about their age, region, position/ responsibility in the organization and years of experience if they have.

5   Analysis and Result

We have analyzed the collected data by utilizing proper and different features of Questback and Excel for the purpose of getting clear results that everyone can understand. We have analyzed data for each question separately, with summary of each one and we have used comparison feature for question itself in order to find interesting results of data collection. We have presented the results by using different types of graphs.

5.1   Main Findings from questionnaire

Among law enforcement users, OSN is widely used for non-investigative activities with 57 % versus 43% for investigative activities. Background investigations for job candidates are top non-investigative activity done via OSN, followed by In-service training. A top investigative activity of OSN is for crime investigation, followed by listening/monitoring for potential criminal activity. Lack of OSNs skills and training is a primary reason of often non-use in investigative activities. In addition OSNs is a new scope work especially for new graduated law enforcement officers.

Identifying persons of interest, identifying criminal activity and identifying/ monitoring person of interest's whereabouts are top investigative activities done through OSN as shown in figure 4. Utilizing OSNs for investigative activities has not used obtained information from OSNs as probable cause for search warrants in Turkey. Currently, OSN is utilized by law enforcement in Turkey just as resource to obtain information that can be only used for intelligence investigations, but cannot be used as evidence in the court of law to get legal search warrant.

The other results that we obtained from the questionnaire are as follows:

— Law enforcement professionals are mostly self-taught and depend on their knowledge from use of OSNs for personal purposes, and corporation with colleagues with experience.
— There is not significant statistics for any formal training seminar or conference that was dedicated to the use OSNs in law enforcements.
— Communal OSNs, such as Facebook are most used in OSNs, followed by YouTube and Twitter. Myspace, LinkedIn, and blogs are less used.
— Top frequent crimes been encountered by law enforcement professionals during their work are, assault, burglary, child abuse, harassment, hate crime, and murder.
— There is infrequent of use of OSNs for investigative activities, approximately half of law enforcement using it less often, and half using it 2-3 times in a month- However the level of usage has grown somewhat compared to the previous year.

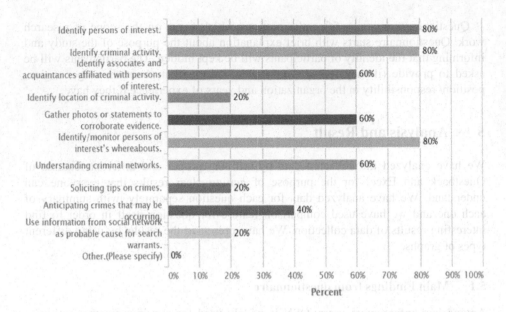

Fig. 4. Types of Investigative Activities Done via OSNs

Forensic Investigation in OSN. Establishing a relationship with the person of interest by creating a fake account is a most used approach among law enforcement to obtain user information from OSNs, followed by request to access into victim's or person of interest account from OSN provider, and request access into associates and acquaintance's affiliated account with person of interest. Photos/videos, location, groups, name are most collected data from OSN by forensics examiner, followed by linked websites, userID, list of friends, status updates, network, and chat.

More than two-third of law enforcement are not using any tools for analyzing OSN activities. Law enforcement believed that visualization is very useful feature to determine the direction of investigation and narrow down the scope of work.

Law enforcement stated that they are following these steps (Identification, Searching, Filtering, and Capturing) in OSN investigations process.

Non-users OSN in Investigations. The main reasons for not using OSN in investigations purpose are the following:

— 33% of law enforcement do not have enough knowledge to use in investigations.
— 33% lack of support from law enforcement leadership.
— 17% Unable to access during working hours.
— 17% Agency policy

Beliefs in OSNs Use

— The value of OSN in investigation will increase in future, and can significantly help to solve crimes more quickly.

— Law enforcement professionals have no worries about the ethics of creating fake profile account as an investigative method.
— Law enforcement believes that information obtained through OSN is credible.
— More than one-third of law enforcement said that they are comfortable to use OSNs, but are not able to use it to its fullest effort due to a lack of proper training. Within age interval 30-39, the law enforcement professionals are more comfortable to use OSNs, but less comfortable to use within the age interval 40-49.

6   Conclusions

The use of OSN in law enforcement agencies has entirely changed in their traditional techniques and procedures in which law enforcement professionals using it in criminal intelligence and investigative activity.

Law enforcement greatly benefited from OSNs and resources as a fruitful tool to prevent, mitigate, respond, and investigate criminal activity. The outline of our work described how criminals committed crimes by using these sites for illegal purposes, and we categorized the crimes that are involving OSNs. Forensics investigators were following two approaches in obtaining data from OSNs; collecting publicly available information of user's subscribers and cooperation with social network provider in order to obtain restricted data of any particular user. There should be transparency in sharing personal information between law enforcement of social networks companies and law enforcement authorizes.

Current approaches in which forensic examiners analyze user interaction vary depending on the types of investigation, such as private (e.g., murder, rape, kidnap crimes), national (e.g., local violence) and global (e.g., organized crime).

Majority of forensic examiners develop their own tools and software that can automatically identify, search, filter, and capture relevant information for investigation. We believe that developing a program that visualizes accurate expression of users feeling and geographically tracking how they develop these feeling in real time and possibility to compare it to time of incidents that happened, can help forensics investigators to identify and predict criminals plans for any actions that represents someone's virtual community. In connection to main findings in questionnaire we discover that primary reason for collecting information from OSNs is just only for investigations intelligence. Law enforcement did not use this information as evidence against the suspects in the court of law in Turkey. In addition to that there is a need for modification in legal jurisdictions in Turkey that can help the law enforcement agencies to use collected information from OSNs as evidence in the court of law.

To the end, OSN will increase in its popularity and usefulness for coming years, especially towards criminal intelligence and investigative activities. Therefore, to ensure that information which is being collected from OSN is vital and legal, there should be a policy on use of OSN for law enforcement and focus and articulating the importance of privacy and how to protect individual's privacy, group's privacy, civil rights, and civil liberties.

References

1. World Map of Social Networks, http://vincos.it/world-map-of-social-networks/
2. Huber, M., Mulazzani, M., Leithner, S.S., Wondracek, G., Weippl, E.: Social Snapshot: Digital Forensics for Online Social Networks. In: 27th Annual Computer Security Applications Conference, pp. 113–122. ACM Digital Library, New York (2011)
3. A Digital Forensic Investigation Model for Online Social Networking, http://www.cms.livjm.ac.uk/pgnet2010/MakeCD/Papers/2010042.pdf
4. Assault Fugitive Who Was Found Via Facebook Is Back In NY, http://newyorkcriminallawyersblog.com/2010/03/assault-criminal-who-was-found-via-facebook-is-back-in-ny.html
5. Facebook status update provides alibi, http://edition.cnn.com/2009/CRIME/11/12/facebook.alibi/
6. A Digital Forensic Investigation Model and Tool for Online Social Networks, http://www.cms.livjm.ac.uk/pgnet2011/Proceedings/Papers/m1569453211-mohd_zainudin.pdf
7. Facebook Sex Trafficking: Social Network Used To Kidnap Indonesian Girls, http://www.huffingtonpost.com/2012/10/29/facebook-sex-trafficking-_n_2036627.html
8. Facebook Sex Trafficking: Social Network Used to Kidnap Indonesian Girls, http://www.sileo.com/facebook-status-update-leads-to-robbery/
9. Burglars Use Social Media to Plan crimes, http://www.blog.littlesafe.co.uk/?p=969
10. Criminal Use of Social Media (2013), http://www.nw3c.org/docs/whitepapers/criminal-use-of-social-media.pdf?sfvrsn=10
11. Digital Crime, http://www.dcrime.com/dcrime.pdf

An Accessibility Evaluation of Social Media Websites for Elder Adults

Jessica Arfaa and Yuanqiong (Kathy) Wang

Towson University, Dept. of Computer & Information Sciences, Towson, MD 21252
jessicaarfaa@yahoo.com, ywangtu@gmail.com

Abstract. Elder adults account for only a small portion of social networking site users despite the numerous benefits provided by social media. Although the number of elder users has grown in the past few years, many are not engaged with social media. Are there any special reasons for the elderly not to take advantage of social media? Are there any accessibility and usability challenges for the elderly to use social media? What are they? How do current social networking sites perform when it comes to accessibility for the elderly? This paper reports the preliminary findings to the above questions based on an instructor's notes on the discussions within an elderly computer class along with an accessibility evaluation of popular social media sites. The results show that many elders struggle with the understanding of Web 2.0 concepts and interpreting the complex layout of the social networking sites. Many sites do not adhere to respected accessibility standards and guidelines. Findings from this study will contribute to the understanding of the elder adults as a user group and improving the design of a more accessible website for the elderly.

Keywords: Social Media, Social Networking, Elder Adults.

1   Introduction

According to the Administration on Aging [1], 39.9 million people in the United States are 65 and older, with the expectation of this demographic to grow to 72.1 million in 2030. As of 2012, 53% of elder adults are engaged online [12] compared to 95% of teens [13]. The number of online elder adults engaged in social networking sites has grown from 7% in 2009 [14] to 34% in 2012 [12]. However, compared to 81% of online teens, elders aged 65 and older still represent the smallest demographic utilizing the internet and social media.

Social media is a popular internet activity because of its collaborative and resource-rich environment. It allows family, friends, and other users to interact synchronously and asynchronously from any device with internet access [10]. Therefore, social media can be beneficial to older adults that can become isolated from family, friends, and society due to health and immobility issues. To reap the benefits of this trend, the reasons behind the low social media participation of elders needs to be investigated.

G. Meiselwitz (Ed.): SCSM 2014, LNCS 8531, pp. 13–24, 2014.
© Springer International Publishing Switzerland 2014

The following research questions should be investigated: (1) Are there any special factors/reasons that prevent elders from using social media? (2) Are there any accessibility and usability challenges for the elderly to use social media? If so, what are they? And, (3) are current social media sites usable and accessible for the elderly? To answer these questions, we conducted discussions with a group of elder adults and an accessibility inspection on some popular social networking sites. This paper reports the preliminary findings of these studies.

This paper is organized as the following: after a brief literature review on social media, elder adults and web usability as well as accessibility guidelines are reviewed. The research design including the class discussion and social media evaluation is discussed in detail. Afterwards, the findings from the class observation and social media site evaluations are presented. To conclude, future research is discussed.

2   Literature Review

2.1   Social Media

Social media is a type of application found within the Web 2.0 trend. Examples of social media include social networking, social bookmarking, blogs, discussion forums, wikis, photo-sharing, and video-sharing sites. These types of sites are characterized by their collaborative and interactive nature and dynamic, user-contributed content. Posting comments, viewing pictures, and connecting with users are just a few activities that can be achieved on these sites. Other unique characteristics include the ability to share, tag, and trend content. According to Alexa.com [2], four of the top ten visited sites on the internet are social media related, including Facebook (Ranked #2), YouTube (Ranked #3), Wikipedia (Ranked #6), and Twitter (Ranked #9).

2.2   Elder Adults

Elder adults can be defined by numerous measures, such as age, legal status, health, dependency, and milestone criteria. An objective way to define an adult is by age. Much research finds an elder adult as being aged 65 and greater, however past and current studies refer to elderly status based on generation, such as Baby Boomers who were born after World War II, from 1946 to 1964 [4]. Legally, an elder can possibly collect social security starting at age 62 or be eligible for Medicare by age 65 [16]. By health or dependence qualifications, elders can be seen as someone with gray hair or wrinkles, or have corrective support devices such as a walker or hearing aid [8]. In addition to age, legal, and physical criteria, elders can be defined by their life milestones, such as having grandchildren, living through the Great Depression, or work retirement [9]. In this paper, adults that are 65 or older are considered.

2.3   Elder Adult Social Media Advantages and Barriers

Elder adults can benefit from engaging in social media activities. Social media can improve self-worth and self-esteem of an elder, empowering them to be self-sufficient and independent [15, 17]. It can also provide a plethora of digital resources for learning found on blogs, wikis, and social bookmarking sites [3]. Contact between elders and others can increase because these types of sites facilitate communication and interactions between other users. Therefore an elder that is immobile or physically bound at a location like an assisted living community or nursing home can still communicate with the outside world.

Despite these advantages, physical impairments and disabilities, computer illiteracy, and negative perceptions may present challenges for elders utilizing social media. The natural aging process can deteriorate the body physically, cognitively, and physiologically [6, 7]. Many elders suffer from arthritis, vision, or memory loss, making it very difficult to use and interact with a computer. Other elders do not engage in internet activities because of computer literacy issues. Elders that were not raised with technology in their daily lives are considered digital immigrants, having to transition their lives from an analog to a digital world. Because of this unfamiliarity, many elders have negative perceptions of computers, the internet, and social media, fearful of breaking something, viewing inappropriate material, and becoming vulnerable with privacy issues.

Although many of these barriers are not easy to fix, there are website mandates and guidelines that address the accessibility issues.

2.4   Interface Design Mandates and Accessibility

There are numerous mandates, standards, and guidelines associated with the disabled to improve the usability and accessibility of computer systems. Although the elderly are not synonymous with the disabled, as discussed above many elders suffer from disabilities due to the natural aging process. Therefore many guidelines available for the disabled can also benefit the elderly.

For evaluation purposes, this study will address the government-mandated Section 508 Compliance, and WCAG 1.0 and 2.0. Section 508 makes it mandatory for government agencies to follow sixteen guidelines related to making webpages accessible and usable to those with disabilities. If any of these guidelines are not met, a site will be deemed as out of compliance. Similar to Section 508, WCAG 1.0 and 2.0 provide guidelines and three conformance levels to ensure a website is usable. WCAG 1.0 has 14 guidelines, including criteria on equivalent alternatives, colors, and language. WCAG 2.0 holds similar, but more detailed criteria that are organized into four principles. Differences between the two versions include inputs, formats, and pre-recordings [18].

Unfortunately, many social media sites do not adhere to these standards. Observations from the class discussion demonstrate how elders interact with social media. These observations provide us with motivation to evaluate current social media sites' compliance with available mandates and guidelines.

3   Class Discussion

To better understand the current state of elders and social media usage, in particular, social networking sites; a class discussion comprising of elderly adults with little computer experience was conducted in May of 2013. In conjunction with a church in the Mid-Atlantic area and an education institution; a free computer class with five sessions was offered to elderly adults with little to no computer experience. Adults accepted in the elderly class were chosen based on age requirement (65 years of age or older). Those that did not meet the age requirement were offered to attend a different class section offered by the same program.

Eight females attended this session. All of them had little to no previous computer and social networking experience. Within this class, students learned how to turn on and off a computer, use the drawing program Microsoft Paint, perform internet searches, and use email. At the end of the program, most of the elderly adults were able to use a mouse, including clicking, scrolling, and moving the cursor, except for those with hand/dexterity issues.

Some adults still had issues on the number of clicks, typing, opening and closing a program, understanding how to use an internet browser, and email. For example, many elder adults did not know when to double click or single click on a page or link. Others did not know how to exit a program, instead, minimizing or maximizing the page after clicking on the wrong button or toggling between applications. Many did not understand the internet browser window, often opting to type search terms in the address bar. Additional issues included elders not understanding the difference between subject lines and the body text of an email. After the final session of review, there was a class discussion on social networking.

During the class discussion, the instructor asked the students to describe what a social networking site is, identify examples of social media, identify and describe the features provided by the social networking sites. The instructor then corrected any misconceptions presented by the students. At the end of the discussion, the instructor conducted a walkthrough of a social networking site (Facebook) with the discussion on how to utilize different features the site has to offer (e.g. viewing a person's timeline, posting and receiving comments).

Throughout this class discussion, the instructor recorded notes regarding student's answers and feedback. The notes were then analyzed after the class to identify any possible issues/challenges that may have prevented elders in using social media/social networking sites.

4   Class Discussion Results

For the start of the class discussion, the instructor asked the students their definition of social media. Instead of giving a clear definition or any characteristics, such as collaboration, tagging, or sharing information; six participants were able to identify YouTube and Facebook as examples of social media applications. Two of the participants assumed that social media was 'the internet' or a chat room.

When asked if they could provide additional examples of social media and the purpose of these sites, most were not able to contribute or had heard of the teacher's suggestions of LinkedIn, Instagram, or Google+. A majority of the adults assumed that social networking sites were geared towards all users for the purpose of sharing pictures with family/friends. After explaining the numerous uses of these sites, the instructor asked if they would be open to utilizing these sites for business connections or current events. Most of the participants were hesitant because of their computer skills and unfamiliarity with social media; however two were willing to use it to find a job and most of the students never thought of using social media for news purposes.

Regarding the features provided, most users did not fully understand Web 2.0 terms such as "wall", "timeline", "instant messaging", "posting", "sharing links", or "tagging". When asked what was "posting to someone's wall or timeline", a participant answered that it is writing on someone's "homepage" (homepage is a term learned in the internet session of class) and that everyone would be able to see what was written. Additionally, the instructor asked what they think is 'sharing a link', and a participant answered that "it's sharing something that is interesting to you." Only three of the eight participants had ever engaged in social media usage for picture viewing purposes. They pointed out that they had received a Facebook link in their email or were told by the poster to navigate to Facebook to view pictures. These terms were further explained in the demo.

After showing how to log into Facebook with the instructor's account, the instructor asked the students their initial thoughts on the main page. Most participants were confused by the layout and did not know where to start or what functions were available on the site. All users asked to enlarge the text on Facebook before continuing. After adjusting the projector to show a larger resolution, the instructor asked the participant's help in completing a few tasks.

The instructor first asked how to view the instructor's main profile page. None of the users knew to click on the instructors name at the top of the page; however seemed to understand after the instructor asked them a few more times after toggling back and forth from the news feed and profile page. When viewing the tagged pictures of the instructor, the participants did not understand that tagging would pull pictures associated with the person. Each user continued to be surprised that the next picture in the series contained the instructor. On the main activity feed, the instructor pointed to a random post and asked the students what the particular fields contained. Most understood that the first line was the poster's name; however, they were confused with the actual post and its purpose, along with the concept of a news feed posting numerous people's posts.

After the teacher explained that the purpose of the particular person's post was for personal reasons, the instructor showed a few more posting examples on the news feed, such as links and images. Most participants did not know if something was a link when there was general text. For posts with links, images, and text, they were not sure where to click to view the entire post (Fig. 1).

Did not
understand
Web 2.0
concepts or
overall layout of
SNS

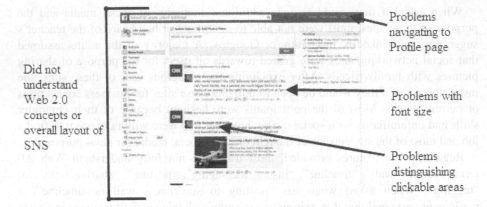

Problems
navigating to
Profile page

Problems with
font size

Problems
distinguishing
clickable areas

Fig. 1. Screenshot of SNS difficulties experienced

After this task, users were asked how to find a friend's profile. Most participants skipped over the search bar in the top-center of the page and told the instructor to click on the "Find Friends" label at the top right of the window.

When asked for additional questions on the demo, a participant asked if the instructor could show her how to view her friend's pictures. After navigating to the photos section, the participant was still confused on how she would be able to complete this task at home without any help. The last task the instructor asked was to sign-out of the website. None of the users were able to find the "log out" button, which was a sub-link after rolling over the settings icon.

At the end of the discussion, the instructor asked how she could encourage the elders to use social networking sites. Their responses included having some sort of support to guide them in using a computer and the internet, as well as having a way to verify that their information is safe without privacy issues. Most users were very interested in learning more about social media, particularly to look at pictures posted by family and friends. It was also suggested that there be a class dedicated to just using social media, so that they could have someone create the account for them and to show them how to view pictures.

5   Social Media Evaluation

Evident by the class discussion results, it is apparent that elder adults encounter a number of hindrances when interacting with a social networking site. Based on these findings, the authors evaluated the accessibility of current social media applications.

The purpose of this assessment is to evaluate the current state of the compliance of the accessibility guidelines, and to identify the most frequently violated accessibility guidelines by social media websites. To evaluate these websites, the automated tool, SiteSort was chosen for its ability to evaluate websites based on Section 508 compliance, WCAG 1.0, and WCAG 2.0 criteria. The results were verified by the author by manually checking the source code of sample pages on each site.

In February 2013, nineteen popular social media websites, ranging from social networking (Facebook, LinkedIn, MySpace, Google+, Meetup), social bookmarking (Delicious, Digg, Reddit), blogs (Twitter, Blogger, WordPress, LiveJournal), photo-sharing (Pinterest, Flickr, Instagram), video-sharing (YouTube, Vimeo), and wiki sites (Wikia, Wikipedia), were reviewed for violations against Section 508 compliance and both versions of WCAG. Within these sites, unauthenticated and authenticated accounts were used to evaluate up to 100 pages of each social media site.

6   Social Media Evaluation Results

The overall results showed that social networking, video-sharing, and image-sharing sites accounted for the most combined violations, while social bookmarking sites and wikis recorded the least amount of infractions (chart). According to the SiteSort report, many disabled users could find it impossible to use some pages of these sites (Fig. 2).

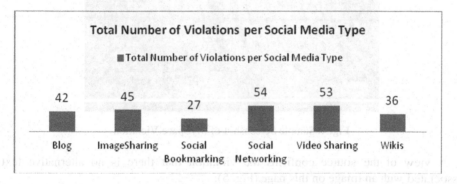

Fig. 2. Total Violations per Social Media Type

Evaluating against Section 508 compliance, video-sharing sites accounted for the majority of violations, followed by social networking sites, image-sharing sites, and wikis (Fig. 3). The social networking sites Facebook and MySpace were the biggest violators, along with Vimeo and YouTube , which was in contrast with the social bookmarking sites Delicious and Digg.

The most violated guideline was Section 508 1194.22 (a), where a text equivalent should accompany a non-text element, either with an alt tag or other type of descriptor, followed by Section 508 1194.22 (n), where electronic forms should be able to be completed by assistive technology.

SiteSort identifies the following page as an example of the Section 508 1194.22 (a) violation: https://myspace.com/onetwowatch?pm_cmp=ed_spl_5top_sky (Fig. 4).

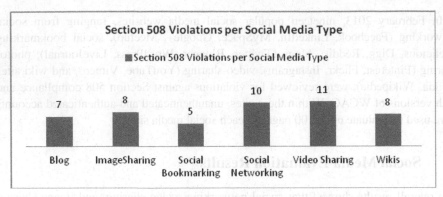

Fig. 3. Section 508 Violations per Social Media Type

Fig. 4. Sample Screenshot of MySpace Violation

A view of the source confirms the violation that there is no alternative text associated with an image on this page (Fig. 5):

Fig. 5. MySpace Source Code

Similar to Section 508, most violations were found for guideline WCAG 1.1, priority 1, suggesting incorporating text equivalents for every non-text element, including images, graphics, image maps, animations, audio, and video files. Another highly violated guideline was priority 2, WCAG 13.1, where each link's target should be clearly identified. SiteSort identifies the following page as an example of a WCAG 1.1 violation, stating that title attributions should be accompanied with each page: http://www.livejournal.com/search/ (Fig. 6).

Fig. 6. Sample Screenshot of LiveJournal Violation

A view of the source confirms that no title was added to the page (Fig. 7):

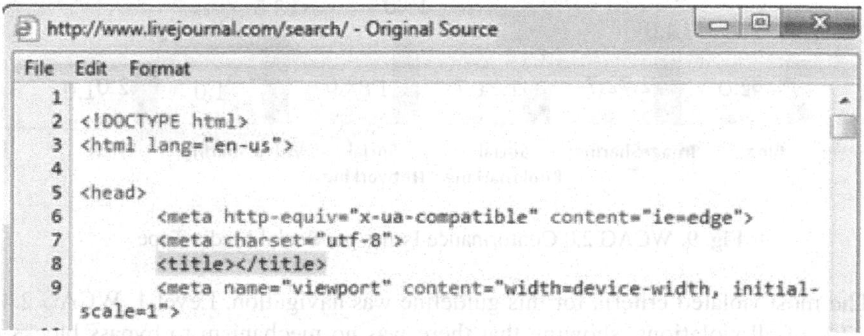

```
http://www.livejournal.com/search/ - Original Source

File   Edit   Format

1
2   <!DOCTYPE html>
3   <html lang="en-us">
4
5   <head>
6          <meta http-equiv="x-ua-compatible" content="ie=edge">
7          <meta charset="utf-8">
8          <title></title>
9          <meta name="viewport" content="width=device-width, initial-
    scale=1">
```

Fig. 7. LiveJournal Source Code

An evaluation of WCAG 2.0 shows similar results. Again, social networking sites and video sharing sites averaged the most number of violations, with the majority of violations from MySpace, YouTube, Facebook, and Flickr , and the least amount found with social bookmarking sites, Delicious and Digg having the least amount of infractions (Fig. 8).

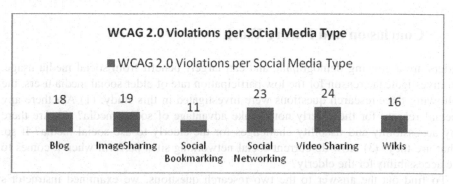

Fig. 8. WCAG 2.0 Violations per Social Media Type

Concerning conformance levels, the social networking sites MySpace and Facebook had the most amounts of level 1 priority violations, with the majority from Facebook and MySpace, in comparison to Blogger and Wiki. For priority level 2, Pinterest and YouTube had 11% of all violations, with the least amount coming from the social bookmarking site Delicious. Flickr and YouTube had the most violations for priority level 3. Overall, social networking sites were the biggest violators of level 1, in comparison to social bookmarking sites (8%). For level 2, video-sharing sites were the biggest offender, followed by wikis and image-sharing sites. Level 3 shows that image-sharing sites had the most violations in contrast to wikis (Fig. 9).

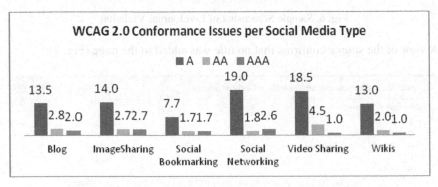

Fig. 9. WCAG 2.0 Conformance Issues per Social Media Type

The most violated criteria for this guideline was navigation. Level 1, WCAG 2.4.1 had 7% of all violations, showing that there was no mechanism to bypass blocks of content that are repeated on other pages. According to the guidelines, there should be a way to skip repetitive links.

The second most violated guidline was priorty 1, WCAG 1.4.4, where content should distinguishable, in particular, text should be able to be resized without assistive technology. The most violated priorty 2 level dealt with predictability, in particular, WCAG 2.0 AA 3.1.2 suggest that content should be readable and understandable.

7   Conclusion and Future Work

Elders are a growing demographic and can largely benefit from social media usage. To investigate the reason for the low participation rate of elder social media users, the following three research questions were investigated in this study: (1) Are there any special reasons for the elderly not to take advantage of social media? (2) Are there any accessibility and usability challenges for the elderly to use social media? If so, what are they? (3) How do current social networking sites perform when it comes to the accessibility for the elderly?

To find out the answer to the two research questions, we examined instructor's notes during the social media discussion in an elderly computer class and a sample social networking site walkthrough exercise. It was noted that many were hindered based on the difficulty of correctly interpreting the page layout and the apprehension of lack of computer skills and computer security. More training on how to use the computer as well as how to interact with the social networking sites is needed to help less experienced users understand the basics.

It is important to note that despite all the issues experienced by the elders, during the class discussion, the majority of students expressed interest in further learning how to use social media. From the class discussion, elder user's motivation in using these types of sites is to stay connected with family and to view family and friend's pictures.

The difficulty in interpreting the page layout led us into the investigation of how well current social media sites are doing when it comes to compliance against accessibility guidelines. We assessed nineteen popular social media sites against Section 508 compliance and WCAG 1.0 and 2.0. Social media usage and elderly computer usage have grown, making it important that these types of sites be usable for this demographic. Although there are many mandates available for the disabled and elderly, this study's results show that many of these highly-used sites do not follow available guidelines and many sites continue to be designed without an evaluation of best practices for those with accessibility issues.

Research show that elder adults already have issues using technology [1], and the violations found in this study could decrease the usability and accessibility of these sites. The websites could improve their websites by adhereing to known guidelines, and correcting issues such as missing labels, titles, headings, and subheadings; providing text-equivalents, identifying all links, creating content that is readable and understandable, and providing pages that can be resized with or without assistive technology.

This paper reported results from a preliminary study on the attempt to help improve the accessibility of the social networking sites. More research using focus groups, usability testing, and other methods of "soliciting unbiased comments" [1] to evaluate usability and accessibility of a website is needed. It is also recommended that the redesigned social media interface should adhere to current mandates and guidelines, paying special attention to criteria regarding text size, layout, and navigation. In addition, it was suggested by the users that to help them be engaged in social media, more classes need to focus strictly on social media. They would also need some type of support while learning how to use these types of sites, as well as verification that their security and privacy would not be compromised.

References

1. Aging statistics (AOA), http://www.aoa.gov/AoARoot/%28S%282ch3qw55k1 qylo45dbihar2u%29%29/Aging_Statistics/index.aspx
2. Alexa.com, http://www.alexa.com/topsites/countries/US
3. Becker, S.: E-government usability for older adults. Communications of the ACM 49, 102–104 (2005)

4. Brossoie, N., Roberto, N., Willis-Walton, S., Reynolds, S.: Report on baby boomers and older adults: Information and service needs. Polytechnic Institute and State University, Center for Gerontology, Blacksburg (2010)
5. Gatto, S., Taka, S.: Computer, internet, and E-mail use among older adults: Benefits and barriers. Educational Gerontology 34, 800–811 (2008)
6. Graf, P., Li, H., McGrener, J.: Technology usability across the adult lifespan. In: HCI, vol. 2 (2005)
7. Hawthorn, D.: Possible implications of aging for interface designers. Interacting with Computers 12(5), 507–528 (2000)
8. HealthyPeople.gov, http://www.healthypeople.gov/2020/topicsobjectives2020/overview.aspx?topicid=31
9. Ke, F., Xie, K.: Toward deep learning for adult students in online courses. The Internet and Higher Education 12, 136–145 (2009)
10. Lerman, K., Jones, L.: Social browsing on Flickr. In: ICWSM (2007); Oblinger, D., Oblinger, J.: Is It Age or IT: First Steps Toward Understanding the Net Generation. EDUCAUSE (2012)
11. Oblinger, D., Oblinger, J.: Is It Age or IT: First Steps Toward Understanding the Net Generation. In: EDUCAUSE (2012)
12. Pew Internet, http://www.pewinternet.org/Reports/2013/Teens-Social-Media-And-Privacy/Main-Report/Part-1.aspx
13. Pew Internet, http://pewinternet.org/Reports/2012/Older-adults-and-internet-use.aspx
14. Pew Internet, http://www.pewinternet.org/Reports/2009/Adults-and-Social-Network-Websites.aspx
15. Saunders, E.: Maximizing computer use among the elderly in rural senior centers. Educational Gerontology 30, 573–585 (2004)
16. Social Security Administration, http://www.socialsecurity.gov/retire2/applying1.htm
17. Wagner, N., Hassanein, K., Head, M.: Computer use by older adults: A multi-disciplinary review. Computers in Human Behavior 26, 870–882 (2010)
18. W3.org, http://www.w3.org/WAI/WCAG20/from10/diff.php

Social Computing—Bridging the Gap between the Social and the Technical

Christoph Beckmann and Tom Gross

Human-Computer Interaction Group, University of Bamberg, Germany
christoph.beckmann@uni-bamberg.de

Abstract. Developing cooperative systems and social media requires taking complex decisions concerning the social interaction to be supported as well as the technical foundation. In this paper we build on the long and successful tradition of design patterns and the social framework of Erving Goffman. We present design patterns that address both challenges of social interaction and technical foundation—they provide input for software developers with respect to structuring software and to providing adequate support for the interaction of users with the environment and with each other.

Keywords: Social Computing, Software Design, Cooperative Systems, Social Media.

1   Introduction

In social computing, systems aim at facilitating communication and cooperation among users who are either at the same location or at different locations. Social media summarises concepts and systems that aim at an active participation of users during an interaction, easy exchange of information, and sophisticated self-presentation [11].

Developing concepts for those systems is a challenging task and has been researched for more than two decades [12] [7]. They often have a strong influence on the structure and flow of the interaction in the group, as Schmidt [18, p. vii] explains: 'the development of computing technologies have from the very beginning been tightly interwoven with the development of cooperative work'. And he [18, p. vii] continues: 'our understanding of the coordinative practices, for which these coordination technologies are being developed, is quite deficient, leaving systems designers and software engineers to base their system designs on rudimentary technologies. The result is that these vitally important systems, though technically sound, typically are experienced as cumbersome, inefficient, rigid, crude'.

Patterns have a long and successful tradition for drafting, for documenting, and for reusing the underlying concepts. Very prominently, Christopher Alexander has suggested and provided design patterns in architecture [2]. He introduced a pattern language to describe solutions that were repeatedly applied to reoccurring challenges in the design of buildings. In software engineering software design patterns have been successfully used for documenting and reusing knowledge and provided a 'way of

G. Meiselwitz (Ed.): SCSM 2014, LNCS 8531, pp. 25–36, 2014.
© Springer International Publishing Switzerland 2014

supporting object-oriented design' [20, p. 422]. With respect to social computing, design patterns can document the knowledge and experience with developing cooperative technology.

All these different types of design patterns provide valuable input for cooperative systems and social media. However, there are also limiting factors: software design patterns primarily help structuring software, and cooperative design patterns are primarily based on the analysis of existing cooperative systems or on some specific ethnographic studies. Therefore, the gap is that the complex task of making both types of patterns compatible is in the hands of software designers and developers.

In this paper we build on the history of patterns and present overarching design patterns for social computing systems. For this purpose we leverage on the works of Erving Goffman who studied social interaction among humans and their use of their technical environment for several decades and derived a framework for social interaction. He uses a metaphor of a performance where everybody is an actor that present her- or himself and acts with others.

In the next section we provide a background of patterns. We then introduce the framework of social interaction of Erving Goffman. We discuss how this framework informs the design of cooperative systems and we derive design patterns for cooperative systems that are modelled in a unified modelling language format for software designers and developers. Finally, we summarise our contribution.

2   Background of Design Pattern

Christopher Alexander et al. [3] were the first to systematically distil patterns from reoccurring solutions to reoccurring problems. In the domain of architecture they identified a language of connected patterns for designing buildings. In this section we introduce patterns related to the design of software in general as well as for cooperative systems and social media in particular that build of Alexander et al.

2.1   Software Design Patterns

Software designers and developers widely use software design patterns. Gamma, Helm, Johnson and Vlissidcs [5] suggested the most notable pattern language for object-oriented software development. They characterise a pattern as a composition of a problem that during the development frequently occurs, a principal solution to the problem, and consequences from applying the solution. Their pattern language includes 23 patterns for classes (i.e., static relationships during compile-time) and objects (i.e., dynamic relationships during run-time) in three categories: creational, structural, and behavioural patterns [21].

Cooperative systems and social media use network-based and distributed software architectures in the background. POSA2 offers a rather technical pattern language addressing the challenges of distributed software architectures especially in the context of object-oriented middleware such as CORBA, COM+, or Jini [17]. It has four categories representing the main challenges of object-oriented middleware: 'Service

Access and Configuration', 'Event Handling', 'Concurrency', and 'Synchronisation'. The description of patterns is extensive and contains precise design implication for the named middleware along verbose source code examples.

While software design patterns are substantial for sustainable software development, they still leave the burden of the complexity of social interactions to software designers and developers of cooperative systems.

2.2   Design Patterns for Cooperative Systems and Social Media

Design patterns for cooperative systems and social media typically focus on human behaviour and interaction. We describe patterns that support designers and developers of cooperative systems and social media.

A pattern language for computer-mediated interaction condenses features and properties of existing cooperative systems [19]. It has three categories: 'community support', 'group support', and 'base technology'. The variety of patterns reaches from simple ones (e.g., the 'login pattern' allows users to interact within a system as individuals with an associated user accounts) to complex ones (e.g., the 'remote field of vision pattern' allows users, which work remotely on shared artefacts to be aware of at which parts others are currently watching at). The description of patterns is very detailed and considers caveats as well as implications for security.

Specific patterns for privacy and sharing provide solutions to problems concerning the quality of use of cooperative systems [4]. They result from field studies, notes, and design sketches that were translated into three patterns: The 'workspace with privacy gradient', the 'combination of personal and shared devices', and the 'drop connector'.

Descriptive patterns have been suggested to allows a better facilitation of the communication in interdisciplinary design teams during the development process [13, 14]. They are comprehensive and express 'generally recurrent phenomena' extracted from ethnographic studies at workplaces. The resulting descriptive pattern language consists of six patterns: 'multiple representations of information', 'artefact as an audit trail', 'use of a public artefact', 'accounting for an unseen artefact', 'working with interruptions', and 'forms of co-located teamwork'. Their patterns are extracted from fieldwork results using two types of properties: 'spatially-oriented features' and 'work-oriented features'. Their patterns can be extended with a 'vignette', which describes real examples as special use cases and provide further design implications.

Despite the fact that patterns for cooperative systems and social media provide detailed insights into practices and requirements of users working together, they mostly lack the dynamic notion of such systems, where users can take advantage of a throughout personalisation of their environment.

3   Goffman's Framework of Social Interaction

We introduce the background and major concepts of Goffman's framework of social interaction that are relevant for designers and developers of cooperative systems.

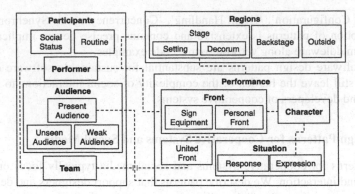

Fig. 1. Major Concepts in Goffman's framework of social interaction

Goffman [6] studied social interaction among humans for several decades and developed a conceptual framework of social interaction among humans in face-to-face situations. It is based on his own observations, on observations of other researchers, and on informal sources. In the following, we describe Goffman's framework in three categories: participants, regions, and performance (cf. Fig. 1).

3.1   Participants

Participants act according to their social status (i.e., socio-economic standing in the society). They present a routine (i.e., a 'pre-established pattern of action which is unfolded during a performance' [6, p. 16]). For Goffman humans follow two types of ideals when interacting with each other: the optimistic ideal of full harmony, which according to Goffman is hard to achieve; and the pragmatic ideal as a projection that should be in accordance with reality and that others can accept—at least temporarily—without showing deep and inner feelings of the self.

In a performance a performer and an audience are involved. A performer defines a situation through a projection of reality as expressions of a character bound to a certain social role in front of an audience. Performers anticipate their audience and continuously adapt their performance according to its responses. Goffman distinguished three audience types. The present audience attends the performance, receives expressions, verifies them according to the projected situation, and responds. The unseen audience is imaginary and used to anticipate a performance. The week audience is real, but not present. It constitutes of other performers giving similar performances. In preparation of a performance, a performer can exchange experiences and responses with the weak audience to improve her own ability to be convincing.

Goffman describes the collaboration of performers as a 'performance team'. Its members ideally fit together as a whole in presenting similar individual performances to amplify a desired projection, or in presenting dissimilar performances that complement to a joint projection.

3.2   Regions

Regions are spatial arrangements used for performances and include specific media for communication as well as boundaries for perception. Goffman names three types of regions: stage, backstage, and outside. A stage provides a setting for the actual performance and is embroidered with decorative properties (i.e., decorum). It supports performers in fostering a situation. Both the performers, as well as the audience can access the stage, having different perspectives. The backstage is a region that performers can access to prepare and evaluate their performance. Also team members suspend backstage. The audience cannot access the backstage. The outside region describes the third type that is neither stage nor backstage. Although it will be excluded from a performance, performers will prepare and use a dedicated front for the outside (e.g., the façade of buildings of a company).

3.3   Performance

For Goffman a performance means social interaction as a finite cycle of expressions to define a situation and of responses as feedback of validity. A performance takes place in a region of type stage. For a performance, each performer prepares a set of fronts, which represents her towards the audience. A front unites material and immaterial parts. Sign equipment is a front's material part and denotes to all properties required to give a convincing performance. The personal front is a front's immaterial part and denotes to certain types of behaviour of a performer (e.g., speech patterns). It combines 'appearance' (i.e., presenting a performer's social status) and 'manner' (i.e., presenting a performer's interactional role).

Characters make the appearance of performers on the stage. A character—as a figure—is composed of a 'front', which is specifically adapted to the audience and performance. In a performance team, the team as whole has a united front (e.g., according to a professional status) and each member has a character with an associated front to invoke during staging. During a performance a character plays routines to convey acceptable and to conceal inacceptable expressions. In a performance team multiple characters will follow this behaviour.

Expressions are information that is communicated by a character using 'sign-vehicles' (i.e., information carriers). There are wanted expressions that are acceptable and foster a situation as a valid projection of reality, and unwanted expressions that are inacceptable and inappropriate for a given performance in front of a particular audience. In order to manifest a performance that is coherent, a performer strives to communicate expressions consistently through their characters towards an audience. Thus a performer's character endeavours to conceal unwanted expressions.

Responses are all kinds of feedback. An audience continuously verifies the performance according to the defined situation and the overall reality as well as to the front of the character. It responds the result to the performer.

In order to manifest a valid performance, performer and audience agree on three principal constructs that prevent a false or doubtful projection of reality based on contradictive expressions or discrediting actions: The 'Working Consensus' is an agreement on the definition of the situation and describes a temporal value system among all participants. The 'Reciprocity' means that performers guise their characters to act according to the situation (i.e., provoke neither intentionally nor factually misunderstandings) and that the audience responds to performance according to the situation (i.e., allege neither consciously nor unconsciously false behaviour). The 'Interactional Modus Vivendi' describes that an individual in the audience only responds to expressions that are important for the individual; the individual in the audience remains silent in things that are only important to others.

Goffman describes additional participants. For instance, the team support, which is one of the following: colleagues that constitute the weak audience, training specialists that build up a desirable performance, service specialists that maintain a performance, confidants that listen to a performer's sins, or renegades that preserve a idealistic moral stand that a performer or team failed to keep. Goffman also defines outsiders as being neither performers nor audience having little or no knowledge of the performance. They can access the type outside region.

4   Informing the Design of Social Computing

In this section we transform Goffman's framework into design patterns. We used three steps. We first identified key statements of Goffman's framework concerning structural aspects (i.e., social entities involved into interactions) and dynamic aspects (i.e., actions of and interactions between social entities). In a second step, we augmented these aspects with literature reviews and lessons learned from conceptualising and developing cooperative systems—especially concerning the transition from physically co-present humans to virtually co-present humans (e.g., [8, 9]). In a third step, we iteratively derived four design patterns for cooperative systems and modelled them in the unified modelling language (UML version 2.4 [16]).

4.1   Structure of Social Computing

The structure of social computing systems refers to entities and their relations as essential ingredients. Our UML class diagrams emphasise entities involved, their compositions, and their dependencies. We use interfaces for modelling general entity behaviour that can be applied to a variety of instances. We use abstract classes for modelling entities that share implementations, and we use standard classes for modelling specific entities.

The first structural pattern we introduce is the *Social Entity Pattern* (cf. Fig. 2). It describes the general setting of people involved in an interaction and their roles. The interface *SocialEntities* refers to humans that are explicitly included in an interaction. A social entity has general knowledge of the world and specific knowledge of particular domains. It relies on *Routines* as 'pre-established pattern of action [...] which may be presented or played...' [6, p. 16]. It conveys information it likes to share with others, and conceals information it likes to hide from others. There are four classes implementing the interface *SocialEntity*: *ActiveIndividuals*, *ActiveTeams*, *PassiveIndividuals*, and *PassiveTeams*.

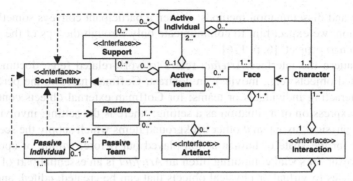

Fig. 2. Social Entity Pattern as UML class diagram

ActiveIndividuals refer to Goffman's performers and are instances of classes with a repertoire of *Faces*. They anticipate the behaviours of others and select as well as fit their faces towards them. An *ActiveTeam* consists of at least two *ActiveIndividuals*: which refers to 'any set of individuals who cooperate in staging a single routine' and '…an emergent team impression arises which can conveniently be treated as a fact in its own right…' [6, p. 79]. Teams have an overall goal. As noted above members of a team can have in individual activity or a shared activity. Since the delegation of an *ActiveTeam's* members can vary from team to team, it is the responsibility of extended classes to implement that behaviour. An *ActiveIndividual* and *ActiveTeam* can rely on their *Support* (i.e., social entities that provide services or feedback).

PassiveIndividuals as an abstract class implements the interface social entity with the ability to observe an action. Further implementations of such passive individuals are the *PassiveTeam*, which refers to the audience that participates in the interaction. About the relationship of active individuals and passive individuals Goffman states: '…the part one individual plays is tailored to the parts played by the others present, and yet these others also constitute the audience' [6, p. xi]. Parallel to the team above a *PassiveTeam* is an aggregation of *PassiveIndividuals*; Goffman writes: 'There will be a team of persons whose activity … in conjunction with available props will constitute the scene from which the performed character's self will emerge, and another team, the audience.' [6, p. 253].

In the pattern a *Face* class lays out the foundation for a distinct configuration of an active individual or team as a prototype to be applied in an interaction. Our notion of a face refers to Goffman's front; it is the 'part of the individual's performance which regularly functions in a general and fixed fashion to define the situation for those who observe the performance' [6, p. 22]. An *ActiveIndividual* can have multiple faces as a repository of communication methods and properties towards passive individuals. Since, in cooperative systems simultaneous interactions are likely, it is important to note that an active individual may have multiple active faces at a time (i.e., a system is required to provide means for the preparation of an interaction as well as means for easy access to the repository of faces to choose from).

A *Character* is a specific configuration of a face. When instantiated in an interaction, an *ActiveIndividual* selects and transforms a face into a *Character* containing information and dissemination methods: 'When a participant conveys something during interaction, we expect him to communicate only through the lips of the character he has chosen to project' [6, p. 176].

In our pattern the interface *Artefact* refers to work-related (e.g., documents) and leisure-related objects (e.g., movies). In contrast, Goffman narrows the performance down to interacting individuals or teams; for Goffman external objects contribute to the overall expression of a situation as a setting: 'there is the setting, involving furniture, decor, physical layout, and other background items which supply the scenery and stage props for the spate of human action played out before, within, or upon it.' [6, p. 22]. However, in social computing often an *Artefact* is an essential part of an interaction. It relates to virtual or physical objects that can be created, edited, and deleted in the course of an interaction.

In a routine, a composition of artefacts that can be involved; in social computing systems this is typically represented as collaborative editing or sharing.

The *Interaction* refers to Goffman's performance. It is a composition of characters of one or more active and one or more passive individuals. It has three phases: in the preparation an active individual sets her role; in the execution a character acts towards passive individuals or a passive team; and in the finalisation an active individual collects responses from its interaction and uses the outcome for further refinements of its faces. A history as set of interactions is important in social computing systems for verifying information and deducing information (i.e., drawing conclusions).

The second structural pattern is the *Region Pattern* (cf. Fig. 3). It maps Goffman's regions into a combination of *Visibility* and *Locality* that can be applied in *Interactions*. Goffman writes: 'A region may be defined as any place that is bounded to some degree by barriers to perception.' [6, p. 106]. As described above, Goffman distinguishes the regions stage, backstage, and outside. However, in our opinion, social computing systems require a more flexible representation that should allow for and contribute to in-between regions.

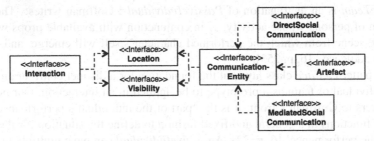

Fig. 3. Region Pattern as UML class diagram

The interface *Visibility* represents filters for types of information and dissemination methods to be applied to interaction with social entities. While active individuals and active teams can access a huge amount of information, passive individuals and passive teams can only access designated information.

The interface *Locality* also refers to filters, but they provide methods as a boundary of real locations (e.g., a display in a shared office space) or virtual locations (e.g. a user's timeline). Combining *Visibility* and *Locality* provides means for sophisticated configurations than the region types proposed by Goffman could cover. The combination reflects individual sharing preferences that also apply during a system's automatic inference of information (i.e., map and reduce). For instance, an interaction can span real and virtual locations at once while communication is still filtered. The filtering can be achieved by matching properties of *CommunicationEntities* (e.g., an *Artefact* as a shared object) towards the properties of passive entities involved into the interaction. Subsequently, we introduce the interfaces *DirectSocialCommunication* and *MediatedSocialCommunication* along their patterns.

4.2   Dynamics of Social Computing

The dynamics of social computing systems refers to the general communication behaviour of humans within the system. The two patterns focus on the interaction between an *ActiveIndividual* and a *PassiveTeam* as the execution of an interaction.

We show two patterns as use cases in UML sequence diagrams. Each diagram shows the entities involved in the execution, and sequences of synchronous and asynchronous calls used in it (please note, we explain an interaction of an individual, for team performances the steps are similar).

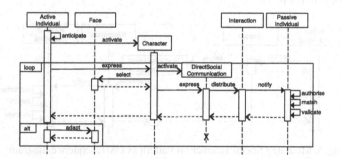

Fig. 4. Direct Social Communication Pattern as UML sequence diagram

The first dynamic pattern is the *Direct Social Interaction Pattern* (cf. Fig. 4). It starts with the path an *ActiveIndividual* executed to setup its *Face* and *Character* and activates a *PassiveIndividual*—summarised as anticipate-call in the diagram. After that, an *ActiveIndividual* instantiates a *Character* object for direct social interaction. According to Goffman, faces are selected and adapted, rather than created; he writes: 'different routines may employ the same front, it is to be noted that a given social front tends to become institutionalised in terms of the abstract stereotyped expectations to which it gives rise, and tends to take on a meaning and stability apart from the specific tasks which happen at the time' [6, p. 27]. This manner of stereotypical selection and adaptation allows *PassiveIndividuals* to recognise familiarity between *Characters* of different *ActiveIndividuals* and thus simplifies the validation process.

The *Character* object creates the *DirectSocialCommunication* object for delivering information. In the loop of direct social communication, a *Character* calls its associated *Face* to obtain valid and appropriate information. It then delegates this information to the *DirectSocialCommunication* object for further distribution in an *Interaction*. Goffman describes direct social interaction as a communication of 'sign-activity'—the transmission of expressions towards the audience relying on 'sign-vehicles'. He distinguishes two 'radically different' types of communication: the given and the given-off [6, p. 2]. In this pattern *DirectSocialCommunication* refers to the type 'given'. It stands for communication in a narrow sense as it consists of verbal or written symbols (i.e., speech and text). All social entities involved in an interaction are familiar with the encoding and decoding these symbols.

The process of delivering *DirectSocialCommunication* occurs frequently in a loop and simultaneously during an interaction, the resulting calls are asynchronous ones. As described previously, a *PassiveIndividual* receives the information and matches its consistency. A *PassiveIndividual* responds accordingly concerning the information's inner validity (e.g., authorisation of sender and contents) as well as regarding previously received ones (e.g., history of the interaction).

An *ActiveIndividual* can emphasise information during sending *DirectSocialCommunication* as it can adapt a *Face* using the responses received—Goffman speaks of governable aspects [6, p. 7].

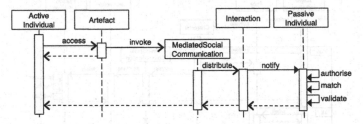

Fig. 5. Mediated Social Interaction Pattern as UML sequence diagram

The second dynamic pattern we introduce is the *Mediated Social Interaction Pattern* (cf. Fig. 5). It reflects the process of accessing an artefact and distributing occurring information of accessing it towards the passive individuals. In cooperative systems and social media applications this type of information is typically used for providing awareness information to the users [10].

MediatedSocialCommunication refers to communication in a broader sense and is related to Goffman's 'given-off'. It consists of a range of behaviours that can hardly controlled or manipulated—Goffman writes of ungovernable aspects and is of 'more theatrical and contextual kind, the non-verbal, presumably unintentional kind, whether this communication be purposely engineered or not.' [6, p. 4]. When accessing an *Artefact* at least one separate object *MediatedSocialCommunication* is created automatically. The *PassiveIndividual* receives information and matches it with previous objects of the type *DirectSocialCommunication* and *MediatedSocialCommunication* and responds accordingly.

5   Discussion and Conclusions

In this paper, we have argued that designers and developers of social computing systems face complex design decisions. To support them, we identified key concepts of Goffman's framework and derived structural and dynamic UML patterns.

Our study of Goffman's framework and the derived patterns relate to some findings of previous work on patterns—corroborating these findings. Our patterns bridge between the artefact-specific patterns of Martin et al. [13, 14] and the collaboration-specific patterns of [19]. The *Social Entity Pattern* represents the typical behaviour of users frequently switching their hats between the two roles of an active individual and a passive individual. The faces they rely on during their performances are diverse in terms of contained information, actions, and reactions. System should address this need for diversity by providing a repository of faces the users can chose from and evolve their characters upon. Yet, our pattern reaches beyond the existing ones, as it allows multiple, persistent, temporal and spatial active characters. The *Region Pattern* addresses the requirement of diverse spaces for preparing, sharing, and acting. Social computing systems should provide these spaces, as users need them for their performance. On the one hand users prepare the interaction using more 'technical standards' in a 'backstage' region where 'the suppressed facts make an appearance.' [6, p. 112]. On the other hand, users interact on 'stage' type regions using more 'expressive standards'. Providing stability of locality and visibility in this pattern is important for preventing users of unmeant disclosures that Goffman calls 'some major forms of performance disruption—unmeant gestures, inopportune intrusions, faux pas, and scenes.' and 'When these flusterings or symptoms of embarrassment become perceived, the reality that is supported by the performance is likely to be further jeopardised and weakened' [6, p. 212]. The *Direct Social Interaction Pattern* and *Mediated Social Interaction Pattern* cope with the performance itself and provide a model for Goffman's two communication types of 'given' and 'given-off'. Users require means of dramaturgical discipline—for instance, the anticipation of the passive individuals—to manage their impression validly. The patterns explicitly inform designers and software engineers of social computing systems to apply the *Region Pattern* in order to consider the hardly to governable type of communication (e.g., when accessing resources within the system or generating meta data). For future work the structural and the dynamic patterns should be applied in the design of social computing systems so their actual benefit for designers and developers in conceptualising and implementing can be measured in empirical studies. Furthermore, Goffman offers detailed descriptions of more social processes (e.g., make work) and best practices (e.g., team collusion) that may supply further patterns towards an extensive language of patterns for social computing systems.

References

1. Alexander, C.: The Timeless Way of Building. Oxford University Press, N.Y. (1979)
2. Alexander, C., Ishikawa, S., Silverstein, M.: A Pattern Language: Towns, Buildings, Construction. Oxford University Press, Oxford (1977)

3. Alexander, C., Isikawa, S., Silverstein, M.: A Pattern Language. Oxford University Press, Oxford (1977)
4. Arvola, M.: Interaction Design Patterns for Computers in Sociable Use. Int. J. of Computer Applications in Technology 25(2/3), 128–139 (2006)
5. Gamma, E., Helm, R., Johnson, R., Vlissides, J.: Design Patterns: Elements of Reusable Object-Oriented Software. Addison-Wesley, Reading (1994)
6. Goffman, E.: The Presentation of Self in Everyday Life. Doubleday Anchor Books, N.Y. (1959)
7. Gross, T.: Supporting Effortless Coordination: 25 Years of Awareness Research. Computer Supported Cooperative Work: The J. of Collaborative Computing 22(4-6), 425–474 (2013)
8. Gross, T., Beckmann, C.: Advanced Publish and Subscribe for Distributed Sensor-Based Infrastructures: The CoLocScribe Cooperative Media Space. In: Proc. of the Seventeenth Conf. on Parallel, Distributed, and Network-Based Processing, PDP 2009, pp. 333–340. IEEE CS Press, Los Alamitos (2009)
9. Gross, T., Oemig, C.: From PRIMI to PRIMIFaces: Technical Concepts for Selective Information Disclosure. In: Proc. of the 32nd Conf. on Software Engineering and Advanced Applications, SEAA 2006, pp. 480–487. IEEE CS Press, Los Alamitos (2006)
10. Gross, T., Stary, C., Totter, A.: User-Centered Awareness in Computer-Supported Cooperative Work-Systems: Structured Embedding of Findings from Social Sciences. Int. J. of Human-Computer Interaction 18(3), 323–360 (2005)
11. Kaplan, A.M., Haenleina, M.: Users of the World, Unite! The Challenges and Opportunities of Social Media. Business Horizons 53(1), 59–68 (2010)
12. Marca, D., Bock, G. (eds.): Groupware: Software for Computer-Supported Cooperative Work. IEEE CS Press, Los Alamitos (1992)
13. Martin, D., Rodden, T., Rouncefield, M., Sommerville, I., Viller, S.: Finding Patterns in the Fieldwork. In: Proc. of the Seventh European Conf. on Computer Supported Cooperative Work, ECSCW 2001, pp. 39–58. Kluwer Academic Publishers, Dortrecht (2001)
14. Martin, D., Rouncefield, M., Sommerville, I.: Applying Patterns of Cooperative Interaction to Work (Re)Design: E-Government and Planning. In: Proc. of the SIGCHI Conf. on Human Factors in Computing Systems, CHI 2002, pp. 235–242. ACM, N.Y. (2002)
15. Martin, D., Sommerville, I.: Patterns of Cooperative Interaction: Linking Ethnomethodology & Design. ACM Trans. on Comp.-Human Interaction 11(1), 59–89 (2004)
16. Object Management Group Inc. Documents Associated With Unified Modelling Language (UML), V2.4 (2011), http://www.omg.org/spec/UML/2.4/ (accessed February 5, 2014)
17. Schmidt, D.C., Stal, M., Rohnert, H., Buschmann, F.: Pattern-Oriented Software Architecture. John Wiley & Sons, Chichester (2000)
18. Schmidt, K.: Cooperative Work and Coordinative Practices - Contributions to the Conceptual Foundations of Computer-Supported Cooperative Work (CSCW). Springer, Heidelberg (2011)
19. Schuemmer, T., Lukosch, S.: Patterns for Computer-Mediated Interaction. John Wiley & Sons, Chichester (2007)
20. Sommerville, I.: Software Engineering 8. Pearson Education Limited, Harlow (2007)
21. Stevens, W.P., Myers, G.J., Contantine, L.L.: Structured Design. IBM Systems J. 13(2), 115–139 (1974)

Taxonomy of Enterprise-Related Mobile Applications

Tobias Brockmann[1], Stefan Stieglitz[1,*], and Christoph Lattemann[2]

[1] University of Muenster, Muenster, Germany
{tobias.brockmann,stefan.stieglitz}@uni-muenster.de
[2] Jacobs University Bremen, Bremen, Germany
c.lattemann@jacobs-university.de

Abstract. The increasing diffusion of mobile devices is changing the working environment and implicating new challenges for enterprises. Mobile applications specifically designed to the enterprises' needs, so-called Enterprise Apps, conquer the market. Enterprise Apps support e.g. enterprise processes to enhance the communication possessing interface to existing enterprise systems, like CRM or ERP. Mobile workers obtain thereby an ideal tool for the accomplishment of their operations in interaction with enterprise system. The applications areas in enterprises throughout Enterprise Apps are complex and widespread. This paper sheds light in the complexity of Enterprise Apps presenting a framework for specific Enterprise Apps. It contributes to research by providing a first approach of a classification scheme to the scenery of Enterprise App usage.

Keywords: Enterprise Apps, Taxonomy, Mobile, Classification.

1 Introduction

On average, each inhabitant of Germany already owns more than one mobile device 17. However, this development is not limited to Germany, smart phones and other mobile devices are widely spread around the world (c. f. table 1). The average penetration and usage rate of mobile devices in major emerging markets, such as Russia, Brazil, China and India and in the developed markets such as United States, Japan, and Germany are between 67 per cent and 130 per cent.

Within the next years the diffusion of mobile devices will further increase worldwide. The traditional feature phone, whose functionality is usually limited to phone calls and short message transmission, is increasingly being replaced by smartphones. Market researchers are forecasting the number of smartphones at one billion in 2016. 350 million smartphone owners will use their devices for business purposes 31. A survey by the University of St. Gallen substantiates this, as 40 percent of respondents state they have used a smartphone for business purposes, and their number is still rising 10.

Consequently, the ubiquitous availability of information due to mobile devices makes employees increasingly independent of their workplace. According to a survey

---

* Corresponding author.

G. Meiselwitz (Ed.): SCSM 2014, LNCS 8531, pp. 37–47, 2014.
© Springer International Publishing Switzerland 2014

Table 1. Average Mobile Device Penetration per Country 19

	Country	Number of Mobile Devices	Population	Percentage	Data exhibited
1	China	916,530,000	1,341,000,000	67.1	July 2011
2	India	858,368,708	1,210,193,422	71.59	July 2011
3	United States	327,577,529	310,866,000	103.9	June 2011
4	Brazil	224,352,712	192 376 496	114.88	Aug. 2011
5	Russia	224,260,000	142,905,200	154.5	July 2011
6	Indonesia	168,264,000	237,556,363	73.1	May 2009
7	Japan	107,490,000	127,370,000	84.1	Mar. 2009
8	Pakistan	108,894,518	171,901,000	65.4	Jun 2011
9	Germany	107,000,000	81,882,342	130.1	Aug. 2009

by BITKOM, 58% of employees prefer flexible working conditions concerning the place of value performance 16. The traditional workplace is becoming less important and an increasing part of the occupational activities occur outside of offices. Enterprises therefore feel the need to attune to these modified conditions and to allow their employees mobile access to enterprise systems 22. CIOs are recognizing this trend. The Gartner CIO Report 2012 states that enterprises now prioritize the adaption of mobile technology and that they are going to invest a large part of their budget in mobile solutions and concepts 23.

Especially the emergence of mobile applications (apps) has created novel applications which enterprises can capitalize on. The survey "Mobile-Web-Watch-2011", released by the consulting company Accenture, proves that 31% of downloaded apps are being used for business purposes. Furthermore, current mobile devices (e.g. smartphones and tablets) have already achieved a high level of maturity concerning their handling and functionalities 24.

Across different platforms, users download apps via so-called app stores and install them on their mobile devices. The amount of applications downloaded is constantly rising. Apple states that in February 2012, 25 billion mobile apps were downloaded via their app store. Nowadays, millions of applications are supporting a huge and complex spectrum of functionalities. The appearance of mobile applications can not only be observed in the private sector. Equally the usage of mobile apps for enterprises shows up an emerging trend. Mobile applications that fulfill the specific needs of an enterprise (e.g. giving access to enterprise information systems) and that are designed to support employees, especially mobile knowledge worker, are understood as "Enterprise Apps". Enterprise Apps exist for various platforms, for various services, and for various business-eco-systems. According to a survey by Research2Guidance, 200,000 enterprise apps were available in consumer app stores in early 2012 29. Their number has doubled since 2011 (Q1) and even there might be a quite large number of enterprise apps in non-public app stores, operated from the enterprise (e.g. SAP Afaria or Appcelerator). Enterprise Apps are promising regarding their ability to increase business values (e.g. increased productivity and higher information flow) on the one hand and to raise the employee's satisfaction on the other hand.

Until now, there hardly exist any research on Enterprise Apps and they have not been classified so far. Therefore, the main research objective of this paper is to define a framework to easily classify the various enterprise applications and to identify use cases for certain contexts. By doing so, we contribute to both the academic discussion and the practical world by providing a framework for other researchers and managers.

In the next chapter the related work is discussed. Based on this, chapter 3 describes the theoretical foundations which are needed to develop a framework for Enterprise Apps. In chapter 4, the framework is presented and different applications scenarios (concepts) are discussed. The article ends with a summary and an outlook on further research.

2   Related Work

The accelerating diffusion of mobile devices, especially of smartphones, have massively influenced business as well as private life 23137 leading to several challenges and opportunities for organizations as well as for employees 1112. Organizations need to manage the transformation into a so-called mobile enterprise 933. The term 'Mobile Enterprise' describes a corporation or large organization that supports business processes by using mobile applications via wireless mobile devices such as smartphones. In this sense, 'Mobile Enterprises' focus on the external utilization with a focal point on marketing and distribution activities as well as on an internal perspective where organizational issues are the focal point of interest 4. Especially the internal perspective can perfectly supported with mobile applications.

Mobile applications (in short: mobile apps) are software applications designed to run on mobile devices such as smart phones and tablet computers. These technologies have come a long way since the opening of the Apple App Store in 2008, especially in its application for business, health, information, communication, and education.

Väätäjä 35 investigated the way mobile devices such as smartphones affect employee's efficiency. She compared the benefits of using mobile devices in everyday work with its costs and asserted that efficiency with regard to the organization (enterprises) is rising. Despite the increase in efficiency in the daily work, she also found that employees are not becoming more satisfied while using Enterprise Apps. Picoto et al. 28 investigated the additional value of mobile applications for enterprises. Supporting mobility is naturally one of the core points of mobile applications. They should help employees in finding assistance to accomplish core objectives and to manage unexpected issues in a flexible and efficient way, like delays or bugs 36.

Key functionalities of Enterprise Apps for mobile workers in terms of time and place are: mobile notifications, a location tracking and navigation system, and mobile, real time assignment of tasks. Furthermore, supporting location-dependent activities (location-based services) potentially generate business values 36. In knowledge-intensive industries, mobile information systems can increase project performance and decrease problem response time 34. By providing information ubiquitously, problems could be identified ans even solved faster than with traditional means for exchanging information.

Bosch 5 suggests that software product integration across enterprise boundaries, e.g. along the supply chain, can improve efficiency. For example, using mobile GPS or RFID modules could establish new perspectives for the interaction of enterprises along their supply chains 15. Moreover, Hislop and Axtell 14 find that mobile devices can be used for managing the work/leisure boundary. They allow employees to organize labor hours individually. Mobile devices can facilitate work outside offices and independent of traditional labor hours to allow personal space at different times. According to boundary theory, they establish the boundary depending on individual interests. Using mobile devices does not only incorporate work topics into the employees' leisure time; rather, the reverse was also observed. In their survey of mobile service engineers, Hislop and Axtell 14 describe that the mobile phone was also used for non-work-related communication during labor time.

Nah et al. 25 characterize business value as profit and cost differences arisen out of the integration of mobile applications when compared to not using them at all. Stieglitz and Brockmann 33 suggested a model that explains how mobile services create business values in enterprises. Their approach describes how private and enterprise mobile IT expenditures could successfully be transformed into overall organizational performance by focusing on the internal perspective of mobile IT usage. A much larger amount of literature focuses on business values that might be created by m-commerce apps 16. M-commerce apps clearly differ from e-commerce apps in consideration of devices and user expectations. Existing e-commerce solutions often consider consumers only as passive receivers of information. To appeal to users with an m-commerce solution, existing e-commerce offers should not only be extended technically onto mobile devices. Moreover users of mobile devices also expect applications to provide individualized subjects and services with a high usability 8. The major advantages of m-commerce, compared to e-commerce, result from the main features of mobile devices, such as ubiquity, comfort, localization, technical advantages and personalization 8.

Kim and Hwang 18 conducted a survey and identified trust and security aspects as the most important factors of success of m-commerce applications. They further mention mobility, devices, quality of subjects, and comprehensibility as relevant parameters. Frequently, m-commerce applications are only noticed in the communication between enterprises and customers (B2C), but additional values are subsumed under the term m-commerce by the communication within enterprises (B2E) and between associate partners. Furthermore, Enterprise Apps can not only be used for exchanging information but to actively support collaboration. Open innovation approaches 7 can now be supported in a mobile and faster way. Customer integration and co-creation approaches 21 are not stationary anymore. E.g. prototypes can now be tested, evaluated and enhanced real-time in a real world setting. Experts are now reachable 24/7 and community members can operate from a mobile device.

Many enterprises begin to develop their own mobile applications which are adapted to their individual needs. By doing so, enterprises aim on facilitating employees' everyday work and enhance their productivity 13. Furthermore enterprises begin to distribute their own apps, via enterprise app stores, which are often part of a mobile device management strategy.

3   Theoretical Background – Developing a Taxonomy

Nickerson et al. 26 suggested a process model for taxonomy development that is based on Bailey's 3 approach, which is called "A Three-Level Measurement Model". According to Nickerson et al. 26, this model is especially useful in the field of information systems for generating taxonomies. Nickerson et al. define a taxonomy T as a set of n dimensions D_i ($i=1,\cdots$, n), each of which consists of k_i ($k_i \geq 2$) characteristics C_{ij} ($j=1, \cdots$, k_i). Additionally, they found that one object has to have exactly one characteristic per dimension, which means that the characteristics have to fulfill the requirements of being mutually exclusive and collectively exhaustive.

A first step that has to be accomplished even before the actual beginning of the taxonomy development starts is the definition of the so-called meta-characteristic. It has to be chosen which function the taxonomy is supposed to cope with. The meta-characteristic therefore represents the basis for the further classification 26. After determining the meta-characteristic, the actual taxonomy is developed via a three-level, iterative process.

The first level of the process model consists of three consecutive sub-steps. Initially, the researcher determines the subset of objects to be analyzed. This subset is usually comparatively delimited and can be identified throughout a literature analysis. Afterwards, distinct features were identified with which the objects can be characterized and differentiated. In the last step of the first level, the identified features are analyzed and appropriate dimensions and characteristics are deduced so that a first concept of the taxonomy is already generated. The entire first level is described as "empirical-to-deductive" because empirical data constitutes the basis of the analysis and are subsequently transformed into dimensions and characteristics by the researcher 26.

The second level is based on the opposite approach and is therefore called "deductive-to-empirical". In the first step of this level, the researcher analyzes his first concept of the taxonomy and aims to deduce new dimensions and characteristics that could not be identified yet because of the comparatively small amount of analyzed objects, but could be relevant according to the determined meta-characteristic. Furthermore, it is possible that not only new dimensions and characteristics are added, but also existing ones modified or combined. Afterwards, the usefulness of these conceptual changes is inspected empirically via devices to be analyzed. On basis of the results of this inspection, a revised version of the taxonomy is established in the last step of the second level 26.

As the process model follows an iterative approach, it is possible (necessary) to return to the first step of the first or second level and hence to develop revised versions of the taxonomy until the result fulfills the criteria of the meta-characteristic and the requirements of a taxonomy. Nickerson et al. 26, however, list several requirements that a useful taxonomy should fulfill. On the one hand, the number of dimensions and characteristics should not be too high as the taxonomy may become unnecessarily complicated and less comprehensible. On the other hand, it should not be too low, so that the taxonomy adequately expresses the differences between the analyzed objects.

Moreover, a useful taxonomy provides the opportunity to allow all objects of the research field to be classified. The taxonomy should be expandable in dimensions and characteristics, so that new items with new features can also be categorized if necessary 26.

The third level of this process model corresponds to the time after the taxonomy development phase and is described as "using taxonomy". After the classification of the investigated objects on basis of their features, it is useful to search for so-called "missing items", which means seeking combinations of characteristics within different dimensions to which no analyzed items can be assigned 26. This paper follows the process model for the development of a taxonomy suggested by Nickerson et al. 26 to classify Enterprise Apps.

4   Framework for Enterprise Apps for Enterprise-Internal Activities

Following the taxonomy development process by Nickerson et al. 26, the literature was first analyzed to find existing categories (meta-characteristic) for the classification of Enterprise Apps. For the review of articles, a period of ten years was defined, and only peer-reviewed IS journals with a strong emphasis on empirical research (for a further discussion on the categories of research in IS see 30) from 2002 to 2012 were considered. The index of information systems journals shows 731 active journals. As quality differs significantly between journals, the search was limited to ten well known IS- and IT-journals (MIS Quarterly, Information Systems Research, Communication of the ACM, Management Science, Journal of Management Information Systems, Artificial Intelligence, Decision Sciences, Harvard Business Review, IEEE Transactions and AI Magazine). Search criteria were, e.g., "apps", "mobile", "business" and "enterprise". Thus, 61 potentially interesting articles were identified.

To identify relevant literature we developed the following definition of Enterprise Apps. "Enterprise Apps support the daily work of mobile worker, whilst offering access to existing enterprise systems or supporting communication and collaboration among the employees".

Based on the literature review we identified a helpful approach categorizing mobile services according to their provided user experience [27]. According to Nysveen et al. mobile apps support user interacts among humans (via a communication medium) or among humans and machines (via interfaces) 27. Huang et al. extended Nysveen et al.'s framework, they identified four unique mobile application services.

- *Mobile Information Services:* Applications supporting users with information. The context of the communication is used to personalize information as much as possible. An example of a goal-oriented information service is a mobile application that connects users with the customer service of an enterprise to solve problems and answer upcoming questions.
- *Mobile Communication Services:* Communication applications of every description, from simple chat or videoconference applications up to ubiquitous communication. Most current experience-oriented communication services are applications of big social networks.
- *Mobile Transaction Services:* Applications for the goal-oriented accomplishment of transactions, especially of finances and other items, services and values.
- *Mobile Interaction Services:* Entertainment applications with video or audio contents as well as games in which users interact with the game themselves.

Nysveen et al.'s 27 and Huang et al.'s 15 works build the basis to define a taxonomy to classify Enterprise Apps (c.f. table 2).

Table 2. Framework for Classifying Enterprise Apps for Enterprise-Internal Activities

Application Area (according to Nysveen, 2005)	Employee 2 Employee (E2E)	Employees 2 Machine (E2M)
Information and Knowledge	**Cluster I – Information Sharing** e.g. Internal Knowledge Management, Context Support, Information Management	**Cluster II- Knowledge Management** e.g. Business Intelligence, Big Data
Transaction and Processes	**Cluster III – Process Support** e.g. Work Flow Management, Ad hoc Process Management, Social BPM	**Cluster IV – Process Management** e.g. Work Flow Management, BPM, Complex Event Processing
Communication	**Cluster V – Communication** e.g. Unified Communication	**Cluster VI – Epistemic Logic** e.g. (Multi-)Agent Systems
Interaction and Collaboration	**Cluster VII – Collaboration** e.g. CSCW, Co-Creation, Social Collaboration	**Cluster VIII - Smart Agents** e.g. Search, Prediction and Analysis (Social Media Analytics), Artificial Intelligence

This framework defines eight distinctive clusters of Enterprise Apps. Generally Enterprise Apps can be differentiated between apps which mediate among employees (E2E) or between employees and machines (E2M). In line with Nysveen et al.'s (2005) concept of mobile applications, - which serve for both before mentioned relationships - the following four purposes of Enterprise Apps could be identified: (1) information and knowledge, (2) transaction and processes, (3) communication, and (4) interaction and collaboration.

In cluster I Enterprise Apps are located which provide information and knowledge services for individuals or for the exchange of knowledge and information among employees. Cluster II consists of Enterprise Apps which enable employees to store, manipulate or analyze data, hence for business intelligence and in the context of big data. Enterprise Apps in cluster III support transactions and processes between employees, e.g. workflow management, ad-hoc process management and business process managements. Mobile apps serve as a medium, not as for transactions, not a medium to transact with. Cluster IV comprises Enterprise Apps which support employees in the workflow management, business process management or complex event processing by providing access to databases and CPU capacities. Cluster V and VI support communication services between employees as well as between employees and computers. Unified communication services and agent systems are well-known concepts which fit into these two clusters. Cluster VII covers mobile enterprise tools for the interaction and collaboration among employees in a company. Known concepts are co-creation and computer supported collaboration cooperative work tools as well as social media applications [38, 39]. Applications in Cluster VIII provide employees with intelligent user interfaces for an effective human-computer interaction. Intelligent search and prediction algorithms are needed. Well-known concepts are Social Media Analytics or Artificial Intelligence [39].

However, it is immediately obvious that concepts involving third parties like supplier or customers for e.g. supply chain management and or more advanced concepts such as open innovation and customer integration cannot be positioned in this framework. This is due to the given, narrow definition of Enterprise Apps (Enterprise Apps support the daily work of mobile worker, whilst offering access to existing enterprise systems or supporting communication and collaboration among the employees). Expanding the definition to Business-to-Business (B2B) and Business-to-Customer (B2C) activities would enable to include the above-mentioned concepts. As this is a first step towards a framework the focus should lie on the support of enterprise-internal work support.

5   Conclusion

The presented framework supports the classification of Enterprise Apps. Build up on the framework of Nysveen et al. 27 the categories information and knowledge, transaction and processes, communication, and interaction and collaboration could be derived. We defined Enterprise Apps as apps who are only used internal in an enterprise and that the must have an interface to existing enterprise systems. Due to this the developed framework finally consists of two dimensions. First the interaction among employees (E2E) and the interaction of employees with machines (E2M).

Generally the framework of Enterprise Apps consists of apps providing mobile access to enterprise systems and able the interaction among colleagues and to access all needed information, as well as to share information. Mobile access and activities might include managing documents, connecting to the enterprise resource planning system (ERP), accessing enterprise communications systems and social business software. Furthermore enterprise apps support workflows e.g. approval processes or the interaction with intelligence enterprise systems.

An integration mobile application into an enterprise's processes and communication is not always expedient and can also imply disadvantages 32. This may cause by problems in case of application failure, network outage, or software bugs. Moreover, it may be more difficult to accomplish changes in enterprise processes with integrated mobile applications because in order to modify a process, the application needs to be changed as well. Additionally, the use of the Enterprise Apps has to be consistent with enterprise security policies and with data protection regulations. Otherwise, the generated business value will easily turn into business damage. Furthermore, Legner et al. 20 state that a major part of research is concerned with the concept and design of mobile business application, whereas the research of their effectiveness and efficiency for the user has not been examined enough so far.

This paper aims on closing a research gap which has arisen through the rise of mobile applications in the last two years. To the author's knowledge, no research had previously been done to categorize Enterprise Apps in the narrow definition of internal usage and an existing interface to enterprise systems. Furthermore a common understanding about the suitable domains for Enterprise Apps is missing. A common framework is needed to come up with a shared understanding and to enable an effective utilization of Enterprise Apps in practice and to build the basis for profound research. The suggested framework is a first step towards classifying mobile enterprise applications. Moreover professionals are provided with a framework to classify mobile applications.

However, the framework still needs to be validated. This could be operationalized by analyzing mobile applications listed in the iTunes or Google Play Store considering only those apps categorized as "business applications" or "productivity applications". Furthermore, it might be helpful to gather information about the distribution of apps among the identified clusters. One research question could be to figure out, if currently mostly "simple" mobile apps are offered more frequently as complex applications (e.g. those of clusters II, VII, and VIII). More research needs to be done in the field of B2B and B2C applications. Moreover it could be investigated whether the use of mobile applications in specific sectors can lead to other dimensions.

References

1. Abdelnasser, A., Hesham, A.: On Incorporating QoS Parameters in M-commerce Applications. In: Proceedings of the 12th Americas Conference on Information Systems, Acapulco (2006)
2. Ahuja, M., Chudoba, K., George, J., McKnight, H., Kacmar, C.: IT Road Warriors: Balancing work-family conflict, job autonomy, and work overload to mitigate turnover intentions. Management Information Systems Quarterly 31(1), 1–17 (2007)
3. Bailey, K.D.: Methods of social research. Free Press, New York (1994)
4. Basole, R.C.: The Emergence of the Mobile Enterprise: A Value-Driven Perspective. In: Proceedings of the Sixth International Conference on the Management of Mobile Business, Toronto (2007)
5. Bosch, J.: Service Orientation in the Enterprise. Computer 40(11), 51–56 (2007)

6. Chau, T., Leung, F., Tang, H., Liao, S.: A Context Information Center for M-commerce Applications. In: Proceedings of the 7th Pacific Asia Conference on Information Systems, Adelaide (2003)
7. Chesbrough, H.W.: The Era of Open Innovation. Sloan Management Review 44(3), 35–41 (2003)
8. Clarke, I.: Emerging Value Propositions for M-commerce. Journal of Business Strategies 18(2), 41–57 (2001)
9. Dery, K., MacCormick, J.: The CIO's management of mobile technology: the shift from mobility to connectivity for executives. MIS Quarterly Executive 11(4), 159–175 (2012)
10. DMI: Smartphones motivate employees. Mobile Business Life, 1–3 (2012)
11. Golden, A.G., Geisler, C.: Work-life boundary management and the personal digital assistant. Human Relations 60(3), 519–551 (2007)
12. Harris, J., Ives, B., Junglas, I.: IT-Consumerization: When Gadgets Turn Into Enterprise IT Tools. MIS Quarterly Executive 11(3) (2012)
13. Hess, B., Sutanto, J., Ameling, M., von Reischach, F.: A Business-to-Business Perspective on Mobile Application Stores. In: Proceedings of the 2012 International Conference on Mobile Business (2012)
14. Hislop, D., Axtell, C.: Mobile phones during work and non-work time: A case study of mobile, non-managerial workers. Information and Organization 21(1), 41–56 (2011)
15. Huang, H., Liu, L., Wang, J.: Diffusion of Mobile Commerce Application in the market. In: Proceedings of the Second International Conference on Innovative Computing, Information and Control (2007)
16. Huth, N.: Netsociety. BITKOM, Berlin (2011)
17. Kaplan, A.M.: If you love something, let it go mobile: Mobile marketing and mobile social media 4x4. Business Horizons 55(2), 129–139 (2012)
18. Kim, J., Hwang, C.: Applying the analytic hierarchy process to the evaluation of customer-oriented success factors in mobile commerce. In: Proceedings of ICSSSM 2005, 2005 International Conference on Services Systems and Services Management (2005)
19. Lattemann, C., Khaddage, F.: A Review of the Current Status of Mobile Apps in Education. In: Alon, I., Jones, V., McIntyre, J.R. (Hrsg.) Innovation in Business Education in Emerging Countries. McMillan-Palgrave (2013)
20. Legner, C., Nolte, C., Urbach, N.: Evaluating Mobile Business Applications in Service and maintenance Processes: Results of A Quantitative-empirical study. In: Proceedings of the 19th European Conference on Information Systems, Helsinki (2011)
21. Lerner, J., Tirole, J.: The Simple Economics of Open Source. The National Bureau of Economic Research, Cambridge (2000)
22. Lünendonk, T.: Themendossier: Mobile Enterprise Erfolgsfaktor Grenzenlosigkeit. Lünendonk GmbH, Kaufbeuren (2011)
23. McDonald, M.P., Aron, D.: Amplifying the Enterprise: 2012 CIO Agenda. Gartner (2012)
24. Mohr, N., Sauthof-Bloch, A.K., Alt, M., Derksen, J.: Mobile Web Watch 2011. Accenture (2011)
25. Nah, F.F., Siau, K., Sheng, H.: The value of mobile applications: a utility company study. Communications of the ACM 48(2), 85–90 (2005)
26. Nickerson, R.C., Varshney, U., Muntermann, J., Isaac, H.: Taxonomy development in Informations Systems: Developing a Taxonomy of Mobile Applications. In: Proceedings of the 17th European Conference on Information Systems (2009)
27. Nysveen, H., Pedersen, P.E., Thorbjørnsen, H.: Intentions to Use Mobile Services: Antecedents and Cross-Service Comparisons. Journal of the Academy of Marketing Science 33(3), 330–346 (2005)

28. Picoto, W., Palma-dos-Reis, A., Bélanger, F.: How Does Mobile Business Create Value for Firms? In: Ninth International Conference on Mobile Business/2010 Ninth Global Mobility Roundtable, Athen (2010)
29. Research2Guidance: The Enterprise Mobile App Market Status Report (2012)
30. Rowe, F.: Toward a richer diversity of genres in information systems research: new categorization and guidelines. European Journal on Information System 21(5), 469–478 (2012)
31. Schadler, T., McCarthy, J.C.: Mobile Is The New Face of Engagement – CIOs Must Plan Now for New Systems of Engagement. Forrester Research (2012)
32. Seo, D., La Paz, A.I.: Exploring the Dark Side of IS in Achieving Organizational Agility. Communications of the ACM 51(11), 136–139 (2008)
33. Stieglitz, S., Brockmann, T.: Increasing Organizational Performance by Transforming into a Mobile Enterprise. MIS Quarterly Executive 11(4), 189–204 (2012)
34. Šuman, N., Pšunder, M.: Mobile Computing Changing the Traditional Ways of Organizing the Construction Company. American Journal of Applied Sciences 5(1), 42–47 (2007)
35. Väätäjä, H.: Mobile Work Efficiency – Balancing between Benefits, Costs and Sacrifices. In: CHI 2011, Vancouver (2011)
36. Yuan, Y., Archer, N., Connelly, C.E., Zheng, W.: Identifying the ideal fit between mobile work and mobile work support. Information & Management 47(3), 125–137 (2010)
37. Willis, D.A.: Bring Your Own Device: New Opportunities, New Challenges, Gartner (2012)
38. Schneider, A.M., Stieglitz, S., Lattemann, C.: Social Software as an Instrument of CSR. In: Transparency, Information and Communication Technology, pp. 124–138. Philosophy Documentation Center, Virginia (2007)
39. Stieglitz, S., Dang-Xuan, L., Bruns, A., Neuberger, C.: Social Media Analytics: An Interdisciplinary Approach and Its Implications for Information Systems. Business and Information Systems Engineering (2014)

Representing Students Curriculum in Social Networks

Habib M. Fardoun[1], Abdullah Albarakati[1], and Antonio Paules Ciprés[2]

[1] King Abdulaziz University, Faculty of Computing and Information Technology,
Information Systems Department,
21589Jeddah, Saudi Arabia
{hfardoun,aalbarakati}@kau.edu.sa
[2] European University of Madrid
Madrid, Spain
apcipres@gmail.com

Abstract. In this paper we are going to use social network for education, focusing the work on the curriculum. To achieve this we need both to work with the curricular structure and a system that let us work with curricular objects. The systems located at the Cloud allow the interaction and combination of different platforms, but we haven't found any social network exclusively defined with the curriculum and which allows the programmed work by the teacher in the session. A structured system like this divides the problem and creates a research line focused on the edition of contents at the Cloud in the shared space.

Keywords: Educative systems, social networks, cloud computing, Web Services, systems architecture, Students Curriculum, Educative Curricula.

1   Introduction

In this paper we are going to capture our idea of design and evaluation in educational methodologies using social networks. Nowadays there are a lot of social networks, either oriented to conventional users or specific to the use by teachers [1] [2] [3]. These social networks are mainly related to share experiences and materials among teachers, without any curricular structure. We can find two well-differenced uses for social networks. In one side we have the social networks for the exploitation of the storage for sharing materials and the distribution of them, and in the other side we have a meeting place between students and teachers where class activities are completed, generally done by mean the Master class method. Currently, the social networks provide a meeting point to exchange experiences.

In previous papers we proposed a curricular structure at the Cloud for educational centres [4] [5], so that it is time to move this curricular system at the Cloud to a curricular system available from social networks. At this start point we have to take into consideration two necessary things for a system of these characteristics: the curriculum and the relation with the authors inside of the system. We want to say with this that the structure of the social network must obey the normative of the scholar organization and the curriculum must be the base of the social network organization.

G. Meiselwitz (Ed.): SCSM 2014, LNCS 8531, pp. 48–58, 2014.

In the future and in other investigations, we will have to keep in mind the researches about interaction and adaptation to the different methodologies, themes in which we also have done previous works.

We are thinking on making a curricular social network, where the teacher's curriculum and the curriculum taught at the class are the central concept of the social network. In this case our beginning point is to create a curricular system at the Cloud to be the social network. The contents' classification of this social network will be agreed with the tags of the curricular classification. As we know the use of social networks in educational environments has well defined limits. For example, in the practical sessions of this study case, primary teachers use the social networks with the target of that students make their expositions to the group at class.

2   State of Art

There are social networks to give services into the human personal relations and into the relations between actors for the exchange of information and products. One of our main goals is to take the curricular structure of the teachers' plan, but we haven't found any social network with those characteristics, therefore the interaction place will be the Cloud.

Due to we have token the curricular structure as one of our goals, we have to take into consideration its structure. It must contain:

- Objectives: Followed by the official curriculum of the academic course, cycle and phase. [7]
- Contents: Contextualization of the concepts that the student has to acquire. [8]
- Evaluation criteria: The consecution level of the targets in the contents understanding. [9]

What it allows:

- Attention to the diversity of procedures with the target of to favour the integration and to reinforce the cooperative work among students. [10].
- To reinforce the principles of the cooperative work, integration and assistance [11].

In addition, we must to take into consideration that:

- The goals must collect the proposals that have been agreed in the educational project of the centre.
- To foresee the diversity of procedures, to favour the interaction and to reinforce the cooperative aspects and the mutual support between students.
- Keeping in mind that the methodology must take care of the activity and the student's role. [13]

As we can see, there isn't any social network that deals with the basic elements of the curriculum, defined from the different educative laws of the countries. On the other hand, we find multitude of web pages and educational platforms oriented to the e-learning, which only let us the distribution of materials and the use of the classic elements of the Web 2.0 and Web 3.0, without take into consideration the central axis of the educational system, the curriculum.

3   System Needs and Definition

Once that we have seen, in the state of art, the necessities of making a social network following the elements of the curriculum, we pass to determine the definition of social network to educational environments. At the following diagram we can observe the organization of the social network and from where the data is taken, because in the educational systems everything starts from the curriculum, the structure of the educational centre and the current legislation.

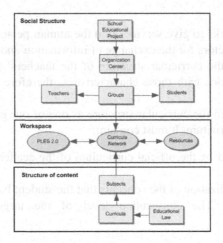

Fig. 1. Parts of the social network

At the previous diagram, we establish how the social network is divided:

- The social structure of the network from the school educational project, the organization of the centre and the groups of teachers and students that belong to that specific school, they give to the social network the social relations determined inside of the educational environment and in a predetermined form. The actions that users make inside of the social structure are associated to the scholar organization and to the administrative interaction of the users, in other words, at this point the interaction between users is done from a non educational point of view. This means that the privacy and data control must be maximum. This is related with the e-government structure that we can find in the states.
- The users' workspace is formed by PLES: personal environments of learning, resources and the curricular network that is the place where users interact and

where takes place the interaction environment formed by User Interfaces distributed in Cloud environments [14]. At this point, the didactical methodologies given by the teacher is where users' interaction is carried out at the different parts of this Cloud.

— Students interact between them and with the teacher, making their activities follow the necessary methodologies offered by the teacher.
— Teachers interact with students and with the other teachers of the group for exchanging students' information.
— The evaluation process is an interaction of the social network evaluation objects, which corresponds with each student and will measure the teaching-learning process.
— The resources are provided by the public administration and the external entities with the target of keeping them updated. In addition, we find the possibility of teachers share their experiences with other teachers.

• The content's structure, from the curriculum, is related to the system's information and the curricular program is the central axis of the teacher's work. From those concepts we take the structure [5]. At this point the system makes constant checks of the curriculums and adapts the legislative changes of them and of the social network contents.

With the goal of clarify the structure of this complex social network, not for the number of users but by its interaction model and by the relation with the rest of entities, we make a IGU diagram where users make their work and where we can see the interface scheme like information flows.

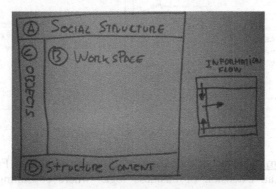

Fig. 2. IGU Curricula Network and Information Flow

As we can see in the IGU, we can find four well-differenced parts, which we organize in different sections of the social network definition. The navigation of these parts condition the objects to insert at the workspace and the interaction of them that will give complete freedom both to the teacher and to the student for making their activities and for the communication among them.

These parts of the social network interact in a work environment. In this work environment we add an extension to the Cloud system for updating it to be a space in the Cloud with all the things that brings with it. Thus, space objects interact in the Cloud from any place and any device, keeping them always synchronized.

Cloud systems are divided in the following categories:

- Software as a Service (SaaS).
- Utility Computing, Web Services, Platform as a Service (PaaS).
- Internet Integration.

As we can observe with these categories, the Cloud system provides the necessary services but in our specific case we miss a service dedicated to the workspace, where the network elements can be edited and stored by the users. This edition service (Software for Edition Integration SEI), is one of the fundamental elements of the social network because it is the workspace where the objects are added and where the daily work is produced by the system's users. Here the objects are added and kept into Cloud containers cached for students can work from their home without internet connection. We can say that this is an storage environment similar to DropBox, where the students work and update their files at the moment of getting internet connection. These containers have the interaction business logic and they don't need a direct connection with the Cloud system because the objects must work in an isolated form.

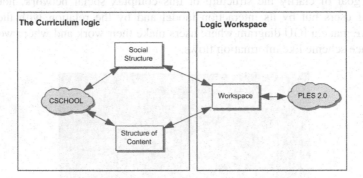

Fig. 3. Curriculum logic and Workspace Logic

- **The curriculum logic** is an extension of the business logic. For us, curricular operations are an extension of business logic, where consulting operations are performed and the insertion of elements from the teacher's plan. In addition, the teacher stores the curricular elements to work with the information at the Cloud (PLES 2.0).
- **The workspace logic** is an extension of the presentation logic. Once the curricular elements are combined, they allow to students and teachers make their daily work independently of where they are because this makes all the interaction and contains the necessary to make the work.

4   System Architecture

For a network of these characteristics, we need flexibility in this architecture and also that it allows the integration. For that reason we think that Cloud systems are the place where we needed to locate the system. At the following diagram we show the different parts of the architecture. The curricular elements depend of the structure and of the curricular organization. At the same time, we structure the elements of the teacher curricular program.

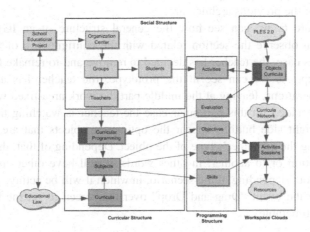

Fig. 4. How it works

At the previous Figure 4, we describe how the architecture is and how it works. Below we explain each one of its parts:

- The Social structure provides the services to configure the system and the data of the educational centre from the management platforms installed on them. Those elements are the organization in groups, teachers, students and timetable.
- The curricular structure. Each teacher generates the curricular program in the server. It contains, default implemented thanks to social structure, the subject given by the teacher at the courses and the students. As we can see the subjects are divided in others, which follow the curricular structure provided by the educative law. These subjects contain: Competences, objectives and contents. With all these elements, teachers generate activities to make at the work sessions and through the curricular objects they pass to students that make the curricular activities for their evaluation.

Each one works independently and we need a workspace where the objects can interact, the students load their activities and the teachers evaluate them with the target of measuring the consecution of their goals. For the communication of all these parts we use web services and RPCs. The curricular objects are activities represented as objects in the presentation logic, how it works and the resolution of the problems proposed are represented in the business logic. The communication and synchronization of the object is made by a data mapping between this object and the object stored in an object oriented data base.

5   Case Study

In this study case we are going to show, through the screen captures, the different structure parts of the previous architecture.

First, in Figure 6, we can see how the general structure of an IGU is and, in addition, we can observe the section related with the configuration of the teacher's timetable. In this case, the teacher has decided to remove and to remake the timetable of the 2B group. As we can see at the prototype, the teacher has access to the conventional operations, leaving at the middle part the work area fixed where the left side objects are added. In this particular case the teacher is watching the beginning screen. In the right side buttons appear the options or objects that are going to be added identifying the container's type of the object. Depending of that, the object will adapt to a situation or to another, in other words, it will have other content with a different behaviour depending of the scenario, in which it will be acting.   In our case, it is performing the event "Drag and Drop" over the screen to set the Mathematics subject into the timetable.

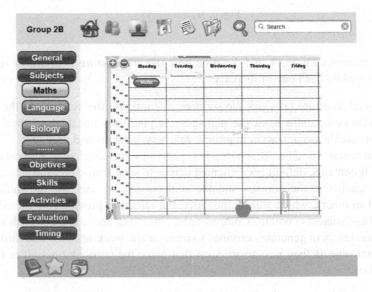

Fig. 5. General structure of the application

Below we are going to describe the interface buttons of the topside and of the bottom side because the buttons of the right side are easy to understand.

Table 1. Buttons of the application

	The teacher will be able to access to the start of the application (main screen).
	Option with which the teachers will be able to search students' data of their classes and to access to their notebooks.
	Hard disk at the Cloud where the teacher s can store their data, files...
	It gives access to the scholar calendar and timetable.
	It gives access to the teacher's program that s/he has opened in the centre.
	This option allows the edition of the screen objects. The activities can be done by other teachers and this one can have access to edit them.
	Advanced search. Through the selected profiles it will search the objects into the system. The simplified search option represented by a text box looks for objects that are shown at the screen.
	It accesses to the section related with the educative legislation and the centre's normative. The teacher can access to repositories of educative information.
	The teacher will have access to the predefined programs for that educative level. These ones can be modified by the teacher and the temporization is already made for this scholar course.
	The teacher accesses to a bank of resources, built by mean of the objectives and basic competences. Thus, s/he can add to the program activities, which are necessary for the goals consecution.

With these objects the teacher composes the educative objects for the didactic units, as we can see in this use case. The teacher selects the didactic unit associated with the adverb, which s/he has predefined, at the right side of the screen, a set of options to complete the task. Finally the teacher selects that s/he wants to add to make that activity.

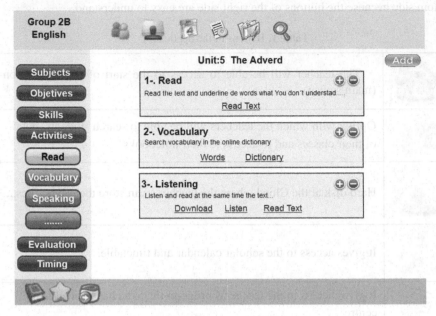

Fig. 6. Creating activities

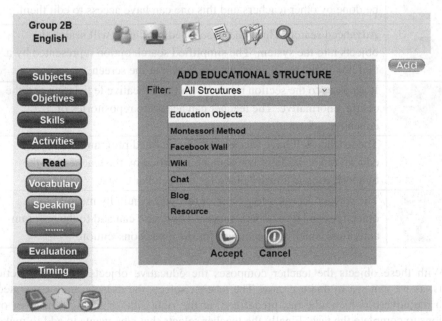

Fig. 7. Adding elements

At the previous figure we see how the teacher can select among different models with the purpose of using every possibility that exists and to include the exercises dynamically. A system of these characteristics allows including new educative models from the server.

6   Conclusions and Future Work

In this paper we have done an approximation to how to work with the social networks from the curricular point of view. Nowadays the social networks are understood as relations of interaction among users through contents. We now extend that definition to the following proposal:

The educative social network can be understood as a curricular relation among users where the contents have educative character.

This is clear but to a system of these characteristics we have to think in adding to it a shared workspace where teachers and students interact in the curricular activities. As we can see, we always keep in mind the curricular activities because the final goal of the teacher's work is to evaluate the consecution level of the objectives.

From a curricular social network we can plan the increase of this social network to the different scenarios of the educational application. We think that the future work in this research field is guaranteed because we have a lot of necessities to investigate and to think inside of a system of these characteristics.

References

1. http://www.teachersn.com/
2. http://www.gnoss.com
3. http://www.teacherssupportnetwork.com/Home.do
4. Fardoun, H.M., Ciprés, A.P., Alghazzawi, D.M.: CSchool: DUI for Educational System using Clouds. In: Proceedings of the 2nd Workshop on Distributed User Interfaces: Collaboration and Usability (May 5, 2012) ISBN: 978-84-695-3318-5
5. Ciprés, A.P., Fardoun, H.M., Mashat, A.: Cataloguing teaching units: Resources, evaluation and collaboration. In: Federated Conference in Computer Science and Information Systems (FedCSIS). IEEE (2012)
6. Definición De Currículo Y Contenidos (Curriculum and contents definition), http://www.uned.es/andresbello/documentos/adaptaciones-tiberio.pdf
7. Bolea, E., Onrubia, J.: Aula de Innovación Educativa. (Versiónelectrónica). RevistaAula de Innovación Educativa 8 La importancia de los objetivos en el curriculum escolar (Class of Innovative education [electronic version]. Journal School of Innovative Education 8: The Importance of Goals Inside of the Scholar Curriculum) (1992), http://aula.grao.com/revistas/aula/008-como-ensenar-ciencias-sociales-la-funcion-de-los-objetivos/la-importancia-de-los-objetivos-en-el-curriculum-escolar
8. http://www.buenastareas.com/ensayos/Definicion-De-Curriculo-y-Contenidos/540674.html

9. Cargo, A.A., Alleva, C.C.: 2.-Unidades Temáticas Unidad 1: Las dimensiones de la evaluación educativa y la evaluación del aprendizaje objetivos (Unit 1: The dimensions of the educative evaluation and the evaluation of learning goals)
10. Concepto de atención a la diversidad, http://www.educantabria.es/atencion
    _a_la_diversidad/atencion_a_la_diversidad/modelo-de-
    atencion-a-la-diversidad-/concepto-de-atencion-a-la-
    diversidad
11. Jose Maria Alonso, A.: La Educacion En Valores En La Institucion Escolar: Planeacion-Programacion (The education in values inside of academic institution: Plan-Program). Ed. Plaza Y Valdes (2004) ISBN 9789707223417, http://www.casadellibro.com/
    libro-la-educacion-en-valores-en-la-institucion-escolar-
    planeacion-pro-gramacion/9789707223417/1051206
12. Poryecto educativo de centro Instituto Nacional de Tecnologías Educativas y de Formación del Profesorado (Educative project of the National Institute of Educative Technologies and of the Teacher's formation), http://www.ite.educacion.es/
    formacion/materiales/72/cd/curso/unidad2/u2.I.1.htm
13. Graells, P.M.: Roles Actuales De Los Estudiantes (Current roles of the students) Departamento de Pedagogía Aplicada, Facultad de Educación, UAB, http://
    peremarques.pangea.org/estudian.htm
14. Fardoun, H.M., Cipres, A.P., Alghazzawi, D.M.: Distributed User Interfaces in a Cloud Educational System

Influence of Interactivity on Social Connectedness

A Study on User Experience in an Interactive Public Installation

Thom van Boheemen and Jun Hu

Department of Industrial Design, Eindhoven University of Technology,
Den Dolech 2, 5612AZ Eindhoven, The Netherlands
j.hu@tue.nl

Abstract. Public installations have the opportunity to influence many people due to their location and the vast amount of people that are exposed to them. New technologies and materials bring new opportunities to the forms of public installations. Many of these installations are interactive. This paper investigates how interaction with public installations affects its users by evaluating the experience of social connectedness with a specially designed prototype.

Keywords: social connectedness, public installation, public arts, interactivity, user experience.

1 Introduction

Looking into the development of public arts or public art installations, especially the introduction of interactivity, based on the work of Edmonds, Turner and Candy [1], Wang, Hu and Rauterberg defined three generations of art installations and generative technology according to the carrying material, technology and interactivity [2, 3]: 1) Static forms: there is no interaction between the art artifact and the viewer, and the artifact does not respond to its context and environment. 2) Dynamic forms: the art artifact has its internal mechanism to change its forms, depending on time or limited to reacting to the changes in its environment such as temperature, sound or light. The viewer is however a passive observer and has no influence on the behavior of the artifact. 3) Interactive forms: the viewer has an active role in influencing the dynamic form of the installation. When interactivity is introduced, the "dialog" between the viewer and the perceived dynamic form of the installation can always vary depending on the difficult-to-predict behavior of the human viewer.

When designing for public spaces it is important to understand what types of activity spaces they are. According to Brignull et al [4] users can find themselves in three types of activity spaces: peripheral awareness activities in which people are peripherally aware of the installation's presence but do not know much about it; focal awareness activities in which people are engaging in socializing activities associated with the installation; direct interaction activities in which an individual (or a group) can

G. Meiselwitz (Ed.): SCSM 2014, LNCS 8531, pp. 59–66, 2014.
© Springer International Publishing Switzerland 2014

directly interact with the installation. This paper focuses on the activities spaces in which people are actively engaged in the installation by either giving it their attention or interacting with it.

Public art installations have the opportunity to reach a large crowd at once, therefore also the opportunity to influence a lot of people at the same time [5]. However, many installations have no interaction with the user, limiting the user in being able to engage with the installation and creating a richer experience, or when they offer the interactivity, many of them can only be interacted with by a single user. This paper reports the research that tries to understand how the user experience with public installations is enriched by different levels of interactivity and especially, the influence of interactivity on the feeling of social connectedness – one of the experiences that many public installations aim at to offer [6-8].

Next we will first introduce the levels or types of interactivity that we are interested in, and the concept of social connectedness. One would assume that having multiple users interacting with an installation would give them more feeling of being socially connected, and having no interactivity at all would give people less feeling of being connected. The experiment to investigation the relation between the interactivity and the social connectedness is described, including the questionnaire, prototype, setup and the procedure, followed by the results and conclusion.

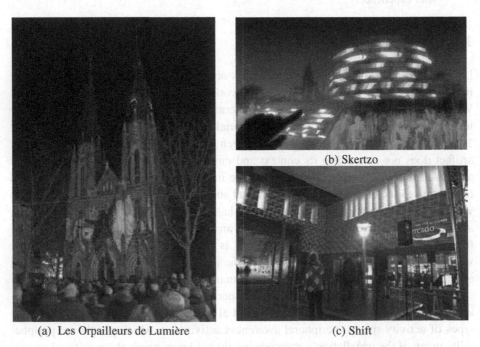

(a) Les Orpailleurs de Lumière   (b) Skertzo   (c) Shift

Fig. 1. Installations at GLOW 2012, Eindhoven, the Netherlands

2   Interactive Installations

As to interactivity of installations in public spaces [2], according to whether an installation is interactive and whether multiple users are involved, interactive public installations can be categorized simply into three types:

1. Non-interactive installations: This category includes both static and dynamic installations, with passive observers who have no influence on the behavior of the artifact. An example is the installation by Les Orpailleurs de Lumière (Fig. 1a), which was a video show on the Catherina church (Eindhoven, the Netherlands) using projection mapping techniques during the GLOW festival in 2012 [9] .

2. Single-User interactive installations.   This category includes installations where the behavior of the installations can be influenced by the observers, but this is limited to one person at the same time. An example is the GLOW 2012 installation by Skertzo (Fig. 1b), where a single user could influence the projected image shown on a public building [10].

3. Multi-User interactive installations: This category includes installations where the behavior of the installations can be influenced by multiple users at the same time. Either multiple users can influence one feature as a group, or every user can influence a different feature while together creating a whole. An example is the GLOW 2012 installation Shift (Fig. 1c), where the public could walk over or stand on a big tilting platform and shifting of the weight influenced the movement of the projections on the surrounding walls and the accompanying sound [11].

3   Social Connectedness

Design of a product, include public installations, should yield not only a usable product but an interaction which is satisfying, if not rich, experience. The term rich experience in this paper means the experience that has a positive and pleasing value for the user, allowing her to perceive beauty in the product and its use. Social connectedness is one of the rich experiences. It is described as the momentary affective experience of belonging by Rettie [12] . Studies by Jose et al. [13] show that a greater social connectedness has a direct correlation with a greater sense of wellbeing. Van Bel [14] described the concept of social connectedness along 5 dimensions: relationship saliency, closeness, contact quality, knowing each other's experiences and shared understanding:

1. Relationship saliency – The prominence of the relationship in one's mind, which is the outcome of thinking of another person or being aware of him/ her.
2. Closeness – The experience of feeling close to another. This does not relate to physical proximity, but rather to the social presence in one's mind.
3. Contact quality – The perceived quality of social contact with another person.
4. Knowing each other's' experiences – being aware of each other's experience, both in terms of subjective experiences (e.g. love, enjoyment, sadness), as well as awareness of things that happen in one's life.
5. Shared understanding – having a similar view on the world, having similar opinions or being "on the same page".

4   Experiment

4.1   Installation

To evaluate the level of social connectedness with different types of interaction, an installation was designed with the focus on producing similar output while the installation is in a non-interactive setting (Fig. 2a), controlled by one user (Fig. 2b) or controlled by multiple users simultaneously (Fig. 2c), providing three experiment setups in which the only variable was the type of interaction.

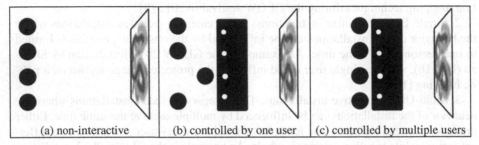

| (a) non-interactive | (b) controlled by one user | (c) controlled by multiple users |

Fig. 2. Experiment setups

The installation itself consisted of four interactive components, which could control a colored dot on a big display (Fig. 3a, the image on the laptop screen is duplicated on the big display). The colored dot was controlled by the four rotatable knobs. Each of the knobs controls one aspect of the colored dot: X and Y positions, the color and the saturation. By the users controlling the X and Y positions, the colored dot would leave a trace on the background, enabling the users to draw on the display. In order to make the system more engaging, the resulting image was continuously scrolling up in such a way that the part which left the display at the top, returned at the bottom. This made it more challenging for the users to actually create something. If the system was in its non-interactive setting, the input was generated randomly.

(a) prototype   (b) users interacting with the installation

Fig. 3. Experiment

4.2   Questionnaire

The Social Connectedness Scale Revised (SCS_R) questionnaire [15] was chosen to measure the level of social connectedness of the participants during this study. SCS-R consists of 20 items (10 positive and 10 negative). All of the questions could be scored from Strongly Disagree to Strongly Agree and had a range from 1 to 6. The negatively worded items are reverse scored and summed with the positively worded items to create a scale score with a possible range from 20 to 120. A higher score on the SCS-R indicates a stronger feeling of social connectedness.

4.3   Participants

24 participants were recruited from a student flat and randomly divided in 6 different groups. The group dynamics were important as a group of friends vs. a group of people who were not familiar with each other could have a different influence on the social connectedness. The random grouping was checked to prevent friends from being in the same group. There were 9 females and 15 males, the age ranged from 18 to 29 and the background was spread over 4 different schools, including Eindhoven University of Technology, Fontys Hogeschool Eindhoven, Summa College Eindhoven and Design Academy Eindhoven.

4.4   Procedure

The experiment took place in one of the rooms in the student flat, where the participants were sat next to each other, in front of the big display where the output was shown (Fig. 3b).

When the participants arrived, they were asked to fill in the SCS-R questionnaire to measure their initial level of social connectedness. The experiment consisted out of 3 different rounds, after each round the students were requested to fill in the questionnaire again.

In every round, the participants engaged with the installation in the 3 different settings as described before. Each of the sessions was filmed for later evaluation of the actions of the users. In order to rule out the influence of the sequence in which the participants were engaging in the different modes, each of the six sessions where done in a different and randomized sequence.

4.5   Results

SCS-R was used to investigate if there was a difference in the level of social connectedness throughout this study. Table 1 shows the descriptive statistical results.

Mauchly's test indicated that the assumption of sphericity had been violated $X^2(5)$ = 24.35, p = <.05. Therefore the results are corrected using the Greenhouse-Geisser estimate of sphericity (e = .603). The results show that the level of social connectedness was significantly affected by the different levels of interaction $F(1.81, 41.64)$ = 8.29, p < .05, w2 = .72.

Table 1. Descriptive statistics

	Mean	Std. Deviation	N
Control Test	96.79	9.948	24
Non-Interactive	99.04	10.063	24
Single-Interactive	98.00	10.138	24
Multi-Interactive	101.13	10.535	24

Using a Helmert contrast revealed that the fact that the user engages with an installations raises the social connectedness significantly $F(1, 23) = 37.40$, $p < .05$ (M = 96,79 vs. M = 99.39) (Table 2). However, using the same contrast also reveals that the change in social connectedness between a not interactive installation and an interactive installation (M = 99,04 v.s. M = 99.57, respectively) is not significant (p = .58).

Table 2. Tests of Within-subjects contrasts

Source	Tests	Mean Square	F	Sig.
Tests	Level 1 vs. Later	161.894	37.403	.000
	Level 2 vs. Later	6.510	.315	.580
	Level 3 vs. Level 4	234.375	9.547	.005
Error(Tests)	Level 1 vs. Later	4.328		
	Level 2 vs. Later	20.663		
	Level 3 vs. Level 4	24.549		

Table 3. Pairwise comparisons

(I) Tests	(J) Tests	Mean Difference (I-J)	Sig.[b]
1	2	-2.250	.070
	3	-1.208	.117
	4	-4.333[*]	.000
2	1	2.250	.070
	3	1.042	1.000
	4	-2.083	.723
3	1	1.208	.117
	2	-1.042	1.000
	4	-3.125[*]	.031
4	1	4.333[*]	.000
	2	2.083	.723
	3	3.125[*]	.031

Finally, a poc hoc test using the Bonferroni correction revealed that the social connectedness improves significantly (p = 0.031) between the single user (M = 98) and the multiple user interaction (M = 101.13) (Table 3).

5   Discussion and Conclusion

During the non-interactive and single user interactive tests, there was little to no engagement between the participants. While during the multiple user tests every group, some sooner than others, ended up interacting with each other in a social way; either by discussing how they should work together in order to create something, or by discussing their opinion about the installation or how and where they would see the installation implemented (for instance up-scaled at the city square, or as a game during a house party).

The experiment was successful in providing evidence that if a public installation is interactive, having the users interact simultaneously increases the level of social connectedness significantly compared to a single user interaction. However, there was no significant difference in the level of social connectedness between having a non-interactive installation and having an interactive installation. Therefore, no conclusions can be drawn from this experiment and this would be a topic for further investigation.

Another topic for further investigation would be a comparison with the interaction as described by Hu et al. [2] in the new generation of public installations, where the installation is not created by the designer as a final result, but as a platform and growing system for the public to participate and for social creativity to contribute to the artifact.

An example of is an installation designed for the Science and Education New Town, Taicang, China. One of the concepts for this installation is a platform where the public is allowed to contribute their photos from social media, for an interactive photo show to induce the feeling of social connectedness, and reinstate the historical values of Taicang as the port to world (Fig. 4).

Fig. 4. Public art installation for Taicang

References

[1] Edmonds, E., Turner, G., Candy, L.: Approaches to interactive art systems. In: Proceedings of the 2nd International Conference on Computer Graphics and Interactive Techniques in Australasia and South East Asia, pp. 113–117 (2004)

[2] Hu, J., Wang, F., Funk, M., Frens, J., Zhang, Y., Boheemen, T.V., et al.: Participatory Public Media Arts for Social Creativity. In: International Conference on Culture and Computing, Kyoto, Japan, pp. 179–180 (2013)

[3] Wang, F., Hu, J., Rauterberg, M.: New Carriers, Media and Forms of Public Digital Arts. Culture and Computing, 83–93 (2012)

[4] Brignull, H., Rogers, Y.: Enticing people to interact with large public displays in public spaces. In: Proceedings of INTERACT, pp. 17–24 (2003)

[5] Zhang, Y., Gu, J., Hu, J., Frens, J., Funk, M., Kang, K., et al.: Learning from Traditional Dynamic Arts: Elements for Interaction Design. In: International Conference on Culture and Computing, Kyoto, Japan, pp. 165–166 (2013)

[6] Funk, M., Le, D., Hu, J.: Feel Connected with Social Actors in Public Spaces. In: Workshop on Computers As Social Actors, co-located with 13th International Conference on Intelligent Virtual Agents (IVA 2013), Edinburgh, UK, pp. 21–33 (2013)

[7] Hu, J., Le, D., Funk, M., Wang, F., Rauterberg, M.: Attractiveness of an Interactive Public Art Installation. In: Streitz, N., Stephanidis, C. (eds.) DAPI 2013. LNCS, vol. 8028, pp. 430–438. Springer, Heidelberg (2013)

[8] Le, D., Funk, M., Hu, J.: Blobulous: Computers As Social Actors. In: Experiencing Interactivity in Public Spaces (EIPS), CHI 2013, Paris, pp. 62–66 (2013)

[9] Les Orpailleurs de Lumière, A sleepless night, in full light Mapping vidéo (2012), http://lesorpailleursdelumiere.com/v3/?p=446

[10] Skertzo, Hello World (2012), http://www.skertzo.fr/en/portfolio/eindhoven/

[11] OpenLight, Intelligent Lighting Institute turns Smalle Haven into an interactive facade for GLOW (2012), http://www.openlight.nl/shift

[12] Rettie, R.: Connectedness, Awareness and Social Presence. In: Proc. PRESENCE 2003, Online Proceedings (2013)

[13] Jose, P.E., Ryan, N., Pryor, J.: Does Social Connectedness Promote a Greater Sense of Well‐Being in Adolescence Over Time? Journal of Research on Adolescence 22, 235–251 (2012)

[14] Van Bel, D.T., IJsselsteijn, W.A., de Kort, Y.A.: Interpersonal connectedness: conceptualization and directions for a measurement instrument. In: CHI 2008 Extended Abstracts on Human Factors in Computing Systems, pp. 3129–3134 (2008)

[15] Lee, R.M., Draper, M., Lee, S.: Social connectedness, dysfunctional interpersonal behaviors, and psychological distress: Testing a mediator model. Journal of Counseling Psychology 48, 310 (2001)

Virtual Homage to the Dead: An Analysis of Digital Memorials in the Social Web

Aron Daniel Lopes, Cristiano Maciel, and Vinicius Carvalho Pereira

Universidade Federal de Mato Grosso (UFMT)
Laboratório de Ambientes Virtuais Interativos (LAVI)
Av. Fernando Corrêa da Costa, n°2367 - Cuiabá/MT - Brazil -78060-000
aronlopes@gmail.com, cmaciel@ufmt.br, vinicius.carpe@yahoo.fr

Abstract. Considering that many real-world cultural practices are now migrating to virtual environments, the expression of mourning and bereavement is also being imported to the virtual world, by means of the so-called digital memorials, supported by increasingly new and complex technologies. In this paper, we undertake a literature review on real and digital memorials, as well as social networks. Then, through empirical observation of digital memorials in Brazil, we investigate if they have characteristics of the social web. Next, by means of an interaction test and a questionnaire, we analyze how users feel when interacting with digital memorials and their evaluation on the functionalities of those applications. Finally, we approach the difficulties found when studying this kind of tools and our perspectives for future works.

Keywords: digital memorials, social web, social networks, death.

1 Introduction

In modern societies, digital technologies are increasingly embedded in our daily activities, thus changing the way we see the world and act upon it. That leads real-world social practices to migrate into virtual environments and acquire new meanings, including cultural expressions triggered by someone's death.

Death is an unavoidable event which entails both sacred and profane rites, most often performed by bereaved people. Among those rites, we can find wakes, funerals, burials, requiem masses, prayers and the building of memorials.

However, as cultural practices migrate from the real world into the virtual one, such rites may change too. Virtual applications that model real memorials in virtual places (herein called virtual memorials, digital memorials or cyber memorials) are becoming more popular, especially in the social web. Such software programs are intended to allow users to pay digital homage to deceased people.

In Brazil, the development of this kind of technology is on the rise, which reinforces the urgent want for more research on this theme. Related discussions must address potential users' needs and wishes concerning those memorials, but it is also necessary to bear in mind that such technologies involve big emotional loads.

G. Meiselwitz (Ed.): SCSM 2014, LNCS 8531, pp. 67–78, 2014.

Through literature review and empirical observation on digital memorials, this paper addresses issues related to the shift of memorials into the digital world, by investigating recent digital memorials in the Brazilian social web. Then, we analyze how those programs work and, by means of an interaction test followed by a questionnaire, we investigate how users feel when interacting with those applications.

After this introduction, we present the results of the literature review concerning digital memorials. Then, we describe the research methodology in detail and we present the results of the investigation on the software programs and the results from the experiments with users. Finally, there are the ending discussions and the references.

2   Digital Memorials

In the physical world, a memorial is "something, such as a monument or holiday, intended to celebrate or honor the memory of a person or an event" [2]. The practice of funeral rites, which involves building memorials in many societies, is considered by Structural Anthropology as the turning point between the state of nature and the state of culture [4]. Therefore, we are no longer common animals and become members of the human culture when we realize death is a different stage in the life cycle, which requires specific practices. These funeral rites have not only hygienic reasons (removing the corpse lest an infection spreads). Instead, they are mingled with many symbolisms, such as fear of spirits, profanation taboos and requests for mercy and protection.

In the virtual world there are many cultural practices about death as well, which involve both the creation of new funeral rites and the migration of those already performed in the physical world. In this context, many social web software applications are being used to express bereavement and mourning, even if they were not designed for this purpose. Two main strategies are performed by users in social networks such as Orkut and Facebook to express sorrow, surprise or missing of a deceased person: a) posting messages on the webpage created by the user before he or she died; or b) creating memorial webpages for the dead [10].

According to [17], although death-related processes are mainly determined by religious and cultural practices, technology may have an important role as well, even if invisibly. "From seeking information online about available burial options to creating multimedia presentations for use at a memorial service, technology can inform, comfort, confront, and connect the bereaved in the years following a death" [17]. In terms of contributions, the authors also make statements that can be translated into guidelines for the design of processes that explicitly consider mortality, death and bereavement in the conception of a system [17].

Besides permitting tributes to people who have passed away, digital memorials provide users with an environment where they can gather and share the deceased person's memories. Relatives may feel comfortable when they visit a social network profile of a lost kin and see there is lots of homage to that person [16] [11]. Furthermore, [29] states that contemporary digital memorials add "the benefits of rich media content and introducing a marked shift of authorship and intent into the process of cultivating and maintaining a postmortem identity".

When it comes to interaction provided by a memorial about someone's death, [23]'s taxonomy must be considered: the bereaved person's self-interaction, the interaction among living people about someone's death, and the interaction between the dead and the alive. Therefore, memorials and the materiality they give to bereavement meet not only the bereaved person's needs. They also meet the dead person's expectations that we should pay attention to him, honor him or simply realize what is happening to him [28].

After this introduction about the digital memorial theme and works related to the area, this research's methodology follows.

3   Methodology

This research began with a literature review on related works and on issues of death and cultural practices on the web, such as posthumous interaction[12], death-related taboos and beliefs [13], Facebook memorial pages [10] and virtual memorials in general [4].

Then, we researched on Brazilian social software applications that work as digital memorials and found the following recent platforms: iHeaven [9], SaudadeEterna [25] (Eternal Missing) and Memorial Digital [18] (Digital Memorial). According to [3], empirical observation on the web, the method we chose for this study, allows the researcher to identify users' expectations for future interactions in new technologies.

We began the observation by registering in the aforementioned social networks, but we were only successful to complete this process in iHeaven and SaudadeEterna. There was no feedback from Digital Memorial as to our registration.

Later on, we investigated iHeaven and SaudadeEterna to identify what characteristics of social web were present in those applications. By means of netethnography [22], we collected data that were quantitatively and qualitatively analyzed in the light of social software elements proposed by [26], [14] and [12].

Next, we applied an interaction test in Heaven with users who had never seen that application before. That test was intended to collect information on how users feel when interacting with the functionalities of such platform. 29 people from Cuiabá (a city in the Middle West of Brazil) aged between 18 and 30 years old participated in this stage of the research. The sample was composed of users from the Y or Internet Generation [27] in accordance with the sample of other researches on posthumous data by [13]. All the participants were undergraduate students in Computer Sciences, Psychology, Social Sciences and Social Communication.

The tests were taken individually and were composed of two steps: the first one consisted of a task-scenario with a set of tasks to be fulfilled by the users in the platform; the second one consisted of a questionnaire.Each guided interaction test took about 20 - 30 minutes and the tasks were divided in three main stages: identifying the tools, interacting with an existing memorial, and creating a memorial.

In the stage of identification of the tools, the user navigated freely in a memorial, by looking at each functionality mentioned in the task-scenario (profile, updates, homage and photos). In the following stage, the user interacted with any memorial he chose by using the tools available on the platform, according to the instructions of the task-scenario. In the last stage, the user was asked to create a memorial in the platform for a friend, a relative or a public person, but only if they felt comfortable do so.

After the interaction test, each user was asked to answer a questionnaire on his socio-demographic profile, his evaluation on the functionalities of the application, how he felt when fulfilling the tasks described in the task-scenario, and how different are physical and digital memorials. The questionnaires were answered in 12.5 minutes in average.All participants in the interaction test and respondents to the questionnaire signed a term of consent, according to the Brazilian Legal Resolution 466/2012 [5]. The data from the questionnaire were analyzed quantitatively and qualitatively, beginning with the socio-demographic profile. Next, the other data were analyzed in two main dimensions: how the users felt when interacting with the memorials and their evaluation on the functionalities of the application.

As mentioned, in this research we investigated the digital memorials provided by the platforms iHeaven and SaudadeEterna, described as follows.

iHeaven: The software iHeaven models the concept of memorials through tombstones (using the Portuguese verb "jaz", which means "here lies" and alludes to the deceased person to whom the memorial was created). In iHeaven, a user can create many memorials, where he must fill in text fields with information on the deceased person, such as name, nationality, place/date of birth and death, and biography. In order to interact with a memorial profile, the user must first add this profile (similarly to adding friends in other social networks). This functionality also requires that the user says which kind of relationship he had with that person (friend, relative etc.). Many photos can be added to a memorial, even organized in galleries. It is also possible to "pray" for that person or leave him a candle or flowers, by clicking the correspondent button.The bereaved user has his own profile and can send messages to other users, add them as friends and see their last updates in the platform. In this platform memorials of public people are especially popular, such as singers and actors.

SaudadeEterna: The platform SaudadeEterna also allows for the creation of memorials for deceased people. In this application, after creating an account and logging in, the user create one or more memorials containing information about the dead person, such as name, date/place of birth and death, and biography, just like in iHeaven. In the digital memorial, it is also possible to add photos and videos.In this platform, the user can pay tributes to the dead person (posts on the memorial profile), send him gifts (hearts, angels and candles, for instance) and express condolences to the family of the dead. However, the user doesn't have a profile of his own: all the interaction takes place in the memorials. Besides, there is no messaging system for users to communicate among themselves.

In the following sections, the results from the research are presented.

4   Analysis of the Platform as to Social Web Elements

In this section, we present the results of our analysis on iHeaven and SaudadeEterna regarding the presence of the following social web elements defined by [26] [14] [12]:

- Identity: in SaudadeEterna, users are not identified by profiles in specific webpages, and all the interaction takes place in the memorials. iHeaven has specific webpages for the tombstones and the users, which emphasizes identity in this social software.
- Relationships: in SaudadeEterna only memorial pages are modeled, thus there are neither relationships between users and memorials nor among users. iHeaven provides friendship relationships among users and, family/friend/idol relationships among users and memorials.
- Conversation: only iHeaven provides users with a messaging system.
- Groups: by means of memorials, both platforms allow users to form communities of interest (in this case, the deceased person).
- Recommendation: in iHeaven, the "score" of the memorial works as a recommendation sign for the users.
- Reputation: in both platforms, homage is paid to the memorials, thus rating them. In SaudadeEterna, reputation comes from the presents a memorial is given, such as hearts, angels, candles etc. The icons for those presents are displayed in the memorial page. In iHeaven, the same functionality is present, although reputation is measured in terms of candles, flowers or prayers to the dead.

The elements Presence, Sharing and Volition could not be found in any of those applications. However, more empirical research on similar platforms is necessary before one can say this is a characteristic of memorial social networks.Table 1 summarizes the analysis of iHeaven and SaudadeEterna as to Social Web Elements.

Table 1. Comparative table of social web elements

Elements	SaudadeEterna	iHeaven
Identity	Memorials	Memorials and users
Presence	Absent	Absent
Relationships	Absent	Relationships between user and memorial and among users
Conversation	Absent	Present
Groups	About memorials	About memorials
Reputation	Present	Present
Sharing	Absent	Absent
Recommendation	Absent	Present
Volition	Absent	Absent

This analysis proves that iHeaven contains more elements of social software. However, in this stage of the research, it proved difficult to identify elements of the social web in these software platforms. As the concepts of "social network for the alive" and "social network for the alive and the dead" are quite different, the categories of analysis of social web elements should be redesigned and broadened, so as to meet the specificities of those applications.

With regard to [23]'s categories of interaction about death, we can see that the two platforms herein analyzed provide interaction between the alive and the deceased and self-interaction for the bereaved. However, interaction among the alive about someone's death is only partially allowed by those applications.

5   Interaction Test

This section presents the results of the interaction test, based on the data from the test and from the subsequent questionnaire.

Each volunteer took the interaction test individually, assisted only by one of the researchers. During the test, some remarks were made by the users and these data are also herein analyzed.The subsequent questionnaire was composed of 23 questions (10 open and 13 closed). 18 of those questions are herein analyzed. We use the letter "U", followed by a number, to refer to a user.

In the following section, all the data collected are analyzed in three categories: users' profile, how the users felt when interacting with the platform and their analysis on the functionalities of the application.

5.1   Users' Profile

82,75% of the users were men. Regarding religion, 44,82% said they did not have a religion, 37,93% were Catholics, 3,44% Buddhists, 6,89% Protestants e and 6,89% choice the option "other". Those who affirmed to have a religion were asked how often they performed rites of that religion. All participants said they sometimes did so.

75,86% of the participants were students of Computer Sciences; 10,34%, of Psychology; and 6,89%, of Social Communication. The other 6,89% took undergraduate courses in different areas. As previously mentioned, all users are part of Generation Y, aged between 18 and 30 years.

5.2   How Users Felt After Interacting with iHeaven

When asked how they felt after interacting with a memorial in iHeaven, 68,96% of the users answered "tranquility"; 44,82%, "uneasiness"; 31,03%, "peace"; 27,58%, "sadness"; 20,68%, "happiness"; 20,68%, "discomfort"; 3,44%, "fear"; and 17,24% "other". In this question, more than one alternative could be chosen.

U06 stated he felt in peace but sad, and added: "I felt as if I were visiting that person's grave, and paying homage to him with flowers and candles makes one think of that environment". U12, who interacted with the memorial with a public person he personally knew, answered that he felt happy and justified: "I felt very well, even because I found some well-known faces of people I miss. Meeting them again, even if in this social network, reminds me of the people I miss". Some users who chose the option "other" said they felt curious when accessing those memorials. U14 stated: "I would like to know the *causa mortis*. I know this is indiscreet, but I feel very curious!"

U20 chose the option "other" and added that he felt "respectful", also saying: "It is interesting to see people paying homage in such an unusual fashion, which must be respected". U29 chose the same option and added he felt "inspired to read about the deeds of an important person".

U5 added that he felt melancholic and "in the beginning, he [I] was uncomfortable, but later on he was tranquil, though a bit scared". Figure 1 depicts how the users felt after interacting with the memorials.

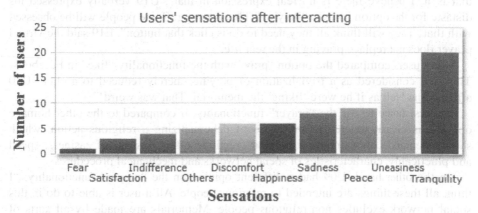

Fig. 1. Graph of how users felt after interacting with a digital memorial

5.3   Users' Evaluation on the Functionalities of iHeaven

In this subsection, we present the users' evaluation on some functionalities of iHeaven, especially focusing on the possibility of paying homage to the deceased person and the creation of a new memorial.

Paying Homage to the Deceased. With regard to homage paid in the memorials, such as messages, prayers, candles and flowers, 65,51% of the users answered all those options had the same symbolic meaning. On the other hand, most of those 34,48% who said they had different values considered the option "message" as the most meaningful. U12 stated: "It was the most common option, I guess! I wrote what I really feel for the person I was paying homage to, instead of simply clicking the candle or prayer button.

U07 added that "messages show there are people who care so much about a dear person's death that they want to show their feelings in a public space". U16, during the interaction test, said the following before writing a message on a memorial: "I will not write that, it is disrespectful". In his speech, that user seems to consider a memorial as something sacred that must not be profaned [13].

There was also some dissension as to what functionalities are proper for a digital memorial. U04 said he "liked messages and prayers, but candles and flowers are needless". This opinion emphasizes the value of immaterial kinds of homage, instead of physical objects, although in iHeaventhere are only icons of those objects on the interface. Possibly, this opinion is related to the fact that messages and prayers can be understood as means of verbal communication someone dead might receive by supersensible means.

On the other hand, U06 affirmed that he "found the option praying superficial, because it was just clicking a button". E15 adds: "By clicking 'pray', you do not pray. You only pray by praying". This is very similar to the opinion of U11: "I found the option 'pray' irrelevant. It has no concrete meaning, it is just clicking a button and that is it, I believe there is no real expression in that". U19 verbally expressed his distaste for the option "pray": "Praying? This is wrong! Some people will be obsessed with that! They will think all they need to do is click that button". E19 said the virtual prayer does not replace praying in the real life.

Many users compared the option "pray" with the functionality "like" in Facebook. This was considered as a trivialization of praying, merely reduced to a click. U10 affirmed he "felt as if he were 'liking' the memorial. That was weird!"

The resistance to use the "prayer" functionality, if compared to the other homage options, is clearly related to the taboo of dehumanizing a religious action, which should demand concentration, time and cognitive effort, instead of easiness, speed and practicality, characteristics of social networks and mechanical procedures.

On the other hand, U09 had a different opinion on the "prayer" functionality: "I think all these things are intended to religious people. All a user is able to do in this social network excludes non-religious people. Memorials are made by all sorts of people, for all sorts of people". U07 added: "As I am an Atheist, it [the prayer option] does not make any sense to me".

Those answers show that even non-religious users do not feel comfortable when the platform addresses religious issues. It is necessary to rethink those functionalities and possibly create new ones to support people in the platform, irrespective of religion, as stated by U05: "All those tools are valid, but they represent only one religion: Christianity. Maybe new kinds of homage are necessary, or the existing ones should be turned into something more neutral".

This matter is twice hard to deal with when it comes to interaction, because it involves two big taboos in western societies: death and religion [13]. Those taboos can be clearly seen in U28's speech: "When accessing this memorial, although it was a fictional one, I felt uncomfortable, as these are very gloomy things".

As to the candles that enhance the reputation of a memorial in iHeaven, U12 said: "I realized different candles had different scores, and I wanted to give the highest scored one". U13 felt the same: "I felt I was contributing to enhance the score of that memorial". On the other hand, U08 criticized this functionality: "I don't think it is right to get points from homage, like a candle. Such a social network should not reward users (…)". This user also said it was disrespectful or incoherent to rate memorials or get score from this kind of interaction, which suggests gamification [1] is not well accepted by all usersin this kind of platform. Once again, death-related taboos influence the way users interacted with this tool, by preventing the association between bereavement and fun through gamification elements.

Creating Memorials. 86,20% of the users fulfilled the task of creating a memorial during the interaction test. Some of those who chose not to do so declared to feel uncomfortable or to be in a hurry. However, the user who said he was on a hurry stayed in the room of the test for many minutes after finishing the task-scenario, which might suggest he was actually uncomfortable or uninterested to create the memorial.

Most users created memorials dedicated to public people or fictional characters. U15 affirmed he "didn't feel he had the right to create a memorial for his dead cousins, even because he wouldn't have the time to administer those profiles and they would remain abandoned on the web". Again, the taboos towards death prevented people from interacting with this functionality of the software. U05 said: "There are people who accept death more easily than others, but for me (and I believe for many people), it is upsetting to think about that. No one thinks of his own grave". U24, when talking about this issue, shows the death-related taboo which founds culture, by separating what is profane and what is sacred [13]: "I felt as if I were doing digitally something that should only be done in the real world".

Many of the users who created memorials for friends said they have a mixed feeling of missing and sadness, for remembering the deceased person. U25 affirmed: "Creating a memorial made me feel very said, as I missed that person". On the other hand, U28 felt consoled when he created a memorial: "I felt as if I were sharing my sorrow for losing someone important, and as if I were giving to others the opportunity to express their feelings too".

Two users created memorials for relatives. U29, who created a memorial for his grandfather, stated: "Creating a memorial was pleasant, as I remembered a dear person. I thought of pleasing other relatives of mine with that deed, as a digital memorial overcomes all distances. However, picking photos was pretty sad". To select those pictures, U29 searched profiles on other social networks and showed on Youtube a song composed by his deceased grandfather.

It is important to say that all those actions were done by free will and were probably triggered by strong emotions raised by the interaction with this application.

Comparison between Virtual and Physical Memorials. The last part of the questionnaire addressed the comparison between virtual and physical memorials. Users were asked about the symbolic value of a virtual memorial if compared to a physical one. 65,51% of the users said both memorials have the same value, whereas 31,03% found the digital ones less symbolic and 3,44% considered the digital ones as more symbolic. About this, U29 said: "In my opinion, a physical memorial has more sentimental value, but there is no conflict with the digital one, which is a complement in fact".

When asked about the comparison between real-world and digital-world homage, 37,93% of the users said they have the same value. On the other hand, 48,27% stated the virtual ones are less meaningful, whereas 13,79% said they have more meaning. Most of those who considered virtual homage as more meaningful explained that this kind of homage rates the image of the deceased, as stated by U02: "It is as if I were telling everyone that person influences/influenced my life". Likewise, U04 said: "It could show other people my feelings for the dead". By their speeches, such users emphasize the wish for eternizing the reputation of the deceased.

The last question posed to users was if they wished for a physical memorial, a digital one, or both, when they died. 27,58% said they did not care about it; 31,03% said they wanted either a physical or a digital one; 10,34% did not want any memorial; 27,58% preferred a digital one; and only 3,44% wished for a physical one. Besides the greater range of people who may access a digital memorial, U06 presented another reason why so many users preferred the digital one: "as for digital memorials, there are no time or distance barriers for paying homage to a dear deceased person".

6   Conclusion

Memorials are traditionally physical constructions or material tributes to the honor of the dead, especially famous people or those who played an important historical role in a society. However, digital memorials provide us with a new device for mourning, which entails different cultural practices, including digital tributes, digital mourning and even digital prayers. They are also more democratic than physical memorials, once any user with access to the internet can create a memorial for a friend, a relative, or a public person. Actually digital memorials can even be created to celebrate the death of someone who did not really exist, like a fictional character, or the fictional death of someone who is still alive in the real world.

Digital memorials also permit that people transcend time and distance limits when it comes to mourning, which warrants the possibility of eternizing someone's memory on an online platform. Most respondents who participated in this research considered this democratic aspect of virtual memorials as something good.

Considering the digital memorials recently launched in Brazil, the respondents said they have some expectations concerning the use of those platforms as social networks. For example, many users said they would be interested in rating the deceased person's reputation, thus showing to others how important that person was. Likewise, if in the past memorials were important for religious and spiritual reasons, nowadays digital memorials allow for the online exposure of the dead persons' legacy, such as photos and videos, which poses privacy challenges to these platforms.

Another challenge we can infer from the data herein analyzed consists in finding an ethical way to approach death and the deep feelings it triggers in the users. For example, after visiting the memorial of a boy, U15 said: "I felt very sad when I saw his mother still posting many messages twenty years after his death". Modeling this kind of application demands a reflection on how far users, designers and researchers can go when dealing with such complex issues.

From the verbal expressions throughout the interaction test and from the answers to the questionnaire, we could gather verbal data on how users felt when interacting with those applications. Many of them called that interaction "weird", or "bizarre", vague expressions for something that may be hard to name. Death-related taboos may hinder users' reflection on those applications or even prevent them from using some of the functionalities. This is what led such a significant amount of users not to create a memorial profile or click the button "pray" in the platform.

Designing virtual applications for users' interaction about death is also challenged by the need to model processes in which most users feel comfortable and satisfied, irrespective of their religion and death-related taboos. Therefore, the cultural diversity inherent to online mourning must be respected. Besides, it is also important to consider how to protect the deceased from libel and how to identify if the virtual death corresponds to a physical one.

The applications herein analyzed model the concept of digital memorials and tributes to the deceased, but they do not provide the user with the volitional element [12]. As it was suggested by U24, "it would be interesting if the user could choose whether or not he wanted that his profile on the social network turned into a memorial profile after his death". So far, if a user of those platforms dies, both his profile and the memorials he administers will be out of administration.

One of the difficulties found in this research is that the users were not bereaved; they were only faced with a platform to pay homage to unknown or public people. Therefore, new researches are necessary with really bereaved users. Besides, the platform iHeaven is a beta version, which caused some bugs and slowness and sometimes hindered interaction.

Future researches must be done with users from different generations, so as to identify whether they have different feelings towards this kind of interaction. Furthermore, it is important to bring other fields to dialogue in this research, such as Theology, Philosophy and Law. These issues demand deeper and more interdisciplinary studies, also employing different methodologies. For example, as many users found it hard to verbally express how they felt when interacting with those memorials, due to the deep feelings they evoke, other techniques must be used to collect data from body and facial language.

References

1. Alves, F.P., Santana, E.C., Maciel, C., Anacleto, J.: A rede social móvel Foursquare: uma análise dos elementos de gamificação sob a ótica dos usuários. In: Workshop Proc. WAIHCWS 2012 (2012) (in Portuguese), http://ceur-ws.org/Vol-980/paper3.pdf
2. American Heritage Dictionary of the English Language, http://education.yahoo.com/reference/dictionary/entry/memorial
3. Barbosa, S.D.J., da Silva, B.S.: Interação Humano-Computador. Elsevier, Rio de Janeiro (2010) (in Portuguese)
4. Braman, J., Dudley, A., Vincenti, G.: Death, Social Networks and Virtual Worlds: A Look Into the Digital Afterlife. In: Proc. SERA 2011, pp. 186–192. IEEE Computer Society, Washington, DC (2011)

5. Brasil: Conselho Nacional de Saúde. Resolução 466/2012. Diretrizes e Normas Regulamentadoras de Pesquisas Envolvendo Seres Humanos (in Portuguese), http://conselho.saude.gov.br/resolucoes/2012/Reso466.pdf
6. Becker, S.H., Knudson, R.M.: Visions of the dead: Imagination and mourning. Death Studies 27, 691–716 (2003)
7. Hallam, E., Hockey, J.: Death, Memory, and Material Culture, Oxford, New York (2001)
8. IBGE: Censo Demográfico (2010) (in Portuguese), ftp://ftp.ibge.gov.br/Censos/Censo_Demografico_2010/Caracteristicas_Gerais_Religiao_Deficiencia/tab1_4.pdf
9. Iheaven (in Portuguese), http://www.iheaven.me
10. Kern, R., Abbe, E.F., Gil-Egui, G.: R.I.P.: Remain in perpetuity. Facebook memorial pages. Telemat. Inf. 30(1), 2–10 (2013)
11. Lopes, A., Maciel, C.: Memoriais Digitais: Morte e manifestação do luto nos ambientes virtuais. In: Anais ERI-MT 2010 (2012) (in Portuguese)
12. Maciel, C.: Issues of the Social Web interaction project faced with afterlife digital legacy. In: Proc. IHC+CLIHC 2011, pp. 3–12. ACM Press (2011)
13. Maciel, C., Pereira: The Influence of Beliefs and Death Taboos in Modeling the Fate of Digital Legacy Under the Software Developers'View. In: CHI 2012 Workshop Memento Mori (2012), https://sites.google.com/site/chi2012eol/accepted-papers/chi2012EAMacielandPereira.pdf?attredirects=0
14. Maciel, C., Roque, L., Garcia, A.C.B.: Interaction and communication resources in collaborative e-democratic environments: The democratic citizenship community. Information Polity 15, 73–88 (2010)
15. Massimi, M., Baecker, R.M.: Dealing with death in design: developing systems for the bereaved. In: Proc. of the CHI 2011, pp. 1001–1010. ACM Press, New York (2011)
16. Massimi, M., Odom, W., Banks, R., Kirk, D.: Matters of life and death: locating the end of life in lifespan-oriented HCI research. In: Proc. of CHI 2011, Vancouver, BD, pp. 987–996. ACM Press (May 2011)
17. Massimi, M., Baecker, R.R.: A death in the family: opportunities for designing technologies for the bereaved. In: Proc. CHI 2010, pp. 1821–1830 (2010)
18. Memorial Digital (in Portuguese), http://www.memorialdigital.com.br
19. Mims, C.: When we Die: The Science, Culture, and Rituals of Death. St. Martin's Press, New York (1998)
20. Nielsen, J.: Why You Only Need to Test with 5 Users, http://www.nngroup.com/articles/why-you-only-need-to-test-with-5-users/
21. Nielsen, J., Landauer, T.K.: A mathematical model of the finding of usability problems. In: Proc. INTERCHI 1993, pp. 206–213 (1993)
22. Pressman, S.R., Lowe, D.: Engenharia Web, 1st edn. Livros Técnicos e Científicos (2009) (in Portuguese)
23. Ricoeur, P.: Memory, History, Forgetting. University of Chicago Press (2004)
24. Riechers, A.: The Persistence of Memory Online: Digital Memorials, Fantasy, and Grief as Entertainment. In: Maciel, C., Pereira, V.C. (eds.) Digital Legacy and Interaction: Post-Mortem Issues. HCI, pp. 49–61. Springer, Switzerland (2013)
25. Saudade Eterna (in Portuguese), http://www.saudadeeterna.com.br
26. Smith, G.: Social software building blocks (2007), http://nform.ca/publications/social-softwarebuilding-Block
27. Tapscott, D.: A hora da geração digital: como os jovens que cresceram usando a internet estão mudando tudo, das empresas aos governos. AgirNegócios, 448 (2010) (in Portuguese)

Deployment, Usage and Impact of Social Media Tools in Small and Medium Enterprises: A Case Study

Eleftherios Papachristos[1], Christos Katsanos[1,2], Nikolaos Karousos[1,2], Ioannis Ioannidis[1], Christos Fidas[1], and Nikolaos Avouris[1]

[1] HCI Group, University of Patras, Patras, Greece
[2] Hellenic Open University, School of Science and Technology, Patras, Greece
{epap,ckatsanos,fidas}@ece.upatras.gr, karousos@eap.gr,
{ioannidg,avouris}@upatras.gr

Abstract. Social media are today engaging millions of users and provide a great venue for various business activities of Small and Medium Enterprises (SMEs). However, many SMEs have been slow to adopt them due to perceived barriers such as lack of resources, negative views about their usefulness, and unfamiliarity with technology. Social Media Tools (SMTs) aim to lift some of these barriers by helping companies monitor, manage and enhance their social media presence. This paper presents a study that investigates the deployment, overall user experience and impact of such SMTs in SMEs. Four SMTs were introduced to three regional SMEs with diverse profiles. The SMEs freely used the tools for a period of one month, and both qualitative (e.g. perceived issues) and quantitative data (e.g. Facebook page fans, Twitter followers) were collected before, during and after the study. Evaluation results are presented per SME and common themes are tentatively discussed.

Keywords: social media, small and medium size enterprises, SME, case study.

1 Introduction

The contribution of information technology in improving and developing business performance has long been recognized [1]. This is certainly the case for social media; a term that was initially considered to be only a "buzz word" but has gradually gained the status of an important strategic tool for any company.

Social media provide businesses with a great opportunity for monitoring customer views about their products or their brand, increasing their customer base, implementing customer relationship management, and targeting advertisement campaigns [2-5]. Before the rise of social media, customers' needs, complaints and opinions about a company or its products could be only gathered through rather expensive and time-consuming methods of traditional consumer/marketing research, such as surveys [6].

However, extracting useful information from the vast amount of unstructured data that users generate daily on Social Networking Sites (SNSs), such as Facebook and Twitter, is by no means an easy and cost-free task. Companies have to dedicate

G. Meiselwitz (Ed.): SCSM 2014, LNCS 8531, pp. 79–90, 2014.

resources and employees with specific expertise or outsource the task to specialized companies offering to provide social media consultancy services. Thus, a need emerged for tools that filter data and enable businesses to extract meaningful information that is often hidden in large amounts of data.

As a result, Social Media Tools (SMTs) have emerged to address the need for customer listening methods, as well as to harness the wealth of information available online in the form of user-generated content [2]. Considering that social media are becoming increasingly important, particularly for the survival of small enterprises [7-9], the proliferation of such tools could be proven to be a critical factor in their competition with the larger ones. Small and Medium Enterprises (SMEs) are usually more limited in their ability to hire additional employees or external help compared to large corporations. Thus, using SMTs effectively could provide opportunities to become more competitive in the landscape created by the rise of social media.

The wealth of information that can be extracted from social media with the help of SMTs can be relevant to many different stakeholders in an enterprise. Examples of insights that can be gained are: overall reputation of a brand, competitor's analysis, feedback about marketing campaigns, current issues and requests in regard to specific products, and new ideas for product development [10]. Stavrakantonakis et al. [2] mention the following application fields for social media monitoring: reputation management; event detection, issue and crisis management; competitor analysis; trend and market research plus campaign monitoring; influencer detection and customer relationship management; product and innovation management. According to [11] companies could benefit from social media monitoring in the areas of: crisis management; influencer identification; building relationships with media and customers; creative feedback and ad-targeting; and competitive monitoring.

More than 200 SMTs are available in the market today [2], and they vary considerably in terms of general scope, functionality, application areas as well as price [12]. To what extend these tools can actually support corporate users, and especially SMEs to adopt, engage and integrate effectively social media in their everyday activities has to be assessed. To this end, case studies on the deployment, usage and impact of SMTs may provide valuable insights on best practices to foster intention to use them, define or re-establish a social media strategy, select tools that would embrace changes in organizational and structural levels and measure their impact [13].

This paper presents such a study that investigates the deployment, overall user experience and impact of SMTs in SMEs. The main goal of the study was to evaluate whether typical regional SMEs could benefit from integrating SMTs into their activities and to identify which specific features or functionalities could adequately support them in achieving their goals. Our efforts were driven by questions such as: "What are the needs of typical regional SMEs in regard to social networking?", "What kind of SMTs could assist them?", "How easy can such tools be integrated into their activities?", and "How much impact can SMTs have on SMEs social presence?".

The paper is structured as follows. First, we elaborate on the case study methodology. In this context, the study phases and procedures, data analysis techniques, profiles of participating SMEs, and the provided SMTs are described.

Next, study results per SME, followed by a discussion of general overarching findings are presented. However, it should be noted that making generalizations from this single study that involved introduction of four SMTs into the business activities of three SMEs should be avoided.

2   Method

2.1   Phases and Procedures

Figure 1 presents an overview of the study methodology. Initially, the participating SMEs were profiled in terms of their overall social media activities, including existing presence, engagement level, goals, strategy, needs, policies and attitude towards social media. The profiles were created using qualitative data collected through a pre-study interview and a set of quantitative metrics gathered from social media analytics tools, such as Facebook Insights, prior the SMTs introduction.

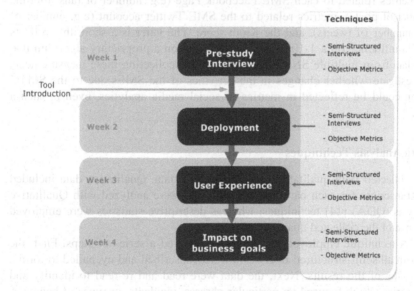

Fig. 1. Overview of the study methodology

Next, a set of SMTs (described in the following) were introduced to the participating SMEs, and concise training material was provided, including contextualized use cases of the tools. Next, the SMEs were left to use freely the provided SMTs for whatever purpose they deemed appropriate and for a time period of one month. During this period and following a ten-day interval, three semi-structured interviews were conducted with each SME in order to collect qualitative data on the tools' deployment process, overall user experience and impact on their business activities.

The interview during the second phase of the study was focused on the deployment process. The SMEs were asked about the level of effort that was required on their part in order to learn and start using the tools, whether changes in their social media policy were necessary due to the tools' deployment, as well to assess the sufficiency of the provided training material. The focus in the third phase was on the participants' user experience with the SMTs introduced in the study. In specific, they were asked to comment about the usefulness, usability, learnability, and functionality of the SMTs. Finally, in the last phase the SMEs were asked to report whether the SMTs supported them in achieving their social media goals, whether they intent to continue using them in the future or recommend them to other SMEs, and to assess the general impact on their business activities. The study concluded with a post-study discussion.

In addition, we collected quantitative data related to the SMEs' social presence before, during and after the study. To this end, we used both tools available through the SNSs themselves (e.g. Facebook Insights), as well as third-party services (e.g. Klout) that were configured to continuously log the SMEs traffic. All in all, we collected metrics related to each SME Facebook Page (e.g. number of fans, lifetime likes, number of posts), metrics related to the SME Twitter account (e.g. number of followers, number of tweets), and the Klout score. The latter is a score that reflects social media influence on a 1-100 scale and is based on a proprietary algorithm that combines data from multiple SNSs. The rationale for collecting these measurements was to investigate whether changes in the activities of the SMEs due to the SMTs' introduction could be reflected in metrics of social media analytics, even in such a short term.

2.2   Data Analysis Techniques

The study collected both qualitative and quantitative data. Qualitative data included interview transcripts for each participating SME and were analyzed with Qualitative Data Analysis (QDA) [14] techniques, whereas descriptive statistics were employed to make sense of the collected quantitative data.

The QDA technique employed in this study followed a series of steps. First, the answers from all semi-structured interviews were transcribed and eyeballed to form a first impression of the results. Next, the data were read and re-read to identify and index categories which focused on particular phrases, incidents, or types of behavior. Each identified category was labeled with a representative word or short phrase. Subsequently, the results were analyzed by summarizing the prevalence of categories and identifying further groupings or relationships through a brainstorming session in which all authors were involved. In addition, various content analysis techniques, such as frequencies or counts of events/mentions, were performed along with correspondence analysis (a technique conceptually similar to principal component analysis) that aimed to create SME profiles in accordance to their responses to the semi-structured interviews. Finally, a technique called Narrative Summary Analysis [15] was performed in which the qualitative data were restructured in a form that resembles a narrative from the points of view of the participating SMEs.

2.3   Participating SMEs

In the context of the European project InterSocial, an exploratory survey on the use of social media in two regions of Greece showed that only 26%-30% of typical regional SMEs had a profile in SNSs, with Facebook being the dominant choice. Study results also showed that social management was usually conducted by company owners and that social media profiles were updated infrequently. These Facebook company pages managed to attract a rather small amount of page likes (range: 41-2588).

According to these findings, three SMEs were recruited as representative regional companies in regard to social media usage and participated in our study. Although all of them were active in the same sector (i.e. information technology), they differed in regard to: business activities and structure; social media strategy, goals, and needs; and initial attitude towards social media. This allowed us to study the effect of SMTs use in different company settings. Finally, the participating SMEs hadn't previously used any SMT.

The first company (SME1) was a Business-to-Business software quality research group primarily engaged in research programs related to software quality assessment and evaluation, with special emphasis on educational technology. Although their workforce entailed 16 employees, only one employee was responsible for the management of the company's social media presence. The company used social media mainly to promote their research effectively, improve their networking and attract new project partners. SME1 was active in three SNSs, which in order of mostly used were: Facebook, Twitter, and LinkedIn. The company created approximately 10 posts per month on their Facebook page and had a total of 119 tweets on their Twitter account. SME1 reported that on average one hour per week was devoted to social media activities. The company's main problem in regard to social media practices was related to time management. The employee responsible for social media management had also other responsibilities and could not find enough time to manage multiple accounts in SNSs and engage more actively in conversations with the SME's followers. In addition, lack of ideas on what to post was also mentioned as a problem.

SME2 was a small Business-to-Business software design and development company with six employees. The company was mainly focused on web development, and their customers were companies and institutions from both the public and private domain. The two owners were responsible for the SME's social media management and they reported using LinkedIn, Facebook, Twitter, and YouTube. However, there wasn't any company page on LinkedIn, which was the network they reported using most frequently. Instead, they used their personal accounts mainly for networking and for monitoring developments in web programming by following specialized groups. On average they reported spending about three hours per week on social media activities, typically reading content created by others and rarely contributing content. The company owners attributed this rather limited social media use to limited human availability, but they also reported that did not believe much in social media Return of Investment (ROI). The main goal they hoped to achieve with their engagement in social media was to establish the company's brand in the market of software houses.

SME3 was a relatively small company mainly focused on web development as well as web and mobile marketing services. Typically, they launched and managed Business-to-Consumer e-commerce projects. An online travel agency and an online coupon and deal offering website were two of these projects they were trying to promote through social media at the time of the study. All employees were actively engaged in social media management. Being strong believers in the social media benefits, they gradually abandoned more traditional web-based marketing strategies (e.g. Google ads, banner campaigns) on which they relied for many years in favor of social media campaigns. The company devoted about an hour everyday posting for each of their projects, mainly on Facebook. In addition to Facebook, they also used Google+ and were eager to start using Twitter and Pinterest in the near future. Their deals-offering website was launched approximately the same time that the study began and therefore started with zero followers and page likes. Their main goal in regard to social media was to increase their reach by widening their customer base. Although the company had an overall strategy for using social media, they did not set measurable goals that would allow them to assess their success. Instead, they occasionally eyeballed Facebook Insights, as they reported.

2.4   Social Media Tools Introduced to the Participating SMEs

Four SMTs were introduced to the participating SMEs. Three of the introduced tools had been developed in the context of the InterSocial project, namely the InterSocial Monitoring tool, Social Network Analytics tool (SONETA), and the Enterprise Social Aggregator (ESA) tool. These tools were created specifically to address the needs of regional SMEs aiming to support them in their social media activities. However, given that the InterSocial project tools had not been extensively tested at the time of the study, we decided to also include HootSuite, a widely-used commercial SMT. In the following, a short overview of the main functionalities of these tools is presented.

The InterSocial Monitoring Tool is a Facebook and Twitter specific search engine, built upon the publicly available APIs of these SNSs. The tool enables the user to search for specific keywords or phrases in the timelines of Facebook and Twitter subscribers that are denoted as being "Public". The tool can retrieve public posts from Facebook, Twitter or both simultaneously.

SONETA [16] is a tool that can be used to monitor and enhance the social media presence of an SME. The tool enables tracking of social media traffic in Twitter for a user-defined set of keywords within a user-specified time period and within user-defined geographical region(s). It can be used to recognize trending conversations in specific geographic regions and returns data visualizations in the form of word clouds, bubble clouds and treemaps.

The ESA [17] tool allows the management and monitoring of Facebook, Twitter, and Google+. Currently the tool is available both as a Wordpress widget and as an Android mobile application. In addition, ESA offers the possibility of calculating statistics of aggregated data from social media using the Facebook and Twitter APIs (e.g. reach, total mentions). It is an open source project and is available for download on Codeplex.

HootSuite is a tool that enables monitoring, searching and custom analysis of social media traffic. Furthermore, it acts as a global aggregator of the most popular social networks (i.e. Facebook, Twitter, LinkedIn, Google+, Foursquare, Wordpress and Mixi) and allows users to participate in their social networks through one single point. In particular, Hootsuite can be used as a Twitter handler to send and schedule Tweets, list and keyword tracking streams, as well as monitor mentions, direct messages, sent tweets, and favorited tweets. Similarly, HootSuite's advanced Facebook functionality enables, inter alia, to post content, edit content and monitor feeds. Finally, HootSuite can also support groups of users through its functionality for role assignment and management. For the purposes of our study, we used the free version of Hootsuite which was sufficient to support the participating SMEs needs.

3   Results and Discussion

3.1   SME1: Business-to-Business, Neutral Initial Attitude Towards Social Media, One Employee Responsible for Social Media

The main characteristic of SME1 was that they followed a single-representative model for their social media management. The most important problem they faced was not having time to post and engage in conversation with their followers as well as difficulties in managing multiple SNSs and finding content to post. When asked about what kind of help they would prefer their answer indicated that they needed tools supporting them in the management of multiple SNSs and tools that could help them understand their customers' needs. Prior to the evaluation study the SME did not have specific measurable goals in order to monitor the success of their social media activities. The only metrics they occasionally checked was the number of views and likes on their Facebook page and general demographic information about their followers.

In general, the SME had no problems deploying and embedding the provided SMTs in the company's activities. However, they did report that learning how to use them effectively was a rather time-consuming task. Analysis of the data collected through the second interview showed that the company was mostly interested in social media aggregators, while they also found the SONETA geo-location monitoring feature very interesting. Interview data also showed that the deployment of the SMTs resulted in new types of social media engagement, such as searching for trends related to the SME's activities and intention to design social media campaigns. In addition, the company realized that their current social media policy was too loosely-defined and that it should be revisited. In the last interview, the SME reported having increased the average time they spend on social media. They also reported that aggregating information from multiple networks and enabling easy posting to multiple networks was the most useful functionality that the tools provided. Even though the geo-location monitoring was perceived as interesting, the SME argued that such functionality was rather inappropriate for its type of activities, but it would be really useful for SMEs that target to sale products or services in specific locations.

Overall findings indicated that the deployment of the tools motivated the staff to increase their company-related social media activities while some of the introduced SMTs or specific features of them had a positive impact on this company. Tools providing management of multiple SNSs solved a real problem for this company and also triggered interest for new activities (trend monitoring, campaigns). In addition, pre-post comparisons of the collected quantitative metrics indicated that the SME gained a small increase in Facebook Page fans (from 69 to 74 page Likes), Twitter followers (from 10 to 12) and Klout score (from from 27.1 to 30.1). In addition, almost all other metrics related to their Facebook Page (e.g. mean daily total reach, reach of page posts) received also a small boost. These metrics showed a small decrease in the third phase of the evaluation study but increased again in the last phase.

3.2 SME2: Business-to-Business, Negative Initial Attitude Towards Social Media, Company Owners Responsible for Social Media

From the initial interview it became apparent that this SME2 was not a very strong believer of social media benefits. They reported spending about three hours per week on social media primarily monitoring content created by others. When asked about what kind of help they would prefer, they expressed their interest for tools that can help in viewing and posting on multiple SNSs, as well as tools that would let them measure their social presence. They had never used Facebook Insights or any other tool to monitor their social presence by studying metrics such as total reach or post effectiveness. The only kind of monitoring they reported doing was checking general metrics such as overall number of page likes. They did not study the demographics of their followers and were not actively searching to identify influencers. In sum, this company was mostly interested in reputation management and in tools that would let them monitor multiple SNSs.

SME2 had no problems deploying and embedding the SMTs in the company's activities. Their involvement in the study gave them a new perspective on social media and contributed in convincing them to take the company's social presence more seriously than before. Analysis of the data collected through the second interview, showed that the company was mostly interested in aggregators that would allow them to monitor multiple SNSs, while tools for enhancing social presence, such as SONETA, also left a positive impression. Usability was highlighted as a very important issue in the deployment. Although most of the SMTs were perceived by the company owners as relatively usable, their perceived usefulness varied considerably. The aggregating functionality in the provided SMTs was perceived as the most useful. Finally, the last interview showed that in the middle of the case study the company had already changed its attitude towards social media. For instance, they reported that the SME's business objectives related to social media should be revisited and specific policies for improving and measuring their social presence should be produced.

All in all, the SMTs introduction had only a marginal motivational effect on SME2. This company needed information and examples about appropriate ways of using SNSs specific to their company domain more than tools. The lack of a general social media strategy resulted in difficulties incorporating the tools in their activities with some exceptions (monitoring multiple SNSs, reputation monitoring). However, pre-post comparisons showed that SME2 had a small increase in Facebook Page fans (from 48 to 53), Twitter followers (from 7 to 9) and Klout score (from 22.4 to 27.0). The frequency that this SME created content did also increase slightly, affecting positively various metrics such as mean daily total reach, reach of page posts and page consumptions. However, the data showed that the positive impact on this measurement peaked immediately after the SMTs introduction and started to slowly decrease after that. It seems that the SMTs introduction resulted in an increased interest in social media engagement by this SME at the beginning of the study. It is, however, doubtful whether the tools will continue to be used in the long term.

3.3   SME3: Business-to-Consumer, Positive Initial Attitude Towards Social Media, All Employees Responsible for Social Media

Before participating in this study, SME3 representatives stated emphatically that they were convinced about the ROI of social media engagement for their kind of business. They had already good results with their Facebook page and were interested in expanding to other platforms. However, their main problem was lack of time and therefore studying how to use new SNSs was postponed perpetually. They stated that it was difficult for them to hire a new employee to work exclusively on social media. The tools that could help them in their activities were those measuring the effectiveness of their posts as well as tools that would help them understand the needs of their followers and build more effective promotions and campaigns. They frequently looked into Facebook post likes in an attempt to understand the effectiveness of certain posts. They expressed their interest about techniques that could help them identify general themes of conversations and learn what their customers are talking about. They frequently launched promotional campaigns, analyzed their audience demographics and created posts targeting specific subgroups (e.g. females only).

The first interview indicated that embedding the provided set of tools in the company's activities was relatively easy. The time spent with the tools triggered a renewed interest in examining more effective ways to use social media. They asked for more information about how to use the tools and identify appropriate ways to use Twitter. During the first phase, they used mainly monitoring functionalities to search for content posted by their competition and form an understanding of appropriate Twitter usage. From the second interview it was found that SME3 was mostly interested in monitoring and enhancement tools. In particular, they found geo-location monitoring conceptually useful, although they faced some usability issues in the provided tools. Tools that did not offer information or functionality in addition to what the company already managed to get through other ways (e.g. Twitter search, Facebook Insights) were evaluated negatively and abandoned quickly. For instance, the company did not use the aggregators in order to post on multiple social networks since they did that already through their RSS feed. They became, however, interested in aggregators for the purpose of monitoring multiple SNSs and their competition, and identifying local trends and relevant conversations. Finally, the last interview showed that the company found ways to use Twitter effectively. They reported that experimentation with the provided SMTs helped them formulate strategies about effective Twitter usage, a SNS that they were not actively engaged before. Apart from that, the deployment of the SMTs did not affect the activities or policies of the company. Even though they found some of the tools interesting, they stated that they intent to use them only infrequently in the future. It seems that for this company information about how to use social media effectively was valued more than specific features of a SMT.

This company needed information about effective ways of using new SNSs more than tools, but their engagement with the provided SMTs triggered an experimentation phase from which the company benefited considerably. In specific, SME3 engaged in Twitter, a new SNS that they were not previously using. Furthermore, this SME became interested in trend, geo-location and competition monitoring through social media analytics. Quantitative data for this SME were analyzed separately for two of their projects. The first project was an online travel agency that had a Facebook Page for more than a year and had a successful social presence as perceived by the SME. Results did not show any substantial change in Facebook followers (from 3418 to 3419) before and after the SMTs introduction, but the Klout score showed some improvement (from 43.0 to 45.2). The second project was a deals-offering website that launched approximately the same time that the study began. Results of the collected one-month data showed an impressive increase in Facebook followers (from 0 to 4649) and Klout score (from 0 to 51.5). However, this impressive increase cannot be solely attributed to the introduced SMTs. The company used various promotion options provided by Facebook (boosting page, advertisement, and boosting posts) during the same period. By contrast, the impact of the SMTs can be clearly observed in the company's engagement with Twitter. In specific, during the first two phases of the study they managed to gain only 6 twitter followers, although they streamlined all their posts to Twitter. After actively using the introduced SMTs to identify appropriate ways to use Twitter they managed to gain 149 followers in ten days.

3.4 Discussion

A general theme that could be identified by looking at the data provided by all SMEs in parallel was that the commercial tool received more positive comments than the tools created in the InterSocial project. One could expect this given that Hootsuite is a well-known tool that is on the market for many years and provides a multitude of functionalities. In addition, the main functionality of the tool is the aggregation of multiple SNSs, which was also the main need of two of the three participating SMEs.

Most negative comments in the study referred to the amount of time required to familiarize with all the concepts and functionalities of the various SMTs. According to the participating SMEs, all the provided tools used unfamiliar words and lacked in concrete information that would enable them to start using them effectively immediately, such as best practices and contextualized examples. For instance, one of the simplest and most common features of SMTs is keyword monitoring, but it was found that companies do not always know what keywords to monitor, as it was the case for SME2 and to some extent SME1. These SMEs felt that their domain or niche market did not have specific keywords that could be tracked in order to gain valuable information. In these situations it would be helpful if case studies about other similar companies or examples about best practices would be provided by these tools.

Trend analysis was particularly useful for SME3 and to some extent for SME2. Finding trending information, especially for specific regions, attracted the interest of all the participating SMEs. It helped them to find and engage in conversations as well as to modify their posts in order to include terms that would receive their customers' attention.

Finally, the participating SMEs did not ask for elaborate reputation measurements, scores or statistics. They were happy with those provided by the SNSs themselves, such as overall page or post Facebook likes. Aggregators that let them view all their SNSs at once were also enough to monitor their social presence by analyzing their customers' comments qualitatively.

4   Conclusions

The results of the study presented in this paper revealed that the usefulness of SMTs as well as intention to adopt and integrate them in future activities varied considerably among the participating SMEs. This was a generally expected result since these companies differed considerably in terms of business activities, organizational structure, social media management needs and initial attitude towards social media.

The main common effect that the introduction of the SMTs had on all SMEs was a renewed interest for engagement with social media in general. However, this could be due to their involvement in the study rather than a genuine impact of SMTs usage. For this reason we intent to revisit all three companies in the future and examine whether they continued to use the tools introduced in the study or other similar ones in their everyday activities. In addition, all SMEs that participated in our study increased their social media presence to some extent either by engaging in new social networks or by increasing their activity on those they were already using. Furthermore, SMTs usage helped all participating SMEs to realize that they were lacking an overall social media strategy with specific objectives and measurable goals.

However, apart from the positive effect in social media presence and intentions to integrate SMTs in their everyday activities, the SMEs confronted difficulties in aligning their business goals with continuous usage of such tools. It also became apparent that these tools need to provide best practices and contextualized usage scenarios so that SMEs can start using them effectively immediately.

The work presented in this paper is primarily driven by an effort to understand the perceived difficulties of SMEs in integrating and adopting SMTs and to describe lessons learned for efficient and effective adoption. A practical implication of this work is the elaboration of an empirical evaluation methodology along with insights related to SMTs' deployment, usage and impact on SMEs with diverse business profiles and objectives.

Acknowledgments. The work reported in this paper was funded by the European Territorial Cooperation Operational Programme "Greece-Italy 2007-2013" under the project Intersocial. We also thank the SMEs who participated in the experiment.

References

1. Hairuddin, H., Noor, N.L.M., Malik, A.M.A.: Why do Microenterprise Refuse to Use Information Technology: A Case of Batik Microenterprises in Malaysia. Procedia - Social and Behavioral Sciences 57, 494–502 (2012)
2. Stavrakantonakis, I., Gagiu, A.-E., Kasper, H., Toma, I., Thalhammer, A.: An approach for evaluation of social media monitoring tools. In: 1st International Workshop Common Value Management, CVM 2012, pp. 52–64 (2012)
3. Zhang, W., Johnson, T.J., Seltzer, T., Bichard, S.L.: The Revolution Will be Networked The Influence of Social Networking Sites on Political Attitudes and Behavior. Social Science Computer Review 28, 75–92 (2010)
4. Bi, F., Konstan, J.A.: Customer Service 2.0: Where Social Computing Meets Customer Relations. Computer 45, 93–95 (2012)
5. Keenan, A., Shiri, A.: Sociability and Social Interaction on Social Networking Websites. Library Review 58, 438–450 (2009)
6. Murphy, J., Kim, A.E., Hagood, H., Richards, A.K., Augustine, C.B., Kroutil, L.A., Sage, A.: Twitter Feeds and Google Search Query Surveillance: Can They Supplement Survey Data Collection? In: Association for Survey Computing 6th International Conference (2011)
7. Copp, C.B., Ivy, R.L.: Networking Trends of Small Tourism Businesses in Post-Socialist Slovakia. Journal of Small Business Management 39, 345–353 (2001)
8. Pitt, L., van der Merwe, R., Berthon, P., Salehi-Sangari, E., Caruana, A.: Global alliance networks: A comparison of biotech SMEs in Sweden and Australia. Industrial Marketing Management 35, 600–610 (2006)
9. Michaelidou, N., Siamagka, N.T., Christodoulides, G.: Usage, Barriers and Measurement of Social Media Marketing: An Exploratory Investigation of Small and Medium B2B Brands. Industrial Marketing Management 40, 1153–1159 (2011)
10. Fensel, A., Fensel, D., Gagiu, A.-E., Kaiser, J., Larizgoitia, I., Leiter, B., Stavrakantonakis, I., Thalhammer, A., Toma, I.: How to Domesticate the Multi-channel Communication Monster. Technical Report, Semantic Technology Institute Innsbruck (2012)
11. Fernandez, L.: 5 Key Benefits of Monitoring Your Client's Brand on Social Media, http://mashable.com/2010/08/15/social-media-monitoring-benefits/
12. Kasper, H., Dausinger, M., Kett, H., Renner, T., Finzen, J., Kintz, M., Stephan, A.: Marktstudie Social Media Monitoring Tools, Fraunhofer-IRB, Stuttgart (2012)
13. Blanchard, O.: Social Media ROI: Managing and Measuring Social Media Efforts in Your Organization. Que Publishing, Indianapolis (2011)
14. Miles, M.B., Huberman, A.M., Saldaña, J.: Qualitative Data Analysis: A Methods Sourcebook. SAGE Publications, Inc. (2014)
15. Gilligan, C., Spencer, R., Weinberg, M.K., Bertsch, T.: On the Listening Guide. Emergent Methods in Social Research, 253–268 (2006)
16. Ioannidis, I., Papachristos, E., Katsanos, C., Karousos, N., Fidas, C., Avouris, N.: SONETA: A Social Media Trend Geo-analysis Tool. In: Meiselwitz, G. (ed.) SCSM/HCII 2014. LNCS, vol. 8531, pp. 186–196. Springer, Heidelberg (2014)
17. Calefato, F., Lanubile, F., Novielli, N.: A Social Aggregator for SMEs. In: Intersocial Workshop on Online Social Networks: Challenges and Perspectives (2012)

Using Ambient Communication and Social Networking Technologies to Reduce Loneliness of Elders

Harri Pensas[1], Antti-Matti Vainio[1], Markus Garschall[2], Tero Kivimäki[1],
Stratis Konakas[3], Socrates Costicoglou[3], and Jukka Vanhala[1]

[1] Tampere University of Technology, Tampere, Finland
{harri.pensas,antti-matti.vainio,
tero.kivimaki,jukka.vanhala}@tut.fi
[2] Center for Usability Research and Engineering, Vienna, Austria
garschall@cure.at
[3] Space Hellas, Athens, Greece
{skona,scostic}@space.gr

Abstract. Online social networks have become part of our everyday lives. However, many elders do not use these networks even though social connections are important for their health and quality of life. To help elders feel more connected to their safety network we have developed an assistive solution based on the elders' requirements that aims at improving their communication and sense of presence. The prototype, consisting of a touch screen device and web services was evaluated in two field trials lasting for 28 weeks in total in Finland and in Austria. In addition to interviews, we used the logged usage data to analyze the user's experience with the system.

Keywords: Online Social Networks, Ambient Communication, Sense of Presence, Ambient Assisted Living.

1   Introduction

Online social networks have become an important part of peoples' everyday lives. Especially, they have gained popularity within the younger and middle aged population that is already used to computers in their lives. However, even though many elders are not used to computers and social networks they would certainly benefit from increased social presence and social connections as elders also often suffer from fears of safety and health [1]. These fears could be reduced by providing a continuous sense of presence [2].

Various reasons keep elders from using social networks. The elders might have misconceptions about nature of online social networks or they might not perceive their usefulness. Fears of privacy may also reduce the interest towards these social networks [3]. However, more than lack of interest might be the lack of suitable solutions for their needs [4]. Elders who have not invested much time in learning the skills to operate such systems or user input methods such as a mouse or a keyboard can find user interfaces and web pages too difficult to use. [5]

G. Meiselwitz (Ed.): SCSM 2014, LNCS 8531, pp. 91–102, 2014.

In this paper we present the AMCOSOP (Ambient Communication for Sense of Presence) platform, which was developed to decrease the elders' loneliness and to encourage communication with their safety net consisting of their friends, families and professional caregivers. AMCOSOP demonstrates how recent research on ambient communication and technical advancement can be used for improving the elders' quality of life and health. A user centered design approach was used to attain user friendliness and to analyze the specific needs of the elderly users.

The system itself is a server-client application that provides different end-user technologies and experiences to different user groups: primary-, secondary- and tertiary users. Primary users represent the elders, whereas secondary users are the elders' families and other close ones. Tertiary users represent other stakeholders such as service providers or care givers. Primary users use the system by Home Terminals featuring touch screens and a novel, pleasant and easy to use-UI. Secondary and tertiary users interact with the system through using a web portal, and in addition secondary users may also use a native mobile phone client with location-based automatic context recognition.

A prototype system was developed based on comprehensive requirements analysis, involving elders and their relatives in Finland, Austria and Greece. The prototype system was then evaluated within two field trials in Finland and Austria. Extensive data was collected from these field trials in order to analyze the usage behavior and to derive design implications for similar systems. Section two of this paper gives and overview on related projects and studies; in sections three and four we provide an overview on the implementation of the prototype; and in sections five and six we discuss the usage logs of the prototype devices.

2   Related Work

Different ICT systems that help and improve the life of elders have been a topic of interest in recent years. The research has been further driven by research initiatives like the AAL JP (Ambient Assisted Living Joint Programme), run by the EU. The AMCOSOP project was funded by the AAL JP. Below we will discuss research that is directed to improving the elders' life quality through communication and sense of presence. Another large group of services are those more related to safety and healthcare, although both goals can be fulfilled in a single system as well.

Many systems propose using a TV set as a communication device. The main argument is that TVs are already present in the elders' lives and they are accustomed to using them. Unfortunate drawback is that TVs are not primarily designed for such a function and usability may be limited with the use of remote controls and long viewing distances. The FoSIBLE [6] project within the AAL JP program provides social games, social sharing and clubs for users based on a TV interface Hybrid Broadcast Broadband TV (HBBTV) platform. In addition to remote controls the user interface is enriched by gestures and the ability to use a tablet as an input device or even independently. TV-Kiosk [7] is another TV-based solution implemented with the Virtual Private Ad-Hoc Network (VPAN) instead of the more traditional client-server architecture. TV-Kiosk allows its users to access information from caregivers or relatives and also some content posted in Facebook using a remote control. Mazadoo [8] circumvents the problem of low social networking activity by using Facebook as the social network. The software is used with remote, but also has a text-to-speech feature to counter the inconvenience of reading long texts from a television display.

Facebook is also used as the social network within ePortrait, an ambient picture frame that aims at improving the social inclusion of elders by showing pictures shared by their relatives in Facebook. This will help the elders to stay up-to-date on events shared by family members in social networks. In addition to ePortrait, eBowl was also designed to complement the ePortrait to allow feedback by putting objects equipped with different RFID tags to this bowl. Any object added to the bowl will trigger a certain action in Facebook [4].

Another direction is to build computer software or a web page which is designed specifically to elder users. The Senior Social Platform [9] is a web application using Googles OpenSocial APIs and RESTful protocol with JSON data format.

Touch interaction is a direct and therefore more intuitive form of interaction compared to traditional point and click systems [10], touch interaction shows high potential for adoption by novice users in general, and specifically by older adults with little to no ICT experience [11] [12] [13].

Mobitable [14] is a touch based gestural interface and device aimed at supporting older adults in social networking. According to Leonardi et al. the touch interface was quickly mastered. However, older users had some exceptions due to unfamiliarity with digital user interfaces. Tapping consistently and quickly proved difficult leading to misinterpretations with the drag operation. Performing actions by moving objects using the drag operation itself was not entirely intuitive for the older users. Finally closing the active area by clicking on the background was surprisingly hard to remember and conceive.

Social Interaction Screen [5] is another AAL project aiming at reducing interaction barriers from elders to participate in social networking services. They created a specific touch tablet for elders and software which may also be used in computers. They use a Social Software Integration Layer to integrate a number of social networks to a single device. Another touch based solution is the Sharetouch [15] device with a large horizontal touch screen. Sharetouch encourages social interaction both locally and via the network as four users may use the device simultaneously. The social network is displayed on the device as fish in pond. Messages may be sent by recording the message and recognizing the sender by the four microphones on the device. In addition to the community pond the Sharetouch system offers a social Waterball game and multimedia sharing functions.

3   AMCOSOP Platform

Major components of the AMCOSOP platform are the Service Platform, the MobSOP mobile client and the Home Terminal. All the user and communication information is

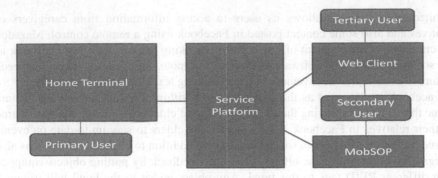

Fig. 1. AMCOSOP top-level architecture

stored on the Service Platform where as the clients; Home Terminal and the MobSOP client, only store relevant information temporally and receive the current configuration state and messaging history during startup. Additionally configuration changes are checked from the server periodically, whereas status changes and messages are sent to the respective clients instantly. The main components of the AMCOSOP system are shown in Figure 1.

The core of the platform's functionality is based on different communication technologies, used for the communication between the AMCOSOP Service Platform and the clients. We use both XMPP (Extensible Messaging and Presence Protocol) and REST (Representational State Transfer)) protocols for communication; additionally JSON (JavaScript Object Notation) is used in encoding the XMPP messages. Communication is secured by using secure SSL connections.

The Service Platform is consists of a database, a messaging server and user interfaces for secondary and tertiary users. The main purpose of the database, using PostgreSQL, is to store the user and service data. In addition, it is used to keep logs about users' activity as well as to store all the possible values of the users' contextual information. User's information stored on the database is managed by a web application. The administrator may use the web application through a simple and user friendly web page to manage user's information and contextual attributes as well as to access statistical information. In addition, the administrator may also manage services that the tertiary user has provided for the AMCOSOP system. The secondary users can access the AMCOSOP by a similar web application as the administrator.

The Secondary user web application is designed for use on both, large display computers and mobile devices. Main functions for secondary users are to interact with the primary users and access their profile and status information. The web application has a simple graphical user interface with a navigation menu on the left side and the content on the right side as shown in Figure 2. On mobile devices the menu is moved to the top and the content is displayed below, as shown in Figure 2 as well. The secondary user web application was implemented with a HTML5-based user interface system, built on a powerful, patterns-based web application engine that enables a clean separation of components enabling fast development.

Communication with other parts of the AMCOSOP platform is implemented by two components: the Instant Messaging Server and an Instant Messaging Client. The Instant Messaging server uses the Openfire Server, a real-time collaboration server which is licensed both with GPL as well as commercially. The Openfire is a powerful instant messaging and chat server that implements the XMPP protocol used in AMCOSOP. The communication between the primary and secondary users is enabled by the Instant Messaging Client.

The Instant Messaging Client connects to the Instant Messaging Server by using the open source XMPP client library Smack, a pure Java library, which can be embedded into the applications to create anything from a full XMPP client to simple XMPP integrations, such as sending notification messages and presence-enabling devices. The messages that this client receives and sends are in JSON format described in more detail in the communications section below.

The User Information Handler is used in order to retrieve and update user's data from the Database. In particular, it is responsible for the communication between AMCOSOP clients (i.e., clients of primary and secondary users) and the Service Platform. It consists of a Web Service implemented with the use of REST technology. The REST service in the AMCOSOP platform uses XML formatted data for exchanging information. The User Information Handler is called by the client applications in the following cases:

- to retrieve user's profile data and user's contact list,
- to retrieve the contextual values from the Database,
- to register a new secondary user in the AMCOSOP system,
- to update user's profile data and user's contacts,
- to retrieve services and messages of services and
- to subscribe a user to an existing service.

The MobSOP mobile client may be used on Symbian^3 smart phones instead of the web application. The application provides mobile phone optimized user interface and automatic context based situation updates based on the phone's location. Unfortunately, the Symbian^3 operating system, which was chosen as a pilot platform in the beginning of the project, is no longer under development. The MobSOP software was implemented using the Qt framework. The user interface is implemented using QML; all views are implemented as separate QML elements. Qt Mobility's Location API is used to get the current phone location. The main view of the MobSOP application is shown in 2.

Fig. 2. Mobile UI of the Secondary User Web Application (left), Standard web UI of the Secondary User Web Application (center) and Secondary user MobSOP mobile application (right)

3.1   Communication

The main communication between the AMCOSOP Service Platform and the clients is performed using the XMPP, an open Extensible Markup Language (XML) protocol for real-time messaging, presence and request-response services. Developed originally as Jabber, XMPP is designed as near real-time instant messaging and presence information. It is defined as an open standard, and it uses open systems approach which enables different implementations to interoperate easily. Since these are exactly the characteristics that the AMCOSOP system was aiming for, XMPP was chosen as the main messaging protocol.

In the AMCOSOP system XMPP is used for all status updates and updates in contextual information such as location, mood, activity etc. Also contact invitations and deletions are handled through the XMPP service. The Home Gateway uses Smack Java API version 3.2.2 for XMPP communication, which is an open source client library by Ignite Realtime community. Normally the contact list is also handled through XMPP, but in AMCOSOP the Service Platform has one XMPP user called "admin", and every Home Terminal has this contact in their contact list. The reason for this is that this way the Service Platform can handle the user management in a more diverse way and keep the records in its own database. Therefore, the contact list is not received through XMPP, but from a REST interface.

REST is a style of software architecture for distributed systems such as the World Wide Web. Over the recent years it has become the most popular web API design model. It aims for scalability, generality of well-defined interfaces and independence of components. It is therefore well suited for AMCOSOP, especially for retrieving user, service and other information. In the AMCOSOP system a REST interface is used using the HTTP methods GET, PUT and POST on the AMCOSOP server port 8080. The data from the REST interfaces is in XML format. The REST interface is used for getting possible types of status and contextual information, to retrieve and edit the contact list of the primary user and to retrieve the list of available third party services.

4   Home Terminal

The primary client software for the elderly is the Home Terminal. It is divided to the Gateway component, responsible for communication, and the Home Terminal part, providing the elder friendly easy-to-use touch screen interface. Both of the components are implemented using Java language; however since the Standard Java Development Kit did not have adequate support for designing modern user interfaces at the time we decided to use an external graphics platform. Therefore the Home Terminal implementation uses JavaFX 2.0 software platform for the UI. Although the second version of JavaFX was still in beta during initial design and in the beginning of the implementation, it was selected for the implementation of the UI. The alternatives were also considered as well, mainly Processing and Piccolo2d, both compatible with Java language. Since then JavaFX has now been bundled with standard Java releases beginning from Java SE 7 update 6.

The Home Terminal UI and the Gateway components can be run separately on different computers using RMI to interact. However, in our pilot installation both parts were run on the same machine, and the ability to separate the parts was made for future flexibility. In addition, a single Gateway could in future serve multiple UI parts instead of all the UI's running their own communication with the server. We also made a version that removed the RMI communication and run both parts in the same virtual machine. This was used during the second part of the user evaluation in order to improve the user experience as there were occasionally some communication problems occurring with the RMI implementation.

The Home Terminal is a straightforward model-view-controller (MVC) application. Most of the implementation of the Home Terminal is for the graphical user interface. The graphical user interface is one of the most important parts of the Home Terminal implementation. Since the targeted users are elder people who have limited or no experience using computers, the UI had to be simple and intuitive. Additionally, designing the UI concept we also paid attention to usability and accessibility aspect, such as the contrast of the UI elements. The screen is divided between the bottom bar and the main view above. From the bottom bar the user can select one of five views. The main view displaying contacts, the management view, which is used to control the contacts and to change their position on the screen, the view for the primary users own profile, the view for accessing the different user controlled settings for the terminal and finally a services view where user can subscribe to third party services and view announcements and descriptions of these services. Additional layers of the UI are reduced to a minimum. Only in the main view a pop-up will be shown in the center of the screen when the user opens up a contact for communication or checking contacts current status. More details of the UI design are available in [16]. An example view of the main user interface of the Home Terminal is shown in Figure 3.

The Gateway part of the Home Terminal, was implemented with a simple messaging architecture. To avoid lockdown, all communication between the Home Terminal and the Service Platform was run on different threads each having its own message queue. Our initial plan to build the Gateway on OSGi framework had to be abandoned because of unsolvable compatibility problems between OSGi and RMI.

Fig. 3. Home Terminal main user interface

4.1 Home Terminal Hardware

Since the Home Terminal was designed to be an ambient display suited in living spaces, instead of constraining it to a desktop like a traditional PC, we wanted a slim aesthetically pleasing touch device resembling of photo frames. However, since such devices were not available and using resources for designing and building a limited number of such devices was not feasible we resorted to using standard PC-computer. Fortunately, the All-in-one PCs manufactured by ASUS with pleasing looks and equipped with touch screens were adequately suitable for deployment for example on bookshelves, dressers or cabinets.

For the pilot we selected the white ET1611 model with 15.6" single touch wide screen display. The device is powered by 1.8 GHz Intel Atom D425 processor and 2GB RAM, which are well enough for running the AMCOSOP Home Terminal application. If needed, the use of Java language gives the benefit of easily porting the system for other devices and operating system providing Java runtime environment.

5 User Evaluation

The AMCOSOP system was evaluated within two consecutive user trials in two countries, Finland and Austria. Between these evaluation phase's the system was updated implementing the tertiary services, not part of the first trial phase, and also integrating improvements based on user feedback after the first trial phase. In total, the trials lasted for 28 weeks and involved 23 primary users. Quantitative and qualitative data was collected in the form of system logs and periodic questionnaires. System logs recorded both, the internal behavior of the Home Terminals and all the interactions that users performed with their terminals.

6   Results

In the following we will analyze the usage data that was extracted from the log files. Most of the users rarely turned the system off, which was encouraged to achieve the ambient communication and ease of use (the display, however could be turned off separately from the device). Almost all users preferred to use only the large text size within the evaluation. The preferred settings for the contrast showed a higher variation between the different users. Background images, an important feature that came up within the initial requirements analysis, were changed occasionally during the first trial phase, but kept mainly unchanged during the second phase.

The users communicated with two main methods status updates and messages. The status was divided into four separate fields: status, mood, location and activity. The messages were person to person communication between primary and secondary users. The secondary users could write their own messages while the primary users had a collection of predefined messages, mostly for requesting for the secondary user to contact the primary user in different ways. In the second phase of the trials the selection of predefined messages was extended as well as giving the primary users an option to use a keyboard for writing free-text messages.

The Figures 4 to 9 below show usage averages for all the users during phase 1 in Finland and phase 2 in Finland and Austria. Status changes depict a change on any of the four status fields. Messages depict any message, predefined or free text, exchanged between the primary user and a secondary user. Blue diamond lines show the messages coming to the Home Terminal from secondary users, whereas the red square lines show messages sent by the primary user with the Home Terminal. The y-axis shows the number of messages or status updates in a week whereas the x-axis shows a week number from the beginning of the evaluation phase.

During the first evaluation phase (shown in Figures 4. and 5.) the usage of the system was relatively constant after the first weeks when the system was introduced to the users. Status updates were used more often than the messages, especially by the elders. This is in line with the original concept of ambient communication, where actual conversations were to be performed with more traditional methods, like visiting and phone calls.

The second evaluation phase in Finland (shown in Figures 6. and 7.) showed a similar amount of activity as the first phase. However, there seems to be an increase in the activity of the secondary users, especially by updating statuses more often. One explanation might be the added e-mail notifications for received messages to secondary users. Even though some primary users were very insistent on having a keyboard (in the beginning not provided because of usability problems) to write free-text messages the average number of sent messages actually declined in the second evaluation phase. Furthermore, in addition to the average, neither any single user was using the message functionality substantially more than others. There is also a large reduction in the communication activity around the 4th week of the test which can be explained by Christmas time. Interestingly the effect is clearer in Finland than in Austria, shown in Figures 8., and 9.

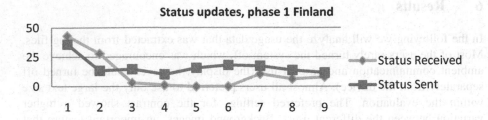

Fig. 4. Status update averages in Finland during first trial phase

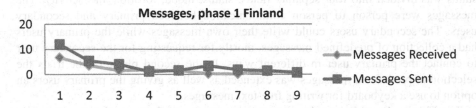

Fig. 5. Message averages in Finland during first trial phase

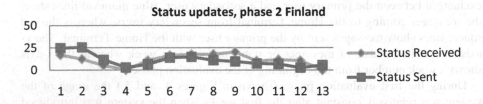

Fig. 6. Status update averages in Finland during second trial phase

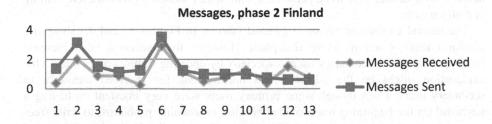

Fig. 7. Message averages in Finland during second trial phase

In Austria the total activity was similar to Finland, however, there was a clear difference in the popularity of messages and status updates. The status updates were used less by both primary and secondary users, but especially by secondary users, whereas messages were used more than in Finland by both user groups.

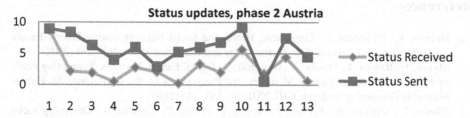

Fig. 8. Status update averages in Austria during second trial phase

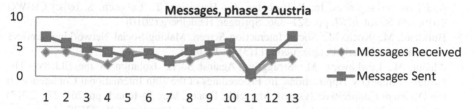

Fig. 9. Message averages in Austria during second trial phase

Conclusion and Future Work

We developed a social networking system based on ambient communication for elders and their safety networks. The elders received a special user-friendly touch screen based Home Terminal device whereas relatives, friends and formal caregivers and local communities can use the provided web based services. A native mobile application was also developed for Symbian^3 devices. The AMCOSOP system is a client-server architecture based on XMPP and REST technologies for communication.

The prototype devices were developed evaluated in user trials in Austria and Finland. The trials were conducted in two phases with a short development period in between. On total the trials lasted for 28 weeks and involved 23 primary users. The usage logs containing records of system activity were analyzed.

In addition to user logs presented in this paper qualitative data was also gathered by questionnaires and interviews. Further review and publication of this data will be an important goal in the future.

The developed prototype system and the results of the user evaluation have shown how modern technology and ambient communication can be used to create solutions that support elders' communication with their safety net. Commercial systems and service providers are needed to bring such technologies to a wider audience, thus making ambient communication and online social networks part of elders' lives.

References

1. Holmén, K., Hidetochi, F.: Loneliness, Health and Social Network among Elderly People – a Follow-up Study. Archives of Gerontology and Geriatrics 35(3), 261–274 (2002)
2. Mynatt, E., Rowan, J., Jacobs, A., Craighill, S.: Digital Family Portraits: Supporting Peace of Mind for Extended Family Members. In: Proceedings of the Conference on Human Factors in Computing Systems, CHI 2001, pp. 333–340 (2001)
3. Gibson, L., Moncur, W., Forbes, P., Arnott, J., Martin, C., Bhachu, A.: Designing social networking sites for older adults. In: Proceedings of the 24th BCS Interaction Specialist Group Conference, BCS 2010, pp. 186–194 (2010)
4. Cornejo, R., Favela, J., Tentori, M.: Ambient displays for integrating older adults into social networking sites. In: Kolfschoten, G., Herrmann, T., Lukosch, S. (eds.) CRIWG 2010. LNCS, vol. 6257, pp. 321–336. Springer, Heidelberg (2010)
5. Burkhard, M., Koch, M.: Social Interaction Screen. Making Social Networking Services Accessible for Elderly People. i-com 11(3), 3–7 (2012)
6. Alaoui, M., Lewkowicz, M.: Struggling Against Social Isolation of the Elderly—The Design of SmartTV Applications. In: Proceedings of the 10th International Conference on the Design of Cooperative Systems, Marseille, France, May 30-June 1, pp. 261–275 (2012)
7. Steenhuyse, M., Hoebeke, J., Ackaert, A., Moerman, I., Demeester, P.: TV-kiosk: an open and extensible platform for the wellbeing of an ageing population. In: Rautiainen, M., et al. (eds.) GPC 2011. LNCS, vol. 7096, pp. 54–63. Springer, Heidelberg (2012)
8. Bothorel, C., Lohr, C., Thépaut, A., Bonnaud, F., Cabasse, G.: From individual communication to social networks: evolution of a technical platform for the elderly. In: Abdulrazak, B., Giroux, S., Bouchard, B., Pigot, H., Mokhtari, M. (eds.) ICOST 2011. LNCS, vol. 6719, pp. 145–152. Springer, Heidelberg (2011)
9. Farkas, A., Schrenk, M., Hlauschek, W.: Senior Social Platform - an application aimed to reduce the social and digital isolation of seniors. In: Proceedings of REAL CORP 2010 (2010)
10. Wood, E., Willoughby, T., Rushing, A., Bechtel, L., Gilbert, J.: Use of computer input devices by older adults. Journal of Applied Gerontology 24(5), 419–438 (2005)
11. Kin, K., Agrawala, M., DeRose, T.: Determining the benefits of direct-touch, bimanual, and multifinger input on a multitouch workstation. In: Proc. GI 2009, pp. 119–124. Canadian Information Processing Society (2009)
12. Stößel, C., Blessing, L.: Mobile device interaction gestures for older users. In: Proc. NordiCHI 2010, pp. 793–796 (2010)
13. Czaja, S.J., Gregor, P., Hanson, V.L.: Introduction to the Special Issue on Aging and Information Technology. ACM Trans. Access. Comput. 2(1), Article 1 (2009)
14. Leonardi, C., Albertini, A., Pianesi, F., Zancanaro, M.: An exploratory study of a touch-based gestural interface for elderly. In: Proceedings of the 6th Nordic Conference on Human-Computer Interaction: Extending Boundaries, pp. 845–850 (2010)
15. Tsai, T., Chang, H., Chang, Y., Huang, G.: Sharetouch: A system to enrich social network experiences for the elderly. J. Syst. Softw. 85(6), 1363–1369 (2012)
16. Kivimäki, T., Kölndorfer, P., Vainio, A.-M., Pensas, H., Vuorela, T., Garschall, M., Vanhala, J.: User Interface for Social Networking Application for the Elderly. In: Proceedings of the 6th International Conference on Pervasive Technologies Related to Assistive Environments, Article 23 (2013)

The Importance of Social Media as Source of Information in the Technology Identification in Dependence of External and Internal Factors

Christian W. Scheiner

Friedrich-Alexander-Universtität Erlangen-Nürnberg, Nürnberg, Germany
christian.scheiner@fau.de

Abstract. Technologies are a key factor in gaining a competitive edge and in ensuring the profitability and survival of a company. Within the last decade a paradigm shift occurred that has placed external sources at the center of identifying technologies. Developments in information technologies have created new external sources of information such as social media, which have enlarged the organizational search field. Social media possess some characteristics which could make them a promising source for technology information. The importance of social media for companies in technology identification has, however, not been examined empirically. This study therefore analyses social media as a source for technological information. The findings of this study show that social media play in comparison to other external sources only a minor role for companies. Additionally, the evaluation of social media does not vary depending on internal or external factors

Keywords: social media, technology identification, sources of information

1 Introduction

Technologies are a key factor in gaining a competitive edge and in ensuring the profitability and survival of a company. Before a company is able to profit from a technology, however, it must become aware of its existence and evaluate its capabilities adequately. Attention to both elements is, however, not always equally and easily given, in particular when technologies are not the result of internal R&D activities but have their origin outside of the organization. Especially within the last decade, a major paradigm shift has occurred that imposes on companies the challenge to consider external sources of information to a greater extent [1]. Chesbrough [2] uses in this context the term open innovation to separate it from the former dominant approach. With the paradigm shift and along its gaining momentum, companies have opened their organizational boundaries (e.g., [1]; [2]; [3]). As a result, search processes and routines have been changed and developed to observe and examine external sources.

Simultaneously, developments in information and telecommunication technologies have created new types of sources. These sources have enlarged the organizational radar and provide relevant information for technologies and technological develop-

G. Meiselwitz (Ed.): SCSM 2014, LNCS 8531, pp. 103–112, 2014.
© Springer International Publishing Switzerland 2014

ments. Among these sources are social media, which have attracted attention among researchers and practitioners alike. Despite the popularity of social media, research has neglected such media as a source for the identification of technologies. This paper therefore examines the importance of social media in the context of technology identification via an explorative quantitative study.

The paper is structured as follows. A definition of social media is given in section 2. Then the research questions are developed (section 3). Following that, the data collection is described and the operationalization of variables is shown (both in section 4). In section 5, the sample is described. Section 6 contains the empirical findings of the study. The findings are then discussed in section 7, their implications are derived and possibilities for future research are indicated.

2   Social Media

Social media subsumes internet-based applications, platforms and other media which aim at enabling the creation and exchange of content, interactions and collaborations among users [4]. Different studies have proposed classification schemes to clarify the meaning of social media and contribute to a common understanding and definition. Kietzmann et al. [5] suggest, for example, that social media be classified according to identity, conversations, exchange, presence, relationships, reputation and groups. The BDW e.V. [6] developed new "Guidelines for Media Type Classification" in order to facilitate the characterization and categorization of social media types for monitoring and analysing purposes. Within these guidelines the essence of social media is defined by the given context and is dependent on the respective subject area. Kaplan and Haenlein [7] point nevertheless to a misunderstanding among researchers and practitioners with regard to what is included under the umbrella term social media. As a consequence, blogs, wikis, podcasts, pictures, video platforms and social bookmarking are seen as expressions of social media. Research on the use of social media has been conducted mainly in marketing and has examined the impact of social media on a company's brand reputation ([8]; [9]). The role of social media as an external source of technology identification has not attracted the attention of scientific researchers.

3   Research Questions

In the context of technology identification, social media are just one possible source. Previous research has highlighted the importance of customers [1], suppliers [10], trade shows, patents [11], magazines, own market research [12], third-party market research, universities [13], blogs [14], trend scouts [12], competitors [15] and the internet. The importance of social media has thus to be examined individually and according to its position relative to these given and established sources. Research question 1 therefore asks:

Research question 1: How are social media evaluated as a source of information for technology identification in relation to other sources and individually?

The importance of social media can be influenced and determined by external and internal company-specific factors. Regarding external influences, research has pointed to the role of technology turbulence [16]. Technology turbulence mirrors the extent to which technology in an industry is in a state of flux and to which a technology offers the possibility to create a competitive advantage. Companies operating in a business environment that is characterized with high technology turbulence, have thus to cope with the necessity of exploring and exploiting technologies quickly. Social media is often associated with up-to-date information and with possibility to access this information without much temporal delay. The evaluation of social media could subsequently be different according to the level of technology turbulence a company is confronted with.

Research question 2a: Do differences exist in the evaluation of social media with respect to technology turbulence?

Regarding internal company-specific factors, scanning and search alertness, number of employees, revenue, product range, range of main technologies and research intensity are examined in this study. Scanning and search alertness mirrors a company's vigilance towards new technologies and developments [17]. A higher alertness could thus result in a distinct evaluation of social media.

Social media are in general seen as a low-cost means of gathering relevant information. Small and medium-sized enterprises in particular could value social media higher than large companies do. The evaluation of social media could thus be influenced by the size of a company [18]. Number of employees and revenue generated are common features for classifying a company's size.

Products consist of a bundle of embedded technologies, of which the main technologies enable differentiation. These technologies can be seen as core capabilities [19]. The more a company has to cope with a broader product range and (subsequently with) different main technologies, the more search and scanning efforts have to be invested to ensure competitiveness. This higher necessity could result in a higher appreciation of social media, as it enlarges the search field and can offer cost-effective immediate access to new information.

The allocation of financial resources reflects the importance of specific functions for a company. Research intensity mirrors as a consequence the value of innovation activities for an organization. The more a budget is spent on R&D, the higher innovation is valued within an organization. Simultaneously, research intensity is seen as a proxy for the ability to evaluate the value of new information, integrate it into the company and commercialize it [3]. Research intensity could hence lead to a different evaluation of social media as a source of information For these reasons, the level of research intensity could lead to a different evaluation of social media as source of information.

Taking these aspects into consideration, the following research questions are raised:

Research question 2b: Do differences exist among companies in the evaluation of social media with respect to scanning and search alertness?

Research question 2c: Do differences exist among companies in the evaluation of social media with respect to number of employees?

Research question 2d: Do differences exist among companies in the evaluation of social media with respect to revenue generated?

Research question 2e: Do differences exist among companies in the evaluation of social media with respect to the existing range of products offered?

Research question 2f: Do differences exist in among companies the evaluation of social media with respect to the spectrum of main embedded technologies?

Research question 2g: Do differences exist among companies in the evaluation of social media with respect to research intensity?

4   Data Collection and Operationalization

For the purpose of this study, a web survey was chosen as a research instrument. The compilation of the web survey was based on the requirements proposed by Schonlau et al. [20] in order to ensure a user-friendly design. The questionnaire was furthermore designed to fulfill the criteria of clarity, clearness and simplicity. The questionnaire was pre-tested by two PhD candidates and one postdoctoral fellow. The survey was conducted between June and August of 2013. The selection of respondents was conducted in a manner to ensure that participants possessed the required knowledge. Additionally, a filter question was embedded in the questionnaire to improve further the selection of appropriate respondents after the survey was completed. As a result, 178 responses could be used for the analysis of this study.

The selection of topics covered and the formulation of questions were based on an extensive literature review and were orientated according to existing surveys in this field. As the role of social media as a source for technological information was examined in this study, several influential factors were included in the questionnaire: technological turbulence, scanning and search alertness, number of employees, revenue generated, product range, range of main technologies and research intensity.

Technology turbulence was measured with the five items of Jaworski and Kohli [16]. A 7-point scoring format (1=strongly agree to 7=strongly disagree) was employed for all items in the questionnaire, which was re-coded in the course of the evaluation (1=strongly disagree to 7=strongly agree). The Cronbach alpha of this construct is higher than 0.7. In order to allow a comparison of companies with respect to their technology turbulence, a new ordinal variable was created according to the level of agreement, categorizing technology turbulence into no technology turbulence (range: 1-1.49), low technology turbulence (range: 1.5-3.49), medium technology turbulence (range: 3.5-4.49), high technology turbulence (range: 4.5-6.49), and very high technology turbulence (range: 6.5-7).

Scanning and search alertness was measured with an adjusted scale which was originally developed by Tang et al. [17]. A 7-point scoring format (1=strongly agree to 7=strongly disagree) was employed for all items in the questionnaire, which was re-coded in the course of the evaluation (1=strongly disagree to 7=strongly agree). Afterwards, the items were summed up and this result averaged to obtain the mean value of the construct. The Cronbach alpha of this construct is higher than 0.7. Based on the calculation, a new ordinal variable was created, categorizing scanning and search alertness into none (range: 1-1.49), low (range: 1.5-3.49), medium (range: 3.5-4.49), high (range: 4.5-6.49), and very high (range: 6.5-7).

Number of employees and annual revenue were measured with closed-ended questions and afterwards grouped together under the following categories: fewer than 50 employees, 50 to fewer than 250 employees, 250 to fewer than 1,000 employees, 1,000 to fewer than 10,000 employees and 10,000 and more employees. Regarding revenue, the following categories were constructed: less than 5 million EUR, 5 to less than 50 million EUR, 50 to less than 250 million EUR, 250 million to less than 1 billion EUR, 1 to less than 10 billion EUR and more than 10 billion EUR.

Research intensity was measured via the average amount spent annually for research in relation to revenue. Accordingly, respondents had to answer the question "What percentage of annual revenues does your company spend on average per year on R&D?" Three reply options were given: less than 3.5%, more than 3.5% but less than 8.5% and more than 8.5%.

Range of products was measured originally with a semantic differential using a single-product company (1) and a multiple-products company (7) as the ends of the continuum. In the course of the evaluation, the responses were grouped as follows: single product (answer option 1), small product range (answer options 2 and 3), middle product range (answer options 4 and 5) and big product range (answer options 6 and 7).

Similarly, respondents could choose within a semantic differential between one main technology (1) and many equally important main technologies (7). Answers were also grouped afterwards into the following categories: one main technology (1), small technology range (answer options 2 and 3), middle technology range (answer options 4 and 5) and big technology range (answer options 6 and 7).

Social media illustrates one possible source of technological information in technology recognition. To gain insight into the research behavior of companies, a list of potential sources was presented to respondents. Participants were asked "Please indicate the importance of the following sources in technology identification" and could evaluate 14 pre-defined sources and add two additional sources if appropriate. Suppliers, professional magazines, trade shows, customers, consulting agencies, patents, social media, a company's own market research, third-party market research, universities, blogs, trend scouts, competitors and the internet comprised the given sources. A 7-point scoring format (1=very high importance to 7=without importance) was employed for all items. To ease the interpretation of the findings, the responses were recoded in the course of the evaluation (1=without importance to 7=very high importance).

In order to identify possible differences in the evaluation of social media as a source of information in technology identification, the non-parametric Kruskal–Wallis test, in which more than two independent group variables can be compared.

5   Description of the Sample

The largest group of companies operates in the sector of mechanical engineering (27.7%), followed by companies focusing on IT, electronics and optics (22.6%), automotive industry(9%), plant engineering (7.7%) and other industries (33%). Companies considered in this study are maneuvering through a competitive environment which is characterized by the majority of respondents as one with a high level of technology turbulence. Companies face as a consequence a high necessity to develop new technologies to ensure competitiveness and increase their competitive advantage. Simultaneously, scanning and search alertness is evaluated generally as high. Only a minority of companies rate their alertness as low or medium. Participating companies have on average 250 to less than 1,000 employees with a mode of more than 10,000 employees. They generate on average revenue of 250 million to less than 1 billion EUR. The mode is from 5 to less than 50 million EUR and the expenditure on average is between 3.5% to less than 8.5% of revenue for R&D.

Regarding product and technology range, companies have on average a medium spectrum of products and main technologies. The numeral biggest group among the participating companies has a high product and technology range (see Figure 1).

6   Findings

Research question 1 examines the importance of social media as a source of information in identifying technologies. Therein, it is necessary to examine the importance of social media both individually and in relation to other sources.

A clear hierarchy is revealed in the evaluation of sources. Respondents assess nine sources as highly important or at least medium important. Customers are seen as the most valuable source for identifying new technologies, followed by competitors and own market research. Trade shows, suppliers, universities, Internet, magazines and patents are also evaluated in average as important. Five sources have a value below four and are subsequently perceived as less or even as unimportant. Social media belongs with a value of 2.9 to group at the bottom of the list together with consulting agencies, 3rd party market research, social media, trend scouts and blogs (see Figure 2).

Other sources, which have been added by respondents are seen in average as important. Respondents mention here for example venture capital, contingencies, economic development schemes, or contact to new ventures.

Research questions 2a–2g examine whether differences related to external and internal factors exist among companies in the evaluation of social media as a source of information in technology identification.

Research question 2a focuses on technology turbulence as an external factor. The Kruskal-Wallis test showed that no difference among companies exists depending on the degree of technology turbulence they experience.

Scanning and search alertness describes the first internal factor, which is examined in research question 2b. The evaluation of social media as a source of information is not dependent on general scanning and search alertness. All companies considered in this study evaluated social media similarly irrespective of their alertness.

Research question 2c examines whether the number of employees affects a company's perception of social media as a valuable tool. The Kruskal–Wallis test also identified no differences among companies in this respect.

Revenue generated describes the third internal factor that could have an influence (research question 2d). Similar to technological turbulence and number of employees no significant difference can be identified.

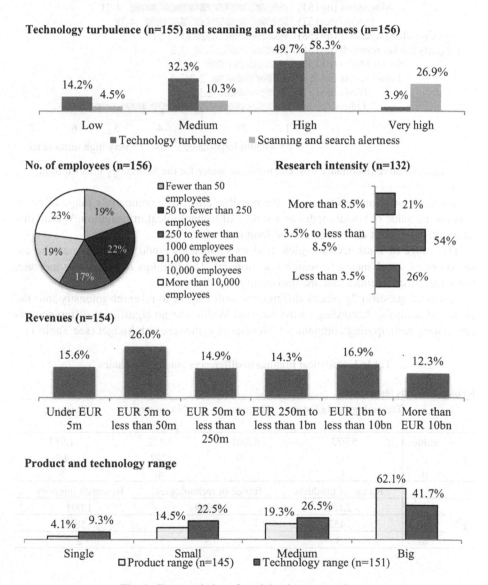

Fig. 1. Characteristics of participating companies

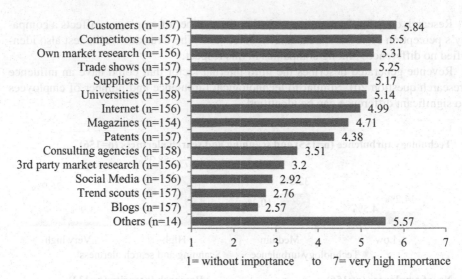

1= without importance   to   7= very high importance

Fig. 2. Relative importance of social media as source for the technology identification

Research question 2e focuses on the possible effect of a company's range of products on the value of social media as a source of technological information. Within this study no significant difference can be found.

The range of main technologies used by companies could also influence the assessment of social media (research question 2f). The findings of this study indicate, however, no differences that are statistically significant.

Research question 2g places differences with respect to research intensity into the center of analysis. According to the Kruskal-Wallis test no significant difference exists among participating companies with respect to the research budget (see Table 1).

Table 1. Statistical findings to differences among companies

Kruskal-Wallis test results					
		Technology turbulence	Alertness	No. of employees	Revenue
χ^2	value	5.972	3.840	5.472	4.813
	p.	.113	.279	.242	.439
	df	3	3	4	5
		Range of products	Range of technologies	Research intensity	
χ^2	value	2.632	1.949	1.091	
	p.	.452	.583	.580	
	df	3	3	2	

7   Discussion, Implications, and Future Research

The findings of this study demonstrate that social media play only a minor role in technology identification and that companies share this evaluation irrespective of external and internal factors. These results can be interpreted in three ways. The first explanation focuses on the stage of development of social media. Sources undergo in general an evolutionary process in which dominant and acknowledged sources emerge over time. Bearing in mind the newness of social media, they could still be in a state of development in which some sources are missing or have not reached a sophisticated level yet. Companies should therefore monitor the development of social media. Future research could examine the state of development of social media and could help companies identify streams in social media which seem to be especially promising for technology identification.

The second explanation is closely linked to the first. When sources are new and still in the early phase of development, the credibility of existing sources is low, or is perhaps evaluated as low, even if the available information is highly accurate [21]. Schmitt and Klein [21] point also to the uncertainty of complex information. In cases where different facets of data have to be integrated, people could be overstrained by or not prepared to cope with the available and perhaps fragmented data. Future research could examine whether and to what extent these aspects are present with respect to social media.

While the first two explanations concentrate on the source of information, the third draws attention to established routines in companies. Companies gain experience and knowledge over time of how to identify technology in external sources. This leads to the improvement of search procedures and processes [22]. At the same time, the spectrum of potential activities can be reduced and can lead to inertia in the exploration of new sources [23]. Companies have to examine whether and to what extent this situation is present and initiate processes that enable them to overcome hindering routines. Future research could examine the level of existing impeding routines in companies with respect to social media and could identify approaches to overcome these hindrances.

References

1. Von Hippel, E.: Democratizing Innovation. MIT Press, Cambridge, MA (2005)
2. Chesbrough, H. W.: The Era of Open Innovation. *MIT Sloan Management Review*, 44(3), 35–42 (2003).
3. Tsai, W.: Knowledge Transfer in Intraorganizational Networks: Effects of Network Position and Absorptive Capacity on Business Unit Innovation and Performance. Academy of Management Journal 44(5), 996–1004 (2001)
4. Richter A, Koch M.: Social software — status quo und Zukunft. Technischer Bericht, Nr. 2007–01, Fakultät für Informatik. Universität der Bundeswehr München (2007)
5. Kietzmann, J., Hermkens, K., McCarthy, I., Silvestre, B.: Social Media? Get Serious! Understanding the Functional Building Blocks of Social Media. Business Horizon, 54 (3), 241–251 (2011)

6. Bundesverband Digitale Wirtschaft e.V. (ed.): Richtlinie zur Medientypeinteilung, (accessed September 5, [available at: http://www.bvdw.org/mybvdw/media/download/ richtlinie-social-media-zur-medientyp-einteilung-2013.pdf?file=2714] (2013)
7. Kaplan, A. M., Haenlein, M.: Users of the World, Unite! The Challenges and Opportunities of Social Media. Business Horizons, 53 (1): 59–68 (2010)
8. Kim, A. J., Ko, E.: Do Social Media Marketing Activities Enhance Customer Equity? An Empirical Study of Luxury Fashion Brand. Journal of Business Research, 65 (10): 1480–1486 (2012)
9. DEI Worldwide: The Impact of Social Media on Purchasing Behavior. Engaging Con su- mers Online. available at www.deiworldwide.com/files/DEIStudy-Engaging% 20ConsumersOnline-Summary.pdf (2008)
10. Lambe, C.J., Spekman, R.E.: Alliances, External Technology Acquisition, and Disconti- nuous Technological Change. Journal of Product Innovation Management 14(2), 102–116 (1997)
11. Basberg, B.L.: Patents and the Measurement of Technological Change: A Survey of the Literature. Research Policy 16(2-4), 131–141 (1987)
12. Bessant, J., von Stamm, B.: Twelve Search Strategies That Could Save Your Organization. AIM Executive Briefing. London Business School, London (2007)
13. Link, A. N., Rees, J.: Firm Size, University Based Research, and the Returns to R&D. Small Business Economics 2(1), 25–31 (1990)
14. Droge, C., Stanko, M.A., Pollitte, W.A.: Lead Users and Early Adopters on the Web: The Role of New Technology Product Blogs. Journal of Product Innovation Management 27(1), 66–82 (2010)
15. Lim, K., Chesbrough, H., Ruan, Y.: Open Innovation and Patterns of R&D Competition. International Journal of Technology Management 52(3-4), 295–321 (2010)
16. Jaworski, B.J., Kohli, A.K.: Market Orientation: Antecedents and Consequences. Journal of Marketing 57, 53–70 (1993)
17. Tang, J., Kacmar, K.M., Busenitz, L.: Entrepreneurial Alertness in the Pursuit of New Op- portunities. Journal of Business Venturing 27(1), 77–94 (2012)
18. Kahle, L.R., Valette-Florence, P.: Marketplace Lifestyles in an Age of Social Media: Theory and Methods. M. E. Sharpe, Armonk, NY (2012)
19. Coombs, R.: Core Competencies and the Strategic Management of R&D. R&D Manage- ment 26(4), 345–355 (1996)
20. Schonlau, M., Fricker, R.D., Elliott, M.N.: Conducting Research Surveys via E-Mail and the Web. Rand, Santa Monica, CA (2002)
21. Schmitt, J.F., Klein, G.: Fighting in the Fog: Dealing with Battlefield Uncertainty. Marine Corps Gazette 80, 62–69 (1996)
22. Mitchell, W.: Whether and When? Probability and Timing of Incumbents' Entry into Emerging Industrial Subfields. Administrative Science Quarterly 34(2), 41–50 (1989)
23. Berthon, P., Pitt, L.F., Ewing, M.T.: Corollaries of the Collective: The Influence of Orga- nizational Culture and Memory Development on Perceived Decision-Making Context. Academy of Marketing Science Journal 29(2), 135–50 (2001)

The Development and Validation of the Social Network Sites (SNSs) Usage Questionnaire

Yuanyuan Shi, Yu L.L. Luo, Ziyan Yang, Yunzhi Liu, and Huajian Cai

Institute of Psychology, Chinese Academy of Sciences,
16 Lincui Road, Beijing, China
{shiyy,luoy,yangzy,liuyz,caihj}@psych.ac.cn

Abstract. Surfing Social network sites (SNSs) has become one of the most popular activity for ordinary people. To date, there has been no satisfactory measure to understand the role of SNSs in daily life. Considering this, we developed a self-report instrument, the Social Network Sites (SNSs) Usage Questionnaire, which included two subscales for featured usage and affective experience, respectively. Factor analysis suggested 3 factors for the subscale of featured usage and 2 factors for the subscale of affective experience. We referred to the Big Five Personality Inventory and a revised version of the Internet Motivation Questionnaire as external criteria to validate our questionnaire. The results indicated that the newly developed questionnaire is of good psychometric characteristics.

Keywords: social network sites (SNSs), affect, personality, motivation.

1 Introduction

We would like to draw your attention to the fact that it is not possible to modify a paper in any way, once it has been published. This applies to both the printed book and the online version of the publication. Every detail, including the order of the names of the authors, should be checked before the paper is sent to the Volume Editors. Social network sites (SNSs) are defined as web-based services that allow individuals to construct a public or semi-public profile and share connections with a certain list of other users [1]. Since the first introduction, SNSs, such as MySpace, Facebook, Cyworld (in Korea), Bebo (in Britain) and Renren (in China), have attracted millions of users. For example, Facebook, the world's most popular SNS, has a total number of 1.3 billion monthly active users (Facebook, 2014). According to China Internet Network Information Center (CNNIC), China, holding the world's most numerous Internet users, has an enormous number of SNSs users, specifically, 281 million users in Weibo and 278 million users in other SNSs [2].

In SNSs, people extended real life to communicate their real personality [3], and profiles can be seen as a form of digital body where individuals write themselves into being [1]. Thus, social network sites provide rich sources of naturalistic behavioral data, and offer a good chance to explore people's personality in the cyber world. SNSs also have attracted numerous researchers, especially personality and social

G. Meiselwitz (Ed.): SCSM 2014, LNCS 8531, pp. 113–124, 2014.

psychologists [4-8]. However, the measures of SNSs usage vary widely. Some of them are lack of reliability and validity, and thus, hard to be used in scientific research. Worse still, most of previous measures ignore the affective experience of SNSs usage. As a result, the primary objective of the present research was to develop and validate a tool for measuring SNSs usage and related affective experience simultaneously.

1.1   Extant Measures

In one line of SNSs research, researchers had participants' SNSs pages saved, gathered information from the pages, and developed comprehensive coding schemes to cover virtually all the major items [9-11]. Thus, researchers would collect some quantitative features that are common to standard SNSs profiles, such as number of friends and number of photos. But a lot of features need subjective coding by research raters, which is labor-intensive and results in limited number of participants. What's more, SNSs, like Facebook and Renren, are multi-audience identity production sites, which means users could control over the privacy settings of their accounts and show different identity to different audiences. Researchers could study only one type of users' performance, thus would be blind to other possible shows users presented in their SNSs accounts [10].

In order to obtain a better measure of Facebook usage, Ellison and his colleague (2007) developed the Facebook Intensity Scale [12]. The scale includes two self-reported assessments designed to measure the extent to which participants actively engage in Facebook, and also includes six attitudinal questions designed to tap the extent to which participants are emotionally connected to Facebook and the extent to which Facebook is integrated into their daily practice [12]. Inspired by their work, Ross and his colleagues (2009) developed a Facebook Questionnaire, which contains three categories of items assessing basic use of Facebook, attitudes associated with Facebook, and posting of personally-identifying information [6]. In this 28-item questionnaire, response alternatives range from multiple choice to yes/no depending on the nature of the item, making it hard to analyze; besides, many items turn out to be useless. Afterwards, researchers have only taken part of the Facebook Questionnaire to measure frequency or preferences for particular Facebook features [7, 13]. In addition, since the questionnaire is designed specifically for Facebook, some of the items are not available for other SNSs, for instance, Wang and his colleagues (2012) picked up 5 important features and changed them into a 5-point Likert scale to measure Renren usage [8].

With these measures, a considerable amount of researches have investigated the relationship between personality, particularly, the Five-Factor Model, and the SNSs usage [4, 5, 14]. However, personality defined by the Five-Factor approach may be too broad and not be the most appropriate way to understand specific Internet behaviors [6]. Researchers have also explored other intrapersonal and interpersonal characteristics, such as motivation [15]. However, not much research queried affective results of using SNSs. According to a recent study, the frequency of updating profiles and giving comments are important predictors of subjective well-being (SWB); meanwhile, caring others' comments could be a negative predictor

[16]. However, the SWB could just be an indirect index to show SNSs users' affective experience. As a result, one important objective of the present research was to directly measure SNSs users' affective experience as well as users' behaviors.

1.2 Current Study

In the present study, we took emotions into consideration and designed a new self-report measure of SNSs usage including two subscales, the SNSs Featured Usage Scale and the SNSs Affective Experiences Scale. Instead of only examining one specific site, we generalized features that were common to standard SNSs sites, and expanded the newly developed scale to a wider application. In order to develop more robust indicators of use from the SNSs Usage Questionnaire, for each subscale, a factor analysis was conducted to extract factors, which would yield data cannot be accurately captured by single items. We computed Cronbach's alpha for each factor and correlations among each factor as indexes of internal consistency. To test external validity, we examined the relations between each factor and important personality characteristics, such as the Big Five personality traits and motivations of Internet usage. We hypothesized that motivations and personality could predict SNSs usage tapped by the questionnaire.

2 Method

2.1 Participants

Four hundred and sixty-four participants took part in the study. The sample was composed of 265 females and 199 males, ranging in age from 17 to 25 (M = 20.26, SD = 1.86).

2.2 Materials

All participants completed the SNSs Usage Questionnaire, a questionnaire for the motivation of Internet usage, a personality inventory, and other tests irrelevant to SNSs. They finished the questionnaires privately, quietly on computer.

The Social Network Sites (SNSs) Usage Questionnaire. The SNSs Usage Questionnaire includes two subscales, the SNSs Featured Usage Scale and the SNSs Affective Experience Scale. At the beginning of the questionaire, participants were asked to recall the daily usage of one SNS they used most frequently. Based on a questionnaire for Facebook usage [6], we developed the SNSs Featured Usage Scale, which includes 13 items to measure featured usage on SNSs, such as updating one's status and visiting friends' homepages (α = 0.82; see the Appendix for the full scale). For 10 items, participants indicated the frequency of their usage of SNSs on 7-point scale (1 = never, 7 = multiple times a day). For the other 3 items, they reported the duration of surfing SNSs each time (1 = less than 15 minutes, 7 = more than four hours), the number of their friends (1 = 1-50, 7 = over 500), and the constitution of their friends (1 = all are friends in real life, 7 = all are strangers in real life).

We also developed an 8-item scale to measure the affective experience of using SNSs (α = 0.82), by adapting the Affective Experience Scale [17] and the Positive Affect and Negative Affect Scale [18]. Participants rated the frequency they experience pleasant affects (happiness, contentment, joy, cheer) and unpleasant affects (depression, anxiety, anger, unhappiness) using SNSs on 7-point Likert scale (1 = never, 7 = always).

Motivation. According to recent studies, people use SNSs mainly to keep up with friends and families, make new friends, record life, show off, relax, and improve daily life [16, 19]. Hence, we asked the participants to indicate whether they endorse those six motivations on 6-point Likert scale (1 = completely disagree, 6 = completely agree). The internal consistency was acceptable (α = 0.69).

Personality. We used a 50-item personality inventory for Big-Five factors [20]: agreeableness (e.g. "I can understand the feelings of others", neuroticism (e.g. "I'm moody"), extraversion (e.g. "I am talkative"), conscientiousness (e.g. "I work meticulously"), and openness to experience (e.g. "I am imaginative"). The inventory consists of ten items for each factor and each item was rated on a 6-point Likert scale (1 = strongly disagree, 6 = strongly agree). The internal consistency was good for each of the subscales: agreeableness (M = 46.49, SD = 5.83, α = 0.80), neuroticism (M = 25.62, SD = 7.59, α = 0.82), extraversion (M = 35.32, SD = 9.01, α = 0.85), conscientiousness (M = 41.55, SD = 7.18, α = 0.80), and openness to experience (M = 41.43, SD = 6.52, α = 0.82).

3   Results

3.1   Dimensionality and Internal Correlations

To develop more nuanced markers of SNSs usage, we carried out a principal component factor analysis with varimax rotation for each subscale (i.e. featured usage and affective experience). We identified three factors from the 13 items of the SNSs Featured Usage Scale (Table 1). According to the content of the items highly loaded on each factor, the three factors represented basic usage (factor I), interactive usage (factor II), and self-display usage (factor III), respectively. The internal consistency of all dimensions was acceptable (0.56 - 0.83). Mean scores were calculated for each dimension (the comp). As for the SNSs Affective Experience scale, the four pleasant affects and the four unpleasant affects, respectively, fell under two factors (Table 2). The internal consistency of each component was high (0.90, 0.85). For each component, we obtained an index by averaging across the four items.

As table 3 shows, the three dimensions of the SNSs Featured Usage Scale (i.e. basic, interactive, and display usage) were significantly correlated with each other (rs > 0.29, ps < .001), and the positive component of the SNSs Affective Experience Scale was negatively related to the negative component (r = -0.14, p = .002). We also correlated the three dimensions of the SNSs Featured Usage Scale with the two components of the SNSs Affective Experience Scale (Table 3). All the three usage dimensions were modestly associated with positive affects (rs ≥ 0.11, ps < .05), whereas only display usage correlated with negative affects (r = 0.16, p < .001).

Table 1. Factor loadings for the SNSs Featured Usage Scale

Item	I	II	III
Frequency of using SNSs	**.75**	.29	.09
Number of friends	**.68**	.24	.02
Duration of using SNSs	**.53**	.09	.51
Making comments	.19	**.82**	.02
Checking other's comments or messages	.23	**.76**	.04
Visiting friends' homepage	.23	**.71**	.03
Sharing or re-send others' profiles	.30	**.69**	.13
Updating status	.18	**.68**	.11
Using private message	.06	**.51**	.27
Updating profile images	.07	.24	**.71**
Constitution of friends	.08	-.12	**.58**
Updating photos	.11	.51	**.55**
Updating notes/blogs	-.33	.45	**.47**

Note: Highest loading of each item is in boldface.

Table 2. Factor loadings for the SNSs Affective Experience Scale

Item	I	II
Joy	**.91**	-.06
Cheer	**.90**	-.06
Contentment	**.88**	-.08
Happy	**.83**	-.05
Depression	-.10	**.84**
Angry	-.03	**.84**
Anxiety	-.04	**.84**
Unhappy	-.06	**.81**

Note: Highest loading of each item is in boldface.

Table 3. Correlations among dimensions of the SNSs Usage Questionnaire

	Cronbach's α	1	2	3	4
1 Basic Usage	0.59				
2 Interact Usage	0.83	.50***			
3 Display Usage	0.56	.29***	.48***		
4 Positive Affects	0.90	.19***	.26***	.11*	
5 Negative Affects	0.85	.02	.03	.16***	-0.14**

Note: *$p < .05$; **$p < .01$; ***$p < .001$.

Table 4. Correlations between the motives of Internet usage and the dimensions of the SNSs Usage Questionnaire

Motive	Basic Usage	Interact Usage	Display Usage	Positive Affects	Negative Affects
Contact family and friend	.18***	.23***	.09+	.33***	-.08+
Make new friend	.08+	.16***	.27***	.16***	.06
Relax	.12**	.10*	-.01	.22***	-.19***
Improve daily life	.22***	.15***	.03	.26***	-.13**
Record life	.13**	.28***	.29***	.22***	.01
Show off	.23***	.31***	.33***	.28***	.06

Note: +p <.1; *p < .05;**p < .01;***p < .001.

3.2   External Validation

Motivation and SNSs Usage. We correlated all the six motivation items with each dimensions of featured usage and affective experience (Table 4). For the featured usage scale, the interactive usage significantly correlated with all the motives (rs $\geq$ 0.10, ps < .05); the basic usage significantly associated with all the motives (rs $\geq$ 0.12, ps < .01) except making new friends (r = 0.08, p = .098); the display usage significantly correlated with making new friends, recording life, and showing off (rs $\geq$ 0.27, ps < .001). As for the affective experience, positive affects were positively correlated with all the motives (rs $\geq$ 0.16, ps < .001); negative affects, however, only significantly correlated with relaxing and improving daily life (rs $\leq$ -0.13, ps < .01), and marginally associated with contacting families and friends (r = -0.08, p = .078).

Table 5. Multiple regression analyses using gender, age, and the Big Five to predict the dimensions of the SNSs Usage Questionnaire

Motive	Basic Usage	Interact Usage	Display Usage	Positive Affects	Negative Affects
gender	-.05	.07	.06	.03	-.08
age	.11*	-.04	-.05	-.03	-.01
Agreeableness	.08	.08	-.05	.18***	-.09+
Neuroticism	.07	.09+	.05	-.07	.34***
Extraversion	.16***	.20***	.20***	.17***	.02
Consciousness	-.10+	-.03	-.05	.10+	-.16**
Openness	.09	.01	-.07	-.04	-.09+
R^2	.05*	.04***	.04***	.09***	.21***

Note: +p <.1; *p < .05;**p < .01;***p < .001.

Personality and SNSs Usage. For each dimension of featured usage and affective experience, we performed a multiple regression analysis with gender, age, and the five personality factors as the independent variables (Table 5). Among the five personality factors, the three dimensions of featured usage could only be predicted by extraversion (βs $\geq$ .16, ps < .001). Agreeableness and extraversion were both predictors of positive affects (βs $\geq$ .17, ps < .001); meanwhile, neurotism, positively (β = .34, p < .001), and conscientiousness, negatively (β = -.16, p = .002), predicted negative affects.

4   Discussion

To understand the role of SNSs in daily life sufficiently, we developed a valid self-report instrument, the Social Network Sites (SNSs) Usage Questionnaire, which included two subscales for featured usage and affective experience, respectively. We introduced factor analysis and distinguished three different featured usages (basic, interactive and display usage) and two affective experiences (positive and negative affects).

For the Featured Usage subscale, different from previous scales examining only one specific site (usually Facebook[6, 12]), we generalized features that were common to standard SNSs sites, and expanded the newly developed scale to a wider application. As expected, the frequency and duration of using SNSs, and the number of friends belong to the basic usage, since they are major indexes of the extent to which the participant actively engages in SNSs [12]. Whereas, constitution of friends belongs to the display factor of SNSs usage, as some researchers lament that friendships in the digital age have somewhat degenerated into a collection of online contacts for others to admire [21]. This could also give an explanation of the high correlation between display factor and the motivation of making new friends. Updating photos and notes (or blogs) had a bit higher factor loadings on the display usage than the interactive usage (0.55 vs. 0.51; 0.47 vs. 0.45). In SNSs, photos and notes are typical means for self-presentation; specially, amongst the various features, the profile image, which is a specific photo and could represent the individual in the online platform, appearing in search results and alongside every turn of online interaction, has been posited as the most important one [10, 22, 23]. Photos displayed on the individual homepage constitute an important way to project the image they wish to present to others [4]. As a result, just like "profile image", we attributed the items "updating photos" and "updating notes" to the factor of display usage, which also making a higher correlation between display usage and showing off motive. Differently, updating status belongs to the interactive factor, which might because unlike photos, which can be constructed and refined to conceal flaws directly [24], status plays as role of blowing off steam to some degree, and users only update status to gain empathy.

Based on these factors, our study revealed behavioral pattern due to different personality. SNSs users with high extraversion and less consciousness tended to use more SNSs basic usage. Users who scored high on neuroticism and extraversion preferred more frequency of interactive usage. Among the three aspects of personality, extraversion counted the most for predicting the interactive behaviors in SNSs. Those using more display features tended to be less agreeable, and more extraverted. These results were consisted with previous study concerned with the Big

Five personality: the extroverts tended to be more active in the SNSs [4, 5, 14, 16]; conscientious individuals tended to spend less time on SNSs [7], because these sites promote procrastination and serve as distraction from more important tasks [25]; individuals high in neuroticism were more likely to use it for instant messaging [5, 26] and updated profiles more frequently as a means of self-presentation aimed at encouraging the responses of others and thereby creating a sense of belongingness and reducing loneliness [8]. Also, like some of former studies [27, 28], our results failed to reveal the relation between openness to experience and SNS featured usage, this might because SNSs are no longer "a new experience" [28].

As for the Affective Experience Scale, the positive affects and negative affects are exactly represented the originally hypothesized dimensions. Using direct measures, our research furthered former study, which indicated SNSs usage was related to both positive and negative affects [16]. Based on these two factors, the present study also investigated the relations between personality and affective experience in SNSs. Users with high level of agreeableness, extraversion and consciousness were more likely to experience positive affects; whereas, negative affects were more likely experienced by users with high neuroticism. Early studies showed an Internet Paradox about computer-mediated communication (CMC). According to Kraut et al.'s (1998) model, the use of the Internet is likely to result in an increase in depression and loneliness, especially for those introverts [29, 30]. Amichai-Hamburger and Ben-Artzi (2003) proposed another model. In terms of this model, for those highly neurotic, increased use of the Internet social services is not a cause, but a result of their loneliness. They also found that for women, loneliness mediates the relationship between neuroticism and Internet use [31].

By combining SNSs featured usage and affective experience, our findings provided a firm proof for the proposition that "both the rich and the poor get richer in the SNSs" [32]. People who scored high on extroversion and narcissism are supposed to have better social skills, and would like to use their advanced social skills to extend their social environment on the internet and use more interactive features; whereas, individuals with high neuroticism, who are supposed to perceived lower level of social support [33], demonstrated a strong interest in using the Internet for communication [26] to avoid loneliness [25] and to make their social needs meet [34], although they still reported plenty of negative experience on SNSs.

5   Implications, Limitations and Future Research

We have presented information regarding the development of 2 subscales to measure SNSs usage, including a 13-item Featured Usage Scales, and an 8-item Affective Experience Scale. The scales correlate at predicted levels, and show the similar relations with external variables as previous studies. Different from extant scales, which are unreliable, or of poor validity, or cumbersome in length, we offered our scales as reliable, valid, and efficient assessment for SNSs user's featured usage and affective experience. More importantly, it was the first trial to measure SNSs users' affective experience directly. And with the combination of behaviors and emotions, we could draw a more complete picture of how SNSs influence daily life.

However, limitation to this study includes lack of comparison with other SNSs questionnaires and examination of the rest-retest reliability. Additionally, personality traits accounted for only a small percentage of the variance in SNS activities, and some of the traits were unrelated to any type of SNS activity in our research. It may be possible that these personality factors do not play a role in directing SNS activities. Further research may extend the present research by examining other intrapersonal or interpersonal characteristics that may have a stronger relationship with SNSs usage, such as narcissism [10, 35] and self-efficacy [11].

References

1. Ellison, N.B.: Social network sites: Definition, history, and scholarship. Journal of Computer - Mediated Communication 13(1), 210–230 (2007)
2. China Internet Network Information Center: Statistical Report on Internet development in China (January 2014), http://www.cnnic.net.cn/hlwfzyj/hlwxzbg/hlwtjbg/201401/P020140116395418429515.pdf
3. Back, M.D., Stopfer, J.M., Vazire, S., Gaddis, S., Schmukle, S.C., Egloff, B., Gosling, S.D.: Facebook profiles reflect actual personality, not self-idealization. Psychological Science 21(3), 372–374 (2010)
4. Amichai-Hamburger, Y., Vinitzky, G.: Social network use and personality. Computers in Human Behavior 26(6), 1289–1295 (2010)
5. Correa, T., Hinsley, A.W., De Zuniga, H.G.: Who interacts on the Web?: The intersection of users' personality and social media use. Computers in Human Behavior 26(2), 247–253 (2010)
6. Ross, C., Orr, E.S., Sisic, M., Arseneault, J.M., Simmering, M.G., Orr, R.R.: Personality and motivations associated with Facebook use. Computers in Human Behavior 25(2), 578–586 (2009)
7. Ryan, T., Xenos, S.: Who uses Facebook? An investigation into the relationship between the Big Five, shyness, narcissism, loneliness, and Facebook usage. Computers in Human Behavior 27(5), 1658–1664 (2011)
8. Wang, J.L., Jackson, L.A., Zhang, D.J., Su, Z.Q.: The relationships among the Big Five Personality factors, self-esteem, narcissism, and sensation-seeking to Chinese University students' uses of social networking sites (SNSs). Computers in Human Behavior 28, 2313–2319 (2012)
9. Zhao, S., Grasmuck, S., Martin, J.: Identity construction on Facebook: Digital empowerment in anchored relationships. Computers in Human Behavior 24(5), 1816–1836 (2008)
10. Buffardi, L.E., Campbell, W.K.: Narcissism and social networking web sites. Personality and Social Psychology Bulletin 34(10), 1303–1314 (2008)
11. Krämer, N.C., Winter, S.: Impression Management 2.0. Journal of Media Psychology: Theories, Methods, and Applications 20(3), 106–116 (2008)
12. Ellison, N.B., Steinfield, C., Lampe, C.: The benefits of Facebook "friends:" Social capital and college students' use of online social network sites. Journal of Computer-Mediated Communication 12(4), 1143–1168 (2007)

13. Smock, A.D., Ellison, N.B., Lampe, C., Wohn, D.Y.: Facebook as a toolkit: A uses and gratification approach to unbundling feature use. Computers in Human Behavior 27(6), 2322–2329 (2011)
14. Wilson, M.: The re-tooled mind: how culture re-engineers cognition. Social Cognitive and Affective Neuroscience 5(2-3), 180–187 (2010)
15. Seidman, G.: Self-presentation and belonging on Facebook: How personality influences social media use and motivations. Personality and Individual Differences 54(3), 402–407 (2013)
16. Shi, Y., Yue, X., He, J.: Understanding Social Network Sites (SNSs) Preferences: Personality, Motivation, and Happiness Matters. In: Ozok, A.A., Zaphiris, P. (eds.) OCSC 2013. LNCS, vol. 8029, pp. 94–103. Springer, Heidelberg (2013)
17. Diener, E.: Assessing subjective well-being: Progress and opportunities. Social Indicators Research 31(2), 103–157 (1994)
18. Watson, D., Clark, L.A., Tellegen, A.: Development and validation of brief measures of positive and negative affect: the PANAS scales. Journal of Personality and Social Psychology 54(6), 1063–1070 (1988)
19. Lenhart, A.: Adults and social network websites. Pew Internet and American Life Project (2009), http://www.pewinternet.org/Reports/2009/Adults-and-Social-Network-Websites.aspx/
20. Goldberg, L.R.: The development of markers for the Big-Five factor structure. Psychological Assessment 4(1), 26–42 (1992)
21. Tong, S.T., Van Der Heide, B., Langwell, L., Walther, J.B.: Too much of a good thing? The relationship between number of friends and interpersonal impressions on Facebook. Journal of Computer-Mediated Communication 13(3), 531–549 (2008)
22. Strano, M.M.: User descriptions and interpretations of self-presentation through Facebook profile images. Cyberpsychology: Journal of Psychosocial Research on Cyberspace 2(2), 5 (2008)
23. Siibak, A.: Constructing the self through the photo selection-visual impression management on social networking websites. Cyberpsychology: Journal of Psychosocial Research on Cyberspace 3(1), 1 (2009)
24. Walther, J.B.: Selective self-presentation in computer-mediated communication: Hyperpersonal dimensions of technology, language, and cognition. Computers in Human Behavior 23(5), 2538–2557 (2007)
25. Butt, S., Phillips, J.G.: Personality and self reported mobile phone use. Computers in Human Behavior 24(2), 346–360 (2008)
26. Wolfradt, U., Doll, J.: Motives of adolescents to use the Internet as a function of personality traits, personal and social factors. Journal of Educational Computing Research 24(1), 13–28 (2001)
27. Hughes, D.J., Brent, L., Beer, J.S.: A tale of two sites: Twitter vs. Facebook and the personality predictors of social media usage. Computers in Human Behavior 28(2), 561–569 (2012)
28. Wilson, K., Fornasier, S., White, K.M.: Psychological predictors of young adults' use of social networking sites. Cyberpsychology, Behavior, and Social Networking 13(2), 173–177 (2010)
29. Kraut, R., Kiesler, S., Boneva, B., Cummings, J., Helgeson, V., Crawford, A.: Internet paradox revisited. Journal of Social Issues 58(1), 49–74 (2002)
30. Kraut, R., Patterson, M., Lundmark, V., Kiesler, S., Mukophadhyay, T., Scherlis, W.: Internet paradox: A social technology that reduces social involvement and psychological well-being? American Psychologist 53(9), 1017–1031 (1998)

31. Amichai-Hamburger, Y., Ben-Artzi, E.: Loneliness and Internet use. Computers in Human Behavior 19(1), 71–80 (2003)
32. Amichai-Hamburger, Y., Kaplan, H., Dorpatcheon, N.: Click to the past: The impact of extroversion by users of nostalgic websites on the use of Internet social services. Computers in Human Behavior 24(5), 1907–1912 (2008)
33. Swickert, R.J., Hittner, J.B., Harris, J.L., Herring, J.A.: Relationships among Internet use, personality, and social support. Computers in Human Behavior 18(4), 437–451 (2002)
34. Amichai-Hamburger, Y.: The social net: understanding human behavior in cyberspace. Oxford University Press (2005)
35. Ong, E.Y., Ang, R.P., Ho, J., Lim, J.C.Y., Goh, D.H., Lee, C.S., Chua, A.Y.K.: Narcissism, extraversion and adolescents' self-presentation on Facebook. Personality and Individual Differences 50(2), 180–185 (2011)

Appendix: Social Network Sites (SNSs) Usage Questionnaire

Social network sites (SNSs) are defined as web-based services that allow individuals to construct a profile and share connections with a certain list of other users. In SNSs, people can establish their own social networks, design their own homepages, post some personal news, photos, audios, and videos, and so on. Some typical and popular SNSs are MySpace, Facebook, Cyworld (in Korea), Weibo and Renren (in China).

Table 6. Part 1. SNSs Featured Usage Scale

Please try to recall the daily usage of one SNSs, and ask the following questions.

1. How frequently do you use SNSs?

Never	Yearly	Monthly	Weekly	Multiple times a week	Daily	Multiple times a day
1	2	3	4	5	6	7

2. On average, each time you visit SNS, how long would you spend on it?

15min or less	15-30min	0.5-1h	1-2h	2-3h	3-4h	More than 4h
1	2	3	4	5	6	7

3. In your favorite SNSs, how many friends do you have?

1-50	50-100	100-200	200-300	300-400	400-500	More than 500
1	2	3	4	5	6	7

4. In your favorite SNSs, the composition of your friends…

All aquentances in reality			Equal			All strangers in reality
1	2	3	4	5	6	7

5. How frequently do you send private message to others?

Never	Yearly	Monthly	Weekly	Multiple times a week	Daily	Multiple times a day
1	2	3	4	5	6	7

6. How frequently do you update your status?

Never	Yearly	Monthly	Weekly	Multiple times a week	Daily	Multiple times a day
1	2	3	4	5	6	7

Table 6. (*continued*)

7. How frequently do you write notes/blogs?						
Never	Yearly	Monthly	Weekly	Multiple times a week	Daily	Multiple times a day
1	2	3	4	5	6	7
8. How frequently do you update your profile image?						
Never	Yearly	Monthly	Weekly	Multiple times a week	Daily	Multiple times a day
1	2	3	4	5	6	7
9. How frequently do you post photos?						
Never	Yearly	Monthly	Weekly	Multiple times a week	Daily	Multiple times a day
1	2	3	4	5	6	7
10. How frequently do you share or re-send others' profiles (e.g. notes or photos)?						
Never	Yearly	Monthly	Weekly	Multiple times a week	Daily	Multiple times a day
1	2	3	4	5	6	7
11. How frequently do you visit your friends' homepage?						
Never	Yearly	Monthly	Weekly	Multiple times a week	Daily	Multiple times a day
1	2	3	4	5	6	7
12. How frequently do you comment on others' notes or photos?						
Never	Yearly	Monthly	Weekly	Multiple times a week	Daily	Multiple times a day
1	2	3	4	5	6	7
13. How frequently do you check others' comments or message on your profiles?						
Never	Yearly	Monthly	Weekly	Multiple times a week	Daily	Multiple times a day
1	2	3	4	5	6	7

Table 7. Part 2. SNSs Affective Experience Scale

Please indicate how frequently you would experiece the following affects when using SNSs (1= never, 7= always).

	Never						Always
Unhappiness	1	2	3	4	5	6	7
Happiness	1	2	3	4	5	6	7
Depression	1	2	3	4	5	6	7
Joy	1	2	3	4	5	6	7
Angry	1	2	3	4	5	6	7
Contentment	1	2	3	4	5	6	7
Anxiety	1	2	3	4	5	6	7
Cheer	1	2	3	4	5	6	7

What Is Beautiful in Cyberspace?
Communication with Attractive Avatars

Sabrina Sobieraj and Nicole C. Krämer

University of Duisburg-Essen, Social Psychology: Media and Communication,
Duisburg, Germany
sabrina.sobieraj@uni-due.de

Abstract. The face with its structural and nonverbal features is the most important cue in interpersonal face-to-face communication (e.g. Dion et al., 1972; Reis et al., 1990). The aim of the presented study is to examine whether physical attractiveness and nonverbal cues in virtual representations can elicit interpersonal effects comparable to those evoked in face-to-face contacts. In a 2 (observer's nationality) x 2 (smiling, non-smiling) x 3 (sender's attractiveness) x 2 (sender's gender) x 2 (observer's gender) experimental design 158 German and 128 Malaysian participants evaluated 18 faces (9 smiling, 9 non-smiling) concerning attractiveness, social competence and dominance. Analyses show several effects, e.g. indicating that the same facial features are attractive in virtual faces and human faces.

Keywords: Attractiveness, avatars, facial features, nonverbal behavior.

1   Theoretical Background

Research on the interaction with virtual figures (avatars or agents) is a field of growing relevance, investigating for instance, what characters gamers create [1] and how these characters influence other gamers/users perception (e.g. [2,3]). However, the impact of the outward appearance was not sufficiently explored so far, although findings in the human context revealed that the attractiveness of a person is decisive for building relationships. Since it was found [4] that the attribution processes induced by virtual figures are generally very similar to those evoked by humans we suggest that attractiveness will be influential in virtual contexts. Additionally, Mühlberger et al. [5] revealed that the neural responses towards virtuals and humans are very much the same.

People derive a lot of information about their interaction partner by looking at his/her outward appearance. One of the most important cues is the face which conveys information on the attractiveness of a person, on someone's gender, cultural background and for instance similarity to oneself or friends.

Especially the facial attractiveness of a person is an important social cue for face-to-face interactions, because it influences interpersonal attraction and the likelihood for interaction. Attractive persons are for instance highly coveted on the dating market (e.g. 6) and the job market (e.g. 7) and receive a lot of beneficial attributions [8].

G. Meiselwitz (Ed.): SCSM 2014, LNCS 8531, pp. 125–136, 2014.
© Springer International Publishing Switzerland 2014

In their seminal study Dion et al. suggested the existence of a "physical attractiveness stereotype"[8, p. 289]. They found their participants to associate attractiveness with several social desirable personality traits (e.g. sensitive, interesting, strong. friendly) and better life experiences (e.g. getting good jobs). Moreover, their participants reported to be even more willing to do life risking actions like donating a kidney for the attractive person and rescuing the person from drowning. These findings were replicated in several studies and confirmed in meta-analyses [9-11]. The attractiveness benefits were also demonstrated for the virtual context [12]. The authors found that attractiveness is associated with social competence, intellectual competence and social adjustment. In line with this Yee, Bailenson and Ducheneaut [2] found that attractive characters in World of Warcraft were rated as more successful, competent and powerful than less attractive characters. Additionally, van Vugt [3] revealed for the e-learning context that the attractiveness of an agent increases the willingness to use it another time under the condition that the agent is generally perceived as supportive.

To examine the triggers for attractiveness Weibel, Stricker, Wissmath, and Mast [13] conducted a study in which they varied virtual character's size of the pupils; blinking frequency and viewing perspective. Results revealed that a higher blinking frequency and bigger pupils enhance attractiveness and perceived sociality. Moreover, a bottom up perspective renders the avatars more social and self-confident than a frontal and top down perspective. This study gives evidence that single features can influence attributions. But it still remains unanswered which facial features in the virtual face are attractive, apart from the width of the pupils.

Ensuing from research on human attractiveness there might be several other attractive facial features in virtual faces. Cunningham [14, 15] detected various facial features which arouse attractiveness ratings. In order to do so, he measured single features' sizes like the length of the nose and correlated measurements with attractiveness ratings made by observers. For female faces he found positive correlations for the size of the eyes, the prominence of the cheekbones and a bright smile with attractiveness ratings, and a negative correlation for the length of the chin and the length of the nose. For male faces very similar results were found [15], indicating that larger eyes, more prominent cheekbones, a long chin, a smaller nose area and a bright smile are rated as attractive. Moreover, to figure out whether ratings on attractiveness are consistent across cultures, Cunningham, Roberts, Barbee, Druen, an Wu [16] conducted another study replicating the earlier study with a multi-cultural sample (US-Americans, Asians, and Hispanics). General attractiveness ratings were highly correlated between the subsamples. Additionally, all subsamples rated large eyes, prominent cheekbones and a short chin to be attractive. Also, high eyebrows and size of pupils were rated as attractive, while smiles' breadth was only attractive for the US-American sample and the Hispanics. Although the study has its weakness with regard to the unequally distributed subsample sizes and the unsystematically distributed facial features in the stimulus material, it indicates that there are on the one hand high consistencies in attractiveness rating, but on the other hand there are subtle differences. Hence we want to examine of whether cultural differences exist for virtual attractiveness.

Besides these static physiognomic features (cheekbones, eyes and chin) the smile is of special importance, because it is a nonverbal behavior, which is usually performed and perceived in a dynamic way. The studies by Cunningham and many other research groups found smiles to be attractive on photographs (e.g. 17, 18). But most recently researcher state that the dynamics of a smile are of particular importance to let it appear authentic and increase attractiveness ratings. Quite slow starting smiles only lasting some milliseconds, for example, evoke high attractiveness ratings [19, 20].

Furthermore, the evaluation of a smile can depend on the sender's sex as well as on the cultural background of the perceiver. Deutsch, LeBaron, and Fryer [21] found non-smiling women to be negatively evaluated compared to non-smiling men, whose attractiveness ratings remain on the same level or even increase. The authors ascribe this difference to gender stereotypes, which suggest that smiling is a normative behavior for women and non-smiling is normative for men. Diekman and Goodfriend [22] even suggest that violating stereotypical norms can provoke penalization. With regard to culture most comparisons were conducted between US-American and Japanese subsamples (e.g. 23-25) followed by comparisons of US-American and Chinese samples (e.g. 26, 27). Less data is available on comparison of other Asian countries than Japan and China with American, European or even African subsamples. Matsumoto [28] states that smiling is an appropriate behavior in America, but not in Asia. However, Matsumoto and Kudoh [24] neither detected an attractiveness benefit for smiling stimuli compared to non-smiling stimuli for Japanese participants nor for Americans, like for instance Reis et al. [18] found it. Finally, Hess, Beaupré, and Cheung [27] suggest that there is no study which directly compares the smiling effect between at least two cultures.

To summarize, general findings suggest that attribution processes towards humans and virtual characters are very similar. Further, attractiveness is correlated with the attribution of beneficial personality characteristics like sociality in face-to-face interactions as well as in the virtual context. However, it remains mostly unanswered which facial features induce the attractiveness attribution. Based on research concerning human attractiveness we want to examine which manifestation of a physiognomic facial feature (cheekbones, eyes, chin) induces the highest attractiveness ratings in the virtual context and whether a dynamic smile can evoke attractiveness ratings. Thus we derive the research question (RQ1): Which manifestations of the cheekbones, the eyes and the chin will be attractive in virtual figures and how do they interact with figure's sex? Furthermore, first data on the different cross-cultural attribution of facial features is available what leads us to ask (RQ2), which facial features will interact with the participant's culture?

Besides the physiognomic facial features smiling is a dynamic nonverbal behavior which can increase attractiveness ratings and is often performed in applied virtual contexts. So we suggest that a smiling figure will be perceived as more attractive (H1). Additionally, research showed that smiling is a behavior which is expected to be performed more by woman than by men [21, 29] and that non-smiling is a correct/norm-conforming male behavior, while the same behavior evokes negative evaluation for women. Therefore, non-smiling female figures will receive lower attractiveness ratings than male figures (H2). Due to the fact that the perception of a dynamic smile is not yet cross-culturally validated we (RQ3) of whether the attractiveness ratings for a smile will interact with the participant's culture?

2   Method

The presented study is a part of a larger research project which was conducted to extensively investigate the influence of physiognomic and nonverbal facial features on attributions of attractiveness, social competence and dominance. Here, we will only report the variables and results which are important for the current research questions.

2.1   Study Design and Stimuli

To test the outlined research questions and hypotheses we conducted an online experiment with a 2 (virtual figures' sex) x 3 (physiognomic facial features) x 2 (nonverbal facial feature) x 2 (participants' sex) x 2 (participants' nationality) mixed-factorial design. While the physiognomic facial features (prominence of the cheekbone, size of the eyes, length of the chin) and nonverbal facial feature (smiling, non-smiling) were varied within subjects, virtual figures' sex, participants' sex and nationality (German, Malay) were varied between subjects.

We created synthetic female and male faces as stimulus material by using the Poser 6 software by Curious Labs. The software enables facial manipulation in a subtle manner (e.g. 19, 20, 30). By referring to Cunningham [14, 15] we decided to vary cheekbones, eyes, chin and smiling, because these features yielded the strongest correlations with attractiveness ratings.   We manipulated the prominence of cheekbones in narrow, middle and prominent cheekbones, the size of eyes in small, middle and large and the length of chin in short, middle, long. The distance between the middle feature and the low feature was the same as the distance between the middle feature to the high feature. In pictures of 13x18 cm size the differences were as follows: in females' faces the width of narrow cheekbones were 11.2 cm, middle cheekbones 11.6 cm and prominent cheekbones were 12.0 cm. The size of eyes, measured from one corner of the eyes to the other, varied from 1.1 cm for small eyes, 1.2 cm for middle sized eyes and 1.3 cm for large eyes. The length of chin measured up from the lower lip ranged from 1.2 cm of the short chin, to 1.3 cm for the middle chin and 1.4 cm for the long chin. Males' facial characteristics were varied accordingly, so the width of cheekbones for narrow cheekbones was 12.4 cm, for middle cheekbones 12.8 cm and for prominent cheekbones 13.2 cm. The size of the eyes ranged from 1.4 cm for small eyes, 1.5 cm for middle eyes and 1.6 cm for large eyes. The length of chin ranged from 1.7 cm of the short chin, 1.9 cm for the middle chin and 2.1 cm of the long chin.

Smiling was varied according to [19, 30]. Thus, we produced short videos (each 3.5 sec) as stimulus material. Smiling was created with a long onset and short apex duration to evoke an authentic impression. In the smiling condition videos started with an eye blinking and then the virtual person started to smile. In the non-smiling condition the figure showed an eye blink and did not smile. For each facial manifestation we produced two different types of faces, which differed in their skin color, their eye color as well as in their hair color and style to avoid confusion on the fact that participants rated the faces with the same physiognomic features twice, once smiling and once not smiling (Table 1, Table 2).

Moreover, to examine differences in the evaluation of the figures we captured participants' gender and nationality.

Fig. 1. Examples for two different types of faces with the same physiognomy

Fig. 2. Examples for a smiling and non-smiling face with the same physiognomy

2.2   Dependent Measures

To test which facial features evoke the highest ratings of attractiveness, we measured attractiveness with a 7-point semantic differential (1= attractive; 7 = unattractive).

2.3   Participants and Procedure

286 participants (N = 164 females) took part in the online experiment. German (N = 159) and Malay (N= 127) participants were acquired by several postings in forums, notices and announcements in foundation courses at the Universities in Western Germany and south Malaysia. Both samples were similar in age and educational background.

Participants were randomly assigned to one of the experimental conditions (i.e. gender of the virtual figure) by activating the survey link. At the first pages they were welcomed and instructed. Each page showed one of the stimulus videos on the top of the page. Below the video the impression was captured, followed by the questions concerning similarity and meeting preference. After evaluating either 16 male or female faces, the experience with virtual figures and demographic information on age, gender and education were captured. Finally, participants were thanked for their participation and were fully debriefed.

3   Results

We conducted ANOVAS with repeated measurement with the manifestations of the facial features (weak, moderate, strong) and figure's nonverbal behavior (smiling, non-smiling) as the within-subject factors and the, figure's sex, participant's culture and participant's sex as between-subject factors. To figure out which manifestations significantly differ we used the Bonferroni post-hoc test and simple contrasts.

RQ1: Which manifestations of the cheekbones, the eyes and the chin will be attractive in virtual figures and how do they interact with figure's sex?

For the comparison of the faces differing in their manifestations of the cheekbones (narrow, middle, prominent) a main effect was found ($F(1.8, 139.85) = 71.55$, $p < .001$, $\eta 2p = .475$). The post-hoc test revealed that the middle cheekbones ($M= 3.65$, $SE= .07$, $p < .001$, $SE= .08$) are more attractive than the narrow cheekbones ($M= 4.04$, $SE= .07$) and the prominent cheekbones ($M= 3.94$, $SE= .09$, $p < .005$, $SE= .09$). No difference was found between the narrow and the prominent cheekbones.

For the comparison of the size of the eyes analyses showed a significant effect ($F(1.92, 534.81) = 44.78$, $p < .001$, $\eta 2p = .139$). The post-hoc test revealed that the middle eyes were more attractive ($M= 3.65$, $SE= .07$, $p < .001$, $SE= .08$) than the small eyes ($M= 4.30$, $SE= .07$), and the large eyes ($M= 4.26$, $SE= .08$, $p < .001$, $SE= .08$). There is no difference between the small and the large eyes.

The analysis of the length of the chin detected a main effect ($F(2, 556) = 26.01$, $p < .001$, $\eta 2p = .086$). The post-hoc test showed that the short chin was perceived as less attractive ($M= 4.19$, $SE= .07$, $p < .001$, $SE= .07$) than the middle chin ($M= 3.65$, $SE= .07$) and the long chin ($M= 3.82$, $SE= .07$)

Furthermore, we found three interaction effects for the facial features and the figure's sex. The evaluation of the cheekbones depends on the figure's sex ($F(2, 556) = 14.47$, $p < .001$, $\eta 2p = .049$). Simple contrasts showed a difference for the narrow and the prominent cheekbones ($F(2, 556) = 14.47$, $p < .001$, $\eta 2p = .049$) as well as for the middle and the prominent cheekbones ($F(2, 556) = 14.47$, $p < .001$, $\eta 2p = .049$). Prominent cheekbones were rated as similarly attractive in females ($M= 3.98$; $SE=.10$) and males ($M=3.95$; $SE=.11$), while narrow cheekbones were perceived as less attractive in females ($M=4.46$; $SE=.10$), but increased ratings of the males ($M=3.61$; $SE=.11$)

Comparing the middle ($M=3.91$; $SE=.11$) and prominent cheekbones revealed that both manifestations are evaluated similarly in females, but that middle cheekbones enhance male's attractiveness ratings ($M=3.40$; $SE=.11$).

Moreover, we found an interaction effect for the size of the eyes ($F(1.92, 534.81) = 4.85$, $p= .009$, $\eta 2p = .017$). Simple contrasts showed a difference for the small and large eyes ($F(1, 278) = 9.51$, $p= .002$, $\eta 2p = .033$). Small eyes were evaluated as quite unattractive in males ($M=4.24$; $SE=.10$) and females ($M=4.35$; $SE=.10$), while large eyes increase ratings for males ($M=4.00$; $SE=.11$) and decrease them for females ($M=4.53$; $SE=.11$). Summarizing, analyses revealed that the middle single features, are attractive in female and male faces, while there are differences in the evaluations for the narrow and the prominent cheekbones and the small and large eyes.

RQ2: Which facial features will interact with the participant's culture?

Concerning RQ2 analyses revealed one interaction effect for the variation of the eyes and nationality ($F(1.92, 534.81) = 8.61$, $p < .001$, $\eta2p = .030$). Simple contrasts detected a difference for the comparison of the small and the large eyes ($F(1, 278) = 8.34$, $p = .004$, $\eta2p = .029$) and for the middle and the large eyes ($F(1, 278) = 14.51$, $p < .001$, $\eta2p = .050$). There is a common thread that small and large eyes are equally attractive, but the Malaysian subsample gave higher ratings on attractiveness (German $M_{small}=4.44$; $SE_{small}=.10$; $M_{large}=4.61$; $SE_{large}=.11$; Malaysian $M_{small}=4.15$; $SE_{small}=.11$; $M_{large}=3.91$; $SE_{large}=.11$). The same trend is observable for the middle and the large eyes (German $M_{middle}=3.69$; $SE_{middle}=.10$; Malaysian $M_{middle}=3.62$; $SE_{middle}=.10$). Moreover, we found an interaction effect for the length of the chin and the figure's sex ($F(2, 556) = 8.80$, $p < .001$, $\eta2p = .031$). Simple contrasts revealed an evaluation difference for the middle and the long chin ($F(1, 278) = 9.74$, $p = .002$, $\eta2p = .034$). While the Malaysian subsample gave similar ratings towards the middle and the long chin ($M_{middle}=3.86$; $SE_{middle}=.10$; $M_{long}=3.62$; $SE_{long}=.10$). Germans perceived the middle chin to be more attractive than the long chin ($M_{middle}=3.69$; $SE_{middle}=.10$; $M_{long}=4.10$; $SE_{long}=.10$). Summarizing analyses detected Malaysian to generally give higher attractiveness ratings and that the attractiveness perception for the middle and long chin differ in dependence of culture.

H1: A smiling figure will be perceived as more attractive than a non-smiling figure.

The conducted ANOVA showed a main effect for smiling over all faces ($F(1, 285) = 53.06$, $p < .001$, $\eta2p = .157$), displaying that smiling faces are more attractive than non-smiling faces ($M_{smiling}=3.90$; $SE_{smiling}=.06$; $M_{non-smiling}=4.27$; $SE_{non-smiling}=.06$). Referring to the ANOVAs with repeated measurements the smiling effect was found the faces in which the cheekbones were varied ($F(1, 278) = 12.57$, $p < .001$, $\eta2p = .043$; $M_{smiling}= 4.02$; $SE_{smiling}= .07$; $M_{non-smiling}= 3.74$; $SE_{non-smiling}= .07$) as well as in the faces with manipulated size of the eyes ($F(1, 278) = 38.34$, $p < .001$, $\eta2p = .121$; $M_{smiling}= 3.84$; $SE_{smiling}= .07$); ($M_{non-smiling}= 4.30$; $SE_{non-smiling}= .07$), and the length of the chin ($F(1, 278) = 25.22$, $p < .001$, $\eta2p = .083$; $M_{smiling}= 3.69$; $SE_{smiling}= .07$; $M_{non-smiling}= 4.08$; $SE_{non-smiling}= .07$).

H2: Non-smiling female figures will receive lower attractiveness ratings than non-smiling male figures.

The analyses revealed two interaction effects for the faces with varied sizes of the eyes ($F(1, 556) = 9.80$, $p = .002$, $\eta2p = .034$) and the faces with a manipulated length of chin ($F(1, 278) = 8.83$, $p = .003$, $\eta2p = .031$) indicating the same pattern of attribution. It hardly makes a difference in the attractiveness ratings for males of whether they laugh ($M_{eyes}= 3.76$; $SE_{eyes}= .10$; $M_{chin}= 3.45$; $SE_{chin}= .10$) or not ($M_{eyes}= 4.00$; $SE_{eyes}= .10$; $M_{chin}= 3.61$; $SE_{chin}= .10$) whereas the attribution changes for smiling ($M_{eyes}= 3.91$; $SE_{eyes}= .10$; $M_{chin}= 3.93$; $SE_{chin}= .09$) and non-smiling ($M_{eyes}= 4.61$; $SE_{eyes}= .10$; $M_{chin}= 4.56$; $SE_{chin}= .10$) females. So do non-smiling females receive declining attractiveness ratings.

RQ3: Will the attractiveness ratings for a smile interact with the participant's culture?

The analyses did not detect any interaction effect for smiling and participant's culture.

4   Discussion

The presented study aimed at identifying what makes a virtual face attractive, because attractiveness is one of the most crucial prerequisites to induce (interpersonal) interaction and relationships. We suggested that characteristics of the virtual figures (physiognomy, nonverbal behavior, sex) as well as characteristics of the user (nationality) would influence the perception of virtual attractiveness. For that reason we systematically varied facial features of the figures.

Our results concerning the physiognomic features indicate that nearly the same facial features as in the human context are attractive in the virtual context. We found that moderately prominent cheekbones, middle sized eyes and a middle chin obtained the highest attractiveness ratings. This is comparable to the results by [14] and [15]. Referring to the effect sizes results indicate that the cheekbones seem to be very important for the attribution of attractiveness followed by the eyes, while the chin has only a weak influence. Thus, to achieve an attractive virtual figure it is more advisable to manipulate the cheekbones than the length of the chin.

Moreover, the influence of the feature's manifestation can depend on the sex of the figure. We found that prominent cheekbones are attractive for virtual females and males, but narrow and middle cheekbones even increase attractiveness ratings for males, while ratings for females decrease. Participants agree that small eyes are unattractive for all figures, but large eyes are attractive in males and unattractive in females. However, these results are not consistent with findings by Cunningham [14, 15], who found positive correlations for the prominence of the cheekbones and the size of the eyes and a gender difference for the length of the chin. Altogether, our findings indicate that the manifestations of the features are not of equal importance for females and males. Thus, when aiming to construct an attractive virtual face, the sex of the figure should be considered: for example, female virtual characters should not have too narrow cheekbones and eyes should not be too large. However, future research would have to show at what point ratings turn from attractive to unattractive in order to have benchmark criteria on what too narrow or too large actually means.

As a consequence of the intercultural study by Cunningham et al. [16], we asked whether the attribution of virtual attractiveness differs across cultures. For that reason we focused on a European and an Asian subsample. Analyses demonstrated that there is a common tendency for what is attractive, as for instance both subsamples perceive a middle size of the eyes as attractive and the small and large eyes as much less attractive. However, the Malaysian sample still attributed more attractiveness to the smaller version of the eyes. Moreover, the Malaysian participants rated the long and middle chins to be attractive, whereas the Germans prefer the middle chin and dislike the long chin. The chin and the cheekbones determine the form of face, for instance the long chin makes the face more oval. Referring to the finding by [31], who revealed that the preference for a hair color increases the more seldom the color is, this tendency might also explain the long chin preference. Because an oval face is not common in the Asian area, the oval face might be exclusive and attractive. These findings suggest that when designing virtual faces for different parts of the world (if there is, for example, the chance to use different virtual agents on consumer websites like ebay or IKEA) cultural preferences for attractiveness should be considered. These preferences must not necessarily entail similarity with the observer and his/her features.

Besides the physiognomic facial features we varied smiling behavior (smiling/non-smiling) and found a strong effect showing that smiling faces are more attractive than non-smiling faces. This is in line with former results achieved in the human context (e.g. 15, 18, 19). Moreover, analyses revealed interactions with the figure's sex. A smile is less important for the attractiveness ratings of a male, but very important for that of females. Non-smiling females are less attractive than their smiling counterparts. This is also consistent with results yielded in the human context [e.g. 21] and might be interpreted as an indication that gender stereotypes are also applied in the virtual context. Indeed, smiling is performed more frequently by women and is also expected of them [32]. Not behaving in the expected way can cause a penalization [22], what our results also indicate. Additionally, we investigated if the smiling attributions interact with the participants' culture. We did not find a difference in the attractiveness attribution, Germans and Malaysians gave similar ratings for the smiling and non-smiling persons. This finding is in contrast to results by Matsumoto and Kudoh [24], who did not detect any increase in attractiveness induced by a smile, but perfectly in line with the general finding that smiling compared to non-smiling enhances attractiveness ratings [14, 15,17,18].

Aside from the theoretical extension concerning attractive virtual features findings have immediate consequences for the applied context, because these findings give worthwhile indications how to design an attractive virtual figure. We assume that attractiveness is not an end in itself, but evoking attractiveness can positively influence users´ perception in the sense of associating beneficial characteristics [8-12] or even influence users´ behavior for instance in the gaming, , e-learning or online-consumer's context.

In the gaming realm, Yee [33] have already found that females are more likely to select elves as gaming characters than ogresses. This could indicate that females or probably also a broader range of gamers like to use attractive avatars more than unattractive ones. In addition, Yee et al. [2] demonstrated that tall attractive avatars outperform their less attractive counterparts in World-of-Warcraft. Tall attractive avatars were suggested to have researched higher levels in the game than tall unattractive characters. Thus, knowing how to create an attractive avatar might enhance playing performance and entertainment experience, what in turn can lead to frequent gaming behavior. Attractiveness could also have a direct effect in the context of digital personal assistances. For instance interfaces like Siri by Apple could get an attractive facial representation, which could be individualized for different user groups. Interfaces should differently look and perform (smiling/non-smiling) in dependence of their sex and possibly in dependence of the country for which they are created. Interacting with an attractive interface might enhance frequency of use and pleasure. In addition to possible direct effects virtual attractiveness might indirectly influence user's behavior with regard to the beneficial attributions caused by the attractiveness stereotype [8, 12]. Attractiveness is for instance associated with integrity and sociality [e.g. 9]. For instance in an online shopping context in which virtual agents are employed as customer service agents this could lead to the perception of trustworthiness and afterwards results in increases purchases. First research in the online shopping context indicated that attractive agents are more result-producing than their unattractive counterparts [34]. Indirect effects might also have an impact in the gaming context, especially for health games or e-learning tutorials. Van Vugt [3] found that perceived attractiveness and utility can indeed enhance the chance to use a fitness agent another time, what in turn can help the user to behave healthier. Furthermore, health games generally use agents which aim to support their players to learn more about a healthy living or more specifically to support diseased persons in their healing process.   In addition Baylor states that "[t]ogether with motivational messages and dialogue (…), the agent's appearance is the most important design feature as it dictates the learner's perception of the agent as a virtual social model, (…)" [35, p. 291]. Thus, knowing how to design an attractive agent for a game might increase the chance that the agents is perceived and accepted as a social entity, which could support learners to improve their performance. Finally all kind of consulting could be supported by attractive agents, since they could evoke trustworthiness and anonymity. The latter might be important for sensitive consultations like in the medical context. Although more variables than the attractiveness, like entertainment or perceived usefulness [3] determine whether the user might use an agent or system again, attractiveness might be one of the most important influencing factors – as it has been shown for the human context. Summarizing, our results give a first answer on the question which facial features are attractive in a virtual face and that the figure's sex certainly is an important moderating variable (for static as well as for dynamic cues) while the observers´ culture was not equally decisive. However, more cross-cultural comparisons should be conducted in the future to also analyze for other countries and cultures whether differences or similarities in the evaluation of attractiveness prevail. It has to be acknowledged that, certainly, the study has its limitations. For instance the varied manifestations might have been too weakly or strongly manipulated resulting in partially incongruent data to for instance Cunningham [14]. Moreover, it would be desirable to test more facial features than the selected three, like the size of the nose or to manipulate more than one feature in each face to derive assumptions on the interactions of features [34]. In sum, the study gives evidence that attractiveness of virtual faces is evaluated based on mechanisms similar to those of the human-human context and thereby a) extends theory concerning virtual figures with regard to physical attractiveness and b) gives valuable advice for the wide field of application, because it provides information on the question what should be considered when creating an attractive virtual figure.

References

1. Bessière, K., Fleming Seay, A., Kiesler, S.: The ideal elf: Identity exploration in World of Warcraft. CyberPsychology & Behavior 10, 530–535 (2007)
2. Yee, N., Bailenson, J.N., Ducheneaut, N.: The proteus effect: Implications of transformed digital self-presentation on online and offline behavior. Communication Research 36, 285–312 (2009)

3. van Vugt, H.C.: Embodied agents from a user's perspective. Ridderprint, Ridderkerk (2008)
4. Bente, G., Krämer, N.C., Petersen, A., de Ruiter, J.P.: Computer animated movement and person perception. Methodological advances in nonverbal behavior research. Journal of Nonverbal Behavior 25, 151–166 (2001)
5. Mühlberger, A., Wieser, M.J., Herrmann, M.J., Weyers, P., Tröger, C., Pauli, P.: Early cortical processing of natural and artificial emotional faces differs between lower and higher social anxious persons. Journal of Neural Transmission 116, 735–746 (2009)
6. Buss, D.M., Shackelford, T.K.: Attractive women want it all: Good genes, economic investment, parenting proclivities, and emotional commitment. Evolutionary Psychology 6, 134–146 (2008)
7. Hosoda, M., Stone-Romero, E.F., Coats, G.: The effects of physical attractiveness on job-related outcomes: a meta-analysis of experimental studies. Personnel Psychology 56, 431–462 (2003)
8. Dion, K.K., Berscheid, E., Walster, E.: What is beautiful is good. Journal of Personality and Social Psychology 24, 285–290 (1972)
9. Feingold, A.: Good-looking people are not what we think. Psychological Bulletin 111, 304–341 (1992)
10. Eagly, A.H., Ashmore, R.D., Makhijani, M.G., Longo, L.C.: What is beautiful is good: a meta-analytic review of research on the physical attractiveness stereotype. Psychological Bulletin 110, 109–128 (1991)
11. Langlois, J.H., Kalakanis, L., Rubenstein, A.J., Larson, A., Hallam, M., Smoot, M.: Maxims or myths of beauty? A meta-analytic and theoretical review. Psychological Bulletin 126, 390–423 (2000)
12. Khan, R., De Angeli, A.: The attractiveness stereotype in the evaluation of embodied conversational agents. In: Gross, T., Gulliksen, J., Kotzé, P., Oestreicher, L., Palanque, P., Prates, R.O., Winckler, M. (eds.) INTERACT 2009. LNCS, vol. 5726, pp. 85–97. Springer, Heidelberg (2009)
13. Weibel, D., Stricker, D., Wissmath, B., Mast, F.W.: How socially relevant visual characteristics of avatars influence impression formation. Journal of Media Psychology 22, 37–43 (2010)
14. Cunningham, M.R.: Measuring the physical in physical attractiveness: Quasi-experiments on the sociobiology of female facial beauty. Journal of Personality and Social Psychology 50, 925–935 (1986)
15. Cunningham, M.R., Barbee, A.P., Pike, C.L.: What do women want? Facialmetric assessment of multiple motives in the perception of male facial physical attractiveness. Journal of Personality and Social Psychology 59, 61–72 (1990)
16. Cunningham, M.R., Roberts, A.R., Barbee, A.P., Druen, P.B., Wu, C.H.: "Their ideas of beauty are, on the whole, the same as ours": consistency and variability in the cross-cultural perception of female physical attractiveness. Journal of Personality and Social Psychology 68, 261–279 (1995)
17. Otta, E., Abrosio, F.F.E., Leneberg Hoshino, R.: Reading a smiling face: Messages conveyed by various forms of smiling. Perceptual and Motor Skills 82, 1111–1121 (1996)
18. Reis, H.T., McDougal Wilson, I., Monestere, C., Bernstein, S., Clark, K., Seidl, E., Franco, M., Giodioso, E., Freeman, L., Radoane, K.: What is smiling is beautiful and good. European Journal of Social Psychology 20, 259–267 (1990)
19. Krumhuber, E., Kappas, A.: Moving smiles: The role of dynamic components for the perception of the genuineness of smiles. Journal of Nonverbal Behavior 29, 3–24 (2005)

20. Krumhuber, E., Manstead, A.S.R., Cosker, D., Marshall, D., Rosin, P.L.: Effects of dynamic attributes of smiles in human and synthetic faces: A simulated job interview setting. Journal of Nonverbal Behavior 33, 1–15 (2009)
21. Deutsch, F.M., LeBaron, D., Fryer, M.M.: What is in a smile? Psychology of Women Quarterly 11, 341–352 (1987)
22. Diekman, A.B., Goodfriend, W.: Rolling with the changes: A role congruity perspective on gender norms. Psychology of Women Quarterly 30, 369–383 (2006)
23. Ekman, P., Friesen, W.W., O'Sullivan, M., Chan, A., Diacoyanni-Tarlatzis, I., Heider, K.: Universals and cultural differences in the judgements of facial expressions of emotions. Journal of Personality and Social Psychology 53, 712–717 (1987)
24. Matsumoto, D., Kudoh, T.: American- Japanese cultural differences in attribution of personality based on smiles. Journal of Nonverbal Behavior 17, 231–243 (1993)
25. Matsumoto, D., Olide, A., Schug, J., Willingham, B., Callan, M.: Cross-cultural judgments of spontaneous facial expressions of emotion. Journal of Nonverbal Behavior 33, 213–238 (2009)
26. Camras, L.A., Chen, Y., Bakeman, R., Norris, K., Cain, T.R.: Culture, ethnicity, and children's facial expressions: A study of European American, mainland Chinese, Chinese American, and adopted Chinese girls. Emotion 6, 103–114 (2006)
27. Hess, U., Beaupré, M.G., Cheung, N.: Who to whom and why-Cultural differences and similarities in the function of smiles. In: Abel, M.H. (ed.) An Empirical Reflection on the Smile, pp. 187–216. Edwin Mellen Press, New York (2002)
28. Matsumoto, D.: Cultural similarities and differences in display rules. Motivation and Emotion 14, 195–214 (1990)
29. Schmid Mast, M., Hall, J.A.: When is dominance related to smiling? Assigned dominance, dominance preference, trait dominance, and gender as moderators. Sex Roles 50, 387–399 (2004)
30. Krumhuber, E., Manstead, A.S.R., Kappas, A.: Temporal aspects of facial displays in person and expression perception: The effects of smile-dynamics, head-tilt and gender. Journal of Nonverbal Behavior 31, 39–56 (2007)
31. Swami, V., Furnham, A., Joshi, K.: The influence of skin tone, hair length, and hair colour on ratings of women's physical attractiveness, health and fertility. Scandinavian Journal of Psychology 49, 429–439 (2008)
32. Briton, N.J., Hall, J.A.: Gender-based expectancies and observers' judgments of smiling. Journal of Nonverbal Behavior 19, 49–65 (1995)
33. Yee, N.: The Norratians Scrolls: A Study of EverQuest (version 2.5) (2001), http://www.nickyee.com/eqt/report.html (retrieved)
34. Holzwarth, M., Janiszewski, C., Neumann, M.M.: The Influence of Avatars on Online Cosumer Shopping Behavior. Journal of Marketing 70, 19–36 (2006)
35. Baylor, A.L.: The design of motivational agents and avatars. Educational Technology Research and Development 59, 291–300 (2011)
36. Sobieraj, S.: What is virtually beautiful is good-Der Einfluss physiognomischer Gesichtsmerkmale und nonverbalen Verhaltens auf die Attribution von Attraktivität, sozialer Kompetenz und Dominanz (2012)

Moderation Techniques for Social Media Content

Andreas Veglis

Media Informatics Lab – School of Journalism & MC
Aristotle University of Thessaloniki
Thessaloniki 54006, Greece
veglis@jour.auth.gr

Abstract. Social media are perhaps the most popular services of cyberspace today. The main characteristic of social media is that they offer to every internet user the ability to add content and thus contribute to participatory journalism. The problem in that this content must be checked as far as quality is concerned and in order to avoid legal issues. This can be accomplished with the help of moderation. The problem is that moderation is a complex process that in many cases requires substantial human resources. This paper studies the moderation process and proposes a moderation model that can guarantee the quality of the content while retaining cost at an affordable level. The model includes various moderation stages which determine the applied moderation technique depending on the publication record of the user that submits the content.

Keywords: Social Media, moderation, hybrid moderation, pre-moderation, post moderation, distributed moderation.

1   Introduction

Since the invention of the WWW, more than 20 years ago we have witnessed a tremendous growth in tools and services. Although at the beginning the internet user was considered to be a passive content consumer, nowadays he has the ability to produce or reproduce and disseminate content. This change took place due to the introduction of social media, which are perhaps the most popular internet services today. Social media can be defined as Internet-based applications that belong to Web 2.0, which support the creation and exchange of user generated content. They include web-based and mobile based technologies which can facilitate interactive dialogue between organizations, communities, and individuals. Social media technologies take on many different forms including magazines, Internet forums, weblogs, social blogs, microblogging, wikis, podcasts, photographs or pictures, video, rating and social bookmarking [1]-[3].

Supported by the evolution of social media, internet users are now generating great amounts of user generated content. This content varies from blog comments and participation in online polls to citizen stories that are usually published in media web sites [4]. The problem is that in the traditional web sites there is quality control of the content. In the case of media web sites journalists act as gatekeepers, ensuring the

G. Meiselwitz (Ed.): SCSM 2014, LNCS 8531, pp. 137–148, 2014.

quality of the news content. Thus the authorities of the web site that publishes user generated content are responsible for users' contributions and attempt to check the validity of the content in order to prevent legal issues that may arise from such content. As far as the methods that can be employed in order to deal with the above issues, they can be summarized in user identification and moderation or other oversight of user material that can guarantee a certain degree of quality. Although user identification is a quite straight forward automatic process, moderation is a complex, costly and time consuming process.

This paper studies techniques for checking the quality of the user generated content in the social media, with emphasis on moderation. More precisely by combining existing moderation techniques (pre-moderation, post-moderation, distributed and automated), hybrid moderation is proposed and discussed in detail. This type of moderation exploits the various types of moderation in order to achieve small publication latency, as well as high quality content. It includes various stages which determine the applied moderation technique depending on the publication record of the user that submits the content. User generated content is subjected to multiple moderation cycles that guarantee the success of the moderation process. The technique is subject to customization depending on the characteristics of web site that adopts it.

The rest of the paper is organized as follows: Section 2 discusses social media as well as user generated content. The types of user generated content are presented in the following section. Section 4 deals with the existing mechanisms that ensure the quality of the user generated content. The proposed moderation model is presented and discussed in section 5. Conclusions and future extensions of this work are included in the last section.

2   The Evolution of Social Media

There is a growing trend of people shifting from the traditional media (newspaper, TV, Radio) to social media in order to stay informed. Social media has often scooped traditional media in reporting current events. Although the majority of original reporting is still generated by traditional journalists, social media make it increasingly possible for an attentive audience to tap into breaking news [1].

A classification scheme for different social media types includes six types: collaborative projects, blogs and microblogs, content communities, social networking sites, virtual game worlds, and virtual social worlds [3].

One of the most widely used types of social media is social networking. A social networking service is a web site that facilitates the building of social networks or social relations among internet users that share similar interests, activities, backgrounds, or real-life connections (http://en.wikipedia.org/wiki/Social_ networking_service). They are web-based services that allow individuals to construct a public of semi-public profile within a bounded system, articulate a list of other users with whom they share a connection, and view and traverse their list of connections and those made by others within the system [5]. Many companies have established a presence in the most popular social networks (for example Facebook) in order to publish their news and attract other members of the social network to their web site. They have also integrated social media links in their web articles in order for users to link to them through their social network profiles. Users have also the ability to interact with the media companies by leaving comments [6]. The most well known and employed social network is Facebook .The latest data indicate that the number of Facebook users is above 1,19 billion and 728 million users login to the system every day (http://thenextweb.com/facebook/2013/10/30/facebook-passes-1-19-billion-monthly-active-users-874-million-mobile-users-728-million-daily-users/#!ubaXH).

Although it appeared later than Facebook, Twitter is another example of social media that became quickly very popular among users [1]. Twitter is a social networking and micro-blogging service that enables its users to send and read other users' updates, known as tweets. Twitter is often described as the "SMS of Internet", in that the site provides the back-end functionality to other desktop and web-based applications to send and receive short text messages, often obscuring the actual web site itself. Tweets are text-based posts of up to 140 characters in length. Updates are displayed on the user's profile page and delivered to other users who have signed up to receive them. Users can send and receive updates via the Twitter web site, SMS, RSS (receive only), or through applications. The service is free to use over the web, but using SMS may incur phone services provider fees. Many media companies are using twitter in order to alert their readers about breaking news [6].

The evolution of the social media created participatory (or citizen) journalism. This concept derives from public citizens playing an active role in the process of collecting, reporting, analyzing, and disseminating news and information [7]. Other term used is user generated content [8]. Information and Communication technologies (social networking, media-sharing web sites and smartphones) have made citizen journalism more accessible to people all over the world, thus enabling them to often report breaking news much faster than professional journalists. Notable examples are the Arab Spring and the Occupy movement. But it is also worth noting that the unregulated nature of participatory journalism has drawn criticism from professional journalists for being too subjective, amateurish, and haphazard in quality and coverage (http://en.wikipedia.org/wiki/ Citizen_journalism).

Bowman and Willis [7] characterize participatory journalism as "a bottom-up, emergent phenomenon in which there is little or no editorial oversight or formal journalistic workflow dictating the decisions of a staff". As a substitute there are various concurrent conversations on social networks, as depicted in figure 1.

The problem is that in the traditional media journalists are responsible for the news. They decide the stories to cover, the sources to use, they write the text and choose the appropriate photographs. Thus they act as gatekeepers, deciding what the public shall receive [9]. But being gatekeepers constitute them responsible for the quality of the news content. The new media gives journalists the possibility to provide vast quantities of information in various formats. But journalists are responsible not only for how much information and in what form they include in the news stories but for how truthful the information is [8].

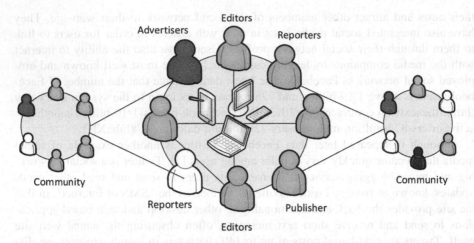

Fig. 1. Participatory journalism [7]

In the case of participatory journalism journalists contribute only part of a news story. Thus they feel responsible for users' contributions and they attempt to check the validity of the user generated content. But that is not an easy task, especially in the case that they receive a substantial volume of information from users [8].

3   Types of User Generated Content

Participatory journalism can be achieved with the variety of tools and services, namely: discussion groups, user generated content, weblog, collaborative publishing, Peer-to-Peer, XML Syndication [7]. The format for the user participation may vary and in the majority of the cases is under some kind of moderation by professional journalists [10]. Next we present and briefly discuss the types of user generated content.

— *User blog:* Users' blogs hosted on the media web site.
— *User multimedia material:* Photos, videos and other multimedia material submitted by users (usually checked by the web sites administrators)
— *User stories:* Users written submission on topical issues, suggestions for news stories (selected or/and edited by journalists and published on the media web site)
— *Collective interviews:* Chats or interviews contacted by journalists, with questions submitted by users (after moderation)
— *Comments:* Views on a story submitted by users (by filling a form on the bottom of the web page)
— *Content ranking:* News stories ranked by users (for example the most read, or the most emailed news story)
— *Forums:* a) Discussions controlled by journalists, with topical questions posed by the newsroom and submissions either fully or reactively moderated (usually available for a limited number of days, b) Forums where users are able to engage in threaded online conversations on debates (usually available for long periods-weeks or even months). The users are given the freedom to initiate these forum topics.

— *Journalists blogs:* Also known as j-blogs, include journalists' posts on specific topics and are open to user comments.
— *Polls*: Topical questions related to major issues, with users asked to make a multiple choice of binary response. They are able to provide instant and quantifiable results to users
— *Social networking*: Distribution of links to stories through social platforms, for example Facebook and Twitter.

4   Mechanisms for Ensuring the Quality of the Content

The introduction of participatory journalism in media organization has resulted in a cost, related to the need of moderation of the content that can guarantee the quality of the content. If we try to outline the basic areas from which problems may arise concerning user generated content we can identify defamation, hate speech, and Intellectual property. As far as the methods that can be employed in order to deal with the above issues, are concerned, these can be summarized in user identification and moderation or other oversight of user material [11].

4.1   User Registration

User registration involves the procedure in which the user provides his credentials, effectively proving his identity upon accessing a web site. Every user can become a registered user by providing some credentials, usually in the form of a username (or email) and password. After the registration of the user, he can access information and privileges unavailable to non-registered users, usually referred to simply as guests. The action of providing the proper credentials for a web site is called logging in, or signing in (http://en.wikipedia.org/wiki/Registered_user). Although user registration is a very common procedure that internet users are familiar with, there is a growing trend of social login or social sigh-in. This is a form of single sign-on using existing login information from a social networking service (Facebook, Google+ or Twitter). By this way logins a simplified for the users and the network administrators are able to acquire reliable demographic information [12].

4.2   CAPTCHA

Another mechanism applied for ensuring the quality of user generated content is CAPTCHA. It is an acronym based on the word "capture" and standing for "Completely Automated Public Turing test to tell Computers and Humans Apart" [13]. It is a type of challenge-response test used in computing as an attempt to ensure that the response is generated by a person. The process usually involves a computer asking a user to complete a simple test which the computer is able to grade. These tests are designed to be easy for a computer to generate, but difficult for a computer to solve, so that if a correct solution is received, it can be presumed to have been entered by a human. A common type of CAPTCHA requires the user to type letters or digits from a distorted image that appears on the screen, and such tests are commonly used to prevent unwanted internet bots from accessing web sites (http://en.wikipedia. org/wiki/CAPTCHA; http://www.captcha.net). This is especially useful in case of comments from unregistered users to blogs, forums, etc. The CAPTCHA technology is widely used in media web sites but sometimes the images that the user is called to identify are much distorted thus resulting in frustration on the part of the user.

CAPTCHA is usually employed in the process of user's registration and in the cases that unregister users are allowed to post comments or upload user generated content in the media web site (see figure 2).

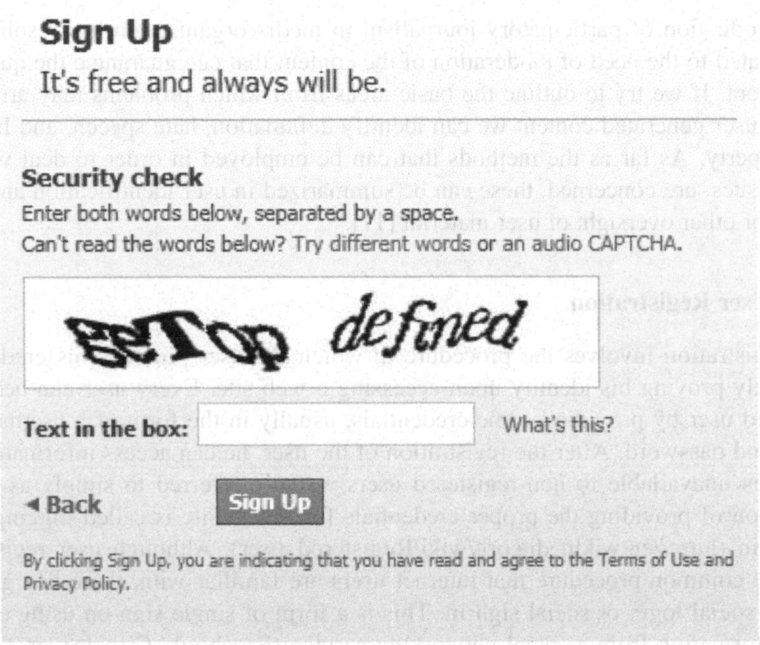

Fig. 2. Captcha identification procedure (depicted from Facebook registration process) (http://www.register-facebook.com)

4.3   Moderation

A moderation mechanism is the method where the webmaster of a media web site chooses to sort contributions which are irrelevant, obscene, illegal, or insulting with regards to useful or informative contributions. In other words he decides if the user generated content is appropriate for publishing or not [14]. Depending on the site's content and intended audience, the webmaster will decide what kind of user content is appropriate, and then delegate the responsibility of sifting through content to lesser moderators. The purpose of the moderation mechanism is to attempt to eliminate trolling, spamming, or flaming, although this varies widely from site to site (http://en.wikipedia.org /wiki/Moderation_system).

There are four types of moderation, namely, pre-moderation, post-moderation, automated moderation, and distributed moderation [15].

Pre-moderation: In this type of moderation all content is checked before publishing. Pre-moderation provides high control of the content that is published on the website. But it can result in a substantial reduction of the mount (40% to 50%) of user generated content. It also creates a lack of instant gratification on the part of the participant, who is left waiting for their submission to be cleared by a moderator. This latency might not create problem in some cases (for example in the case of a citizen story) but it will create an inconsistency in the case of a blog post or a forum when users interact with each other in almost real time. Another disadvantage of pre-moderation is the high cost involved especially if the user generated content is of high volume [15].

Post-moderation: This method involves publishing the content immediately and moderating it within the next 24 hours. All user generated content is replicated in a queue for a moderator to pass or remove it afterwards. The main advantage of this moderation type is that conversations may occur in real time, based on the immediacy offered by the direct publication of the content. Of course this advantage may cause many problems since there is no initial screening of the user generated content, which may include inappropriate material.

Automated moderation: This type of moderation differs from the previous types since it does not involve human intervention. It consists of deploying various technical tools (mainly filters) to process user generated content and apply pre-defined rules in order to reject or approve submissions. One of the most typical tool used is the word filter, in which a list of banned words is entered and the tool either stars the word out or otherwise replaces it with a defined alternative, or blocks or rejects the content altogether. A similar tool is the IP ban list which deletes inappropriate external links, or deletes content that comes from banned IPs. Of course there are other more sophisticated filters. Overall automated moderation is a valuable tool that involves an initial cost, but includes no operational cost [15].

Distributed moderation: One other type of moderation is Distributed moderation. This is a form of comment moderation that allows users that participate in the process of participatory journalism to moderate each other. Distributed moderation can be distinguished in two types: *User Moderation* and *Spontaneous Moderation* or *Reactive moderation* [15], [16].

User moderation allows any user to moderate any other user's contributions. This method works fine in web sites with large active population (for example Slashdot). More precisely each moderator is given a limited number of "mod points," each of which can be used to moderate an individual comment up or down by one point. Comments thus accumulate a score, which is additionally bounded to the range of -1 to 5 points. When viewing the site, a threshold can be chosen from the same scale, and only posts meeting or exceeding that threshold will be displayed (http://en.wikipedia.org/wiki/Moderation_system).

In the case of spontaneous moderation no official moderation scheme exists. Users spontaneously moderate their peers through posting their own comments about others' comments. One variation of spontaneous moderation is meta-moderation. This method enables any user to judge (moderate) the evaluation (voting) of another user [17]. Meta-moderation can be considered as a second layer of moderation. It attempts to increase fairness by letting users "rate the rating" of randomly selected comment posts.

Many media companies use pre and post moderation and others outsourced moderation, by enlisting journalists to moderate the vast amount of content users post on various services (blogs etc) offered by the media companies. In many cases the approach is to over-moderate the user generated content in order to avoid being criticized for trying to manipulating the conversation on various subjects [11].

It is obvious that moderation is a complicated issue. Media companies usually employ various types of moderation depending on the type of user participation. Automated moderation should be employed in every kind of user generated content. Table I includes the types of user generated content versus the moderation type that can be employed. It is worth noting that for certain types of user generated content in which the probability of arising legal issues is high, pre-moderation is the ideal type of moderation. On the other hand in types of user generated content that do not usually arise legal issues, distributed moderation can be applied. In any case all types of distributed moderation can be applied in case that the media web site has a large active population of users [17].

Table 1. Types of user generated content versus type of moderation

Type of user generated content	Type of moderation
User blog	Distributed moderation or post moderation
User multimedia material	Pre-moderation
User stories	Pre-moderation
Collective interviews	Pre-moderation
Comments	Distributed moderation
Content ranking	Spontaneous moderation
Forums	Pre-moderation
Journalists blogs	Pre-moderation
Polls	Spontaneous moderation
Social networking	Not applicable*

any comments that may accompany a link to a news article can be moderated only by the social network. Usually social network moderate user content only after a user's complaint.

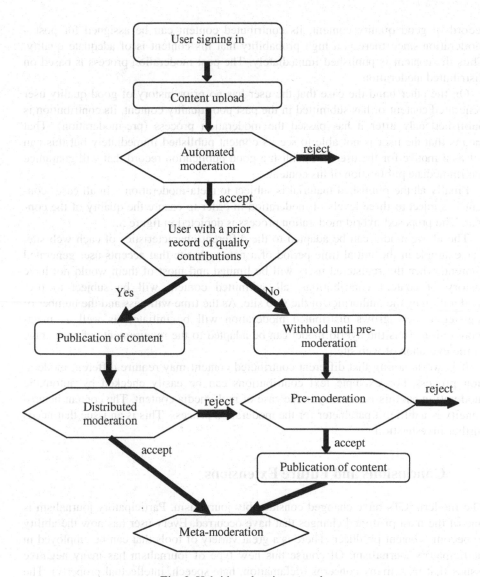

Fig. 3. Hybrid moderation procedure

5   Hybrid Moderation

Based on the types of moderation previously presented, we propose a mixed approach. This hybrid moderation method involves all moderation types. Next we briefly describe the proposed method. Users who are interested in contributing content will be obliged to register to the web site. When a registered user adds content the content is submitted immediately to automated moderation. Subsequently the moderation process is determined by the user's record. More precisely, in case that the user has a

record of good quality content, its contributed content can be assigned for post –
moderation since there is a high probability that his content is of adequate quality.
Thus the content is published immediately. The post moderation process is based on
distributed moderation.

On the other hand the case that the user has no prior history of good quality user
generated content or has submitted in the past poor quality content, its contribution is
published only after it has passed the moderation process (pre-moderation). That
means that the user is not able to see its content published immediately but this can
act as a motive for the user to establish a good publication record that will guarantee
the immediate publication of his content.

Finally all the published material is subject to meta-moderation. In all cases content is subject to three levels of moderation in order to ensure the quality of the content. The proposed hybrid moderation process is depicted in figure 3.

The above model can be adapted to the different characteristics of each web site.
For example in the initial time period of a new web site that accepts user generated
content, when the registered users will be limited and most of them would not have
history of content contributions, all submitted content will be subject to pre-
moderation by the authorities of the web site. As the time will pass and the number of
registered users grows distributed moderation will be initiated as well as meta-
moderation. Thus the hybrid model can be adapted to the requirements of each stage
of the evolution of web site.

It is worth noting that different contributed content may require different moderation process. For example text contributions can be easily checked by automatic
moderation but this is not easy in the case of multimedia content. The content heterogeneity is a difficult parameter for the moderation process. This is an issue that needs
further investigation.

6   Conclusions and Future Extensions

The modern ICTs have changed considerably journalism. Participatory journalism is
one of the most profound changes that have occurred. Every user has now the ability
to become content producer. There is a great variety of tools that can be employed in
participatory journalism. Of course this new type of journalism has many negative
issues that raise many concerns (defamation, hate speech, intellectual property). The
solution to these problems is the control of the user generated material. This can be
achieved with the registration of the users that contribute material and with the moderation of the user generated material. The registration process is a well known
process to the users, since it has been employed for many years in many internet services (for example, e-mail services, social networks, etc.). On the other hand moderation can be very time consuming and the media company may have to dedicate many
human recourses to this task. Of course there are many different types of moderation
(post-moderation, distributed moderation, or even the proposed hybrid moderation)
that may alleviate to some extent this problem. The proposed hybrid moderation
model combines all existing moderation techniques and applies them based on the

publication record of the user. Thus it is able to overcome in many cases the necessary latency that is required in order for the user generated content to be checked. The model also guarantees that all content is subject to three moderation stages.

There is no doubt that participative journalism is an issue that no media company can choose to adopt or disregard without great consideration. As usual the solution to this problem is a compromise. The media company chooses to implement some type of citizen participation, usually gradually by imposing strict moderation in order to prevent legal issues. Of course this means that a great deal of user generated material that may be rejected will be of good quality, but will be rejected just in case it might produces legal problems for the media company, thus resulting in a negative effect on its credibility.

One solution to this problem is the training of the users that contribute in participative journalism, in order to act as responsible e-citizens. Another proposal involves the careful selection of the issues that are being developed with user generated content. Future extension of this work will involve the detail study of the moderation mechanism employed in participative journalism in order to locate steps in the process that may be improved.

One other issue that demands further study is the automatic moderation of multimedia material. Applicable video indexing can be deployed taking advantage of motion and/or color features, while the interaction with audio parameters is very powerful towards multimodal event detection, and summarization [18]. This is also fuelled by the evolution of machine learning algorithms and hybrid expert systems that facilitate many interdisciplinary research topics and knowledge management application areas [19]. However, there are many difficulties in such content recognition and semantic analysis scenarios, which are related with content massiveness and heterogeneity, especially in user contributed content [20]. Nevertheless such focused approaches in such orientation already have been initiated and look promising [21].

References

1. An, J., Cha, M., Gummadi, K., Crowcroft, J.: Media landscape in Twitter: A world of new conventions and political diversity. Artificial Intelligence 6(1), 18–25 (2011)
2. Spyridou, L.P., Veglis, A.: Political Parties and Web 2.0 tools: A Shift in Power or a New Digital Bandwagon? International Journal of Electronic Governance 4(1/2), 136–155 (2011)
3. Kaplan, A.M., Haenlein, M.: Users of the world, unite! The challenges and opportunities of Social Media. Business Horizons 53(1), 59–68 (2010)
4. Veglis, A., Pomportsis, A.: The e-citizen in the cyberspace – a journalism aspect. In: Texts and Articles from the 5th International Conference on Information Law (ICIL 2012) (2013)
5. Boyd, D.M., Ellison, N.B.: Social Network Sites: Definition, History, and Scholarship. Journal of Computer-Mediated Communication 13(1), 210–230 (2008)
6. Veglis, A.: Journalism and Cross Media Publishing: The case of Greece. In: Siapera, E., Veglis, A. (eds.) The Wiley-Blackwell Handbook of Online Journalism. Blackwell Publishing (2012)

7. Bowman, S., Willis, C.: We Media: How Audiences are Shaping the Future of News and Information. The Media Center at the American Press Institute (2003), http://www.hypergene.net/wemedia/download/we_media.pdf

8. Singer, J.B., Hermida, A., Domingo, D., Heinonen, A., Paulussen, S., Quandt, T., Reich, Z., Vujnovic, M.: Participatory Journalism-Guarding Open Gates at Online Newspapers. Willey-Blackwell (2011)

9. White, D.M.: The gatekeeper: A case study in the selection of news. Journalism Quarterly 27, 383–96 (1950)

10. Hermida, A., Thurman, N.: A clash of cultures: the integration of user generated content within professional journalistic frameworks at British newspaper web sites. Journalism Practice 2(3), 342–356 (2008)

11. Singer, J.B.: Taking Responsibility: Legal and ethical issues in participatory journalism. In: Singer, J.B., Hermida, A., Domingo, D., Heinonen, A., Paulussen, S., Quandt, T., Reich, Z., Vujnovic, M. (eds.) Participatory Journalism-Guarding Open Gates at Online Newspapers. Willey-Blackwell (2011)

12. Prescott, B.: Social Sign-On: What is it and How Does It Benefit Your Web Site? Social Technology Review (January 10, 2011), http://www.socialtechnologyreview.com/articles/social-sign-what-it-and-how-does-it-benefit-your-web-site

13. Grossman, L.: Computer Literacy Tests: Are You Human? Time (magazine) (2008), http://www.time.com/time/magazine/article/0,9171,1812084,00.html

14. ABC, Moderating User Generated Content, Guidance Note (2011), http://www.abc.net.au/corp/pubs/documents/GNModerationINS.pdf

15. Grimes-Viort, B.: 6 types of content moderation you need to know about, Blaisise Grimes-Viort – Online Communities & Social Media (December 6, 2010), http://blaisegv.com/community-management/6-types-of-content-moderation-you-need-to-know-about/

16. Lampe, C., Resnick, P.: Slash(dot) and Burn: Distributed Moderation in a Large Online Conversation Space. In: Proc. of ACM Computer Human Interaction Conference 2004, Vienna Austria (2004)

17. Momeni, E.: Semi-Automatic Semantic Moderation of Web Annotations. In: WWW 2012 Companion, Lyon, France, April 16-20. ACM 978-1-4503-1230-1/12/04 (2012)

18. Dimoulas, C., Avdelidis, A., Kalliris, G., Papanikolaou, G.: Joint Wavelet video denoising and motion activity detection in multi-modal human activity analysis: Application to video – Assisted bioacoustic/psycho-physiological monitoring. EURASIP Journal on Advances in Signal Processing (2008), doi:10.1155/2008/792028

19. Dimoulas, C., Papanikolaou, G., Petridis, V.: Pattern classification and audiovisual content management techniques using hybrid expert systems: a video-assisted bioacoustics application in abdominal sounds pattern analysis. Expert Systems with Application 38(10), 13082–13093 (2011)

20. Kotsakis, R., Kalliris, G., Dimoulas, C.: Investigation of broadcast-audio semantic analysis scenarios employing radio-programme-adaptive pattern classification. Speech Communication 54(6), 743–762 (2012)

21. Chen, T.M., Wang, V.: Web filtering and censoring. Computer 43(3), 94–97 (2010)

Analysing, Visualising, and Modelling Social Networks

Use of Twitter Stream Data for Trend Detection of Various Social Media Sites in Real Time

Sapumal Ahangama

MillenniumIT, Sri Lanka
sahangama@gmail.com

Abstract. Emergence of social networks such as Twitter has enhanced communication among large proportions of participants sharing enormous volumes of data. Categorization and analysis of the data in-depth will enable to generate valuable insights and information. In this paper, a new method is presented to find the trending content and trending topics of various social media networks using real time data shared on Twitter. The insights on current trending content generated by the proposed system will be of high importance as majority of the external social media networks doesn't directly publish any real time data related to trends or most interesting content within itself.

Keywords: Trend Detection, Social Media, Social Computing.

1 Introduction

Social networks are a framework used worldwide to share personal views, ideas, debate on various topics and exchange personal experiences. The use and penetration of popular social networks in societies have grown rapidly during the past few years.

Among popular social media networks, Twitter can be considered as a great reservoir of information with nearly 200million Twitter users worldwide. The users engage with nearly 400million micro blogging posts ('Tweets') published daily [1]. Within such information, trends or popular topics are driven by emerging events, breaking news and general topics that attract attention of many Twitter users. Since the data originates mainly from human users scattered worldwide and as the tweets would display the direct personal opinion on a topic, the data can be of immense value in decision making and generating foresights. Understanding and identifying the important topics in these social networks will give insights on how the society gives value to various issues. In addition, structured analysis could lead to arriving at definitions on how people in various segments would respond to an issue in the social media domain. Such an analysis could lead to understand how a community would come into a conclusion or a decision based upon a news outbreak. Also, such intelligence would be important in commercial as well as in political aspects. Having an understanding on the reaction and impact of a political decision taken by a main stream political party would enable to improve the decisions such that the positive sentiment among the public can be increased. Similarly, commercial enterprises would be able

G. Meiselwitz (Ed.): SCSM 2014, LNCS 8531, pp. 151–159, 2014.

to assess the success of a commercial campaign by determining the popularity strength of the keywords the campaign created. Availability of a proper model would enable fine tuning of such a commercial campaign to attain higher popularity with a greater positive sentiment.

With the increase in popularity of social media networks, various new social media sites emerge with sharing limited to a specific type of content such as social media networks specializing on sharing solely the images, videos or location based information. Since these social media networks specialize in a specific type of content being shared, understanding the patterns of the data will add more value. For example in the most simplest form, identifying the trends in a video sharing social media network in real time will enable to determine the   videos creating the highest social impact at the time indicating the success of such videos. Further, the identification of user behavior patterns would enable to target and produce the videos in the specific user interest areas.

Various attempts have been previously made to derive intelligence, conclusions and behavior models using Twitter real time data in different fields with satisfactory results. In this paper, we look in to an indirect method, where the trend analysis in external social media networks will be carried out using the twitter real time stream data. Since many of the current social media networks do not provide at least the basic real time content analytics data such as trending or most talked about content, it is intended to bridge this gap with the indirect method proposed.

In this paper, Section 2 describes the related work where Twitter data has been purely used to generate various conclusions. Section 3 describes the content categories in Twitter as well as the methodology used to derive trends of external social media sites. An analysis of the data and results are done in Section 4 and Section 5 deals with the concluding remarks with an explanation of limitations of the system.

2   Related Work

Basic location based trend identification on Twitter would provide an insight into the most talked about topics in a specific geo location. Further in-depth analysis has proved that Twitter data can be used in a variety of other fields as well. Various studies on Twitter data has been carried out beyond mere identification of worldwide trends or location based trends of overall Twitter data. Becker et al. [2] demonstrated on improving such generic real time analysis of 'trending topics' to identify real world events using Twitter data.

Further, studies have successfully displayed how Twitter data can be used to generate foresights in a specific domain such as entertainment, medical, disaster recovery etc. Sitaram et al. [3] displayed how user chatter on Twitter could be used in a real world scenario. It was shown how the chatter can be used to generate forecasts of box office performances of movies. Sakaki et al. [4] demonstrated how real time algorithmic analysis of Twitter data can be used to generate location estimations of earthquakes in Japan. Vieweg et al. [5] analyzed the Twitter data published during natural disasters and proposes a framework such that the important information could be extracted where the emergency responders could use it. In the medical field, Achrekar et al. [6] have gone to the level of predicting flu trends by analyzing real time Tweets which can be used to identify flu outbreaks and contain them.

The above approaches are of great use as the information generated directly from people can be obtained in real time which is not possible in traditional methods of data collection via manual or online surveys. In addition, no previous attempts were found where Twitter data was used to derive content analytics of external social media networks which is the intention of this paper.

3   Methodology

A variety of studies have been carried out on the content categories shared on the micro-blogging platform. Naaman et al. [7] analyzed Tweets originating from a random set of users other than re-Tweets. In this study, data was collected from the Twitter API and categorized into various segments based on the content of the Tweet.   In the categorization, a vast majority of the Tweets fell in categories such as the current state of the user and self-promotion of the user (Categories Current State and Self-Promotion in Figure 1).   Content shared on external social media sites such as for image or video sharing consist mainly of content that is about the user's current state or content with intention of self-promotion. Hence there is a high content category correlation among overall Twitter content and the content on external social media sites.

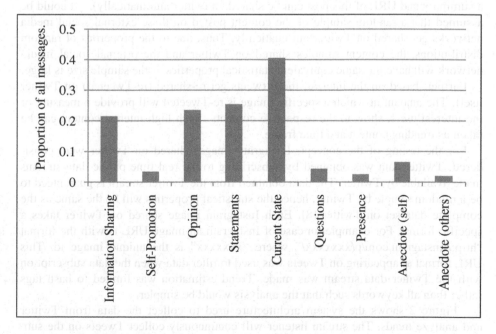

Fig. 1. Twitter Content Category Frequency Source Naaman et al. (2010)

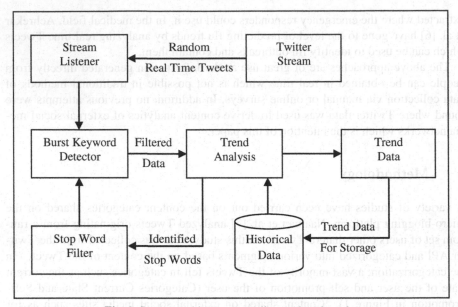

Fig. 2. System architecture to collect and analyze data

Majority of the external social media sites are provided with the feature to share the content in Twitter alongside the original post. The Tweet would provide a link to the original post with a short description (e.g. When an image is posted on Instagram, a summary and URL of this post can be shared on twitter automatically).   It could be assumed that a random sample of the content posted on these external social media networks get shared on Twitter automatically. Thus, due to the properties of random distributions, the content samples shared on Twitter and the original social media network will have the same equivalent statistical properties as the sample size is large.

Further, based on the interest, these tweets get re-shared (re-Tweeted) on Twitter itself. The amount at which a specific image is re-Tweeted will provide a measure of the interest users, show to the respective content.   Such high interest content can be taken as trending content at a time frame.

For the testing of the concept, Instagram images shared on Twitter were considered. Twitter data was obtained by subscribing to the real time public data streams made available by Twitter. The data obtained from the Twitter stream is guaranteed to be a random sample by Twitter, hence the statistical properties will be the same as the complete data set on Twitter [8]. Each Instagram image shared on Twitter takes a specific format. For example, in case of Instagram an image URL is with the format "http://instagram.com/p/xxxxxxx/" where "xxxxxxx" is the unique image id. This URL format as appearing on Tweets was used to filter data when the data subscription with the Twitter data stream was made. Trend estimation was limited to hash tags rather than all keywords such that the analysis would be simpler.

Figure 2 shows the system architecture used to collect the data from Twitter and analyze trends. The stream listener will continuously collect Tweets on the subscribed topic from the public Twitter stream. The listener further filters for Tweets with Instagram images. Each of the hash tags reported of the collected tweets is then analyzed for a burst within the time frame. The burst keyword detector uses a stop word filter. The stop word filter will filter any common hash tags that report large data counts, but the count is within the average count reported in a time frame. The filtered data is then analyzed to detect any trends. For trend analysis a database stores the historical data such that the system can maintain a state.

4   Analysis of Data

Table 1 summarizes the data collected from Twitter. Since the sample obtained from Twitter is guaranteed to be random [8] and can be considered as a large sample, it can be assumed that the analyzed data set represents the original data set in statistical properties.

Table 1. Summary and analysis of data collected

Average number of images posted on Instagram daily	55,000,000 [9]
Average rate of Tweets collected (per second)	50
Average daily Tweets processed	4,320,000
Average number of Instagram images processed from Tweets (daily)	3,850,000
Average unique number of Instagram images processed from Tweets (daily)	3,210,000

Table 2 shows the distribution and breakdown of all collected hash tags during a 1 hour time window. Hash tags collected had a positively skewed distribution with vast majority of the hash tags reporting a very few occurrences within the time frame while a few displaying relatively larger numbers of occurrences. These hash tags were filtered to identify any tags that report in bursts which may turn out as trends.

Upon filtering for stop words and trend detection, many of the hash tags identified as trending, coincided with top news stories and events around the world that are currently taking place. Sports events, award ceremonies, deaths of popular people and protests are few examples. Hash tags of these events became trends with people sharing images related to the event in bursts during the event. Figure 3 shows the general life time pattern of a hash tag trend over time. In addition the figure shows an example hash tag trend where counts are plotted every ten minutes. In the graph pattern, the number of occurrences in a time interval and the time taken for the trend to fade away is a direct measure of the strength of the trend. Highly talked about and highly interesting tags tend to show higher bursts. Stories which tend to develop further with new sub events showed to last longer in the time axis.

Table 2. Number of occurrences of a hash tag within a 1 hour time frame

Number of occurrences within time frame	Number of hash tags
1	51,443
2	8,352
3 – 10	7,766
11 – 20	1,101
21 – 1000	948
> 1000	7
Total	**69,617**

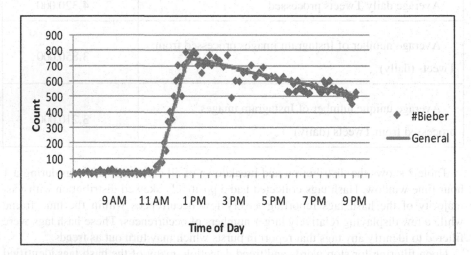

Fig. 3. Generalized life time pattern of a trending hash tag with an example (#Bieber)

An example set of such tags trending related to an event identified by the system are given in Table 3.

Table 3. Example trending events and popular event hash tags

Hash Tags	Event
#Egypt, #TharirSquare, #ByeByeMorsi	During 2013 Egypt uprising.
#NelsonMandela, #Madiba	During the mourning period of Nelson Mandela.
#4thofjuly, #America, #July4, #independence-dayusa	During July 4th Independence celebrations in USA.
#princesskate, #royalbaby, #boyorgirl	During the period where Royal Baby was expected in UK.
#wimbledon, #murray, #AndyMurray, #tennis, #champion,#77years	During 2013 Wimbledon Championship.
#runningofthebulls	During Running of the Bulls event in Spain.
#UnitedforMar-riage,#Equality, #EqualityForAll, #prop8	During 2013 Equal Marriage Supreme Court hearing in Washington, USA

During the analysis of Instagram images collected, nearly 5% of the images collected during a day accounted to reporting multiple times as a result of re-Tweets or re-sharing of the same image. Table 4 demonstrates the distribution of images reported more than once in the time period. The images which recorded highest number of re-Tweets were shared by popular personalities on Instagram such as celebrities and sports stars. These users had large number of followers as well as the images received large number of likes. As a result of their popularity, the images recorded a large number of re-Tweets resulting in certain hash tags of the images identified as trending.

Table 4. Repeat count of images within a time frame of 1 day

Repeat Count	No of Images
2	121,522
3 – 10	42,930
11 – 20	3460
21 – 100	2956
101 – 1000	588
> 1000	32
Total	171,488

5   Conclusion

In the analysis of results for Instagram, it was found that trends directly coincided with major news and other popular events taking place in the time frame. Reasons for image trends fall into 2 main categories. Firstly, major social events such as protests, civil unrests, and festivals create image trends with many people sharing images related to the event. The second category is when a popular person posts a controversial or a unique image, tags of the image became a trend with many re-sharing the same image in quick succession due to the high interest. It is assumed that a random sample of the content originally shared on the external social media site is shared on Twitter. It could be said that Twitter stream can be successfully used to generate insights on Twitter connected external social media sites if the assumption holds true. This assumption is a limitation of the system when expanding to monitor trends of external social media networks which are not highly integrated with Twitter. In addition, due to text content length limitations in Twitter, certain parts of the original post may get truncated leading to incomplete data. Also the method cannot be verified accurately as various social media sites use proprietary algorithms and custom variables to calculate their own trends and most information is not published openly.

References

1. The Official Twitter Blog, Celebrating #Twitter7, https://blog.twitter.com/2013/celebrating-twitter7
2. Hila, B., Naaman, M., Gravano, L.: Beyond Trending Topics: Real-World Event Identification on Twitter. In: ICWSM (2011)

3. Sitaram, A., Huberman, B.A.: Predicting the future with social media. In: 2010 IEEE/WIC/ACM International Conference on Web Intelligence and Intelligent Agent Technology (WI-IAT), vol. 1, pp. 492–499. IEEE (2010)
4. Takeshi, S., Okazaki, M., Matsuo, Y.: Earthquake shakes Twitter users: real-time event detection by social sensors. In: Proceedings of the 19th International Conference on World Wide Web, pp. 851–860. ACM (2010)
5. Sarah, V., Hughes, A.L., Starbird, K., Palen, L.: Microblogging during two natural hazards events: what twitter may contribute to situational awareness. In: Proceedings of the SIGCHI Conference on Human Factors in Computing Systems, pp. 1079–1088. ACM (2010)
6. Harshavardhan, A., Gandhe, A., Lazarus, R., Yu, S., Liu, B.: Predicting flu trends using twitter data. In: 2011 IEEE Conference on Computer Communications Workshops (INFOCOM WKSHPS), pp. 702–707. IEEE (2011)
7. Naaman, M., Boase, J., Lai, C.: Is it really about me?: message content in social awareness streams. In: Proceedings of the 2010 ACM Conference on Computer Supported Cooperative Work, Savannah, Georgia, USA, February 6-10 (2010)
8. Twitter Developers, Frequently Asked Questions, How are rate limits determined on the Streaming API?, https://dev.twitter.com/docs/faq#6861
9. Instgram Press Page, http://instagram.com/press/

Social Network Representation and Dissemination of Pre-Exposure Prophylaxis (PrEP): A Semantic Network Analysis of HIV Prevention Drug on Twitter

Zheng An, Margaret McLaughlin, Jinghui Hou, Yujung Nam,
Chih-Wei Hu, Mina Park, and Jingbo Meng

University of Southern California, Los Angeles, United States
zan@usc.edu

Abstract. Daily oral pre-exposure prophylaxis (PrEP) is a new approach to HIV prevention. The study aims to examine how PrEP has been represented and disseminated on one of the most popular social networking sites - Twitter. We collected 1435 public tweets containing the word "Truvada." After computer-mediated and manual de-duplication, we analyzed 447 unique tweets and calculated weights between two words to measure their co-occurrence in 7-word windows. Semantic networks of PrEP-related tweets were constructed. We found that Twitter was used to generate public discussions and collectively interpret new medical information, especially in frequently propagated tweets and from users with more followers. In the meantime, the results revealed the presence of illicit online pharmacies that marketed and sold PrEP without the need for a prescription. We discussed implications for public health and made urgent call for better regulation of online pharmacies.

Keywords: PrEP, HIV, Twitter, Semantic Network, Illicit Online Pharmacies.

1 Introduction

1.1 Social Media Representations of Health Issues

Social media is becoming a popular platform to disseminate and discuss health information [1-3]. Twitter has emerged as one of the most popular online social networking and micro-blogging sites that enable users to share their perceptions and experiences within 140 characters. The National Research Corporation [4] reported that about 18% of nearly 23,000 respondents has used Twitter to seek health-related information. Health information can be quickly spread to a potentially enormous audience by tweeting and re-tweeting.

Recent studies have monitored public perceptions and social media representations of health topics on Twitter. Twitter is not only a venue for news media and public agencies to disseminate health information, but also a platform to generate discussions on various health topics [5,6]. For instance, Scanfeld, Scanfeld, and Larson content analyzed antibiotic-related Twitter status updates and found that Twitter provided a space for sharing health information and advice [7]. Among the

G. Meiselwitz (Ed.): SCSM 2014, LNCS 8531, pp. 160–169, 2014.
© Springer International Publishing Switzerland 2014

randomly selected 1000 status updates, 289 updates were about commenting generally on taking antibiotics, followed by offering advice and explanations (157), claiming side effects (113), mentioning reasons for taking antibiotics (102), discussing resistance (92), and other categories. Robillard et al. analyzed Twitter content about aging and dementia and showed that the majority of Tweets generated discussions of recent research findings related to prediction and risk management of Alzheimer's disease [6]. Love et al. studied Tweet content about vaccination and reported that Twitter users frequently discussed the development of new vaccines and collectively interpreted updated research findings about vaccine effectiveness [5]. A more recent study examined social media representation around pre-exposure prophylaxis for HIV prevention (PrEP) [8]. The results reveal that PrEP-related Tweets covered a wide range of issues, such as side effects, adherence issues, risk compensation, moral judgments, and targeted recipients.

1.2   Misuse of Health Information on Social Media

In the meantime, the participatory nature of social media may increase the possibility of misuse and misinterpretation of health information [1, 5, 7]. Purchasing drugs from illicit Internet pharmacies has received an increasing attention since this behavior raises significant public health risks. Illicit Internet pharmacies refer to "those marketing and offering for sale prescription pharmaceutical products without the need for a prescription [9]." Prescription drugs are marketed as generic or no prescription needed. Sometimes, prescription can be also substituted by unsubstantiated medical questionnaires. The illicit Internet pharmacies may sell potentially dangerous, counterfeit or unapproved drugs.

There is a high volume of social media (e.g. Twitter) content about prescription drugs sold illegally online [10,11]. Prescription drugs are advertised or linked to websites where users make purchases from illicit Internet pharmacies. Liang and Mackey found that the majority of the top 20 drug brands by direct-to-consumer advertising (DTCA) spending were marketed by illicit online pharmacies [12]. Out of the 20 drugs, 11 had Facebook page links and 16 had Twitter/Friendster links that directed users to illicit online pharmacies. According to the 2007 National Center on Addiction and Substance Abuse at Columbia University, about 85 percent of their monitored websites that sold prescription drugs did not require a doctor's prescription [13]. In June 2013, the U.S. Food and Drug Administration, in partnership with international regulatory and law enforcement agencies took actions (i.e. issued regulatory warnings or shut down) towards more than 9,600 websites that illegally sold medical products [14].

Illicit online pharmacies are easily accessible to the public through social media. Mackey and Liang created a fictitious advertisement about purchasing prescription drugs online on the top four social media platforms (Facebook, Twitter, Google+, and MySpace) [9]. The advertisement was linked to a website with an error page. They tracked the user traffic and found 2795 visits over a 10-month period in 2011. The U.S. Food and Drug Administration sampled 6090 adults who lived in the U.S. and have made purchases online. About 17% of surveyed adults reported purchasing a prescription drug from online pharmacies that were not associated with their health insurance or a local pharmacy [15].

Illicit Internet pharmacies are becoming a global public health threat. Misuse of prescription drugs can lead to overdose death, drug-impaired driving, and other serious consequences [16]. For instance, drug overdose attributed to a total of 15,323 deaths (9.8% per 100,000 population) in 2010 [17]. The actual number is estimated to be higher since many death certificates do not provide information about the specific type of drug that causes overdose death. Despite the insufficient research on social media and illicit online pharmacies, the association between Internet/social media and nonmedical use of prescription drugs began to emerge [18]. Jena found that as the high-speed Internet use increased for every 10 percent, admissions for prescription drug abuse increased 1 percent [19]. Some studies show that as many as 11% drug abusers got their drugs online. The actual prevalence should be higher since drugs that are easier to get online have lower risks for abuse and these studies did not include local drug dealers and street distributors who got their drugs online [19].

1.3   Semantic Network Analysis

Social network analysis has been recently introduced to media studies to identify key themes or attributes emerged from semantic networks [20-22]. Building upon research in cognitive mapping and scheme analysis, this approach assumes that individuals use networks of words or concepts to construct meanings in thought. Schemas are formed to reduce cognitive load and enhance information processing capabilities [23]. Certain attributes and meanings are highlighted in media content, and therefore translated into individuals' mental representations of social reality [24]. For instance, Tian and Stewart examined 332 news reports from CNN's website and 408 reports from BBC's website on SARS-related issues [25]. They identified clusters of words that frequently appeared in those news reports and looked at their semantic relationships. They found that both media outlets focused on reporting the SARS outbreak and public health effects from a global perspective, and CNN adopted a more economic perspective compared to BBC. Murphy analyzed testimonies and identified major themes on how entrepreneurs, bureaucrats, and egalitarians framed the nicotine debate using the semantic network analysis and the cluster analysis [26]. They found that all three interest groups shared concerns about the association between advertising and tobacco use, especially for minors. Recently this approach was introduced to the agenda setting research and used to examine meanings revealed by network structures [20]. Schultz et al. looked at newspaper reports about BP oil spill crisis [22]. They identified key clusters such as oil spill problem, cause, solution, and consequences. These reports revealed that BP successfully dissociated itself from being responsible for this crisis.

To expand this line of research to social media in the health context, this study aims at examining social media representation of PrEP. Daily oral pre-exposure prophylaxis (PrEP) is a new approach to HIV prevention currently being evaluated globally. In July of 2012, the U.S. Food and Drug Administration approved emtricitabine/tenofovir disoproxil fumarate (Truvada) as an antiretroviral PrEP to prevent HIV infection in populations at high risk (e.g. men who have sex with men and those who have sex with HIV infected individuals. However, the effective implementation of PrEP is a complex subject [27]. Among the various influencing factors, individuals at high risk of HIV infection need comprehensive and accurate information about PrEP.

Individuals need to be carefully screened and monitored by healthcare providers if they want to take PrEP for HIV prevention. An individual is required to be tested of being completely HIV negative before he starts to take PrEP. He should also be tested regularly (every 3 months) to confirm that he is HIV negative. He needs to practice safer sex, such as using a condom, getting tested for other sexually transmitted diseases, and limiting contact with body fluids. An individual at high risk cannot take PrEP to prevent HIV infection through sex if he does not know his status [28].

PrEP can cause serious side effects, such as lactic acidosis, kidney problems, changes in body fat, symptoms of inflammation and serious liver problems, which may lead to serious or fatal medical emergency. Individuals should consult their healthcare providers about other medications they take simultaneously. Women who are pregnant or breastfeeding also need to speak to their healthcare provider before taking PrEP as it can harm the unborn baby or pass the drug to the baby through breast milk [28].

Given the complex nature of HIV prevention, our study aims at examining how Twitter users understand and disseminate information about PrEP-related issues. Although tweets that are frequently retweeted or disseminated by popular users have potentially bigger influence [29,30], little is known whether the content of the message differ by propagation rate and source popularity. We specifically examine the following research questions:

RQ1: What are the major themes emerged from PrEP-related tweets?

RQ2: Do the themes vary significantly by propagation rate on Twitter?

RQ3: Do the themes vary significantly by the number of followers of the Tweet source?

2   Method

2.1   Sample

A total of 1435 public tweets containing the word "Truvada" were collected between November 15 and December 27, 2012 through a cloud-based text analytics software. The sample consisted of 774 (53.94%) English tweets and 661 (46.06%) non-English Tweets. Only the English Tweets were subject to further analysis. Since a great proportion of Tweets contained duplicated texts, we performed some procedures to cluster Tweets with the same or highly similar content. First, we removed hashtags, ReTweets (RTs), and URLs of each Tweet. Tweets were clustered together if they contained exactly the same content. This computer-assisted de-duplication did not produce a satisfactory dataset since Tweets with highly similar content were assigned to different clusters. For example, "an HIV treatment medication, to be taken by uninfect.." and "an HIV treatment medication, to be taken by uninfected people to protect..." were assigned to different clusters. In the next step, five graduate students manually clustered highly similar Tweets that conveyed the same meaning (e.g.

omission of a comma). Tweets with differences in title length and comments (e.g. "Truvada, HIV Prevention Drug, Divides The Gay Community (VIDEO) Huffington Post" and "Truvada, HIV Prevention Drug, Divides The Gay Community: Truvada, a new drug which is said to knock out the HIV virus before it can ...") were coded into different clusters since each might contain additional information and convey different meanings. Each Tweet was coded by at least two graduate students. Discrepancies were discussed until reaching agreement. Table 1 presents the number of Tweets in each cluster. Tweets in each cluster were sorted alphabetically. The first Tweet in each cluster was taken out to construct a new dataset.

Table 1. Number of tweets in each cluster

Cluster ID	# of Tweets	Cluster ID	# of Tweets	Cluster ID	# of Tweets
1	37	8	13	18-27	4
2-3	24	9	11	28-47	3
4-5	19	10	8	48-91	2
6	18	11-14	7	92-447	1
7	14	15-17	5		

2.2   Procedure

The final sample consisted of 447 unique English Tweets that were converted to a set of tokens. A weight was calculated between two tokens to measure their co-occurrence in 7-word windows [26]. The tokens (nodes) and weights (edges) were further analyzed in semantic networks to capture the semantic representation of PrEP related words. The sample contained 1268 nodes and 15385 edges. Separate semantic networks were constructed for highly propagated Tweets (from clusters that contained three tweets or more) and infrequently propagated Tweets (1 or 2 tweets) respectively. The average number of followers was calculated for each cluster (ranged from 1 to 21,170, $M = 1.431.34$, $SD = 2,653.03$). Missing values (n = 111) were treated as "0" since the Twitter account was either suspended or had no followers. Separate semantic networks were prepared for Tweets posted by users with more followers (above median) and with fewer followers (below median).

3   Results

QAP and MRQAP tests detected moderate correlations between highly and infrequently propagated Tweets (QAP Correlation Pearson's $r = .35$, MRQAP $F(1,28054) = 3948$, $R^2 = .12$, $p < .001$). A similar pattern was found when examining Tweets by number of followers of the users (QAP Correlation Pearson's $r = .32$, MRQAP $F(1,78678) = 8904$, $R^2 = .10$, $p < .001$). Table 2 reports clusters of words with high centrality measures that revealed two predominant themes about representation of PrEP on Twitter.

The first theme – public discussions about PrEP-related topics – was found in highly propagated Tweets and from users with more followers. Users tweeted and retweeted a wide range of PrEP-related topics, such as spreading the news (e.g. "US

Approved HIV Prevention Pill Truvada."), mentioning insurance plans (e.g. "Interesting thing I learned today: PrEP (Truvada) is now covered if you're under the Healthy SF plan. Kudos to SF fo ..."), expressing moral judgements (e.g. "Truvada Whores?"), expressing opinions (e.g. "My Perspective of (Truvada) as a Method to Prevent Infection: A Blog Entry by ..."), and discussing the targeting recipients ("The HIV Prevention Pill: How Is Truvada Taking Root in Black Communities?").

The second theme – illicit online pharmacies – appeared in infrequently propagated Tweets and in Tweets from users with fewer followers. For instance, a number of tweets contained information about purchasing PrEP without a doctor's prescription, such as "Cheap truvada online drug free shipping Wyoming in case of can I buy truvada tenofovir online coupon no script Mississ," "Where To Order Truvada Online No Script Required, Buy Cheap Truvada Free Fedex Ship seimon," and "Cheap truvada online paypal fast delivery Indiana by way of buy truvada in internet tablets without prescription Miss." Figure 1 presents the semantic network of PrEP-related words that appeared in infrequently propagated Tweets.

Table 2. PrEP-related themes and clusters of words on Twitter

Themes	Clusters of words
Public discussions about PrEP-related topics	"HIV," "drug," "prevention," and "pill," "PrEP," "FDA," "Virus," "patient," "perspective," "learned," "how," "immunodeficiency," "liked" "they" "see" "transmission" "cure" "community" "talk" "discussion" "efficacy" "read" "dose," "medication," and "treatment."
Illicit online pharmacies	"HIV," "drug," "prevention," "pill," "online," "buy," "order," "Internet," "get," "pharmacy," "no" "prescription" "without" "free" "fast" "shipping" "delivery" "Saturday" "purchase" "Fedex" "cheap" "price" "shop" "brand" "overnight" "paypal" and "cost."

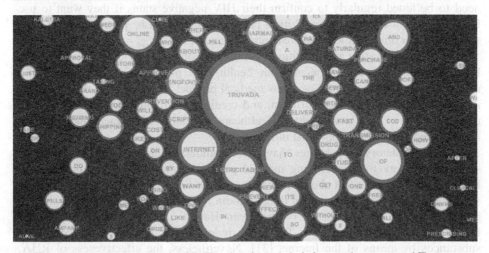

Fig. 1. The semantic network of PrEP-related words in infrequently propagated Tweets

4   Discussion

The purpose of this study is to examine how PrEP-related issues are represented and disseminated on one of the most popular social networking sites – Twitter. The results reveal two major themes. Twitter has been used as a platform to (1) generate public discussions about PrEP, and (2) market and sell prescription drugs without the need of a prescription by illicit online pharmacies. First, frequently propagated Tweets and Tweets posted by users with more followers centered on discussions about various aspects of PrEP, such as side effects and targeted recipients. The results also show consistency with previous literature that news and updates about health information are more likely to be retweeted [32].

Second, online marketing and selling of prescription drugs from illicit online pharmacies are prevalent. Our results show recurrence of issues surrounding online pharmacies, including the dispensing of drugs without prescriptions, the importation of prescription drugs from overseas, and the endorsement of such practices by health professionals without proper credentials. Although this theme appeared more often in infrequently propagated Tweets and in those posted by users with fewer followers, the overall proportion of Tweets with this theme was high. This trend is in line with other studies that show similar concerns about illicit online pharmacies posing a public health threat [12,16,18]. Purchasing PrEP from illicit online pharmacies without a doctor's prescription may lead to detrimental health consequences. Without appropriate screening and monitoring from healthcare providers, efforts to prevent HIV infection may be failing and posing health threats to both uninfected and infected individuals. Advertisements of PrEP from illicit online pharmacies may attract individuals who are HIV infected. PrEP alone is not a complete treatment for HIV infection. Developing resistance will make the infection harder to treat [28]. Uninfected individuals should adhere to PrEP daily dosing schedule. Adherence failure may increase the possibility of HIV infection. Uninfected individuals also need to be tested regularly to confirm their HIV negative status if they want to use PrEP to prevent HIV infection. Critical health problems can be posed to individuals where PrEP or other medications are contraindicated [33].

Healthcare educators and practitioners should encourage individuals at high risk of HIV infection to seek treatment from health care providers. It is possible that uncertainty is high at the start of a new medical product (e.g. PrEP). In this situation, individuals at high risk need sufficient and credible information to develop a better understanding of the new product. Healthcare educators and practitioners should make a greater effort to supply that information.

Several regulatory approaches have been underway to address legal issues surrounding marketing and selling medical products from illicit online pharmacies. For instance, a tragic event about the overdose death of an 18-year-old honors student who purchased opioid prescription drug Vicodin from an online pharmacy without a prescription led to the passage of the Ryan Haight Online Pharmacy Consumer Protection Act (RHA) in 2008. The RHA regulates the dispensing of controlled substances by means of the Internet [31]. Nevertheless, the effectiveness of RHA, especially for regulating nonmedical use of prescription medicines, has not been established [9]. Our results and several other studies [9,16,18,19,] have provided further evidence to show the ineffectiveness of enforcement and coverage of existing regulations. Therefore, there is an urgent need for better regulations and enforcement to protect online consumers.

This study has several limitations. We only analyzed English Tweets, which may limit our understanding of the social media representation of PrEP within English-speaking users. In our non-English sample, we identified 19.5% Spanish Tweets. Future studies should expand the scope to non-English Tweets. Furthermore, our study is descriptive. We showed the prevalence of illicit online pharmacies that marketed and sold prescription drugs through social media. Future studies could monitor the traffic and estimate people's exposure to illicit online pharmacies. Finally, we found quite a few Tweets emphasizing the gay and the Black communities. Future studies could investigate HIV-related stigma and cultural identities on social media.

5   Conclusion

Dissemination of health information and distribution of health care products are changing rapidly. For decades, patients consult health professionals to obtain information about the newest medicine. Patients are subsequently prescribed that medicine after a differential diagnosis. Newly approved prescription-only medicines are closely monitored and carefully regulated by authorities for specified prescribing indications and for its cost-effectiveness. Social networking sites such as Twitter have empowered disenfranchised patients and lowered the barriers of exchanging health information and accessing the medicine. However, emergence of marketing and selling prescription drugs without a prescription has led to serious bypass of government rules and regulations. Our semantic network analysis of PrEP-related tweets shows the presence of illicit online pharmacies. High-risk prescription medicines such as PrEP are aggressively marketed and sold without requiring a prescription and without requiring a visit to a doctor. This may pose a public health threat. We make urgent call for better regulation of online pharmacies.

References

1. Chou, W.Y.S., Hunt, Y.M., Beckjord, E.B., Moser, R.P., Hesse, B.W.: Social media use in the United States: implications for health communication. Journal of Medical Internet Research 11(4) (2009) Clarke, J. N. (1992)
2. Fox, S., Duggan, M.: Health online 2013. Pew Internet Project (2013), http://pewinternet.org/Reports/2013/Health-online.aspx (retrieved)
3. Vance, K., Howe, W., Dellavalle, R.P.: Social Internet sites as a source of public health information. Dermatologic Clinics 27(2), 133–136 (2009)
4. CNN. Patients use Facebook, Twitter, to get health information (2011), http://thechart.blogs.cnn.com/2011/03/04/patients-use-facebook-twitter-to-get-health-information/ (retrieved)

5. Love, B., Himelboim, I., Holton, A., Stewart, K.: Twitter as a source of vaccination information: Content drivers and what they are saying. American Journal of Infection Control 41(6), 568–570 (2013)
6. Robillard, J.M., Johnson, T.W., Hennessey, C., Beattie, B.L., Illes, J.: Aging 2.0: Health Information about Dementia on Twitter. PloS One 8(7), e69861 (2013)
7. Scanfeld, D., Scanfeld, V., Larson, E.: Dissemination of health information through social networks: Twitter and antibiotics. American Journal of Infection Control 38(3), 182–188 (2010)
8. McLaughlin, M.L., Hou, J., Park, M., Hu, C., Meng, J.: Dissemination of Truvada-related health information through Twitter. In: American Public Health Association, 141st Annual Meeting (2013)
9. Mackey, T.K., Liang, B.A.: Global Reach of Direct-to-Consumer Advertising Using Social Media for Illicit Online Drug Sales. Journal of Medical Internet Research 15(5) (2013)
10. Hanson, C.L., Burton, S.H., Giraud-Carrier, C., West, J.H., Barnes, M.D., Hansen, B.: Tweaking and tweeting: exploring Twitter for nonmedical use of a psychostimulant drug (Adderall) among college students. Journal of Medical Internet Research 15(4), e62 (2013)
11. Kemp, C.: Mid-term Prescription Drug Abuse: Does Social Media Play a Role? (2012), http://cathykemp.blogspot.com/2012/03/mid-term-prescription-drug-abuse-does.html (retrieved)
12. Liang, B.A., Mackey, T.K.: Prevalence and global health implications of social media in direct-to-consumer drug advertising. Journal of Medical Internet Research 13(3) (2011)
13. National Center on Addiction and Substance Abuse. "You've got drugs!" V: Prescritipon drug pushers on the Internet (2008), http://www.casacolumbia.org/addiction-research/reports/youve-got-drugs-perscription-drug-pushers-internet-2008 (retrieved)
14. FDA. FDA takes action to protect consumers from dangerous medicines sold by illegal online pharmacies (2013a), http://www.fda.gov/NewsEvents/Newsroom/PressAnnouncements/ucm358794.htm (retrieved)
15. FDA. Survey highlights (2013b), http://www.fda.gov/Drugs/ResourcesForYou/Consumers/BuyingUsingMedicineSafely/BuyingMedicinesOvertheInt ernet/BeSafeRxKnowYourOnlinePharmacy/ucm318497.htm (retrieved)
16. DuPont, R.: Prescription Drug Abuse: An Epidemic Dilemma. Journal of Psychoactive Drugs, 127–132 (June 2010)
17. CDC. Vital signs: Overdoses of prescription opioid pain relievers and other drugs among women – United States, 1999-2010 (2013), http://www.cdc.gov/mmwr/preview/mmwrhtml/mm6226a3.htm (retrieved)
18. Mackey, T.K., Liang, B.A., Strathdee, S.A.: Digital social media, youth, and nonmedical use of prescription drugs: the need for reform. Journal of Medical Internet Research 15(7), e143 (2013)
19. Jena, A.A.: Growing Internet Use May Help Explain the Rise in Prescription Drug Abuse in the United States. Health Affairs, 1192–1199 (June 2011)
20. Guo, L.: The Application of Social Network Analysis in Agenda Setting Research: A Methodological Exploration. Journal of Broadcasting & Electronic Media 56(4), 616–631 (2012)
21. Ognyanova, K., Monge, P.: A Multitheoretical, Multilevel, Multidimensional Network Model of the Media System. Communication Yearbook 37, 67 (2013)
22. Schultz, F., Kleinnijenhuis, J., Oegema, D., Utz, S., van Atteveldt, W.: Strategic framing in the BP crisis: A semantic network analysis of associative frames. Public Relations Review 38, 97–107 (2012)

23. Kitchin, R.M.: Cognitive maps: What are they and they study them? Journal of Environemntal Psychology 14(1), 1–19 (1994); McCombs, M.E., Shaw, D.L.: The agenda-setting function of the mass media. Public Opinion Quarterly 36, 176–187 (1972)
24. Clarke, J.N.: Cancer, heart disease, and AIDS: What do the media tell us about these diseases? Health Communication 4, 105–120 (1992)
25. Tian, Y., Stewart, C.: Framing the SARS crisis: A computer-assisted text analysis of CNN and BBC online news reports of SARS. Asian Journal of Communication 15(3), 289–301 (2005)
26. Murphy, P.: Framing the nicotine debate: A cultural approach to risk. Health Communication 13(2), 119–140 (2001)
27. Katz, M.H.: Pre-exposure prophylaxis for HIV: Can it be implemented in the real world? American Journal of Preventive Medicine 44(1), S161–S162 (2013)
28. Gilead Sciences Inc. Medication guide Truvada (2013), http://www.gilead.com/~/media/Files/pdfs/medicines/hiv/truvada/truvada_medication_guide.pdf (retrieved)
29. Cha, M., Haddadi, H., Benevenuto, F., Gummadi, P.K.: Measuring User Influence in Twitter: The Million Follower Fallacy. In: ICWSM, vol. 10, pp. 10–17 (2010)
30. Westerman, D., Spence, P.R., Van Der Heide, B.: A social network as information: The effect of system generated reports of connectedness on credibility on Twitter. Computers in Human Behavior 28(1), 199–206 (2012)
31. Ryan Haight Online Pharmacy Consumer Protection Act of 2008 (2008), https://www.govtrack.us/congress/bills/110/hr6353/text (retrieved)
32. Suh, B., Hong, L., Pirolli, P., Chi, E.H.: Want to be retweeted? Large scale analytics on factors impacting retweet in twitter network. In: 2010 IEEE Second International Conference on Social Computing (SocialCom), pp. 177–184. IEEE (August 2010)
33. Eysenbach, G.: Online Prescribing of Sildanefil (Viagra [R]) on the World Wide Web. Journal of Medical Internet Research 1(2), e10 (1999)

Identifying Locations of Social Significance: Aggregating Social Media Content to Create a New Trust Model for Exploring Crowd Sourced Data and Information

Al Di Leonardo, Scott Fairgrieve Adam Gribble, Frank Prats, Wyatt Smith, Tracy Sweat, Abe Usher, Derek Woodley, and Jeffrey B. Cozzens

The HumanGeo Group, LLC
Arlington, Virginia, United States
{al,scott,adam,frank,wyatt,tracy,abe,derek}@thehumangeo.com

Abstract. Most Internet content is no longer produced directly by corporate organizations or governments. Instead, individuals produce voluminous amounts of informal content in the form of social media updates (micro blogs, Facebook, Twitter, etc.) and other artifacts of community communication on the Web. This grassroots production of information has led to an environment where the quantity of low-quality, non-vetted information dwarfs the amount of professionally produced content. This is especially true in the geospatial domain, where this information onslaught challenges Local and National Governments and Non-Governmental Organizations seeking to make sense of what is happening on the ground.

This paper proposes a new model of trust for interpreting locational data without a clear pedigree or lineage. By applying principles of aggregation and inference, it is possible to identify locations of social significance and discover "facts" that are being asserted by crowd sourced information.

Keywords: geospatial, social media, aggregation, trust, location.

1 Introduction

Gathering geographical data on populations has always constituted an essential element of census taking, political campaigning, assisting in humanitarian disasters/relief, law enforcement, and even in post-conflict areas where grand strategy looks beyond the combat to managing future peace. Warrior philosophers have over the millennia praised indirect approaches to warfare as the most effective means of combat—where influence and information about enemies and their supporters trumps reliance on kinetic operations to achieve military objectives. This approach can assist in the perpetuation and management of peace easier. However, successful indirect means are only as good as the human geographical data assembled.

Aggregating, categorizing, and interpreting geo-referenced or geo-located data on a specific population lies at the heart of contemporary counter-insurgency, counter terrorism, and nation-building and good governance. Western military campaigns in Afghanistan and Iraq are obvious examples as well as intensifying conflict scenarios

G. Meiselwitz (Ed.): SCSM 2014, LNCS 8531, pp. 170–177, 2014.

throughout Africa pose looming future challenges. Isolating insurgents and terrorists from populations and potential recruits is essential to winning at war's 'moral' level—inextricably linked to a grand strategy—but this cannot be accomplished using biased, insufficient, or conversely, unwieldy amounts of socio-cultural data. Unfortunately for military planners, this is often the nature of information found in the open source domain.

This paper discusses how simplified and trustworthy human geography data sources and fusion methodologies can empower U.S. military planning by analyzing Open Source Information/Intelligence (OSINT) from social media to generate significant human geography data on populations amidst a dense stream of Web-based community communication. In so doing, it proposes a new model of trust for interpreting locational data—one that involves applying principles of aggregation and inference to identify locations of social significance and discover 'facts' asserted by a collective of independent data producers. This approach is critical to winning indirect battles and 'doing no harm' in non-Western human terrains vulnerable to exploitation by terrorists and insurgents. This model has other applications such as assisting people and property before, during and after disasters or helping law enforcement agencies mitigate criminal activities by analyzing gang online and offline presence.

2   Value of Crowd-sourced Data

Data sources continually evolve and change. Social movements are rarely characterized by known 'knowns'; shifting online commentaries, or the capture and upload of a singular event, can precipitate sudden and massive human change (the Arab Spring is perhaps the most prominent recent example). By the time data has been validated, verified, synthesized with other government sourced information, it may no longer be relevant to analysts, planners or decision-makers because the event might have al-ready occurred, names have changed, or the meaning of an observation has been completely altered. The shifting social and geopolitical environment is, in sum, constantly redefining and challenging analysts' observational capabilities.

However, crowd-sourced information—that is, social media data used for analysis—is of great analytical value because it presents data snapshots of specific spaces, places and times. Harnessed efficiently and effectively, it allows analysts to identify important socio-cultural landmarks (observations) at any given moment. This analyzed crowd-sourced information can help make sense of a wide variety of human events of interest (such as disaster response) for governments, first responders, politicians, international organizations, and many others.

Present in social media data is the latent capability to update changes to previously defined socio-cultural landmarks, including highly relevant places that may not have been recognized by decision makers, military personnel or diplomats. For instance, captured near real-time crowd source updates can lead to a better understanding of culturally significant artifacts, institutions and landmarks that might help facilitate or strengthen partnerships with regional actors.

3   Military Planning Using Social Media: A Matter of Trust

Western militaries' planning lifecycles revolve around geospatial intelligence systems designed to interpret socio-cultural data. However, these systems often demand too much from analysts in order to reach their potential. Many expert analysts do not have the fundamental Geographic Information Systems (GIS) skills (or resource-intensive training) required to ask informed questions and properly interpret GIS system responses. Further, it is much easier for analysts to 'connect the dots' and understand the associations and relationships between various data when using highly structured, well-formatted information. Disparate human geography data derived from social media is a different story. Analysts experience a fundamental trust challenge with social media data at a time when the volume, dispersion, and discrepancies of grassroots information increase by the second.

What is required of the human geography community to effectively support the US military's indirect planning approaches and the 'do no harm' principal when dealing with non-Western foes in their own at-risk communities? HumanGeo has developed a simple, non-parametric approach to socio-cultural data mining built around the National Geospatial-Intelligence Agency's (NGA) "Thirteen Themes of Human Geography" to provide precisely this type of support.[1] HumanGeo's quantitative and predictive solution, is based on a simplified fusion of geography feature data using variable precision data encoding known as "geohash" that allows social patterns to more easily emerge from voluminous data sets [2]. Consequently, this provides immediate answers from crowd-sourced data for planners concerned with generating socio-cultural queries along the lines of "where, when, who, what, why?"

Invented in 2008 by Gustavo Niemeyer, the geohash is a latitude/longitude geocode system that combines decimal degrees latitude and longitude annotations into a single string-variable that defines a certain size box. These synthetic boxes are described as a centroid point and a value range of latitude, with a value range of longitude. By looking at the world as a series of boxes (geohashes) and the attributes that pertain to these boxes (e.g. places of interest (transportation, religious, political, economic, etc), events [sporting, political, violent, economic, etc.], the presence of national interests and/or those of allies, etc.), various types of planners are able to more efficiently fuse disparate data sources into a single, unified view. This approach empowers analysts by providing them with simplified tools that allow them to explore data based on their own expert hypotheses.

---

[1] NGA's thirteen Themes of Human Geography include the following: Transportation, Significant Events, Religion, Medical/Health, Language, Land-Use, Groups, Ethnicity, Education, Economy, Demographics, Communications, and Climate (water).

[2] The best summary description of geohash is found on Wikipedia:
http://en.wikipedia.org/wiki/Geohash (accessed 13 October 2013).

4   Aggregation Models

HumanGeo has developed a four-step methodology for applying this variable encoding scheme to human geography data. The process is detailed below:

- Aggregate
- Annotate
- Automate
- Analyze

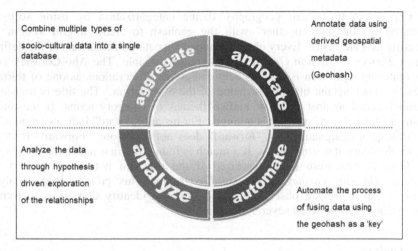

Fig. 1. HumanGeo's Four-Step Process for Social Media Data Retrieval and Enrichment

This four-step process (Figure 1 above) describes how the data was retrieved and enriched in a recent three-country study examining social media in Mexico, Syria, and Nigeria:

4.1   Aggregate

HumanGeo's data aggregation process is unique due to its ability to identify and aggregate disparate geo-located/geo-referenced human geography data from multiple crowd sourcing mediums using algorithms to identify those observations in numerous languages. The aggregation process combines multiple types of data into a single database. Social media data, in its typical state, is otherwise too disparate and cumbersome to be analyzed in aggregation without tools to organize and categorize it—precisely what HumanGeo does. In other words, one cannot simply download Wikimapia, Google Places, or Panoramio to create visualizations or databases for easy assessment.

4.2   Annotate

Annotation involves synthesizing metadata with each dataset using the geohash to encode location data, and adding additional geospatial metadata to each point (i.e. observation or raw data). This is where HumanGeo adds the *Thirteen Themes of Human Geography* to the individual observations (e.g. an identified geo-located or geo-referenced social cultural landmark).

4.3   Automate

This step refers to human geography theme categorization by using software automation to "tie data together" with the geohash to create a grid system for connecting data elements. Every observation is then categorized as one of the defined *Thirteen Themes of Human Geography* whenever possible. The Aho-Corasick sub-string matching algorithm is used to help categorize observations as one of thirteen themes by matching the title and/or name of the observation.[3] The title is translated and transliterated against a list of known themes or category terms. If the match contains a known "stop" word, it is ignored. For instance, "ward" indicates a possible medical/hospital designation, but "forward" does not; therefore, "Forward" is in the set of medical/hospital stop words. If a match is found, the first matching category is used. Observations were not categorized if the title did not match one of the designated *Thirteen Themes of Human Geography*. This process helps analysts because it can aggregate observations and possibly identify clusters of activities and/or relationships between several observations.

4.4   Analyze

This step allows for the analysis of data through hypothesis-driven exploration of the data relationships, enabled by Google Earth Keyhole Markup Language (KML) exports of the fused/combined data layers. As in step three (automate), each dataset is simplified into a "data layer" that is represented as a series of geohash boxes. These data layers are then combined into a "context lens"—user-specific data layers related to a particular analytic hypothesis.

This process, in summary, provides a mechanism for annotating disparate human geography datasets with a geohash format, fusing the data together (at different levels of precision) using the geohash as a connecting key, and projecting patterns and relationships of the data into Open Geospatial Consortium (OGC) formats for visual analytics. For example, one could portray macro-level indicators of violent events by breaking the world up into squares of approximately 150 km each (geohash 3), affording analysts a view of the attributes of each square to enable inference-making. Used differently, one could examine criminality in subdivisions of major cities by encoding crime locations into a geohash string of length six or seven, thereby breaking up the city up into squares of approximately 610 meters or 118 meters,

---

[3] See Aho, Alfred V.; Margaret J. Corasick (June 1975). "Efficient string matching: An aid to bibliographic search". *Communications of the Association for Computing Machinery* 18 (6): 333–340. More details at: http://xlinux.nist.gov/dads/HTML/ahoCorasick.html Accessed on 18 September 2013.

respectively, then analyzing the event characteristics of each square. Further, the application can draw out (and visualize) critical socio-cultural anomalies in specific regions in a scalable manner using crowd-source data, as the Syria case demonstrates.

Case Study: Syria. HumanGeo applied its crowd source data analysis methodology to Syria in September 2013. The scalable test assessment generated and visualized critical socio-cultural observations on 92,012 resolved entities (combinations of similar observations) at the national, regional and local levels using data from Wikimapia, Google Places and Panaramio.

The national level assessment visualized social media activity throughout Syria, noting spikes in usage along the Mediterranean coast (as anticipated), as well as in historic tourist destinations like Palmyra—essentially an oasis of social media in an otherwise barren area. This highlights the methodology's ability to identify socio-cultural anomalies in a region or country.

Regionally, the data used highlighted a cluster of social media activity along the Euphrates river in the Dayr az Zawr region—another seemingly desolate locale. However, visualization of social media in the form of bar graphs created a pictorial narrative highlighting the importance of the Euphrates as a metric for mapping social development over time. Such data can also lead to making inferences about why social media growth is occurring in the absence of additional infrastructure development.

Data sources used were from the town of Palmyra. The visualizations demonstrated their utility in identifying landmarks of socio-cultural significance that may have been previously unknown. Such discoveries could enhance previously weak knowledge of important local artifacts, institutions or traditions, thereby facilitating or strengthening relationships with local actors.

Fig. 2. HumanGeo's National level assessment of crowd source data in Syria (Google Earth view). Palmyra is highlighted in the circle.

5   Geospatial Entity Resolution

Lise Getoor and Ashwin Machanavajjhala note that entity resolution is essentially a method of entity disambiguation.[4] Entity resolution, for the purposes of HumanGeo's social media data sets and enrichment process, also means identifying similar entities—an entity being a set of one or more geo-located observations—and combining and categorizing them with confidence for purposes of inference-making. HumanGeo's geospatial entity resolution algorithm and resulting confidence score methodology—developed from a number of academic resources, especially the Stanford Entity Resolution Framework[5]—is unique in this respect.

When applying HumanGeo's methodology for entity resolution, observations from multiple sources undergo an entity resolution process using the following algorithm: every defined observation is allocated a Geohash bounding box and is at the center of nine Geohash bounding boxes. The surrounding Geohash bounding boxes are called 'neighbors'.

Step one involves finding all observations within a 3x3 Geohash box. Once all obser-vations have been defined within the box, the jaro-winkler string-matching algorithm is used to compute the similarity of titles (names) between the observations. Any observation with a similarity equal to or greater than 0.9 is resolved by combining similar observations as one.

Spatial data can be analyzed to verify and validate geospatial coordinates, and conversion occurs to make spatial coordinates available in latitude/longitude, Military Grid Reference System (MGRS), and geohash formats. Data that is inherently non-spatial in nature is aggregated and fused, but no spatial attributes are assigned to the records. However, for non-spatial full-text data sources, HumanGeo applies place-name extraction software to isolate place-names when referenced within the text. For example, if a full-text field of a data source references "Washington, DC," or "White House," that place-name will be added as a geospatial attribute of the data and will include latitude/longitude, MGRS and geohash coordinates associated with it.

Measuring confidence in entity resolution

HumanGeo measures confidence in the entity resolution process by multiplying three factors: the number of sources, the average jaro-winkler[6] score, and the dispersion—the maximum distance between two observations within an entity. A weighted value system has been applied to account for the number of sources used: one source identifying an entity has a confidence interval rating of 0.6; two sources identifying an entity has a confidence interval rating of 0.8; three sources identifying an entity has the highest confidence interval rating of 1.0.

---

[4] See Lise Getoor and Ashwin Machanavajjhala, "Entity Resolution: Tutorial" (2012), at:
http://www.umiacs.umd.edu/~getoor/Tutorials/ER_VLDB2012.pdf
[5] See Stanford Entity Resolution Framework (Stanford University), at:
http://infolab.stanford.edu/serf/#motivation. Accessed 18 September 2013.
[6] See http://xlinux.nist.gov/dads/HTML/jaroWinkler.html
(accessed 18 September 2013).

6   Conclusion

A simplified and trustworthy human geography analysis methodology as employed by HumanGeo can empower end users (based on their legal authorities) in using OSINT from social media to generate significant human geography data on populations amidst a dense stream of Web-based community communication. This enables analysts to put rich socio-cultural data at their fingertips, highlighting significant social activity and previously unknown, but germane, socio-cultural nodes. This approach is strategically important to helping win indirect battles and 'doing no harm' in non-Western human terrains vulnerable to exploitation by terrorists and insurgents.

Beyond the social media retrieval, enrichment, and visualization capabilities discussed here, companies such as HumanGeo are developing other systems to capture enriched (i.e. with administrative boundaries, language identification, sentiment, etc.) social media data in near-real-time. HumanGeo's system also tags data with one or more event topics from a set of event categories tailored to client analysts using simple keyword matching. This event detection capability is pushing back boundaries using unstructured topic learning as a means of developing even greater insights. This system makes it easier and faster for analysts to find and assess data, since data are pre-categorized in a variety of ways optimized for searching by end-users. Cascading political and security-related events in the Middle East and Africa demonstrate the requirement for such a capability and furthering this line of research.

Living in the Era of Social Media: How the Different Types of Social Media May Affect Information Acquisition Process

Katerina Fraidaki, Katerina Pramatari, and George Doukidis

Athens University of Economics and Business, Greece
{fraidaki,k.pramatari,gjd}@aueb.gr

Abstract. The main objective of this research is to study the role of social media in the information acquisition process. We study social media as "information sources" and we give answer to the question: Do consumers use different types of social media when they seek for pre-purchase information? In order to address this question, firstly we investigate the existence of a typology of social media based on their characteristics as information sources; and we study the factors that affect consumers to use different types of social media during their pre-purchase information acquisition process.

Keywords: social media, typology, factors.

1   Introduction

Social media have attracted a lot of research attention over the last years as sources of information. For Mangold & Faulds, (2009)"... social media have become Internet users' number one choice of gathering information". The results of a recent study (Brenner, 2013) have shown that 89% of Internet users spend at least 3 hours per day in order to communicate with friends via facebook; in the same research, 76% of the respondents mention that they spend at least four hours per day in order to search information about products in social media. Academics from the areas of Marketing ((Jepsen, 2007); (Grant, Clarke, & Kyriazis, 2007); (Putrevu & Ratchford, 1997)), Sociology ((Sciglimpaglia, 2013); (Cole, 2011)), Psychology ((Peterson & Merino, n.d.); (Kim & Eastin, 2011).) and Information Systems ((Lee, Kim, & Chan-Olmsted, 2011); (Niu & Hemminger, 2012)) study their effect on consumer behavior and make comparisons with the offline environment.

The main objective of this research is to study the role of social media in the information acquisition process. In this context, we study social media as "information sources" and we try to give answers to two questions: (1) Do different types of social media exist, based on their characteristics as sources of information, and (2) which are the factors that affect the use of different types of social media?

G. Meiselwitz (Ed.): SCSM 2014, LNCS 8531, pp. 178–185, 2014.

2   Background and Hypotheses

2.1   The Role of "Sources" in the Information Acquisition Process

The information acquisition process has been studied by numerous academics during the last decades (e.g.(Klein & Ford, 2003), (Jacoby & Szybillo, 2013), (Tidwell, 2005)). In this paper the following definition is adopted, which is most commonly used in the pertinent literature:

"Information acquisition is the stage of the decision making process wherein consumers actively collect and integrate information from numerous sources, both internal and external, prior to making a choice" (Klein & Ford, 2003).

The information acquisition process consists of three parts (Dickson & Wilkie, 2013): the source, the message and the receiver. The majority of literature is focused "on the exploration of (1) the needs that make a consumer search for information, (2) the sources that have been visited in order for the consumer to collect the information, and (3) the factors that influence seeking information in different sources" (Vogt & Fesenmaier, 1998).

The following research is focused on the *sources* that have been used by the receivers of the message. Since 1996, the pertinent literature has studied the electronic sources. In the beginning, academics considered as electronic sources the websites of the firms, the newsletters and the emails ((Van Rijnsoever, Castaldi, & Dijst, 2012); (Mourali, Laroche, & Pons, 2005)). Since 2002, academics have focused on electronic word of mouth (e-wom); they study the role of e-wom in consumer behavior ((J. Brown, Broderick, & Lee, 2007); (J. J. Brown & Reingen, 2013)). *Social Media* consist the mean of transferring e-wom; their official definition mentions that they are *sources with user-generated content.*

The basic areas of study in the literature of social media are: the factors that influence consumers in order to participate in social media (Tidwell, 2005), the factors that influence consumers to express themselves positively or negatively(Bagozzi & Dholakia, 2002), the way that consumers choose their "electronic friends" (Niu & Hemminger, 2012).

The main gap in the literature exists in the study of social media as sources of gathering pre purchase information. Which are the factors that affect consumers to visit social media during the pre-purchase phase of their decision process? The basic objective of our research is to investigate this gap.

Our research is divided into two parts: in the former we analyze the term social media and we discover the possibility of existence of different types of social media, based on their characteristics as sources of information. Based on "uses and gratification theory", *purpose of use* consists the most important characteristic of a source. The question that arises in this part of the study is:

Question 1: Can we develop a typology of social media based on their purpose of use?

In the latter, we study the factors that affect the use of every type of social media, by consumers who seek pre purchase information. Based on the literature the factors that influence the use of a source are separated into three groups: individual characteristics, situational characteristics and product characteristics (Morrison, 2000). Thus, the research questions that arise are:

Question 2: How consumers' individual characteristics may affect the use of different types of social media, when they seek for pre-purchase information?.

Question 3: How the product characteristics may affect the use of different types of social media, when consumers seek for pre-purchase information?.

Question 4: How the situational characteristics may affect the use of different types of social media, when consumers seek for pre-purchase information?.

3   Methodology

3.1   Developmentnof the Typology

In order to develop the social media typology, we use Hunt's theory (1991). In the first step we study the literature and understand the axes on which the typology may be based on. Studying the pertinent literature, we identify the existence of different definitions about the phenomenon. Their difference is based on the different functionalities of the "brands" (e.g. facebook, twitter, flickr, etc) which are described by the authors. Collecting the basic characteristics of the definitions, we identify the existence of three types of social media (based on their functionalities): social networking sites, blogs and review pages. Our goal is to study, if the different functionalities make consumers use the different types of social media for different purposes . "Uses and Gratification" theory (Quan-Haase & Young, 2010) help us to define the *purpose of use* of information sources. In the second step we visit the 44 most popular brands of social media, and we try to recognize their functionalities; the objective of this step is the recognition of the three types of social media, based on actual data. In the third step, we conduct a survey in order to investigate the purpose of use of each type of social media. We use "Uses and Gratification theory" items in order to develop our questionnaire; we collect 1096 answers by internet users. The results of the survey show that consumers use the different types of social media for different purposes. More specific, they use social networking sites for entertainment and communication; they use blogs in order to collect information about specific general topics (e.g. health); and review pages in order to collect information about transactions. This step proves the existence of the typology of social media, based on perceived data. In order to complete all the steps of Hunt's methodology we evaluate the typology based also on actual data. In the final step, we visit the most popular "brand" of each type of social media and we analyze 1000 movements (e.g posts, comments, uploads etc) by each one. The analysis is also based on the items of "Uses and Gratification Theory". The results of the procedure evoke the existence of three types of social media: social networking sites, blogs/ forums and review pages, based on their purpose of use.

3.2   Factors that Affect the Use of Different Types of Social Media

In the second part of our research, we study the factors that affect the use of different types of social media, when consumers search for pre-purchase information. In this part of the study we want to answer the questions 2, 3 and 4. For this reason, we conduct a quasi experiment, in which we use two different services: gathering health information vs gathering travel information

Definition of the Situation. Wilson (1994) declares that in order to study information acquisition process, it is important to define the "the situation within a need arises". Moreover, he mentions that in every situation "the person who searches for information performs a role in an environment". Based on Wilson, in order to design our research, we should define the following variables:

- The Environment (= context) in which the research will take place
- What kind of information do the person need
- What is the role of the person

The Environment/ Context. Morisson (2000) mentions that information acquisition process may differ between the commerce and the non-commerce environment. For this reason, in order to study the role of social media as sources of information, we will conduct two different studies: in the first one the participants should search information about products/ services that they intend to buy (Chapter 6.1). In the second one the participants should find information about a non-commercial topic. Regarding the second study of the non-commerce environment, many academics have focused their research on the search of information of health issues (Cotten, 1998; Morisson 2008). ELTRUN research (2012) shows that the 84% of internet users use Internet in order to find health information. For this reason, the second part of our research will be focused on the healthcare environment (Chapter 6.2). In order to be able to manipulate the variables, in two studies we will conduct quasi experiments.

Type of Information need. In order to develop the scenarios of each quasi experiment, we should define the type of information that the person will look for. Weights (1993) proves that three types of information need exist:

- Need for new information
- Need to elucidate the information held
- Need to confirm information held

In parallel, Peterson and Merino (2003) two types of information search exist:

- Specific Information search: In this type of search, the information characteristics are: extremely motivated, having instrumental orientation, situational involvement, seeking utilitarian benefits, focusing on goal oriented choices

- General Information search: In the second type of search the information characteristics are: intrinsically motivated, having ritualized orientation, enduring involvement, hedonic benefits, non-directed search.

The previous types of search would involved in the description of the scenarios. The role of the perceived benefits received by the use of the product/ service has been studied as a factor that affect the use of a source (Sojung et al, 2011). In our study, we will investigate the role of hedonic/ utilitarian benefits as a factor which affect the use of different types of social media.

Research Model. In order to study the research questions, we develop the following research model.

Individual Characteristics. Beatty and Smith (1987) mention that the term ""individual characteristics" consists of three basic sub-categories of factors: demographic characteristics (gender, age, etc), socio-economic characteristics, and cognitive traits (ability, experience, expertise). In this research we focus our study in the third sub-category (cognitive characteristics). More specific we study the factor "user's experience"; how familiar is the consumer with the product.

Product Characteristics. Peterson and Merino (2013) mention that the type of information that consumers search for, is based on the type of the product. They assume that two types of information search exist: specific information search which is characterized as extremely motivated, with utilitarian benefits, being focused on goal directed choices; general information search, which is characterized as intrinsically motivated, with hedonic benefits. For this reason in our study we focus our research in the perceived benefits of the product (hedonic/ utilitarian)

Situational Characteristics. Ashfor et al (1983) develop Feedback Seeking Behavior Model. "This model conceptualizes information seeking as a process of uncertainty reduction in the specific situation" (Ashfor et al, 1983). In their model, the most important characteristic is perceived value of the feedback that the consumer gets from the source. Fedor (1992), studies the importance of source credibility. In our research we study the role of source credibility in our model.

Based on the previous analysis the hypotheses of the research are formed as follow:

H1: Users' experience affect the use of different types of social media

H2: Hedonic/ Utilitarian benefits of the product affect the use of different types of social media

H3: The credibility of the source affect the use of different types of social media

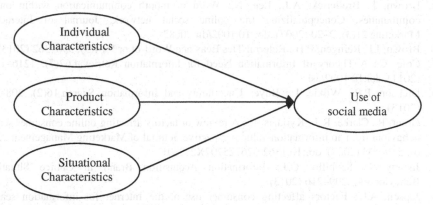

Fig. 1. Factors that affect the use of different types of social media- General model

4   Results and Discussion

The results of the quasi experiment are based on 1.105 answers and show that:

- When the consumer is familiar with the service/product, (s)he uses blogs and review pages (sig. 0.001)
- When a consumer searches information about services/ products with hedonic perceived benefits, (s)he uses review pages and social networking sites. On the other hand, when the consumer searches information for services/ products with utilitarian benefits, (s)he uses review pages and blogs. (sig. 0.000)
- Finally, the source credibility influences the use of all types of social media. (sig. 0.000)

The implications of our study in the academic sector is the existence of a social media typology, which is based on the variable "purpose of use". We study social media as sources of information and we recognize factors that affect the use of different types of social media. Academics have the opportunity to study more factors from the different groups and analyze their influence on the different types of social media. On the other hand, as for the business implications of our study, we may help marketers to develop a more specific and effective social media strategy for their products. Using the previous results marketers have the opportunity to design a social media strategy more focused to their needs and their products.

References

1. Bagozzi, R.P., Dholakia, U.M.: Intentional social action in virtual communities. Journal of Interactive Marketing 16(2), 2–21 (2002), doi:10.1002/dir.10006
2. Brenner, J.: The Demographics of Social Media Users — 2012 (2013)

3. Brown, J., Broderick, A.J., Lee, N.: Word of mouth communication within online communities: Conceptualizing the online social network. Journal of Interactive Marketing 21(3), 2–20 (2007), doi:10.1002/dir.20082
4. Brown, J.J., Reingen, P.H.: Referral Ties Beav and Word-of or * 14(3), 350–362 (2013)
5. Cole, C.: A Theory of Information Need for Information Retrieval 62(7), 1216–1231 (2011), doi:10.1002/asi
6. Dickson, P.R., Wilkie, L.: Buyer Uncertainty and Information Search 16(2), 208–215 (2013)
7. Grant, R., Clarke, R.J., Kyriazis, E.: A review of factors affecting online consumer search behaviour from an information value perspective. Journal of Marketing Management 23(5-6), 519–533 (2007), doi:10.1362/026725707X212801
8. Jacoby, J., Szybillo, G.J.: Information Acquisition Brand in Choice Situations Behavior 3(4), 209–216 (2013)
9. Jepsen, A.L.: Factors affecting consumer use of the Internet for information search. Journal of Interactive Marketing 21(3), 21–34 (2007), doi:10.1002/dir.20083
10. Kim, S., Eastin, M.S.: Hedonic Tendencies and the Online Consumer: An Investigation of the Online Shopping Process. Journal of Internet Commerce 10(1), 68–90 (2011), doi:10.1080/15332861.2011.558458
11. Klein, L.R., Ford, G.T.: Consumer search for information in the digital age: An empirical study of prepurchase search for automobiles. Journal of Interactive Marketing 17(3), 29–49 (2003), doi:10.1002/dir.10058
12. Lee, C., Kim, J., Chan-Olmsted, S.M.: Branded product information search on the Web: The role of brand trust and credibility of online information sources. Journal of Marketing Communications 17(5),   355–374   (2011),   http://www.tandfonline.com/doi/abs/10.1080/13527266.2010.484128
13. Mangold, W.G., Faulds, D.J.: Social media: The new hybrid element of the promotion mix. Business Horizons 52(4), 357–365 (2009), doi:10.1016/j.bushor.2009.03.002
14. Morrison, E.W.: Within-Person Analysis of Information Seeking. The Effects of Perceived Costs and Benefits 26(1), 119–137 (2000)
15. Mourali, M., Laroche, M., Pons, F.: Antecedents of consumer relative preference for interpersonal information sources in pre-purchase search. Journal of Consumer Behaviour 4(5), 307–318 (2005), doi:10.1002/cb.16
16. Niu, X., Hemminger, B.M.: A Study of Factors That Affect the Information-Seeking Behavior of Academic Scientists 21669(2), 336–353 (2012), doi:10.1002/asi
17. Peterson, R.A., Merino, M.C. (n.d.): Consumer Information Search Behavior and the Internet 20, 99–121 (February 2003), doi:10.1002/mar
18. Putrevu, S., Ratchford, B.T.: A Model of Search Behavior with an Application to Grocery Shopping 73(4) (1997)
19. Quan-Haase, A., Young, A.L.: Uses and Gratifications of Social Media: A Comparison of Facebook and Instant Messaging. Bulletin of Science, Technology & Society 30(5), 350–361 (2010), doi:10.1177/0270467610380009
20. Sciglimpaglia, D.: The Traits Influence and of Cognitive Personality Consumer on Demographics Information Acquisition 8(2), 208–216 (2013)
21. Tidwell, M.: Personality and Information Seeking: Understanding How Traits Influence Information-Seeking Behaviors. Journal of Business Communication 42(1), 51–77 (2005), doi:10.1177/0021943604272028

22. Van Rijnsoever, F.J., Castaldi, C., Dijst, M.J.: In what sequence are information sources consulted by involved consumers? The case of automobile pre-purchase search. Journal of Retailing and Consumer Services 19(3), 343–352 (2012), doi:10.1016/j.jretconser.2012.03.008
23. Vogt, C.A., Fesenmaier, D.R.: Expanding the Functional Information Search Model 25(3), 551–578 (1998)
24. Xiang, Z., Gretzel, U.: Role of social media in online travel information search. Tourism Management 31(2), 179–188 (2010), doi:10.1016/j.tourman.2009.02.016

SONETA: A Social Media Geo-Trends Analysis Tool

Ioannis Ioannidis[1], Eleftherios Papachristos[1], Christos Katsanos[1,2], Nikolaos Karousos[2], Christos Fidas[1], and Nikolaos Avouris[1]

[1] HCI Group, University of Patras, Patras, Greece
[2] Hellenic Open University, School of Science and Technology, Patras, Greece
{Ioannidg,avouris}@upatras.gr,
{epap,ckatsanos,fidas}@ece.upatras.gr, karousos@eap.gr

Abstract. Social media are used for expressing thoughts and opinions. Finding information hidden inside the vast amount of social media data is an overwhelming task especially for Small and Medium Enterprises (SMEs) that have limited resources. In this paper, we present an early prototype of SONETA, a social media geo-trend analysis tool that supports users, and specifically SMEs, by helping them detect social media trends in specific geographic areas. First, its architectural design and development process is delineated, followed by the presentation of a study that evaluated SONETA in terms of its usefulness and usability. Three SMEs participated in the SONETA evaluation study. Evaluation results showed that SONETA can be used in order to help SMEs in engaging social media more effectively.

Keywords: social media tools, geo-location analysis, visualization, Twitter.

1   Introduction

From the beginning of Web 2.0 and subsequently the rise of Social Networking Sites much has changed in the way that the Web works. Social media transformed users from passive consumers to active generators of information. People participating in social media comment about virtually any aspect of their lives, they share personal moments, they discuss breaking news, and they express their thoughts and feelings about products or people. The wealth of information that is created by the millions of users that participate on a daily basis in social media poses an immense research opportunity for a variety of disciplines.

Social media research has been used in a variety of contexts, for example it has been successfully used in journalism in order to discover breaking news faster than it was previously possible with traditional media [1]. A variety of tools have been created to aid journalists in their work as for example applications that can help them identify and highlight interesting and trustworthy sources in the Twitter stream [2]. Emergency situations and crisis management is another field in which social media have been used with great success. For example social media has been used in order to support emergency planning, risk and damage assessment as well as for enhancing awareness about emergency situations. Social media data have also been proven to be

G. Meiselwitz (Ed.): SCSM 2014, LNCS 8531, pp. 186–196, 2014.
© Springer International Publishing Switzerland 2014

valuable in helping emergency operators to navigate through areas with heavy traffic [3]. In Japan it has been demonstrated that earthquake alerts could be created faster by using data derived from social media than official announcements from government agencies [4].

Much attention has been recently devoted to examine whether the business sector can gain value from social media [5-8]. For many years corporations and institutions relied on traditional structures and were content with a model in which the image of a company was controlled by their marketing and public relation department. The companies have gradually lost some of this control since social media enables consumers to talk freely to each other about products or services and express their opinions or complains [9]. Although companies cannot control or intervene in conversations about their products or services that happen in various social media platforms they nevertheless can gain extremely valuable feedback by listening carefully to what their customers have to say about them [10].

Listening to customer conversations in order to gain feedback about their own or their competitors' products as well as monitoring the reputation of their brand is not an easy task for companies considering the large amount of data that is generated on social media daily. Twitter alone is being used by 190 million users many of which are posting multiple times per day [1]. Taking into account the multitude of social media platforms it becomes apparent that in order gain valuable information companies have to examine large amounts of unstructured data. However, many companies are reluctant or unable to develop strategies and allocate resources in order to engage effectively with social media [9]. Social media engagement requires time, as well as commitment in personnel and financial resources, which can be difficult even for large companies, but even more difficult for Small and Medium Enterprises (SMEs) [6]. Although, social media present SMEs with excellent opportunities to compete with larger companies, SMEs are severely limited by their inability to acquire the necessary skills, hire additional employees or external help in order to learn use them effectively.

The need for new methods and technologies that could help companies harness the power of social media has led to the profusion of social media tools. These tools can be used among others for event detection, crisis management as well as for trend and campaign monitoring. The majority of them perform some kind of filtering to a vast amount of social media data in order to present only relevant information to its user promising increased efficiency. According to [11], more than 200 social media tool are available in the market today that vary considerably in terms of general scope, functionality, application areas as well as on the matter of price; ranging from zero to several thousand Euros per month [12]. The main problem with the commercials tools is that although they typically provide a wide range of functionalities their price often exceeds the budgets of most SMEs. On the other hand low-budget or free tools usually provide only basic functionality, they focus on single Social Networking Sites and don't offer adequate support to their users [11]. Social media tools are also developed for academic research but these tools are usually created as a proof of concept and are not available to the general public to be used in an applied setting.

Considering the multitude of social media tools available today it is surprising that none has been created specifically to address the needs of SMEs, which represent a large percentage of the economic power of most countries [13]. The main barriers that hinder SMEs to adopt social media are scarcity in time, financial resources and technology skills [14] as well as negative views about their usefulness, or unfamiliarity with a particular technology. In this paper we present the development process of a social media tool called SONETA[1] (Social Networks Analysis Tool) that aims to help SME's lift such barriers. We describe the initial assumptions that have been made in order to create a first version of the tool as well as the results of a first evaluation iteration that was conducted involving three typical regional SMEs.

The rest of the paper is structured as follows. In section 2 of the paper we discuss how SONETA addresses the specific needs of SMEs and the conceptual design of the tool. In section 3 of the paper we discuss the main components of the system from an architectural point of view, and in section 4 we describe a typical usage scenario of the tool. Next, we describe a study in which usability experts and end-users (three SMEs) evaluated SONETA in terms of its usability and usefulness in actual practice. The paper concludes with a discussion on the implications of this research and directions for future work.

2   Conceptual Design

Time and money constraints as well as lack of IT expertise [14] are special characteristics of SMEs that could hinder them in adopting and using social media as effectively as large corporations. These characteristics have been taken into consideration during the creation process of SONETA.

Browsing social networking sites in order to monitor customer opinions and conversations relevant to a specific business domain can be a tedious and time-consuming task. Outsourcing the task, hiring new or training existing personnel to be responsible for social media management is typically not an option for SMEs. Thus, appropriate social media tools that can support the task of data filtering would be of great value for SMEs. For this reason, the highest priority in terms of functionality that has been given to SONETA was to enable users to navigate the unstructured stream of social media and to help them extract useful and relevant to their business information. Various data visualizations techniques have been considered that could help the user quickly recognize relevant information as well as to facilitate further exploration of the data. The lack of IT expertise, which is another characteristic of SMEs, has been addressed by giving special emphasis on creating a usable and intuitive user interface that would not require time consuming training sessions and lengthy instructional material.

Geographic location of customers is considered as an important factor for businesses [15]. Geographic segmentation helps marketers identify the specific needs of their customers. This is true for multi-national businesses as well as for SMEs.

---

[1] http://soneta.hci.ece.upatras.gr/

Even though SMEs may not use geographic segmentation marketing, geo-location still remains an important factor for SMEs since they often have local clientele and are not attempting to broaden their business beyond their own region [14]. SMEs are probably interested in monitoring only social media data that originate in a specific and confined geographic location and not in a specific country or even the entire world. However, since not all SMEs have their customers confined in specific geographic regions, restriction of social media results should be an optional feature that the user could choose to use or not.

In order to meet the above requirements, we created an experimental prototype that is able to detect social media trends for specific keywords in specific geographic areas, entitled SONETA. These trends are defined as the most important related terms around a user-defined topic, keyword, phrase or geographic region. In this initial development phase SONETA extracts information only from the Twitter stream.

3   Architectural Design

The SONETA system architecture is consisted of four main layers (Fig. 1): the communication layer that is responsible for querying Twitter, the storage layer where all the data (processed and raw) are stored, the preprocessing layer that transforms the unstructured data into top-level keywords, and the presentation layer that visualizes the top keywords. In the next paragraphs we provide a brief technical description of each layer.

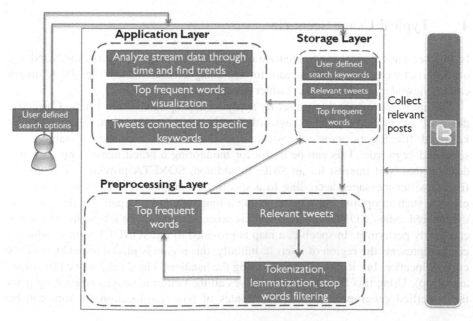

Fig. 1. Architectural design

Communication Layer: SONETA communicates with the Twitter Search API 1.1 in order to retrieve tweets related to user-defined keywords. To this end, we used a PHP library[2] as a client for accessing Twitter resources. SONETA asks for tweets containing specific keywords posted from a specific location.

Storage Layer: Results from the communication layer are stored in the storage layer. The storage layer consists of two main components: a MySQL Database and a data directory. The database stores the user-defined keywords, the results from the Twitter stream and the user credentials. It has been designed in such a way that new components and services can be easily added later. The data directory stores the results from the preprocessing layer.

Preprocessing Layer: Stored tweets are the input of the preprocessing layer. The preprocessing layer is implemented in PYTHON with the help of the NTLK package. For each tweet, external links, mentions and stop words of different languages are removed since they don't provide any useful information for the purposes of our system. Retrieved results are tokenized and the most frequently appearing ones are stored in the data directory component of the Storage layer using a JSON format.

Presentation Layer: Processed results are visualized at the presentation layer. Visualizations are implemented with the D3.JS[3], a javascript library for data visualizations. Using this library, we developed a timeline graph, a word cloud, a bubble chart and a treemap visualization. In addition, Google maps was used for building the geolocation feature.

4   Typical Usage Scenario

In this section a typical usage scenario of SONETA is presented. First, the SONETA user starts by creating a new stream for searching across Twitter (Fig. 2). A stream can be viewed as a subset of the Twitter stream.

The user can restrict this subset by applying appropriate search filters. Currently, the tool offers two options: keyword filtering and geo-location filtering. When keyword filtering is active, the steam includes Twitter messages containing the specified keywords. This can be useful for monitoring a brand name, a product or a domain that is of interest for an SME. In addition, SONETA provides the option to filter Twitter messages according to a specific geographic region. Other tools also provide such an option, but require setting a longitude-latitude pair and the length of the desired radius. SONETA simplifies this process, so that even less tech-savvy users can easily perform it. In specific, a map is provided to the SONETA user, in which a circle represents the region of interest. Initially, this region is placed around the user's current location, but it can be resized (using the handlers; Fig. 2) and moved (by drag-and-drop). Using this filter the user retrieves all the twitter messages originating from the specified geographic location. Examples of how geo-location filtering can be

---

[2] https://github.com/abraham/twitteroauth
[3] http://d3js.org/

useful for an SME are: understanding trend topics in customer conversations located in specific regions, estimating the impact of targeted advertising campaigns, and collecting ideas for new user products or services customized to a specific region. Finally, both filters can be combined in order to receive messages that contain a user-specified keyword in a specific region.

Fig. 2. New stream creation interface

Figure 3 presents an example of the output produced by SONETA. The timeline presents two bar charts of the total number of tweets per day that are contained in the user-defined stream. The bottom bar chart provides a bird's-eye-view and helps the user to easily identify areas of interest, whereas the top bar chart displays an adjustable zoomed portion of the bottom bar chart. Timeline representation was used in order to provide a spatial perspective of the trends [16].

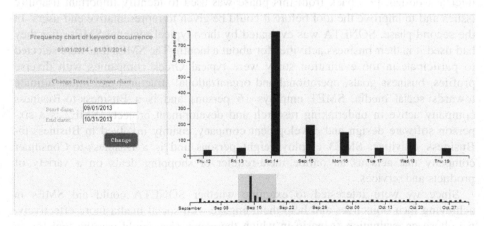

Fig. 3. An example of the SONETA output: total numbers of tweets per day

For each day, the SONETA user can see the most frequent words for the selected stream by clicking on the respective bar of the timeline. The initial representation of the most frequent words is a word cloud (Fig. 4, left), which is considered a powerful representation of textual data [17]. Monochromatic color combination and size are used to denote the frequency of the words appearing in the selected stream. SONETA provides two additional data visualizations: a) a bubblecloud in which the size and the color represent word frequency (Fig. 4, mid), and b) a treemap that uses the size and the color of the rectangles to represent word frequency (Fig. 4, right).

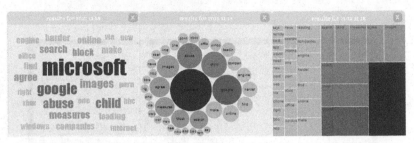

Fig. 4. An example of the SONETA output: top keywords and the available visualizations

5   Evaluation Study

This section presents an evaluation study of SONETA in terms of its usefulness and usability.

5.1   Method

The evaluation methodology we followed had two phases. During the first phase, a formative usability evaluation of SONETA was conducted by three usability experts. The experts performed heuristic evaluations to review the tool's interaction and interface design. Feedback from this phase was used to identify important usability issues and to improve the tool before it could be given to representative end-users. In the second phase, SONETA was evaluated by three typical regional SMEs after they had used it in their business activities for about a month. The SMEs that were selected to participate in the evaluation study were typical Greek companies with diverse profiles, business goals, operational and organizational structures and initial attitude towards social media. SME1 employs 16 persons and is a Business-to-Business company active in undertaking research and development projects. SME2 is a six-person software design and development company, mainly involved in Business-to-Business activities. SME3 employs eight persons and is a Business-to-Consumer company that acts as an online meta-retailer of shopping deals on a variety of products and services.

Since we were interested to examine whether SONETA could aid SMEs in achieving their objectives and help them engage with social media more effectively, we chose an evaluation scenario in which the companies would use the tool for an extended period with as little intervention from us as possible. First, a pre-study interview was conducted with the SMEs in order to profile them and identify their needs and problems in regard to social media usage. After the initial interview, SONETA was introduced to the participants followed by a training session in which instructional material was given to each SME. Subsequently, the participating SMEs were left to use SONETA for a period of one month for whatever reason they deemed appropriate. During this period and following a ten-day interval, three semi-structured interviews were conducted with each SME in order to collect qualitative feedback about whether and how they used SONETA, as well as to collect suggestions for improvement. Each interview placed emphasis on a different aspect. The first interview focused on the deployment process (e.g. level of effort required, training quality), the second interview on the user experience (e.g. usability, usefulness, learnability) and the final interview on overall impact (e.g. business goals support, change in policies). Apart from evaluating the features and functionalities that SONETA currently provides, a secondary objective was to identify future directions for improvement

5.2   Results and Findings

The pre-study interview showed that all three SMEs were primarily active in Facebook, which is typical for Greek companies. All of them had Twitter accounts but they were considerably less active in Twitter compared to Facebook. Two of the participating SMEs just mirrored Facebook posts on Twitter, whenever possible, while the third one used Twitter mostly to monitor content posted by others. SME3 reported being particularly interested to learn how to use Twitter effectively for the purpose of promoting their business. In the pre-study interview, no SME mentioned the importance or the need of geo-location as a feature of a social networking tool. Finally, even though all SMEs mentioned that they had problems to find interesting content to post they did not mention the need for tools that could help them find relevant to their business information in the social media stream.

Even though in the pre-study interview the SMEs did not mention the need for tools that filter data from the Twitter stream and identify information relevant to their businesses trends, their engagement with SONETA made them realize the potential of this feature. The participating SMEs reported that the possibility to restrict results in a specific geographic location was very interesting conceptually. All SMEs experimented with this SONETA feature, but their perceptions about the usefulness of the results varied considerably among them. SME1 and SME2 struggled to find appropriate ways to use it in their specific business domain. They reported having difficulties in formulating strategies on how to act upon information they extracted through SONETA and difficulties in finding appropriate keywords in order to create relevant streams. They asked about examples or good practices of using SONETA in similar to their own domains. On the other hand, SME3 found SONETA extremely useful. In contrast to the other participating companies, SME3 was active in a more consumer oriented sector. In addition, they were more motivated compared to the other two SMEs, since they explicitly stated in the pre-study interview that they wanted to learn to use Twitter more effectively and that they strongly believed in the power of social media. They used various keywords as well as the geo-location feature to find trending conversations that were particularly useful to them. The following excerpt from the transcribed interviews indicates that they did find SONETA useful:

"It [SONETA] helped me increase my followers on Twitter by looking for trending conversations in specific areas as well as in Greece in general. Taking part in these conversations allowed me to create 115 followers in a matter of two weeks. The tool allowed me to find what the competitions is tweeting about and to identify what topics are gaining attraction. This helped me make decisions about what to tweet myself."

In regard to the tool's usability the users reported at the beginning of the evaluation that they faced difficulties in learning how to use it. They reported that they would most likely not be able to use SONETA without the introductory material that was given to them at the beginning of the study. User comments helped us realize some moderate user interface problems that were resolved as soon as possible. In addition, we included supplementary instructions for first-time users, describing the main components of a stream creation process as well as how results can be further explored. We also added functionalities for the management of the streams as suggested by the participating SMEs. They confirmed that the word cloud visualization was particularly useful because it helped them to explore specific domains and identify important keywords and trends in a straightforward and quick manner. However, SMEs asked for the additional possibility to see specific Tweets, apart from the word cloud. This request was also implemented at a later time, allowing users to see all tweets that contain a certain keyword by simply clicking on it on the word cloud.

6   Conclusions and Future Work

In this paper we described the need for social media tools that specifically address SMEs because of their increased constraints, such as lack of resources and IT expertise, compared to larger corporations. To that end, we developed SONETA, a tool that filters information from the Twitter stream.

SONETA was introduced to three typical SMEs who used it for a period of one month in the context of an evaluation study that was designed to maximize ecological validity. The main goal of the evaluation was to understand if such a tool can support SMEs in engaging effectively with social media data. Evaluation showed that in general, SONETA was perceived by the participating SMEs as a reasonably useful tool. More specifically it was found that:

(a) SONETA can be particularly useful for SMEs that are mostly engaged in Business-to-Customer activities.
(b) There is a need for exemplary scenarios and case studies of using SONETA in specific domains.

(c) Attitude towards social media in general, and Twitter in particular, conditioned the perceived quality of the tool.

The feedback that was received from the evaluation study was used to further improve the tool, and will guide the development of future versions. For instance, the next version of SONETA will provide the option to retrieve data from multiple social networking sites. In addition, we plan to examine how such data can be integrated and summarized in order to help users gain insights from different perspectives. Future work also involves investigating how various types of visualizations may help users gain insight from social media data that originate from different domains. Finally, considering the real time nature of social media, the visualization layer in the SONETA system architecture could also be modified to support real time updates.

Acknowledgments. The work reported in this paper was funded by the European Territorial Cooperation Operational Programme "Greece-Italy 2007-2013" under the project Intersocial. We also thank the SMEs who participated in the experiment.

References

1. Brett, M., Kevin, B., Yamara, S., Beomjin, K.: Twitterreporter: Breaking News Detection and Visualization through the Geo-tagged Twitter Network. In: Li, W. (ed.) CATA, pp. 84–89. ISCA (2011)
2. Diakopoulos, N., De Choudhury, M., Naaman, M.: Finding and Assessing Social Media Information Sources in the Context of Journalism. In: Proceedings of the SIGCHI Conference on Human Factors in Computing Systems, pp. 2451–2460. ACM, New York (2012)
3. Best, D., Bruce, J., Dowson, S., Love, O., McGrath, L.: Web-based Visual Analytics for Social Media. In: AAAI ICWSM SocMedVis: Workshop on Social Media Visualization, pp. 2–5. AAAI Technical Report WS-12-03 (2012)
4. Takeshi, S., Makoto, O., Yutaka, M.: Earthquake Shakes Twitter Users: Real-time Event Detection by Social Sensors. In: Proceedings of the 19th International Conference on World Wide Web (2010)
5. Mangold, W.G., Faulds, D.J.: Social Media: The New Hybrid Element of the Promotion Mix. Business Horizons 52(4), 357–365 (2009)
6. Bulearca, M.: Twitter: A Viable Marketing Tool for SMEs? Global Business Management Research 2(4), 296–309 (2010)
7. Bughin, J., Manyika, J.: How Businesses Are Using Web 2.0: A McKinsey Global Survey. McKinsey Quarterly Web Exclusive, McKinsey and Company (2010)
8. Hawn, C.: Take Two Aspirin and Tweet Me in The Morning: How Twitter, Facebook, and Other Social Media are Reshaping Health Care. Health Affairs 28(2), 361 (2009)
9. Kietzman, J.H., Hermkens, K., McCarthy, I.P., Silvestre, B.S.: Social media? Get serious! Understanding the functional building blocks of social media. Business Horizons 54(3), 241–251 (2011)
10. Chamlertwat, W., Bhattarakosol, P., Rungkasiri, T., Haruechaiyasak, C.: Discovering Consumer Insight from Twitter via Sentiment Analysis. Journal of Universal Computer Science 18(8), 973–992 (2012)

11. Stavrakantonakis, I., Gagiu, A.-E., Kasper, H., Toma, I., Thalhammer, A.: An approach for evaluation of social media monitoring tools. Common Value Management, 52–64 (2012)
12. Kasper, H., Dausinger, M., Kett, H., Renner, T., Finzen, J., Kintz, M., Stephan, A.: Marktstudie Social Media Monitoring Tools. Fraunhofer-IRB, Stuttgart (2012)
13. Michaelidou, N., Siamagka, N.T., Christodoulides, G.: Usage, Barriers and Measurement of Social Media Marketing: An Exploratory Investigation of Small and Medium B2B Brands. Industrial Marketing Management 40, 1153–1159 (2011)
14. Stockdale, R., Ahmed, A., Scheepers, H.: Identifying Business Value from the Use of Social Media: An SME Perspective. In: PACIS 2012 Proceedings, Paper 169 (2012)
15. Broderick, A., Pickton, D.: Integrated Marketing Communications, 2nd edn. Edinburgh Gate Pearson Education Ltd. (2005)
16. Heer, J., Bostock, M., Ogievetsky, V.: A Tour through the Visualization Zoo. Communications of the ACM 53(6), 59 (2010)
17. McNaught, C., Lam, P.: Using Wordle as a Supplementary Research Tool. The Qualitative Report 15(3), 630–643 (2010)

Seed-Centric Approaches for Community Detection in Complex Networks

Rushed Kanawati

University Paris 13, Sorbonne Paris Cité
LIPN, CNRS UMR 7030, Villetaneuse, France,
rushed.kanawati@lipn.univ-paris13.fr
http://www-lipn.univ-paris13.fr/~kanawati

Abstract. Seed-centric algorithms constitue an emerging trend in the hot area of community detection in complex networks. The basic idea underlaying these approaches consists on identifying special nodes in the target network, called seeds, around which communities can then be identified. Different algorithms adopt different seed definitions and apply different seed selection and community construction approaches. This paper presents a first survey work on this type of algorithms.

Keywords: Community detection, complex networks, seed-centric algorithms.

1 Introduction

Complex networks are frequently used for modeling interactions in real-world systems in diverse areas, such as sociology, biology, information spreading and exchanging and many other different areas. One key topological feature of real-world complex networks is that nodes are arranged in tightly knit groups that are loosely connected one to each other. Such groups are called *communities*. Nodes composing a community are generally admitted to share common proprieties and/or be involved in a same function and/or having a same role. Hence, unfolding the community structure of a network could give us much insights about the overall structure a complex network. Works in this field can be roughly divided into two main classes:

- Computing a network partition into communities [12,39], or possibly detecting overlapping communities [31,41].
- Computing a local community centered on a given node [8,6,19].

Recently, an increasing number of work has been proposed with the idea of merging both kind of approaches. The basic idea is to identify some particular nodes in the target network, called *seed nodes*, around which local communities can be computed [18,32,36]. The interest in seed-centric approaches has been boosted in the recent years following the demonstration of serious limitations of *modularity optimization* based approaches considered till lately as the most efficient approaches for community detection [16,24].

G. Meiselwitz (Ed.): SCSM 2014, LNCS 8531, pp. 197–208, 2014.

Different algorithms adopt different seed definitions and apply different seed selection and community construction approaches. To the best of our knowledge, this paper provides the first survey study on this promising type of community detection algorithms.

The reminder of this paper is organized as follows. Next in section 2 we propose a set of criteria for classifying seed-centric algorithms. Some exemples are given in section 3. Performances, on benchmark networks, of a representative selection of some seed-centric algorithms and top state of the art algorithms (mainly based on modularity optimization) are compared and commented in section 4. Finally we conclude in section 5.

2   Seed-Centric Algorithms: A Classification Study

2.1   General Description

Algorithm 1 presents the general outlines of a typical seed-centric community detection algorithm. We recognize three principal steps:

1. Seed computation.
2. Seed local community computation
3. Community computation out from the set of local communities computed in step 2.

Algorithm 1 General seed-centric community detection algorithm

---

Require: $G =< V, E >$ a connected graph,
1: $C \leftarrow \emptyset$
2: $S \leftarrow$ **compute_seeds(G)**
3: **for** $s \in S$ **do**
4:     $C_s \leftarrow$ **compute_local_com(s,G)**
5:     $C \leftarrow C + C_s$
6: **end for**
7: **return compute_community(C)**

Each of the above mentioned steps can be implemented applying different techniques. A quick survey of existing approaches allows to identify five main criteria that can be used to classify seed-centric approaches. These criteria are detailed in next section

2.2   Classification Criteria

Five criteria has been identified for classifying seed-centric approaches. The first three criteria are relative to the step of seed computation. The two last ones are relative to the two last steps : seed local community computation and community computation steps. The five identified criteria are the following:

1. **Seed nature**: Form a pure topological point of view, a single seed can be: a single node [21,36,40], a set of nodes (not necessarily connected)[18], or a set of nodes composing a subgraph that is densely connected [5,32]. Concerning the role that a seed plays in a network, most existing algorithms search for seeds that are likely to be at the core of communities to be detected. This is mainly the case of leader-based approaches [18,36,21] and set-seeds based approaches [33]. One exception is the Yasca algorithm that search for seeds playing various roles in the target network [20].

2. **Seed number**: The number of seed nodes can be given as an input to the algorithm. This is much a classical approach similar to the use of the standard k-means data clustering algorithm [1]. In most situation, it is hard to know the number of communities to discover. Some heuristics have been proposed in order to automatically compute the set of all possible seeds. For exemple, in leader-based algorithms (where seeds are supposed to be community leaders), nodes that have a higher centrality than their direct neighbors are considered as leaders (i.e. seeds) [18,36].

3. **Seed selection policy**: We can distinguish here between two main approaches for seed selection: random election and informed selection. Applying a random selection consists on selecting randomly a set of eligible seeds. For exemple in [21] authors propose to select K-top central nodes as leaders. Algorithms applying a random selection strategy often apply an iterative process, where communities discovered by the ned of a first iteration are used to selecte new set of leaders and the algorithm iterates, and thus until convergence [21]. Algorithms defining seed as a groupe of nodes or as a subgraph apply mainly an informed selection policy such as the one cited above (selecting nodes with higher centrality that direct neighbors) [18].

4. **Seed local community computation**: One first classical approach for seed local community computation consists on applying an *expansion approach*. Local (or ego-centered) community detection algorithms can simply be applied for that purpose [3,6,10,27,19]. One major drawback of expansion strategy is that it does not ensure covering all nodes of the network in the set of detected communities. To overcome this problem, one can add outliers node to the most *near* community as proposed in [40]. Another approach, is to apply an *agglomerative approach* where each node in the network search to join the community of the *nearest* detected seed [18,21].

5. **Community computation**: Once all local communities of all seeds have been identified, a global decomposition of the network into, eventually overlapped, communities should be computed. In most existing approaches The final result is simply taken to be the set of seed communities. This is natural when seeds are selected as nodes at the core of theirs communities. In [20], authors propose an alternative approach where an ensemble clustering approach is applied [37]. This will be detailed in section 3.2.

Table 1 summarizes the characteristics of major seed-centered algorithms. In section 3 we describe in more details two different seed-centric algorithms that we have implemented: the Licod algorithm [18] and Yasca algorithm [20].

Table 1. Characteristics of major seed-centric algorithms

Algorithm	Seed Nature	Seed Number	Seed selection	Local Com.	Com. computation
Leaders-Followers [36]	Single	Computed	informed	Agglomerative	-
Top-Leaders [21]	Single	Input	Random	Expansion	-
Licod [18]	Set	Computed	Informed	Agglomerative	-
Yasca [20]	Single	Computed	Informed	Expansion	Ensemble clustering
[33]	Subgraph	Computed	Informed	Expansion	-
[40]	single	Computed	informed	Expansion	-
[5]	Subgraph	Computed	informed	expansion	-

3 Selected Exemples

In this section we detail two selected algorithms that we have implemented using the *igraph* graph analysis library [9]. Performances of these algorithms are evaluated and compared with those obtained by top algorithms of the state of the art on benchmark networks. Results are reported in section 4

3.1 LICOD

The algorithm is initially introduced in [18] as a framework for implementing leader-based community detection algorithms. Algorithm 2 gives the outline of the approach.

- Seed computation: The seed set computation is done in two steps. First all nodes having a centrality higher than $\sigma\%$ of the centrality of their direct neighbors are elected as a seed. Let $\mathcal{L}$ be the set of identified leaders. In algorithm 2 this step is achieved by the function $isLeader()$ (line 3).The list $\mathcal{L}$ is then reduced by grouping leaders that are estimated to be in the same community. This is the task of the function $computeCommunitiesLeader()$, line 7 in algorithm 2. Let $\mathcal{C}$ be the set of identified communities.
- Seed local community computation: this is also done in two steps. First, each node in the network (a leader or a follower) computes its membership degree to each community in $\mathcal{C}$. A ranked list of communities can then be obtained, for each node, where communities with highest membership degree are ranked first (lines 9-13 in algorithm 2). Next, each node will adjust its community membership preference list by merging this with preference lists of its direct neighbors in the network. Different strategies borrowed form the social choice theory can applied here to merge the different preference lists [2,11,7,38] . This step is iterated until stabilization of obtained ranked lists at each node. The convergence towards a stable sate is function of the applied voting scheme.
- Community computation: Finally, each node will be assigned to top ranked communities in its final obtained membership preference list.

Algorithm 2 LICOD algorithm

Require: $G = <V, E>$ a connected graph
1: $\mathcal{L} \leftarrow \emptyset$ {set of leaders}
2: **for** $v \in V$ **do**
3:    **if** $isLeader(v)$ **then**
4:       $\mathcal{L} \leftarrow \mathcal{L} \cup \{v\}$
5:    **end if**
6: **end for**
7: $\mathcal{C} \leftarrow computeComumunitiesLeader(\mathcal{L})$
8: **for** $v \in V$ **do**
9:    **for** $c \in \mathcal{C}$ **do**
10:      $M[v, c] \leftarrow membership(v, c)$
11:    **end for**
12:    $P[v] = \mathbf{sortAndRank}(M[v])$
13: **end for**
14: **repeat**
15:    **for** $v \in V$ **do**
16:      $P^*[v] \leftarrow \mathbf{rankAggregate}_{x \in \{v\} \cap \Gamma_G(v)} P[x]$
17:      $P[v] \leftarrow P^*[v]$
18:    **end for**
19: **until** Stabilization of $P^*[v] \forall v$
20: **for** $v \in V$ **do**
21:    /* assigning v to communities */
22:    **for** $c \in P[v]$ **do**
23:      **if** $|M[v, c] - M[v, P[0]]| \leq \epsilon$ **then**
24:        $COM(c) \leftarrow COM(c) \cup \{v\}$
25:      **end if**
26:    **end for**
27: **end for**
28: **return** $\mathcal{C}$

3.2 YASCA

Algorithm 3 sketchs the outlines of proposed approach. This is structured into three main steps:

Algorithm 3 The Yasca community detection algorithm

Require: $G = <V, E>$ a connected graph,
1: $\mathcal{C} \leftarrow \emptyset$
2: $S \leftarrow \mathbf{compute\_seeds(G)}$
3: **for** $s \in S$ **do**
4:    $C_s \leftarrow \mathbf{compute\_local\_com(s, G)}$
5:    $\mathcal{C} \leftarrow \mathcal{C} + (C_s, \overline{C_s})$
6: **end for**
7: **return** $\mathbf{Ensemble\_Clustering}(\mathcal{C})$

---

1. Seed computation: This is the role of the **compute_seeds()** function (line 2 in algorithm 3). The algorithms searchs to locate seeds as nodes having various positions in the graph. The seeding strategy is inspired form the work of [26] that show that real complex networks are often structured in one huge *bi-connected core* linked to number of small-sized sub-graphs named *whiskers* by a set of *bridges*. Nodes connecting the bi-connected core to whiskers are called *articulation nodes*. In Yasca, seeds are taken to be the set of articulation nodes plus the top $\sigma\%$ high central nodes belonging to the biconnected core.

2. For each seed node $s \in S$ we compute its local community C_s. This is the role of **compute_local_com()** function (line 4 in algorithm 3). Different algorithms can be applied for local community detection [6,8,3]. We mainly apply here a recent algorithm proposed in [19] that apply a multi-objective greedy optimization approach. The set of vertices V can then be partitioned into two disjoint sets : $P_v = \{C_s, \overline{C_s}\}$ where $\overline{C_s}$ denotes the complement of set C_s.

3. Finally, we apply an ensemble clustering approach [37] in order to merge the different bi-partitions obtained in step 2. This is the role of the **Ensemble_Clutering()** function (line 7 in algorithm 3). The output of this process is then taken to be the final decomposition of the graph into communities.

The overall complexity of the algorithm is determined by the highest complexity of the three above described steps. This depends on specific algorithms applied for implementing each step. However, the ensemble clustering step is usually the most expensive step, computationally speaking. In this work, we apply a classical cluster-based similarity partitioning algorithm [37] that have the following complexity in our case $\mathcal{O}(n^2 \times 2 \times |S|) \sim \mathcal{O}(n^2)$, where n is the number of nodes of the graph, 2 is the number of clusters in each clustering and $|S|$ is the number of different partitions to merge.

4 Experiments

In this section we evaluate a selection of seed-centric approaches on a set of classical benchmark networks for which a ground-truth decomposition into communities era known. First we described the used datasets. Then we explicit the applied evaluation criteria and lastly we compare results of selected seed-centric approaches along with some classical community detection algorithms mainly based on the principle of modularity optimisation.

4.1 Datasets

A set of three widely used benchmark networks for which a ground-truth decomposition into communities are known are used:

- **Zachary's karate club:** This network is a social network of friendships between 34 members of a karate club at a US university in 1970 [43]. Following a dispute the network was divided into 2 groups between the club's administrator and the club's instructor. The dispute ended in the instructor creating his own club and taking about half of the initial club with him. The network can hence be divided into two main communities.

- **Dolphins social network:** This network is an undirected social network resulting from observations of a community of 62 dolphins over a period of 7 years [28]. Nodes represent dolphins and edges represent frequent associations between dolphin pairs occurring more often than expected by chance. Analysis of the data revealed two main groups.

- **American political books:** This is a political books co-purchasing network. Nodes represent books about US politics sold by the online bookseller *Amazon.com*. Edges represent frequent co-purchasing of books by the same buyers, as indicated by the "customers who bought this book also bought these other books" feature on Amazon. Books are classified into three disjoint classes: liberal, neutral or conservative. The classification was made separately by Mark Newman based on a reading of the descriptions and reviews of the books posted on Amazon.

Next figure shows the structure of the selected networks with real communities indicated by the color code. In table 2 we summarize basic characteristics of selected benchmark real networks.

(a) Zachary Karate Club Network [43]   (b) US Politics books network [22]

(c) Dolphins social network [28]

Fig. 1. Real community structure of the selected benchmark networks

Table 2. Characteristics of some well-known benchmark networks

Network	# nodes	# edges	# com	reference
Zachary club	34	78	2	[43]
Political books	100	441	3	[22]
Dolphins	62	159	2	[28]

4.2 Evaluation Criteria

Th problem of community evaluation is still to be an open and difficult problem in spite of huge amount of work addressing this issue [42,23,14,25]. In this work we apply much a classical approach based on computing the similarity of computed partitions (communities) with ground-truth partitions. This is a classical issu in the field of data clustering [1] from which we borrow main evaluation indices: Adaptive Rand Index [17], Normalized Information Index (NMI) [37]. Other mutual infirmation based indices can also be used [30,13,13]. In this paper we mainly used the NMI index.

The ARI index is based on counting the number of pairs of elements that are clustered in the same clusters in both compared partitions. Let $P_i = \{P_i^1, \ldots, P_i^l\}$, $P_j = \{P_j^1, \ldots, P_j^k\}$ be two partitions of a set of nodes V. The set of all (unordered) pairs of nodes of V can be partitioned into the following four disjoint sets :

- $S_{11} = \{$ pairs that are in the same cluster under P_i and P_j $\}$
- $S_{00} = \{$ pairs that are in different clusters under P_i and P_j $\}$
- $S_{10} = \{$ pairs that are in the same cluster under P_i but in different ones under P_j $\}$
- $S_{01} = \{$ pairs that are in different clusters under P_i but in the same under P_j $\}$

Let $n_{ab} = |S_{ab}|, a, b \in \{0, 1\}$, be the respective sizes of the above defined sets. The rand index, initially defined in [35] is simply given by :

$$\mathcal{R}(P_i, P_j) = \frac{2 \times (n_{11} + n_{00})}{n \times (n-1)}$$

In [17], authors show that the expected value of the Rand Index of two random partitions does not take a constant value (e.g. zero). They proposed an adjusted version which assumes a generalized hypergeometric distribution as null hypothesis: the two clusterings are drawn randomly with a fixed number of clusters and a fixed number of eleme nts in each cluster (the number of clusters in the two clusterings need not be the same). Then the adjusted Rand Index is the normalized difference of the Rand Index and its expected value under the null hypothesis. It is defined as follows:

$$ARI(P_i, P_j) = \frac{\sum_{x=1}^{l} \sum_{y=1}^{k} \binom{P_i^x \cap P_j^y}{2} - t_3}{\frac{1}{2}(t_1 + t_2) - t_3} \tag{1}$$

Table 3. Comparison of performances of different community detection algorithms

Dataset	Algorithm	NMI	ARI	Q	# Communities
Zachary	Newman	0.57	0.46	0.40	5
	Louvain	0.58	0.46	0.41	4
	Walktrap	0.50	0.33	0.35	5
	Licod	0.60	0.62	0.24	3
	YASCA	**0.77**	0.69	0.34	2
US Politics	Newman	0.55	0.68	0.51	5
	Louvain	0.57	0.55	0.52	4
	Walktrap	0.53	0.65	0.50	4
	Licod	**0.68**	0.67	0.42	6
	YASCA	0.60	0.62	0.24	3
Dolphins	Newman	0.55	0.39	0.51	5
	Louvain	0.51	0.32	0.51	5
	Walktrap	0.53	0.41	0.48	4
	Licod	0.41	0.32	0.35	2
	YASCA	**0.58**	0.59	0.53	3

where :

$$t_1 = \sum_{x=1}^{l} \binom{|P_i^x|}{2} , t_2 = \sum_{y=1}^{k} \binom{|P_j^y|}{2} , t_3 = \frac{2t_1t_2}{n(n-1)}$$

This index has expected value zero for independent clusterings and maximum value 1 for identical clusterings.

Another family of partitions comparisons functions is the one based on the notion of mutual information. A partition P is assimilated to a random variable. We seek to quantify how much we reduce the uncertainty of the clustering of randomly picked element from V in a partition P_j if we know P_i. The Shanon's entropy of a partition P_i is given by:

$$H(P_i) = -\sum_{x=1}^{l} \frac{|P_i^x|}{n} log_2(\frac{|P_i^x|}{n})$$

Notice that $\frac{|P_i^x|}{n}$ is the probability that a randomly picked element from V be clustered in P_i^x. The mutual information between two random variables X,Y is given by the general formula:

$$MI(X,Y) = H(X) + H(Y) - H(X,Y) \qquad (2)$$

This can then be applied to measure the mutual information between two partitions P_i, P_j. The mutual information defines a metric on the space of all clusterings and is bounded by the entropies of involved partitions. In [37], authors propose a normalized version given by:

$$NMI(X,Y) = \frac{MI(X,Y)}{\sqrt{H(X)H(Y)}} \qquad (3)$$

4.3   Comparative Results

Next figure shows the obtained results on the three datasets compared to state of the art algorithms : Louvain [4], Infomap [29], Walktrap [34] and edge-betweenness based modularity optimisation algorithm (denoted Newman algorithm in the table) [15].

Evaluation is made in function of the normalized mutual information NMI, ARI index, the modularity Q [15]. These results needs confirmation on large-scale datasets. The problem to cope with is to find large-scale networks with reliable known ground-truth partitions.

5   Conclusion

Seed-centric algorithms constitute an merging and promising trend in the active area of for community detection in complex networks. In this paper, we've provided a quick survey of existing approaches. Performances caparison with top algorithms in the state of the art show the Results obtained on both small benchmark social network and on clustering problems argue for the capacity of the approach to detect real communities. Future developments we are working include: testing the algorithm on further large scale networks, develop a full distributed self-stabilizing version exploiting the fact that major part of computations are made in a local manner and finally adapt the approach for K-partite and for multiplex networks.

References

1. Aggarwal, C.C., Reddy, C.K. (eds.): Data Clustering: Algorithms and Applications. CRC Press (2014)
2. Arrow, K.: Social choice and individual values, 2nd edn. Cowles Foundation, New Haven (1963)
3. Bagrow, J.P., Bollt, E.M.: A local method for detecting communities. Phys. Rev. E 72, 046108 (2005)
4. Blondel, V.D., Guillaume, J.I., Lefebvre, E.: Fast unfolding of communities in large networks, pp. 1–12 (2008)
5. Bollobás, B., Riordan, O.: Clique percolation. Random Struct. Algorithms 35(3), 294–322 (2009)
6. Chen, J., Zaïane, O.R., Goebel, R.: Local community identification in social networks. In: Memon, N., Alhajj, R. (eds.) ASONAM, pp. 237–242. IEEE Computer Society (2009)
7. Chevaleyre, Y., Endriss, U., Lang, J., Maudet, N.: A short introduction to computational social choice. In: van Leeuwen, J., Italiano, G.F., van der Hoek, W., Meinel, C., Sack, H., Plášil, F. (eds.) SOFSEM 2007. LNCS, vol. 4362, pp. 51–69. Springer, Heidelberg (2007)
8. Clauset, A.: Finding local community structure in networks. Physical Review E (2005)
9. Csardi, G., Nepusz, T.: The igraph software package for complex network research. InterJournal Complex Systems 1695 (2006), http://igraph.sf.net

10. Danisch, M., Guillaume, J.-L., Le Grand, B.: Unfolding ego-centered community structures with a similarity approach. In: Ghoshal, G., Poncela-Casasnovas, J., Tolksdorf, R. (eds.) Complex Networks IV. SCI, vol. 476, pp. 145–153. Springer, Heidelberg (2013)
11. Dwork, C., Kumar, R., Naor, M., Sivakumar, D.: Rank aggregation methods for the Web. In: WWW, pp. 613–622 (2001)
12. Fortunato, S.: Community detection in graphs. Physics Reports 486(3-5), 75–174 (2010)
13. Fred, A.L.N., Jain, A.K.: Robust data clustering. In: CVPR (2), pp. 128–136. IEEE Computer Society (2003)
14. Giatsidis, C., Malliaros, F.D., Vazirgiannis, M.: Advanced graph mining for community evaluation in social networks and the web. In: WSDM, pp. 771–772 (2013)
15. Girvan, M., Newman, M.E.J.: Community structure in social and biological networks. PNAS 99(12), 7821–7826 (2002)
16. Good, B.H., de Montjoye, Y.A., Clauset, A.: The performance of modularity maximization in practical contexts. Physical Review E(81), 046106 (2010)
17. Hubert, L., Arabie, P.: Comparing partitions. Journal of Classification 2(1), 192–218 (1985)
18. Kanawati, R.: Licod: Leaders identification for community detection in complex networks. In: SocialCom/PASSAT, pp. 577–582 (2011)
19. Kanawati, R.: Empirical evaluation of applying ensemble ranking to ego-centered communities identification in complex networks. In: Zaz, Y. (ed.) 4th International Conference on Multimedia Computing and Systems. IEEE, Marrakech (April 2014)
20. Kanawati, R.: Yasca: A collective intelligence approach for community detection in complex networks. CoRR abs/1401.4472 (2014)
21. Khorasgani, R.R., Chen, J., Zaiane, O.R.: Top leaders community detection approach in information networks. In: 4th SNA-KDD Workshop on Social Network Mining and Analysis, Washington, D.C. (2010)
22. Krebs, V.: Political books network, http://www.orgnet.com/
23. Labatut, V.: Generalized measures for the evaluation of community detection methods. CoRR abs/1303.5441 (2013)
24. Lancichinetti, A., Fortunato, S.: Limits of modularity maximization in community detection. CoRR abs/1107.1 (2011)
25. Lee, C., Cunningham, P.: Community detection: effective evaluation on large social networks. Journal of Complex Networks 2(1), 19–37 (2014)
26. Leskovec, J., Lang, K.J., Dasgupta, A., Mahoney, M.W.: Community structure in large networks: Natural cluster sizes and the absence of large well-defined clusters. Internet Mathematics 6(1), 29–123 (2009)
27. Lim, K.H., Datta, A.: A seed-centric community detection algorithm based on an expanding ring search. In: Proceedings of the First Australasian Web Conference, AWC 2013, Adelaide, Australia (2013)
28. Lusseau, D., Schneider, K., Boisseau, O.J., Haase, P., Slooten, E., Dawson, S.M.: The bottlenose dolphin community of doubtful sound features a large proportion of long-lasting associations. Behavioral Ecology and Sociobiology 54, 396–405 (2003)
29. Rosvall, M., Axelsson, D., Bergstrom, C.T.: The map equation. Eur. Phys. J. Special Topics 13, 178 (2009)
30. Meilă, M.: Comparing clusterings by the variation of information. In: Schölkopf, B., Warmuth, M.K. (eds.) COLT/Kernel 2003. LNCS (LNAI), vol. 2777, pp. 173–187. Springer, Heidelberg (2003)
31. Palla, G., Derönyi, I., Farkas, I., Vicsek, T.: Uncovering the overlapping modular structure of protein interaction networks. FEBS Journal 272, 434 (2005)

32. Papadopoulos, S., Kompatsiaris, Y., Vakali, A.: A graph-based clustering scheme for identifying related tags in folksonomies. In: Bach Pedersen, T., Mohania, M.K., Tjoa, A.M. (eds.) DaWak 2010. LNCS, vol. 6263, pp. 65–76. Springer, Heidelberg (2010)

33. Papadopoulos, S., Kompatsiaris, Y., Vakali, A., Spyridonos, P.: Community detection in social media - performance and application considerations. Data Min. Knowl. Discov. 24(3), 515–554 (2012)

34. Pons, P., Latapy, M.: Computing communities in large networks using random walks. J. Graph Algorithms Appl. 10(2), 191–218 (2006)

35. Rand, W.M.: Objective criteria for the evaluation of clustering methods. Journal of the American Statistical Association 66, 846–850 (1971)

36. Shah, D., Zaman, T.: Community Detection in Networks: The Leader-Follower Algorithm. In: Workshop on Networks Across Disciplines in Theory and Applications, NIPS (2010)

37. Strehl, A., Ghosh, J.: Cluster ensembles: a knowledge reuse framework for combining multiple partitions. The Journal of Machine Learning Research 3, 583–617 (2003)

38. Subbian, K., Melville, P.: Supervised rank aggregation for predicting influencers in twitter. In: SocialCom/PASSAT, pp. 661–665. IEEE (2011)

39. Tang, L., Liu, H.: Community Detection and Mining in Social Media. Synthesis Lectures on Data Mining and Knowledge Discovery. Morgan & Claypool Publishers (2010)

40. Whang, J.J., Gleich, D.F., Dhillon, I.S.: Overlapping community detection using seed set expansion. In: He, Q., Iyengar, A., Nejdl, W., Pei, J., Rastogi, R. (eds.) CIKM, pp. 2099–2108. ACM (2013)

41. Xie, J., Kelley, S., Szymanski, B.K.: Overlapping community detection in networks: The state-of-the-art and comparative study. ACM Comput. Surv. 45(4), 43 (2013)

42. Yackoubi, Z., Kanawati, R.: Applying leaders driven community detection algorithms to data clustering. In: The 36th Annual Conference of the German Classification Society on Data Analysis, Machine Learning and Knowledge Discovery (GfKI 2012) (2012)

43. Zachary, W.W.: An information flow model for conflict and fission in small groups. Journal of Anthropological Research 33, 452–473 (1977)

Visualizing Impression-Based Preferences
of Twitter Users

Tadahiko Kumamoto, Tomoya Suzuki, and Hitomi Wada

Chiba Institute of Technology, Narashino, Chiba 275-0016, Japan
kumamoto@net.it-chiba.ac.jp

Abstract. Twitter is extremely useful for connecting with other users, because, on Twitter, following other users is simple. On the other hand, people are often followed by unknown and anonymous users and are sometimes shown tweets of unknown users through the tweets of the users they follow. In such a situation, they wonder whether they should follow such unknown users. This paper proposes a system for visualizing impression-based preferences of Twitter users to help people select whom to follow. The impression-based preference of a user is derived based on the impressions of the tweets the user has posted and those of the tweets of users followed by the user under consideration. Our proposed system enables people to select whom to follow depending on whether or not another user adheres to the user's own sensibilities, rather than on whether or not another user provides valuable information.

1 Introduction

A number of social networking services (SNS), such as Twitter and Facebook, are actively used. Twitter is superior to other SNSs as a tool for connecting with famous people, on-screen talent, and strangers, as well as with friends and acquaintances, because it makes following any user simple. Many users post daily tweets with topics ranging from political and economic events to events concerning themselves. Obtaining such information routinely requires following users who are posting the information. However, the type of tweets that users normally post can be judged by reading a large number of users' tweets carefully. Some users may always tweet only somber messages, and other users may always express anger in their tweets. Many users prefer not to receive negative tweets.

This paper proposes a system for visualizing impression-based preferences of Twitter users to help people select whom to follow. Usually, Twitter users view tweets posted by someone they follow voluntarily, or post tweets with the awareness that the tweets are viewed by their followers. Therefore, we consider that the impression-based preferences of Twitter users can be derived based on the impressions of the tweets they have posted and those of the tweets the users they follow have posted. People can use the proposed system to determine the type of tweets Twitter users usually view or post by visually checking the impression-based preferences of the users. The system also extracts keyphrases,

G. Meiselwitz (Ed.): SCSM 2014, LNCS 8531, pp. 209–220, 2014.

or characteristic character strings, from each set of tweets and presents the commonalities and differences among the sets. This helps people identify the topics that interest the users.

When people specify the account name of a Twitter user as input to our proposed system, the system uses the Twitter API [1] to collect tweets posted by the specified user and her or his following users. Then, it rates each tweet based on three distinct impressions, using the impression mining method that the authors have proposed [2]. The target impressions are limited to those represented by three bipolar scales of impressions [3], "Happy – Sad," "Glad – Angry," and "Peaceful – Strained." The strength of each impression is computed as an "impression value," *i.e.* a real number between one and seven denoting a position on the corresponding scale. For example, on the scale "Happy – Sad," the score one indicates "Happy," the middle score four denotes "Neither happy nor sad," and the score seven equals "Sad." If the impression value of a tweet is 2.5, then the average person will experience an intermediate impression between "Comparatively happy (2)" and "A little happy (3)" from reading the tweet. In addition, the system uses the Yahoo! Keyphrase Extraction API [4] to extract keyphrases from each set of tweets. Last, the system uses the Google Chart API [5] to visualize the results of the previous processing and presents it to the user. Using our proposed system, people can visually grasp the impression-based preferences of their specified users, that is, the type of tweets the specified users usually view or post and the topics that interests them.

2   Related Work

Many systems have been developed for using information on Twitter effectively including a system that detects trends over the Twitter stream [6], a system that recommends news articles based on Twitter-based user modeling [7], and a system that detects earthquakes by monitoring tweets [8].

Studies of ways to recommend users as candidates to follow are also ongoing, with the goal of supporting the making of connections with other Twitter users. Weng et al. proposed a Pagerank-like algorithm, called TwitterRank, for identifying influential Twitter users and recommending them as users to follow [9]. Sadilek et al. proposed a system for suggesting users to follow by inferring friendship in the physical world [10]. Pennacchiotti et al. proposed a method that suggests users who have a similar latent interest based on information extracted from their tweets [11]. In Japan, a method for recommending users to follow was proposed based on how many of the user's tweets were registered in "Favorites" regarding a topic [12]. On the official Twitter website, several users are suggested as "Who to follow" based on whom other users follow and other criteria. In addition, users can easily follow popular users in the field of a topic by clicking on "Popular accounts" on the official website and selecting a topic that interests them. Our proposed system enables people to select whom to follow depending on whether or not they adhere to their own sensibilities, rather than on whether or not they provide valuable information, by incorporating information on their sensibilities or impression-based preferences of users.

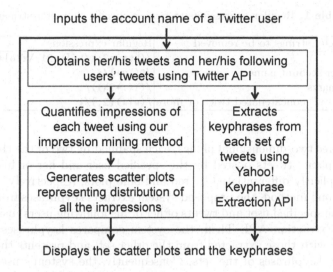

Fig. 1. Architecture of our proposed visualization system

In research on affective computing and sentiment analysis, studies on extracting subjective information, called sentiment, emotion, or impression, from text data, such as reviews, news articles, and web pages, are ongoing, and their results have been applied to various task domains, for example, sentiment analysis [13], information visualization [14], annotation of impression tags [15], and the like. However, these studies only classify text data into emotion classes or attach impression tags to text data, without quantifying impressions of those data.

3 Design of the Visualization System

3.1 System Architecture

We show the architecture of our proposed system in Figure 1. First, the system's users are asked to specify a Twitter user by entering her or his account name. Using the Twitter API, the system then obtains tweets posted by the specified user and tweets posted by her or his following users. These two sets of tweets are analyzed in the following two ways:

In the first method, the system computes three impression values of each tweet using the impression mining method we proposed previously [2]. This method generates word unigrams from an input tweet and obtains values representing the effect of each word unigram, based on the impression lexicons we constructed from a newspaper database. The method then computes and outputs the three impression values of the tweet based on these values. This method is highly accurate even for unlearned data, and our experimental results show that the average root-mean-square errors (RMSE) for unlearned data were 0.69, 0.49, and 0.64 on the respective scales. Last, the proposed system plots the impression

Table 1. Regular expressions to remove specific character strings

Character strings to be removed	Regular expressions
URLs	`/(https?:\/\/[\x21-\x7e]+)/i`
Twitter account names	`/@(\w+)/i`
Face marks	`/(\(.*?\))/`
Letter "w" concatenated twice or more	`/(w|w){2,}/i`

values on three two-dimensional planes, each spanned by two of the three scales. In each 2D plane, tweets posted by the specified user and her or his following users are explicitly differentiated by red and blue plots, respectively.

In the second method, the proposed system extracts keyphrases from each set (tweets of the specified user and tweets of her or his following users) using Yahoo! Keyphrase Extraction API. Then, the system compares keyphrases extracted from one set with those extracted from the other set, and presents the common and different keyphrases of the sets. Consequently, the system's users become aware of the strong and weak interests of the specified user.

The following subsections will describe in detail the main parts of the system.

3.2   Collecting Tweets on User and Home Timelines

Users are asked to input a Twitter user's account name to the system. First, the system obtains user and home timelines (User TL and Home TL, respectively) of the specified user from Twitter using the Twitter API. In this paper, the former timeline consists of the tweets the specified user posted, and the latter timeline consists of the tweets the users, or followees, whom the specified user has followed posted. A user's User TL can be obtained using the API for getting User TLs. On the other hand, only the Home TL of a user authenticated in advance can be obtained using the API for getting Home TLs; the Home TLs of arbitrary users are not available. The system must reconstruct the Home TL of an arbitrary user artificially. First, the system gets an ID list of the specified user's followees using the Twitter API, and then it checks the newest date and hour posted in each ID. Any ID in which the newest date and hour is older than the base date set in advance is removed from the ID list. The base date is set to one, representing "yesterday" as a default value, after which it can be changed freely by the system's users. Next, the system gets the User TL of each followee who has an ID in the remaining ID list, and then reconstructs the Home TL of the specified user. Note that tweets for which the date and hour are older than the base date are not collected.

3.3   Removing Noise

The system removes character strings, such as face marks and Uniform Resource Locators (URLs), from every tweet, because the current version of the impression mining method cannot analyze these character strings adequately. Character strings to be removed and regular expressions for removing them are enumerated in Table 1.

3.4   Quantifying Impressions of Tweets

Determining Target Impressions. We designed six bipolar scales suitable for representing impressions of news articles, "Happy – Sad," "Glad – Angry," "Interesting – Uninteresting," "Optimistic – Pessimistic," "Peaceful – Strained," and "Surprising – Common." First, we conducted nine experiments, in each of which 100 subjects read ten news articles and estimated their impressions on a scale from one to five for each of 42 impression words. These 42 impression words were manually selected from a Japanese thesaurus [16] as words that can express impressions of news articles. Next, factor analysis was applied to the data obtained in the experiments, and the 42 words were divided into four groups, negative words, positive words, two words that were "uninteresting" and "common," and two words that were "surprising" and "unexpected." In the meantime, after cluster analysis of the data, the 42 words were divided into ten groups. The results of the two analyses were used to create the six bipolar scales mentioned above. We showed that impressions on the "Surprising – Common" scale differed greatly among individuals in terms of their perspective. We also showed that processing according to the background knowledge, interests, and characters of individuals was required to deal with the impressions represented by the two scales "Interesting – Uninteresting" and "Optimistic – Pessimistic." Therefore, we decided not to use these three scales at the present stage, and adopted the remaining three scales, "Happy – Sad," "Glad – Angry," and "Peaceful – Strained."

Constructing Impression Lexicons. An impression lexicon plays an important role in computing impressions of text data. In this paper, we describe the implementation of a method for automatically constructing an impression lexicon.

First, two contrasting sets, each consisting of multiple reference words, are used to construct an impression lexicon for each scale. Next, we let the set of reference words that expresses an impression at the left of a scale be S_L, and we let the set of reference words that expresses an impression at the right of the scale be S_R. Articles including one or more reference words in S_L or S_R are extracted from a newspaper database, and the number of reference words belonging to each set is counted in each article. For this we use the 2002 to 2006 editions of the Yomiuri Newspaper Text Database as the newspaper database. Then, we let A_L be the articles that each contains a number of reference words belonging to S_L larger than the number of reference words belonging to S_R, and we let the number of articles in A_L be N_L. We let A_R be the articles that each contains a number of reference words belonging to S_L smaller than the number of reference words belonging to S_R, and we let the number of articles in A_R be N_R. Next, all words are extracted from each of A_L and A_R except for

Table 2. Specifications of our impression lexicons

Scales	# of entries	W_L	W_R
Happy – Sad	387,428	4.90	3.80
Glad – Angry	350,388	4.76	3.82
Peaceful – Strained	324,590	3.91	4.67

Table 3. Reference words prepared for each scale

Scales	Reference words
Happy	tanoshii (happy), tanoshimu (enjoy), tanosimida (look forward to), tanoshigeda (joyous)
– Sad	kanashii (sad), kanashimu (suffer sadness), kanashimida (feel sad), kanashigeda (look sad)
Glad	ureshii (glad), yorokobashii (blessed), yorokobu (feel delight)
– Angry	ikaru/okoru (get angry), ikidooru (become irate), gekidosuru (get enraged)
Peaceful	nodokada (peaceful), nagoyakada (friendly), sobokuda (simple), anshinda (feel easy)
– Strained	kinpakusuru (strained), bukimida (scared), fuanda (be anxious), osoreru (fear)

particles, adnominal words[1], and demonstratives, and the document frequency of each word is measured. Then, we let the document frequency in A_L of a word w be $N_L(w)$, and we let the document frequency in A_R of a word w be $N_R(w)$. The revised conditional probabilities of a word w are defined as follows.

$$P_L(w) = \frac{N_L(w)}{N_L}, \qquad P_R(w) = \frac{N_R(w)}{N_R}$$

In these equations, only articles that satisfy the assumptions described above are used to calculate $P_L(w)$ and $P_R(w)$.

Finally, the impression value $v(w)$ of a word w is calculated using these $P_L(w)$ and $P_R(w)$ as follows.

$$v(w) = \frac{P_L(w) * W_L}{P_L(w) * W_L + P_R(w) * W_R}$$

$$W_L = \log_{10} N_L, \qquad W_R = \log_{10} N_R$$

That is, a weighted interior division ratio $v(w)$ of $P_L(w)$ and $P_R(w)$ is calculated using these formulas and stored as an impression value of w in the scale "$S_L -$ S_R" in an impression lexicon. Note that W_L and W_R denote weights, and that the larger N_L and N_R are, the heavier W_L and W_R are.

---

[1] This part of speech exists only in Japanese, not in English. For example, "that," "so called," and "of no particular distinction" are expressed using adnominal words in Japanese.

The numbers of entries in the impression lexicons constructed as above are shown in Table 2, together with the values of W_L and W_R obtained. Further, the two contrasting sets of reference words[2] used in creating the impression lexicons are enumerated in Table 3 for each scale. These words were determined after some trial and error and are based on two criteria: (i) a word is a verb or adjective that expresses either of two contrasting impressions represented by a scale, and (ii) as far as possible, the word does not suggest other types of impressions.

Computing Impression Values of News Articles. For each scale, the impression value of a news article is calculated as follows. First, the article is segmented into words using "Juman" [17][3], one of the most powerful Japanese morphological analysis systems, and an impression value for each word is obtained by consulting the impression lexicon constructed for the scale. Seventeen rules that we designed are then applied to the Juman output. For example, there is a rule that a phrase of a negative form such as "sakujo-shi-nai (do not erase)" should not be divided into a verb "shi (do)," a suffix "nai (not)," and an action noun "sakujo (erasure)," but should be treated as a single verb "sakujo-shi-nai (do-not-erase)." There is also a rule that an assertive phrase such as "hoomuran-da (is a home run)" should not be divided into a copula "da (is)" and a noun "hoomuran (a home run)," but should form a single copula "hoomuran-da (is-a-home-run)." Further, there is a rule that a phrase with a prefix, such as "sai-charenji (re-challenge)" should not be divided into a prefix "sai (re)" and an action noun "charenji (challenge)," but should form a single action noun "sai-charenji (re-challenge)." All the rules are applied to the Juman output in creating impression lexicons and computing the impression values of articles. Finally, an average of the impression values obtained for all of the words except for particles, adnominal words, and demonstratives is calculated and presented as the impression value of the article.

Correcting Computed Impression Values. We considered that some gaps would occur between impression values computed by an unsupervised method such as the one we used and those of the readers. Therefore, we conducted experiments with a total of 900 people participating as subjects and identified the gaps that actually occurred.

First, we conducted experiments with 900 subjects and obtained data that described correspondence relationships between news articles and impressions to be extracted from the articles. That is, the 900 subjects were randomly divided into nine equal groups, each group consisting of 50 males and 50 females, and 90 articles selected from the 2002 edition of the Mainichi Newspaper Text Database[4]

---

[2] These words were translated into English by the authors.

[3] Since there are no boundary markers between words in Japanese, word segmentation is needed to identify individual words.

[4] This database is different from the Yomiuri newspaper database we used in creating impression lexicons.

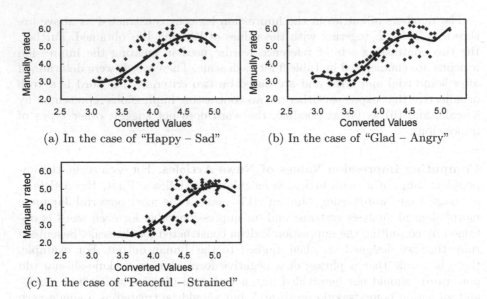

(a) In the case of "Happy – Sad"   (b) In the case of "Glad – Angry"

(c) In the case of "Peaceful – Strained"

Fig. 2. Scatter diagrams and regression equations

were randomly divided into nine equal parts. Then, each subject was asked to read the ten articles presented in a random order and rate each of them using three seven-point bipolar scales presented in a random order. The scales we used were "Happy – Sad," "Glad – Angry," and "Peaceful – Strained," and the subjects were asked to assess, on a scale from one to seven, the intensity of each impression, represented by each scale, from reading a target article. After the experiments, for each scale, we calculated an average of the 100 values rated for every article. We regarded this average as the impression value to be extracted from the article. Note that in these experiments, we presented only the first paragraphs of the original news articles to the subjects. This procedure was based on the fact that people can understand the outline of a news article by just reading the first paragraph of the article.

Next, impression values for the first paragraphs of the 90 articles were computed using the method we implemented in 3.4, where the first paragraphs were identical to those presented to the subjects in the experiments. Note that according to the definition of our equations, these impression values are close to one, when impressions on the left of a scale are felt strongly, and are close to zero, when impressions on the right of a scale are felt strongly. We therefore used the following formula to convert the computed value into a value between 1.0 and 7.0.

$$Converted = (1 - Computed) * 6 + 1$$

Next, for each scale, we drew a scatter diagram to identify the potential correspondence relationship between these converted values and the averages

Table 4. Regression equations designed for impression data of ninety articles

Scales	Regression equations (x: converted values)
Happy – Sad	$-1.6355586x^3 + 18.971570x^2 - 70.68575x + 88.5147$
Glad – Angry	$2.384741939x^5 - 46.87159982x^4 + 363.6602058x^3 -$
	$1391.589442x^2 + 2627.06261x - 1955.3058$
Peaceful – Strained	$-1.7138394x^3 + 21.942197x^2 - 90.79203x + 124.8218$

obtained in the experiments, as illustrated in Figure 2. We can see from any of the scatter diagrams that the impression values manually rated by the subjects are positively correlated with those automatically computed by the method we implemented. In fact, from the case at the top of the figure, their coefficients of correlation are 0.76, 0.84, and 0.78, which are all high. This not only means that as an overall trend, the underlying assumption of this paper is confirmed, but also indicates that the correspondence relationships can be represented by regression equations.

Next, we applied regression analysis to the converted values and the averages, where the converted values were used as the explanatory variable, and the averages were used as the objective variable. Various regression models, such as linear function, logarithmic function, logistic curve, quadratic function, cubic function, quartic function, and quintic function, were used in this regression analysis on a trial basis. As a result, the regression equation with the highest coefficient of determination was determined to be an optimal function denoting the correspondence relationship between the converted values and the averages in each scale. This means that for each scale, the impression value of an article was obtained more accurately by correcting the value computed by the method we implemented using the corresponding regression equation.

The regression equations obtained here are shown in Table 4 and are already illustrated on the corresponding scatter diagrams in Figure 2. Their coefficients of determination were 0.63, 0.81, 0.64, respectively, which were higher than 0.5 in all scales. This means that the results of regression analysis were good. In addition, we can see from Figure 2 that each regression equation fits the shape of the corresponding scatter diagram.

The impression mining method described above is applied to tweets, and three impression values of each tweet are computed.

3.5 Extracting Keyphrases

Keyphrases are extracted from the tweets from which noise was removed. The system extracts keyphrases from two sets of tweets, those of the specified user and those of the specified user's followees using the Yahoo! Keyphrase Extraction API. Last, twenty keyphrases extracted from each set of tweets are presented to the system's user in a tag cloud form.

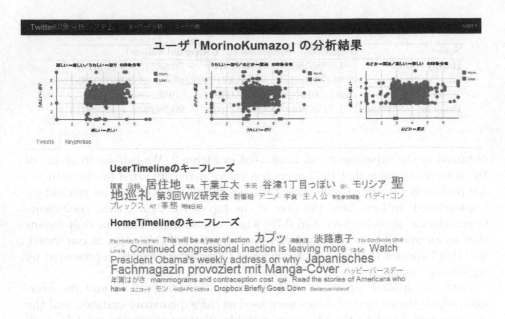

Fig. 3. Results of user analysis

3.6 Generating Scatter Plots

The system generates three scatter plots from the impression values of the tweets using the Google Chart API to visualize the impression-based preference of a Twitter user. That is, a plot for impression values in "Happy – Sad" and "Glad – Angry," one for "Glad – Angry" and "Peaceful – Strained," and one for "Peaceful – Strained" and "Happy – Sad" are generated. In each scatter plot, tweets on a User TL are indicated by red plots, and those on a Home TL by blue plots.

4 Implementation as Web Application

Our proposed system has been implemented as a web application system. This section provides a snapshot to show how the proposed system works.

A snapshot of the screen displayed when we specified @MorinoKumazo, one of the authors, as the target user is shown in Figure 3. Three scatter plots are displayed at the top of the screen. Scatter plots for impression values in "Happy – Sad" and "Glad – Angry", for impression values in "Glad – Angry" and "Peaceful – Strained," and for impression values in "Peaceful – Strained" and "Happy – Sad" are on the left, in the middle, and on the right, respectively. Keyphrases extracted from User and Home TLs are displayed separately in tag cloud form at the lower part of the screen. The system's user can view the tweets that were classified into the impression scale she or he selected, instead of using keyphrases.

5   Conclusion

In this paper, we presented a web application system for visualizing impression-based preferences of Twitter users. When a person specifies the account name of a Twitter user as input to the system, the system checks and visualizes the type of tweets the specified user usually views or posts. The target impressions are limited to those represented by three bipolar scales of impressions: "Happy – Sad," "Glad – Angry," and "Peaceful – Strained." With the system, a person can easily grasp the impression-based preferences of the specified user. The system also extracts twenty keyphrases from each of the user and home timelines of the specified user and presents the commonalities and differences of the two timelines. This helps people to identify the topics that interest the specified user.

Our future work is as follows. Since the impression mining method we used in the proposed system was designed for quantifying impressions of news articles [2], the effectiveness of the method for tweets has not been verified. Many ungrammatical sentences, short sentences consisting of one or two words, and Twitter-dependent expressions, such as face marks and Internet slang words, are observed in tweets. We therefore consider that the current lexicon-based approach to impression mining is not suitable for such tweets. Now we are planning to design and develop an impression mining method suitable for tweets. Impression scales should also be redesigned according to impressions to be extracted from tweets. In addition, we will design a followee recommendation system by expanding the proposed system.

Acknowledgment. This work was supported by JSPS KAKENHI Grant Number 24500134 and donations from Masaharu Fukuda.

References

1. Documentation — Twitter Developers, https://dev.twitter.com/docs
2. Kumamoto, T., Kawai, Y., Tanaka, K.: Improving a Method for Quantifying Readers' Impressions of News Articles with a Regression Equation. In: Proc. of the 2nd Workshop on Computational Approaches to Subjectivity and Sentiment Analysis, Portland, Oregon, USA, pp. 87–95 (2011)
3. Kumamoto, T.: Design of Impression Scales for Assessing Impressions of News Articles. In: Yoshikawa, M., Meng, X., Yumoto, T., Ma, Q., Sun, L., Watanabe, C. (eds.) DASFAA 2010. LNCS, vol. 6193, pp. 285–295. Springer, Heidelberg (2010)
4. Yahoo! Keyphrase Extraction API – Yahoo! Developers, http://developer.yahoo.co.jp/webapi/jlp/keyphrase/v1/extract.html
5. Google Charts – Google Developers, https://developers.google.com/chart/
6. Mathioudakis, M., Koudas, N.: TwitterMonitor: Trend Detection over the Twitter Stream. In: Proc. of the ACM SIGMOD International Conference on Management of Data, Indianapolis, USA, pp. 1155–1158 (2010)
7. Abel, F., Gao, Q., Houben, G.-J., Tao, K.: Twitter-Based User Modeling for News Recommendations. In: Proc. of the 23rd International Joint Conference on Artificial Intelligence, Beijing, China, pp. 2962–2966 (2013)

8. Sakaki, T., Okazaki, M., Matsuo, Y.: Earthquake Shakes Twitter Users: Real-time Event Detection by Social Sensors. In: Proc. of the 19th International Conference on World Wide Web, Raleigh, North Carolina, USA, pp. 851–860 (2010)
9. Weng, J., Lim, E.-P., Jiang, J., He, Q.: TwitterRank, Finding Topic-Sensitive Influential Twitterers. In: Proc. of the Third ACM International Conference on Web Search and Data Mining, New York, USA, pp. 261–270 (2010)
10. Sadilek, A., Kautz, H., Bigham, J.P.: Finding Your Friends and Following Them to Where You Are. In: Proc. of the Fifth ACM International Conference on Web Search and Data Mining, Seattle, USA, pp. 723–732 (2012)
11. Pennacchiotti, M., Gurumurthy, S.: Investigating Topic Models for Social Media User Recommendation. In: Proc. of the 20th International Conference Companion on World Wide Web, Hyderabad, India, pp. 101–102 (2011)
12. Watabe, S., Miyamori, H.: Twitter User Recommender: The User Recommendation System Using the Favorite Function of Twitter. In: Proc. of the Forum on Data Engineering and Information Management, No. B3-4, Kobe, Japan (2012)
13. Pang, B., Lee, L.: Seeing Stars: Exploiting Class Relationships for Sentiment Categorization with Respect to Rating Scales. In: Proc. of the Annual Meeting on Association for Computational Linguistics, Morristown, USA, pp. 115–124 (2005)
14. Lin, K.H.-Y., Yang, C., Chen, H.-H.: Emotion Classification of Online News Articles from the Reader's Perspective. In: Proc. of the IEEE/WIC/ACM International Conference on Web Intelligence and Intelligent Agent Technology, vol. 1, pp. 220–226 (2008)
15. Kiyoki, Y., Kitagawa, T., Hayama, T.: A Metadatabase System for Semantic Image Search by a Mathematical Model of Meaning. ACM SIGMOD Record 23(4), 34–41 (1994)
16. Ohno, S., Hamanishi, M. (eds.): Ruigo-Kokugo-Jiten. Kadokawa Shoten Publishing Co.,Ltd., Tokyo (1986)
17. Kurohashi, S., Nakamura, T., Matsumoto, Y., Nagao, M.: Improvements of Japanese Morphological Analyzer JUMAN. In: Proc. of the International Workshop on Sharable Natural Language Resources, Nara, Japan, pp. 22–28 (1994)

A New Approach to Exploring Spatiotemporal Space in the Context of Social Network Services[*]

Jae-Gil Lee[1], Kun Chang Lee[2,**], and Dong-Hee Shin[3,**]

[1] Department of Interaction Science, Sungkyunkwan University, Seoul, Republic of Korea
firstmage@skku.edu
[2] Business School, Sungkyunkwan University, Seoul, Republic of Korea
kunchanglee@gmail.com
[3] Department of Interaction Science, Sungkyunkwan University, Seoul, Republic of Korea
dshin@skku.edu

Abstract. This paper proposes a new approach for exploring contextual information in social network services (SNS) such as Facebook. With the explosion of SNSs on the internet, it is becoming increasingly necessary for users to search for appropriate information in the contextual space of SNSs. However, conventional methods to accomplish this task, which are based on 2D browsing mechanisms, are inefficient for those attempting to find the right information in the contexts of SNSs in a timely manner. To help users overcome this inefficiency, this paper proposes TARDIS (Time and Relative Dimension in Space), where a 3D hand gesture interface is available to enhance users' perceived satisfaction.

Keywords: Social network, 3D gesture, Space-time cube, HCI.

1 Introduction

In this age of mobile access to the internet, the amount of data that contain both temporal and spatial properties has increased. Many services, such as locally-based services, life-tracking services, and social network services (SNSs) are good examples. The latter are especially popular and it is likely that the SNS phenomenon will continue to expand. Therefore, it is useful to discuss how to display such information on the screen and how to interact with it.

Traditionally, most services display spatiotemporal data separately. Temporal data are displayed as a virtual line on the screen (Fig. 1a). In most cases, the upper portion of the screen represents current time and the lower portion represents past time, because humans typically think about time in terms of space. Spatial data are displayed directly on a geographical map (Fig. 1b) and location-based events are represented by markers on the map. This method is widely used and intuitive. However, it can be a problem

---

[*] This research was supported by the Ministry of Education, Korea, under the Brain Korea 21 Plus Project (Grant No. 10Z20130000013).
[**] Corresponding authors.

G. Meiselwitz (Ed.): SCSM 2014, LNCS 8531, pp. 221–228, 2014.

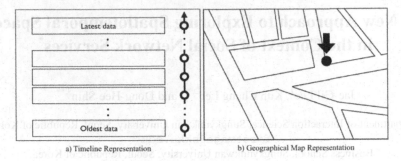

a) Timeline Representation   b) Geographical Map Representation

Fig. 1. Methods for displaying time and location

when temporal data are added to a geographical map, as the upper section of a map usually represents north rather than current time. This can produce cognitive interference.

Some methods are widely used to display time and location data concurrently. Sequential selection or filters are the most common techniques. In this model, the user has to first select location data on the map (Fig. 2a), and then search related data that are filtered by the first selection. While this is a logical process, it is not a convenient one, as it may require considerable time to find exactly what the user wants to see. It is also possible to display both types of data on a divided screen (Fig. 2b). In this model, the user can select a specific time from a concise timeline in one part of the screen. At the same time, the user can explore locations on another part of the screen. This method appears to be ideal; however, the timeline occupies a huge part of the screen and the similar interfaces used to control time and location also may interfere with each other.

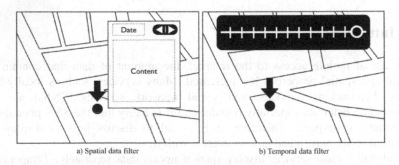

a) Spatial data filter   b) Temporal data filter

Fig. 2. Spatial and temporal data filter

Because temporal and spatial data are both located in the same virtual plane, there is an inevitable interference when both kinds of data are displayed on the same screen. This interference originates from its own information space. In this paper, we propose an efficient way to display both types of data via the construction of a new information space. We also present an intuitive interface for interaction in this information space.

2   Literature Review

2.1   Information Space

As stated above, temporal data are typically represented as a conceptual line on the screen. This is a traditional information space for temporal data. To construct an intuitive information space for data that have spatiotemporal properties, we need to discuss how people recognize time. The domains of space and time are similar in their conceptual structure. People usually think about time using space as a metaphor. The spatial time metaphor is a one-dimensional, rather than a multidimensional, space. This metaphor provides the relational information needed to organize events in time [1]. In our minds, past, present, and future occupy different positions on the line. This can be an intuitive and effective solution for displaying time on a screen. When time is mapped onto the spatial dimension, its distance represents temporal duration, which allows people to estimate temporal duration using spatial distance [2]. It is also possible to predict a specific moment of time using a specific point in the spatial dimension. This means that people do not need to see a visual timeline at all times in order to estimate events in time. Partial information, such as hidden timelines and a midpoint, are sufficient to recognize an event in time. This notion provides a guideline for constructing a timeline in information space.

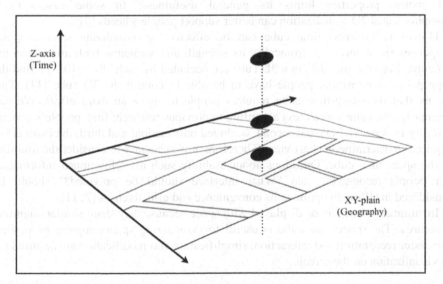

Fig. 3. Concept of 3D space-time cube

A space-time cube (Fig. 2) is a well-known solution for visualizing time on a geographical map. In 1970, Torsten Hägerstrand suggested a framework that used time geography to analyze human activities in a spatiotemporal context. This framework used the concept of a space-time cube. To treat time as essential as space, the framework adopts a 3-dimensional orthogonal coordinate system with time as the third dimension added to a 2D spatial plane [3]. In addition to the 3D framework, the space-time cube consists of an XY-plane geographical map and a Z-axis time line. While traditional geographic information systems (GIS) cannot analyze temporal data due to their limited capability to deal with that dimension, the space-time cube provides a visual relationship between time and space [4]. This benefit makes the space-time cube a useful tool that has been used in many studies to analyze human activity [5, 6, 7].

A specific point in the space-time cube represents a specific event in a database. Data in SNSs that have spatiotemporal properties represent individual human activities. Therefore, SNS databases that represent human activities can be located easily in the space-time cube. In contrast to the traditional space-time cube, in SNSs, the cube must be focused on the visual aspect rather than on the analysis. People who use SNSs should be able to recognize and interact easily with these data.

However, there are some studies that have pointed out the difficulty of using the space-time cube. Gatalsky and his colleagues conducted a study with the space-time cube. Problems arose from the difficulty of detecting the specific data that they wanted, which required much time and concentration [7]. Compared to 2D plane representations, the space-time cube can provide a faster response time in selecting specific data in a complex information space. However, it caused higher error rates than baseline 2D representations [8]. People's general inability to precisely perceive 3D metric properties limits its general usefulness. In some cases, fairly unsophisticated 2D visualization can better support people's needs [9].

However, the space-time cube can be effective in visualizing spatiotemporal properties simultaneously. Ironically, its strength and weakness both arise from the 3D cube. For example, data in a 3D cube are occluded by each other [10]. To find the appropriate composition, people have to be able to control the 3D cube [11]. This means that the space-time cube requires people to make an extra effort. We can summarize the cube's weakness according to previous research: first, people's general inability to perceive 3D data; second, occluded information; and third, the extra effort required to determine the best view. Therefore, it is necessary to consider the usability of the space-time cube. Questions about usability such as: "How much information can people recognize?" and "What interface should be provided?" should be considered in efforts to optimize its convenience and effectiveness [7, 11].

In summary, time can be displayed with space because they share similar cognitive structures. The space-time cube is useful for visualizing spatiotemporal properties. For easier recognition and interaction, simplification and modification are required for its visualization on the screen.

2.2   Interface

It is obvious that current interfaces, such as the mouse and touch screen, are suitable for use in a 2D information space that follows a 2D desktop paradigm. In most cases, they provide an intuitive way to control an information space because such spaces are already optimized for 2D interfaces. However, when these information spaces collide with each other, their interfaces also interfere with each other. At this time, we do not have an effective technology with which to simultaneously interact with time and space. Because we have chosen a 3D concept for information space, it is logical that we need to find an alternative interface, rather than following the traditional 2D-based interface. It is worth mentioning the properties that must be considered for interfaces that control 3D information space.

For decades, direct manipulation has been a fundamental concept in interface design. We believe this is a powerful concept that we would like to use to develop a new form of data interaction. Many useful interfaces, such as the scrollbar, were developed by following this concept. The success of direct manipulation comes from the close relationship between the object that people want to control and the interface used to achieve that control. Thus, objects that are displayed on the screen react to operations through people's physical actions rather than through complex commands. People can see comprehensible and highly related results of their actions immediately. This visibility helps people learn easily. It is also clear that the close relationship reduces people's cognitive effort [12].

The instrumental interaction concept derives from direct manipulation and focuses on experiences in the physical world. It is based on how we naturally use tools to manipulate objects. In this concept, these experiences are applied similarly to information space. It also suggests three properties as criteria: indirection, integration, and compatibility. The degree of indirection means the distance between a person's action and an object's reaction. The degree of integration means how interface is provided naturally. If we use a separated 2-way scrollbar to move a document, it can be scored lower than a touch-screen panning interface. This can be applied to 3D information space and a 3D hand gesture interface. The degree of capability means the similarity between a person's physical action and an object's reaction. For example, if people want to move something to the right, it is better to require a physical trajectory with the same direction [13, 14].

Both methods emphasize the reflection of the user's actions. From these viewpoints, current 2D-based interfaces are not intuitive in controlling a 3D information space. Particularly when people are interacting with spatiotemporal data that have two major properties on a conflicting axis, those axes interfere with each other. This causes cognitive interference and confusion. We propose that a 3D hand gesture interface can provide a more natural and intuitive interaction than a 2D-based interface. Therefore, we chose this interface and demonstrated that it can be suitable for manipulation of data in 3D information space.

To our knowledge, even though there have been many studies to empirically determine intuitive gestures [15, 16], there is no golden rule for intuitive 3D hand gesture interfaces. This might be obvious, because in developing a gesture interface, the objective should not be "to make a generic gesture interface". A gesture interface is not universally the best interface for every application. The objective must be "to develop a more efficient interface" for a given application [17]. This means that custom 3D hand gestures are required to control information space within a specific application.

3   Research Proposal

Based on previous research, we propose to use TARDIS to interact with time in a spatial context. As mentioned above, the 3D cube provides an intuitive concept for spatiotemporal property visualization. It is indisputable that the space-time cube is a powerful tool, but its complexity makes it difficult to use. To compensate for the complexity of the cube, we accepted its concept, but not the entire 3D visualization. Rather than a cube, we chose 2D static maps for visualization with the time axis standing upright on the map. Unlike information space in a traditional space-time cube, we use TARDIS, which has a conceptual time axis that is not displayed directly. Only events on the time axis that are represented as marker icons are displayed.

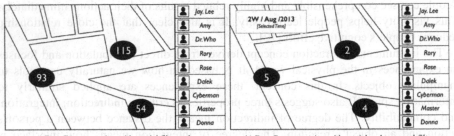

a) Data Representation with spatial filter only   b) Data Representation with spatial and temporal filter

Fig. 4. Displaying data with spatiotemporal filter

A large database is another primary factor in complexity. If all data are displayed on the screen simultaneously, people become confused and may fail to recognize certain data because they cannot be distinguished from others on the screen. To reduce the amount of data displayed simultaneously, spatiotemporal data can be classified by their properties. The goal is to focus on relevant data and omit those that are less important [11]. In many services, the spatial property works as a filter (Fig. 4a). Data are located on a map via the spatial property. When people select a specific location, data that match this spatial property are displayed. It can help people to find entire events that happened at a specific place through time. But people have to search other location points to find specific data, which may require too much effort. For example, the question "Where were you last summer?" cannot be answered easily. In contrast, we propose using the temporal property as a primary data filter (Fig. 4b). Temporal filtering is helpful with numerous events [7]. When only the portion of data matching a selected temporal property is displayed on a map, it reduces complexity and compensates for information loss. In temporal filtering, people see only a portion of the data at each selected time. Moreover, the time axis in TARDIS does not occupy space on the map because it is located vertically on the screen. Finally, it is important to determine the direction of time. In TARDIS, time is moving forward and backward form the user's viewpoint because it is a service to explore the user's past. This means the past is located far from the user.

We chose a 3D hand gesture interface with which to interact with TARDIS. A 3D hand gesture consists of two main aspects: posture and trajectory. We tried to make the best use of trajectory, rather than specific posture, because people have to memorize specific postures to control the data presentation. This also causes physical stress to make its static form [20]. Therefore, the use of posture increases the user's cognitive and physical effort, no matter how simple it is. In contrast, trajectory alone does not require cognitive effort, although fatigue remains a problem. However, fatigue can be relieved via a natural movement of the arm. We simply refer to the hand's position to explore time in TARDIS. Because its movements and the reaction of the information space are so closely linked, people do not have to memorize specific gestures. They simply move their hand and see the relevant result.

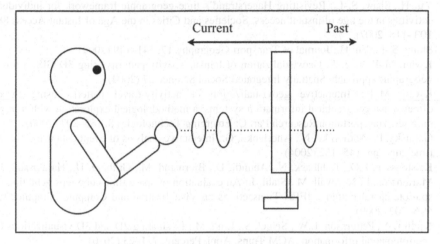

Fig. 5. Concept of TARDIS gesture interface to control timeline

Three types of actions are needed to control maps, content, and time in TARDIS. In this paper, we focus on the time interface because it is the core of the TARDIS interface. When people "grab" the conceptual timeline and pull it from the screen, past data will be displayed on the screen by following its time axis (Fig. 5). The opposite action is also possible. When people push their hand across the screen, current data will be displayed. This gives a more realistic experience of the form of our physical world than does the traditional 2D interface.

4   Concluding Remarks

We have identified a problem in interacting with spatiotemporal data that arises from discordance between an information space and its interface. We discussed the compatibility of the space-time cube in displaying and interacting with spatiotemporal data in SNSs. Moreover, we suggested a way to optimize the method of visualization to provide easier recognition and combined that with a 3D gesture to achieve intuitive interaction. The importance of this study is that its focuses on the usefulness of the space-time cube structure to manage a complex information space on a 2D screen. Future research may be required to verify its efficiency because, currently, TARDIS is simply a conceptual methodology. Development of the actual software and experimental verification of its effectiveness are needed.

References

1. Boroditsky, L.: Metaphoric structuring: Understanding time through spatial metaphors. Cognition 75, 1–28 (2000)
2. Casasanto, D., Boroditsky, L.: Time in the mind: Using space to think about time. Cognition 106, 579–593 (2008)
3. Yu, H., Shaw, S.-L.: Revisiting Hägerstrand's time-geographic framework for individual activities in the age of instant access. Societies and Cities in the Age of Instant Access 88, 103–118 (2007)
4. Shaw, S.-L., Yu, H.: Journal of Transport Geography 17, 141–149 (2009)
5. Kwan, M.-P., Lee, J.: Geovisualization of human activity patterns using 3D GIS: a time-geographic approach. Spatially Integrated Social Science 27 (2004)
6. Kwan, M.-P.: Interactive geovisualization of activity-travel patterns using three-dimensional geographical information systems: a methodological exploration with a large data set. Transportation Research Part C: Emerging Technologies 8, 185–203 (2000)
7. Gatalsky, P., Andrienko, N., Andrienko, G.: Interactive analysis of event data using space-time cube, pp. 145–152 (2004)
8. Kristensson, P.O., Dahlback, N., Anundi, D., Bjornstad, M., Gillberg, H., Haraldsson, J., Martensson, I., Nordvall, M., Stahl, J.: An evaluation of space time cube representation of spatiotemporal patterns. IEEE Transactions on Visualization and Computer Graphics 15, 696–702 (2009)
9. Kjellin, A., Pettersson, L.W., Seipel, S., Lind, M.: Evaluating 2D and 3D visualizations of spatiotemporal information. ACM Trans. Appl. Percept. 7, 1–23 (2010)
10. Tominski, C., Schulze-Wollgast, P., Schumann, H.: 3d information visualization for time dependent data on maps, pp. 175–181 (2005)
11. Kraak, M.-J., Koussoulakou, A.: A visualization environment for the space-time-cube. In: Developments in Spatial Data Handling, pp. 189–200 (2005)
12. Shneiderman, B.: Direct Manipulation: A Step Beyond Programming Languages. Computer 16, 57–69 (1983)
13. Beaudouin-Lafon, M.: Instrumental interaction: an interaction model for designing post-WIMP user interfaces. Presented at the CHI 2000: Proceedings of the SIGCHI Conference on Human Factors in Computing Systems, New York, USA (April 2000)
14. Beaudouin-Lafon, M.: Designing interaction, not interfaces. In: Conference on Advanced Visual Interfaces (2004)
15. Bordegoni, M., Hemmje, M.: A Dynamic Gesture Language and Graphical Feedback for Interaction in a 3D User Interface. Computer Graphics Forum 12, 1–11 (1993)
16. Epps, J., Lichman, S., Wu, M.: A study of hand shape use in tabletop gesture interaction. Presented at the CHI 2006 Extended Abstracts, New York, USA (April 21, 2006)
17. Nielsen, M., Störring, M., Moeslund, T.B., Granum, E.: A procedure for developing intuitive and ergonomic gesture interfaces for HCI. In: Camurri, A., Volpe, G. (eds.) GW 2003. LNCS (LNAI), vol. 2915, pp. 409–420. Springer, Heidelberg (2004)

How Do Users Express Their Emotions Regarding the Social System in Use? A Classification of Their Postings by Using the Emotional Analysis of Norman

Marília S. Mendes[1], Elizabeth Furtado[2], Vasco Furtado[2], and Miguel F. de Castro[1]

[1] Federal University of Ceará (UFC), Fortaleza, CE, Brazil
[2] University of Fortaleza (Unifor), Fortaleza, CE, Brazil
{mariliamendes,elizabethsfur,furtado.vasco}@gmail.com,
miguel@great.ufc.br

Abstract. Social Networking Sites (SNS) allow users to post messages about any event which has occurred with them, including the system itself. In this study, we conducted two experiments with postings of users on SNS in order to investigate (i) how users express their emotions regarding the use of the system, and (ii) how to assess the user experience by using their postings during the system interaction. The results showed some characteristics of postings related to the use which may be useful for UX evaluation in SNS.

Keywords: Human Computer Interaction, User eXperience, Natural Processing Language, Social Network Sites.

1   Introduction

The field of Human Computer Interaction (HCI) has suggested various methods for evaluating systems in order to improve their usability and User eXperience (UX). The advent of Web 2.0 has allowed the development of applications marked by collaboration, communication and interaction among their users in a way and on a scale never seen before [4]. Social Networking Sites (SNS) (e.g. Twitter, Facebook, MySpace, LinkedIn, etc.) are examples of such applications. These are websites which allow users to create their own profile page with information about themselves (either real or virtual), in order to establish public connections and communicate with other members [7].

SNS have features such as: frequent exchange of messages, spontaneity and expression of feelings [26]. Such aspects have even encouraged the creation of new features in these systems in order to encourage the expression of emotions by its users. Facebook, for instance, has recently released a new tool for inserting emoticons into status updates [11]. The idea is to let users express their emotions (what they are feeling) in a more visual way. Twitter, meanwhile, has provided new search options, including searching for positive or negative   postings[1].

---

[1] https://twitter.com/search-advanced

G. Meiselwitz (Ed.): SCSM 2014, LNCS 8531, pp. 229–241, 2014.

According to Zhao, Sosik and Cosley [34], the opportunities and challenges posed by these types of applications require the traditional evaluation methods to be reassessed, considering these new characteristics. For instance, the postings of users on SNS reveal their opinions on various issues, including on what they think of the system [25]. In [24, 26], a collection of postings from users is presented as an interesting technique for supporting the evaluation of UX in SNS. Such technique has as major advantage to capture the user spontaneity at the moment they are using the system. Although several studies have worked on the evaluation of UX in SNS, no studies were found directing their focus towards analyzing the postings of users about the system in use.

The objective of this work is to investigate how users express their emotions regarding the system through their postings in order to support the UX evaluation in SNS. Such postings have been freely and spontaneously made by users while they were using the system. In order to achieve this goal, we conducted two research studies in three SNS, and some characteristics of postings related to the use were found relevant for the UX evaluation in SNS.

This paper is organized as follows: in the next section, the UX evaluation techniques during the use of the system are presented. In the third section, the postings regarding the system in use in SNS are described. In the fourth section, the emotional analysis in SNS is addressed. In the fifth and sixth sections, the investigative studies are described, followed of results, discussion, conclusions and future work.

2   UX Evaluation During the Use of the System

As reported by ISO 9241 - 210:2008 [20], UX is defined as: "the perceptions and responses of users resulting from the use and / or anticipated use of a product, system or service". Some studies [5, 14, 31] have raised questions about the difference between the concepts of usability and UX, stressing that the usability techniques make use of metrics which are difficult to define in UX reviews [5, 31], thus leading to different concerns during the development phase. For Bevan [5], the typical concerns of usability include: assessing the efficacy, efficiency, comfort, satisfaction and learning ability of users, in order to identify and correct problems of usability to make the product easy to use. On the other hand, UX is concerned with understanding and designing the user experience with a product and with identifying and evoking emotional responses from users [5, 13].

Based on this context and focusing on the techniques for evaluating UX, particularly those evaluating the UX at the time when it is being used in the system, the following techniques are used [6]: Experience Sampling Method (ESM), Activity Sampling Experience, Experience sampling triggered by events, Tracking Real Time User Experience (TRUE) and Sensual Evaluation Instrument (SEI). These will be discussed in the next paragraphs.

ESM is a technique which requests participants to stop at certain points so that they can make notes about their experience in real time [9]. One of its features consists in contacting users at various unexpected times and not necessarily with the same frequency, promoting a more realistic view of the interaction with the system, thus preventing the user from "preparing to conduct a test". As reported by the site All about UX [1], a drawback of this technique is that the break point may be inappropriate to report the user experience. At this point, the user cannot use the system, and disrupting their experience can trigger negative emotions for them.

The Activity Experience Sampling method collects samples of momentary experiences in the natural environment of the user, such as, for instance, the use of diaries reporting their experience [30]. The Experience sampling triggered by events technique is a variation of these techniques, but it captures users events during their use by means of a tool [12, 21, 27].

TRUE assists the assessor in tracking user behavior, by digitally monitoring the interaction between the user and the system, through recording on video, and can merge behavioral data and user attitudes regarding the system [22].

SEI is a technique designed to provide a flexible non-verbal communication channel between user and designer during the system development. Users express their feelings through hand carved objects, indicating how they feel when interacting with a system [19].

Although the aforementioned techniques are interesting for evaluating the UX during its use, this work considers the context of use in SNS, in which there are features such as frequent and spontaneous exchange of messages between users. In ESM technique, users will report the use to experts. It is believed that the spontaneous way of describing a use problem to a friend is different from a description to an expert. Moreover, the SNS predominant language consists of written texts. The events collected from users may be interesting for analysis of characteristics such as metrics for satisfaction, efficacy or errors in the system, but the texts may allow the expression of emotions of users [2, 8].

3   Postings Regarding the System in Use in SNS

In previous studies [24, 25], experiments on Twitter were performed in order to examine the postings related to the use of the system. In these studies, a tool for extracting postings was used [24] and the following extraction patterns were proposed: the name of the system or of its features, both isolated and in combination with nouns, adjectives, adverbs and question marks. Related and unrelated postings as for the use of the system were returned. For instance, by using the patterns: "system name = Twitter" + "noun =   problem", the following posting regarding the use of the system was obtained: "*My **Twitter** has some **problem** - it's repeating my tweets*", but also a posting not related to the use of the system was returned: "*I'd love to spend more time on **Twitter**, but the **problem** is that I have to study*".

In [25], 5 types of postings related to the use of the system are noted: complaints, compliments, questions, suggestions and comparisons. Such postings reveal several user intentions, such as: the user will either criticize or praise the system, or they will make questions, or suggest or give solutions or even compare the system to another system they know. In the postings, they generally use the name of the system or of its features, although such patterns not always characterize a posting about the use of the system.

However, more information is still needed in order to understand **how** users express their emotions regarding the system in use through their postings outlined in this system. What are their goals when making a posting about the system in use? Venting? Finding a solution? How to evaluate their experience through their postings? Therefore, the need came for a deeper search for postings regarding emotional characteristics.

4   Emotional Analysis

Emotions are an important factor of life and play an essential role for understanding user behavior when interacting with the computer [18]. Hume [17] made a distinction between affect, emotions and moods, as follows: Affect is a generic term that covers a broad range of feelings that people experience. It is an umbrella concept that encompasses both emotions and moods; Emotions are intense feelings that are directed at someone or something; and Moods are feelings that tend to be less intense than emotions and that often (though not always) lack a contextual stimulus [17].The author also states that there are dozens of emotions, including anger, contempt, enthusiasm, envy, fear, frustration, disappointment, embarrassment, disgust, happiness, hate, hope, jealousy, joy, love, pride, surprise, and sadness.

Ekman [10], on the other hand, limits the amount of emotions to six basic emotions: Happiness, Sadness, Surprise, Fear, Disgust and Anger, readily accepted by other authors, considering that the others are combinations of these [32]. Thelwall, Wilkinson and Uppal [32] observed that, from the perspective of felt human experiences rather than at the neurological or descriptive levels, it seems there are two fundamental dimensions rather than a range of differing kinds of emotions. The authors state that the valence of an experienced emotion is the degree to which it is strongly positive or negative and that the level of arousal felt is the amount of energy perceived (e.g., from lethargic to hyperactive) [32]. Voeffray [33] considers that positive and negative emotions influence products consumption and decision-making understanding, thus being crucial for measuring emotional expression.

Another view of emotion is presented by Norman [28]. In his studies on emotion, the author characterized the affective behavior of humans in three levels of processing: Visceral, Behavioral and Reflective. Since the Visceral level is automatic, pre-programmed and fast, it quickly distinguishes what is good or bad, safe or dangerous, and sends the appropriate signals to the muscles, alerting the rest of the brain; Behavioral level is where one finds the greatest part of human behavior, responsible for performing activities of daily behavior; and the reflective level is the highest layer (contemplative part) of the brain, which reflects on the behavioral level and tries to influence it [28].

According to Maitland and Chalmers [23], the motivation of users to post messages is based on the support received by their contacts, such as advice in difficult times. On the other hand, Preece, Rogers and Sharp [29] state that, when users are annoyed or angered by something new, they tend to overreact, by typing things they would not even dream of saying in person. According to Norman [28], a user first reacts emotionally to a situation before evaluating it cognitively. In this sense, would a posting of the user regarding the system come before or after the user reflection?

In the next sections, the two investigations carried to analyze users' postings will be described. The first research aims to differentiate postings according to their expressed emotions, considering the following question: In systems review, would only the postings expressing some kind of emotion be useful? The second investigation has a relationship with the emotional model of Norman, sorting postings according to their intentions in the system, by using the following question: what behavior motivates the user to post a message about the system?

5   First Investigation

The first investigation of this work was to examine postings related to the use of the system from users in SNS, aiming to distinguish postings expressing some (positive or negative) sentiment from those not expressing any (neutral). The objective of this investigation was to assess the need for further study in order to analyze how users express their emotions regarding the system through their postings during the system use.

5.1   Participants

Three experts at usability (active researchers in academia) were requested to read and classify users postings.

5.2   Procedure

The research was conducted with three SNS: Twitter[2], Facebook[3] e Virtual Fans[4]. Twitter and Facebook are two popular SNS covering users who have distinct objectives and post messages regarding various topics. The Virtual Fan (VF) gathers fans of Brazilian soccer teams, providing its users with tools for mapping, interaction and search for relevant information about their team. In the three websites there is a main page ("Home" for Twitter, "home" or "News Feed" for Facebook, and "teasing zone" for VF) in which users post messages (on any subject) to all their contacts.

Data collection was performed as follows: from the main page of each SNS, we extracted public postings from users by using a data extraction tool [24] in April

---

[2] https://twitter.com/
[3] https://www.facebook.com/
[4] http://torcidas.esporte.ig.com.br/

2013. The filters used were the name of the system or of its features, for instance: in order to extract postings from Twitter, we used Twitter, Tweets, Followers and Following; as for Facebook, we used: Facebook, timeline, events and photo; as for Virtual Fans, we used: Virtual Fans, fans, virtual, VF, points, website and friends. Not all postings obtained were related to the use of the system, so we selected the first 100 postings related to the use for each of the three systems. Each participant was designated to one of the three systems and analyzed 100 postings, classifying them into two categories: with and without emotion.

5.3   Results

As a result, we obtained postings with the following characteristics (See Table 1):

Table 1. Classification of postings according to the emotion level observed

SNS	With emotion	Without emotion
Twitter	**71% of the postings** *"I looooooove it when I feel like making my postings, and then I get a server error!"* *"HATE the new Twitter feel!!!"*	**29% of the postings** *"My Twitter has a problem. It doesn't let me put a gif into the icon."* *"When will we have the edit function on twitter?"* *"I always type everything with errors and only see them after posted";*
Facebook	**69% of the postings** *"This is torture!! Such a wonderful tool for what it could provide us, but its usability is terrible!!!!!!! Wake up Facebook!!"*	**51% of the postings** *"How can I hide this time line?"* *"Hey guys, how do I filter my feed to only see moments from my Inner Circle?"*
Virtual Fans	**37% of the postings** *"I'm already in love with this website!!"* *"<bad language> the Virtual Fans was the best site in Brazil!! What happened to the website???"*	**63% of the postings** *"Does anybody know how to get points by inviting friends?"*

In the three systems analyzed, we obtained postings both with and without emotional content.In this analysis, we observed that those messages with greater emotional content are usually meant to criticize or praise the system, but generally without explaining why. Postings with lower emotional content (neutral) are those in which users report the system problems.

Based on the postings analyzed and by creating a relationship with emotional analysis of Norman, we reach the following relationship (See Table 2).

Table 2. Postings classification according to the emotional analysis of Norman

Emotional processing level	Classification of postings about the use of SNS
Visceral	Impulsive Posting, generally more emotional, with the primary purpose to criticize / praise the system or its functionalities.
Behavioral	Postings more focused on the use of the system, aiming to report precisely the problem or question solutions.
Reflective	Postings with lower emotion level and more focused on finding a solution to a problem or on providing use suggestions to the system.

Based on this result, we initiated a second investigation, explained in the next section.

6   Second Investigation

Our second investigation aimed to classify postings related to use of the system into the following types: Visceral, Behavioral and Reflective, by following the rules explained in Table 2.

6.1   Participants

The participants team was composed of four experts at usability. Three of them were the same who worked in the first investigation, and the fourth one was invited to participate in the second investigation.

6.2   Procedure

The research was conducted on 1452 postings related to the system in use, made by Twitter public users and obtained from a previous work [25]. The postings had been classified into 5 pre-defined categories: complaints, compliments, questions, suggestions and comparisons, and had the following number of postings: 944, 212, 60, 58 and 178, respectively. The classification process was as follows: 2 participants classified the postings separately, and the other two analyzed both classifications and validated the results.

6.3   Results

As a result of the 1452 postings analyzed, the type of postings with the highest proportion was Visceral (61%), followed by Behavioral (33%) and Reflective (5%) (See Figure 1). Some examples of postings for each processing level are shown in Table 3.

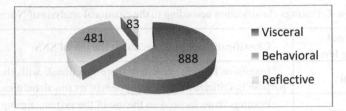

Fig. 1. Postings obtained through processing levels

Table 3. Emotional processing level in postings regarding the use of SNS

Type of Posting	Representation of the analyzed postings
Visceral	*(P1) "I'm upset by Twitter, it's been returning errors all day long :("* *(P2)"Ahhh, I'd rather use Twitter!!! I don't even care about the other social media anymore!!!"* *(P3) "Is it only over here that Twitter's been returning error?"* *(P4) "Is Twitter full of bugs today, or am I going crazy?"* *(P5) "My twitter doesn't work, what the <bad language>"* *(P6) "Twitter has been even more unbearable lately.."*
Behavioral	*(P7) "Twitter, what's the matter with you... Why don't you simply let me use the question mark!!!"* *(P8) "Few things get me upset as much as this message: The following download is not available"* *(P9) "Cool thing being able to press enter on Twitter"* *(P10) "It's been a while since Twitter interface has changed and I still can't find where to click"* *(P11) "Yesterday I was checking the people I follow and I realized I'm not following a lot of people I used to over here. Is that a bug on Twitter?"* *(P12) "My twitter is very bad today, I sometimes can't RT and I gotta refresh the page all the time"* *(P13) "It's been returning errors whenever I try to tweet from my cell phone"* *(P14) "My Twitter has a problem, it's been repeating my tweets"* *(P15) "How many followers does it show that I have? Because there's a bug here"*
Reflective	*(P16) "You know what I miss on Twitter? An easy way to find the first tweets of each account."* *(P17) "I think it wouldn't be bad if they changed twitter interface on android, would it?"* *(P18) "Does anybody know a website or app for making postings simultaneously on twitter, google+ and facebook?"* *(P19) "Suggestion for Twitter: provide an edition button. This way we won't need to erase everything just because of a single mistake."* *(P20) "I guess I'm in love with Twitter rather than with facebook, since there on facebook I don't express myself soooo much *-*"*

All of the 1452 postings were classified into types of postings at each level, as shown in Figure 2.

Visceral postings P1 - P6 in Table 3 had the following types (See Figure 2): complaints (586), compliments (157), comparisons (135) and questions (10). No suggestion fit at this level. Users complain, praise or make comparisons in the system demonstrating emotion, but usually without specifying what the error is (P1, P3) / what the problem is (P4), why they prefer Twitter (P2), why the system does not work (P5) or why the system is unbearable (P6). Throughout the postings, users did not express any need to find a solution / or for an explanation.

As examples of behavioral postings, P7-P15 (Table 3), we found the following types (See Figure 2): complaints (348), compliments (61), comparisons (24) and questions (10). Again, no postings regarding suggestions were classified at this level. However, in postings (P7, P8 and P12), users show some emotion as for the system use and explain the problem (P7, P14), the error (P12, P13), the reason for satisfaction (P9) or dissatisfaction (P10), or even to express the need to find a solution (P11, P15).

As examples of reflective postings, we have postings P16-P20. At such level, we found the following types of postings (See Figure 2): comparisons (15) and suggestions (58). These suggestions are based on the reflection of the system use. In posting P20 we can still see the added value the system provides and which was described by the user.

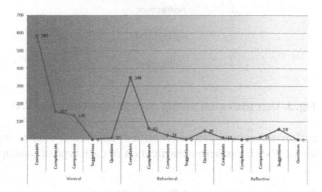

Fig. 2. Users goals when posting messages regarding the system in use

7   Implication for the UX Analysis

Based on these investigations, in this section we analyze the implication of the results of this study for the development of a new model of UX emotional evaluation in SNS. This model would provide the perceptions and needs of users as for the system examined through textual analysis of their postings.

A possible research would be on the more relevant type of posting, depending on the objectives of the system assessors, which could be:

- In order to identify the user satisfaction/dissatisfaction level as for the system, postings with higher emotion content, of visceral type, would be more relevant;

- as for identifying the problems of use of the system under analysis, the postings of behavioral type would be more important; and
- for analysis of suggestions or solutions, postings of reflective type would be more significant.

The results used for the analysis of this new model are:

All of these three levels of postings representing the user emotional behavior are important for emotional evaluation of SNS, specifically the emotions that the system evokes to its users. Even though the emotional field is stronger in the visceral level, a lot of visceral postings may not have efficient results for problem identification. In this analysis, we observed that people express their emotion regarding the system or a system error, but not always specify this error. It is an outburst, an impulsive posting with the sole purpose of representing their emotions at that time. One characteristic observed by analysis of the postings was that the more the user expresses their emotion in a post, the less they demonstrate interest in obtaining a solution; otherwise, when they focus on reaching a solution, they do not show much emotion, characterizing reflective postings (See Figure 3).

Fig. 3. User goals when posting messages about the use of SNS

Other types of investigations can be identified, but further studies are still needed on the interaction of SNS for pattern classification of each type of posting.

8   Final Considerations and Future Work

This study aimed to investigate how users express their emotions through their postings regarding the system. To this end, we conducted two studies with SNS in order to find relevant features for UX in SNS. We observed that users, when posting on the system in use, have distinct objectives, such as: venting, finding a solution or even suggesting solutions to the system. It is up to the evaluators to decide the purpose of the assessment system.

Hedegaard and Simonsen [16] propose a tool for evaluating the usability and UX of products from reviews websites. We believe that the user posture in a website for products evaluation is different from that when they are using a system and then face a problem and decide to report it to vent or even to suggest a solution. The authors stated that, from their study, revisions from the Internet, in general, possibly do not seem to contain very detailed information on specific situations of use or measurements. They state that no critic will ever write as follows: *"The number of mouse click to navigate from the start screen to the functionality I want is 7, and that this is an-noying"*. However, in our experiments, we found postings relating exactly specific information about the use, such as: *"Folks, sorry, but I've just had a problem here on Twitter and since then I can't use punctuation once it opens a Twitter menu whenever I try to"*, which also characterizes the fact that the user may report the error in the own system in use.

Another important point to be considered in UX evaluation for the collection of postings on SNS is the possibility that a comment from a user encourages other users to comment as well. We refer to the "emotional contagion" [15, 3]. Such factor can have its advantages and disadvantages. A disadvantage is the possibility that some comments do not represent the real motivation of the user while posting, but an advantage is that it would allow more descriptions of problems of use.

Also, no study was conducted as for identifying the type of user who posts visceral messages, or as for those who are more interested in solving problems and providing solutions to the system. In future work, we will study these users, as well as their characteristics (age, gender and preferences). We also intend to include the features found through our extraction tool in order to automatically select these data and perform validation testing with users.

References

1. All about UX - Information for user experience professionals, http://www.allaboutux.org/
2. Asiaee, T.A., Tepper, M., Banerjee, A., Sapiro, G.: If you are happy and you know it.. tweet. In: 21st ACM International Conference on Information and Knowledge Management, Maui, USA (2012)
3. Barsade, S.G.: The ripple effect: Emotional contagion and its influence on group behavior. Administrative Science Quarterly 47(4), 644–677 (2002)
4. Becker, K., Tumitan, D.: Introdução à Mineração de Opiniões: Conceitos, Aplicações e Desafios. In: Simpósio Brasileiro de Banco de Dados (2013)
5. Bevan, N.: What is the difference between the purpose of usability and user experience evaluation methods? In: 12th IFIP TC13 Conference on Human-Computer Interaction, Uppsala, Sweden (2009)
6. Bollena, J., Maoa, H., Zengb, X.: Twitter mood predicts the stock market. Journal of Computational Science (2011)
7. Boyd, D., Ellison, N.: Social network sites: Definition, history, and scholarship. Journal of Computer-Mediated Communication (2007)
8. Brooke, J.: A semantic approach to automated text sentiment analysis. PHD Thesis, Simon Fraser University (2009)
9. Consolvo, S., Walker, M.: Using the Experience Sampling Method to Evaluate Ubicomp Applications (2003)
10. Ekman, P.: An argument for basic emotions. Cognition and Emotion 6(3/4), 169–200 (1992)
11. Engadget, http://www.engadget.com/2013/04/09/facebook-emotion-selection-tool/

12. Fetter, M., Gross, T., Schirmer, M.: CAESSA: Visual Author-ing of ContextAware Experience Sampling Studies. In: ACM SIGCHI Conference on Human Factors in Computing Systems, Vancouver, BC, Canada (2011)
13. Furtado, E., Furtado, V., Vasconcelos, E.: A Conceptual Framework for the Design and Evaluation of Affective Usability in Educational Geosimulation Systems. In: Baranauskas, C., Abascal, J., Barbosa, S.D.J. (eds.) INTERACT 2007. LNCS, vol. 4662, Part I, pp. 497–510. Springer, Heidelberg (2007)
14. Hassenzahl, M., Tractinsky, N.: User experience - a research agenda, Behaviour & Information Technology (2006)
15. Hatfield, E., Cacioppo, J.L., Rapson, R.L.: Emotional contagion. Current Directions in Psychological Sciences 2, 96–99 (1993)
16. Hedegaard, S., Simonsen, J.G.: Extracting usability and user experience information from online user reviews. In: Proceedings of the SIGCHI Conference on Human Factors in Computing Systems (2013)
17. Hume, D.: Emotions and Moods. In: Robbins, S.P., Judge, T.A. (eds.) Organizational Behavior, pp. 258–297
18. Cristescu, I.: Emotions in human-computer interaction: the role of non-verbal behavior in interactive systems. Revista Informatica Economica (2008)
19. Isbistera, K., Hook, K., Laaksolahtib, J., Sharpa, M.: The sensual evaluation instrument: Developing a trans-cultural self-report measure of affect. Elsevier (2006)
20. ISO DIS 9241 - 210:2008. Ergonomics of human system interaction - Part 210: Human - centred design for interactive systems (formerly known as 13407). International Standardization Organization (ISO). Switzerland
21. Khan, V.J., Markopoulos, P.: Experience Sampling: A workbook about the method and the tools that support it - Eindhoven (2009)
22. Kim, J.H., Gunn, D.V., Schuh, E., Phillips, B.C., Pagulayan, R.J., Wixon, D.: Tracking Real-Time User Experience (TRUE): A comprehensive instrumentation solution for complex systems. In: SIGCHI Conference on Human Factors in Computing Systems (2008)
23. Maitland, J., Chalmers, M.: Designing for peer involvement in weight management. In: SIGCHI Conference on Human Factors in Computing Systems, Vancouver, BC (2011)
24. Mendes, M.S., Furtado, E., Castro, M.F.: Uma investigação no apoio da avaliação da usabilidade em Sistemas Sociais usando Processamento da Linguagem Natural. In: IX Brazilian Symposium in Information and Human Language Technology, Brazil (2013)
25. Mendes, M.S., Furtado, E., Castro, M.F.: Do users write about the system in use? An investigation from messages in Natural Language on Twitter. In: 7th Euro American Association on Telematics and Information Systems, Valparaiso, Chile (2014)
26. Mendes, M.S., Furtado, E., Theophilo, F., Castro, M.F.: A Study about the usability evaluation of Social Systems from messages in Natural Language. In: Congreso Latinoamericano de la Interacción Humano-Computadora, Guanacaste, Costa-Rica (2013)
27. Meschtscherjakov, A., Reitberger, W., Tscheligi, M.: MAESTRO: Orchestrating User Behavior Driven and Context Triggered Experience Sampling. In: Proceedings of the 7th International Conference on Methods and Techniques in Behavioral Research (2010)
28. Norman, D.A.: Emotional Design: Why We Love (or Hate) Everyday Things. Basic Books, New York (2004)
29. Preece, J., Rogers, Y., Sharp, H.: Interaction design: Beyond human-computer interaction. John Wiley & Sons, Inc., New York (2002), ISBN: 0-471-49278-7
30. Riediger, M.: Experience Sampling, http://library.mpib-berlin.mpg.de/ft/mr/MR_Experience_2009.pdf

31. Roto, V., Obrist, M., Väänänen-Vainio-Mattila, K.: User Experience Evaluation Me-thods in Academic and Industrial Contexts. In: User Experience Evaluation Methods in Product Development (2009)

32. Thelwall, M., Wilkinson, D., Uppal, S.: Data mining emotion in social network communication: Gender differences in MySpace. Journal of the American Society for Information Science and Technology 61(1), 190–199 (2010)

33. Voeffray, S.: Emotion-sensitive Human-Computer Interaction (HCI): State of the art - Seminar paper, http://diuf.unifr.ch/main/diva/teaching/seminars/emotion-recognition

34. Zhao, X., Sosik, V.S., Cosley, D.: It's complicated: how romantic partners use facebook. In: ACM SIGCHI Conference on Human Factors in Computing Systems is the Premier International Conference on Human-Computer Interaction, Austin, Texas (2012)

Modelling of Excitation Propagation
for Social Interactions

Darius Plikynas[1], Aistis Raudys[1], and Šarūnas Raudys[2]

[1] Kazimieras Simonavicius University, Research and Development Center
J. Basanaviciaus g. 29A, LT-03109 Vilnius, Lithuania
[2] Vilnius University, Faculty of Mathematics and Informatics
Didlaukio g. 47, LT-08303 Vilnius, Lithuania
darius.plikynas@ksu.lt

Abstract. This paper investigates regularities in excitation information propagation in social interaction. We use cellular automaton approach where it is assumed that social media is composed from tens of thousands of community agents. Each agent can transmit and get a signal from several nearest neighbours. Weighted sums of input signals after reaction delay are transmitted to the closest agents. The model's originality consists in the exploitation of neuron-based agent schema with nonlinear activation function employed to determine the reaction delay, the agent recovery period, and algorithms that define cooperation of several excitable groups. In the grouped model, each agent group can send its excitation signal to other groups. The agents and their groups should acquire diverse media parameters of social media in order to ensure desirable for social media character of excitation wave propagation patterns. The novel media model allows methodical analysis of propagation of several competing novelty signals. Simulations are very fast and can be useful for understanding and control of the simulated human and agent-based social mediums, planning and performing social and economy research.

Keywords: agents based modelling, social medium, excitation waves, grouped populations, propagation of novelties.

1 Introduction

Human beings and the communication instruments' network surrounding them are coming together at various stages, starting from low-level connectivity at verbal or cellular automaton level, to the highest echelons of achieving collective actions. One may hope humans and communications means will coexist as an entangled web in future. The implications of excitation propagation modelling in the simulated agent-based social mediums have a paramount role for the better understanding of modern digitally interconnected social systems behaviour. It provides a possibility to define and find some ways to manage the core digital network parameters, which impede or enable observed local and nonlocal emergent complex social phenomena. For instance, such modelling provides means to simulate and investigate information

G. Meiselwitz (Ed.): SCSM 2014, LNCS 8531, pp. 242–252, 2014.

diffusion properties (e.g. spread of novelties, political campaigns, social norms, etc) in the social-technological mediums depending on the characteristics of the simulated simple agents and their connections [1, 2, 3, 9, 15].

For that reason, a need arises to analyze outcomes of such coexistence just now. One of the possible models for communication network analysis is the excitation wave propagation model already considered earlier in the Chaos theory. To our best knowledge, such approach was not used in social interactions research. This almost universal methodology of signal propagation in an excitable media is the bottom-up approach that is successfully employed in many research disciplines, such as particle physics, micro and cell biology, chemistry, medicine, meteorology, and astrophysics [4], [5], [12], [13], [23], [24], [25]. We propose that this kind of model can be used in analysis of information propagation processes in human-agent based social media too, and can lead to deeper conceptual understanding of the fundamental nature of information dissemination in virtual agent societies. To demonstrate this statement is an objective of the present paper.

This paper is organized as follows. For a simpler explanation of virtual agent population model and for visualization purposes, we describe and extend two-dimensional (2D) cellular grid based, social medium model and its modifications (Section 2). Diverse excitation signal propagation patterns are demonstrated. In Section 3 we introduce a group-based agent model where the agent population is split into the groups. Inside the single group the excitation signals are transmitted only to the neighbouring nodes. Limited interaction of groups, as well as propagation of diverse informational signals, is allowed. In Section 4 we consider propagation of two competing excitations in the grouped agent population. Section 5 summarizes the simulation results and discusses perspectives for the further studies.

2   The Basic Model

2.1   Hexagonal 2 Dimensional Cellular Automaton Model

Below we provide a general type of model. Like in the cellular grid based models, each node is summing input signals transmitted from neighbouring nodes. In the nature inspired model, however, magnitudes of the output signals and their release times depend on sums of the accumulated inputs nonlinearly. To understand main properties of the model easier, at first we present its simplified version: 2-dimensional (2D) hexagonal model (see information transmission schema bellow).

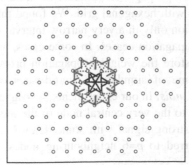

The signal transmission starts from central node as blue marked line arrows show. After refractory period ends, the excitation signals are transferred to further 12 nodes (doted arrows, magenta). In the hexagonal model, each element of the grid is represented by the single layer perceptron (SLP) with six inputs that use weights (connection strengths between the nodes) to calculate a weighted sum of inputs in each node ([8, 16]). In the output of the nodes we have nonlinear sigmoid activation functions that restrict outputs between 0 and 1 (for details see [18]). After refractory period ends each unexcited node can be excited only in cases where the sum of input signals exceeds *apriori* defined sensitivity threshold. A novelty of the model is that the refractory period depends on the magnitude of the node's outputs. It makes the model's behaviour to differential equation and biology inspired excitable medium models that claim "the longer is delay in transfer of the excitation, the greater the node-to-node strength of the signal" [23]. Reaction to the excitation signal and refractory periods are necessary, e.g. to verify obtained information or get used to it. In order to ensure chaotic behaviour of the agents we introduce additional noise while determining coordinates of the nodes and calculation of the nearest neighbours. It is worth noting, that the SLP is a nature inspired model of information processing and has several universality properties [17]. For that reason, on may say that excitable media model considered is partially inspired by nature. Main media parameters are: N_y, a number of nodes in each edge of the hexagonal media, w_1, w_2, ... , w_6, the connection weights, θ^* , sensitivity threshold, the rule and its parameters that determines the refractory period. To realize human-information agent based social media, parameters just mentioned can be common for a group of nodes, or specific for each node, that represents an element of social community (in different applications it can be human being, a group of individuals, economy or political unit, or even a network of information processing and transmitting computer). Depending on the weights, initial excitation, excitation threshold, refractory period, etc. we obtained various excitation propagation patterns.

2.2 Excitation Signal Propagation Patterns in 2D Space

In economy and social hybrid human-computer agent based systems three, four or higher-dimensional models are preferable. Higher dimensionality of the space aggravates visualisation of the wave propagation. Two dimensional illustrations show interesting excitation wave propagation patterns. In simulation studies we performed hundreds of experiments with hexagonal grid. We found that some of the parameters affect the wave propagation only in a very narrow interval of their variation. Outside the interval the wave propagation ceases. In some cases, adequate selection of other parameters value can restore the weight propagation process. In order to introduce non-homogeneity, in some of simulations, coordinates of the model nodes were affected by a small noise, *nois*. In our experiments the triggering of the social medium ($arg_{start} = 0.7$) was made to the very central node of the media model. If excitation is sufficiently powerful, a strong signal with some delay (inspect the basic hexagonal model above) is transferred to $p=6$ neighbouring nodes. Then, each of p already excited nodes transfer their output signals further to 1, 2 or even 3 non-excited nodes. In Fig. 1 *a*, *b*, *c*, and *d* we show four wave propagation patterns. The media models 1*b* and 1d were strictly hexagonal, while coordinates of nodes in models 1a and 1c were shifted randomly in horizontal and vertical directions (level of noise – up to 50% of distances between two adjacent nodes in hexagonal grid) *c*) – non-uniformly. Other parameters of four media models: N = [182, 184, 180 and 178; *weights* = 0.82, 0.7, 0.7, 0.7; refractory period *refr* = [5 29 4 3]; excitation threshold θ*=[0.5 0.6 0.45 0.5]. More examples of excitation wave patterns can be found in figures 2 and 3.

If the weights and initial excitation are small and the excitation threshold is too high (or very small), the wave propagation can cease. In intermediate situations, gaps (non-excited nodes) appear in a circle of excited nodes. If refractory period is lengthy, the gap is fulfilled quickly by excitations from neighbouring nodes. If refractory period is brief, after the excitation the nodes can be excited without lengthy delay. In such cases, the number of non-excited nodes increases quickly and the wave can start propagating backwards. Such situation we observe in the propagation patterns depictured in Fig. 1 *a*, *c* and *d*. In Fig 1*b* we have regular wave propagation starting from the centre towards borders of the media model.   The smaller wave corresponds to t = 100 signal propagation steps, while the outer wave corresponds to t = 300. After reaching the border, this wave ceases.

If weights values are close to 1, almost entire incoming signal can be transferred further. Then we have regular hexagonal-formed signal propagation even in situations where the refractory period is short. Such situation we have in Fig. 2*d*. Dark colour shows freshly (two most recent time periods) excited nodes and lighter colours indicate cells still being in refractory period. Depending of parameters of the media we can observe oscillating wave propagation (Fig.1*a*), chaotic (Fig. 1*c*), or complex regular patterns (Fig. 1*d*).

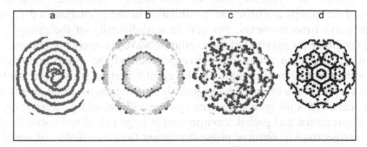

Fig. 1. Diverse wave propagation patterns after *a*) – 160 and 300; *b*), *c*), and *d*) – 215 wave propagation steps in four social medium examples differing in size and other model parameters

For testing these and other simulation results, please, visit our on-line virtual lab (V-lab) at http://vlab.vva.lt/ ; MEPSM1 model, login: Guest, Passw.: guest555). In short, novel for social media investigations approach allowed us to obtain numerous diverse wave propagation patterns observed in the real-world experiments [11], [22].

3   Social Medium Model Composed Of Several Agent Groups

3.1   Multi-Layer Media Model

Analysis of cell behaviours in biology and social organizations of human beings and enterprises show the clustered structure, even their synchronized behaviours. The same is confirmed by theory and by simulations of wave propagation processes (see Section 2.3, also [6]) and other approaches [10]. It is believed that "group interests" are driving forces of evolution in biology and human society. In general, many aspects of nature, biology or even from society have become a part of the techniques and algorithms used in the computer science or they have been used to enhance or hybridize several techniques through an inclusion of advanced evolution, cooperation or biology (see review [7]).

Having this knowledge "in mind" we expanded a *structured schema of agent society*. The socio-technological agents (the nodes in the model) are split into groups with diverse characteristics (parameters of the social medium model). It is assumed that the groups in the different populations are partners and share novel excitation information they get from outside. Inside the single group, the wave excitation and propagation is performed in the way described in Section 2. If a great number of nodes in the single medium (group) exceed a *certain level*, the "group leader" transmits excitation (novelty) signal to "leaders" of other groups of the agent populations (central nodes in the group's media). To determine the "certain level", we selected a fraction $T_{excitation}=0.02$ of the recently excited nodes in a central part of the medium as a criterion to transmit excitation information to other partner groups. The "central part" was characterized by a fraction of total number of the agents to be found excited in this area. In simulations we used $N_{closest}=0.8$. In Fig. 2 we present the wave distribution patterns after $t=200$ and $t=500$ wave propagation steps. In this experiment, we have one group (b) where signal does not fade, and three groups where the signals after reaching the medium edges - vanished. Since the model parameters of the groups are different, annihilation of the excitation in diverse groups occur at different time moments. For that reason, diversity of the groups is almost obligatory condition for survival of the excitation waves in agent population.

Mathematical notation aside, the motivation behind the group approach is very simple. For the simulation of complex social agent-based systems explicit information encoded in the properties of individual agents is not enough, as social agents are not so individual after all. Social agents are open systems influenced by external, i.e. not only local, but also regional and global, environment at large [3]. Novel social media model gives new perspectives to observe phase dependent field-like reality of social medium excitations [22], [14], [3], [15]. These findings guide us to the idea that contextual (implicit) information via mechanism of excitation waves dissipation is distributed in the fields and that fields – although expressing some global information – are locally (mostly unconsciously) perceived by the agents. Based on the above considerations, we foresee further expansion of present information transmission model. One needs to introduce global variables and states of the whole system. In such a simulation, not only local explicit but also global implicit level of contextual information could be captured and effectively exploited [3].

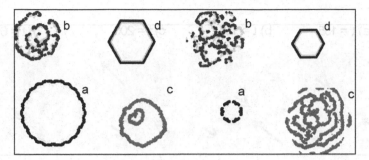

Fig. 2. Wave patterns in 4 (*NG* = 4) agent groups after A) – 200, B) – 500 wave propagation steps. Parameters: sizes N_y =[184 146 124 104]; *weights*=[0.7 0.8 0.7 0.9]; *refractory period refr* =[29 5 4 5]; excitation threshold θ^*=[29 5 4 5].

4 Propagation of Two Competing Signals in Populations of Agents

Evidently, single stimulus excitation is mere simplified?? of the social multi-modal reality. Nevertheless, such reductionism helps us to observe the basic features of the excitation propagation dynamics. In fact, two competing excitation modes are often perceived in social mediums, for instance, competing two major parties, presidential candidates, opposite opinions, genders, states of faith, etc. This naturally happens even in the complex heterogeneous agents' environments, where extreme competition (or cooperation) boils down to only two dominating social excitation states. Hence, two-stimulus modelling reveals from "bottom to top" agents' parameters, which foster observed social behavioural patterns.

4.1 Two Colliding Waves and Their Breakdown

Up to now we considered propagation of the innovation (excitation) signals in an unexcited social medium. In reality, everybody, the human beings, economy and social organizations are already excited by some previous "innovations". In fact, competitive dissemination of innovations takes place, when one innovation is replaced by another one. In order to meet such a multi-excitatory reality, we have to enrich single excitation model with multi-excitatory properties, where several competing signals could be modelled.

Let, for the start, consider single excitable medium model where two signals are starting propagating from different nodes. In the 2D example in Fig. 3 *a* (after *t* =155 propagation time steps) we see two *vis-a-vis* propagating excitation (novelties) waves. Both excitation signals are propagating in strictly hexagonal medium. Relatively short refractory period usually causes chaotic, however periodic, patterns for both propagating signals. After the wave colliding (Fig. 3 *b*, after *t* =161 propagation time steps) almost all nodes near collision area are in their refractory period. Due to small refractory period the excited nodes of both signals can find some nodes just after their

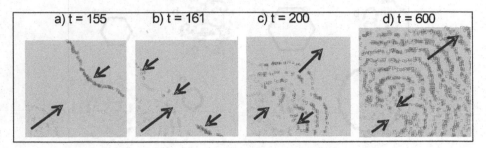

Fig. 3. Annihilations of two colliding waves and their breakdown

refractory period ends. In Fig. 3 *b* we see that signal of red (dark) "squares" "wins" and "cyan (gray) signal is almost dying. In Fig. 3 *c* shows that rotating red (dark) wave is generated and the excitation signal waves are going back. After 600 time periods the red (dark) excitation signal starts dominating almost in all area of the medium space. Wave propagation character remains the same during subsequent 10000 time steps (Fig. 3 *d*).

By changing parameters of the social medium one can watch enormous variety of wave propagating patterns, with one signal outperforming another and one of them dying, slow or rapid swinging of borders between two differently excited areas. Simulations analysis of great entity with a variety of models' parameters can let towards better understanding of wave colliding mechanisms.

4.2 Propagation of Two Signals in the Grouped Population

Like in [10] the authors of this paper assumed at first that novelties signals were rare. In Sections 2, 3 we considered excitation wave propagation in empty non-excited social medium. In previous grouped agent population models, the novel excitation from outside arose just after the end of refractory period in the central area of the nodes. At the present time scientific, technological, political, economy novelties appear rather often. In practical situations, we do not have unexcited economy or social medium. All of them are "full of activity" with some of previous "fruitful" idea.

In order to analyze propagation of two (*EXS*=2) or more excitation signals that appear in different time moments, we expanded the grouped structure of the agent population. In analysis of two, the old and new, excitation signals we considered population composed of *NG* = 4 agent groups. Each group control two excitable social mediums, one medium for propagation for each single innovation signal. Totally, we had to examine wave propagation patterns in 2×*NG* = 8 group medium. To create the model closer to reality problems, we introduced mutual influence of the two groups parameters allocated to each solitary agent group. We supposed that propagation of alternative signal (first four groups of the medium) influences the media parameters of remaining four groups: excitation threshold refractory period, and magnitudes of the weights. In such a way one excitation signal is disturbing propagation of another one. We inspected a variety of scenarios and found a wide assortment of innovative information propagation patterns:

    1) both signals propagate in the population of the groups;

    2) new signal wins or loses, etc.

Variety of possibilities requires a separate large scale study. Two-fold analysis of information propagations in the grouped excitable social media model, however, shows that wave propagation approach can be useful for understanding of distribution of a variety of innovations and controlling their dissemination processes.

5   An Example

As an example of concrete social phenomena we examine high-dimensional financial data used in automated trading [20], [21]. We considered high frequency automated trading systems (ATS) where for decision making we use hundreds or even thousands of investments. In such a case, to develop and train a multi-agent trading system we need thousands of training vectors [21]. Exclusive feature of this financial time series that ATSs sometimes refuse from active investments: a very large part of data consists of zeros. In Fig. 4a we see an example of two trading series, A (stock returns), and B (ATS returns), where up to 70% of days have zero profit and loss.

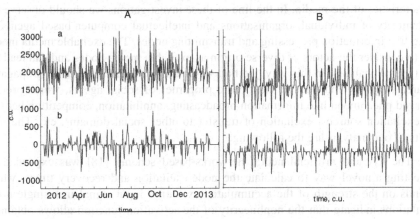

Fig. 4. A - fluctuations of robots' (ATSs'), where a and b profits and losses during 15 months; B - fluctuations of profits simulated by means of excitable media model

Unfortunately, nowadays economic and financial situation is changing very rapidly and two years history (less as 500 trading days) is too long (contains old data). To test primary versions of multi-agent trading schemas we used artificial data generated by using the wave propagation model described in above chapter. Generation of artificial time series was based on the hypothesis that economy and financial world is composed of large number mutually communicating human and computer based actors that interchange novel information in a similar way as considered above in this paper. The excitable media model was composed of six mutually cooperating agent groups of size N_y= 184 with media parameters ensuring steady chaotic behaviour. The example is depictured in Fig. 1c and Fig. 2a. There you see differences between two sums of excitations in two small subgroups of agents (~140 nodes each) represented the financial profit. After introducing the risk factor and ability to refuse from trading we obtained time series (Fig. 4b) similar to that used in real trading (Fig. 4a).

The use of the excitable media model to generate financial time series allows better understanding automated trading. We found that synthetic data is useful for comparison of different decision making schemas. Most important it provides the instrument that can be used for better understanding economical and financial problems. In this task, the connection weights, $w_1, w_2, \ldots, w_p$, characterise influence of discipline in economy and finance. Reaction to the excitation signal and refractory period characterizes eagerness and capability of media to react to the novel information and ability to use it in practice. These subjects will be presented in subsequent publications.

6   Concluding Remarks

In this paper, we have presented a novel information interchanging approach developed to simulate large human-computer interaction social media. Our model provides a bottom-up means to simulate and investigate novel information diffusion properties in the complex human-technology agent media depending on the characteristics of the media. In the line of these investigations we should observe that the majority of individual, organisations and intellectual computer based agents are acting like information processing and transmitting nodes. The excitable media models help to consider the actors of diverse origin as excitable media nodes and can lead to a new type of analysis. In this way, the bottom-up and wave-like excitation propagation research helps to find out the most basic properties of social agents, which produce observed phenomena like information broadcasting, annihilation, competition between few excitation sources, excitation of transfer to other social domains, etc. The main results of our analysis are the following:

1. The CA and artificial neural networks-based schema [18] was expanded by suggesting a novel way to calculate the node excitation and recovery times, which depends on the strength of the accumulated excitation input signal in a single node. Simulations indicate that the nonlinearity of the activation function allows obtaining wave propagation patterns modelled by more complex and more computer time demanding systems of differential equations based model.

2. We broadened the homogeneous medium model to the heterogeneous, which revealed population clustering dynamics and cooperation conditions between different groups. We showed that clustered and diverse nature of population is vital for the overall performance of society.

3. We suggested a structure and the model of the population groups for analysis of dissemination of two or more competing innovation signals. It provides new possibilities to understand which kinds of social media characteristics influence domination of one or another signal.

Our analysis supports the conclusion concerning the branching process of a speciation observed in databases and theoretically explained as a branching process in [10]. In sum, this paper presents a mechanism to parameterize and explore regular uniform, chaotic, spiral, rhythmic oscillations and bursting excitation propagation patterns, which have originated from essentially similar basic properties, namely, agents' propensity to adopt a new behaviour depending on the proportion of some neighbouring reference group that have adopted it before. Modelling excitation wave propagation can be used to generate and analyse various wave propagation patterns in order to determine a set of attributes necessary to register while performing real world sociological surveys.

The agent groups and wave propagation-based model can be expanded in a number of ways. Various agent proximity measures can be applied, simultaneous propagation of several dissimilar information waves can be considered. In joint analysis of human being and computerized agents media we can introduce the global variables and states of the whole system to transmit excitations to distant neighbours. The agents can differ in size, refractory period, importance. The agent groups can be joined into subpopulations with essentially different characteristics. We can form more complex, the multilevel, hierarchical structures of the agent groups and populations. An important, up to now untouched task, is an automated evaluation of the model's parameters. Simulation of media evolution during long sequences of innovations can become a useful instrument here [19].

In the prospective research, though, we plan to simulate and examine concrete social phenomena and seek for task dependant interpretations of single model's parameters or sets of them. We intend to bring into play 2D and 3D visualizations of excitation propagation patterns in the analysis of time series of high-dimensional financial data used in automated trading [20], [21].

Acknowledgments. The research was funded by the European Social Fund following the Global Grant measure program; project No. VP1-3.1-SMM-07-K-01-137.

References

1. Acemoglu, D., Ozdaglar, A., Yildiz, E.: Diffusion of innovations in social networks, Technical Report. Massachusets Institute of Technology (2012)
2. Alkemade, F., Castaldi, C.: Strategies for the diffusion of innovations on social networks. Computational Economics 25, 3–23 (2005)
3. Bandini, S., Federici, M.L., Vizzari, G.: Situated cellular agents approach to crowd modelling and simulation. Cybern. and Syst.: Int. J. 38(7), 729–753 (2007)
4. Ben-Jackob, I.E., Cohen, I.: Cooperative self-organization of microorganisms. Advances in Physics 49(4), 395–554 (2000)
5. Berestycki, H., Rodriguez, N., Ryzhik, L.: Traveling wave solutions in a reaction-diffusion model for criminal activity (2013), http://arxiv.org/ftp/arxiv/papers/1302/1302.4333.pdf

6. Chua, L.O., Hasler, M., Moschyt, G.S., Neirynck, J.: Autonomous cellular neural networks: a unified paradigm for pattern formation and active wave propagation. IEEE Transactions on Circuits and Systems I: Fundamental Theory and Applications 42(10), 559–577 (1995)
7. Cruz, C., González, J.R., Pelta, D.: Optimization in dynamic environments: a survey on problems, methods and measures. Soft Computing - A Fusion of Foundations, Methodologies and Applications 15, 1427–1448 (2011)
8. Haykin, S.: Neural Networks: A comprehensive foundation, 2nd edn. Macmillan College Publishing Company, New York (1998)
9. Helbing, D., Grund, T.U.: Editorial: agent-based modelling and techno-social systems. Advances in Complex Systems 16(04n05), 1303002 (2013)
10. Keller-Schmidt, S., Klemm, K.: A model of macro-evolution as a branching process based on innovations. Advances in Complex Systems 15(7), 1250043 (2012)
11. Litvak-Hinenzon, A., Stone, L.: Epidemic waves, small worlds and targeted vaccination, Biomathematics Unit, Faculty of Life Sciences, Tel Aviv University (2013)
12. Martin, P.M.V., Granel, E.M.: 2,500-year Evolution of the term epidemic. Emerging Infectious Diseases 12(6), 976–980 (2006)
13. Moe, G.K., Rheinbolt, W.C., Abildskov, J.: A computer model of atrial fibrillation. Am. Heart J. 67, 200–220 (1964)
14. De Paoli, F., Vizzari, G.: Context dependent management of field diffusion: an experimental framework. In: Proc. WOA (Pitagora Editrice Bologna 2003), pp. 78–84 (2003)
15. Plikynas, D.: A virtual field-based conceptual framework for the simulation of complex social systems. Journal of Systems Science and Complexity 23(2), 232–248 (2010)
16. Raudys, S.: Statistical and Neural Classifiers: An integrated approach to design. Springer (2001)
17. Raudys, S.: On the universality of the single-layer perceptron model. In: Neural Networks and Soft Computing. AISC, vol. 19, pp. 79–86. Springer, Wien (2003)
18. Raudys, S.: Information transmission concept based model of wave propagation in discrete excitable media. Nonlinear Analysis: Modelling and Control 9(3), 271–289 (2004)
19. Raudys, S.: A target value control while training the perceptrons in changing environments. In: Guo, M., Zhao, L., Wang, L. (eds.) Proc. of the 4th Int.l Conf. on Natural Computation, pp. 54–58. IEEE Computer Society Press (2008)
20. Raudys, S., Raudys, A.: Three decision making levels in portfolio management. In: Proc. IEEE Conf. Computational Intelligence for Financial Engineering and Economics, pp. 197–204. IEEE Computer Society Press, NYC (2012)
21. Raudys, S.: Portfolio of automated trading systems: Complexity and learning set size issues. IEEE Transacions on Neural Networks and Learning Systems 24(3), 448–459 (2013)
22. Reber, A.S.: Implicit learning and tacit knowledge: an essay on the cognitive unconscious. Oxford University Press (1996)
23. Spach, M.S.: Discontinuous cardiac conduction: its origin in cellular connectivity with long-term adaptive changes that cause arrhytmias. In: Spooner, P.M., Joynes, R.W., Jalife, J. (eds.) Discontinuous Conduction in the Heart, pp. 5–51. Futura Publ. Company, Inc, Armonk (1997)
24. Steele, A.J., Tinsley, M., Showalter, K.: Collective behaviour of stabilized reaction-diffusion waves. Chaos 18, 026108 (2008)
25. Yde, P., Jensen, H., Trusina, A.: Analyzing inflammatory response as excitable media. Physical Review E 84, 051913 (2011)

Agent-Based Nonlocal Social Systems:
Neurodynamic Oscillations Approach

Darius Plikynas[1] and Saulius Masteika[1,2]

[1] Research and Development Center, Kazimieras Simonavicius University,
J. Basanaviciaus 29a, LT-03109, Vilnius, Lithuania
darius.plikynas@ksu.lt
[2] Department of Informatics, Faculty of Humanities, Vilnius University,
Muitines g. 8, LT-44280, Kaunas, Lithuania
saulius.masteika@khf.vu.lt

Abstract. This work addresses a conceptual problem – the lack of a multidisciplinary connecting paradigm, which could link fragmented research in the fields of neuroscience, artificial intelligence (AI), multi-agent systems (MAS) and social simulation domains. The need for a common multidisciplinary research framework arises essentially because these fields share a common object of investigation and simulation, i.e. individual and collective behavior. Based on the proposed conceptually novel social neuroscience paradigm (OSIMAS), we envisage social systems emerging from the coherent neurodynamical processes taking place in the individual mind-fields. For the experimental validation of the biologically inspired OSIMAS paradigm we have designed a framework of EEG based experiments. Some benchmark EEG tests for the chosen mind states have been provided in the current paper.

Keywords: oscillating agent, group neurodynamics, social neuroscience, multi-agent systems.

1   Introduction

The complexity of individual and collective human behavior permits myriad theoretical, simulational and experimental ways of investigation. This naturally deepens, but also fragments and specializes our knowledge. Therefore, this paper first strives to find a common a priori denominator as regards deductive reasoning. Only then does it offer some experimental approaches to validate the proposed nonlocal simulation aaproach. In this way, we strive to escape the loss of a general overview, and retain the necessary precision and scrutiny of investigation a posteriori. Below, in a few paragraphs, we briefly review the chosen research domains in order to emphasize some recent common trends, which in our understanding connects them all.

Lately new opportunities for multidisciplinary integration have emerged following technical neuroscience advancements in the research area of brain activity mapping. This has enabled a qualitatively new level of cognitive, behavioral and computational neuroscience (Bunge and Kahn 2009, Haan and Gunnar 2009). With the increase of

G. Meiselwitz (Ed.): SCSM 2014, LNCS 8531, pp. 253–264, 2014.
© Springer International Publishing Switzerland 2014

computing power neuroscience methods have crossed the borders of individual brain and mind states research. Hardware and software, used for mapping and analyzing electromagnetic brain activations, has enabled measurements of brain states across groups in real time (Nummenmaa 2012, Lindenberger et al. 2009, Newandee et al. 1996, Grinberg-Zylberbaum and Ramos 1987). This research frontier has made room for emerging multidisciplinary research areas like field-theoretic modeling of consciousness (McFadden 2002, Vitello 2001, Travis and Orme-Johnson 1989, Travis and Arenander 2006, Thaheld 2005, Pribram 1991, Pessa and Vitello 2004, Libet 1994), social neuroscience, neuroeconomics, and group neurodynamics (Cacioppo and Decety 2011, Haan and Gunnar 2009), see Table 1.

From the other side, some perspicacious biologically–inspired simulation approaches have emerged in the areas of computational (artificial) intelligence and agent-based and multi-agent systems research (Pérez et al. 2012, Raudys 2004, Qi and Sun 2003, Nagpal and Mamei 2004). In turn, these advances have laid the foundations for simulation methods oriented towards intelligent, ubiquitous, pervasive, amorphous, organic computing (Poslad 2009, Hansmann 2003, Servat and Drogoul 2002) and field-based coordination research (Mamei and Zambonelli 2006, Paoli and Vizzari 2003, Bandini et al. 2007, Camurri 2007), see Table 1.

A closer look at applied social networks research also reveals some related approaches, which deal, in one way or another, with simulations of field-like information spreading in social networks. For instance, behaviors spread in dynamic social networks (Zhang and Wu 2012), spread of behavior in online social networks (Centola 2010), urban traffic control with coordinating fields (Camuri et al. 2007), mining social networks using wave propagation (Wang et al. 2012), network models of the diffusion of innovations (Valente 1996), a virtual field-based simulation of complex social systems (Plikynas et al. 2014, Plikynas 2010), etc.

Table 1. Emerging field-theoretic research approaches in various domains and scales of self-organization

Research domains	Emerging field-theoretic research approaches	
	Individual level	*Social level*
Neuroscience	Consciousness as coherent electromagnetic field (e. g. represented by the Δ, θ, α, β, γ brain waves)	• Social neuroscience • Neuroeconomics • Group neurodynamics
AI/MAS	Artificial intelligent agent	• Field-based coordination • Intelligent ubiquitous • Pervasive/amorphous computing
Social networks	Social networking agent	Social mediums as excitatory systems, distributed cognition, etc

In sum, research trends in neuroscience, AI/MAS and social networks are leading to increasingly complex approaches, pointing towards oscillations or field-theoretic representations of individual and collective mental and behavioral phenomena as well. Hence, the major value of this paper is derived from our earlier proposed Oscillation-Based Multi-Agent System (OSIMAS) social simulation paradigm (Plikynas et al. 2014), which links above mentioned emerging research domains via stylized neurodynamic oscillations-based representation of human mind[1] and society (as collective mind) states as well.

Major conceptual implications of the paradigm presented here essentially provide field-theoretic ways of modeling and simulating individual and collective mind states. Major practical implications of the OSIMAS paradigm are targeted to the applied simulations of some real social phenomena[2] using agent-based and multi-agent systems (ABS and MAS respectively) research. However, it is a long way from the theory presented here to its practical applications, which are of most importance. Hence below, in a few paragraphs, we introduce how the conceptual ideas presented here can find their way in ABS and MAS applications.

This article is organized as follows. In the Section 2, we explain nonlocal approach in the agent based social modeling. Section 3 provides empirical premises of the EEG experimental setup and some results. Finally, section 4 concludes.

2   Local vs. Nonlocal Agent Based Social Modeling

Current ABS and MAS applications are famous for their construction based on the so-called 'bottom to top' principle, which in essence is explicitly agent-centric, with pair-based communication protocols between separate agents. Such models are used for the simulation of local pair-to-pair interactions, which are similar to cellular automata models, except that more sophisticated communication protocols and some intelligent decision algorithms are usually employed (Perez et al. 2012).

Nevertheless, in order to achieve substantial progress in the simulation of complex social phenomena, such models are usually enriched with some 'top to bottom' construction principles like the belief-desire-intention (BDI) approach, agent selection criteria, higher emotional states, altruism, a credit/fines system, added noise in the inputs and outputs, confines for learning speed and acceleration, etc. These principles are applied from some meta-level – in other words, a nonlocal organizational level – which cannot be deduced from the simple agent properties. In this way, the pure 'bottom to top' self-organization principle is lost. This obviously shows that explicit information encoded solely in the properties of individual agents is not enough for the

---

[1] Some electroencephalographic (EEG) experimental evidences provided in the sections below lead to an idea of interpreting human basic behavioral patterns in terms of mind states, which can be characterized by a unique electromagnetic power spectral density distributions (Alecu 2011, McFadden 2002, Plikynas et al. 2014).

[2] Like previously mentioned modeling of contextual (implicit) information spread in social networks, network models of the diffusion of innovations, models of self-excitatory wave propagation in social media, etc.

simulation of complex social agent-based systems, as social agents are not so individual after all. They are open systems influenced by the external, i.e. not only local but also regional and global environments at large (Raudys 2004).

In one way or another, this nonlocal (or 'implicit') self-organizational level is introduced artificially, following observed social behavioral patterns (Qi and Sun 2003). For instance, in communication theory and practice it is well known that tacit (informal, officially unrecorded) information like emotional 'atmosphere', working environment, moods, mimicry, gestures, media stories, weather conditions, etc. prevail in social organizations, which all profoundly influence human decisions and social wellbeing in general on an unconscious level (Lam 2000). This unconscious (implicit) level of self-organization is working in a form of contextual (nonlocal) information shared by all.

The closest empirical confirmations come from the fundamental sciences, e.g. quantum nonlocality phenomenon, which refers to the quantum mechanical predictions of many-systems measurement correlations for the entangled quantum states (Oppenheim and Wehner 2010). The issue has also been raised that we may have to differentiate between two different types of nonlocality: one related to quantum mechanics and the other to what is termed 'biological nonlocality' (Thaheld 2005).

To date, very few experiments that attempt to explore the possibility of a quantum physics–biology interrelationship have been conducted. The first experiment utilized pairs of human subjects in Faraday cages, where just one of the pair was subjected to photo stimulation, and possible electroencephalographic (EEG) correlations between human brains were investigated (Grinberg-Zylberbaum et al. 1994). Later experiments, building upon this pioneering research, continue to corroborate the findings with increasing experimental and statistical sophistication [Standish et al. 2004, Radin 2004].

Experiments which revealed evidence of correlated functional magnetic resonance imaging (fMRI) signals between human brains have also been conducted (Wackermann et al. 2004). These correlations occurred while one subject was being photostimulated and the other subject underwent an fMRI scan. Research is also ongoing at the University of Milan (Pizzi et al. 2004, Thaheld 2005) utilizing pairs of 2 cm diameter basins containing human neurons on printed circuit boards inside Faraday cages placed 20 cm apart. Laser stimulation of just one of the basins reveals consistent waveform autocorrelations between the stimulated and unstimulated basins[3].

All of these experiments, when taken together, seem to be pointing us in an unusual direction by implying that biological entanglement and nonlocality effects take place between human brains (Travis and Orme-Johnson 1989, Orme-Johnson and Oates 2009). These findings direct us to the idea that contextual implicit information is distributed in fields, and that fields – although expressing some global information – are locally (unconsciously) perceived by agents. It also leads us to the totally novel

---

[3]   Researchers at the University of Milan state, "Despite [the fact that] at this level of understanding it is impossible to tell if the origin of this non-locality is a genuine quantum effect, our experimental data seem to strongly suggest that biological systems present non-local properties not explainable by classical models" (Pizzi et al. 2004).

understanding of agents as an oscillating entity, which is capable of absorbing and emitting contextual fields (Plikynas 2010, Plikynas et al. 2014).

The current ABS and MAS have been unable to incorporate this huge amount of informal (contextual) information. This is due to the associated complexity and informal information intangibility, and the lack of a foundational theory that could create a conceptual framework for the incorporation of implicit information in a more natural way. Hence, there is a need to expand prevailing ABS/MAS conceptual frameworks in such a way that nonlocal (contextual) interaction and exchange of information could be incorporated.

Hence, the idea is to incorporate implicit information in the form of nonlocal (contextual) information, which, as in the case of natural laws (e.g. the laws of gravity, entropy, symmetry, energy conservation, etc.), would affect an entire system of social agents at once. Following such an analogy with natural laws, we assume that explicit local activities of social agents can be similarly influenced by implicit (contextual or nonlocal) social information. This could influence entire system of agents in a form of social laws (Reimers 2011). Each agent would respond to this contextual (nonlocal) information in a different way depending on individual characteristics.

Therefore, we should introduce local MAS_L and nonlocal MAS_N layers of self-organization in the prospective ABS/MAS simulation platforms:

$$MAS = (1 - \eta)MAS_L + \eta MAS_N,$$ (1)

Where $0 \leq \eta \geq 1$ denotes the degree of nonlocality:

$\eta \Rightarrow 0$, then $MAS = MAS_L$,

$\eta \Rightarrow 1$, then $MAS = MAS_N$.

In this way, we expand the concept of the ABS/MAS through nonlocal levels of self-organization. Thus, starting with $\eta \to 0$, self-organization could be observed (i) at the local single-agent level; (ii) on the intermediate scale $0 < \eta < 1$ it could be observed in coherent groups and organizations of agents; and (iii) on the global scale ($\eta \to 1$) it could be observed in coherent societies of agents.

The theory naturally follows from real life observations, where agents interact locally (interchanging information with neighbors), but also are affected by the nonlocal states of the whole system (e.g. traditions, cultures, fashions, national mentalities, political situations, economical/financial situations, etc.). Here the term 'nonlocality', which we borrowed from quantum physics, could have many social interpretations, but we prefer to understand it as Jung's archetypes of the collective unconscious, which can be thought of as laws of nature in terms of structures of consciousness (Laszlo 1959).

In fact, recent advancements of brain imaging techniques allow to measure and differentiate human mind states (Bunge and Kahn 2009, Haan and Gunnar 2009). Hence, new niches are opening up for the group-wide brain activations research, which allows to model and simulate individual and nonlocal, i.e. collective mind states (Nummenmaa 2012, Lindenberger et al. 2009, Newandee et al. 1996, Grinberg-Zylberbaum and Ramos 1987). Following this line of thought, we designed for the experimental validation a framework of EEG based experiments. Some benchmark EEG tests for the chosen mind states have been provided in the current paper below.

3   Empirical Premises and EEG Experimental Setup

While formulating our experimental framework, we faced some challenging fundamental questions - like how to bring human interaction, occurring in a complex social environment, under the scrutiny of laboratory testing and how to identify human interaction itself, i.e. what are the most basic social communication artifacts to measure? Obviously, human external behavior shows only the tip of the iceberg and can only vaguely represent the states of individual and collective mind-fields. Hence, we had to look for more fundamental, i.e. brain waves activation artifacts, which lead to various external behavioral patterns.

Because of the immense complexity of such a research framework, we identified and cross-correlated various mental states of temporally separated individuals in terms of their characteristic brain wave patterns (delta [1-4 Hz], theta [4-8 Hz], alpha [8-12 Hz], beta [13-30 Hz], and gamma [30-70 Hz] frequency ranges), which were recorded using EEG (electroencephalograph) methods. In this way, we defined mind-field states in terms of the EEG spectra for different people and mind states. The main purpose of the proposed experimental EEG framework was to find out whether brain wave patterns, i.e. EEG-recorded mind-fields, can demonstrate mutually correlated features (Plikynas et al. 2014). Hence, the main experimental hypothesis consisted of two parts - H0(1) and H0(2), see Fig. 1 for an illustration of experimental research stages.

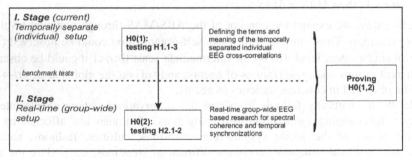

Fig. 1. Experimental research stages and series of tests

In this short paper, we mostly discuss hypothesis *H0*:

H0.1: EEG recordings of different consciousness states for different individuals have the fewest cross-correlations and thus have less similar spectral patterns.
H0.2: Temporally separate EEG recordings of the same consciousness states for different individuals have statistically significant cross-correlations and have more similar spectral patterns.

Hence, we were looking for the cross-correlations of brain wave signals for temporally separate individuals in the same mind states (like meditation, meditation with noise, counting with noise, thinking, thinking with noise). Saving up space, we will illustrate just few results below, see Fig. 2.

Thus, a more detailed analysis of the EEG-recorded differences (see diagrams A, B, C, and D in Fig. 2) between the meditation and thinking states has revealed results, which well correspond with other observations (Travis and Arenander 2006, Newandee et al. 1996):

1. In the meditation state, the Δ (delta) frequency range dominates
2. In the thinking state the α frequency range is dominant.
3. In the meditating and thinking states, the Θ and β frequency ranges are activated considerably less than the Δ and α ranges respectively.
4. For experienced meditators, the topological distribution of activated brain zones on the surface of the skull is almost identical in the Δ, Θ, and α ranges.

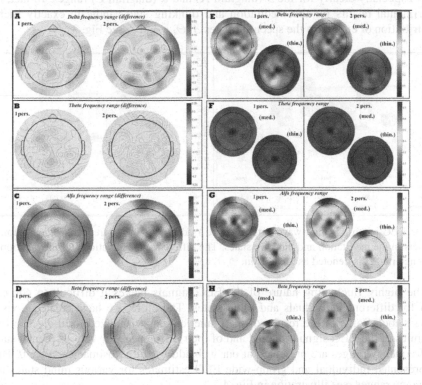

Fig. 2. Differences in the EEG-recorded electric field potentials between meditation and thinking states for experienced meditators in the Δ, Θ, α, and β frequency ranges (diagrams A, B, C, and D respectively). EEG diagrams E, F, G and H show actual activations of the corresponding mental states for the chosen frequency ranges. All power spectra are normalized (c.u.).

It is important to discuss in more detail an experimental observation regarding the inverse activation of different frequency ranges in the same brain areas depending on the mental states, see diagrams A and C in Fig. 2. In fact, this observation can be inferred from the OSIMAS paradigm (Plikynas et al. 2014), where different mental states are perceived as part of one and the same multivariate mental field composed of a set of dominant frequencies which are called natural resonant frequencies in the OSIMAS paradigm (biological system stores free energy in these superimposed spectral bands). Apart from any mathematical calculations, we argue that the theoretically inferred dominant frequencies of the mind-field correspond to the experimentally observed Δ, Θ, α and β brain waves.

Moreover, the OSIMAS paradigm envisages that various combinations of activated dominant frequencies in the common mind-field will yield unique mental states. As a matter of fact, experimental data for the meditation and thinking states validate exactly this assumption. We observe an equivalent spectral energy redistribution over frequency ranges for mental states like meditation vs. thinking, as these two states are opposite in nature. We can see this spectral energy redistribution effect especially clearly for the Δ (diagram A) and α (diagram C) ranges. In fact, our experimental results for the meditation and thinking states indicate exactly such a redistribution of energy in the spectral ranges Δ, Θ, α and β, see Fig. 3.

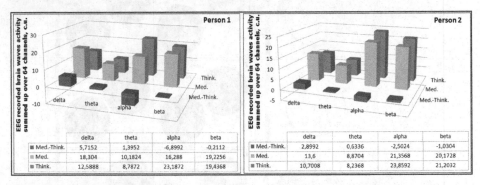

	delta	theta	alpha	beta
■ Med.-Think.	5,7152	1,3952	-6,8992	-0,2112
■ Med.	18,304	10,1824	16,288	19,2256
■ Think.	12,5888	8,7872	23,1872	19,4368

	delta	theta	alpha	beta
■ Med.-Think.	2,8992	0,6336	-2,5024	-1,0304
■ Med.	13,6	8,8704	21,3568	20,1728
■ Think.	10,7008	8,2368	23,8592	21,2032

Fig. 3. EEG-recorded brain-wave activity (c. u.) added up in all frequency ranges for 64 channels in the meditation and thinking states. The difference in activations for the appropriate frequency ranges is denoted as Med.-Thin.

The highly fluctuating nature of the EEG signals makes it difficult to compare them for different individuals and mind states. Therefore, we have created a visual analysis tool. Some of the results of the numerical and visualized local electric field dynamics of the EEG signals studied and of their differences for various mental states and frequency ranges are presented at our web address http://osimas-eeg.vva.lt/. Here are presented individual and group-wide EEG estimates for various mind states and frequency ranges, see illustration in Fig. 4.

Such a visualization of brain wave dynamics is very helpful for the recognition of group synchronization patterns for different persons, mind states, and frequency ranges. For the sake of clarity, we have added smaller head-maps that show direct differences in brain wave activation patterns (for the mind state chosen) between pairs of people, e.g. for persons I-IV, I-II, III-IV, etc. If brain wave activations for the pair of people chosen are dissimilar, the corresponding differences between activations produce a color and intensity-rich activation pattern in the difference head-map.

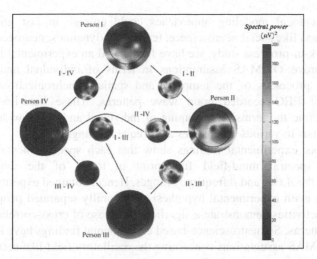

Fig. 4. Spectral power activation of brain wave dynamics for 4 persons in chosen mind state and spectral range. Smaller diagrams and connecting lines indicate spectral power differences between respective persons.

This approach helps greatly to distinguish similar brain activations when both activation patterns are very different and tend to have rapidly changing dynamics. In fact, our proposed group-wide mind-field visualization approach extends well-known brain-imaging techniques (BIT). Therefore, we named it the group-wide mind-field imaging method - GMIM.

4   Concluding Remarks

Major contribution of this paper comes from the provided conceptual and experimental framework of nonlocal field-based social simulation approach. In the presented conceptual framework, we envisage human society as a complex system of neurodynamically entangled mind-fields that together form a superposed and multifaceted collective mind-field. In this way, instead of a mechanistic pair-to-pair based communication approach, we provide a vision of social processes as collective mind-field effects emerging from the coherent field-like behavior of individual mind-fields. In other words, we propose to envisage societies as wave-like nonlocal processes emerging from the coherent behavior of the conscious and subconscious mind-fields of the individual members of a society.

Such a paradigmatic shift fosters new ways of designing nonlocal models of emergent systems of agents and complex social phenomena as well. We argue that simulation systems based on our proposed conceptual framework will make it possible to study the collective mind-field basis of social distributed cognition and interaction in terms of two- or multi-person neuroscience - an approach that could shift the focus of traditional social communication research from basic sensory functions in individual subjects toward the study of interconnected mind-fields. In this way, novel nonlocal modeling approaches could emerge in fast growing social research domains like social neuroscience, team neurodynamics, neuroeconomics, etc.

In this work-in-progress study, we have formulated an experimental framework to prove or disprove OSIMAS assumptions in terms of individual and group-wide neurodynamic processes of the temporal and spatial synchronizations and cross-correlations of EEG-recorded brain wave patterns. These base-line tests were designed to define the terms and meaning of individual and group-wide brain wave cross-correlations in various mind states and frequency ranges.

In short, our experimental findings show that each specific mental state has a characteristic spectral mind-field fingerprint in terms of the total activation distribution in the Δ,Θ,α and β frequency ranges. Hence, obtained experimental results confirmed our main experimental hypothesis: temporally separated people doing the same mental activities demonstrate a significant increase of cross-correlations in their brain wave patterns. So, neuroscience-based experimental findings have not disproved the major OSIMAS assumptions concerning the oscillatory field-like nature of mental states and consciousness in general.

Like all pioneering studies, proposed novel research framework needs thorough further investigation and statistical validation. This work-in-progress, however, provides some clear outlines with explanatory sources and initial testing for further fundamental, experimental and simulation-oriented investigation.

Acknowledgments. The research was funded by the European Social Fund following the Global Grant measure program; project No. VP1-3.1-SMM-07-K-01-137.

References

1. Alecu, L., Frezza-Buet, H., Alexandre, F.: Can self-organisation emerge through dynamic neural fields computation? Connection Science 23(1), 1–31 (2011)
2. Bandini, S., Manzoni, S., Vizzari, G.: Toward a platform for multilayered multi-agent situated system based simulations: focusing on field diffusion. Applied Artificial Intelligence: An International Journal 20(2-4), 327–351 (2007)
3. Bunge, S.A., Kahn, I.: Cognition: An Overview of Neuroimaging Techniques. Encyclopedia of Neuroscience, 1063–1067 (2009)
4. Cacioppo, J.T., Decety, J.: Social neuroscience: challenges and opportunities in the study of complex behavior. Annals of the New York Academy of Sciences (special issue), 162–173 (2011)
5. Camurri, M., Mamei, M., Zambonelli, F.: Urban Traffic Control with Co-Fields. In: Weyns, D., Van Dyke Parunak, H., Michel, F. (eds.) E4MAS 2006. LNCS (LNAI), vol. 4389, pp. 239–253. Springer, Heidelberg (2007)
6. Centola, D.: The spread of behavior in an online social network experiment. Science 329(5996), 1194–1197 (2010)
7. Grinberg-Zylberbaum, Ramos: Patterns of inter-hemispheric correlation during human communication. International Journal of Neuroscience 36, 41–53 (1987)
8. Grinberg-Zylberbaum, J., Delaflor, M., Attie, L., Goswami, A.: The Einstein-Podolsky-Rosen Paradox in the Brain: The Transferred Potential. Physics Essays 7(4), 422–428 (1994)

9. Haan, M., Gunnar, M.R.: Handbook of Developmental Social Neuroscience. The Guilford Press (2009)
10. Hansmann, U.: Pervasive Computing: The Mobile World, 2nd edn., p. 448. Springer (2003)
11. Lam, A.: Tacit Knowledge, Organizational Learning and Societal Institutions: An Integrated Framework. Organization Studies 21(3), 487–513 (2000)
12. Laszlo, V.S.: The Basic Writings of C. G. Jung. The Modern Library (1959)
13. Libet, B.: A testable field theory of mind-brain interaction. Journal of Consciousness Studies 1(1), 119–226 (1994)
14. Lindenberger, U., Li, S.C., Gruber, W., Muller, V.: Brains swinging in concert: cortical phase synchronization while playing guitar. BMC Neuroscience 10(22), 1471–2202 (2009)
15. Mamei, M., Zambonelli, F.: Field-Based Coordination for Pervasive Multiagent Systems. Springer, Berlin (2006)
16. McFadden, J.: Synchronous Firing and Its Influence on the Brain's Electromagnetic Field. Journal of Consciousness Studies 9(4), 23–50 (2002)
17. Nagpal, R., Mamei, M.: Engineering amorphous computing systems. In: Methodol. Softw. Engin. Agent Systems, p. 505. Springer (2004)
18. Newandee, D.A., Stanley, M.S., Reisman, S.: Measurement of the Electroencephalogram (EEG) Coherence in Group Meditation. In: Bioengineering Conference Proceedings of the IEEE Twenty-Second Annual Northeast, pp. 95–96 (1996)
19. Nummenmaa, L., Glerean, E., Viinikainen, M., Joskelinen, I.P., Hari, R., Sams, M.: Emotions promote social interaction by synchronizing brain activity across individuals. PNAS 109(24), 9599–9604 (2012)
20. Oppenheim, J., Wehner, S.: The uncertainty principle determines the non-locality of quantum mechanics. Science 330(6007), 1072–1074 (2010)
21. Orme-Johnson, D.W., Oates, R.M.: A Field-Theoretic View of Consciousness: Reply to Critics. Journal of Scientific Exploration 23(2), 1–28 (2009)
22. Paoli, F.D., Vizzari, G.: Context dependent management of field diffusion: an experimental framework. In: Proc. of the Workshop from Object to Agents, WOA (2003)
23. Pessa, E., Vitello, G.: Quantum noise induced entanglement and chaos in the dissipative quantum model of brain. Int. J. Mod. Phys. B 18(6), 841–858 (2004)
24. Pérez, J.B., et al. (eds.): Highlights on Practical Applications of Agents and Multi-Agent Systems. In: 10th International Conference on Practical Applications of Agents and Multi-Agent Systems. Springer (2012)
25. Plikynas, D.: A virtual field-based conceptual framework for the simulation of complex social systems. Journal of Systems Science and Complexity 23(2), 232–248 (2010)
26. Plikynas, D., Masteika, S., Basinskas, G., Kezys, D., Kumar, P., Laukaitis, A.: Social Systems in Terms of Coherent Individual Neurodynamics: Conceptual Premises and Experimental Scope. In: International Journal of General Systems (2014), doi:10.1080/03081079.2014.888552
27. Poslad, S.: Ubiquitous Computing: Smart Devices, Environments and Interactions, p. 502. Wiley (2009)
28. Pribram, K.H.: Brain and Perception: Holonomy and Structure in Figural Processing. Lawrence Erlbaum Associates, Hillsdale (1991)
29. Qi, D., Sun, R.: A multi-agent system integrating reinforcement learning, bidding and genetic algorithms. Web Intelligence and Agent Systems 1(3-4), 187–202 (2003)
30. Radin, D.I.: Event-related electroencephalographic correlations between isolated human subjects. The Journal of Alternative and Complementary Medicine 10(2), 315–323 (2004)

31. Raudys, Š.: Survival of intelligent agents in changing environments. In: Rutkowski, L., Siekmann, J.H., Tadeusiewicz, R., Zadeh, L.A. (eds.) ICAISC 2004. LNCS (LNAI), vol. 3070, pp. 109–117. Springer, Heidelberg (2004)

32. Reimers, M.: Local or distributed activation? The view from biology. Connection Science 23(2), 155–160 (2011)

33. Servat, D., Drogoul, A.: Combining amorphous computing and reactive agent-based systems: a Paradigm for Pervasive Intelligence. In: Proc. first Int'l Joint Conf. on Autonomous Agents and Multiagent Systems, pp. 441–448 (2002)

34. Standish, L.J., Kozak, L., Johnson, L.C., Richards, T.: Electroencephalographic evidence of correlated event-related signals between the brains of spatially and sensory isolated human subjects. The Journal of Alternative and Complementary Medicine 10(2), 307–314 (2004)

35. Thaheld, F.H.: An interdisciplinary approach to certain fundamental issues in the fields of physics and biology: towards a unified theory. BioSystems 80, 41–56 (2005)

36. Travis, F.T., Orme-Johnson, D.W.: Field model of consciousness: EEG coherence changes as indicators of field effects. International Journal of Neuroscience 49, 203–211 (1989)

37. Travis, F., Arenander, A.: Cross-sectional and longitudinal study of effects of transcendental meditation practice on interhemispheric frontal asymmetry and frontal coherence. Intern. J. Neuroscience 116, 1519–1538 (2006)

38. Valente, T.W.: Network models of the diffusion of innovations. Comput. Math. Organ. Theory 2(2), 163–164 (1996)

39. Vitello, G.: My Double Unveiled: The Dissipative Quantum Model of Brain (Advances in Consciousness Research). John Benjamins Pub. Co., Amsterdam (2001)

40. Wang, X., Tao, H., Xie, Z., Yi, D.: Mining social networks using wave propagation. Comput. Math. Organ. Theory (2012), doi:10.1007/s10588-012-9142-x

41. Zhang, Y., Wu, Y.: How behaviors spread in dynamic social networks. Comput. Math. Organ. Theory 18, 419–444 (2012), doi:10.1007/s10588-011-9105-7

Enhancing Social Media with Pervasive Features

Ioanna Roussaki[1], Nikos Kalatzis[1], Nicolas Liampotis[1], Edel Jennings[2],
Pavlos Kosmides[1], Mark Roddy[2], Luca Lamorte[3], and Miltiades Anagnostou[1]

[1] National Technical University of Athens, Athens, Greece
{ioanna.roussaki,nikosk,nicolas.liampotis,pkosmidis,miltos}@cn.ntua.gr
[2] TSSG, Waterford Institute of Technology, Waterford, Ireland
{ejennings,mroddy}@tssg.org
[3] Telecom Italia, Innovation & Industry Relations, Milano, Italy
luca.lamorte@telecomitalia.it

Abstract. During the last decade, social media have enjoyed meteoric success in bringing people together online. On the other hand, pervasive computing assists users in their everyday tasks, in a seamless unobtrusive manner exploiting the resources available in the user's environments focusing on the needs of individuals. The time is ripe for the two paradigms to converge. This paper presents research work undertaken to integrate pervasive computing with various social computing systems, including enterprise social media, aiming to contribute to the emergence of the next generation of social media systems.

Keywords: social networking, pervasive computing, pervasive communities, enterprise social media.

1 Introduction

Web and mobile technologies and devices have rapidly evolved and have known extensive market penetration to the majority of potential users. This fact, along with the inherent need of humans to communicate, socialise and share, have been the driving forces behind the rise of social media [1] and their meteoric success in enabling them to virtually socialise, interact and network, to share multimedia (user generated) content, to generate collective knowledge, etc. A wide variety of existing applications and services have already been integrated with social media and have evolved based on them, while new attractive applications have been enabled via social networking means, very often exploiting the vast wealth of information and content made available by social media facilities [2]. However, the wide spectrum of services provided via social networking systems (SNSs) do not integrate well or not at all with the variety of services, devices and resources in general that the users have access to locally or remotely.

On the other hand, there is ambient intelligence and pervasive computing [3] that aim to unobtrusively assist users in their everyday lives, by transparently and ubiquitously embedding numerous computing, communication and sensing resources in their surrounding environment and mobile devices. Up to this point,

G. Meiselwitz (Ed.): SCSM 2014, LNCS 8531, pp. 265–276, 2014.

Smart Spaces and pervasive computing systems in general have been built so that they primarily serve the requirements and desires of individual users. Compared to the success of social media, the products and services enriched with pervasive features or designed specifically to support the establishment of smart environments have known limited penetration in the wide market.

The SOCIETIES project (http://www.ict-societies.eu) investigates approaches to enable the convergence of social computing and pervasive computing. Integrating current pervasive computing systems with social networking services allows users to communicate and socialise, while it facilitates their everyday activities by supporting their interaction with other users that have similar interests, preferences and expectations, and in general, the same or similar context. The most popular SNSs do not exploit such information explicitly, but rather rely on the users' actions and intentions on describing their situation, their relationships with the other users, their preferences, etc. Nevertheless, lately there have been observed some social networking services that gradually exploit location information. But this is a very limited usage of a single type of context information and is still very far from the establishment of actual pervasive social media.

This is more intense for the Enterprise Social Media [4], where no such attempts to exploit pervasive information or enable pervasive computing facilities have taken place. However, there are numerous reports that enterprise social media will re-shape corporate culture forming the new paradigm that leverage the knowledge of employees, customers, and partners [5]. Social media enhance the exposure of enterprises reducing at the same time their overall marketing expenses. In addition, social technology may substitute companies' traditional intranets allowing employees to efficiently collaborate via innovative means. Mobile service provision and intelligent behaviour of services are two crucial aspects of pervasive computing that need to integrate with emerging enterprise social media technologies. Exchanging ideas, managing resources and locating people are only few of the aspects that will be improved. On the other hand, as emerging social media technologies should be highly interoperable, the need for standardisation is raising.

The framework proposed in this paper aims to contribute to enriching social networking systems, including enterprise social media, with pervasive computing features. This is accomplished via the notion of the Cooperating Smart Space (CSS) [6] that extends pervasive systems beyond the individual to dynamic pervasive communities of users. A Pervasive Community, modelled as a Community Interaction Space (CIS), is a group of, two or more, individuals who have agreed to share some, but not necessarily all, of their pervasive resources with other members of that community [6].

The remainder of this paper is structured as follows. In Sect. 2, a state-of-the-art review is presented with regards to pervasive features provided by social computing systems in general and in enterprise social media in particular. In Sect. 3, the implemented architecture is described focusing on the integration of our platform with existing social networking systems. Subsequently, Sect. 4

elaborates on the manner that social media data are modelled to be treated as pervasive information (context data in particular) so that they can further enhance the perceived experience of SNS users. Section 5 provides information on the enterprise user trials that have already taken place and have enabled validation of our system by enterprise users. Finally, in Sect. 6, the paper conclusions are drawn.

2   State of the Art on Pervasive Social Media

Social Networks have evolved dramatically during the last decade and pervasive computing is becoming part of today's Social Networks. Such an approach, of pervasive social networks is presented by the WhozThat system [7]. In this system, the users are interconnected based on their location proximity and their personal interests, while initially the user is notified for the identities of their proximal users and if they share some common interest, social communities are formed on the fly, exploiting information gathered from popular social media (e.g. Facebook) automatically.

Another effort of using pervasiveness in SNSs is presented in [8], where a friend recommendation approach for mobile Social Network Sites is proposed. The authors integrate community discovery with context-awareness and ontology modelling technologies. Although the system recognises the variety of context information around users, it mainly sets the user location, the social network and the personal information as the basis for supporting dynamic recommendation in mobile communities.

An effort to retrieve users' behaviour from location habits has been presented in [9]. The authors use Foursquare, a Location-based Social Network, to derive user behaviours and specifically the activity duration. The activity duration, is approximately calculated using a method based on statistics from real users' activity. The system avoids the use of external location-purpose devices like GPSs in order to reduce the power consumption of smartphones.

Another important factor in pervasive computing is the use of sensors. In this respect, the authors in [10] try to recognise emotions of the user by collecting and analysing user-generated data from different types of sensors on the smartphone. To evaluate the proposed approach, they developed a social network service client for Android smartphones classifying seven types of emotions: happiness, surprise, anger, disgust, sadness, fear, and neutral.

Recently, in addition to being part of users' personal lives, social networks have also been adopted for business purposes. In particular, social networks are being used in order to build someone's professional profile, such as in LinkedIn [11] and Xing [12]. Leaving aside the use of social networks by individuals, many recent studies indicate the benefits that can be accomplished by the use of social networks inside modern enterprises. Some of the most know Enterprise Social Networks are IBM Social Business [13], Jive [14], Coyo [15] and Yammer [16].

The use of Enterprise Social Networks is valuable irrespectively of the company size, as both small/medium-sized and international enterprises may benefit.

In [17], the authors analyse specific decisions and approaches regarding the social media adoption in enterprises. In this process, they also consider the high cultural diversity and independence of the local entities.

Similarly, the authors in [18], examine the adoption, usage and benefits of social media in Small and Medium-sized Enterprises (SMEs), as well as, potential concerns that may prevent a wider adoption of social media in SMEs. According to their research, SMEs started to use internal social media (e.g. wikis, blogs) in order to support collaboration among employees and to improve knowledge management.

Though there are many studies proposing social network approaches in the business sector, to the best of our knowledge, there has been no effort to combine Enterprise Social Networks with Pervasive Computing.

3   Architectural Approach

This section initially provides an overview of the functional architecture of the SOCIETIES platform and, subsequently, elaborates on the integration of the platform with existing social network services.

3.1   High-level Architecture View

The overall system architecture encompasses the SOCIETIES platform services, third party (3P) services that utilise the platform, as well as, software and hardware elements, such as, sensors, devices, web interfaces and social networks. Figure 1 depicts a functional viewpoint of the implemented architecture, where platform services are grouped in different layers according to the logical deployment they support [19]. These layers are outlined hereafter.

Multi CSS/CIS Layer: Services contained in this layer support federated search, identity, and domain administration functions, and store public information referring to multiple CSS or CISs. Each administrative domain maintains one instance of these services that may be utilised by other federated domains.

CIS Layer: Services contained in this layer support the members of a community and the respective CIS. Every CIS maintains at least one instance of these services, and an instance of these services can be used by multiple CISs.

CSS Layer: Services contained in this layer support an individual participant and the respective CSS. The word "participant" is used to refer to a single user or organisation. There is at least one instance of these services per participant, and an instance of these services can be used by multiple participants. This layer also maintains the necessary components that allow the integration of existing social networking systems (SNSs), enabling the extraction of public information available in SNSs, as well as, access/update of non-public information for the CSS owner. This functionality is provided by the *Social Network Connectors* component depicted in Fig. 1, which will be described in the following subsection.

Node Layer: Services contained in this layer are characterised as core services and are available per node. A CSS node is a logical node/device/cloud instance

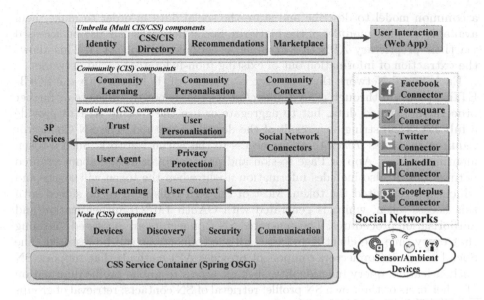

Fig. 1. High-level functional architecture

running CSS software that coordinates with other CSS nodes to form a participant's CSS. There is an instance of these services per CSS node.

3.2   Integration with Social Media

An important aspect of the pervasive community vision is to seamlessly capture
and facilitate Social Web interactions. SOCIETIES is not providing another Social Network in its common definition, but a bridging scheme between the Social
Web and pervasive communities. Our first step is to link the profiles and activities
of users in our pervasive communities with those in their online social networks
(e.g., Facebook, LinkedIn, Google+, Twitter, Diaspora, etc.). Interoperability
with Social Web initiatives needs to be taken into account, with regards both to
standards work on federation, as well as, to non-standardised approaches given
their popularity. Towards this approach, common representation of people, profiles, and activities is necessary. Another key step is to facilitate the exchange of
information between both systems, for example, details such as the name of the
pervasive community, the participants' identities and the activities of individual
participants.

The *Social Network Connectors* component provides a proxy between the
SOCIETIES Platform and the user's social network communities. Using this
subsystem, the platform is able to connect to one or more social networks and
fetch most of the user's profile information, plus his/her behaviour on the social
network. It also provides an API to push data through one or more social channels. The component hides the details of each social network API and provides

a common model to describe and store the social data in order to make them available to other modules of the platform. Social networks can also be accessed via their proprietary APIs (for example, FaceBook's Graph API). This allows the extraction of information out of existing (non-federated) social networks.

Each Social Network that the user is member of, is linked with the SOCIETIES platform through a *SN Connector*. Its goal is not to translate or further process the fetched data, but to aggregate or use the specific API to provide a full JSON [20] string as a result of the described method. The SN Connector requires an *Access Token* to secure access to the Social Network. Such a token identifies a User, App or Page session and provides information about granted permissions. It also includes information about when the token will expire and which app generated the token. Most of the API calls need to be signed with this access token, which is generated with OAuth 1.0/2.0 authentication and authorisation procedures. The generated SN Connectors are persisted, meaning that every time the client is restarted all the connections can be restored. The Social Network Connectors component provides API methods that support: SN authentication; query functionality, such as, access to public profile information of other users or their own SN profile; retrieval of SN contacts; retrieval of groups the user belongs to/follows/likes; retrieval of activities performed within SNs; and publishing of content on the SN (e.g., posting a textual message on the SN, performing a check-in or posting an event).

The most valuable piece of functionality exposed by this component is data abstraction. Each active SN connector is periodically called, and the extracted raw data are passed to a converter. In order to support interoperability among the different information items originating from each source, the converter translates the specific social network language into a common object according to the OpenSocial specification [21] which has been introduced by Google. OpenSocial is an open set of programming interfaces for building web-based social network applications. It encompasses several aspects of Social Networking Applications including Profiles, Relationships, Activities, Shared applications, Authentication and Authorisation. The following three OpenSocial data objects are of particular interest: (i) *Person* (OpenSocial defines many common attributes associated with a person and is aligned with the Portable Contacts specification), (ii) *ActivityEntry* (consists of an actor, a verb, an object, and a target; it can, thus, describe a person performing an action *on* or *with* an object), and (iii) *Group* (OpenSocial Groups are owned by people, and are used to tag or categorise people and their relationships).

The mapping between the information retrieved and the OpenSocial object is not always complete, as it relies on what the user has provided on their profile, as well as, the type of social network that the data are coming from. The strength of this approach is that an application, which needs to consume such data, is not required to understand different languages or dialects for the same information type, but just one, and is, thus, able to handle them in a uniform fashion. This allows for incorporating social media data from heterogeneous sources into the CSS Context Management system which serves a twofold purpose: on the one hand, to enrich the SOCIETIES user profile information, while on the other, to make these data available to other components of the platform or interested 3P services.

4   Modelling of Social Media Data as Context Information

A dominant feature of pervasive computing is the provision of mechanisms that support proactive and intelligent platform behaviour. User/community personalisation, context management and learning are some of the facilities offered by the SOCIETIES architecture, as illustrated in Fig. 1. Such facilities rely on a variety of data that need to be derived from heterogeneous sources (e.g. hardware sensors, social networks, user feedback) in order to provide an enhanced user experience for both individuals and entire user communities establishing proactive smart space behaviour [22].

It is, therefore, necessary to integrate all this information, including data originating from social media, into a common data model. This was one of the core design principles for the SOCIETIES Context Model (SCM) [23]. The SCM data model comprises the following core classes: CtxEntity, CtxAttribute, CtxAssociation, CtxHistoryAttribute, CommunityMemberCtxEntity, IndividualCtxEntity, CommunityCtxEntity and CtxBond. The first four of these classes serve as the basis for the representation of context data pertaining to individuals. As it is obvious, an entity–attribute–value model is adopted, where an entity is assigned with various attribute types and respective values detailing the properties of the entity. Relations among entities are expressed by the CtxAssociation class that has a crucial role in modelling Social Network data. An association may entail a parent CtxEntity and various child entities and hence, it is characterised as directed or may relate two or more peer entities forming an undirected association. A predefined but extendable taxonomy semantically describes the types of entities, attributes and associations. SCM supports the modelling of information referring to communities of individuals, communities that consist of other sub-communities forming community hierarchies and even complex structures, where community members are a mixture of both individuals and subcommunities. The CommunityMemberCtxEntity, IndividualCtxEntity, CommunityCtxEntity and CtxBond classes tackle the added complexity imposed by the representation requirements of community context [23].

In Fig. 2, an example data object diagram is presented. A person is modelled as an IndividualCtxEntity that is assigned with various attributes describing the current situation of the user (e.g., user status, location, etc.). Each social network account that the person maintains is modelled as a distinct CtxEntity, where the type of the social network service is stored as a CtxAttribute value. Additional data derived from the social network (e.g., "interests", "books", "movies") are represented as extra CtxAttributes of the respective type. Complicated Social Network data structures that cannot be mapped to simple attribute–value objects, are modelled as CtxEntities assigned to a CtxAssociation. For example, each SN connection (Facebook friend or Twitter follower) is represented as

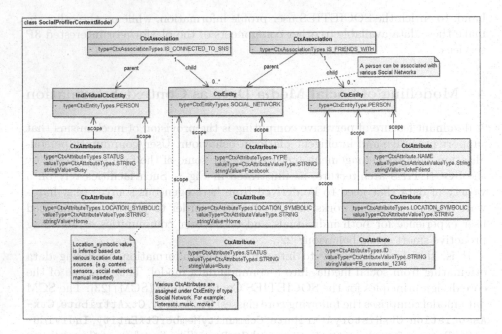

Fig. 2. The social profile context model

a distinct `CtxEntity` escorted by a number of `CtxAttributes` that correspond to the profile information being shared (e.g., name, location, social network user ID).

5   Enterprise User Trial

The SOCIETIES platform is intended to be used by both individuals and entire communities. It is, thus, imperative that the design is user-centred and, wherever possible, user-driven. The SOCIETIES methodology [24] is based on the inclusion of three different user communities, which have engaged continually in the design and development process from initial user requirements gathering and early concept creation, through to scenario refinements and feature revisions via early prototype evaluations. These are an Enterprise community, a Student community, and a Disaster Management community. Early user requirements were elicited via ethnographic techniques, involving close observation of each community in their real-world environment, combined with questionnaires and participatory discussions.

The remainder of this section focuses on the Enterprise users for whom the above methodology indicated a profound interest in pervasive community services, which could enhance the workflow of their daily lives, with additional features for more selective relevant communications. Enterprise communities play an important role in bringing together people, goods and services within global markets, local ecosystems or large organisations. These busy executives, in several cases, reported being over-loaded with communications and information, and the automatic filtering of both, without missing opportunities for useful connections, would be attractive to them.

5.1   Trial Outline

The SOCIETIES prototype Enterprise user trial took place in the Intel Campus in Leixlip, Ireland, during April 2013. The trial participants were Intel employees who elected to partake in the trial following a SOCIETIES Innovations presentation. Participants were given a mobile device with the prototype applications installed. The trial activities included a participatory demo and playful context discovery games, followed by role–playing conference scenarios and open discussion sessions. All of these trial participants were technology literate men, who work in technology research and development, and therefore did not have unrealistic expectations about the maturity of trial prototypes. In addition, all participants as frequent conference organisers, and/or attendees, were familiar with the conference settings for the trial scenarios, and each one brought his particular knowledge, expectations, experience and preferences about such events to the trial.

5.2   The Conference Scenario

Early in the project lifecycle, SOCIETIES chose to focus on conference scenarios in order to investigate novel social and pervasive concepts and services for the Enterprise community. These enterprise scenarios aim at supporting the formation of relevant context-aware communities in a conference environment, and as such, assume a large number of users, who are willing to share information, to access a wide range of integrated dynamic context and community aware services, including the following: pre-conference planning, personalised agendas, ad-hoc meetings, post-conference reviews, and tailored peripheral services, such as, organising menus and taxi sharing.

At the time of the prototype trial, two of the five conference services in development were selected for inclusion, along with the main SOCIETIES application:

– *Networking Zones:* The service provides backend and client components that enable users to detect a virtual networking zone, based on their location, which informs them with details on a 'topic of interest' for each zone, other users (and relevant details) who have agreed to share these details in the zone, and existing social network connections between users in the various zones.

– *Context-Aware Wall:* The service allows users to post messages in the area (zone) they are in. The message stays in the zone—or on the wall for a while, is visible to others who walk in to the same zone, and are in the intended group/community for which the posting user selected.

– *SOCIETIES Application:* Provides end users with web and mobile interfaces to the platform and services. It enables users to: join communities, control which information to share, access context-aware services and review their interactions with the system through an activity feed.

5.3 Role–Play

Role–play was adopted as an evaluation tool for the trial. This is a powerful and flexible tool as described in [25], which has been employed in several HCI studies from early design to evaluation. Role–play allows for complex socio technical experiences to be modelled. This facilitated giving trial participants access to particularly interesting aspects of SOCIETIES innovations, whilst protecting them from having to share personal information. The functioning and benefits of the system required existing social network connections, which could be better managed through preloaded personas and pre-configured social media identities. Inviting participants to act out characters with such personas allowed them to get a condensed complex view inside a situated staging of the system in a conference setting, at no personal risk.

Another objective that role–playing fulfilled, was to direct trial activities to interesting and innovative aspects of the projects' enterprise applications. The restricted number of trial participants enabled detailed character development into new personas and improvised ideas which evolved into outline scripts. Pre-existing relationships and links from private and professional social networks were assigned to each character in the script and set up explicitly in actual social media accounts. The scripts were devised to motivate participants to engage with the trial system, thus allowing them to experience creating groups, making friends, and organising meetings, and to understand the unique innovations of the SOCIETIES system with regards to: personalisation, social network integration, context-awareness, and discovery of relevant friends and communities. Finally, a System Usability Survey was conducted and a post role–play discussion was facilitated.

5.4 Findings

Despite some software bugs and the controlled environment of the trial scenario, participants were clearly willing and inspired to imagine the potential for the types of services made feasible by a system such as SOCIETIES. They were intelligent about the possible risks and the assurances they would require with regard to the management of their data, but enthusiastic about the reach of services which link social networks, relevant contacts and communities with pervasive features. Discovering relevant connections, while still protecting one's identity or detail of organisation from others was considered very useful. There are potential drawbacks in including both SOCIETIES researchers, and trial participants in a set of participatory exercises. More specifically, the participants could be reluctant to criticise the proposed technologies for fear of offending developers; or they might vocalise their own presumptions of confusion or frustration even before attempting to perform a task, so perceived flaws may gain greater significance than they otherwise would. The emotional responses and instincts of participants are understood in a more meaningful way by direct observation and engagement. Also as everyone in the participatory discussions understood that these are prototype trials and there is scope for improvement, it allowed for a more honest discussion. Finally, it should be emphasised that the findings that emerged, have led to design and development refinements for the final prototype.

6 Conclusions

This paper elaborated on the SOCIETIES vision and concepts that allow the integration of social media with full-scale pervasive functionality. Social media have already penetrated a wide spectrum of applications and are expected to revamp corporate culture by leveraging the knowledge of employees, customers, and partners. In this respect, services and products enriched with pervasive features need to amalgamate with these emerging enterprise social media technologies. The framework presented in this paper, provides innovative mechanisms that are able to support the incorporation of social media data into the intelligent facilities of the SOCIETIES platform. The implemented architecture has been evaluated through a series of user trials from different domains in realistic environments. The evaluation results from the Enterprise trial verify the potential for the types of services made feasible by a system such as SOCIETIES, which links social networks, relevant contacts and communities with pervasive services.

Acknowledgement. The research leading to these results has received funding from the European Community's Seventh Framework Programme [FP7/2007-2013] under grant agreement no. 257493 of the *SOCIETIES* (Self Orchestrating CommunIty ambiEnT IntelligEnce Spaces) Collaborative Project.

References

1. Lietsala, K., Sirkkunen, E.: Social Media: Introduction to the tools and processes of participatory economy. Tampere University Press, Findland (2008)
2. Kaplan, A.M., Haenlein, M.: Users of the world, unite! The challenges and opportunities of Social Media. Business Horizons 53(1), 59–68 (2010)
3. Hansmann, U., Merk, L., Nicklous, M.S., Stober, T.: Pervasive Computing: The Mobile World, 2nd edn. Springer, Berlin (2003)
4. Klososky, S.: Enterprise Social Technology: Helping Organizations Harness the Power of Social Media, Social Networking, Social Relevance. Greenleaf Book Group, LLC (2010)
5. Fidelman, M.: The rise of enterprise social networks. White paper, Microsoft (2013)
6. Doolin, K., et al.: SOCIETIES: Where pervasive meets social. In: Álvarez, F., et al. (eds.) FIA 2012. LNCS, vol. 7281, pp. 30–41. Springer, Heidelberg (2012)

7. Beach, A., Gartrell, M., Akkala, S., Elston, J., Kelley, J., Nishimoto, K., Ray, B., Razgulin, S., Sundaresan, K., Surendar, B., Terada, M., Han, R.: Whozthat? evolving an ecosystem for context-aware mobile social networks. IEEE Network 22(4), 50–55 (2008)
8. Qiao, X., Li, X., Su, Z., Cao, D.: A context-awareness dynamic friend recommendation approach for mobile social network users. International Journal of Advanced Intelligence 3(2), 155–172 (2011)
9. Melià-Seguí, J., Zhang, R., Bart, E., Price, B., Brdiczka, O.: Activity duration analysis for context-aware services using foursquare check-ins. In: 2012 International Workshop on Self-aware Internet of Things, Self-IoT 2012, pp. 13–18. ACM, New York (2012)
10. Lee, H., Choi, Y.S., Lee, S., Park, I.: Towards unobtrusive emotion recognition for affective social communication. In: 2012 IEEE Consumer Communications and Networking Conference (CCNC), pp. 260–264 (January 2012)
11. LinkedIn: World's Largest Professional Network, http://www.linkedin.com
12. XING: For a better working life, http://www.xing.com
13. IBM Social Business, http://www.ibm.com/socialbusiness
14. Jive Software: Social Business Software for the Modern Mobile Workforce, http://www.jivesoftware.com
15. Coyo: Enterprise Social Network, http://www.coyoapp.com
16. Yammer: Enterprise Social Network, http://www.yammer.com
17. Stieglitz, S., Schallenmuller, S., Meske, C.: Adoption of social media for internal usage in a global enterprise. In: 27th International Conference on Advanced Information Networking and Applications Workshops, Los Alamitos, CA, USA, pp. 1483–1488. IEEE Computer Society (March 2013)
18. Meske, C., Stieglitz, S.: Adoption and use of social media in small and medium-sized enterprises. In: Harmsen, F., Proper, H.A. (eds.) PRET 2013. LNBIP, vol. 151, pp. 61–75. Springer, Heidelberg (2013)
19. Doolin, K., Taylor, N., Crotty, M., Roddy, M., Jennings, E., Roussaki, I., McKitterick, D.: Enhancing mobile social networks with ambient intelligence. In: Chin, A., Zhang, D. (eds.) Mobile Social Networking. Computational Social Sciences, pp. 139–163. Springer, New York (2014)
20. JSON: JavaScript Object Notation, http://www.json.org
21. OpenSocial: Social Data Specification 2.0, http://opensocial-resources0. googlecode.com/svn/spec/2.0/Social-Data.xml
22. SOCIETIES Magazine: Issue 1, http://www.ict-societies.eu/magazine
23. Kalatzis, N., Liampotis, N., Roussaki, I., Kosmides, P., Papaioannou, I., Xynogalas, S., Zhang, D., Anagnostou, M.: Cross-community context management in Cooperating Smart Spaces. Personal and Ubiquitous Computing 18(2), 427–443 (2014)
24. Jennings, E., Madden, E., Roddy, M., Roussaki, I.: Participative user research and evaluation methodologies for pervasive communities. In: 5th Irish Human Computer Interaction Conference, iHCI 2011, Cork, Ireland (2011)
25. Thoring, K., Müller, R.: The role of role–play: Intagible systems representations for business innovations. In: 2012 International Design Management Research Conference, Leading Innovation Through Design, Boston, MA, USA, pp. 537–545 (August 2012)

Social Robots as Persuasive Agents

Evgenios Vlachos and Henrik Schärfe

Aalborg University, Department of Communication and Psychology,
Nyhavnsgade 14, 9000, Denmark
{evlachos,scharfe}@hum.aau.dk

Abstract. The topic of human robot interaction (HRI) is an important part of human computer interaction (HCI). Robots are more and more used in a social context, and in this paper we try to formulate a research agenda concerning ethical issues around social HRI in order to be prepared for future scenarios where robots may be a naturally integrated part of human society. We outline different paradigms to describe the role of social robots in communication processes with humans, and connect HRI with the topic of persuasive technology in health care, to critically reflect the potential benefits of using social robots as persuasive agents. The ability of a robotic system to conform to the demands (behaviors, understanding, roles, and tasks) that arise from the place the robot is designed to perform, affect the user and his/er sense of place attachment. Places are constantly changing, and so do interactions, thus robotic systems should continually adjust to change by modifying their behavior accordingly.

Keywords: human-robot interaction, persuasive agent, social robots, ethics, place attachment.

1 Introduction

Until very recently, robots were limited to industrial environments, and research facilities. Only lately did they migrate to our daily life, and became more social, user friendly, communicative and interactive. In most of the cases of social HRI the user is not able to distinguish clearly the entities that are embodied within the robot when interacting with it. Is the robot completely autonomous and self-oriented, or is it semi-autonomous? Is it controlled by a human, by a team of humans, or by other robots? What kind of information is the robot storing? Why and for what purpose? Does it share information with third parties, and who are they? A precondition needed for establishing a trusting relationship between the user, and the robotic system prior to interaction, is to have an answer for each of the risen questions above, meaning that the robotic system should be completely overt. For that reason, HRI could borrow the Code of Ethics from Information and Communication Technology (ICT) called PAPA, acronym of privacy, accuracy, intellectual property, and access [1]. Indeed, HRI and ICT share a plethora of common ethical issues; however, a robot's physical representation is a decisive factor in the argument in favor of determining new ethics for robots, the robo-ethics.

G. Meiselwitz (Ed.): SCSM 2014, LNCS 8531, pp. 277–284, 2014.
© Springer International Publishing Switzerland 2014

The majority of the published research findings in HRI deal with the target group of children and elderly people. On the one hand, there is a growing body of research presenting fruitful interactions between children and robots in the home, and in the classroom, specifically when the subject matter is related to science and engineering [2, 3]. Robots have also been shown to have a positive outcome in therapeutic applications for children [4]. On the other hand, according to the Population Division of the United Nations the population ageing is unprecedented, pervasive, enduring, and has profound implications for many facets of human life [5]. Therefore, ageing population is expected to need physical and cognitive assistance. Moreover, space and staff shortages at health care facilities are already an issue. Assistive robotic systems and companion robots for the elderly could be a solution provided that technologies are capable of being commanded through natural communication (e.g., facial expressions, speech, non-verbal communication, gestures,), of grasping and lifting items, and of assisting with daily chores and tasks (e.g., moving, feeding) if they are to improve the physiological and psychological health of the ageing population.

In the following sections we will discuss the notion of social robotics, present the key principles of persuasive technology, explain how the displayed behavior of a robot can affect the requirements for place attachment, and finally investigate the relationships between a user, a robot, and the robot's operator in a HRI scenario taking place in a health facility.

2   Social Robotics

Robots that are able to interact and communicate with humans in a human-like manner, but also with other robots, as well as with their environment, respecting the existing social and cultural norms are called social robots [6]. When interacting with such robots we apply social rules, and act on inherited behavioral guidelines, expecting that the robots will have the ability to understand, and follow them. Notable instances of social robots around us are the Geminoid-DK android when it took up the role of a university lecturer, or the role of a business man offering deals in an office [7], the Geminoid-F android when it performed in theatrical plays around the world [8], the Telenoid teleoperated humanoid when used for facilitating communication with elderly people suffering from dementia [9], the Kaspar humanoid robot when fostering cooperative dyadic play among children with autism [10], the Rofina teleoperated robot when it helped children with special needs to understand play behaviors [11], and the Zeno child-like humanoid when it assisted physical therapists to treat sensor-motor impairments [12]. Several researchers have also explored interactions with zoomorphic robots like the robot dog AIBO that uses body language and simple musical melodies to communicate with people [13], the robotic creature Kismet that engages physically, affectively, and socially with humans so as to learn from them [14], the seal robot Paro when used to improve the lives of elderly dementia patients [15], the Nabatzag rabbit that augments audio messages with display of non-verbal expressions [16], or the robotic cat NeCoRo whose behavior depends on the history of its interactions and can recognize its name [17].

Robots were not initially created to deceive, but to be trusted. After all, the term robot comes from the Czech word *"robota"* which means forced labor, or servitude and firstly appeared in the play R.U.R. (Rossum's Universal Robots) by the author Karel Čapek in 1921 [18]. Their purpose was, and still is, to serve the human either by handling situations, data, or by dealing with various tasks.

3   Persuasive Technology

If we assume that social robots bare strong similarities to traditional media, they should be defined as a medium that connects users to a source of a message. Under the view of computer-as-medium paradigm [19], the robot is the mediator of communication between the users, and the robot programmer or/and the robot operator. Therefore, HRI can be considered as human-human interaction. On the contrary, paraphrasing the computer-as-source unmediated perspective users respond to social robots as a source of information by following unintentionally the Media Equation formula (convenience to perceive robots as humans) [20]. There is strong evidence that in HCI users communicate directly with the computer, and not with a vague persona of a programmer behind it. If we apply these results to the area of HRI, then users should relate directly to the social robot, and not to the person behind it, either this person holds the position of a programmer, a designer, an operator, or embodies a whole organization, or a brand. But, is that the case? Ambient intelligence, multi-Intelligence (draw on multiple sources of intelligence, including big data, cloud and crowd resources), and networked robotics (share sensory input, solutions and problems across many locations and application areas), are three popular research topics among roboticists that enable robots to be more than mediating artifacts. Hence, robots include in their definition and the other two aspects of Fogg's Functional Triad [21] namely the notion of social actor, and the notion of tool. Robots, and especially social robots, encompass much more qualities than a computer does, and since they are a relatively new field of technology, people have not yet conceptualized their full range of abilities. In order to minimize the amount of false information such robots transmit, either intentionally for the greater good of the mixed initiative team comprised of the user, the robot and its operator, or unintentionally due to the effects of the Media Equation formula, the user should in advance be informed of what the robotic system is capable of doing, and equally important of not doing.

According to the Greek philosopher Aristotle persuasion was the art of convincing people to accept something, or do something they would normally not otherwise. The three modes of persuasion introduced by Aristotle are Ethos (ethical character of the source of information), Pathos (emotional state of the receiver), and Logos (argument) [22]. For a persuasive message a blend of all three is needed. The definition of persuasive technology (PT) includes robotic systems that are *"designed to change people's attitudes or behaviors or both without using coercion or deception"* [21]. Gass et al. [23] proposed that *"persuasion involves one or more persons who are engaged in the activity of creating, reinforcing, modifying, or extinguishing beliefs, attitudes, intentions, motivations, and/or behaviors within the constraints of a given communication context"*. The ultimate goal of PT is to promote wellbeing, health, quality of life, and a more sustainable lifestyle, but requires awareness of the user that it is an intentional act, and at all times he/she has the choice to decline. Trust in robotic systems directly influences both the interactions, and the overall acceptance of robotic agents. A user's trust, or distrust, towards a robot is expanded towards the entities that are embodied in the robot, which might be the programmer, the operator, the organization, or company the robot is located in, and even the brand of the robot (e.g., Honda Motor Co. in the case of Asimo, Kokoro Co. ltd in the case of the Geminoids, and Hanson Robotics in the case of Zeno).

What nearly all of the social robots have in common is the –most of the times- false message they transmit concerning two features that make their character being perceived more believable, and encourage interaction; the freedom of their actions, and their degree of autonomy. In [24], due to false attribution of robot capabilities, the children were expecting the robot to play along with them, while researchers were expecting the children to play along with the robot. Hiding or showing false information can be regarded as manipulation of the truth. This kind of deceit takes unintentional advantage of the effects of the Media Equation [20] and tricks the human mind by letting it treat machines in the same way as towards other people.

4   Place Attachment

"The structure of the space around us moulds and guides our actions and interactions", S. Harrison and P. Dourish [25]. The place a user is located frames his/er behavior, and automatically creates a mental icon concerning both the properties of the robotic system, and the type of HRI that would take place in case a robot was present. Therefore, even before real time HRI occurs, the user might have already categorized the expected-to-be-there robot by following unintentionally a robotic version of the HCI Paradigms; robot categorized as a tool (extending the abilities, strength, competence, intelligence of the human), robot categorized as a medium -or avatar [6]- (being a mediator of interpersonal communication and intentionality), robot categorized as a partner (embodying anthropomorphic features, humanlike properties, behavioral characteristics, and emotional/mental states) [26-28]. It seems that the HCI paradigms are identical to the Fogg's Functional Triad that was discussed earlier.

Places are constantly changing as they are continuously enacted by people [29]. Being part of the material topography of a place, the robotic system should be readjusted according to these changes either by being reprogrammed manually, or by being able to detect them through its sensory input and modify its behavior. The character of HRI can only be understood, and thereafter evaluated, if linked to a place. Thus, the evaluation criteria for a competent robotic system are limited to only one; how well it conforms to the user's perspective, meaning how well it fits the place. This criterion can be subdivided into smaller segments that represent each task, and each task can also be decomposed to smaller components in relation to the objectives of the task.

While place plays an essential role in human life, it is equally important in robotics, and often takes precedence over all other aspects of HRI. Place attachment is defined as the bond a person develops for a place that *"evolves from specifiable conditions of place and characteristics of people"* [30]. Extending that definition towards the field of HRI we suggest that robotic behavior should be added to the key factors that affect place attachment. Social robots are structurally coupled with their operational environment, and are connected to it with channels of mutual perturbation [31].

Hence, negative attitudes toward a robot, might lead to negative attitudes toward the people, the organization, the brand, or the company the robot embodies. We hope our statement to stimulate further research in order to avoid being confronted with the phenomenon of place aversion (including brand, company, and organization aversion) due to prejudice against interacting with robots in the near future.

5   Ethical Concerns in a HRI Scenario

Let us consider the scenario where a hospital makes use of a toy-robot companion for hospitalized children to play with. The robot is monitoring the child, observing every move, collecting personal information and, sending them to a system supervised by an operator. Figure 1 depicts the interactions between the user, the robot, and the robot's operator. The default situation would be the autonomous circle, where the

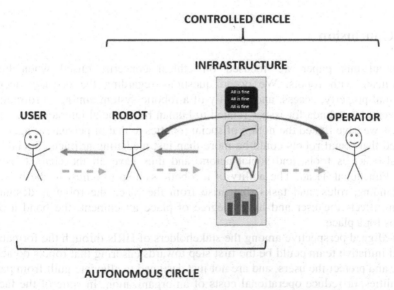

Fig. 1. Interactions between the user, the robot, and the operator featuring the Autonomous Circle (operator does not intervene in the HRI) and the Controlled Circle (operator intervenes in the HRI)

robotic system supervises and communicates with the user without the intervention of an operator. The operator would only override the autonomous circle in case of emergency, and take control. The toy-robot holds three roles; (i) is the mediator of communication between the operator (the doctors, and the hospital;) and the hospitalized child, (ii) is a tool measuring temperature, pulse rate, blood pressure, and whatever else is needed according to the situation, and (iii) serves as a companion partner to the child, where the child is speaking to, sharing personal stories, and maybe information that even his/her parents are not aware of. The toy-robot exhibits all of the persuasive characteristics in Fogg's Functinal Triad, but the cognitive and/or mental state of the child might not be sufficient to understand the roles of the involved stakeholders, including that of the robot. Is a consensus between the parents and the hospital about using a toy-robot enough? The toy-robot should neither be used as a justification for leaving the child on its own for longer time since it could lead to malformed development and emotional problems [2], nor as an excuse to migrate the responsibility from humans to robots [32]. One can imagine the same scenario with people suffering from dementia.

Another ethical concern is the liability of the robotic system. In case of a malfunction we have to be consistent with where to place responsibility. It could be the ethics of the operator, the ethics of the designer, the embedded ethical system of the robot, or the ethics of the user. According to [33], the wisest decision is to either avoid blaming anyone, or blame everyone. To prevent such a dramatic turn of events from happening, the stakeholders (user, operator, organization) should form a mixed initiative team having one common goal aligned and oriented towards one direction; to **protect the user, and secure his/er interests**.

6   Conclusion

Throughout this paper we focused on ethical concerns raised when humans communicate with robots. We posed questions regarding the privacy, accuracy, intellectual property, access, and liability of a robotic system aiming to formulate an ethical research agenda for issues related to human robot social interaction. In a brief overview we have linked the notion of social robotics to that of persuasive agents, and proposed that social robots could be more than just mediating artifacts. Social robots could also act as tools, and social actors, and thus have all the characteristics in Fogg's Functional Triad. The ability of a robotic system to adjust to the behaviors, understanding, roles, and tasks that arise from the place the robot is designed to perform, affects the user and his/er degree of place attachment, the bond a person develops for a place.

An aligned perspective among the stakeholders of HRIs through the formation of a mixed initiative team could be the first step towards ensuring that robots do actually benefit, and protect the users, and are not just designed to alleviate guilt from parental personalities, or reduce operational costs of an organization. In spite of the fact that robotic systems are designed by humans, and have more human values inherited than expected, the engagement of a human operator is a reassuring act indicating that robots are not here to substitute us, but to assist us.

Acknowledgement. Financial support was provided by the Department of Communications and Psychology, Aalborg University.

References

1. Veruggio, G., Operto, F.: Roboethics: a bottom-up interdisciplinary discourse in the field of applied ethics in robotics. International Review of Information Ethics 6, 2–8 (2006)
2. Sharkey, N., Sharkey, A.: The crying shame of robot nannies: an ethical appraisal. Interaction Studies 11(2), 161–190 (2010)
3. Kanda, T., Nishio, S., Ishiguro, H., Hagita, N.: Interactive Humanoid Robots and Androids in Children's Lives. Children, Youth and Environments 19(1), 12–33 (2009)
4. Liu, C., Conn, K., Sarkar, N., Stone, W.: Online affect detection and robot behaviour adaptation for intervention of children with autism. IEEE Transactions on Robotics 24(4), 883–896 (2008)
5. World Population Ageing: 1950-2050, http://www.un.org/esa/population/publications/worldageing19502050
6. Breazeal, C.: Social interactions in HRI: the robot view. IEEE Transactions on Systems, Man, and Cybernetics 34(2), 181–186 (2004)
7. Vlachos, E., Schärfe, H.: The Geminoid Reality. In: Stephanidis, C. (ed.) HCII 2013, Part II. CCIS, vol. 374, pp. 621–625. Springer, Heidelberg (2013)
8. Paré, Z.: Robot Drama Research: From Identification to Synchronization. In: Ge, S.S., Khatib, O., Cabibihan, J.-J., Simmons, R., Williams, M.-A. (eds.) ICSR 2012. LNCS (LNAI), vol. 7621, pp. 308–316. Springer, Heidelberg (2012)
9. Yamazaki, R., Nishio, S., Ogawa, K., Ishiguro, H.: Teleoperated android as an embodied communication medium: A case study with demented elderlies in a care facility. In: RO-MAN 2012, pp. 1066–1071 (2012)
10. Wainer, J., Dautenhahn, K., Robins, B., Amirabdollahian, F.: Collaborating with Kaspar: Using an autonomous humanoid robot to foster cooperative dyadic play among children with autism. In: IEEE-RAS 2010 Inter. Con. on Humanoid Robots, pp. 631–638. IEEE Press (2010)
11. Wong, A., Tan, Y.K., Tay, A., Wong, A., Limbu, D.K., Dung, T.A., Chua, Y., Yow, A.P.: A User Trial Study to Understand Play Behaviors of Autistic Children Using a Social Robot. In: Ge, S.S., Khatib, O., Cabibihan, J.-J., Simmons, R., Williams, M.-A. (eds.) ICSR 2012. LNCS (LNAI), vol. 7621, pp. 76–85. Springer, Heidelberg (2012)
12. Ranatunga, I., Rajruangrabin, J., Popa, D.O., Makedon, F.: Enhanced therapeutic interactivity using social robot Zeno. In: Proc. of the 4th International Conference on Pervasive Technologies Related to Assistive Environments, pp. 57–62. ACM (2011)
13. Kaplan, F.: Talking AIBO: First experimentation of verbal interactions with an autonomous four-legged robot. In: Learning to behave: interacting agents CELE-TWENTE Workshop on Language Technology, pp. 57–63 (2000)
14. Breazeal, C.: Toward sociable robots. Robotics and Autonomous Systems 42(3), 167–175 (2003)
15. Calo, C.J., Hunt-Bull, N., Lewis, L., Metzler, T.: Ethical Implications of Using the Paro Robot. In: 2011 AAAI Workshop (WS-2011-2012), pp. 20–24 (2011)
16. Rist, T., Wendzel, S., Masoodian, M., André, E.: Creating awareness for efficient energy use in smart homes. In: Intelligent Wohnen. Zusammenfassung der Beiträge zum Usability Day IX, pp. 162–168 (2011)

17. Libin, A., Cohen-Mansfield, J.: Therapeutic robocat for nursing home residents with dementia: preliminary inquiry. American Journal of Alzheimer's Disease and Other Dementias 19(2), 111–116 (2004)
18. Gupta, A.K., Arora, S.K.: Industrial automation and robotics. Laxmi Publications (2007)
19. Sundar, S.S., Nass, C.: Source Orientation in Human-Computer Interaction Programmer, Networker, or Independent Social Actor. Communication Research 27(6), 683–703 (2000)
20. Reeves, B., Nass, C.: The Media Equations: How People Treat Computers, Television, and New Media Like Real People and Places. CLSI Publications (2002)
21. Fogg, B.J.: Persuasive Technology: Using Computers to Change what We Think and Do. Morgan Kaufmann (2003)
22. Aristotle's Ethics, http://plato.stanford.edu/entries/aristotle-rhetoric
23. Gass, R.H., Seiter, J.S.: Persuasion, social influence, and compliance gaining, 2nd edn., p. 34. Allyn & Bacon/Longman, Boston (2003)
24. Strommen, E.: When the interface is a talking dinosaur: learning across media with ActiMates Barney. In: Proceedings of the SIGCHI Conference on Human Factors in Computing Systems, pp. 288–295. ACM Press/Addison-Wesley Publishing Co. (1998)
25. Harrison, S., Dourish, P.: Re-place-ing space: the roles of place and space in collaborative systems. In: Proceedings of the 1996 ACM Conference on Computer Supported Cooperative Work, pp. 67–76. ACM, New York (1996)
26. Beaudouin-Lafon, M.: Designing Interaction, not Interfaces. In: Proceedings of the Working Conference on Advanced Visual Interfaces, pp. 15–22. ACM (2004)
27. Kuzuoka, H., Yamazaki, K., Yamazaki, A., Kosaka, J., Suga, Y., Heath, C.: Dual Ecologies of Robot as Communication Media: Thoughts on Coordinating Orientations and Projectability. In: Proceedings of the SIGCHI Conference on Human Factors in Computing Systems (CHI 2004), vol. 6(1), pp. 183–190 (2004)
28. Epley, N., Waytz, A., Cacioppo, J.T.: On Seeing Human: A Three-Factor Theory of Anthropomorphism. Psychological Review 114(4), 864–886 (2007)
29. Cresswell, T.: Place. Blackwell Pub. (2004)
30. Shumaker, S.A., Taylor, R.B.: Toward a clarification of people-place relationships: A model of attachment to place. In: Feimer, N.R., Geller, E.S. (eds.) Environmental Psychology: Directions and Perspectives, pp. 219–251. Praeger, New York (1983)
31. Dautenhahn, K., Ogden, B., Quick, T.: From embodied to socially embedded agents– implications for interaction-aware robots. Cognitive Systems Research 3(3), 397–428 (2002)
32. Sharkey, A., Sharkey, N.: Granny and the robots: ethical issues in robot care for the elderly. Ethics and Information Technology 14(1), 27–40 (2012)
33. Reason, J.T.: Human error. Cambridge University Press (1990)

Online Communities and Engagement

Worker-Community: Using Crowdsourcing to Link Informal Workers with Potential Clients

Rocío Abascal-Mena, Erick López-Ornelas, J. Sergio Zepeda-Hernández,
Bárbara E. Gómez-Torrero, Gilberto León-Martagón, and Héctor Morales-Franco

Universidad Autónoma Metropolitana – Unidad Cuajimalpa
Departamento de Tecnologías de la Información,
Avenida Vasco de Quiroga 4871, Colonia Santa Fe Cuajimalpa,
Del. Cuajimalpa de Morelos, Distrito Federal, C.P. 05300, México
{mabascal,elopez,jzepeda}@correo.cua.uam.mx,
{barb.torrero,leon.gilberto,hubein2}@gmail.com

Abstract. Crowdsourcing is an emerging paradigm that is changing the way people establishes contact and works with others. The crowd is used to make people collaborate and solve problems that are difficult to answer without having many brains working together. Some of the applications of crowdsourcing include the capacity to create new employment opportunities to informal workers who seek for potential clients in the street. This paper presents Worker-Community, a new platform to link informal workers with potential clients in Mexico City. Our approach is based on the study of informal workers in order to know how they reach potential clients and the study of these clients to know their needs. A contextual study was carried to propose a prototype to create employments and assure security to all the people involved.

Keywords: crowdsourcing, Human Computer-Interaction, usability, recruitment system, collaboration.

1   Introduction

Nowadays, we find that all around the world there are millions of people unemployed. Part of this problem comes from the recent global economic crisis but also to the lack of connection between workers and potentials job opportunities.

A recent study made by the Statistic and Geographic National Institute of Mexico (INEGI)[1], in 2012, showed that about 21 millions of Mexican people are part of the informal economy, unemployment and low job conditions. In 2013, 830,000 people joined this group having precarious conditions in their works: unstable salaries, no social security services, no job benefits and lack of health care. From the previous study, the amount of people that work in the informal economy is around 14.2 millions, a quantity close to the number of regular registered workers (15.2 millions of Mexicans). This is not a small problem considering that, if there are not solutions,

---

[1] Instituto Nacional de Estadística y Geografía, http://www.inegi.org.mx/.

G. Meiselwitz (Ed.): SCSM 2014, LNCS 8531, pp. 287–297, 2014.

Mexico will become a country where informal economy is bigger than registered economy. Also, this problem has some social consequences: informal workers are victims of corruption, insecurity and social distrust. The society needs programs to help informal workers such as plumbers, construction workers, carpenters, electric workers, welders and others (that are out of the big companies but that have the skills to serve well to society) to get jobs in a more organized and secured way.

To help to solve this problem we have created a prototype named Worker-Community, a crowdsourcing project to link informal workers with potential users around Mexico City. Our solution envisages a design problem related to Human Computer Interaction (HCI), where two disciplines were involved (Design, and Information Technology) to get a solution for it.

The rest of the paper is organized as follows. Section 2 describes what is crowdsourcing and we present some examples of systems that are oriented to the recruitment of workers. In section 3, we focus on explaining the main problem and the application of the User-Centered Design Methodology to solve it. Section 4 presents the usability testing and the results that were obtained. Finally, we present the conclusions and the future work in section 5.

2   Crowdsourcing to Guarantee New Employment Opportunities

Collective intelligence is a form of intelligence that emerges from the collaboration of many individuals. It is a distributed intelligence that is constantly coordinated in real time and which leads to effective mobilization of competencies. In the field of human computation, this kind of human mobilization is being exploited to enable humans and computers to work together and solve hard problems that neither of them can solve alone [1]. This is known as crowdsourcing. Often, this kind of cooperation is given by open calls trying to recruit people in order to achieve an objective in common. In reality, the most prominent examples of crowdsourcing platforms, that we find, allow the people that participate to be encouraged by something that they are going to get or win at the end of the task. This gain can be to earn money (real or virtual), have fun, socialize with others, obtain social recognition or prestige, do altruism, learn something new or even create self-serving resources. Crowdsourcing has been used for a wide variety of applications like: open innovation markets and prices [2], competition markets [3], collaborative knowledge creation (like Wikipedia) [4], citizen science [5], social search and polling [6], human sensing [7], gamification [8], prediction markets [9], and others. In this paper, we focus on the use of crowdsourcing to facilitate the recruitment of workers. We present some of the most famous applications around the use of crowdsourcing to recruit workers.

Global crowdsourcing is emerging in order to impact poor communities in developing regions [10]. Even if crowdsourcing has not yet delivered all its potential it is a new way to empower people and to make the things work by enabling collaboration. The most prominent example is Amazon Mechanical Turk[2] (AMT), a

---

[2] http ://www.mturk.com

marketplace for work where businesses and developers ("requesters") can get access to an on-demand, scalable workforce ("workers") [11]. These requesters use AMT to post "Human Intelligence Tasks" (or "HITs") which typically involve basic computing and language skills – such as tagging photos according to their contents, rewriting sections of prose, transcribing audio, choosing representative screenshots from a short video clip, responding to survey questions, or performing internet research. The results are returned to the system. Requesters gain a task realized and workers gain a payment corresponding to their work. In this system, in difference with traditional works, we don't find long-term contracts or payments based on the hours that were worked.

Paid crowd work offers remarkable opportunities for improving productivity, social mobility, and global economy by engaging a geographically distributed workforce to complete complex tasks on demand and at scale [12]. Also, it enables the improvement of existing services and the creation of new ones. Reducing task completion time has become one of crowdsourcing's holy grails. Increased payment leads to higher work output, which translates to faster completion times [13]. An example of this is VizWiz that allows blind people to take a picture and ask questions that are answered in nearly real-time by asking multiple people on the web [14].

We also find ChaCha[3] a search service that uses humans to interpret search queries and select the most relevant results. As well as AMT, others crowdsourcing systems allowing the recruitment of workers are Rent-A-Coder[4] which provides a ready labor pool of software coders to firms seeking discrete and fairly straightforward coding projects. In the case of oDesk[5] and Elance[6] crowdsourcing platforms offer a wide array of professional services, including design, engineering, writing, web development and administrative support. Other kind of crowdsourcing company is OnForce[7], which maintains a network of information technology professionals who can be dispatched to needy companies, on demand.

As crowdsourcing marketplaces grow, requesters face new challenges to recruit good workers for their work and to establish rules to have productive results. This is the main problem of our work where requesters need to recruit somebody but also it is important to preserve their integrity by applying rules from the beginning of the establishment of the contact.

3   Applying User-Centered Design Methodology (UCD) to Implement a Crowdsourcing Solution

The development and research of our project is based on the User-Centered Design Methodology (UCD), comprising five stages. By using this methodology we created a prototype based on the needs of the users. In this way, we have carried out interviews

---

[3] http://www.chacha.com
[4] http://www.rent-acoder.com/
[5] https://www.odesk.com/
[6] https://es.elance.com/
[7] http://www.onforce.com/

with two kinds of users: (1) the informal workers and (2) the potential clients. As well, we have made a research in order to know the statistics of informal workers in Mexico City. Based on these interviews, we have applied an ethnographic study to understand in a better way our users. The results lead us to the development of a prototype that was evaluated and tested using the Wizard of Oz experiment. We also made a usability study that shows the interaction between the users (informal workers and potential clients) and the prototypes.

In our approach, we chose a place in Mexico City where we find an example of a need of collaboration between people in order to improve economy stability. The selection was easy because, despite of all, there are many places where informal workers offer their services. The center of the Mexico City, better known as Zocalo, has a long reputation of being a meeting point where informal workers and potential clients can get an agreement. We interviewed the workers by asking them about their social and economical situation.

We found out the fact that the number of workers has been reduced because of two reasons: (1) the lack of job offers to people and (2) a government regulation that allows to establish at the Zocalo to only the people that belong to a small and bad organized syndicate. Despite many critics, many of the workers are happy with this regulation because it avoids to strangers and not trusted people to offer their services without any guaranty of their job. This eliminates the possibility to find people that are part of criminal groups and pretend to be workers. We find, from the interviews, that some years ago the Zocalo was invaded with criminal groups that wanted to cheat potential users. This problem motivated them to get together and fight against it. Now, the honest workers try to regulate their own work using a membership. For example, if they know that one of their members has done a bad job, the rest of the workers fix it up. Sometimes the worker with a bad job is ejected from the Zocalo. This is a "solution" to try to convince potential clients of their security.

3.1   Interviews with the Users: Workers and Potential Clients

In this section, we present the interviews carried out with the two kinds of users: workers (Fig. 1 shows an example) and potential clients.

User 1- Workers. When we asked to the workers about their professions we found: plumbers, construction workers, electrics, welders, carpenters, domestic workers, taxi drivers and more. These were the most common professions but there are workers that have several skills, they can either work as a plumber or as a carpenter. Other interesting information was the fact of the spot's workplace rotation: when a worker gets a job opportunity by a pedestrian or a phone call he goes to attend the call and let one member of his family in their spot workplace. With this action they make sure that there is always somebody of his family ready to get another job opportunity. Unfortunately, there is no way to know how many workers really are. Neither them nor the government can say the exactly amount of workers because of the lack of communication between them. However, many of the workers estimate that they are about 300 workers that use this area (even if they are the real owner of the place or just a family member).

Fig. 1. Workers waiting for potential clients

In the place we find that there is a difference between the ages of the workers. We can find people of 60 and 70 years old, that refuses to leave their place because of the job opportunity or just the spot workplace they have. An example is Mr. Venustiano Martínez (76 years old construction worker) he has been working for almost 30 years in that place. We also met some younger workers like M. Federico Cansino (27 years old). He left his home to study a career on mechanics but, still now, he had not yet found any stable job opportunity. So, we find that there are workers with studies and others that have learned from the experience all over the years. In the study area we saw that the oldest workers are the ones with less job opportunities (clients). The main reason seems to be their age. Potential clients prefer to employ younger workers in order to avoid any accident of these workers.

As well as the case of ages, the interviews showed a big difference between workers education levels. There are many of them that only have the elementary school, third grade mostly (oldest workers), while others have high-school grades and a few of them have a professional training.

The workers experience with technology is linked to the previous results, one part of the workers (60 to 70 years old) have not experience with computers while the youngest ones have it, at least the essential. In the case of mobile phones, many of them don't have one, while others have at least a cheap one. It is important to say that we could not find any Smartphone. Although the fact that not everybody has mobile phones all of them were willing to try to buy and use one in order to be connected with potential clients.

This kind of workers cannot afford any publicity service like the yellow pages, web page or other way that could help them to get new clients. The only thing they have, are recommendation from others clients and cardboard signs they made with their phone number, their profession and skills. This is not trivial because many of the signs they made do not inspire the people to trust and employ them.

User 2- Potential Clients. Our potential clients or social group is the Mexico City's low middle class. From INEGI information we know that 35% of the Mexico's population belongs to the low middle class. In Mexico City the middle class is about the 32%. The income of this social group is about $500.00 to $666.00 US Dollars by month. These salaries are not enough to support a family. Some experts in the study of social groups coincide in saying that middle class could disappear in the future if their economical situation continue in the same way. For this social group it is very hard to search for workers by using services provided by big companies because of the expensive bills. This social group always needs to hire workers to do maintenance of their houses and small business. Because of their economic situation they require of informal workers to reduce the costs of the work. We interviewed many potential clients and they wanted to try the program Worker-Community (our proposal), especially because of the fact that they can hire people from their computer or mobile phone.

The low middle class is composed of several kinds of people: we can find members of these families with university degrees, but also with just the elementary school. Because of their salary, many of them can get mobile phones or even smartphones. Also, lot of them have the elemental experience with computers, they use Internet, whether in their house or in a cybercafé. All these facts show that they can use the Worker-Community program and we do not have to worry about any special training for them. We just need to remember that the low middle class in Mexico City is more than 3 million people that could be our potential clients to this program, this support the idea of our crowdsourcing system.

In the next section we present our crowdsourcing system, which enables the collaboration between informal workers and potential clients by preserving security and quality.

3.2   Design of Worker-Community

Analyzing the interviews and comparing them with the contextual inquiries carried out at the Zocalo of Mexico City, we could see that potential workers are afraid to make a recruitment of somebody that they don't know. Trust is important in order to establish collaboration and enable new jobs. It is therefore evident that our help is needed.

The design of the system, based on the UCD Methodology, had to be functional and attractive to both users. Our application has two types of interfaces: one for informal workers and the other for potential clients. The first interface is an Internet terminal booth so informal workers can interact with it (Fig. 2). The second interface consists of a web page where the clients are going to be able to get information about the services and personal information about the workers that they can recruit. As we saw previously, a big percent of low middle class can have Internet, either by their mobile phone, computer at home or a cybercafé. The web page allows the access to the list of services, the possibility to describe their problem as well as they can have a closer look to the workers they are going to hire.

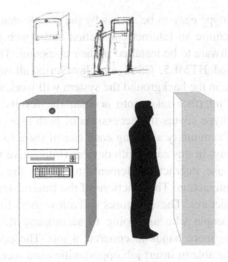

Fig. 2. Internet terminal booth for informal workers

Our decision of using an Internet terminal booth, that will be located in strategic points of the Zocalo, is an answer to the insecurity situation that we find at Mexico City. By using the contextual information that we got at the Zocalo, we know that the informal workers don't have a mobile phone or neither computer experience (only a small number of them have). Also, informal workers don't want to leave their place. So, the idea of an Internet terminal booth close to them (in the Zocalo) seems to be promising. In this way, workers can be alert about any job opportunities at the same time that they can watch their place, besides they can do the registration process on site. In this way, our proposition lets the workers, to make a registration in one side of the module and on the other side they will be able to see the job opportunities appearing as the potential clients insert them.

The Internet terminal booth will be a structure that allows us to move it because, as we remember, the Zocalo is a crowded place, and everyday we can find hundreds of people with different purpose: tourists, protesters, normal citizens doing their everyday activities, festivals visitors and many more. In this way, we need a flexible booth to be placed from 9:00 a.m. to 5:00 p.m. from Monday to Friday. On Saturday it will be placed only from 9:00 a.m. to 2:00 p.m. This is the time and days that normally the workers are in that place. After that, the booth could be taken to a more secure place (we propose a control office where personal must be capable to resolve basic computers problems and to talk with the users if they have a problem with the system).

We propose a web interface in order to interact with all the sections of the system. This decision was made from the results of our contextual study with the users. In this way, we made a prototype easy to be access by the people that will order a work. In this case, they only require an Internet connection and a web browser, this is better than giving them a software to be installed in their computer. The development of the project's interface used HTML5, CSS3 and JavaScript allowing us to generate a simple interface, while in the background the system will work with PHP and Myself.

The design of the interface takes into account the results of the Wizard of Oz experiment. Our prototype covers the necessities of both users that will be operating the program Worker-Community allowing each one of them to do his operations in a secure and efficient way. In this case, both devices (interactive web page and Internet terminal booth) will use interactive elements to attract the attention of the user contributing to keep interaction. The functions of the Internet terminal booth interface are: text capture and pictures. These features will allow users to select a proposed job but also insert new people who are going to accompany the worker. Sometimes, informal worker needs more hands to concrete a job. The potential clients, on the other hand, will also be able to insert job opportunities and receive information about the worker assigned. Both users will be able to share their opinions or ask questions about the collaboration that was established.

As a result of our contextual studies we were able to identify the main features of each interface. For the Internet Terminal Booths - initial settings; enter personal information, personal skills, photo, fingerprint, to explore job opportunities with description and address. It is possible to grade the attitude of the client once the work is finished. For the Interactive web page - initial settings; user authentification, enter job opportunity, specify characteristics of the job, specify payment, and add information about the client and address. For the design of the interfaces we relied on the study of our users' needs. The colors, shapes and style of the interfaces were created focused on users who would use these interfaces. These elements are important for the interface to be functional and usable (see Fig. 3).

4   Usability Testing Evaluation and Results

For our project it was necessary to evaluate the two user groups, informal workers and potential clients. For the informal workers the usability tests took place at the Zocalo; for the potential workers the tests were taken in their houses and cybercafés.

The usability tests (Wizard of Oz prototyping) were done using a simulated touch screen (see figures 4 and 5).

Fig. 3. The first 3 icons were selected at the beginning of our project. The last 3 icons correspond to those that were redesigned after the usability test.

Fig. 4. First contact of informal workers with the system

Fig. 5. First contact of potential clients with the system

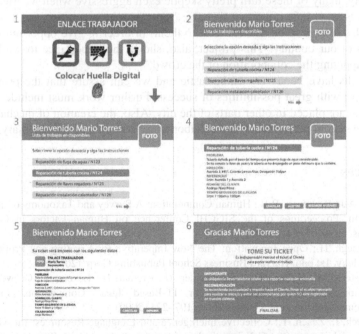

Fig. 6. Interface of the Internet terminal booth to access job offers at the same time that it prints a ticket with the name of the client, address and security information

For the booth the problems mentioned by the users were: problems with the use of the icons, however 80% could understand the iconography used; having no contact with the technology, the users were afraid to interact with the interfaces; but they approved the steps of the process. Improvements were made to the system based on the results of usability testing. Icons were changed in order to be more understandable (see Figures 3 and 4).

In the case of the potential clients, the majority of users thought that the Worker-Community system was easy to use.

5   Conclusions and Further Work

In this research we presented one problem that occurs in Mexico City: people are more and more seeking for job opportunities but the way to seek is not the better one. We need to support projects, like this one, to help improve the lives of millions of people that are in unfavorable conditions. Worker-Community Project (see Fig. 6) is a program that wants to achieve this goal; this can be used to eliminate unemployment and informality.

Our program use technology to enable collaboration between two different groups of people: informal workers and potential clients. Besides, we have understood the complexity of trying to help groups of workers that have been exploited and excluded from society, many of these turn pretty skeptic even aggressive when we tried to help them. In this way, it is important to have a government supporting for this kind of projects, also it have to be free (no cost to them) in order to give opportunities to all the sectors of our country. This project, also, shows the importance to work in real problems applying the collaboration of the crowd.

Our results have been very enthusiastic and we can assure that the project it is ready to start with great possibilities of success. Further work must include informal workers that are placed in other parts of the city. Also, the creation of mechanisms to monitor the system performance and collaboration between users is necessary.

References

1. Quinn, A.J., Bederson, B.B.: Human Computation: A Survey and Taxonomy of a Growing Field. In: Proceedings of the SIGCHI Conference on Human Factors in Computing Systems, pp. 1403–1412 (2011)
2. Chesbrough, H.: Open Innovation: The New Imperative for Creating and Profiting from Technology, 1st edn. Harvard Business School Publishing Corp. (2003)
3. Leimeister, J.M., Huber, M., Bretschneider, U., Krcmar, H.: Leveraging Crowdsourcing: Activation-Supporting Components for IT-Based Ideas Competition. Journal of Management Information Systems 26(1), 197–224 (2009)
4. Gurevych, I., Zesch, T.: Collective Intelligence and Language Resources: Introduction to the Special Issue on Collaboratively Constructed Language Resources. Language Resources and Evaluation, pp. 1-7 (2013)
5. Robson, C., Hearst, M., Kau, C., Pierce, J.: Comparing the Use of Social Networking and Traditional Media Channels for Promoting Citizen Science. In: Proceedings of the 2013 Conference on Computer Supported Cooperative Work, pp. 1463–1468. ACM (2013)
6. Brambilla, M., Mauri, A.: Model-Driven Development of Social Network Enabled Applications with WebML and Social Primitives. In: Grossniklaus, M., Wimmer, M. (eds.) ICWE Workshops 2012. LNCS, vol. 7703, pp. 41–55. Springer, Heidelberg (2012)

7. Srivastava, M., Abdelzaher, T., Szymanski, B.: Human-Centric Sensing. Philosophical Transactions of the Royal Society A: Mathematical, Physical and Engineering Sciences 370(1958), 176–197 (2012)

8. Prpic, J., Shukla, P.: The Theory of Crowd Capital. In: Proceedings of the 46th Hawaii International Conference on Systems Sciences, pp. 3505–3514. IEEE (2013)

9. Venanzi, M., Rogers, A., Jennings, N.R.: Trust-Based Fusion of Untrustworthy Information in Crowdsourcing Applications. In: Proceedings of the 2013 International Conference on Autonomous Agents and Multi-Agent Systems, AAMAS, pp. 829–836 (2013)

10. Gupta, A., Thies, W., Cutrell, E., Balakrishnan, R.: mClerk: Enabling Mobile Crowdsourcing in Developing Regions. In: Proceedings of the 2012 ACM Annual Conference on Human Factors in Computing Systems, pp. 1843–1852. ACM (2012)

11. Schulze, T., Krug, S., Schader, M.: Workers' Task Choice in Crowdsourcing and Human Computation Markets. In: Thirty Third International Conference on Information Systems, Orlando (2012)

12. Kittur, A., et al.: The Future of Crowd Work. In: Proceedings of the 2013 Conference on Computer Supported Cooperative Work (CSCW), pp. 1301–1318. ACM (February 2013)

13. Mason, W., Watts, D.J.: Financial Incentives and the Performance of Crowds. ACM SigKDD Explorations Newsletter 11(2), 100–108 (2010)

14. Bigham, J.P., Jayant, C., Ji, H., Little, G., Miller, A., Miller, R.C., Tatarowicz, A., White, B., White, S., Yeh, T.: VizWiz: Nearly Real-Time Answers to Visual Questions. In: Proceedings of the 23rd Annual ACM Symposium on User Interface Software and Technology, pp. 333–342. ACM (2010)

Revolutionizing Mobile Healthcare Monitoring Technology: Analysis of Features through Task Model

Supunmali Ahangama, Yong Sheng Lim, Shun Yuan Koh,
and Danny Chiang Choon Poo

Department of Information Systems, School of Computing,
National University of Singapore, 13 Computing Drive, Singapore 117417
supunmali@comp.nus.edu.sg,
{a0067398,a00750272,dannypoo}@nus.edu.sg

Abstract. Proliferation of health information and patient communication had allowed patients to have deeper understanding of their ailments leading to positive effects on personal health management (PHM). There are many PHM systems developed in the form of web and mobile applications to cultivate personal responsibility for one's own health. Thus, this paper aims to explore the alternatives and avenues available in the form of mobile PHM applications utilized by patients, caregivers and medical professionals that can provide value-adding initiatives to improve the process of personal medical care. A Task model for the development of a mobile PHM will be discussed based on six factors, namely (1) subject; (2) objective; (3) control; (4) tool; (5) context; and (6) communication.

Keywords: Friends and family groups, healthcare communities, task model.

1 Introduction

According to WHO statistics [1] government spending on healthcare is escalating more rapidly than the growth in gross national domestic product (GDP). For example it is expected that change in public health expenditure in USA for 2011-2030 is expected to be 5.1% as a percentage of GDP. This indicates that people spend a greater proportion of their wealth on health to be healthy. Present day people are taking a proactive attitude towards their own health as well as that of their family [2]. With the proliferation of health information and patient communication, patients have gained deeper understanding of their ailments leading to positive effects on self-efficacy [3]. However, the prevailing scenario of unequal growth of demand and supply of medical service, may lead to an eventual decline of quality and service provided to the patients [4].

With the rapid technological advancements in smart phones and other mobile technologies, management of one's personal health is no longer an onerous task and could be carried out while on the go [5]. Moreover, ever increasing availability of smart phone users provides us an opportunity to diffuse mobile personal health management (mPHM) among these users [6]. The void of inadequate communication highlighted by both the patients and the doctors during our preliminary study could be filled by

G. Meiselwitz (Ed.): SCSM 2014, LNCS 8531, pp. 298–305, 2014.

the integration of technology and especially mobile applications in their daily lives. There seems to be a strong demand for professional and personal healthcare services on mobile applications. Factors enriching the mobile environment, like convenience, increased motivation, and capability of controlling and reminding patients can be considered as value addition to PHM mobile applications.

We will be using the Task model proposed by Sharples and Taylor [7] as the theoretical framework. Even though this model had been proposed for mobile learning environments, the framework could be adopted in mPHM environment as well. The mPHM platform named "SerpentPole" will be proposed to cater to all the requirements of the task model. Our study develops a mobile application for both patients and physicians based on the OSGi framework [8] and web client technologies.

The rest of this paper will deal with a description of the task model for patients followed by a more detailed description of application of the task model in PHM application named SerpentPole mobile app development. Finally, the discussion and conclusion will be presented highlighting the limitations and future directions of this study.

2   Theoretical Framework

Task Model from Sharples and Taylor [7, 9] is an interconnected framework of six factors used to design and analyze projects on a detailed level and Meta level of projects. This model is commonly used in mobile learning environment [10] to understand the design functions of projects and later on to analyze them. We believe that a similar model could be applied in the context of mobile health for capturing of its functions better when designing the architecture of the system and to compare with other available systems to differentiate the application from others. This is mainly composed of three standard factors namely, subject, objective and tool. The subject in a learning process is a learner or the student. Then the objective is moving the learner from novice stage to a trained stage or an advanced knowledgeable stage. Tools can be distinguished as any device, instrument, medium, material or content used to educate students in learning process. In this study, patient is considered as the subject, health management goals are objectives and tools used to mediate objectives to the patient (e.g. doctor, monitoring device, a text) are considered under tools. Then the model is extended by three other influencing factors, namely the context, control and communication. Control can be defined as setting the right aims and meaningful process for leaning. This could be varying from full teacher control to full learner control. In a learning process, this is the responsibility of the teacher or the l earner. Context is defined as the relationship between the context of learning and environment of the learner. This could be independent, formalized or socializing. Communication describes the interaction and communication with other persons of the learning group. For mobile health, we could see that these functions are important. Subsequent sections will deal with each function based on mobile health.

This model appears as two layers as it is considered on dialectic [9]. They are technological and semiotic. The technological layer considers learning as an engagement with technology. Thus, in mobile health, it represents health management as an engagement with technology, where mobile phone functions as an interactive agent. The semiotic layer considers learning as a semiotic system in which learner's objective actions are mediated by tools. Thus, technology is an enabler for semiotic layer.

Sharples and Taylor's Task model is used to analyze the context, subjects and objectives, tools, control and communication of mobile health applications [10]. Though there are many mPHM applications (e.g. health buddy, iDAT, healthDiary, medscape, iTriage), they have not considered a model like Task model giving a pragmatic and comprehensive view in designing and developing the applications. Moreover, this will provide a common ground to compare with other applications i.e. can look into similarities, differences and contradictions based on this model.

3   Usage of Task Model in PHM Application

First we develop 3 instantiations of the Task model, namely (1) patient who is undergoing medication for a certain condition; (2) caregiver who is looking after the patient and (3) physician who he is diagnosing and prescribing. The semiotic components could be found in Table 1.

Table 1. Semiotic components for patient, caregiver, provider

Semiotic Components		Required features
	Patient	• Maintain record of condition, medication and interactions;
Object		• Promote healthy diet and behavior by tracking daily food intake, exercise and encouraging to maintain wellness goals
		• Provide healthcare services like managing appointments, get map of nearest hospital or clinic
		• Maintain a repository of medical records, prescriptions and other image files (x-ray images)
		• Demonstrate change in pattern of measurements in condition (e.g. blood pressure)
		• Recommendation of peers based mutual similarities and location
	Caregiver	• Manage multiple number of patients
		• Monitor changes in conditions and interactions for medication
		• Send reminders to perform certain actions (e.g. medication, appointments)
		• Keep track of location of the patient
		• Encourage and remind to maintain wellness goals

Table 1. (*continued*)

	Physician	• Monitor changes in conditions and interactions for medication of patients • Determine the current status of the patient • Facilitate patient collaboration and discussion
Subject	Patient	• Patients taking medication for a certain condition
	Caregiver	• Caregiver who is looking after the patient. Caregiver could be a family member or an employed person to look after the patient.
	Physician	• Physician who is diagnosing conditions and prescribing medications to cure or control the condition.
Tool	Patient Caregiver Physician	• Device independent PHM • Real-time update of data collected from measuring instruments to reflect actual changes in symptoms
Control	Patient	• Patient retains the full control of what to share with others and whether to join public groups • Patient has control in deciding the level of participation in group discussions • Patient derives various wellness goals
	Caregiver	• No control over the content unless patient has allowed
	Physician	• Physician maintains control over the content shared in a private group (moderation) • No control over the content unless patient has allowed (e.g. personal medical condition)
Context	Patient Caregiver Physician	• Able to participate in informally structured groups exchange and reflect with users having common interests • Location independent where current place of being has no issue with using the application • Dependent on the context where it has a relationship to current issue of health
Communication	Patient Caregiver Physician	• Enable one-to-one communication between patients, patient-caregiver and patient-doctor to discuss on symptoms, medication etc. • Enable group communication to share experiences and for emotional support • Enable sharing of conditions or certain files in the repository with doctors or other particular user

Based on the instantiations for semiotic components, we built a general list of technological components (Table 2).

Table 2. General list of requirements for technlogical compoenets

Technological Components	Required features
Tools	• Sufficient power and network access to sustain uninterrupted usage
Object	• Personal health management on mobile platform
Communication	• Mobile network access via internet • One-to one messaging • Multi user messaging and collaboration • Posting of updates by users
Context	• Role-based control panels • Geo-location services to allow geo-tagging • Informal discussion space for user created groups
Control	• Hide/show of blocked components

3.1   Application Architecture

SerpentPole system as mPHM platform is architected to provide condition, medication tracking and collaborative features to patients, caregivers and physicians. The architecture of the system is discussed in another paper of the authors [11]. Nevertheless, technologies employed will be discussed briefly (Fig 1). First, SerpentPole mobile application is platform independent. Today mobile applications are highly segregated based on the mobile operating systems as Apple iOS, Google Android, Blackberry OS, and Microsoft Windows Phone. Considering the heterogeneity of these platforms and smart phone brands, it is important to provide the users with similar standard support. Thus, it is important to consider the development of a platform that allows these necessities. Our application is developed using HTML5, CSS5 and JavaScript and PhoneGap is used as the development framework. Furthermore, JqueryMobile is used to develop the responsive mobile client application. Thus, these technologies and frameworks guarantee the cross platform usage.

Location based services are used in this context for several reasons. It assures to keep track of the patients; this is especially useful for the caregivers. Moreover, when recommending fellow patients as friends to other patients, geo-location of the patients will also be taken into consideration. As a social media application, geo-tagging is allowed when interacting with peers, thus, to indicate the access environment to others. To render maps and to get the shortest path to the nearest clinics or hospital or the preferred hospital, our platform is using Google Maps API.

The server side platform is developed using OSGi framework [8] to assure the modularity and extensibility and coded in Java. Each server side component works as plug-in.

This application allows management of multiple profiles. That is multiple user profiles could be maintained in a single user account. This is especially useful for caregivers as they could log in from their personal account and could link with user profiles of the patients. Thus, they can oversee the conditions and other records of the other patient from the same user account, rather than re-logging over and over again from different accounts.

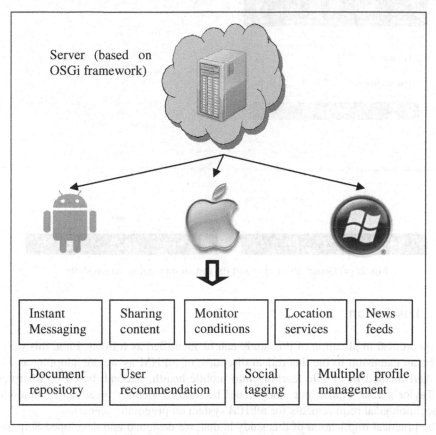

Fig. 1. Overview of SerpentPole platform

Social interaction (Fig 2) is allowed in this application where the user can create and interact as peer-to-peer and with multiple peers. The users can create private and public groups where, first only the invited users can join and contribute while anyone can search for the group and can join the groups later. These groups are segmented based on topics. If a certain comment is useful, then the users can like or unlike those posts and vice versa.

The SerpentPole application will act as a repository of medical documents. The users can upload images of prescriptions, discharge reports, medication labels etc. The documents will be classified based on user tags and users can create folders and store them for letter reference. This is especially useful when seeing a doctor, where one can show all the necessary documents rather than worrying about any important documents left at home. Moreover, these records can be linked with data entry records. For example, particular condition could be linked with the set of documents.

Fig. 2. (a) Group discussion and (b) instant messaging screen shots

4   Discussion

The theoretical implication of this study can be identified as follows. First, this study will be an extension to the theoretical discourse of mPHM as we are adopting an established method in mobile learning into mobile health. Second, based on Sharples and Taylor's Task model, our study could be used to identify broad set of semiotic and technological requirements for mPHM system on pragmatic scenarios.

The practical implication of this study is that, we designed and developed Serpent-Pole mobile application for PHM as a complete platform for formalized health management and structured for ad-hoc social interaction. The system is composed of social media components like instant messaging, social tagging and social networking. The system allows extensibility for different instances of the context. The initial application is developed and anyone interested, could contact the authors for further information.

5   Conclusion

On a meta-level, we can identify necessary requirements we need to consider when developing a mobile application to facilitate PHM. It is important to consider about object, subject, tool, control, context and communication. Based on these categories, users are able to create different instantiations of the Task model to achieve an application to meet different contexts, subjects or other requirements. This paper is the beginning of further research into mPHM. In future we are considering means of interfacing with input devices (hardware) and also with the electronic health records (EMR). Furthermore, we plan to perform user experiments to evaluate the effectiveness of SepentPole application.

References

1. WHO, World health statistics. World Health Organization (2012)
2. Hesse, B.W., et al.: Social participation in health 2.0. Computer 43(11), 45–52 (2010)
3. Pratt, W., et al.: Personal health information management. Communications of the ACM 49(1), 51–55 (2006)
4. Unruh, L., Spetz, J.: A primer on health economics. Policy and Politics in Nursing and Healthcare-Revised Reprint (2013)
5. Eysenbach, G.: CONSORT-EHEALTH: improving and standardizing evaluation reports of Web-based and mobile health interventions. Journal of Medical Internet Research 13(4) (2011)
6. Kahn, J.G., Yang, J.S., Kahn, J.S.: 'Mobile'health needs and opportunities in developing countries. Health Affairs 29(2), 252–258 (2010)
7. Taylor, J., et al.: Towards a task model for mobile learning: a dialectical approach. International Journal of Learning Technology 2(2), 138–158 (2006)
8. Lee, C., Nordstedt, D., Helal, S.: Enabling smart spaces with OSGi. IEEE Pervasive Computing 2(3), 89–94 (2003)
9. Sharples, M., Taylor, J., Vavoula, G.: Towards a theory of mobile learning. In: Proceedings of mLearn 2005, vol. 1(1), pp. 1–9 (2005)
10. Frohberg, D., Göth, C., Schwabe, G.: Mobile learning projects–a critical analysis of the state of the art. Journal of Computer Assisted Learning 25(4), 307–331 (2009)
11. Ahangama, S., Poo, D.C.C.: Mobile Social Media Platform for Personal Health Management. In: 24th Workshop on Information Technologies and Systems (WITS), Milano, Italy (2013) (accepted for poster presentation)

Feedback Platform for Community Colleges:
An Approach to Knowledge Excellence

Habib M. Fardoun and Abdullah Al-Malaise Al-Ghamdi

Information Systems Department,
King Abdulaziz University (KAU),
Jeddah, Saudi Arabia
{hfardoun,aalmalaise}@kau.edu.sa

Abstract. This proposal describes a feedback system based on a virtual platform between the cloister, which connects theoretical and practical imbalances taught for adapting them to new needs. This allows an increase in efficiency in the quality of teaching and that students get involved in improving their own training, by making the dynamism and interaction two fundamental pillars.

This feedback can improve the quality of academic material and facilitate students' adaptation to their practical preparation and their incorporation into the workplace. This fact is complemented with the use of the feedback system by the technical department of the companies associated with training centers, which communicate to them their needs and improvement suggestions based on the needs that they experience.

Keywords: community college, education, feedback, e-learning, adaptability.

1 Introduction

In the era of rapid changes in the workplace, the development is a key factor that cannot be stopped, and it is necessary to allow the growth and expansion of our knowledge. Our society inconstantly changing, so what facilitated our access to the work market yesterday, maybe it will be obsolete tomorrow [1] [2].

The change in the workplace, which exerts its influence on students' training, and future professionals to be inserted in the labor market, based on three fundamental reasons, which are: technology, increasing competition, and globalization. The rapid and constant progress of technology, which surprises us daily with new developments, helps us in our spare time or in the workplace [3]. It is not enough to use the programs we learnt in schools where we began our learning period, but the latest news and developments compel us to hone our skills and expand our knowledge. The second reason is the growing competition between firms in the workplace. We live in a time of crisis, where each company has to fight for survival from the plurality of supply and demand, which requires us to use new technologies, inventions and knowledge to continue in the workplace [3].

G. Meiselwitz (Ed.): SCSM 2014, LNCS 8531, pp. 306–313, 2014.
© Springer International Publishing Switzerland 2014

The last reason and perhaps the most important is globalization. The contact with different cultures occurs regularly and we must know how to handle these experiences [4]. It is very important to follow the progress and development to be able to move up at the profession and gain professional knowledge. Community Colleges, gives us the opportunity to achieve our own goals and to continue the development work, which happens very fast in our time. To be in constant evolution and to grow, allows us to be part of this progressive world.

2   State of Art

Students and instructors need new and flexible tools [5] that can help students engage with relevant learning and depth so they can obtain better results in life and professional senses.

Today, due to the teacher's work, the role of technology has been appreciated as a mean of transforming education. Using it in the right way, technology can expand the impact of good teachers, motivate students and connect faster than ever to the world of information and provide them the support they require, thus creating a powerful learning environment. The importance of using technology in community college nowadays depends on the academic education type [6], which is taught in different ways:

- **Classroom:** Teaching takes place in facilities intended for it. The physical presence of the student is required for this purpose.
- **Virtual:** In this case, the use of online teaching platforms [7], reaches its maximum development. The teaching process relies exclusively on the use of technology as a mean of learning, supporting and developing the contents offered to the student.
- **Hybrid:** As its name suggests, it is the mix result of the above two methods, as a flexible mean of learning within the classroom facilities or home / work student.

The teaching process includes theoretical lectures, simulations [8], laboratory practices, use of management programs or theories which represent the academic contents offered to the student. Gradually, during training, or near the end of the degree, business practices take place for the achievement of academic degree. Subsequently, the employment would occur with more or less success by the student, and in the professional labor market, being able to do their work.

During these two possible contacts with the company, the student suffers an adaptive process as a result of the application of their theoretical knowledge, that lacks accuracy when we consider the specific activities to be performed at the enterprise level [9][10] or the use of market management applications or implementing activities in handling instrumentation. All of them are determined by supply and demand offers that govern the labor market needs.

3   Teaching Quality VS Successful Job Placement

Regardless the type of community colleges, we are going to focus on the teaching quality, and a supplement to help improve the educational process through using virtual platforms. Despite the use of technology in virtual or hybrid classroom teaching, there are difficulties in the employment of graduated students as a result of the mismatch between the learning content and its practical application, starting from the practices in different companies, they perform as part of their training [11].

This imbalance not only exists in community colleges, but also at any training center, particularly by the very practical and flexible sense of community colleges, we propose to implement it, because of its proximity to the professional environment which students have to adapt with. A successful education, connected to the labor market, reduces academic failure caused by the theoretical complexity and distance of teaching contents to the reality that surrounds the pupil. A successful education more adapted to the student's immediate future, allows a satisfactory employment and greater understanding and assimilation of the information he will apply in the market.

Therefore, the quality of education provided in the Community Colleges, affects the medium-long term academic success and the student's profession [12]. But how can we combine higher quality teaching with the practice that students should do?

4   Feedback Virtual Platform (FVP)

For these differences are minimal and adaptation in practice or as a professional, be the less aggressive and the most pleasant possible, we propose a virtual platform that facilitates communication between the training centers, students and companies in which the student perform his practices or work as newly professional.

Once the student takes his first contact with the labor market, he can perceive the difficulties experienced due to theoretical gaps, lack of accuracy in laboratory practices concerning management programs or instrument manipulation, which is not adjusted to the existing market. [9] Similarly, the company's supervisors may appreciate such difficulties from their experience so they could transmit their suggestions to the teachers in the Community College, for a greater efficiency, by preventing students or professionals from repeating the concepts that need revision.

The platform is constituted by three communication channels we describe below.

4.1   Company – Community College

For this purpose the virtual platform fully provides the teaching materials used in the student training:

- Theoretical material.
- Audiovisual material.
- Computing resources.
- Teaching methodology.

These files represent the academic contribution of the community college for students and can be exclusively accessed by the company that they gave it the permission for such purpose. Each section above can be viewed and reviewed by the company's supervisors after detecting the deficiencies in the implementation by a specific professional or apprentice in practices. This platform provides a registration area where the company once has logged and in contact with the teaching load, can interact with it through:

- **Suggestions' and comments' form:** it's attached right after the visualization of each training material and methodology. The companies can notice specific improvements to the information exposed in the platform.
- **Forms uploading files:** companies can share with Community Colleges, attachments or documents that complement the teaching information, or reflect a more accurate view of the proposed changes.

The contribution of the company is publicly available to all Community Colleges associated with the platform, so that the experience of improvement towards a center can be shared and used by others.

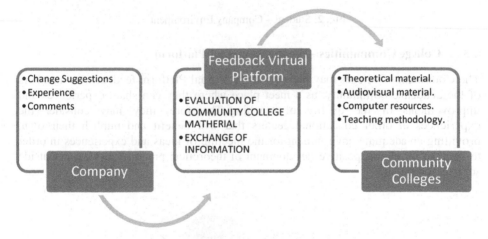

Fig. 1. Company – Community College Environment

4.2   Student/Professional – Company

In this section the intern or recent graduate who joins the business world may notify the supervisors, aspects they see appropriate to be communicated by the company to the Community College, so that, once received, these aspects can be incorporated into the teaching content in short term for their benefit, or the benefit of future students. That would result in a better use of their adapting time in companies. For this purpose, once the students logged in the platform, they can interact with it through:

- **Suggestions and comments form:** it's attached right after the visualization of each training material and methodology. The students, like previously in the case of the companies, can notice specific improvements regarding the information exposed in the platform.

- **Forms uploading files:** it would allow students to upload academic material or documentation for a better exhibition of their view, so that it may be assessed by the company and the Community College.

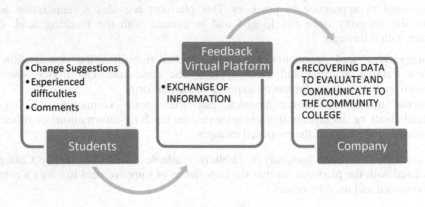

Fig. 2. Student – Company Environment

4.3   College Communities –Feedback Virtual Platform

The Community Colleges may register on the Virtual Platform feedback, as members of the academic community, as a meet place where they can share experiences and improvements in the quality of teaching. Therefore, they may consider the experiences of other educational centers that will benefit and publish their own, providing an adequate environment for the meeting of ideas and experiences in order to achieve together a positive development of theoretical practice, inside and outside schools formation.

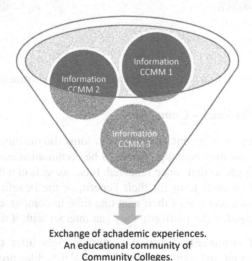

Exchange of achademic experiences.
An educational community of
Community Colleges.

Fig. 3. Community Colleges – Feedback Virtual Platform

Beside the platform we are proposing in this paper, researches prove the practical use of the social networks as a tool to create a participation e-learning environment between the students and the teachers, such as Facebook with the help of plugins specifically designed for educative purposes, as it has been presented in last studies [13]

5   How does Feedback Virtual Platform (FVP) Work?

The virtual platform feedback is an educational web platform, which is like another already existing academic platforms, provides an intuitive and basic functionality, summarized in the following points:

5.1   The Front Page

- The front-page of the platform – the web page accessed by your web browser - usually includes information about the site and can be highly customized.
- The users (Community Colleges, students or companies) proceed to log into the platform, through the accounts provided previously or the individual registering on the platform or after authentication from other system.

5.2   Inside the Feedback Virtual Platform (FVP)

- The basic structure of the FVP platform is organized round the different Community College courses in which they are associated by the student or the company. These are basically web pages or areas, where teachers can submit their resources and activities for students. They may have different rules, but usually include a number of central sections where the materials are shown and where side modules offer information or additional characteristics. Attached to the sections mentioned above, we can find the comment-suggestions web forms and the file upload section, the students and companies may use to transmit their contributions.
- Courses may contain a yearly academic content, according to specialty and the Community College. They may be used by a teacher or group of teachers.
- The way students or companies enroll in courses depends on the establishment, for example, through self-inscription, manual registering by the Community College or automatically by an administrator.
- The courses are organized into categories according to the area they belong to.
- The forum which forms the virtual community where Community Colleges share or exchange ideas and experiences, provides an alert notification area, that is activated right after the remittance of information between a company and a learning center. This can be publicly viewed if the contacted learning center allows it, so that other centers (Community Colleges) can take advantages of the suggestions and contributions made by a particular company.

5.3   Teachers, Students and Companies

• Access to the FVP platform can be performed in the role of   "teacher" or "student" or "company"
• Whoever logs into platform disposes a special privilege according to the needs previously defined by the administrator.

5.4   Finding the Way

• A logged user can access FVP platform areas such as Community College courses associated to a certain profile through navigation and administration sides. The content of these sides depends on the user role and the privilege granted by the administrator.
• Each user has its own customizable page, which can be acceded through the Home menu navigation.

6   Conclusions

We note that the discrepancies between the information provided in the Community Colleges and the experience received in the labor market are significantly reduced, making the academic experience a satisfactory approach towards the future work performance, as we improve the quality of education.

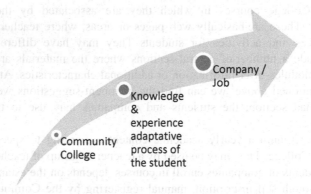

Fig. 4. Student – Professional gradual process

Thus, after adding a more practical teaching component, the Community Colleges become closer to real life experience through gradual approaches thanks to the feedback provided by the platform, in a way that can be warranted at the same time, that the transition to the professional life market by the students is satisfactory and not traumatic due to the labor-academic mismatches.

References

1. Briceno-Leon, R.: El autor responde, vol. 12(1). Saúde Pública, Rio de Janeiro (March 1996)
2. Mashat, A.S., Fardoun, H.M., Gallud, J.A.: Interaction Design in Educational Environments J. UCS Special Issue. Journal of Universal Computer Science 19(7), 851–853 (2013)
3. Jackowski, M.B., Akroyd, D.: Technology Usage Among Community College Faculty. Community College Journal of Research and Practice 34(8), 624–644 (2010)
4. Guenther, C.J.: Globalization and the Community College. Bulletin of Science, Technology & Society 21(4), 267–271 (2001)
5. Fardoun, H.M., Montero, F., López Jaquero, V.M.: Diseño de sistemas de e-learning para el soporte de nuevas técnicas de enseñanza. Avances en Sistemas e Informática 6(3), 181–187 (2009)
6. Rosales–Gracia, S., Gómez–López, V.M., Durán–Rodríguez, S.: Margarita Salinas–Fregoso y Sergio Saldaña–Cedillo. Modalidad híbrida y presencial. Comparación de dos modalidades educativas. Rev. Educ. Sup. 37(148) (2008)
7. Ciprés, A.P., Fardoun, H.M., Mashat, A.: Cataloging teaching units: Resources, evaluation and collaboration. In: Federated Conference on Computer Science and Information Systems, FedCSIS (2012)
8. Salas Perea Ramón, S., Ardanza Zulueta, P.: La simulación como método de enseñanza y aprendizaje. Educ. Med. Super
9. López, M.R.: Un análisis del desajuste educativo en el primer empleo de los jóvenes. Principios: estudios de economía política (11), 45–70 (2008) ISSN 1698-7616
10. Fardoun, H.M., Mashat, A.S., González, L.C.: New subject to improve the educational system: Through a communication channel betwen educational institution-company. In: Federated Conference on Computer Science and Information Systems (FedCSIS) 2013, pp. 709–712 (2013)
11. Deming, W.E.: Calidad, productividad y competitividad: la salida de la crisis. EdicionesDíaz de Santos (1989)
12. Sprouse, M., Ebbers, L.H., King, A.R.: Hiring and Developing Quality Community College Faculty. Community College Journal of Research and Practice 32(12), 985–998 (2008)
13. Fardoun, H.M., Zafar, B., Ciprés, A.P.: Using facebook for collaborative academic activities in education. In: Ozok, A.A., Zaphiris, P. (eds.) OCSC 2013. LNCS, vol. 8029, pp. 137–146. Springer, Heidelberg (2013)

Useful Educational Exercises for the Community

Habib M. Fardoun, Daniyal M. Alghazzawi, and Lorenzo Carretero González

Information Systems Department,
King Abdulaziz University (KAU),
Jeddah, Saudi Arabia
{hfardoun,dghazzawi,lgonzalez}@kau.edu.sa

Abstract. In a lot of cases, the contents given by the educational system don't leave a mark on students due to that it doesn't reach to pay enough attention for it has a positive effect on the learning. For that reason, we propose a system able to help for carrying the learning task out and for solving the problem raised with the lack of students' attention related to the lack of awareness of the place to apply the new taught contents. That makes necessary the incorporation of new technologies, like the use of a Cloud system and the communication via of Web Services when users access by mean of mobile devices, which provide a global site of consults that helps to students to understand contents given and associate them to the real world.

Keywords: Cloud, Web Services, e-Learning, Educational System, practical exercises.

1 Introduction

The academic failure of a determined student is not only associated to the student in particular, but also to the context into that student is. In this global context coexist familiar factors, friends, educational system and teachers. If we focus on the academic field, in a lot of cases the contents given by the system don't reach students' mind due to that those contents don't call enough the attention to have a positive effect on the learning. Part of it occurs because exposed information is, in some cases, too theoretical; and in other cases it doesn't show a practical situation where use it in the future.

If we put as example the Mathematics subject, we can check that when we work with derivatives, the academic staff often limit themselves to explain how it must be done and the basic rules to do it. However, as much as students know how to derivate perfectly, it won't have any sense nor utility if they don't know for what and where, inside of real life, they can use those formulas. For that reason, the ideal form to make the learning task is to show a real situation with images, which are close to students' life; joined to it to represent, in a graphical form, the scenario as it is usually represented on any problem; And lastly to make the exercise solving the problem described.

G. Meiselwitz (Ed.): SCSM 2014, LNCS 8531, pp. 314–321, 2014.

Because of that, we propose a system able to help to carry the learning task out and to solve the problem related with the lack of students' attention associated to the lack of awareness of the place where to apply the contents given. For that reason, it is necessary the incorporation of new technologies to provide a global site for consulting doubts about the material that students are studying and thus to associate it to the real world. This system located at the Cloud consists of the storage of practical examples, which follow specific steps previously commented. Each exercise should be composed by:

- A video, images or any other material that shows its application on the real world.
- A graphical representation of the content for its resolution.
- The problem resolution.

The users of the system give points to the exercises such that the most valued are shown at the first positions because their use helps, in a clearly form, to understand the didactical material taught. In addition, all of these examples serve to the teaching community as assistance for teaching to their students the appropriate didactical contents. Thus, any teacher from any place of the world can show to the students through a projector, TV screen, laptop or mobile device, the activities that help more to understand the subject contents. Anyone is able to consult by mean of his/her personal computer or mobile device, the different topics in the system, finding exercises about derivatives, electronic circuits, etc., taking into consideration that the fact of that every resolved problem is associated to a real problem where it is understandable its use, is a very important factor.

2 Exercise Structure

As we have talked previously, to that an exercise can be suitable enough for the target of call the student attention and so can keep it in the memory, it must accomplish a structure, whose content resemble to a real situation and whose resolution is clear. Thus, the main elements inside of this structure are as follow:

- **Area**. It is the topic related to the exercise content. So, if we are treating an exercise where, the physical principles of the bodies' movement without take into consideration the forces where they come from, are evaluated, then we were talking about kinematic. Thus, the area would be "Physics – Kinematic".
- **Statement**. Detailed explanation of a real situation close to the students where the variables to take into consideration or the phrases to evaluate are described.
- **Resource**. It contains a video, image or another element that shows the situation described in the statement.
- **Representation**. Graphical element that shows the problem from a practical point of view to evaluate, in a easier way, the elements that take part of the suggested situation.

With all this information, the system's users have everything that they need to understand the explained things and thus to learn the contents related with that scope in particular. Following, in the figure 1, we show an example where we put in practice the detailed structure previously treated and where we can observe each of the described sections.

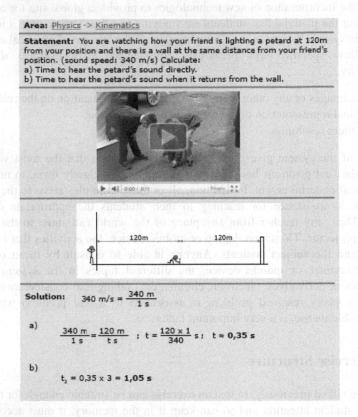

Fig. 1. Example of exercise

As we can see, the example is a very easy problem but it contains every part of the structure. With it any user will have access to a complete exercise and with a big similarity to situations that users can find in their real life. However, the exercise of the previous example doesn't suppose a total innovation due to that for any exercise of the Physics subject is necessary a lot of information and, in most cases, daily life examples are used. Instead, when we are talking about certain elements of the Mathematics subject, like derivatives or integrals, something changes. In that case, most current exercises that teachers propose come determined by the resolution of concrete equations or formulas each time more complex for evaluating the students' ability to solve them. In that moment we are creating users with a big ability to resolve equations but with little ability for applying them into the real life.

Due to previous facts, in the figure 2, we can observe an exercise where we put in practice the resolution of derivatives applied to real situations, which show to the user the utility of them in a concrete scope.

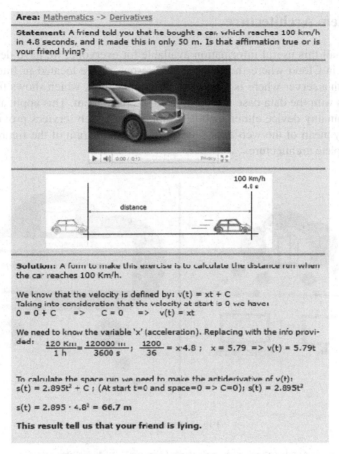

Fig. 2. Example of exercise with derivatives

As we can see in the previous example, all the provided information has a goal: to convince to the user that the exercise done has a real application, which could be useful in a future. Thus, in a unconscious form, the user assimilates better the concepts given, needing so of less time to teach a specific theme and keeping that information more time into the students' mind. This is because of they don't see the content as an ephemeral thing that they will use only for an exam or an evaluation in particular.

Although into the structure are the resources and the graphical representation, these are not necessary. However, they are useful when we want that the user associates the theoretical world with the real world.

3   System Architecture

As we want all this useful information available for everyone, we have developed an architecture in Cloud where the services and resources are located in Internet[4][5]. We start with a server where is stored the web application, which shows the contents and contacts with the data base to obtain them or create them. This application can be accessed from any device either mobile or not, through web services provided by the system or by mean of the web application [6]. At the diagram of the figure 3 we can see the complete architecture.

Fig. 3. Architecture

As we can see in the figure above, the elements inside of the server are divided in function of their labour into the system. Below, we are going to explain in detail each one of these elements:

- **Web Services.** They are the entrance gate to the services that the system offers to users. Thus, a particular student, with the application installed at his/her mobile device, will be able to access to the resources and information needed without make use of the web site directly.
- **Web Application.** The web application is the whole system, but in the figure is shown as the presentation layer where a user can access to create or to obtain information.
- **Logic layer.** It is the layer in charge of storing and treating the application's objects. In this layer is developed the system's functionality.
- **Data Access layer.** Through this layer we perform the exchange of data between the system and the data base, in other words, this layer is in charge of translate the data from the data base to recognizable objects for the system.
- **Data Base.** Into the data base is stored all the information related to users, exercises, themes, areas, stars, etc.

This type of architecture is ideal due to we don't need too much resources; in consequence the cost is so reduced. In addition, as we commented previously, it provides an isolated access to devices, which facilitates the user's work.

4   Exercise Evaluation

Once defined the structure of the exercises to store and the architecture of the system, next thing to do is the exercise evaluation. This point will determine what exercises are more intuitive to users, and due to that, more voted. All the registered users have the opportunity to vote the exercises that they see into the system to determine which ones are the exercises that are more identified with the philosophy, in other words, the best resolved exercises must be the ones that are closer to the user's reality, the most intuitive and better explained.

The voting system is defined by a stars system. A similar method is used in [7] where stars are used for evaluating specific characteristics. The most valuated will have five stars and the less valuated will have zero. Thus, an exercise with two stars and a half will mean that is a medium quality exercise. The figure 3 shows how this classification based on stars is visualized into a determined exercise.

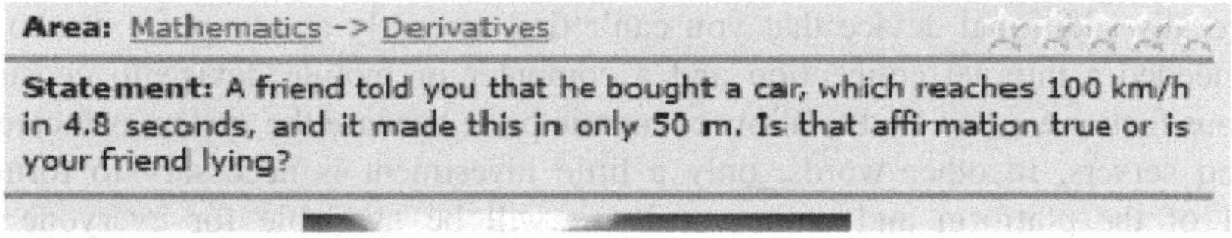

Area: Mathematics -> Derivatives

Statement: A friend told you that he bought a car, which reaches 100 km/h in 4.8 seconds, and it made this in only 50 m. Is that affirmation true or is your friend lying?

Fig. 4. Exercise score based on the stars system

Basing the exercises on this type of classification, it is easier and quicker for users and/or students to find examples that are really useful, avoiding thus an exhaustive search that expends time and moral. For this motive, it is essential that the exercise is scored by a quantity of people as greater as possible to adjust its mark. In addition, if the mouse is maintained over the stars (PC users) or if someone makes click on them (mobile device users), the number of users, who have voted the exercise will be shown. It is useful to evaluate this score. Besides the previous facts, we have to take into consideration that the exercises are divided in different themes to facilitate the search labour.

5   Repercussions into the Educational System

Due to the global character of the system, any teacher has access to the uploaded exercises in the data base. Thus, these examples can be shown to the students for bracing their knowledge about a subject in particular. For that reason, it helps to teaching staff at time to find adequate and useful material that can call the students' attention and with it, to improve the learning. In relation with students, they have also access to the platform, so that the learning followed by the studies plan is accompanied by the realization of exercises that show to the student a reality where to use the concepts studied[8][9][10].

Inside of educative infrastructure, the inclusion of this new system doesn't generate a revolutionary impact due to we don't need make big changes that can destabilize the system and to provoke mistrust. The cost in infrastructures of the implantation of this system into the academic center is non-existent because it doesn't depend of hardware that the center has to buy or of classes used as storage or where to put in practice the new methodologies. The only necessary thing is to have a internet connection for accessing the platform. Once into it, each teacher/user will have access to material that they need to their class. Thus, the impact of the implantation of this system is close to 0.

6   Conclusions

With the proposed environment we improve the learning and the aid to teachers for making their work, getting that students show a bigger interest as a consequence of the examples have a real practical application. In addition, the impact that the incorporation into the class of this system suppose is minimum because it doesn't require any additional device that you can't find currently at any place due to it is only needed a internet connection and a computer or mobile device to consult it. Previous facts are associated to a low economic price because the system is located on isolated servers, in other words, only a little investment is necessary to form the kernel of the platform and automatically it will be available for everyone (this investment is only necessary in case of a private platform).

However, not only the teaching staff is benefited, but also the students and users that want to use the platform, are be able to do it. Thus, using the platform helps to keep in mind the contents learned and to consult real use cases where to apply the concepts. Moreover, through the exercises' marks the platform generates a sort system where the best exercises are the most valuated by the users and, as consequence, the first ones to appear in searches. It decreases the searching time of exercises that can be useful for the student.

References

1. Sarason, S.B.: The Predictable Failure of Educational Reform: Can We Change Course before It's Too Late? The Jossey-Bass Education Series and the Jossey-Bass Social and Behavioral Science Series (1990) ISBN-1-55542-269-1
2. Noddings, N.: The Challenge to Care in Schools: An Alternative Approach to Education. Advances in Contemporary Educational Thought 8 (1992) ISBN-0-8077-3177-3
3. Duttweiler, P.C., Mutchler, S.E.: Organizing the Educational System for Excellence: Harnessing the Energy of People (1990)
4. Sultan, N.: Cloud computing for education: A new dawn? International Journal of Information Management 30(2) (April 2010)

5. Ercan, T.: Effective use of cloud computing in educational institutions. Procedia - Social and Behavioral Sciences 2(2) (2010)
6. Giurgiu, I., Riva, O., Juric, D., Krivulev, I., Alonso, G.: Calling the Cloud: Enabling Mobile Phones as Interfaces to Cloud Applications. In: Bacon, J.M., Cooper, B.F. (eds.) Middleware 2009. LNCS, vol. 5896, pp. 83–102. Springer, Heidelberg (2009)
7. Fardoun, H.M., Alghazzawi, D.M., González, L.C.: Improving learning methods through student's opinion into teacher's curricula Using graphical representations. In: Federated Conference on Computer Science and Information Systems, FedCSIS (2013)
8. Inan, F.A., Lowther, D.L., Ross, S.M., Strahl, D.: Pattern of classroom activities during students' use of computers: Relations between instructional strategies and computer applications. Teaching and Teacher Education 26(3), 540–546 (2010)
9. Brown, S., Bull, J., Race, P.: Computer-assisted Assessment of Students. British Library Cataloguing in Publication Data. ISBN 0-7494-3035-4
10. de Jong, F., Veldhuis-Diermanse, E., Lutgens, G.: Computer-Supported Collaborative Learning in University and Vocational Education. In: CSCL2 Carrying Forward the Conversation ch. 3
11. del Jesús, V.: Elementos Básicos del Cálculo Diferencial (Basic Elements of Differential Calculus). Ude@ (2007) ISBN 958-665-961-0
12. AL-Malaise, A.S., AL-Ghamdi, Fardoun, H.M., Antonio Paules, C.: Tutor Platform for Vocational Students Education. In: Federated Conference on Computer Science and Information Systems, pp. 703–707 (2013)
13. Fardoun, H.M., Mashat, A.S., González, L.C.: New subject to improve the educational system: Through a communication channel betwen educational institution-company. In: Federated Conference on Computer Science and Information Systems (FedCSIS), pp. 709–712 (2013)
14. Fardoun, H.M., Mashat, A., López, S.R.: Applying Professional Solutions within the Educational Environments by Means of Cloud Computing: Coaching for Teachers. Journal of Universal Computer Science 19(12), 1703–1717 (2013)
15. Romero, S., Fardoun, H.M., Penichet, V.M., Gallud, J.A.: Tweacher: New proposal for Online Social Networks Impact in Secondary Education. ADCAIJ: Advances in Distributed Computing and Artificial Intelligence Journual, 9–18 (2013)

An Investigation into Gender Role Conformity in an Online Social Networking Environment

Alexander Fawzi and Andrea Szymkowiak

University of Abertay Dundee, Dundee DD1 1HG, UK
{a.fawzi,a.szymkowiak}@abertay.ac.uk

Abstract. Social networking sites (SNS) offer a relatively novel arena in which to display and investigate social behavior. The study investigated consistency between social behaviors typical of traditional (offline) social interactions and those online by examining conformity to gender stereotypes in an online social networking environment. Findings from gender role conformity research based on traditional approaches provided a framework for analyzing online social interactions. Three predictions were derived: 1) females will display higher expression in status updates than males; 2) there will be a relationship between status update frequency and the amount of friends in an individual's network; and 3) there will be an effect of gender on concentration of emotional expression within status updates. All three predictions were at least partially supported with significant differences apparent between males' and females' online behavior. The findings are discussed with respect to theories on gender differences.

Keywords: Social behavior, gender role, conformity, internet-mediated research, social networking.

1 Introduction

The current research investigated conformity to gender stereotypes in an online social networking environment. Traditionally, research regarding gender differences has been carried out in controlled studies and has been reliant on participant feedback to form the data for analysis [1]. The unobtrusive observation of expressions of gender might present a more natural way of investigating how gender affects behavior, as it is less subjected to reporting biases. The justification for the current research lies in the lack of consistency of previous findings on gender differences [1] and the availability of new methodologies (observational through IMR) with which to approach this research. In the following sections, we will review theories of gender and research on stereotyping, with a particular focus on emotional expression. Next we briefly examine methodological aspects of IMR, followed by a description of our study.

1.1 Theories of Gender

The term sex is used typically to refer to the biologically determined aspects of an individual, i.e. we are described as male or female depending on our chromosomal

G. Meiselwitz (Ed.): SCSM 2014, LNCS 8531, pp. 322–330, 2014.

make-up. The term gender is used to refer to the patterns of behavior and typical personality characteristics associated with the sex of an individual, for example, masculine or feminine [2].Social role theory represents a social perspective on gender differences which, although heavily debated and researched, conjures great interest. Social role theory reflects the idea of males and females having differing behavioral norms due to historically divergent roles ingrained through social models of learning [3, 4]. The segregation of roles based on sex seems apparent throughout human history and societies. Evidence of a gender split can be seen as stemming from the biologically determined division of labor in Man's primitive days when males' superior upper-body strength favored them in roles as hunters and ploughmen, both being systematic, labor-intensive tasks [5]. These tasks would have required them to be instrumental, aggressive, and assertive. However, females, with reproductive responsibility, were more physically suited to supportive, interpersonal tasks such as child-rearing [5], requiring them to be communal, expressive, and empathic to the needs of others [4, 6, 7]. Thus, divergent gender roles and associated behavioral norms may be considered both biologically and socially influenced. Given the vast plethora of personality and behavioral differences amongst people, it may seem superficial to separate and analyze individuals based on gender. However, the huge amount of research into gender differences makes it an ideal area from which to draw benchmarks and comparisons for investigating congruency between online and already researched, offline behaviors. Between 1967 and 2002, over 50,000 articles were published regarding inter-gender differences [8]. However, a lack of consistent findings means that this is still an area which warrants investigation. This prompts the need to examine the methodology of previous research to highlight potential comparative shortcomings and to carry out further research, minimizing as far as possible any identified limitations in methodology or interpretation of results, such as those encountered in laboratory settings (e.g., social desirability in participant responses).

1.2   Stereotypes and Their Influence on Behavior

An understanding of gender stereotypes, stereotype-conformity, and attitudes towards stereotype-conformists provides insight into one possible mechanism by which gender differences are promoted and maintained [9]. With specific regard to conforming to sex related norms, Wood, Christensen, Hebl and Rothberger (1997) examined participants' reactions to an experience involving "dominance, power and assertiveness over others" or "warmth, caring and concern for others" [9, p.525]. These represented a stereotypically male (dominance behavior) scenario and stereotypically female (communal behavior) scenario, respectively [3, 4]. Men reported having significantly higher positive feelings during the dominance interactions than females. Females reported marginally greater positive feelings than males during the communal experience. These results, coupled with the participants' ratings of their ideal self as holding attributes being stereotypically of their gender in accordance with social role theory, yield some interesting implications. Primarily, the research indicates a participant's bias towards conformity to the stereotypes associated with their gender due to positive reinforcement received through positive feelings. That is to say, we are rewarded for behaving in accordance with societally imposed stereotypes, which extend to patterns of behavior, associated with whichever role we assume. These patterns differ from role to role, such as differences in emotional expression for males and females [9].

1.3   Gender Differences in Emotion

Emotion can be defined as processes encompassing "...physiological arousal, expressive behaviors, and conscious experience." [10]. It is these expressive behaviors which normally constitute the main measurable variable as an indicator of emotionality amongst individuals [1, 11, 12]. Based on the stereotypical assumption that women are the more emotional sex, Feldman Barrett et al. (1998) carried out an investigation using self-descriptive, retrospective, measures compared with data collected from momentary ratings of emotion. The results indicated that during self-descriptions, females rated themselves as having felt significantly higher emotional intensity, overall, as well as rating themselves higher in the specific areas of openness to feelings, anxiety, sadness, and positive emotion compared to male participants. Interestingly, these findings were not reflected in the results obtained from the momentary emotion ratings which indicated no statistically significant emotion-based differences between males and females [1]. The question arises whether this difference is due to an incorrect recollection of emotion, i.e. faulty memory, and/or associated with it, an exaggeration of stereotypical emotional expression on the part of the participants.

Other work [12] examined gender differences in expression of emotion in an online social network environment; drawing results from text-analysis of dyadic interactions between network-linked individuals on Twitter. Kivran-Swaine et al. (2012) found the highest rates of positive emotional expression in female-female interactions. This coincides with the stereotypical view of females being more emotional than males who were shown to be least emotionally expressive, especially in male – male dyadic interactions. This study differs from the current study in the nature of the units of analysis. Whereas Kivran-Swaine et al. analyzed dyadic conversations, the current study investigated behavior based on one-to-all public communications, potentially allowing for a more generalized supposition of adherence to traditionally held stereotypes, regardless of the composition of the interaction.

1.4   Research Using Online Social Networking Sites

Since the advent of the Internet, SNSs have undeniably flourished [13]. Facebook represents the largest social networking site with over 1 billion active users as of October 2012, accumulating an approximate 10.5 billion minutes of time logged on to Facebook per day [14, 15]. Findings of a recent SNS-user survey indicated 39% of users spend more time interacting socially online than they do in traditional settings and are more comfortable talking to new people online than in real life [14]. Given the popularity of SNSs, research using this platform provides great potential to reach participants on an unprecedented scale.

In addressing the validity of results drawn from data collected in an online social network environment, there are several factors that need to be considered to minimize false interpretation. Primarily, the level of accuracy in a self-representing profile on a social networking site is an important aspect in determining whether data collected from said profile is a true reflection of an individual or a projection of how they wish to be perceived. Research has found varying figures relating to the accuracy of information displayed online. Gross and Acquisti (2005) found evidence suggesting 89% of identified profiles displayed the profile owner's real first and second names, with 3% displaying first names only, and 8% being obviously fake. A further report indicated that 28% of British SNS-users admit to exaggerating the information they display on SNS [13].

Despite the inaccuracies highlighted above, the figures do indicate the majority of information displayed by SNS users might be a true reflection of themselves [14]. However, care must be taken and measures implemented to address the occurrence of false information wherever possible, such as excluding obviously 'fake' information.

1.5   Current Research

The aim of the current research was to investigate gender differences based on traditionally held gender stereotypes through analysis of emotional expression and recording of social behavior in an online setting (Facebook). We used an observational design, falling into the category of Internet Mediated Research [16]. An observational study eliminates experimenter effects, such as those occurring through reliance on self-reports and factors which may promote social desirability in participant responses [1]. In line with the reviewed findings and theories, indicating the perception of the female gender role to be more communally oriented, it is expected that females will display a higher volume of expression in status updates than males, and that these status updates will contain a higher concentration of emotionally expressive language [1, 12]. In line with findings indicating endorsement or antipathy for adherence to or deviation from stereotypical behavior [17], it is expected that females who display more status updates, as it might be indicative of communal behavior, will have more friends in their network than females who display fewer status updates. These expectations are summarized in the hypotheses below:

- Hypothesis 1: Females will display higher expression in status updates than males. For the study, two dependent measures of expression were analyzed. The first being status update frequency and the other being mean word count for the period of data collection.
- Hypothesis 2: There will be a relationship between status update frequency and the amount of friends in an individual's network, especially for females.
- Hypothesis 3: There will be an effect of gender on concentration of positive and negative emotional expression in status updates, as indexed by a linguistic content analysis.

2   Method

The study took the form of naturalistic observation with data being collected from publicly viewable social network sources on Facebook. The profiles for 300 Facebook users were monitored for a period of 4 weeks. Public one-to-all status updates and communications were collated and linguistically analyzed. In addition, a Facebook users' number of friends was recorded. For the linguistic analysis, two measures of expression were analyzed, i.e., status update frequency and mean word count. Content analysis of emotional expression was carried out using Linguistic Inquiry and Word Count software [18], which analyzes text files to provide outputs on 80 linguistic dimensions. We investigated total emotional expression, positive emotions, negative emotion, sadness, anxiety and anger.

3   Results

Hypothesis 1: Females will display higher expression in status updates than males. Visual inspection of Fig. 1 (A) shows that, on average, females had a higher frequency of status updates than males (confidence intervals (CI) for females being 25.87 and 19.14 and for males being 19.61 and 14.37), but not significantly so, as established by a Mann Whitney U test (two-tailed) [U=10034, N1=134, N2=166, p=0.145].

Fig. 1 (B) shows that females had a higher average word count (mean = 481.39) than males (mean = 344.20). The upper and lower CIs for females were 556.67 and 406.10 and for males were 403.13 and 285.27. A Mann Whitney U test (two-tailed) confirmed that this difference was significant at the 5% level [U=9526, N1=134, N2=166, p=0.04].

Hypothesis 2: There will be a relationship between status update frequency and the amount of friends in an individual's network. Fig. 2 shows significant positive associations between frequency of status updates and number of Facebook friends for both males [rs(120)=0.239, p=0.017] and females [rs(147)=0.254, p=0.004].

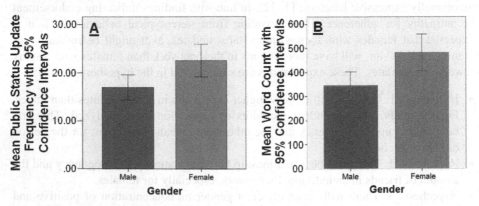

Fig. 1. Bar charts showing mean status update frequencies (A) and mean word count for collated status updates (B) with 95% confidence intervals for males and females

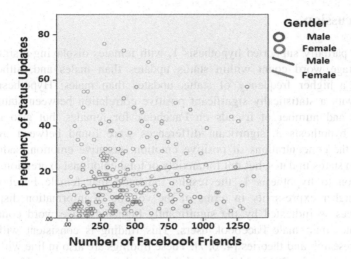

Fig. 2. Scatterplot showing relationship between frequencies of status updates and number of Facebook friends for males and females

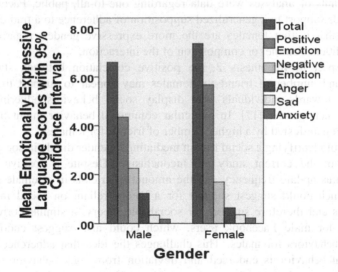

Fig. 3. Bar chart showing mean concentration of emotional expression in status updates for various emotional dimensions for males and females

Hypothesis 3: There will be an effect of gender on concentration of emotional expression in status updates. To examine the observed differences between males' and females' mean concentrations for the various dimensions of emotional expression (Fig 3), Mann Whitney U tests (two tailed) were carried out and were found to be significant at the 5% level for concentrations of positive emotion (p<0.001), negative emotion (p<0.001), sadness (p=0.042) and anger (p<0.001).

4   Discussion

The results partially supported hypothesis 1, with females displaying a significantly higher average word count within status updates than males and, although not significant, a higher frequency of status updates than males. Hypothesis 2 was supported with a statistically significant positive correlation between status update frequencies and number of friends on Facebook for females, but also males. In relation to hypothesis 3, significant differences were found between males and females in the concentrations of positive emotion, negative emotion, sadness, and anger within status updates, but not for anxiety or total emotional expression.

In relation to hypothesis 1, the results indicated that female Facebook users displayed higher expressivity in terms of the volume of information displayed in status updates as indicated by the significantly higher average word count within status updates than male Facebook users. This finding is consistent with that of traditional research and theories [4, 6, 7]. These findings are also in line with those of Kivran-Swaine et al. (2012) who used dyadic gender-composition of bi-directional interactions on twitter. With this in mind, similar findings in the current study in which the units of analyses were data regarding one-to-all, public, Facebook status updates lends support to a generalized supposition of adherence to a traditionally held stereotype (that is that females are the more expressive gender) regardless of the setting (traditional/online) or composition of the interaction.

With respect to hypothesis 2, the positive correlation between status update frequency and number of friend for females may appear to support the theory of favorability towards individuals who display social behaviors adhering to those ascribed to their gender [17]. In particular communal behavior might be met with endorsement manifested by a higher number of friends for females.

In terms of identifying a social role in mediating a gender divide in social behavior, the results of the current study are inconclusive. Despite a positive correlation between status update frequency and the amount of friends in a female's Facebook network which could suggest support for a theory reliant on social mediation of gender roles and therefore support for social-role theory, a similar correlation was also found for male Facebook users, which could also suggest endorsement of communal behaviors for males. This challenges the idea that adherence to gender-stereotypical behavior is endorsed and deviation from such behavior is met with antipathy. However, a lack of control measures to identify the gender composition of an individual's Facebook friends may have masked any significant associations, which could be investigated in future studies. Thus, although the current findings do concur in general with the stereotypical gender-oriented behaviors associated with social-role theory, they do not provide insights into the possible mechanisms through which a gender divide is promoted or maintained.

Regarding hypothesis 3, there were several significant differences identified in concentrations of emotional expression by use of emotionally charged language. Primarily, and in line with Feldman Barrett et al.'s (1998) findings with respect to *retrospective* measures of emotionality, the results indicate that females displayed significantly higher concentrations of positive emotion and sadness in their status updates compared to males. These findings challenge the lack of significant differences found by Feldman Barrett et al. (1998) between males and females for *momentary* ratings of emotion [1], if one assumes that Facebook users update their profiles frequently, and thus, do not rely on retrospection extensively. In the context of the current study this retrospective bias may play a role in emotional expression depending on the duration a memory is held before being used prior to the creation of the measurable data. Due to the observational design of the current study it was not possible to monitor the time between a preceding event and the genesis of a status update.

Males expressed a significantly higher concentration of negative emotion and anger compared to females. Although this may seem to contradict the theory of females being more emotionally expressive than males, this may not be the case when we consider the dimensions of emotion concerned. Within the variable category of Anger, LIWC includes several target words which may also relate to aggression, such as 'kill'. Taking this into consideration, this finding may be extrapolated to at least partially reflect findings relating to aggression. Daly and Wilson (1988) [19] suggested that the masculine gender role includes higher aggression than the feminine gender role. Taken together with our findings this is consistent with observations of the need for some species of male animals to display higher aggression in order to be selected by females in mating, an integral aspect of the biological perspective of gender roles [20].

5 Conclusion

With a view to the generalized stereotypes associated with typically male or typically female social behaviors, the findings of the current study generally support the persistence of gender-based differences in terms of emotional expression across research platforms. In addition, the positive correlation between status update frequency and number of friends for females is consistent with the findings from traditional research, highlighting the role of IMR as a viable tool for investigating human behavior. However, a positive correlation between status update frequency and number of friends was also found for males, which might indicate endorsement of communal behaviors within an online forum, which is not consistent with traditional (offline) research on stereotypical behaviors for males. This begs the question to which extent deviations from stereotypical roles are acceptable in an online forum, opening up an interesting area for future studies, challenging the persistence of gender stereotypes in this domain.

References

1. Feldman Barrett, L., Robin, L., Pietromonaco, P.R., Eyssell, K.M.: Are Women the "More Emotional" Sex? Evidence from Emotional Experiences in Social Context. Cognition and Emotion 12(4), 555–578 (1998)

2. Nobelius, A.: What is the difference between sex and gender? Faculty of Medicine, Nursing and Health Sciences, http://www.med.monash.edu.au/gendermed/sexandgender.html

3. Eagly, A.H.: Sex Differences in Social Behavior: A Social-role interpretation. Erlbaum Associates Inc., New Jersey (1987)

4. Brannon, L.: Gender Stereotypes: Masculinity and Femininity. In: Gender: Psychological Perspectives. 4/E, pp. 159–185. Pearson (2004)

5. Eagly, A.H., Wood, W., Diekman, A.: Social role theory of sex differences and similarities: A current appraisal. In: Eckes, T., Trautner, H.M. (eds.) The Developmental Social Psychology of Gender, pp. 123–174. Psychology Press (2000)

6. Archer, J.: Sex Differences in Social Behaviour: Are the Social Role and Evolutionary Explanations Compatible. American Psychologist 51(9), 909–917 (1996)

7. Hess, N.H., Hagen, E.H.: Sex differences in indirect aggression: Psychological evidence from young adults. Evolution and Human Behavior 27, 231–245 (2006)

8. Howe, J.: An Investigation into the Discourses of Secondary Aged Girls' Emotions and Emotional Difficulties. University of Birmingham Research Archive: E-theses repository (2009), http://etheses.bham.ac.uk/325/1/howe09EdPsychD.pdf

9. Wood, W., Christensen, P.N., Hebl, M.R., Rothberger, H.: Conformity to Sex-Typed Norms, Affect and the Self-Concept. Journal of Personality and Social Psychology 73(3), 523–535 (1997)

10. Myers, D.G.: Theories of Emotion. In: Psychology: 7/E. Worth Publishers, New York (2004)

11. Snell Jr., W.E., Miller, R.S., Belk, S.S., Garcia-Falconi, R., Hernandez-Sanchez, J.E.: Men's and Women's Emotional Disclosures: The Impact of Disclosure Recipient, Culture, and the Masculine Role. Sex Roles 21(7/8), 467–486 (1989)

12. Kivran-Swaine, F., Naaman, M., Brody, S., Diakopoulos, N.: Of Joy and Gender: Emotional Expression in Online Social Network. Squarespace (2012), http://funda.squarespace.com/storage/CSCW2012Poster.Pdf

13. Gross, R., Acquisti, A.: Information Revelation and Privacy in Online Social Networks (The Facebook case). In: Proceedings of the 2005 ACM Workshop on Privacy in the Electronic Society, pp. 71–80 (2005)

14. Pring, C.: 216 Social Media and Internet Statistics, http://thesocialskinny.com/216-social-media-and-Internet-statistics-september-2012/

15. Facebook Newsroom, http://newsroom.fb.com/Key-Facts

16. The British Psychological Society. Report of the Working Party on Conducting Research on the Internet: Guidelines for Ethical Practice in Psychological research online (2007)

17. Glick, P., Fiske, S.T.: An Ambivalent Alliance: Hostile and Benevolent Sexism as Complementary Justifications for Gender Inequality. American Psychologist 56(2), 109–118 (2001)

18. Pennebaker, J.W., Booth, R.J., Francis, M.E.: LIWC2007: Linguistic Inquiry and Word Count, Austin, Texas (2007)

19. Daly, M., Wilson, M.: Evolutionary Social Psychology and Family Homicide. Science 242, 519–524 (1988)

20. Cialdini, R., Kenrick, D., Neuberg, S.: Chapter 1 Introduction to Social Psychology (1999), http://www.scribd.com/doc/44045375/Introduction-to-Social-Psychology

Can Network Help Chinese Microblogs Diffuse? Analyzing 118 Networks of Reposts About Social Issues in China

King-wa Fu

Journalism and Media Studies Centre, University of Hong Kong
kwfu@hku.hk

Abstract. The use of microblog, i.e. Twitter, in politics and social issues has been broadly studied. But research into the role of microblog in China's unique socio-political context is still limited and empirical data remain inadequate. In this study, we conceptualize the process of diffusion of microblogs in China as a "social network" and deploy social network analysis to operationalize the network characteristics of such process. Using Sina Weibo's Open API, we collected 118 networks of reposts related to various social issues in China. While our findings describe the network characteristics of the samples, we reveal that decentralized network is a key contributing factor for diffusion of microblogs in China. The implication of the result is then discussed.

Keywords: China, microblog, social network analysis, information diffusion.

1   Background

Broadly speaking, social media is a newer digital communication technology designed for facilitating human interactions and social connectivity. While its formal definition remains contestable [1], social media can be generally characterized by their capacity to produce and exchange user-generated content, participate in collaborative projects, and connect with one another in a variety of social communities [2]. Real life examples of social media applications include the online encyclopedia Wikipedia, video-sharing website YouTube, content sharing sites Flickr, Instagram, and Pinterest, social networking sites Facebook and Google Plus, microblogs such as Twitter or Chinese Sina Weibo or Tencent Weibo. (Remark: Throughout the text, Weibo is referred to the company or the title of Chinese microblog service; weibo is referred to a unit of message or post of the microblog service in China)

Microblog service is a self-publishing online application that enables Internet users to communicate with each other by posting or sharing short messages, say up to 140 characters in length in Twitter. Functionally, it allows users to subscribe the posts (or "tweets" in Twitter parlance) made by other users ("friends"), to be followed by others ("followers"), to forward message to one's followers ("retweet" or "repost" throughout the text), and to create searchable "hashtags" preceded by the pound sign

G. Meiselwitz (Ed.): SCSM 2014, LNCS 8531, pp. 331–341, 2014.
© Springer International Publishing Switzerland 2014

(#). Microblogging is characterized by its rapid diffusion of short messages through social networks comprising clusters of interconnected friends/followers relationships, i.e., friends, friends of friends, and so on. Such human connectivity has demonstrated powerful mass communication capacity during a variety of social and political incidents [3, 4], natural disasters [5-8], general elections [9-11], and political uprisings [12, 13].

In China, mass communication is vigorously controlled by the governments. Chinese traditional news media are subject to heavy-handed government monitoring and regulation. Much essential information on the newspaper or the Internet, which are not permissible by the government, is censored [14]. As a result, the country ranks at the bottom (173 out of 179) in the international rankings of freedom of the press and speech [15]. However, even though Chinese Internet platforms remain to be regulated and monitored [16], Internet users in China seem to possess greater autonomy over what they read and say concerning public affairs than they enjoy in their engagement with the traditional media and the public sphere [17]. Chinese microbloggers have successfully made local issues become international agenda, for example the "My father is Li Gang," "Guo Meimei," and "Wenzhou high-speed train crash" incidents were widely reported in the Western media after appearing in Chinese microblogs.

According to the China Internet Network Information Center [18], the number of Chinese microbloggers reached 331 million in mid-2013, accounting for 56% of the total Internet population. The two leading Chinese microblog platforms are Sina Weibo and Tencent Weibo, each of which claims to have 500 million registered accounts [19]. Nevertheless, our study reveals an alternative picture [17]: about 60% of Sina Weibo registered accounts are inactive and never make a post; the weibo contents are unevenly distributed among users and about 5% of whom create over 80% of the overall original posts.

1.1   Diffusion of Microblogs in China

The propagation of emerging social topics or critical novel ideas on the Internet can be conceptualized as a process of diffusion of innovations [20], under which is defined as "the process by which an innovation is communicated through certain channels over time among the members of a social system" (p. 5), where an innovation is defined as "an idea, practice, or object that is perceived as new by an individual or other unit of adoption" (p. 11). The process of a successful diffusion of innovation is determined by the following factors [21]: characteristics of the innovations (e.g., whether they have public consequence), characteristics of the innovators (e.g., their personal characteristics and position in the social network), and environmental and contextual setting (e.g., political conditions and societal culture).

Chinese microblogs are known to be a powerful tool for amplifying local incidents and setting the public agenda [22]. In a controlled media environment such as China's, local journalists and foreign correspondents alike rely on popular microblogs and social media as sources of information on breaking news. The use of microblogs in China thus has clear public consequence. Microblog opinion leaders are identified as information hubs when reposting significant messages [17], thereby serving as "innovators" in this context. The heavily regulated media environment in China is a unique political and social setting that contextualizes the process of diffusion of novel information.

1.2   A Network Perspective on Microblogs

Human communication via the Internet has long been thought as a form of social network [23]. According to Manuel Castells [24], the widespread use of information and communication technology has given rise to the formation of a basic mode of social organization, namely "network society", along with the state and the capitalist market. Yochai Benkler puts forward the notion of the "networked information economy," [25] suggesting that decentralized individual actions can be interconnected by the network technologies for cooperative and coordinated work facilitated by advances in digital communication and computing technology.

Technological advances and the growing popularity of social media applications enable online users to be situated within a set of interconnected social networks that constitute the "dominant form of social organization (p. 11)" [26]. The networked individuals within such an organization (who are known as the nodes of the network) are able to take advantage of their connections with close friends, acquaintances, and friends of friends (represented by an edge between two nodes) to extend their ability to reach beyond a densely knit group, communicate effectively with the society at large, and become ubiquitously accessible [26]. Under such conception, social networks can be multi-dimensional in essence: behavioral (tweeting, retweeting, and following), semantic (sharing topics of interest, hashtags, or media content), cognitive (value or attitude), affective (emotion or happiness), or societal (reflection of real-life relationships) and various dimensions are distinct but are interlinked. As Rainie and Wellman put it, "the lines between information, communication, and action have blurred: Networked individuals use the Internet, mobile phones, and social networks to get information at their fingertips and act on it, empowering their claims to expertise (p.14)" [27].

With such backdrop of network perspective, we extend the idea to conceptualize the interconnections among microbloggers. The notion of community network has been used to describe the formation of a network of interlinked personal Twitter accounts [28]. Studies analyzing data collected from Twitter have consistently identified the characteristics of human social network such as scale-free and power-law distribution, homophily, and small world phenomenon [29, 30]. These previous works provide empirical support for our attempt to theorize Chinese microblogs as a social network.

Conventional social networks are mainly connected by weak ties [31], where the strength of a tie is "a combination of the amount of time, the emotional intensity, the intimacy (mutual confiding), and the reciprocal services which characterize the tie (p.1361)." Weak ties are thus those with casual acquaintances, not very close friends, neighbors, and co-workers. Granovetter [31] shows that weak ties can actually be quite strong in the sense that a weak-tie interpersonal network is more helpful than a closed group in diffusion of information, e.g., information on job opportunities. Weak ties can bring new and diverse information from other social circles into a strongly connected relationship cluster. A recent study demonstrates that removing weak ties from a social network reduces the effectiveness of information diffusion to a considerable degree [32]. However, another study argues that Twitter networks do not fall perfectly within the scope of weak ties since the emotional intensity and reciprocal relationships among Twitter users are weak [33].

1.3   Research Question

The use of microblog, i.e. Twitter, in politics and social issues has been broadly researched. But study on the role of microblog as well as the formation of network in the Chinese context is still limited. While empirical evidence remains inadequate, the use of the notion "social network" in the Chinese context is still debatable [2]. Another challenge in research is the ubiquity of the mechanisms by which the Chinese authorities control the flow of public information [17].

Previous studies have found the rate of information diffusion via online network is influenced by the network structure [34, 35]. In this study, we seek 1) to describe the network characteristics of the flow of microblogs in China; 2) to examine the relationships between various network characteristics of repost networks in China.

2   Method

2.1   Data Collection

We make use of Sina Weibo's Open API (http://open.weibo.com/) to access raw microblog data in China. To gather the complete set of reposts of a list of original microblogs, we obtained an exhaustive set of reposts using Sina Weibo's repost timeline API (http://open.weibo.com/wiki/Statuses/repost_timeline/en). When the identity code of an original post is given as a parameter, the repost timeline API returns the list of reposts originated from that post. Since Sina imposes a limit of 200 reposts per API call, the whole list of reposts can be obtained by multiple calls of the repost timeline API.

To study the pattern of repost network, we extracted the user names contained in the message content of the reposts. When copying a post, a reference in the form of '@XYZ', where XYZ is the displayed name of a user account, is offered by default by the system as a part of the reposting text and the entire form is preserved in the repost text if it is not deleted or modified by the user. We took advantage of this property to trace back the pattern of reposting.

We then collected 118 sets of reposts of Chinese microblogs in August 2012. The original posts were identified by keyword search in our Weiboscope database [17]. The samples covered a wide spectrum of social issues ranging from anti-corruption (keywords 贪污 or 腐败), housing demolition (拆迁 or 迁拆), misbehavior of city administrators (城管), and campaign calling for finding lost children ([失踪 or 寻人]

and 小孩). Because of political sensitivity of certain topics, some posts found in the Weiboscope database had been removed from the user timeline. However, the whole list of reposts was still accessible by using the repost timeline API even the original post no longer existed (remark: Since 2013, the updated version of Sina API does not allow access to censored reposts anymore). As the time stamp was attached with the returned data, cumulative distribution of each set of reposts was devised for the analysis. Their descriptive statistics were also calculated and were presented in table format.

2.2 Modelling Network Characteristics of Reposts

The network connectivity of microbloggers is represented by a directed social graph indicating the flow of repost messages between microbloggers, in which a link (an arrow) between two nodes signifies a microblogger forwarding another user's post. For example, If User B reposts a received message sent from User A, such relationship is represented by an arrow pointing from User A (a node) to User B (another node). In this way, microblog data are mapped into a network data structure in which a node represents a microblogger, the node attributes denote one's characteristics, e.g., sex, province, and follower count, and an edge between two nodes stands for a repost from one microblogger to another.

For instance, each individual node represents a microblogger who reposts a message, say microblogger M with a list of followers $F(M)=[FM_1, FM_2,..... FM_f]$, where f is the total number of followers of M. The out-degree centrality of User M means the number of M's followers who eventually repost the message after receiving the message from M. Like in Figure 1, if M has 10 followers $F(M)=[FM_1, FM_2,.....$ $FM_{10}]$, and the followers FM_1, FM_3, FM_8, FM_9, and FM_{10} repost the message sent by M, the out-degree centrality of M is then 5. Only one follower of FM_1, namely FFM_1, reposts the message again and thus the out-degree of FM_1 is 1. Two followers of FM_9, FFM_{91} and FFM_{92}, reposts the message and thus the out-degree of FM_9 is 2.

The out-degree centrality serves as an indicator of the strength of the microblogger in propagating the message. The in-degree centrality of M represents the number of times that M reposts the same message received from other microbloggers and usually it is one time. When following a list of microbloggers, M does possibly receive the same message from multiple sources and thus M can still repost more than one time; The betweenness centrality of M represents the total count of pairs of nodes in the network whose shortest path between them consists of M, denoting the relative importance of the position where M is located as a bridging tie to link up different clusters within the network; Betweenness centrality is an indicator of the intermediary power of a node (microblogger) [36]. In this study, we deploy betweenness centralization to measure the extent to which the most central node in the network differs from all other nodes. Moreover, the proportion of out-degree of the maximum degree node to total number of edges, i.e. denoting as Degree (Max), is computed to indicate the role of the highest out-degree microblogger in the network. Therefore the higher value of the Degree (Max), the more important role of the highest out-degree microblogger one has (centralized network).

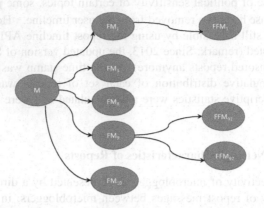

Fig. 1. Reposting Messages as a Network

Some additional network properties were measured [36]. The average path length is the average over all shortest paths between any pair of nodes in a network. The global cluster coefficient is an indicator of the extent to which a network's nodes cluster together, i.e. how many nodes form triangular connections with their adjacent nodes. The diameter of a network represents the longest path between any two nodes in the network. The entropy of degree sequence of a network is a measure of network randomness. For the sake of comparison across networks, the standardized entropy is computed by dividing the entropy by the maximum entropy, i.e. evenly distributed degree sequence. Therefore, the closer the standardized entropy to one, the higher randomness (even distribution) of the degree distribution. Lastly, the degree sequence of a network is fitted to power-law distribution and the power-law exponent is estimated.

2.3   Statistical Analysis

To analyze the set of social networks, we deployed the statistics software package R [37] and its network research package igraph [38]. Network-based commands, including the average shortest path length, standardized entropy, global cluster coefficient, diameter, power-law-fitted, out-degree, and betweenness centralization were used to measure the network characteristics of the samples [36].

Pearson correlation coefficients were used to test the associations between network characteristics. Because of multiple statistical tests between pairs of variables, p values were set as 0.001, 0.01, and 0.05 to indicate different levels of statistical significance.

3   Result

Totally 118 repost networks were analyzed. Their network size ranged from 102 nodes to 63,068 nodes (mean = 5,873, standard deviation = 8,745) and the number of edges varied from 101 edges to 63,368 edges (mean = 5,898, standard deviation = 8,807). The time duration between the first repost and the last repost made (based on the time stamp of the data collected by the API) varied from 17 hours to 5,450 hours (mean = 1,820 hours, standard deviation = 1,463 hours).

Table 1 presents the descriptive statistics of the network characteristics of the samples. A few points are worth noting. First, the mean diameter and average path length were 8.85 and 1.98 respectively, indicating that on average each network had at least a microblogger who was about 9 steps away from the author of the original message. The central tendency of the networks' average shortest path between all microbloggers was about 2 steps. These results seem to suggest that the path of diffusion of reposts is highly efficient.

Second, on average 58% of the network connections were generated by the largest out-degree microblogger in the network and only a tiny proportion of the network, i.e. 3.04×10^{-5} as the mean cluster coefficient, was clustered.

Third, the mean and the standard deviation of the standardized entropy were 0.21 and 0.07 respectively, suggesting that the degree distribution of the sampled networks were mostly nonrandom. The mean betweenness centralization was found as 3.67×10^{-4}. These findings were consistent with the large value of maximum out-degree because of the central role of the key microblogger. Last, the average power-law exponent was 2.37, which is surprisingly close to the one estimated for Twitter connections [30]. This also suggests that a small group of high-out-degree microbloggers contributes the majority of network connections.

Table 1. Descriptive statistics of the network characteristics (n=118)

	Minimum	First quartile	Median	Mean	Third quartile	Maximum	Standard deviation
Diameter	2	5	8	8.85	12	34	5.10
Average Path Length	1.02	1.35	1.65	1.98	2.29	6.53	1.04
Cluster Coefficient	0.00	1.66E-7	3.31E-6	3.04E-5	1.32E-5	5.65E-4	9.30E-5
Degree (Max)	0.21	0.38	0.62	0.58	0.77	0.98	0.22
Betweenness	4.75E-7	1.66E-5	6.39E-5	3.67E-4	1.95E-4	8.33E-3	1.09E-3
Standardized Entropy	0.07	0.16	0.20	0.21	0.26	0.49	0.07
Power-law exponent	0.00	2.18	2.40	2.37	2.62	3.30	0.45

Table 2. shows the Pearson correlation coefficients between the network characteristics of the 118 repost networks.

Table 2. Pearson correlations between the network characteristic (n=118)

	No. of microbloggers	Diameter	Average Path Length	Cluster Coefficient	Degree (Max)	Betweenness	Standardized Entropy	Power-law exponent
No. of microbloggers	1	0.52***	0.33***	ns	-0.29**	ns	-0.19*	ns
Diameter		1	0.85***	ns	-0.66***	0.42***	0.25**	0.18*
Average Path Length			1	ns	-0.68***	0.59***	0.27**	ns
Cluster Coefficient				1	-0.19*	0.43***	0.4***	ns
Degree (Max)					1	-0.27**	-0.4***	ns
Betweenness						1	0.26**	ns
Standardized Entropy							1	0.2*
Power-law exponent								1

Remark: p<0.001***; p<0.01**; p<0.05*; "ns" stands for "non-significance"

The number of microbloggers in the network and the network diameter are the two measures for the extent to which the diffusion of microblogs reached out, i.e. effectiveness of the process of diffusion. As shown in the Table 2, the number of microbloggers in the network who reposted the original message was positively associated with the network diameter (r=0.52, p<0.001) and the average path length (r=0.33, p<0.001) but was negatively correlated with the maximum degree of network (r=-0.29, p<0.01) and the standardized entropy (r=-0.19, p<0.05).

For the network diameter, it was positively associated with the average path length (r=0.85, p<0.001), the standardized entropy (r=0.25, p<0.01), the betweenness centralization (r=0.42, p<0.001), and the power-law exponent (r=0.18, p<0.05) but was correlated negatively with the maximum degree of network (r=-0.66, p<0.001).

4   Discussion

In this study, we attempt to conceptualize the process of diffusion of reposting microblogs in China as a "social network" and deploy social network analysis to operationalize and describe the network characteristics of such interconnections between "networked" microbloggers who involve in reposting an original message.

Based on our findings, we identify some network characteristics that are conducive to the spread of messages about social issues via microblogs in China. While the presence of highly centralized microbloggers is essential [39], say higher betweenness centralization, our study finds that a lower ratio of maximum degree to total number of edges in the network, i.e. a less dominant position of the highest out-degree microblogger or a relative decentralized network, is a key contributing factor for information diffusion. It suggests that the effectiveness of microblog diffusion is not overly dependent on a dominant "online opinion leader", but rather a number of players who have high power to generate reposts and subsequent reposts. Moreover, our study finds a conflicting result on the role of randomness in information diffusion, despite previous finding that randomness helps diffuse information [35]. This part of question requires further investigation.

The finding of this study is particularly timely under the circumstance that the Chinese government has enacted a new regulation to control the spread of "rumor" via reposting weibos (being reposted 500 times) and subsequently some well-known "online opinion leaders" were allegedly targeted [16]. Since the implementation of the real name registration system for microbloggers in 2012 [17], such measures of Internet regulation may be another political intervention of the Chinese government that could limit the free flow of information in China.

Our findings provide an empirical base to understand the role of network characteristics in diffusion of microblogs and we have demonstrated that the conception of "social network" can be applied to theorize and operationalize the flow of microblogs. Nevertheless, our analysis is preliminary and exploratory. Future research is warranted to investigate the information diffusion as a function of time and its association with a broader range of network characteristics.

References

1. Dijck, J.V.: The culture of connectivity: A critical history of social media. Oxford University Press, Oxford (2013)
2. White, J., Fu, K.-W., Benson, B.: Social Media: An Ill-Defined Phenomenon. In: Ozok, A.A., Zaphiris, P. (eds.) OCSC 2013. LNCS, vol. 8029, pp. 422–431. Springer, Heidelberg (2013)
3. Efron, M.: Information search and retrieval in microblogs. Journal of the American Society for Information Science and Technology 62, 996–1008 (2011)
4. Thelwall, M., Buckley, K., Paltoglou, G.: Sentiment in Twitter events. Journal of the American Society for Information Science and Technology 62, 406–418 (2011)
5. Mendoza, M., Poblete, B., Castillo, C.: Twitter under crisis: Can we trust what we RT? In: Social Media Analytics, KDD 2010 Workshops. ACM, Washington, DC (2010)
6. Preis, T., Moat, H.S., Bishop, S.R., Treleaven, P., Stanley, H.E.: Quantifying the Digital Traces of Hurricane Sandy on Flickr. Sci. Rep. 3 (2013)
7. Qu, Y., Huang, C., Zhang, P., Zhang, J.: Microblogging after a major disaster in China: A case study of the 2010 Yushu earthquake. In: CSCW 2011, pp. 25–34. ACM (2011)
8. Vieweg, S., Hughes, A., Starbird, K., Palen, L.: Microblogging during two natural hazards events: What Twitter contribute to situational awareness. In: Proceedings of the 28th International Conference on Human Factors in Computing Systems, pp. 1079–1088. ACM (2010)
9. Adamic, L., Glance, N.: The political blogosphere and the 2004 US election: Divided they blog. In: Proceedings of the 3rd International Workshop on Link Discovery, pp. 36–43. ACM (2005)
10. Burns, A., Eltham, B.: Twitter free Iran: An evaluation of Twitter's role in public diplomacy and information operations in Iran's 2009 election crisis. Communications Policy & Research Forum 2009, University of Technology, Sydney (2009)

11. Lassen, D.S., Brown, A.R.: Twitter: The electoral connection? Social Science Computer Review 29, 419–436 (2011)
12. Castells, M.: Networks of outrage and hope: social movements in the Internet age. Polity, Cambridge (2012)
13. Grossman, L.: Iran protests: Twitter, the medium of the movement. Time Magazine (2009)
14. OpenNet Initiative: China (2009)
15. Reporters Without Borders, http://en.rsf.org/press-freedom-index-2013,1054.html
16. Chin, J.: China Intensifies Social-Media Crackdown. The Wall Street Journal (2013)
17. Fu, K.W., Chan, C., Chau, M.: Assessing Censorship on Microblogs in China: Discriminatory Keyword Analysis and the Real-Name Registration Policy. IEEE Internet Computing 17, 42–50 (2013)
18. China Internet Network Information Center: 32nd statistical report on Internet development in China. China Internet Network Information Center (2013)
19. Mozur, P.: How many people really use Sina Weibo? Wall Street Journal China, Beijing (2013)
20. Rogers, E.M.: Diffusion of innovations. Free Press, New York (1995)
21. Wejnert, B.: Integrating models of diffusion of innovations: A conceptual framework. Annu. Rev. Sociol. 28, 297–326 (2002)
22. Fu, K.W., Chau, M.: Use of Microblogs in Grassroots Movements in China: Exploring the Role of Online Networking in Public Agenda-Setting. Journal of Information Technology & Politics (online first, 2014)
23. Wellman, B.: Computer Networks As Social Networks. Science 293, 2031–2034 (2001)
24. Castells, M.: The rise of the network society. Blackwell Publishers, Cambridge (1996)
25. Benkler, Y.: The wealth of networks how social production transforms markets and freedom. Yale University Press, New Haven (2006)
26. Wellman, B.: Little boxes, glocalization, and networked individualism. In: Tanabe, M., van den Besselaar, P., Ishida, T. (eds.) Digital Cities 2001. LNCS, vol. 2362, pp. 10–343. Springer, Heidelberg (2002)
27. Rainie, L., Wellman, B.: Networked: The new social operating system. The MIT Press, Cambridge (2012)
28. Gruzd, A., Wellman, B., Takhteyev, Y.: Imagining Twitter as an Imagined Community. Am. Behav. Sci. 55, 1294–1318 (2011)
29. Huberman, B., Romero, D., Wu, F.: Social networks that matter: Twitter under the microscope. Available at SSRN 1313405 (2008)
30. Kwak, H., Lee, C., Park, H., Moon, S.: What is Twitter, a social network or a news media? In: WWW 2010, pp. 591–600. ACM (2010)
31. Granovetter, M.S.: The strength of weak ties. Am. J. Sociol. 78, 1360–1380 (1973)
32. Zhao, J., Wu, J., Xu, K.: Weak ties: Subtle role of information diffusion in online social networks. Physical Review E 82, 016105 (2010)
33. Takhteyev, Y., Gruzd, A., Wellman, B.: Geography of Twitter networks. Social Networks 34, 73–81 (2012)
34. Opuszko, M., Ruhland, J.: Impact of the Network Structure on the SIR Model Spreading Phenomena in Online Networks. In: ICCGI 2013, The Eighth International Multi-Conference on Computing in the Global Information Technology, pp. 22–28 (2013)
35. Watts, D.J.: The "New" Science of Networks. Annu. Rev. Sociol. 30, 243–270 (2004)
36. Lewis, T.G.: Network science: Theory and practice. John Wiley & Sons, Hoboken (2009)

37. R Development Core Team: R: A language and environment for statistical computing. R Foundation for Statistical Computing (2011)
38. Csardi, G., Nepusz, T.: The igraph software package for complex network research. Inter. Journal, Complex Systems, vol. 1695 (2006)
39. Guan, W., Gao, H., Yang, M., Li, Y., Ma, H., Qian, W., Cao, Z., Yang, X.: Analyzing user behavior of the micro-blogging website Sina Weibo during hot social events. Physica A: Statistical Mechanics and its Applications 395, 340–351 (2014)

On the Design of Trustworthy Compute Frameworks for Self-organizing Digital Institutions

Thomas Hardjono[1], Patrick Deegan[2], and John Henry Clippinger[2]

[1] MIT Kerberos & Internet Trust Consortium
Massachusetts Institute of Technology, Cambridge, MA 02139, USA
hardjono@mit.edu
[2] ID3 & MIT Media Lab
Massachusetts Institute of Technology, Cambridge, MA 02139, USA
patrick@idcubed.org, john@idcubed.org

Abstract. This paper provides an overview of the *Open Mustard Seed* (OMS) project that seeks to develop a social interaction platform to facilitate *group affiliations* based on Reed's Law [1]. Reed posits that the value of a network soars when users are given the tools for free and responsible association for common purposes. The OMS as tool for common association supports the ability for people to form self-organizing groups following the notion of the *data commons* put forward by Elinor Ostrom [2]. The data commons in OMS consists of various personal data which the owner has agreed to contribute into what Ostrom calls the common-pool resource, and which is to be managed by the self-organized group or institution. This paper discusses some design considerations of the OMS platform from the perspective of the privacy and security of the personal data that participate in the common-pool resource. The technical core value of the OMS lies in its construction of the *Trusted Compute Cells*, which are intended to be recombinable and embeddable units of logic, computation and storage.

Keywords: Reed's Law, personal data, open data commons, social computing, virtualization, cloud computing.

1 Introduction: Authority and Governance in the Next Generation Internet

The Internet offers a new opportunity for individuals, communities and societies to interact based on self-organized network governance. Currently there is arguably inequitable access to resources on the Internet, where incumbent service providers and digital technology providers seek to resist open network dynamics and maintain the old business models that in the long term benefit only a fraction of the Internet population [3,4]. Current social networking platforms typically rely upon proprietary business models that collect and sell personal information about users, inducing social distrust in these business models.

G. Meiselwitz (Ed.): SCSM 2014, LNCS 8531, pp. 342–353, 2014.

The *Open Mustard Seed* (OMS) is a project at the ID3 organization [5] and the MIT Media Lab. The mission of the ID3 is to develop new social ecosystems consisting of trusted self-healing digital institutions [6,7]. This mission is being realized through the development of an open data platform to enable people to share all their personal data within a legally constituted *trust framework*. This framework will allow people to have their own personal data service that can securely store and process static and dynamic data about themselves. Governed by privacy by design principles, all agreements of the trust framework support open authentication, storage, discovery, payment, auditing, market making and monetized "app store" services. These aims are in alignment with the growing quantified-self movement occurring today via the Internet.

1.1   Group Forming Networks

Today the various social network services on the Internet can be considered still rudimentary and in their infancy in the face of the promise of Reed's Law [1]. Reed posits that the value in a network increases exponentially as interactions move from a "broadcasting model" that offers "best content" (in which value is described by the number of consumers n) to a network of "peer-to-peer transactions" (where the network's value is based on "most members", mathematically denoted as n^2). However, by far the most valuable networks are based on those that *facilitate group affiliations*. When users have tools for "free and responsible association for common purposes" the value of the network soars exponentially to 2^n. This is the foundation of Reed's *Group Forming Networks* (GFN).

The work of Reed points to the need for a new *network architecture* and tools that facilitates GFNs. Such a network architecture and software systems should allow the establishment of trust and social capital in a user-centric and scalable way. This leads, furthermore, to the promise of *self-organized network governance* as a manifestation of GFNs and which holds a great deal of appeal when it comes to "Big Data". Networked technologies in the sense of Reed's GFN could enable individuals to negotiate their own social contract(s) and meet their needs more directly and responsively. It would enable the emergence of new sorts of effective, quasi-autonomous governance and self-provisioning. And it could achieve these goals without necessarily or directly requiring government. Online communities working in well-designed software environments could act more rapidly, and with more legitimacy than conventional government institutions [6].

1.2   Data Commons and Digital Law

This scenario is inspired not just by Reed's analysis of how to reap value from networks, but by the extensive scholarship of Elinor Ostrom, the Nobel Laureate in economics in 2009. In this new network architecture, self-organizing groups identified by Ostrom [2] could emerge.

Ostrom identified key principles by which self-organized groups can manage common-pool resources in fair and sustainable ways. If data were to be regarded as a common-pool resource, Ostrom's research shows how it would be possible for online groups to devise their own *data commons* to manage their personal data in their own interests. This opens the possibility for the data commons to be the basis for self-organizing digital institutions, where "law" would have a very different character from the kinds law we know today. The development of "digital law" in self-organizing digital institutions would enable users to devise new types of legal contracts that are computationally expressible and executable.

Such an innovation would make institutional corruption and insider collusion far easier to detect and eliminate. Arcane systems of law – once based on oral traditions and printed texts – could make the great leap to computable code, providing powerful new platforms for governance. Law that is dynamic, evolvable and outcome-oriented would make the art of governance subject to the iterative innovations of Moore's Law. Designs could be experimentally tested, evaluated by actual outcomes, and made into better iterations [6].

1.3   Data Driven Societies

Fair access to data shared within "data commons" – as a manifestation of Ostrom's common-pool resources – will have tremendous economic impact, as societies today are increasingly reliant on data as the basis for economic interactions and decisions.

Today "Big Data" offers a way to examine the detailed patterns occurring within the billions of individual exchanges occurring in the Internet and other digital medium. Data such as the billions of telephone call records, credit card transactions and GPS location fixes allow us to precisely measure patterns of interaction between people. These individual exchanges lead to the realization that social influence is the most important phenomenon emerging from these exchanges [8,9].

People are highly influenced by the actions of others. It is the patterns that have to do with the flow of information between people that can provide us with the best insight. These patterns range from telephone calls, social media "tweets" to purchasing behaviors. These flows of information are central not only to the functioning of efficient systems, but key also to innovation. The spread and combination of information is the basis for innovation.

The patterns of information flow underscore the promise of data driven governance and policy. The use of Big Data to examine the fine-grain patterns of information exchanges promises greater transparency, control and stability in market behaviors as well improved social outcomes. Thus the vision of the *data driven society* assumes that we have continual access to Big Data. However, such access must be fair to all and must protect the personal privacy of individuals.

In the remainder of the current paper we provide a semi-technical discussion regarding the OMS platform design (Section 2) which seeks to provide a new infrastructure to let people build their own highly distributed social ecosystem for reliably governing shared resources or data commons, including controlling access to personal data. The OMS could be viewed as a component of a new kind of "social stack" of protocols, software and legal trust frameworks for self-organized digital institutions. Section 3 discusses the groups based on contextual affinities within OMS. The paper is closed in Section 4 with a description of future work.

2   Design of Open Mustard Seed

In this section we discuss the two main building blocks of the OMS, namely the TCF and TCC constructs.

2.1   OMS Building Blocks: TCC and TCF

The design of OMS distinguishes two types of constructions that support the creation and management of digital representations of individuals, groups and institutions. These are the *Trusted Compute Frameworks* (TCF) and *Trusted Compute Cells* (TCC).

The TCC can be considered as a *cell* unit that can be replicated, enjoined with other cells and enhanced with capabilities that are context-specific. The TCF is a larger unit of computational capability that is designed to operate in the virtual environment atop a virtual machines layer.

Figure 1 attempts to illustrate a generic virtualization stack with a TCF environment containing the TCCs. Figure 1 (a) illustrates a TCF with multiple TCCs, where the TCF and the TCCs are viewed as a portable constructs that are moveable from one virtualizatin stack to another. Figure 1 (b) shows abstractly both TCF#2 and TCF#3 running multiple TCC cells with relationships or links among them (within the same TCF and across TCFs). A summary of the functions inside the TCC is shown in Figure 2.

Using the TCF and TCC constructs the OMS project seeks to explore the possibility of a TCF design that can support millions of TCCs, where each TCC represents an individual or a community. In this way the OMS platform can be used not only peer-to-peer interactions, but also peer-to-community and peer-to-business relationships.

2.2   Trusted Compute Frameworks (TCF)

The TCF is a portable compute unit which can be spun-up (and shut-down) by its owner at a TCF-compliant cloud provider (or self-operated infrastructure). The TCF is portable in that it can be relocated from one TCF-compliant cloud provider to another using a trustworthy migration protocol.

One useful way to view the TCF is as a *virtual resource container* within which one or more TCC operates. The primary concern of the TCF is (a) to support the secure and uninterrupted operations of the TCCs and (b) to ensure the TCF as compute unit can operate atop the virtualization stack (e.g. hypervisor layer, security monitor layer, hardware abstraction layer, etc) operated by the cloud provider.

The TCF implements a number of functions related to supporting itself as a virtual resource container:

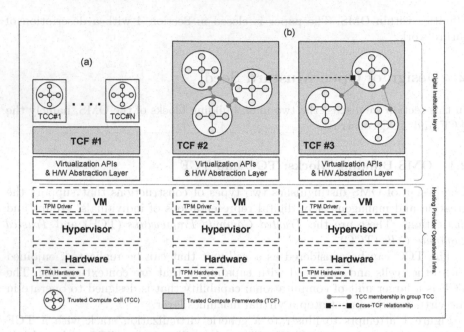

Fig. 1. Overview of TCC and TCF

- *TCF administration*: As a compute unit operating atop a virtualization stack, there are administrative tasks pertaining to the operations of the TCF itself. These include, but not limited to secure boot-up and shut-down under the owner's control, migration and the secure archiving of one or more TCC inside a TCF.
- *VM provisioning & management*: When a TCF is to be launched, a virtual machine (VM) must first be provisioned that suits the desired TCF. These include processes that interact with the underlying layers (e.g. hypervisor layer), processes for memory management, processes related to security management, and others.
- *Framework bootstrapping*: Inside the TCF, there are several processes that need to be started and managed related to the support of the TCC. These include shared databases, API end-points, registries, and so on. Some of these processes will be utilized by the applications that are run by the TCC.
- *Portal, policy & applications management*: Since the TCF by design supports the importation and the running of applications as part of the TCC these applications must be instrumented and managed through the TCF. It is envisioned that much of the social network supporting applications will operate inside the TCC, allowing the TCC to support virtual individuals, groups and institutions.
- *Security & self-protection*: As an infrastructure supporting TCCs, the TCF must provide security and resiliency against possible attacks (e.g. DDOS attacks from external sources, interference from adjacent VMs in a multi-tenant environment, etc).

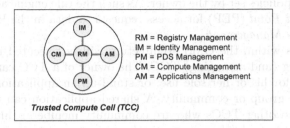

RM = Registry Management
IM = Identity Management
PM = PDS Management
CM = Compute Management
AM = Applications Management

Trusted Compute Cell (TCC)

Fig. 2. Overview of functions of the Trusted Compute Cell (TCC)

2.3   Trusted Compute Cells (TCC)

The Trusted Compute Cell (TCC) is best seen from the perspective of the *social functions* it seeks to provide (as a service) to its owner. When the owner of a TCC is an individual that represents himself or herself in the virtual space, the TCC acts among others as an identity manager, personal data manager, registry of his or her connections (to other TCCs), applications execution manager and other functions.

When a TCC is created to serve as an organizational unit (e.g. social group or digital institution), the TCC has the capability to provide services that pertain to groups and group-behaviors. In this case the TCC establishes a group-identity, and also performs membership management, collective data store management, shared applications management and other group-supporting services.

In designing the TCC, the OMS project seeks to use the TCC as a cell unit from which larger "organisms" and social constructs can be created in the digital world. From the perspective of technological functions, the capabilities of the TCC are grouped under five (5) categories (see Figure 3):

1. *Identity Management*:
   The function of identity management includes authentication, authorization, audit and log, core-identity and persona management [11,12], group identity management, assertions and claims management [13], single-sign-on (SSO) establishment, and others.
2. *Personal Data Store (PDS) Management*:
   The PDS system [3,14] is a component inside the TCC which collects data (or receives streams of data) coming from the owner's devices, either generated by the device (e.g. GPS data) or proxied by the device (e.g. device pulling down copies of the owner's postings on external social network sites). The PDS system also exposes a number of APIs to external readers or consumers of the de-personalized data, such as analytics organizations and data brokers that make available the de-personalized data to the market [4,12]. An important sub-component of the PDS system is the *dynamic rule engine* which performs the role of a filtering gateway for access requests to the TCC owner's data in the PDS. The rule engine receives queries and returns answers to the querier, all the while ensuring that the responses follows the

data access policies set by the owner. As such the rule engine acts as a *Policy Enforcement Point* (PEP) for access requests to data in the PDS system.

3. *Applications Management*:
Applications within the OMS architecture will be executed in the context of the calling (and managing) TCC. The owner of a TCC can stand-up an application for his or her sole use, or stand-up an application that will be shared by a group or community. A shared application can then be made accessible (to other TCCs who are community members) through its published APIs. As such, the management and instrumentation of applications is a core requirement of TCCs.

4. *Compute Power Management*:
Related to applications management is the need for compute power to be expanded or reduced in an elastic manner depending on the current demand of the TCC. Elastic compute capability is particularly relevant in the case of community-shared applications, which may be shared by hundreds to millions of TCCs.

5. *Registry & Cell Management*:
The registry in the TCC is the component that keeps track of identities, relationships, access policies, the TCC's memberships (to communities or institutions), and others. The registry also aids in the day-to-day management of the TCC by its owner. The registry acts as a *Policy Administration Point* (PAP) where the owner of a TCC can set policies regarding access to applications in the TCC (which is relevant in community-shared applications) and access to the owner's data in the PDS.

2.4   Security and Privacy Considerations

There are a number of security and privacy requirements for a TCF/TCC design and implementation. These arise from the need to protect the user's personal data in the PDS inside the TCC and from the need for the TCF as a virtualized resource container to operate in the manner for which it was designed, regardless of the cloud provider's platform on which it is running. Some key security and privacy requirements [10,15,16] include *unambiguous identification* of each TCC instance, *unhindered operation* of a TCC instance and its enveloping TCF, and *truthful attestations* reported by a TCC instance regarding its internal status.

There are a number of new and emerging trustworthy computing technologies that can be used to address some of the security and privacy requirements of the TCC and TCF design. For example, a hardware-based root of trust could be used as the basis for truthful attestations regarding not only the TCF (and the TCCs it supports), but also for the entire virtualization stack. The wide availability of hardware such as *Trusted Platform Module* (TPM) [10] on both client and server hardwares can be used as a starting point to address the security needs of the TCF and TCC. Cloud providers that seek to provide high assurance services could make use of these technologies to increase the security of their virtualization infrastructure [16]. Features such as "trusted boot" of a TCF could

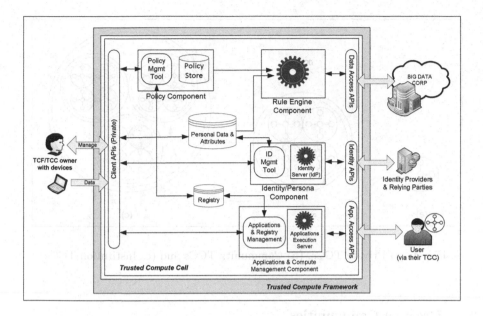

Fig. 3. Overview of Components of the Trusted Compute Cell (TCC)

be deployed more widely if these trustworthy computing hardware were deployed by cloud providers.

A number of features of the TPM hardware could be used today to increase the security of the TCF and TCC. For example, the "sealing" capability of the TPMv2.0 hardware could be used to provide data-at-rest security to a TCF. In such a scenario, when in-rest (not in operation) a TCF could be encrypted and the keys then be bound to a given hardware platform (e.g. bound to the TPM hardware belonging to the cloud provider or the TPM hardware in the owner's portable device). In this way, the launching of the TCF can only be cryptographically possible with the presence of the TCF-owner (i.e. a human owner). Similarly, a secure "TCF migration" protocol could be envisaged based on the migration protocol designed for the TPM hardware [17]. Such a migration protocol would allow a TCF-owner to safely move their TCF from one cloud provider to another with a higher degree of assurance [18].

3   OMS Communities

One of the key aims of the OMS project is to make available new infrastructure on the Internet to allow people to create their own highly distributed social ecosystems for governing shared resources, including their personal data. The OMS uses the notion of *manifests* to express modes of operations of a given TCF as well as the rules of behavior for a community that has been established using a TCF.

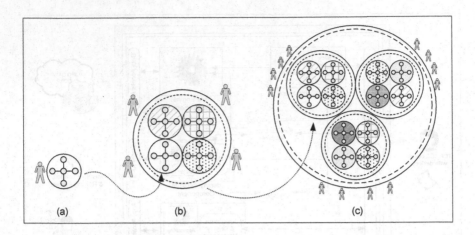

Fig. 4. (a) Private TCCs, (b) Community TCCs and (c) Institution TCCs

3.1   Creating Communities

When one or more users seek to establish a self-organizing community, they must define the purpose of the community and a number of "operating rules" for the community which are expressed internally within the TCF as manifests. Some of these operating and behavioral rules can be complex. Some examples are as follows:

- How the group is to be formed, governed, managed and evolved.
- How users interact and share information based on individual consent.
- What data is collected, and how they are accessed, stored and logged/audited.
- Access policies and access-control mechanisms by which the data is protected.
- How a user may join, suspend or withdraw from the community or institution, and how their personal data can be extracted upon departure.
- What data is retained regarding a departed user and the fact of his/her participation in the community or institution.

It is worth emphasizing here that a human person may participate in several digital communities, own and operate multiple TCFs, and thereby have "slices" of their personal data spread across several digital communities. In all these instances the common requirements include individual consent, control over personal data, and data sharing as an opt-in choice. These personal data stores should be heterogeneous distributed repositories to protect the individual against unauthorized collection of data, inference and linking of data that violates the privacy of the individual [8,4].

3.2   Private and Portal TCCs

The design of the TCC is intended to allow TCCs to be recombinable and embeddable units of logic, computation and storage. An individual person at minimum can represent himself or herself as a solitary unit by creating a lone or private TCC cell contained within a TCF (see Figure 4(a)).

However, life becomes more interesting for that person if he or she participates in a digital community through the use of one or more TCCs that he or she owns and controls. Using the same cell paradigm, the person can launch another distinct TCC that he or she can then use to establish a community-shared TCC. We refer to this as a *Portal TCC* because it represents an entry-point or portal to a shared TCC running shared applications. This is abstractly shown in Figure 4(b).

A portal TCC allows its creator to pre-define the purpose of the TCC, the applications allowed to operate in the TCC and the rules-of-operation (manifests) that govern the TCC. A complete and functioning portal TCC is thus referred to as a *Community TCC*. In order to be accepted into and participate within a Community-TCC (Figure 4(b)), an individual newcomer must agree (opt-in) to the terms of participation of the community as expressed in that TCC's manifest. Such manifests are accessible through public-APIs as a means for "discovery" of resources in that Community-TCC.

Figure 4(c) attempts to illustrate the situation where the community shown in Figure 4(b) participates in a larger community or what we refer to as an *Institution TCC*. Such an Institution-TCC also has its manifests that must be accepted by Community-TCCs and individual TCCs before they can join the Institution-TCC.

4   Future Work

There are a number of future challenges that we want to address, using the OMS as a platform for research:

- *A new Internet stack for Digital Institutions*: There is a need to broaden the notion of "layers" of the (future) Internet by introducing a new "stack". Such a stack should identify distinct layers pertaining to the personal data ecosystem, the open data commons, and digital institutions (see Figure 5). Just as in the Internet stack of today, in the *Digital Institutions Stack* each layer makes use the of "services" of the layer below it, while exposing new services and APIs to the layer above it. We envision that new Internet services will appear in each of the layers, and that each layer will evolve to become an ecosystem in itself.
- *Computational law*: The notion of self-governance is core to the value proposition of communities operating using the TCF and TCC constructs. As such, there needs to be a new perspective regarding "law as algorithm" where rules could be automatically enforced by the TCCs. In other words, law could be self-enforcing in a community that operated the TCFs and TCCs. The rule

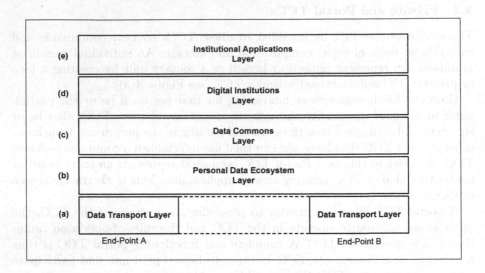

Fig. 5. A New Internet Stack for Digital Institutions

engine inside the TCC could be developed into a digital "law enforcement engine".

– *Protocols for personal data exchange*: A new generation of "protocols" need to emerge that view personal data stores (contained within TCCs) as legitimate end-points. Such a protocol would be key to making personal data a true digital asset [4]. These new protocols would not only exchange data but also observe, negotiate and enforce the legal trust frameworks governing the usage of personal data.

Acknowledgments. We thank Professor Alex (Sandy) Pentland from the MIT Media Lab for his support in this work. We also thank Stephen Buckley from the MIT Kerberos and Internet Trust (MIT-KIT) consortium for his ongoing support.

References

1. Reed, D.P.: That Sneaky Exponential – Beyond Metcalfe's Law to the Power of Community Building (1999), http://www.reed.com/dpr/locus/gfn/reedslaw.html
2. Ostrom, E.: Beyond Markets and States: Polycentric Governance of Complex Economic Systems. Nobel Prize Lecture (December 8, 2009), http://www.nobelprize.org
3. Pentland, A.: Reality Mining of Mobile Communications: Toward a New Deal on Data. In: Dutta, S., Mia, I. (eds.) The Global Information Technology Report 2008-2009: Mobility in a Networked World, World Economic Forum 2009, pp. 75–80 (2009), http://hd.media.mit.edu/wef_globalit.pdf

4. World Economic Forum, Personal Data: The Emergence of a New Asset Class (2011), http://www.weforum.org/reports/personal-data-emergence-new-asset-class
5. ID3, Institute for Data Driven Design (2013), http://www.idcubed.org
6. Clippinger, J.: The Next Great Internet Disruption: Authority and Governance. ID3 (2013), http://idcubed.org
7. Clippinger, J.: A Crowd of One: The Future of Individual Identity. Public Affairs/Perseus Group (2007)
8. Pentland, A.: Data Driven Societies (2012), http://media.mit.edu/pentland
9. Mani, A., Ozdaglar, A., Pentland, A.: Stable, Fair Societies as the Natural Product of Local Exchange Networks. In: Proceedings of the 2010 Workshop on Information in Networks (2010), http://media.mit.edu/pentland
10. Trusted Computing Group, TPM 1.2 Specifications (2011), http://www.trustedcomputinggroup.org
11. The Jericho Forum, "Identity Commandments," The Open Group (2011), http://www.opengroup.org
12. Hardjono, T., Greenwood, D., Pentland, A.: Towards a trustworthy digital infrastructure for core identities and personal data stores. In: Proceedings of the ID360 Conference on Identity, University of Texas (April 2013)
13. OASIS, "Assertions and Protocols for the OASIS Security Assertion Markup Language (SAML) V2.0 (March 2005), http://docs.oasis-open.org/security/saml/v2.0/saml-core-2.0-os.pdf
14. de Montjoye, Y.A., Shmueli, E., Wang, S., Pentland, A.: openPDS: Regaining ownership and privacy of personal data (2013) (Submitted for publication)
15. Trusted Computing Group, Trusted Computing Group Web Site, http://www.trustedcomputinggroup.org
16. Zic, J., Hardjono, T.: Towards a cloud-based integrity measurement service. In: Journal of Cloud Computing: Advances, Systems and Applications (February 2013)
17. Trusted Computing Group, TCG Interoperability Specifications for Backup and Migration Services (v1.0), Trusted Computing Group, TCG Issued Specification resources (June 2005), http://www.trustedcomputinggroup.org/
18. Berger, S., Caceres, R., Goldman, K.A., Perez, R., Sailer, R., van Doorn, L.: vTPM: Virtualizing the Trusted Platform Module. In: Security 2006: 15th USENIX Security Symposium, Vancouver, Canada (July-August 2006), http://www.usenix.org

Health Slacktivism on Social Media:
Predictors and Effects

Chih-Wei Hu

Annenberg School for Communication, University of Southern California, USA
huchihwe@usc.edu

Abstract. The present study examined predictors, moderators, and effects of health slacktivism, which is characterized as individuals' effortless acts in supporting health causes primarily through Internet and social media. Findings revealed that issue-involvement and self-presentation were two underlying predictors of slacktivism. Specifically, ingratiation self-presentation was found to be a significant predictor of slacktivism among slacktivists, while enhancement self-presentation predicted slacktivism among activists. Results imply that strategic impression-management types were associated with health slacktivism among particular sub-groups. It is also found that health slacktivists and activists differed by relational connection. Slacktivists tended to be people who were remotely related to the health issue advocated, while activists were people who had closer relational connection to the health issue. Health consciousness, however, was not a significant predictor of slacktivism nor a differentiating factor between slacktivists and activists. Consistent with the Transtheoretical Model, slacktivism was found to have positive effects among participants in terms of awareness, psychological wellbeing, behavioral intention and behavior adoption. Individuals' low-threshold engagement as slacktivism also predicted their high-threshold engagement (activism), implying that getting involved in slacktivism does not substitute for offline forms of participation but may increase the possibility of offline engagement instead.

Keywords: slacktivism, activism, social media, health campaign, health consciousness, issue-involvement, self-presentation.

1   Introduction

Web 2.0 has changed the way people engage in social activism in that the Internet have opened up a new world for quick access and connection to online campaigns of various social causes [1-2]. Social media allows people to "collaborate, coordinate, and give voice to their concerns" in a convenient and effortless way [3, p.2]. Nonetheless, "slacktivism" emerges as online activism increases through social media [4-7]. The term, slacktivism, combining slacker and activism, refers to acts of participating in effortless activities as an expedient alternative to expending effort to support a social cause [4-5]. In other words, social media allows people to take a stance and participate in social issues with minimum effort. For example, people

G. Meiselwitz (Ed.): SCSM 2014, LNCS 8531, pp. 354–364, 2014.

cartooned their Facebook profile picture to support the anti-child abuse campaign [8] or greened their Twitter profile to support democratic elections in Iran [1]. Slacktivists are thus characterized as individuals who are generally "happy to click a 'like' button about a cause" but "hardly inspired with the kind of emotional fire that forces a shift in public perception" [9, p.18]. The term implies that this kind of supporters is lazy and their actions are not very helpful [10]. Criticism about slacktivists is thus that they do not really advance activism to make any real change, which is considered as the most critical goal of any activism [9]. Nonetheless, proponents of slacktivism regard slacktivist activities as indicators of growing support, such as website traffic numbers generated, e-petition signatures delivered, "like" counts, etc. [9].

Despite it's a growing trend, slacktivism has received little research, particularly in the health domain. There is a lack of knowledge about the potential benefits and factors associated with slacktivism [1]. The present study attempts to fill in the gap by exploring predictors of individuals' participation in health slacktivism and potential effects.

2   Literature Review

2.1   Issue-Involvement and Relational Connection

Research [3] suggests that activism taking place on social media is primarily built around weak ties, while conventional activism usually entails greater bonding/ face-to-face connections to make a spark to a real change, and thus is mostly built around strong ties. In a similar vein, McCofferty [9] argues that conventional activism requires "strong, robust or organizational structure," and is usually "built upon strong tie personal connections," but activism on social media is deemed to be "relying on individuals' weak ties which are less related and loosely connected" (p.18). In other words, social media, which connects people with weak ties, is suitable for finding people sharing the same concerns and spreading the ideas, but may not necessarily for "high-risk activism"[3, p.5]. Connection is a way to understand supportive activities to health causes [11]. It is thus hypothesized that issue-involvement will be a predictor of activism/slacktivism, and relational connection to the addressed cause can differentiate how much effort a person will put in to a health cause:

H_1: Issue-involvement positively predicts low-threshold engagement (H_{1a}) and high threshold engagement (H_{1b}) in health causes.

H_2: Slacktivists exhibit lower issue-involvement (H_{2a}) and have less close relational connection (H_{2b}) with the health issue advocated than their activist counterparts.

H_3: Participants who have close relational connection to the health issue advocated have higher issue-involvement (H_{3a}), low-threshold engagement (H_{3b}), and high-threshold engagement (H_{3c}) than those who have remote relational connection.

2.2   Self-presentation and Slacktivism

Studies have shown that individuals are aware of their presentation online for a pleasing impression [12,19]. People try to influence the perception of their image and create a good impression by regulating and controlling the information on social media [13]. Self-presentation, which is defined as the types of behavior by which people communicate what they want to deliver and to control how others see them, is associated with self-esteem maintenance and goal-relevance of impressions [14-15]. Lee at al. [16] extended the concepts into ten strategies and developed a Self-presentation Tactics Scale (SPT). Among the ten tactics, four types of self-presentation were selected and examined by the researcher, including ingratiation, supplication, enhancement, and exemplification self-presentation.

Ingratiation self-presentation refers to the strategy to increase one's likability by intentionally doing positive things to make others feel good (e.g., saying positive things about others, doing favors for others, etc.). It could be associated with slacktivism in that people want to increase their likability by "appearing" to be supportive and attentive to health causes, but they may not be actually concerned enough to sacrifice more. Supplication self-representation refers to the strategy of presenting oneself as weak and dependent on others in order to "get others' care, protection, help and support" [17]. Supplication could be associated with slacktivism in that individuals may want to get help from others by associating themselves with a health cause and engaging in activities (e.g., sharing sympathetic photos or messages related to the health causes) to highlight their needs, draw attention, or gain support. Enhancement refers to the strategy to increase others' perception of one's knowledge, status, or success by presenting oneself as knowledgeable, competent or resourceful in front of others. It could be associated with slacktivism in that individuals may want to participate in health campaigns through social media in order to show their capacity to access, manage, and refer resources to those who are in need of them. As Hansen, Shneiderman, and Smith[18] mentioned, some functions afforded on social media (e.g., a "retweet" or a "share" from someone else) allow people to "show off the cool people they know." Lastly, exemplification self-presentation refers to the strategy to increase positive impressions by presenting one's behavior as "morally worthy and as having integrity" [19]. It is associated with slacktivism in that slacktivists may engage in supportive acts of health campaigns in order to be seen as role models by others. Taken together, the following research question was brought up with respect to self-presentation:

RQ$_1$: How is self-presentation associated with slacktivism? Do slacktivists exhibit certain type of self-presentation compared to their activist counterparts?

2.3   Health Consciousness and Slacktivism

Researchers have defined health consciousness as "a tendency to focus attention on one's health" [20, p.603]. It generally refers to an individuals' orientation toward preventing possible illness and improving wellness. The orientation is believed to be important to initiate health-promoting behaviors and activate health information seeking. Kraft and Goodell [21] suggested that health consciousness comprises sensitivity to health hazards, physical fitness, stress, and nutrition, and it also signals individuals' "readiness to undertake health actions" [22-23, p.4]. Health conscious individuals were believed to be more concerned about their health, more knowledgeable about health issues, more likely to take actions to improve their health quality of life, and were shown to have better wellness [24]. Given so, it is thus hypothesized that health slacktivists, compared with their activist counterpart, may possess lower health consciousness. The following hypothesis was proposed:

H$_4$: Health consciousness positively predicts the level of engagement in online health activism (H$_{4a}$). Plus, slacktivists will have lower level of health consciousness than activists (H$_{4b}$).

2.4 Slacktivism and the Stages of Change

Based on the Transtheoretical Model [25-29], health behavior change unfolds over time through a temporal sequence of stages, including precontemplation, contemplation, preparation, action, maintenance, and termination. In this model, "processes of changes" are believed to be associated with progress people make through stages, including consciousness-raising, dramatic relief, self-reevaluation, and environmental reevaluation [28]. The stages of change are associated with slacktivism in that, compared with their activists counterpart, slacktivists could be people who are not concerned enough about a health cause due to a lack of consciousness, a lack of emotional arousal, or a lack of information to commit actions beyond a certain level. As a result, they are not motivated enough or not become concerned enough about a health issue to consider a new behavior [27]. Given so, the last research question concerning the effects of slacktivism was proposed in terms of awareness, psychological wellbeing, behavioral intention, and behavior adoption. Uncovering these subsequent effects caused by engaging in slacktivist activities would help understand potential benefits/costs of the phenomenon and explain it through a theoretical lens.

RQ$_2$: What are the effects of slacktivism in terms of awareness, psychological wellbeing, behavioral intention, and behavior adoption?

3   Methods

3.1   Recruitment

This study was developed using Qualtrics online survey software. Participants were recruited on Amazon Mechanical Turk at time 1 (April 2013) and time 2 (July 2013). Participants who were over 18 years old and currently resided in the United States were eligible to participate in the survey. Incomplete surveys and cases with incorrect answers for validation questions were excluded (n_1=6, n_2= 10), and this resulted in a total of 156 (n_1=63, n_2= 93) respondents retained for subsequent analyses. Responses in the study were examined for normal distribution, skewness, and outliers. All variables in this study met the assumption of parametric tests. They were normally distributed and outlier-free. Case-wise method was used to deal with missing values in subsequent analyses.

3.2   Measures

Health slacktivism was measured by a set of items assessing participants' *types of engagement* in health campaigns (i.e., slacktivists or activists) and their *amount of engagement* in each level of engagement (i.e., low- and high-threshold engagement). The first variable, *types of participation* (slacktivists vs. activists), was measured by a nominal question asking participants in what way they usually involved in health campaigns. The question presents three levels of engagement using the concepts from Neiger et al. [30]. A sample option is "I usually engage in online health campaigns/advocacy by acknowledging agreement or showing preference for the content shared using the 'Like' function, the 'Favorite' function, or the rating system on the social media." Participants were further asked with three sets of items about the *amount* of their participation in health causes on a 5-point scale from "never" to "almost always". The first two levels were further designated as "low-threshold engagement" (slacktivism), and the third level was labeled "high-threshold engagement" (activism). The 9 items measuring low-threshold engagement had a Cronbach's alpha of 0.895, and the 6 items measuring high-threshold engagement had a Cronbach's alpha of 0.834.

The second variable, *relational connection*, was measured by asking about participants' relationship with the health cause with nominal options. A sample question is "I identify myself as the patient of the health causes/problem."

The third variable, *issue-involvement*, was measured by four items representing different reasons for showing support to the health cause on a 5-point scale from "not at all true of myself" to "true of myself". A sample item was "I am motivated to learn more about the health issue advocated". The scale had a Cronbach's alpha of 0.885.

Self-presentation was measured by the adapted version of the Self-presentation Scale[16]. Ingratiation was measured by five items (Cronbach's α= .819), such as "I use flattery to win the favor of others." Supplication was measured by three items (Cronbach's α= .846), such as "I tell others they are stronger or more competent than me in order to get others to do things for me." Enhancement was measured by three items (Cronbach's α= .839) such as "When I succeed at a task, I emphasize to others how important the task was." Examplification was measured by three items (Cronbach's α= .831) such as "I try to set an example for others to follow." All 13 items were rated by participants on a 5-point scale from "never" to "always". The Cronbach's alpha for the overall 13-item scale is 0.869.

Health consciousness was measured by 6 items adapted from previous health consciousness scales [21, 24, 31]. A sample items was "I am aware of the state of my health as I go through the day." Response options ranged from "strongly disagree" to "strongly agree". The scale had a Cronbach's alpha of 0.799.

Effects. Awareness items (Cronbach's α= .776) asked participants whether they perceived themselves as becoming aware of the health issue advocated after their participation in to online health campaign/advocacy, such as "I became aware of the health issue after my responding to the online health campaign." Psychological wellbeing was measured by five items (Cronbach's $\alpha = .871$) such as "I feel more empowered after my online participation in the health campaign." Behavioral intention was measured by one item "I intended to adopt behavior advocated in the online health campaign/advocacy." Behavior adoption was measured by three items (Cronbach's $\alpha = .721$) asked participants' behavioral change related to the health issue advocated, such as "I made changes of my lifestyle/habits as what is advocated in the health campaign." All items were rated on a 6-point scale from "strongly disagree" to "strongly agree."

4   Results

4.1   Participants Demographics

Participants were 156 adults recruited from Mechanical Turk. There were 39.2% males ($n=62$), and 60.3 % were females ($n=94$). The mean age was 35.5 ($SD=13.99$), ranging from 19 to 85 years old. Approximately 69.9% ($n=109$) of participants were White/Caucasian, 12.2% were Asian ($n=19$), 7.1% were Black/African American ($n=11$), 6.4% were Hispanic/Latino ($n=10$), and 3.8% marked "other" ($n=6$). As for marital status, 43.6% of participants were single ($n=68$), 34.6% were married ($n=54$), 2.6% were widowed ($n=4$), 6.4% were divorced or separated ($n=10$), and 12.8% were living with a partner ($n=20$). Thirty-three percent of respondents had children ($n=52$), and 66.7% of respondents did not have children ($n=104$). About 82% ($n=128$) indicated that they primarily had low-threshold engagement in health campaigns/advocacy, who were characterized as "slacktivists" in the study, and 16% ($n=25$) had high-threshold engagement, who were labeled as "activists" in the present study.

4.2   Main Results

A series of chi-square analyses on demographics were firstly conducted to examine differences between slacktivists and activists. No significant differences were found for gender ($p=0.12$), marital status ($p=0.57$), ethnicity ($p=0.97$), schooling ($p=0.99$) and income ($p=0.63$).

In order to test H_1 which proposed that issue-involvement positively predicts individuals' low- and high- threshold engagement, simple regression analyses were conducted. Results showed that issue-involvement was positively associated with low-threshold engagement and also a significant predictor of both low-threshold engagement ($\beta=0.43$, $p=0.000$) and high-threshold engagement ($\beta=0.33$, $p=0.000$). H_{1a} and H_{1b} were supported. In addition, it was found that there was a strong, positive link between low- and high-threshold engagement. Low-threshold engagement (i.e., slacktivism) was a strong predictor of high-threshold engagement (i.e., activism) ($F(1,147)=94.32$, $\beta= 0.63$, $p=0.000$, $R^2= 0.39$), indicating that the more an individual participate in slacktivist activities, the more likely the person will be involve in offline support which entails greater costs.

In addition, results of t-tests confirmed that slacktivists had significantly greater participation in low-threshold health activism (M=2.44, SD= 0.77) than activists (M=2.07, SD= 0.83) (t(146)= 2.102, p=0.04); and activists had significantly greater participation in high threshold health activism (M=2.27, SD= 0.68) than slacktivists (M=1.89, SD= 0.72) (t(148)= -2.339, p=0.02). Results indicated that there was no significant difference in issue-involvement between slacktivists and activists (t(151)= 0.484, p=0.629). H_{2a} was rejected. Nonetheless, there were significant differences in relational connection existed between slacktivists and activists (χ^2= 14.17, p=0.015). Significantly higher proportion of slacktivists indicated that "none of people around me is related to health issue advocated" (14.1%, compared to 0% of activists). H_{2b} was accepted.

To examine H_3 which proposed that issue-involvement is influenced by individuals' relational connection to the health issue advocated, a t-test indicated a significant differences in issue-involvement between close and remote relational connection groups (p= 0.000; t(154)= 3.96. Participants who identified themselves as patients/ friends or family members/caregivers with respect to the health issue advocated had significantly higher scores on issue-involvement (M=3.80, SD= 0.87) than those who were remotely related to the health issue (e.g., "None of people around me are related to the health issue advocated" (M=3.18, SD=1.00). H_{3a} was supported. The close relational connection group also had significant (t(151)=2.127; p=0.035) higher high-threshold engagement (M=2.02, SD=.76) and low-threshold engagement (M=2.45, SD=.77) than the remote relational group (M=1.76, SD=.63 and M=2.17, SD=.82 respectively). H_{3b} and H_{3c} were supported.

Furthermore, the first research question concerned the association between self-presentation and slacktivism. No significant differences in any of the four types of self-presentation between slacktivists and activists (ingratiation: t(150)=-0.96, p= 0.34; supplication: t(149)=0.28, p= 0.78; enhancement: t(151)= 0.13, p=0.90; exemplification: t(150)= -0.69, p=0.50). Nonetheless, results of a multiple regression analysis with stepwise method indicated that, among slacktivists, ingratiation self-presentation was found to be a significant predictor of low-threshold engagement (F(1,120)=14.53, p=0.000, β= 0.33). For activists, enhancement self-presentation was found to be a significant predictor of their low-threshold engagement with a very high coefficient (F(1,20)=5.04, p=0.036, β= 0.449). Interestingly, relational connection was found to moderate the relationship between self-presentation and slacktivism. Among those who were remotely related to the health issue advocated, ingratiation self-presentation significantly predicted low-threshold engagement (F(1,48)=21.80; β=0.56, p=0.000). On the contrary, among those who were personally related to the health issue advocated, enhancement self-presentation significantly predicted their low-threshold engagement (F(1,95)=7.71; β=0.27, p=0.007).

H_4 concerned health consciousness as a predictor of level of engagement in health campaigns/advocacy (H_{4a}), and it proposed that slacktivists would have a lower level of health consciousness than activists (H_{4b}). Regressional analyses indicated that health consciousness was significantly associated with and was a predictor of both low-threshold engagement $(F(1,148)=8.88, p= 0.003, \beta=0.24)$ and high-threshold engagement $F(1,151)=8.04, p= 0.005, \beta=0.23)$. While there was no significant difference in health consciousness between slacktivists and activists $(t(150)= -0.89, p=0.37)$, the scores were in the right direction (activists: $M=4.43, SD= 0.78$; slacktivists: $M=4.28, SD= 0.74$). A multiple regression analysis with stepwise method was conducted to examine the model fit with the inclusion of the three predictors and low-threshold engagement as the dependent variable. Results were shown in Figure 1:

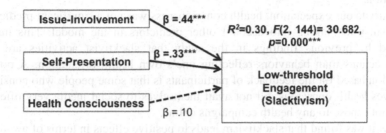

Fig. 1. Predictors of low-threshold engagement using multiple regression (stepwise method)

The last research question concerned the effects of slacktivism in terms of awareness, psychological wellbeing, behavioral intention, and behavior adoption. A series of regression analyses revealed that low-threshold engagement was a significant predictor of awareness $(F(1,149)=63.19, \beta= 0.55, p=0.000)$, psychological wellbeing $(F(1,149)=54.63, \beta= 0.52, p=0.000)$, behavioral intention $(F(1,149)=23.55, \beta= 0.37, p=0.000)$, and behavioral adoption $(F(1,149)=65.22, \beta= 0.55, p=0.000)$. Our findings revealed that participants gained awareness, psychological and behavioral benefits by engaging in slacktivist activities, which may disprove negative claims about slacktivism.

5   Discussion

To sum up, issue-involvement and self-presentation were found to be the best underlying predictors of slacktivism in the study. Relational connection and income level were found to be important moderators between issue-involvement and slacktivism. The findings reaffirm the assumption that stronger ties (i.e., close relationships) serve as a mechanism to increase individuals' issue-involvement in a health cause, which in turn is transformed into both online and offline support to health campaigns. Also, income was found to be a moderator between issue-involvement and slacktivsm, revealing the importance of financial factor in determining one's participation in health campaigns.

Noticeably, self-presentation was found to be associated with slacktivism and activism in particular ways. Ingratiation self-presentation was found to be a significant predictor of slacktivism among slacktivists, implying that slacktivists who had greater desire to gain liking from others engaged more in health campaign online even it's remotely related to them. Among activists, on the other hand, enhancement self-presentation was found to be a strong predictor of slacktivism, indicating health activists engaged in online activities with the hope of enhancing their self-image (e.g., perceived as credible, influential). The results address the importance of social media as a recognized public sphere where individuals can build positive self-images by performing "seemingly" altruistic behaviors, which particularly manifests among those who have little to do with the health cause advocated. In other words, slacktivism, which relies on less related ties [9], is a function of strategic self-presentation.

Contrary to our expectation, health consciousness was not a significant predictor of slacktivism when taking into account other predictors in the model. This may be explained by previous findings in the study that slacktivist activities are more strategic actions than behaviors reflecting one's own health orientation. A possible explanation based on the feedback of participants is that some people who considered themselves health conscious did not avail themselves to social media very often and thus do not expose to any health campaigns online.

Lastly, it was found that slacktivism leads to positive effects in terms of awareness, psychological wellbeing, behavioral intention, and behavioral adoption. It was also found that slacktivism was a strong predictor of activism, implying that getting involved in health slacktivism online did not replace traditional forms of participation, but can actually reinforces one's offline engagement. To conclude, it may not be necessary to hold a skeptical view about slacktivism [9]. As proponents suggest, slacktivism may be just a reflection of human nature to utilize handy, available resources and tools [10]. Slacktivism could be seen as "approaches to exploit technology in ways previously not conceived to advance a cause" [9, p.19]. At best, it helps promote health behavioral change as revealed by current study; at worst, it may not achieve what it claims but it is harmless [10, 33].

6   Limitations

There are several limitations in this study. Firstly, the sample was a convenience sample recruited from Mechanical Turk. A random sampling is desired in the future work in order to have better generalizability. In addition, as a preliminary study, this paper is meant to explore underlying factors that were assumed to bear an influence on slacktivsm, whereas there would be more potential factors differentiating slacktivists from activists. There is also a need to explore the mechanisms turn slacktivists into activists. Adding these elements to the study would yield more abundant findings that help theorize on health slacktivism/activism. Future studies could consider using an experimental design which incorporates pre- and post-measurement to compare the effects of slacktivism and activism. However, measuring efficaciousness of health slacktivism versus activism is not easy and may require long-term observation and repeated measures. There is much research that needs to be done to assess the impact of slacktivism.

References

1. Rotman, et al.: From slacktivism to activism. Participatory culture in the age of social media. In: Proceedings from CHI EA 2011: The 2011 Annual Conference Extended Abstracts on Human Factors in Computing Systems, Canada, Vancouver (2011)
2. Middaugh, E.: Service & Activism in the Digital Age: Supporting Youth Engagement in Public Life. DML Central Working Papers (2012)
3. Gladwell, M.: Small change: Why the revolution will not be tweeted, New Yorker (October 4, 2010), http://www.newyorker.com/reporting/2010/10/04/101004fa_fact_gladwell (retrieved April 3, 2013)
4. Davis, J.: Cause marketing: Moving beyond corporate slacktivism (November 22, 2011), http://evidencebasedmarketing.net/cause-marketing-moving-beyond-corporate-slacktivism (retrieved April 2, 2013)
5. Whipple, T.: The rise of slacktivism. The Times (February 9, 2011), http://search.proquest.com.ezp01.library.qut.edu.au/docview/850108467 (retrieved April 3, 2013)
6. Shirky, C.: The Political Power of Social Media. Foreign Affairs 90(1), 28–41 (2011)
7. Kain, E.: Time 'Person' of the year prediction: The slacktivist. Forbes (April 3, 2012), http://www.forbes.com/sites/erikkain/2012/04/03/2012-time-person-of-the-year-prediction-the-slacktivist/ (retrieved April 15, 2013)
8. Slacktivism: Know Your Meme (n.d.), http://knowyourmeme.com/memes/slacktivism (retrieved April 16, 2012)
9. McCofferty, D.: Activism vs. Slacktivism. Communications of the ACM 54(12), 17–19 (2011)
10. Bailyn, E.: The Difference between slacktivism and activism: How 'Kony 2012' is narrowing the gap. Huffington Post (March 29, 2012), http://www.huffingtonpost.com/evan-bailyn/kony-2012-activism_b_1361791.html (retrieved April 20, 2013)
11. Saxton, G.D., Wang, L.: The social network effect: The determinants of giving through social media. Nonprofit and Voluntary Sector Quarterly, 1–35 (2013)
12. Ellison, N., Heino, R., Gibbs, J.: Managing impressions online: Self-presentation processes in the online dating environment. Journal of Computer-Mediated Communication 11(2), article 2 (2006), http://jcmc.indiana.edu/vol11/issue2/ellison.html (retrieved April 2, 2013)
13. Birnbaum, M.G.: Taking Goffman on a Tour of Facebook: College students and the presentation of self in a mediated digital environment. Dissertation Abstracts International Section A 69 (2008)
14. Goffman, E.: The presentation of self in everyday life. Doubleday, New York (1959)
15. Leary, M.R., Kowalski, R.M.: Impression Management: A literature Review and Two-factor Model. Psychological Bulletin 107, 34–47 (1990)
16. Lee, S.J., et al.: Development of a Self-presentation Tactics Scale. Personality and Individual Differences 26(4), 701–722 (1999)
17. Wang, K.W.: Faces on Facebook: A study of self-presentation and social support on Facebook. SS Student E-Journal 1, 184–214 (2012)
18. Hansen, D., Schneiderman, B., Smith, M.A.: Analyzing social media networks with NodeXL: Insights from a connected world. Morgan Kaufmann (2011)
19. Jones, E.E., Pittman, T.S.: Toward a general theory of strategic self-presentation. In: Suls, J. (ed.) Psychological Perspectives on the Self. Erlbaum, Hillsdale (1982)

20. Iversen, A.C., Kraft, P.: Does socio-economic status and health consciousness influence how women respond to health related messages in media? Health Education Research 21(5), 601–610 (2006)
21. Kraft, F.B., Goodell, P.W.: Identifying the health conscious consumer. Journal of Health Care Marketing 13(3), 18–25 (1993)
22. Becker, M.H., Maiman, L.A., Kirscht, J.P., Haefner, D.P., Drachman, R.H.: The health belief model and prediction of dietary compliance: a field experiment. Journal of Health and Social Behaviour 18, 348–366 (1977)
23. Michaelidou, N., Hassan, L.M.: The role of health consciousness, food safety concern and ethical identity on attitudes and intentions towards organic food. International Journal of Consumer Studies 32(1), 163–170 (2008)
24. Hu, C.W.: A New Measure for Health Consciousness: Development of A Health Consciousness Conceptual Model. Unpublished paper presented at National Communication Association 99th Annual Convention, Washington, D.C. (November 2013)
25. DiClemente, C.C., Prochaska, J.O.: Self-change and therapy change of smoking behavior: A comparison of processes of change in cessation and maintenance. Addictive Behaviors 7, 133–142 (1982)
26. Prochaska, J.O., DiClemente, C.C.: Stages and processes of self-change of smoking: Toward an integrative model of change. Journal of Consulting and Clinical Psychology 51(3), 390–395 (1983)
27. DiClemente, C.C.: The Transtheoretical Model of intentional behaviour change. Drugs and Alcohol Today 7(1), 29–33 (2007)
28. Prochaska, J.O., Redding, C.A., Evers, K.E.: The transtheoretical model and stages of change. In: Glanz, K., Rimer, B.K., Viswanath, K. (eds.) Health Behavior and Health Education: Theory, Research, and Practice, pp. 97–102. Jossey-Bass, San Francisco (2008)
29. Prochaska, J.O.: Decision making in the Transtheoretical Model of behavioral change. Medical Decision Making 28, 845–849 (2008)
30. Neiger, et al.: Use of Social Media in Health Promotion: Purposes, Key Performance Indicators, and Evaluation Metrics. Health Promotion Practice 13, 159–164 (2012)
31. Gould, S.J.: Consumer attitudes toward health and health care: A differential perspective. The Journal of Consumer Affairs 22(1), 96–118 (1988)
32. Christensen, H.S.: Political activities on the Internet: Slacktivism or political participation by other means? First Monday (2011), http://firstmonday.org/ojs/index.php/fm/article/view/3336/2767 (retrieved April 21, 2013)

Exploring Health Care Professionals' Attitudes of Using Social Networking Sites for Health Care: An Empirical Study

Zhao Huang[1] and NanNan Gai[2]

[1] School of Computer Science, ShaanXi Normal University, 710062, P.R. China
zhaohuang@snnu.edu.cn
[2] Xi'an No. Five Hospital, 710049, P.R. China
nannangai1122@stu.xjtu.edu.cn

Abstract. Evidence from relevant studies show that the use of social networking sites or Web 2.0 portals in health care provide huge potential to transform traditional health care services, generating great collaboration, participation and openness. However, challenges of employing Web 2.0 for health care still exit. This empirical study uses semi-structured interview approach to explore health care professionals' attitudes towards using Web 2.0 portals for health care, especially focusing on specific social networking sites for chronic health care in China. Results present a range of positive attitudes of using the social networking sites to health professionals' clinical practice. Meanwhile, the opportunities and barriers related to use of such social networking sites into clinical practice are presented and discussed.

Keywords: E-health, health care services, Web 2.0 portals, Social media, Social networking sites.

1 Introduction

Today, for people with a chronic health problem, such as rheumatic diseases or diabetes, the Internet has evolved from being a source for health information presentation (Web 1.0) to being a collaborative resource for connecting with social experiences (Web 2.0) [1]. This change is driven not only by the popularity of Web 2.0, but because user participation. It can strengthen the connections between users (e.g., doctors, nurses and patients) and form a complex network of relation, which in turn enables collaboration, increases user engagement, and promotes service openness [2]. For example, it enables users to access to a peer community where they can discuss their treatment with doctors, nurses and other fellow patients [3]. This means delivers open health information and services, addressing attention to continuous support and problem-based learning for people living with a chronic health problem. On the other hand, the development of medical information on the Internet towards openness and quality control reflects the transformation of health service organizations, where quality surveillance becomes more significant [4], generating

G. Meiselwitz (Ed.): SCSM 2014, LNCS 8531, pp. 365–372, 2014.
© Springer International Publishing Switzerland 2014

great cooperation, openness, participation and quality information [5]. Such a new approach echoes the modern management of the chronic health that addresses open education activities and initiatives implemented by health care professionals to help patients with chronic diseases and health conditions to understand their condition and live successfully [6]. For instance, those with rheumatic diseases need to take care of daily physical movement, struggling with undesirable Erythrocyte Sedimentation Rate and the risk of complications, such as interstitial lung disease and primary sjogren syndrome. Long-term assessment of rheumatic treatment addresses the importance of rheumatoid factor changes so as to measure the severity level of rheumatic diseases [21]. Therefore, finding the means to educate and support patients and their families is paramount.

Many studies address the patient perspective, indicating that chronic health care needs improvement of patient information and their accessibility (e.g., [1]). While, some find that effective use of interactive telecare, Internet-based approaches and Web 2.0 applications in health care can promote user access to health services, increase the service delivery as well as information quality, and support patient education (e.g., [7]). Others demonstrate the effects of Web 2.0 on chronic patients' perception, behaviour, attitudes, knowledge, and skills. Although the benefits of using Web 2.0 in health care are recently reviewed (e.g., [8]), only a few studies explore the improvement of quality of life, especially focusing on the health professionals' perspectives. To this end, this paper reported an empirical study that investigates health professionals' attitude towards using Web 2.0 portals, focusing on specific social networking sites for chronic health care in China. Meanwhile, the opportunities and barriers related to use of such social networking sites into clinical practice are presented and discussed.

Accordingly, the paper is presented as follows: Section 2 presents related studies from literature to demonstrate the opportunities and benefits of Web 2.0 applications in health care services. In section 3, an empirical study is designed to explore health care professionals' attitude towards using social networking sites. This allows the detection of opportunities and barriers related to use of social networking sites which are discussed in section 4. Finally, conclusions are drawn and possibilities for future study are recommended in section 5.

2   Related Work

Web 2.0 is a notion where users utilize the web to participate and collaborate using existing web applications and the technologies [9]. Since this concept emerges within the e-health context, the terms Health 2.0 or Medicine 2.0 have been widely used. Eysenbach [2] defines Medicine 2.0 as Web-based services for health care, leveraging Web 2.0 tools, applications and technologies to enable and facilitate social networking, participation, apomediation, openness and collaboration between user groups (including consumers, caregivers, patients, health professional and biomedical researchers). Additionally, Belt et al. [10] use a systematic approach to view the difference between Health 2.0 or Medicine 2.0. The findings indicate that as Health

2.0 and Medicine 2.0 are still developing areas, there is still no general consensus regarding the definitions of Health 2.0 and Medicine 2.0. These results are also supported by Hughes [11], who state that these concepts seem to have evolved together with the increased use of the definitions and the different parties involved in Healath 2.0 and Medicine 2.0. Hence, no relevant differences exist between Health 2.0 and Medicine 2.0. Although there are no clear definitions of Medicine 2.0 and Health 2.0, or sometime the concepts are exchangeable, it can be argued that Web 2.0 is changing medical practice, transforming traditional health care services and empowering health care users [12].

Jackson et al. [13] investigate interactive computer-assisted technology in diabetes care. The results show that information technology provides an avenue for the rapid and easy dissemination of information to patients and clinicians as well as allowing interactive communication between the patients and their health care provider teams. Moreover, Harno et al. [14] explore diabetes care using an e-health application. They find that the patients start involving e-health because use of e-health in diabetes care for 12 months was able to provide equivalent diabetic control to usual care, and improved cardiovascular risk factors. Such an approach provides the patients with a convenient way to their usual care without physical space and time limitations. Similarly, McMahon et al. [15] assess the effects of web-based care management on glucose and blood pressure control patients. The results present that persistent website users had greater improvement in A1C when compared with intermittent users. Therefore, Web-based care management may be a useful adjunct in the care of patients with poorly controlled diabetes. The above studies suggest that Internet-based interventions have a profound impact on diabetic patients' health care utilization, behaviour, attitude, knowledge and skills.

Existing research investigated the patient views [1], examined e-health service quality [7], and analysed the effects of Web 2.0 on metabolic control with better quality of life [16], while, obtaining limited attention to the health professionals' perspective. It can be argued that without understanding health professionals' attitude toward using Web 2.0 for health care, Health 2.0 or Medicine 2.0 will not reach its full potential. In this vein, this empirical study aims to explore health professionals' attitude toward using Web 2.0 portals, focusing on specific social networking sites for chronic health care in China. By doing so, we hope to contribute to better insights into social networking sites usage in health care by health professionals.

3   Methodology

To conduct the study, semi-structured interviews were employed as the research technique with purpose of capturing participants' perception and attitudes of the target social networking sites. The interview was developed based on a set of pre-defined questions. These questions were developed by reviewing relevant evaluation criteria in social media studies in health care (e.g., [17];[19]), and electronic health studies (e.g., [18];[20]). Based on these identified criteria, relevant interview questions were developed and grouped into corresponding question categories. By doing so, we are able to provide a step-by-step approach to closely focus on health professionals' attitude towards using target social networking sites.

Two social networking sites (or Web 2.0 portals) were selected as representatives of current social health systems, and targeted to assess health professionals' perception of using them in the study: Huayi.com and Medlive.cn. The former is the one of the most popular social networking sites for health care services in China, involving about two millions health professionals in online health care education, while the latter one is the Chinese largest and most influential medical specialty websites, encouraging social communication and interaction between health professionals and patients. In total, twenty five health care professionals (twenty doctors and five nurses) from three rheumatic diseases units in Xi'an No. Five Hospital took part in this study on a voluntary basis. They all have good knowledge of electronic health systems and experiences using social networking sites. Each participant followed the same interview process consisting of: (1) a free review of the assigned social networking site; (2) answering the interview question. During the interview, the target social networking sites are still available for interviewees to review. Finally, qualitative data were obtained and analyzed.

4   Results and Discussion

Overall, the results of our study show that there are a range of positive attitudes towards using the target social networking sites to health professionals' clinical practice. Most interviewees were satisfied with the peer community established through the target social networking sites. Using social networking sites provides health professionals with huge opportunities for health information sharing, communication as well as continuous support for problem-based learning. However, problems were given to being familiar with the target social networking sites, showing that interviewees thought they may need to learn more about working with the portals. Furthermore, the findings also identify some major barriers related to utilizing the social networking sites into clinical practice. For example, the process of using social networking sites requires health professionals to offer active contributions from the experience of the present care process in order for them to play a key role in the improvement of care. Nevertheless, most health professionals have had limited computer training either from their prior education or their professional life. Therefore, the requirements of computer training for health professionals become necessary. Furthermore, the results show that health professionals are recently familiar with the rapidly emerging social networking tools on the Internet. In particular, the young health professionals are more likely to accept and use the social networking sites or Web 2.0 portals for health information exchange and communication, but they expect to have more comprehensive understanding or specialized knowledge of using social networking sites or Web 2.0 tools into health care systems. Additionally, since patients' participation and patient generated content, it draws health professionals' greater attention in terms of real-world cases. Several health professionals regard such interactive activities as a valuable source. Hence, a need for close collaboration between health care professionals and patients are pointed out when health professional access to the social networking sites.

Moreover, some interviewees described the dissatisfaction with their interaction with the target social networking sites due to the limited time, the lack of the Internet knowledge and insufficient information in the course of the writing process. Although health professionals' experience with the writing process varies, they still feel that a sort of community was built after working with the target social networking sites. Most of them believe that the use of these social networking sites in chronic health could expand health knowledge beyond the clinics, offering more detailed help, support and information for patients. As such, these interviewees are willing to continue working on these social networking sites and expect that more active activities can be involved, as indicated by the following participants' responses:

> *"I feel confident that such portals become very useful when health professionals and patients work on it......and we are going to use it......I would like to be involved and participate in it in the future."*

Regarding the provision of information on the social networking sites, a few interviewees concerned the importance of information quality over the sites, and suggested relevant responsibility from health professionals. They required professional control in order to avoid harmful advice delivery or presenting incorrect references relating to the management of chronic health. A common point made by participants is that access to regularly updated content would encourage patients to take an active role in using the sites as well as learning more about their diseases. The following quotes from the participants' responses indicate their views:

> *"Site update is used to maintain information and services regularly and keep them up-to-date. A recently updated date is regarded as a key visual cue offering significant reference, which helps patients to determine the quality of information received"; "the last update date indicates regular attention to the site, such a way is beneficial for those who can judge whether information or services obtained are current."*

Based on the participants' responses, a significant benefit of the social networking sites is that it enables health professionals to closely communicate and interact with patients and their families. In particular, it is more important for those living with chronic diseases, such as rheumatic diseases, who expect to have continuous support, long-term progress evaluation and problem-based learning. The following quotes indicate the views of the participants:

> *"I thought the key thing of the Web 2.0 applications in health care is to provide a new way that has the huge potential to change the working environment of the traditional health services to enhance access and patient interaction."*

In addition, some interviewees expressed their concern about the responsibility of acquiring health information. In other words, some patient's parents or family members take more active role in searching for medical advice as well as communicating with health professionals through the social networking sites. To consider the essence of the social networking sites in health care services that emphasize on open education initiatives conducted by health care professionals to help patients with chronic diseases and health conditions to understand their condition and live successfully, there is also a need that involves patients themselves engagement, especially for young patients. After that, several interviewees emphasized that an authorized source of credible health information, for example, references to reliable medical websites, could be very useful support to their work with patients. Such information can provide more detailed health care information, focusing on the specific chronic health problems, as responded in the following: "I like a function on the portals that provides a shared source linking with a number of useful information for the specific chronic health problems. It makes me easier to start working with patients, offering great support, even if I am not familiar with these problems".

5   Conclusion

As indicated by recent studies, using social media or Web 2.0 technologies is becoming as a new phenomenon in health care. It brings huge benefits for user groups, such as increased participation and greater collaboration as well as health care organizations, for example accelerating openness health service process and strengthening patient relationships. More importantly, such a way reflects open health service organization perspectives that advocate the modern management of the chronic health, paying more attention to patient continuous support and problem-based learning. This empirical study explore health professionals' attitude towards using the social networking sites for chronic health care. The results indicate that health care professionals point to a number of positive attitudes towards employing the social networking sites for health care. Moreover, the findings encourage close collaboration with all user groups when implementing social networking sites for the care of patients with chronic diseases, particularly rheumatic diseases. This study also highlights the need for efforts to educate health professionals in the use of Web publishing, social networking sites, and other Web 2.0 resources. The value of our study lies in the guidance for designers to improve social networking sites for health care, as well as in the help to health service organizations in developing their health care systems.

However, this study is only a small step. There are some important limitations that need to be taken into account when interpreting the findings. First, this study only presents qualitative information about attitudes of health care professionals, which may provide the limited viewpoint of exploration. In order to obtain a more comprehensive research, both qualitative and quantitative data are recommended. Future studies will combine the questionnaire, semi-structure interview and observation approach to deeply explore health care professionals' attitudes and task performance when they interact with the social networking sites. In addition, the results show that there is a need to have deep insights into other attitudes of health care team. Such information is beneficial for identifying the specific functions of social networking sites for daily use.

References

1. Eysenbach, G.: From intermediation to disintermediation and apomediation: new models for consumers to access and assess the credibility of health information in the age of Web 2.0. Stud. Health Technol. Inform. 129(pt. 1), 162–166 (2007)
2. Eysenbach, G.: Medicine 2.0: social networking, collaboration, participation, apomediation, and openness. J. Med. Internet Res. 10(3), 22 (2008)
3. Zrebiec, J.F.: Internet communities: do they improve coping with diabetes? Diabetes Educ. 31(6), 825–828, 830–832, 834, 836 (2005)
4. Nordqvist, C., Hanberger, L., Timpka, T., Nordfeldt, S.: Health Professionals' Attitudes Towards Using a Web 2.0 Portal for Child and Adolescent Diabetes Care: Qualitative Study. J. Med. Internet Res. 11(2), 240–247 (2009)
5. Booth, R.G.: Educating the future eHealth professional nurse. Int. J. Nurs. Educ. Scholarsh. 3, Article 13 (2006)
6. Eysenbach, G.: An Ontology of Quality Initiatives and a Model for Decentralized, Collaborative Quality Management on the (Semantic) World Wide Web. J. Med. Internet Res. 3(4), 34 (2001)
7. Kerr, C., Murray, E., Stevenson, F., Gore, C., Nazareth, I.: Internet interventions for long-term conditions: patient and caregiver quality criteria. J. Med. Internet Res. 8(3), 13 (2006)
8. Eysenbach, G., Köhler, C., Yihune, G., Lampe, K., Cross, P., Brickley, D.: A framework for improving the quality of health information on the world-wide-web and bettering public (e-)health: the MedCERTAIN approach. Stud. Health Technol. Inform. 84(pt. 2), 1450–1454 (2001)
9. Wigand, R.T., Benjamin, R.I., Birkland: Web 2.0 and beyond: implications for electronic commerce. Presented at the 10th International Conference on Electronic Commerce (2008)
10. Van De Belt, T.H., Engelen, L.J., Berben, S.A., Schoonhoven, L.: Definition of Health 2.0 and Medicine 2.0: A Systematic Review. J. Med. Internet Res. 12(2), 18 (2010)
11. Hughes, B., Joshi, I., Wareham, J.: Health 2.0 and Medicine 2.0: Tensions and Controversies in the Field. J. Med. Internet Res. 10(3), 23 (2008)
12. Juzwishin, D.W.M.: Political, policy and social barriers to health system interoperability: Emerging opportunities of Web 2.0 and 3.0. Healthc. Manage. Forum 22(4), 6–10 (2009)
13. Jackson, C.L., Bolen, S., Brancati, F.L., Batts-Turner, M.L., Gary, T.L.: A systematic review of interactive computer-assisted technology in diabetes care. Interactive information technology in diabetes care. J. Gen. Intern. Med. 21(2), 105–110 (2006)
14. Harno, K., Kauppinen-Mäkelin, R., Syrjäläinen, J.: Managing diabetes care using an integrated regional e-health approach. J. Telemed. Telecare 12(suppl. 1), 13–15 (2006)
15. McMahon, G.T., Gomes, H.E., Hickson Hohne, S., Hu, T.M.-J., Levine, B.A., Conlin, P.R.: Web-based care management in patients with poorly controlled diabetes. Diabetes Care 28(7), 1624–1629 (2005)

16. Hoey, H., Aanstoot, H.J., Chiarelli, F., Daneman, D., Danne, T., Dorchy, H., Fitzgerald, M., Garandeau, P., Greene, S., Holl, R., Hougaard, P., Kaprio, E., Kocova, M., Lynggaard, H., Martul, P., Matsuura, N., McGee, H.M., Mortensen, H.B., Robertson, K., Schoenle, E., Sovik, O., Swift, P., Tsou, R.M., Vanelli, M., Aman, J.: Good metabolic control is associated with better quality of life in 2,101 adolescents with type 1 diabetes. Diabetes Care 24(11), 1923–1928 (2001)
17. Nordfeldt, S., Johansson, C., Carlsson, E., Hammersjö, J.-A.: Use of the Internet to search for information in type 1 diabetes children and adolescents: a cross-sectional study. Technol. Health Care Off. J. Eur. Soc. Eng. Med. 13(1), 67–74 (2005)
18. Falkman, G., Gustafsson, M., Jontell, M., Torgersson, O.: SOMWeb: A Semantic Web-Based System for Supporting Collaboration of Distributed Medical Communities of Practice. J. Med. Internet Res. 10(3), 25 (2008)
19. Eysenbach, G., Diepgen, T.L.: Towards quality management of medical information on the internet: evaluation, labelling, and filtering of information. BMJ 317(7171), 1496–1500 (1998)
20. Eysenbach, G.: Credibility of Health Information and Digital Media: New Perspectives and Implications for Youth. In: Digital Media, Youth, and Credibility. The John D. and Catherine T. MacArthur Foundation Series on Digital Media and Learning (2008)
21. Brummaier, T., Pohanka, E., Studnicka-Benke, A., Pieringer, H.: Using cyclophosphamide in inflammatory rheumatic diseases. Eur. J. Intern. Med. 24(7), 590–596 (2013)

E-Democracy and Public Online Budgeting

An Empirical Case Study of Deliberation in Social Media

Alice Katharina Pieper[1] and Michael Pieper[2]

[1] Institute for Political Science and Media Science
Johannes Gutenberg University Mainz
Frankfurter Str. 9, D 55252 Mainz-Kastel, Germany
alpieper@students.uni-mainz.de
[2] Fraunhofer Institute for Applied Information Technology – FIT
Schloss Birlinghoven, 53754 Sankt Augustin, Germany
michael.pieper@fit.fhg.de

Abstract. If social media are to reinforce sustainability of political decisions their design has conceptually to take into account the implications of deliberative democracy, which stresses the active co-operation of virtually all citizens of a democracy for the purposes of participatory involvement. Essential to deliberative e-democracy is therefore a technologically supported comprehensive discourse about political subjects which is also called Deliberation. Theoretical implications of Deliberation are discussed from the angle of political science and social psychology. Finally, the practical implications of Deliberation rooted in social media are exemplified by an online citizen involvement for the public budgeting purposes of the city of Frankfurt/Main (Germany).

Keywords: impact research, sustainable systems design, conceptual models, deliberation, social media, social capital, collective intelligence, e-democracy, Web 2.0.

1   Introduction

As this paper deals with the merits of collective intelligence by means of user generated content via the Internet, it starts with a definition derived from WIKIPEDIA, the best known user generated website at all: "Sustainability is the capacity to endure". For humans, sustainability is the long-term maintenance of responsibility with - besides environmental and economical - also social dimensions. In this respect the use of social media follows the mission of participation. Social problems are to large extent mass problems. As sustainability also encompasses the responsible management of resource use, sustainable policy making, significantly supported by a society, can thus only take place if just these masses actively and consciously participate as resources in generating sustainable impact. In this respect a technologically supported comprehensive discourse about political subjects which is also called Deliberation becomes meaningful.

G. Meiselwitz (Ed.): SCSM 2014, LNCS 8531, pp. 373–384, 2014.

Doubtlessly, to ensure sustainability the political sphere needs to respond to the long basic and structural changes of mass communication that go hand in hand with the emergence of social media. In this context however the general research question remains: Are the discussions of deliberative quality?

The democratic implications of structural media changes are obvious. They comply with so called "deliberation theorists" thinking, which requests maximum participation as well as comprehensive freedom of speech in political discourses, in which citizens not inhibited by external circumstances and across temporal and spatial distances agree in a rationally motivated way about the justification of political projects and decisions. However, for one of the leading exponents of deliberation theory, Jürgen HABERMAS, this 'ideal speech situation' cannot be approached by new social media [1]. On the contrary: They rather promote the "collapse of public structures", as HABERMAS quotes, and undermine the normative claim of a deliberative democratic ideal [5], rather than to move closer to it. HABERMAS thus clearly belongs to the fraction of the skeptics regarding the usage of new media under the structural conditions of sustainable political participation. The media philosopher Stefan MÜNKER however can be regarded as a prominent scientific representative of the opposing camp [6]. He describes the ever larger growing circles of Web 2.0 implementations as a historic step towards a culture founded on participatory interaction. MÜNKER opposes HABERMAS' skepticism about the "fragmentation of the public" by the theorem of the "emergence of digital publics" and attaches with it explicitly its functional implications for political participation.

In the following the practical implications of Deliberation rooted in social media are exemplified by an online citizen involvement for the public budgeting purposes of the city of Frankfurt/Main (Germany). Before it is described in more detail, a general definition of (online) citizen budgeting explains why it is relevant to the investigation and how it is currently scientifically evaluated with respect to Web 2.0.@

2   Citizen Budgeting: Definition and Relevance

Citizen budgeting is a municipal-political participation instrument by which citizens of a municipality or a city can advise deliberatively through the use of budget proposals and exert influence. A three-stage procedure was carried out concerning the participation phases of the overall budgeting process: An intensive phase of information in which the administration reports about the financial state of affairs follows a consultation phase in which the opinions and suggestions of the citizens are caught up, before administration reasonably accepts or declines them in the account phase. The investigation of the Frankfurt 2013 citizen budgeting process deals especially with the consultation phase.

2.1   Frankfurt 2013 (online) Citizen Budgeting

The first Frankfurt citizens' budget deliberations for the financial year 2013 launched its consultation phase titled 'Frankfurt asks me' on November 18th, 2011. Up to the

11th of December 2011the citizens had the possibility to submit suggestions in particular online, but also traditionally by mail and phone. Budgetary administration transmitted those analog proposals into online versions. Until December 18, so even a week longer, all the proposals could online be assessed and discussed. In total, 2751 Internet users registered. There were 1328 proposals on which a total of 46135 reviews and 6904 comments have been delivered. Before in October 103 best of all valued suggestions were introduced into the consultations of the town municipal council, the consultations had been extended by two additional phases. On one hand the City Council evaluated the feasibility and the financial consequences of the single suggestions. On the other hand a one-day public forum convened on March 24, 2012, in which a jury of citizens deliberated to foster individual proposals on the basis of the city council's feasibility evaluations. A total of 1200 citizens applied for the formation of the jury of which 300 participants were representatively selected and invited. Ultimately, 92 citizens as well as an administrative staff of 14 and 13 moderators participated in the forum. Finally, the citizens forum favored 25 proposals. Since October, 2012 the town parliament discussed the top 103 suggestions of the online phase taking into account the favored proposals of the civil forum and the feasibility analysis of the city council. Frankfurt's citizen budgeting process 2013 was finished with the publication of the decisions of the town delegate meeting on March 21st 2013. Then a new (online) citizens budgeting process started for 2014.@

2.2 Description of the Online System

Description of the online system refers to its configuration during the one-month online consultation phase from the 18th of November to the 18th of December 2011. The web application „Frankfurt asks me" (WWW.FFM.DE) allowed the user to submit suggestions to value them positively or negatively by clicking a button and to comment on them. Besides, users had the possibility to refer by sub comment especially to contributions of other participants from which often originated independent communication chains. Users needed to register themselves with name or pseudonym so that the word contributions could unambiguously be assigned. Direct feedback on part of the budgetary administration did not take place at this stage. Furthermore moderators intervened regularly as actors in the communicative process. They first and foremost ensured compliance with discursive conditions of the so-called 'Netiquette'. These are conventional rules for social communication behavior in the Internet which were available under the menu item 'Rules of the game' (WWW.FFM.DE/INHALT/SPIELREGELN). They can already be understood as basic rules of discourse. Amongst other basic rules of discourse, it is requested to "respectfully deal with each other", "write what you mean" or "stick to the topic". However, here and there the moderators also answered on issues of content or procedure criticism. In these cases and for procedural understanding questions they referred the users to the separate forums 'praise and criticism' (WWW.FFM. DE/LOB_UND_KRITIK) and 'frequently asked questions' (WWW.FFM.DE/ HAEUFIGE_FRAGEN).

3   Realization of the Study

The case study of political communication in Web 2.0 in the context of online deliberations of the Frankfurt 2013 citizens' budget is exploratory. A quantitative content analysis shall yield insights about the way how the offer is used and whether implications for the ideal of deliberative democracy can be revealed.

3.1   Methodology and Research Objectives

To get a first impression in this regard, it will be checked how many discussions have been carried out as a whole and which in turn meet the necessary condition for deliberation, "Dialogicity": A discussion will be designated as dialogic if a participant pipes up at least twice and additionally makes reference to the utterance of another participant. Subsequently, the actual analysis is carried out on a case example, namely the longest discussion that has taken place. It comprises 112 comments concerning the proposal to cover the grandstands of a Frankfurt soccer stadium. All single comments form the units of analysis. They are encoded using a self-developed category scheme, which already proved to approach the 'discourse quality index (DQI)', the 'coding scheme 2.2' and 'Contrasting content analysis'.

By means of the category scheme it should be detected, whether the online discussions of 'Frankfurt asks me' show some kind of collective reasoning on a constructive level, as it is described as a normative ideal by HABERMAS, or whether it is mostly mixed with personal sensitivities and irrelevant contributions. At the same time the antagonism between the theorem of the "emergence of the digital general public" according to Münker[6] and the "fragmentation of the general public "[5] according to HABERMAS should be taken into account.

3.2   Swarm Intelligence or Shitstorm: A Category Scheme

Thus the design of the category scheme follows on one hand a deductive approach according to the theorems of Münker and HABERMAS, but also an inductive approach on the other as a result of the first sighting of the examination material. Thereby a controversy about the installation of so-called 'occupy corners' was particularly outstanding. The proposal dealt with the installation of speaker-pulpits and venues throughout Frankfurt for members of the anti-capitalism movement 'Occupy Germany'. It was observed that the discussions in places deviated from the real subject. Partly, one author was ironically attacked because he proved to be a controversial lord mayor candidate. Accordingly, the discussion took a momentum that threatened to break the above mentioned rules of Netiquette, which is why straightway moderators intervened in the communication process.

Against this background, two diametrically opposed measurement constructs were designed for political communication, to be named after two currently popular phenomena: 'Swarm intelligence' and 'shitstorm'. Both constructs are to be understood as ideal types. 'Swarm intelligence' indicates the highest degree of deliberation, whereas 'shitstorm' is intended to alert on missing deliberation. Four indicators which form together likewise contrast pairs were assigned to both constructs in each case. Swarm intelligence comprises the indicators focus, dispassion, intersubjectivity and constructivity. Shitstorm encloses the dimensions capture, irony, subjectivity and stagnation (see fig.2).

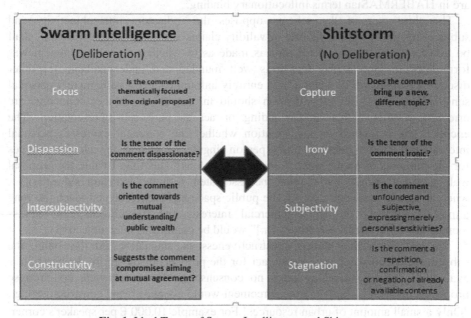

Fig. 1. Ideal Types of Swarm Intelligence and Shitstorm

The first dichotomy focus vs. capture takes into account the antagonism between fragmentation and emergence of the public sphere. Here, it should be decided whether a comment relates to the original proposal or whether a new, different topic comes up. In the first case the necessary focusing of the general public can be assumed, which according to HABERMAS is needed to ensure productive deliberation on the Internet at all. The latter defines a so-called 'capture' of the discussion. The comment feeds subjects foreign to the original suggestion into the communicative process which may interest only a fraction of the participants, thereby provoking a disintegration of the debaters into partial public spheres. In the above example that would be the following criticism of the lord mayor's candidate: " […] is this the attempt to pretend there are other more people (except yourself) who would elect you lord mayor?!?" His candidacy was not the subject of the proposal to be debated.

The indicators dispassion and irony form the second contrast pair. It refers to the criterion of the illocutionary binding effect of speech acts demanded by HABERMAS. As already mentioned, in the general rules of the discussions of 'Frankfurt asks me' it is also explicitly prompted to make no ironic or sarcastic contributions because these could be misread. At times irony is registered in several comments , such as: „ […] can we agree on a pillory instead of a speaker-pulpit ? […] ". People do not really say what they mean but refer to backround knowledge or even a shared sense of humor that tends to exclude other members of discussion. In contrast to that a phrase like "The city should only spend money on sports events if children, youngsters and amateurs benefit from it but not professional players [...]" would be considered comprehensible, unagitated and therefore dispassionate as they are in HABERMASian terms inllocutionary binding.

The third pair of the scheme opposes the indicators intersubjectivity and subjectivity. At this point the role of validity claims according to HABERMAS shall be taken into account. A distinction is made as to whether or not a comment was formulated in such a way that it is well founded and understandable for other discourse participants or whether it is entirely unfounded, expressing merely personal sensitivities. Thus, this classification should inform about whether comments are oriented towards mutual understanding or act as pure self-representation. The encoders are istructued to pay attention whether the comment expresses personal interests and is often held in the first person singular or whether the annotator argues for the purposes of public weal. A statement such as "This time I value my proposal well-reasoned" would for example be associated with the indicator subjectivity , whereas speech acts such as "[...] The public space has been occupied much too long almost exclusively through commercial interests and the citizens can express themselves so far hardly effectively [...]" would be counted as intersubjectivity.

The last contrasting pair is constructiveness vs. stagnation. At this point, the substantive added value in a speech act for the progress of the entire deliberation is evaluated. Because in reality often no consensus is to be achieved, compromise proposals oriented towards mutual agreement would count as being constructive, e.g.: "Only a small amount of urban resources! For example 10,000 € per speaker's corner. The rest can be privately financed ... [...]" Repetition, confirmation or negation of already available contents would be valued as stagnation. A few special cases could also be observed in which disjointed, meaningless one-word comments did not even have illocutionary meaning and therefore no acceptability condition could be assumed to be known. Naturally they would also fall under the category "stagnation".

The category scheme assumes that the mentioned four opposed indicator pairs between the dimensions of 'Swarm Intelligence' and 'Shit Storm' are disjunctive with each other. That is: a comment cannot be at the same time focused and captured, dispassionate and ironic, inter-subjective and subjective or constructive and stagnative. Thus only one value per opposites is assigned to any comment. Conversely this means that the values must not be consistent concerning the ideal types. The implication of the typology is not that the measuring constructs 'Swarm Intelligence' and 'Shit Storm' appear empirically only in pure form. On the contrary: The draft implies that in reality many hybrid forms unfold between these ideal types. Consequently a comment could be focused but nevertheless ironic; intersubjective but nevertheless stagnative. At this point once again the above mentioned example comment shall be taken into reference: „ [...] Can we agree instead of a speaker-pulpit on a pillory? -with ecological tomatoes and rotten organic eggs? I have in mind there a self-administered, spontaneous free throwing. [...]". The irony absolutely focuses on the subject speaker's-pulpit. The word "we" implies that the speech act is addressed towards enraged discussion partners, thus being intersubjective. The content of the comment has certainly no added value, if at all entertainment value. It is thus stagnative.

Furthermore, it is well conceivable that a thematic subject is captured, about that, however, still essentially is discussed intersubjectively and constructively. To illustrate the varied possible combinations, it is useful to arrange the dimensions of the ideal constructs in form of a two-factorial matrix design.

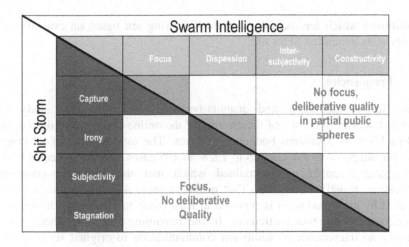

Fig. 2. Communication Style and Deliberation Quality

Depending on whether and where in the matrix mixed combinations frequently occur, investigative statements about the deliberative quality of the underlying debate as a whole can finally be derived. The diagonal divides the matrix into two halves. Thereby the left lower half is dominated by the factor 'Shit Storm', however, the dimension focus of the factor 'Swarm Intelligence' is of highest relevance in this field. Should the higher proportion of encoded cases fall into this lower half of the matrix, this indicates that the discussion has not run off in direction of sustainable deliberation. Still it can count as approximately focused. This would comply with the theorem of the 'emergence of the digital general public' but rather deny deliberative quality of internet-based communication in this point.

In contrast, the upper right half of the matrix is dominated by the factor 'Swarm Intelligence'.,This time the dimension capture of the factor 'Shit Storm' is simultaneously of highest relevance in this field. If the higher proportion of encoded cases falls into this upper half of the matrix, it can be concluded that the discussions tend to have been carried out in the sense of deliberation, however mainly in partial public spheres. This would support the fragmentation theory of HABERMAS but would not diminish the deliberative quality of these small-scale communication processes per se. Would the frequencies of encoded cases become equally distributed over both halves, distinguishing between fragmentation and emergence quality of the general digital public would be a too weak explanation for online-deliberation.

Ultimately the category scheme should indeed serve to distinguish how deliberative quality of online discussions is affected by a trade-off between fragmentation and emergence of the general public. Pointedly expressed a response to the question has to be made who is right: HABERMAS or Münker? Or perhaps both?

4   Findings

All numbers which are mentioned in the following are based on evaluations of an appropriately generated SPSS file.

4.1   Frequencies

Before further qualitative and quantitative analyses of the case study will be presented, a brief overview of the entirety of the online communication processes in the Frankfurt 2013 citizens budgeting is given. The total number of all potentially debatable suggestions amounts up to 1328. In 405 cases an interconnected additional communication could be ascertained which met the necessary condition for deliberation, namely dialogicity. That means in these 405 discussions a participant indicated by his pseudonym is reported at least twice to comment with reference to the utterance of another participant. In the remaining 923 cases there was either generally no interconnected additional communication to original suggestions, or it was commented merely once without entering into a dialog. A proportion of approximately 30.5% of original proposals was thus at least rudimentarily discussed dialogically.

The longest discussion with 112 comments was selected from these 405 cases for the analysis. In it, several participants including three moderators piped up even more than two times. The proposal's subject area was 'sports and culture' and focused on covering the grandstand of a Frankfurt soccer stadium. The basic argument was that the city should finance the roofing of the grandstands so that soccer fans do not have to stand in the rain when they watch a game in the stadium. It was thus an issue of expenditure. The original suggestion was rated 184 times. The comments including the original proposal were top down numbered in the order of their listing on the Web site. Altogether they totaled up to 113 analysis units. They were, as already described, associated with the binary categories focus vs. capture, dispassion vs. irony, intersubjectivity vs. subjectivity and constructiveness vs. stagnation. With every comment all four categories were encoded; within the binary categories only one value was ascribed in each case.12

To begin with the pure types of political communication in the web 2.0: A substantial amount of 36.6 percent of the comments turn out to be focused,

---

[1] Besides, there is in the category *dispassion* versus irony in three cases an exception, where the comments contained ironic, as well as dispassionate elements. A single-sided predominance of objectivity or irony could not be identified, which is why both forms were encoded.

[2] Inter-coder reliability was tested: Krippendorff's Alpha coefficient= .782.

dispassionate, intersubjective and constructive; that is absolutely equivalent to 41 comments. Only 8 comments are to be arranged as a pure Shit Storm; thus share of 7.1%. With 56.6% more than half of the comments turned out to be hybrid combinations of Shit Storm as well as Swarm Intelligence indicators. Taking into account the frequency distributions within the hybrid types, the following picture emerges (see table 1):

Table 1. Swarm Intelligence vs. Shit Storm: Frequencies of Hybrid Combinations (in % of total research units)

Swarm Int. 36,3% / 7,1% Shit Storm	Swarm Intelligence			
Shit Storm	Focus	Dispassion	Inter-subjectivity	Constructivity
Capture	0 %	10,6%	9,7%	9,7%
Irony	11,5 %	(2,7%)	4,4%	4,4%
Subjectivity	37,2%	31,9%	0%	5,3%
Stagnation	39,8%	34,5%	8,0%	0%

It is evident that hybrid combinations between Swarm Intelligence and Shit Storm indicators appear heaped in the left lower part of the matrix. The majority of the comments seem to show focus and dispassion on the one as well as subjectivity and stagnation on the other side. These circumstances state that the investigated discussion is characterized by a loss of deliberative quality but proceeds at least in a focused and dispassionate manner. At this point it must explicitly be pointed out not conclude the fallacy that, discussions focused on the Internet would in general proceed in a focused, dispassionate, subjective and stagnative way. Such an inference on the basis of the present frequency observations alone is statistically invalid. However it can be checked by correlation analyses, whether the observed correlations occur more than randomly and thus exhibit statistical significance.

4.2   Correlations

The present data set presents binary encoded, nominal-scaled variables. Their relationships are therefore based on a two-factorial crosstab design and can be calculated by means of the correlation algorithms Chi-square, or Phi. The objective is to examine to what extent the values of variables more often appear together than would be expected at random distribution. Therefore, in a first step, the internal relationships of the indicators focus, dispassion, intersubjectivity and constructiveness are determined on the one, as well as capture, irony, subjectivity and stagnation on the other side. This gives evidence about how consistently the constructs Swarm Intelligence and Shit Storm are in themselves.

The intra-correlations of Swarm Intelligence manifest themselves first between the indicators focus and dispassion. Furthermore dispassion, intersubjectivity and constructivity correlate significantly (p<0.05).. However, no appreciable correlation could be ascertained between focus and intersubjectivity as well as focus and constructivity.

With Shit Storm it is mirror-image. Capture correlates significantly with irony. Equally significantly correlated are irony, subjectivity and stagnation (p<0.05). Again no appreciable correlation exists between capture and subjectivity as well as capture and stagnation. This circumstances show that the focus of a discussion on a certain topic is not necessarily an indication for their deliberative quality. Vice versa, the capture of a topic is not inevitably tied to a deliberative quality loss.

Also the inter-correlations support these assumptions. They now indicate, to what extent the indicators of the constructs vary amongst each other; or in other words, which communicative hybrid types appear being systematic. For that purpose, the sample was first cleaned from all ideal cases which indicated perfect Swarm Intelligence, or perfect Shit Storm. Then all types of hybrid combinations between two indicators with its binary values (0=not existent, 1=existent) were analyzed. The correlations are listed in the table below (see table 2).

Significant findings, as it implies the presumption based on the frequency distribution, could only partially be registered. Obviously within the mixing type combinations the indicators focus and subjectivity are highly correlated, focus and stagnation even higher. Just the same appears with the contradicting arrangement between capture, intersubjectivity and constructivity. Nevertheless, a significant correlation between dispassion and subjectivity or stagnation does not appear.

Table 2. Swarm Intelligence vs. Shit Storm: Inter-correlation of hybrid combinations (Phi coefficient on significance level 0,01)

		Swarm Intelligence			
		Focus	Dispassion	Inter-subjectivity	Constructivity
Shit Storm	Capture	-1*	-	0,581*	0,664*
	Irony	-	-0,903*	-	-
	Subjectivity	0,581*	-	-1*	-0,434*
	Stagnation	0,664*	-	-0434*	-1*

The contributions are above-average subjective and stagnative and thus have small deliberative quality. If the comments are however thematically captured and thus fragmented, they are exceptionally often intersubjective and constructive and show high deliberative quality. As has already been shown by the intra-correlations, it is here again noticed that capture or focus is fairly irrespective of whether the discussion has deliberative quality. These findings may seem trivial; they confirm however the basic assumption that with the communicative hybrid type combinations there must be a certain tradeoff between deliberative quality and fragmenting public spheres. All in all it can be stated, that with the longest discussion of the Frankfurt 2013 citizen budgeting process no appreciable fragmenting of the general public could be ascertained. Subject and purpose of the discussion are clearly contoured. The municipal reference and the overarching aim of the allocation of resources seem to discipline the debate from the outset. Certainly, it would be interesting to check these conditions for federal political issues in which the direct relationship to everyday life is less tangible. Furthermore, there might be special factors that are more likely to accelerate a 'Shit Storm' versus a 'Swarm Intelligence' than others and vice versa. Stagnation for instance might not as heavily support Shit Storm-tendencies as irony does. Stagnative phrases can in parts be helpful to keep already achieved aspects of agreement in mind even if it might not bring forward the whole discussion as effectively as a constructive speech act could. A factor analysis could help further research to find more about this aspect.

5   Conclusions

It was the ultimate purpose of this study to investigate by means of a case example whether and how deliberation sustainably takes place in political discussion processes carried out via the social media of web 2.0. Furthermore, it should also be contributed to conceptual theory in this field. It was to investigate the extent to which the HABERMAS' concept of the ideal speech situation can be matched with the structurally new qualities of social media.

If one applies HABERMAS' rules for succeeding deliberation as a basic framework and extends it by the concepts about fragmenting or emergence of a rational general public, which were especially formulated for the communicative conditions of web 2.0, rather positive case-study results arise for the present online discussion within the scope of the Frankfurt 2013 citizens budgeting process.

A good third of the comments proves to be highly deliberative. They are clearly associated with the pure type of Swarm Intelligence and resist the danger of fragmentation. Only a vanishing small percentage of the comments proves to relate to Shit Storm and is completely useless for deliberative purposes. This is not all too surprising. Citizens budgeting are a communal participation tool that requires the involvement of its citizens. The use of this participation instrument is highly auto selective. In other words: It can be assumed that anyway only persons take part who are politically interested and want to argue accordingly focused.

However,, the discussion is not consistently deliberative. Central findings of the investigation are that the discussion is dominated predominantly by a communicative hybrid form between the poles Swarm Intelligence and Shit Storm. It predominantely proceeds in a focused and dispassionate, but also subjective and stagnative manner. Thus, the discussion is interspersed by a majority of pure statements. The participants comment dispassionately on the subject. They bring in their personal opinions in response to other opinions but do not claim to advance the overall discussion. This emphasizes the fact that the user feels motivated to articulate his opinion without wanting to impress necessarily with constructive suggestions oriented to public weal. By the majority the comments thus relieve themselves from the intellectual claim to be totally deliberative but do indeed testify a will for political participation. It is to be supposed that specific Internet-related circumstances favor this trend. A speech act which will be made online cannot be interrupted. The user has longer time to ponder his word contribution than with analogous face to face discussions in which he acts under time pressure.

The citizens appear to see the first-time offer to consult online about the budget of their home town predominantly as an additional option to make their personal view known to the public. In the coming financial years shall be observed whether more citizens get used to this additional participation option and if so, which implications for the deliberative quality of the discussions this may have. Does more experience with online communication at the same time lead to more active, critical reasoning? Will the currently high level of communicative hybrids be pushed back in favor of pure deliberation?

Or unzips the habituation of the political Web 2.0 the borders unto much more irrelevant criticism than is currently the case? These questions can be answered only in quite some time and increasingly be investigated by quantitative inference-statistical means. In any case, the snapshot undertaken here absolutely justifies the application of online-deliberation within the scope of citizens budgeting processes. It allows the assumption that the Web 2.0 in the sense of a functional add-on option for political participation can be evaluated as a progress towards the ideal of deliberative democracy.

References

1. Habermas, J.: Die Einbeziehung des Anderen. Studien zur politischen Theorie. Suhrkamp, Frankfurt a.M. (1999)
2. Habermas, J.: Faktizität und Geltung. Beiträge zur Diskurstheorie des Rechts und des demokratischen Rechtsstaats. Suhrkamp, Frankfurt a.M. (1994)
3. Habermas, J.: Moralbewusstsein und kommunikatives Handeln. Suhrkamp, Frankfurt a.M. (1984)
4. Habermas, J.: Theorie des kommunikativen Handelns, Band 1, 4. Aufl. Suhrkamp, Frankfurt a.M. (1981)
5. Habermas, J.: Strukturwandel der Öffentlichkeit. Untersuchungen zu einer Kategorie der bürgerlichen Gesellschaft. Luchterhand, Neuwied (1968)
6. Münker, S.: Emergenz digitaler Öffentlichkeiten. Die Sozialen Medien des Web 2.0. Suhrkamp, Frankfurt a.M. (2009a)
7. Nietzsche, P., et al.: Development of an Evaluation Tool for Participative E-Government Services. A Case Study of Electronic Participatory Budgeting Projects in Germany. Administration and Public Management 18, S.6–S.25 (2012)

Reasons for Using Social Networks Professionally
The Influence of User Diversity on Usage Motivation

Anne Kathrin Schaar[1], André Calero Valdez[1], Martina Ziefle[1],
Denise Eraßme[2], Ann-Kathrin Löcker[2], and Eva-Maria Jakobs[2]

[1] Human-Computer Interaction Center and Chair for Communcation Science,
RWTH Aachen University, Campus Boulevard 57, 52074 Aachen, Germany
schaar@comm.rwth-aachen.de
[2] Human-Computer Interaction Center and Chair for Textlinguistics and Technical
Communication, RWTH Aachen University, Campus Boulevard 57, 52074 Aachen,
Germany

Abstract. Since the success of social media in private usage settings,
social media applications spread rapidly in the working context. In business internal contexts these applications seem useful as a measure for
strategic knowledge management. Social media in this context promises
to offer adequate facilities to support a systematic storage of knowledge
as well as a support of knowledge exchange and communication in enterprises. But since social media is only successful when used, the usage
motivation of employees is one central key for their success. Therefore
this paper focusses on the motivation to use social media professionally.
To achieve this we are investigating the influence of user diversity factors
such as age, gender, and social media expertise on aspects of usage motivation. In a study with N=84 the employees of an enterprise were asked
which reasons for using social media are relevant to them. Findings show
that both factors age and gender reveal a relatively low influence on the
factors evaluation of usage motives, tools (as a measure for motivation),
and incentives/reinforcements for social network usage. In contrast both
expertise with social media and achievement motivation revealed many
correlations with both usage motives and tools as well as incentives and
reinforcements.

Keywords: social media, technology acceptance, motivation,
user-centered design, incentivation.

1 Introduction

The integration of online social network approaches or comparable social media applications in corporate settings has started. This was triggered by the
enormous success of these applications within the private utilization context[1].
According to the designation of these new forms of media as Web 2.0[2] or Social
Software[3] corporate activities in the field of social media were labeled as *Enterprise 2.0*[4] or *Social Business*[5]. Where first forms of social media integration

G. Meiselwitz (Ed.): SCSM 2014, LNCS 8531, pp. 385–396, 2014.
© Springer International Publishing Switzerland 2014

were predominantly focused on business external marketing purposes, internal approaches of social media integration were more and more realized during the last 8 years e.g. the integration of social networks, wikis[6], or blogs[7, 8]. Perceived goals of internal social media integration in a corporate setting are mostly named in the context of knowledge transfer and collaboration[9] thus in line with the goals of knowledge management[10, 11].

The approaches to use social media as a new measure to support knowledge management even becomes more relevant when looking at current societal changes in big economies: Almost all big economies have to face the challenge of the so-called demographic change. A large part of the workforce of an aging population is retiring, with a shrinking workforce supplying for the elderly part of the population[12]. This does not only increase the burden on the younger part of the population to maintain a high tax volume to pay for pensions, but the upcoming generations will also have to acquire business critical knowledge from the baby boomer generation before they retire. This phenomenon is especially threatening for economies that are based on service providers. As knowledge is the central good for them[13]. Without the knowledge of experts, existing systems cannot be maintained and will deteriorate. Furthermore knowledge is required in the process of innovation[14]. Granovetter[15] proposed that the weak-ties in a social network (e.g. employee network) are the sources of information, innovation and, opportunity. Making them available is a central need of any knowledge intensive enterprise today.

From this perspective social media applications seem to be even more interesting as a support for weak-tie networks in enterprises or a room for systematic storage of knowledge as a sensitive and important good. But although business executives are highly interested in success factors or deployment strategies, so far there is only little valid knowledge about these aspects. One approach that aims to make a contribution to these questions is the user-centered community design approach that is based on knowledge from technology acceptance research.

The Approach of User-Centered Community Design. The approach of user-centered community design was developed in the research project *iNec*. An interdisciplinary team of researchers from social sciences, computer science, economists and partners from industry investigates how to develop a social community concept that fits the needs of all involved stakeholders successfully. One central aspect of the overall approach is the user-centered perspective. This facet is based on the assumption that technology acceptance benefits from an early integration of potential users. Understanding which factors are relevant for potential users in the context of using technology, is essential for a successful technology implementation within any setting[16–19]. In the context of this paper especially the motives behind a professional use of technology are of interest. In contrast to the private usage of technology, professional usage may reveal other conditions. For example using technology for work relevant purposes may not always be voluntarily but obligatory.

The research field of technology acceptance originated from research in social psychology, when researchers tried to understand which factors are influencing voting behavior and social behavior. Early research in this context was predominately focussed on predicting social behavior in general (Theory of Reasoned Action[20], and Theory of Planned Behavior[21]). Newer models and theories in the context of technology acceptance research focussed on the intention to use information systems within the working context. For example the Technology Acceptance Model (TAM) aims to explain behavioral intention to use an information system predicted by two factors – compatibility and relative advantage (i.e. perceived ease of use and perceived usefulness). In tradition of the TAM Venkatesh et al.[16] reformed the model into the Unified Theory of Acceptance and Use of Technology (UTAUT). The UTAUT predicts behavior using four perceptions about a system – the expected performance (i.e. perceived usefulness), expected effort (i.e. perceived ease of use), social influence (i.e. perception of a system in the peer group), and facilitating conditions (i.e. availability of support). These factors are moderated in regard to their importance by gender, age, experience and voluntariness of use.

In this context the question remains how these models can be applied to social media applications. The approach of user-centered community design tries to apply the insights from technology acceptance research with focussing on two central key aspects: a) The comprehension of employees cognitive skills, their emotional-, motivational-, and knowledge-related needs in their working environment. b) The understanding of communicative usability in the context of social media. The approach is focussed on the influence of diversity factors age, gender, social media expertise, personality, technical expertise and educational level on motivation[17], matching of incentives, and usability and design criteria.

In this paper only selected aspects of this model are investigated: age and gender, and social media expertise and achievement motivation.

Motivation to Use Social Media in Corporate Settings. In addition to general information about social media usage in corporate settings (see Section 1.1) and the presentation of the approach of user-centered community design this section deals with motivation to use social media.

It is essential to learn more about the motives behind social media usage in corporate settings, because human activity is always triggered by underlying motivation. In this context Holtzblatt et al. investigated perceived benefits and utility of wikis in 2010[11]. Three central categories that influenced people to use or not use wikis within a corporate setting were be revealed: a) the *reluctance to share*, which addresses the tension between necessity to share expertise across individuals and individual aspects that hinder this exchange, b) *reliance on the channels of communication* and c) *sensitivities*[11].

The first category *reluctance to share* consists of five factors: The *extra costs of sharing information* is the first aspects that influences knowledge exchange. People mentioned that strategic information sharing takes too much time and effort, because more editorial effort is necessary. The second aspect that influences the willingness to disclose information was *sensitivity of information*. In this context especially the specific culture (e.g. strictly separated business units) in an enterprises hindered exchange. The *unwillingness to share unfinished work* was another aspect that results from a feeling of indisposition when presenting unfinished work. A similar correlating aspect for this aspect introduced by Holtzblatt et al. was *sensitivities to the openness of information*, which especially focusses on hierarchy. People reported to feel uncomfortable when superiors are looking on a status quo reports. This aspect was confirmed by a study at IBM, where Danis and Singer also could reveal that people were not willing to disclose unfinished work in a wiki[22].

Reluctance to share as a more affective aspect is contrasted with *reliance*, which focusses on workflow aspects. Here one factor was *work practice*. This describes that people are not willing to learn new tools, because time is scarce or the wiki does not match their work practice. *Lack of guidelines and standards* irritated people when deciding which information to disclose and which not to. The third factor introduced by Holtzblatt et al. was *sensitivities*. It refers to cultural sensitivities according to cooperation. Holtzblatt et al. revealed the general habit that data is owned by the person who had generated it. Based on this assumption people reported that they do not want others to edit their documents or were afraid of editing other contributions.

In general we ca say that individual or cultural influences are relevant for using wikis (or other social media applications) and the way they are used. Hence it is necessary to learn more about the motives and motivation behind the scenes. The next section presents the main focus and central questions addressed in this paper.

2   Main Focus of the Study and Questions Addressed

In order to find out which factors impact social media usage in professional settings, we conducted this research focusing on the influence of user diversity factors on motives to use social media professionally. According to the user-centered community design approach (see Section 1.2), we focus on the influence of age, gender, and social media expertise, as well as an slightly amended short version of the Achievement Motivation Inventory (AMI)[23]. In this context the following research questions are relevant:

- Does *age,gender*, and *level of achievement motivation* influence the motives to use social media professionally?
- Does *age,gender*, and *level of achievement motivation* influence the evaluation of motivational effects of social media tools?
- Does *age,gender*, and *level of achievement motivation* influence the evaluation of incentives and reinforcements?

Overall, the impact of user diversity factors is investigated in regard of their influence on three dependent variables: general motives to use social media, tools as a motivator to use social media, and incentives and reinforcements, which might support motivation to use social media in professional usage settings.

3   Method

In order to reach a large number of participants, the questionnaire method was chosen. The questionnaire was provided paper based in one manufacturing company. The questionnaire was distributed during lunch breaks, on two consecutive days and collected after lunch. Before distribution, differently aged adults examined the questionnaire to avoid misunderstandings and possible lack of clarity. Completing the questionnaire took between 25 and 30 minutes. In the following subsections the design of the study is presented: Section 3.1 contains the central variables of the study and Section 3.2 presents a description of the questionnaire instrument.

3.1   Variables

As *independent variables* we have chosen age, gender, number of contacts in most used social network, social media usage frequency, and a slightly modified short version of the Achievement Motivation Inventory (AMI).

As *dependent variables* we have chosen motives to use social networks professionally (see Section 3.2). In this context the participants were asked to evaluate six motives for social media usage (see Table 1). Additionally participants were asked to evaluate different social media tools according to the level they could enhance motivation social media usage. Furthermore a set of possible incentives and reinforcements for social media usage were chosen as independent variables.

3.2   Questionnaire Instrument

The questionnaire was divided into six main parts: (a) demographic data (b) social media experience (c) AMI (d) usage motives (e) tools and (f) possible incentives and reinforcements for social media usage. More information about the topics and the scales used are given in the subsections below:

Demographic data. In order to get general information about user diversity factors each participant was asked to state their age and gender.

Social Media Experience. This part of the questionnaire aimed to find out how experienced the participants are in using social media. Therefore the frequency of using exemplary social media applications (i.e. Facebook, Xing, Twitter, LinkedIn, Blogs, forums, Wikis, in-house network) were asked. Answers had to be selected from of a 6-point-Likert scale (daily, 2-3x/week, once a week, once a month, 2-3x/year, rarer). Asking for the degree of liking social media the participants could choose answering options from 1=very unwillingly to 6=very willingly and 7=I dont use this product. As an additional information in this context the participants were asked for the number of contacts in the Social Network the participant uses the most.

Usage Motives. To find out more about the motives behind social media usage in professional settings the participants were asked under which conditions they would use an internal social network (*"I would use an in-house network, if ..."*). Possible motives for social media use were measured by a 6-point Likert scale (1 = totally disagree – 6 = totally agree) with 3 items for 6 different motives. All items used are presented in Table 1. All scales showed high reliability with alpha ranging from .72 to .88 and were summarized to factors for the analysis.

Table 1. List of motives for social network use in the working context

I would use a social network in the working context, when ...	
Motive	**Items**
Information	...I get information about activities in my business unit
	...I could get information easier
	...I could get information relevant for me
Importance	...my work within the network is valued
	...my contributions matter for progress at work
	...my contributions are useful for other members
Contact	...my colleagues are immediately available for me
	...I can stay in contact with my colleagues via the network
	...I can socialize with my colleagues
Self-potrayal	...it increases my visibility of what my skills and competences are
	...I can present new ideas
	...I can present my achievements
Autonomy	...I can work independently within the network
	...I can work at any time and at any location
	...I can plan my work more independently
Feedback	...I get feedback from my colleagues
	...I get feedback for my work
	...I get responses according to my work

Tools. This part aimed to explore tools, which are likely to increase the use of in-house Social Networks (e.g. groups, chat function, personalized profile, etc.). For this purpose the participants were asked to rate on a 6-point Liker Scale if their motivation to use such a network would 1 = strongly decrease to 6 = strongly increase depending on integrated tools. In sum 27 different tools were rated.

Incentives and Reinforcements. The questionnaire presented a list of possible incentives and reinforcements that could be relevant for for the motivation to use a social network within a professional context. A list of 21 items was presented including among others financial incentives as well as gamification elements but also options on how to get feedback (e.g. only private feedback). All incentives and reinforcements had to be evaluated on a 6-point Likert scale (1 = totally disagree – 6 = totally agree).

4   Results

The following section presents first the description of the sample (see Section 4.1). And second the empirical results of the study (Section 4.2 and 4.3) are presented. Results are presented according to the independent variables of the study (gender, age, social media experience, achievement motivation). As statistical methods, Mann-Whitney U, and bivariate correlation analysis were used. The level of significance was set to $\alpha = .05$. Effect sizes, if applicable, are reported using Pearson's r.

4.1   Sample

A total of $N = 84$ took part in the study. Our sample consisted of 53 male and 31 female employees. Participants were recruited to voluntary complete the questionnaire in paper form during lunch break. The age ranges from 16 to 58 years ($M = 36.06$, $SD = 12.32$). We found a wide dispersion concerning the job tenure. Some of the younger participants just started apprenticeship (some months of occupation), while the eldest employee has been working for 43 years in the company. The general job tenure was $M = 14.8$ years ($SD = 12.66$) and M=9.87 years ($SD = 10.74$). Referring to the social media expertise we can report that the sample uses especially Facebook ($M = 3.25, SD = 2.51$) and the in-house community ($M = 4.07, SD = 2.19$).

4.2   The Influence of User Diverstiy on Motives to Use Social Media Professionally

First of all the overall evaluation of otives to use social media professionally is presented (see Fig. 1). As Fig. 1 presents information, autonomy, and importance are the top motives behind social media usage. These four reached means above 4. So did also contact and feedback that were both additionally evaluated above neutral ($= 3.5$).

Gender. In the context of *motives* we could not reveal any influence of gender. In the context of *tools* that might enhance the motivation to use social media applications professionally, we could reveal a correlation between gender and the evaluation of an *email distribution list* as a motivator for social media usage ($U = 519.000$, $Z = -2.045$, $p = .041$). In the context of *incentive and reinforcements* evaluation we could reveal significant gender differences for *public feedback* within the community ($U = 547.000$, $Z = -2.562$, $p = .010$), the option to form *virtual teams* that compete with each other ($U = 554.500$, $Z = -2.223$, $p = .026$) and an *individual performance evaluation* ($U = 537.000$, $Z = -2.309$, $p = .021$).

We can say that women reported to be more motivated by functions that support communication than male participants ($M_{\female} = 4.4, M_{\male} = 4.0$). Additionally females stated that an individual performance evaluation is more important for them ($M_{\female} = 3.3, M_{\male} = 3.9$). Males in contrast reported to prefer incentives and reinforcements that allow public feedback ($M_{\female} = 2.2, M_{\male} = 2.9$) as well as competitive reinforcements like virtual teams ($M_{\female} = 2.3, M_{\male} = 3.0$).

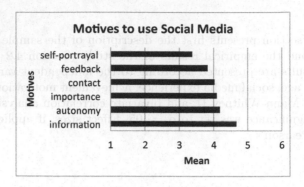

Fig. 1. Comparison of mean evaluation of motives to use social media for profssional reasons

Age. According to age we could reveal a significant correlation with the motive *importance* (see Table 2). For *social media tools* we could reveal five functions with significant correlations: There is a negative correlation between age and *groups, birthday lists, messaging,* and *chat.* For the effectiveness of incentives in the context of age we could reveal a correlation with *financial incentives,* which means the older a person the less open for financial incentives.

In conclusion we hold, that the older a person the more motivating the feeling of being important in the context of professional social media usage. Furthermore we can state that the older a person the less functions that could enhance communication (e.g. messaging and chat), are perceived to be motivating professional social media usage. According to incentives and reinforcements we can say that financial incentives are becoming less important with increasing age.

Social Media Experience. Correlation analysis between *usage motives* and social usage frequency revealed significant influences on the motives *information, autonomy, contact* as well as *importance* (see Table 2). The more often a person uses social media, the higher their agreement with the notion these motives are relevant in the context of using social media at work. Additionally we could reveal a negative correlation between the number of contacts a person has in social networks and the motive importance. Correlation analysis between *social media tools* and social media usage frequency revealed correlations with three functions (see Table 2). In addition to that we could reveal five correlations between *number of contacts within social networks* and functions. In the context of incentives and reinforcements we could not reveal any correlations with social media expertise.

Concluding we can say that the level of expertise with social media influences most motives (we investigated) to use social media. Furthermore we can say that with a higher level of social media expertise comes a more positive evaluation of tools that address personal portrayal facilities (personal profile page and upload of CV and business cards) as well as social media specific forms of communication

Table 2. Bivariate correlations of Age, Social Media Expertise (SME), Number of Contacts (NOC), Achievement Motivation (AMI) and dependent variables.

Dependent variable	Age	SME	NOC	AMI
Motives				
Importance	.238*	.265*	-.271*	
Information		.378**		
Autonomy		.283*		
Contact		.220*		
Self-Portrayal				.294**
Tools				
Forming groups	-.255*	.300**		.300**
Birthday lists	-.248*		.353**	
Messaging	-.289*		.364**	.492**
Chat	-.236*		.259**	
Personal Profile Page		.231*	.284**	.317**
Upload of CV and Business cards		.231*	.297**	.223*
Make Contacts			.302**	.238*
Privacy Settings				.273*
Mailing Lists				.293**
Comments				.416**
Posting Articles				.238*
Document Upload				.290**
Calendar				.290**
Surveys				.232*
Search				.354**
Incentives and Reinforcements				
Financial Incentives	-.276*			.255*
Only Positive Feedback				.230*
Virtual Team Competitions				.272**
Virtual Badges and Medals				.230*
Unlock additional functions				.335**
Compensatory Time Off				.226*
Constructive Comments				.248*
Thank-You function				.348**
Exchange Points for Awards				.248*
Virtual Favors				.318**

Levels of significance * $p < .05$, ** $p < .01$

(e.g. chat, personal messaging). Additionally functions that facilitate the social aspect of social media like e.g. groups or birthday lists also revealed correlations with social media expertise.

Achievment Motivation (AMI). The correlation analysis of achievement motivation and *usage motives* revealed significant correlations for the motive *self-portrayal*. The higher a persons level of achievement motivation the higher the evaluation of the motive self-portrayal.

Correlation analysis with achievement motivation and *social media tools* revealed significant correlations for thirteen social media tools (see Table 2). In general we can say that the higher the achievement motivation the higher the evaluation of social media functions. For *incentives and reinforcements* we could reveal ten correlations with achievement motivation.

Summarizing we can say that the higher the achievement motivation the more important the motive self-portrayal becomes. Additionally we can state that the higher the level of achievement motivation the higher the evaluation of several social media functions as motivators and incentives and reinforcements.

Interim Summary. Finishing the result section we can summarize that *gender* has a relatively low influence on the motivation to use social media professionally. We can say that women are less motivated by competitive elements of social media and more open to cooperative tools. For the diversity factor *age* we can state that the older a person the more important the need for importance in the context of social media. Additionally we could reveal, that the older a person is, the less they are open to social media functions as motivators for a usage. Especially new communication functions that could support information exchange within a social community were negatively correlated with age. According to *social media expertise* we can report that many correlations could be revealed. The expertise with social media showed correlations with four usage motives (information, autonomy, contact, importance). Additionally the factors of social media expertise also revealed manifold influence on the evaluation of social media functions that addresses forms of self-portrayal and social media specific forms of communication (i.e. chat, messaging, etc.). As a third aspect we investigated the correlations between ones *achievement motivation* and usage motives, social media tools, and incentives and reinforcements. For *motives* we found the higher the level of achievement motivation the higher the assessment of the motive self-portrayal. Further more we could reveal the general trend that people with a higher level of achievement motivation showed a higher affinity to social media functions and incentives and reinforcements in general. Hence we can say that expertise with social media seems to weigh much more than other diversity facets.

5 Discussion and Conclusion

As social media integration into the working context promises to be a benefit for knowledge management and thus a possible answer to the challenges of knowledge intense economies in the times of demographic change, this research focussed on reasons for social network usage in professional settings. Taking for granted the principles of the current technology acceptance research we focussed on the influence of diversity facets (age, gender, social media (technology) experience short and modified version of achievement motivation) and their influence on motives and motivation to use social media professionally. As presented the empirical results indicate, that motives to use social media professionally are less influenced by the general diversity factors age and gender, which play an important role in other contexts, but by more specific characteristics like expertise with the specific technology and a persons immanent achievement motivation. Hence one key finding of this study is that the framework conditions of technology use are the most important groundwork for the usage motivation. Especially the non-voluntary character of professional technology use implies focussing on job specific diversity factors like achievement motivation. The classical diversity factors age and gender are therefore of only secondary importance. As limitations of this research we have to name the small sample of the study as well as the branche specific view. That is why future research activities should focus on other industry branches to avoid selective results. Additionally we are working on studies that focus on people that are working with social media systems at work everyday, to get more information whether the attitude and motivation might change over time.

Acknowledgments. We would like to thank the anonymous reviewers for their constructive comments on an earlier version of this manuscript. Furthermore we would like to thank our student assistants Tatjana Hamann and Juliana Brell for their support. The studies from the "iNec" project have been funded by the German Ministry of Education and Research (BMBF) and the European Social Fund (ESF) within the program "Innovationsfähigkeit im demographischen Wandel" under the reference number 01HH11045.

References

1. Stocker, A., Müller, J.: Exploring factual and perceived use and benefits of a web 2.0-based knowledge management application: The siemens case references+. In: Proceedings of the 13th International Conference on Knowledge Management and Knowledge Technologies, p. 18. ACM (2013)
2. O'Reilly, T.: What is web 2.0 (2005)
3. Coates, T.: An addendum to a definition of social software 27, 2009 (2005) (retrieved on August)
4. McAfee, A.P.: Enterprise 2.0: The dawn of emergent collaboration. Management of Technology and Innovation 47(3) (2006)

5. Kiron, D., Palmer, D., Phillips, A.N., Kruschwitz, N.: Social business: What are companies really doing? MIT Sloan Management Review (2012)
6. Arazy, O., Gellatly, I., Jang, S., Patterson, R.: Wiki deployment in corporate settings. IEEE Technology and Society Magazine 28(2), 57–64 (2009)
7. Efimova, L., Grudin, J.: Crossing boundaries: A case study of employee blogging. In: 40th Annual Hawaii International Conference on System Sciences, HICSS 2007, p. 86. IEEE (2007)
8. Müller, J., Stocker, A.: Enterprise microblogging for advanced knowledge sharing: The references@ bt case study. J. UCS 17(4), 532–547 (2011)
9. Paroutis, S., Al Saleh, A.: Determinants of knowledge sharing using web 2.0 technologies. Journal of Knowledge Management 13(4), 52–63 (2009)
10. Richter, A., Stocker, A., Müller, S., Avram, G.: Knowledge management goals revisited – a cross-sectional analysis of social software adoption in corporate environments. In: ACIS 2011 Proceedings (January 2011)
11. Holtzblatt, L.J., Damianos, L.E., Weiss, D.: Factors impeding wiki use in the enterprise: a case study. In: CHI 2010 Extended Abstracts on Human Factors in Computing Systems, pp. 4661–4676. ACM (2010)
12. Bloom, D.E., Canning, D.: Global demographic change: Dimensions and economic significance. Working Paper 10817, National Bureau of Economic Research (October 2004)
13. Sturgeon, T.J.: Does manufacturing still matter? The organizational delinking of production from innovation (1997)
14. Maier, R.: Knowledge management systems: Information and communication technologies for knowledge management. Springer (2007)
15. Granovetter, M.S.: The strength of weak ties. American Journal of Sociology, 1360–1380 (1973)
16. Venkatesh, V., Morris, M.G., Davis, G.B., Davis, F.D.: User acceptance of information technology: Toward a unified view. MIS Quarterly 27(3), 425–478 (2003)
17. Schaar, A.K., Calero Valdez, A., Ziefle, M.: The impact of user diversity on the willingness to disclose personal information in social network services. In: Holzinger, A., Ziefle, M., Hitz, M., Debevc, M. (eds.) SouthCHI 2013. LNCS, vol. 7946, pp. 174–193. Springer, Heidelberg (2013)
18. Calero Valdez, A., Ziefle, M., Alagöz, F., Holzinger, A.: Mental models of menu structures in diabetes assistants. In: Miesenberger, K., Klaus, J., Zagler, W., Karshmer, A. (eds.) ICCHP 2010, Part II. LNCS, vol. 6180, pp. 584–591. Springer, Heidelberg (2010)
19. Arning, K., Ziefle, M.: Understanding age differences in PDA acceptance and performance. Computers in Human Behavior 23(6), 2904–2927 (2007)
20. Ajzen, I., Fishbein, M.: Attitude-behavior relations: A theoretical analysis and review of empirical research. Psychological Bulletin 84(5), 888 (1977)
21. Ajzen, I.: The theory of planned behavior. Organizational Behavior and Human Decision Processes 50(2), 179–211 (1991)
22. Danis, C., Singer, D.: A wiki instance in the enterprise: opportunities, concerns and reality. In: Proceedings of the 2008 ACM Conference on Computer Supported Cooperative Work, pp. 495–504. ACM (2008)
23. Schuler, H., Prochaska, M.: Leistungsmotivationsinventar, hogrefe (2001)

Antecedents and Consequences of Online Campaign Engagement of Greek College Students

Amalia Triantafillidou[1], Prodromos Yannas[2], and Georgios Lappas[1]

[1] Technological Institute of Western Macedonia, Digital Media and Communication,
Kastoria, Greece
amtriantafil@aueb.gr, lappas@kastoria.teikoz.gr
[2] Technological Institute of Piraeus, Business Administration, Athens, Greece
prodyannas@teipir.gr

Abstract. This study measured college students' engagement with official online campaign tools of political parties and politicians during the pre-election period in Greek Parliamentary elections in May 2012. Furthermore, the antecedents and consequences of voters' online campaign engagement were examined. Findings indicate that Greek college students are not digitally mature in using various online platforms for political information and engagement. The engagement with official campaign tools is affected by the interest of young voters in politics as well as their level of political cynicism. Based on the findings, only Facebook interaction of Greek college students with the profile of political party/politicians can influence their voting intentions.

Keywords: online campaign engagement, young voters, Greek Parliamentary Elections 2012, political interest, distrust in politics, political cynicism, voting intention.

1 Introduction

The increased use of Internet as a means of political campaigning along with the high levels of young voters' apathy and political cynicism are the most important challenges that political parties and politicians are currently facing. Until now, candidates had come to the realization that web tools could be a cost-effective way of mobilizing voters. The aim of this paper is two-fold: to measure Greek college students' engagement with official web tools and social media used by political parties/politicians; and through a series of hypotheses testing, to investigate the antecedents (i.e. interest in politics, political cynicism) as well as the consequences (i.e. voting intention) of Greek youth engagement with the official web tools of political parties/politicians during the pre-election period of Greek Parliamentary Elections in May 2012.

2 Literature Review

Few studies have tried to measure in a reliable and valid way the level of voters' engagement in online campaign activities of candidates. For example, Gil de Zúñiga

G. Meiselwitz (Ed.): SCSM 2014, LNCS 8531, pp. 397–407, 2014.
© Springer International Publishing Switzerland 2014

et al. (2009) measured the level of online political engagement of citizens by constructing three scales: online political discussion, online political campaign and online participation. Online political discussion scale estimated citizens' participation in online political discussions and chat rooms whereas the online political campaign construct captured online activities of citizens to promote candidates and persuade others to vote for them by sending e-mails. In addition, the online participation scale measured the level of citizens' participation in activities such as reading a post of discussion forums, signing online petitions and making online donations.

Using factor analysis, Kushin and Yamamoto (2010) constructed a multi-dimensional scale to capture online political activity of voters in the 2008 US elections. Their scale was comprised of three factors: attention to social media, attention to traditional internet sources, and online expression. The factor named attention to social media captured voters' activities regarding personal blogs, online forums and social networking sites. Attention to traditional internet sources scales comprised of items that measured voters' involvement with political parties/candidates' websites and other news sites, whereas the online expression factor reflected more active types of online political involvement such as creating content sharing and exchanging information via emails and social networking sites.

Gibson et al. (2010b), conducting exploratory as well as confirmatory factor analysis, developed and validated a four-dimensional scale for measuring online participation of UK voters to official and unofficial campaign activities. The four dimensions of this scale were e-communication, e-targeted involvement, e-formal campaigning and e-informal campaigning. E-communication consisted of items that estimated voters' visits to online news sites and official websites of political parties as well as views of unofficial video content. The e-targeted involvement factor consisted of items that reflected the active online engagement of voters through activities such as making online donations, signing e-petitions and communicating online with government. The e-formal campaigning factor referred to the proclivity of voters to join official social networking sites of politicians/parties. Furthermore, the e-informal campaigning dimension measured the level of forwarding and posting unofficial campaign content.

Finally, Dimitrova et al. (2011) using exploratory factor analysis measured online campaign involvement in the Swedish elections in 2010. Their measurement consisted of three factors, namely: online news, party websites and social media. Online news measured the frequency of visiting online news pages. The party websites scale estimated the frequency of visiting a number of official websites of political parties while the social media construct measured the level of engagement with activities like reading and writing on a blog, following politicians or political party's profiles on Facebook, Twitter and YouTube.

Yannas et al. (2013) investigating college engagement revealed that online official campaign engagement is a multi-dimensional concept consisting of six factors, namely: Twitter engagement, Facebook interaction, e-negative content generation, e-deliberating, e-voluntary expression of interest, and e-visiting. The above factors could be positioned along a continuum based upon the negative or positive valence of the activity as well as the level of the engagement (see Figure 1).

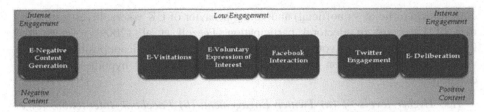

Fig. 1. Continuum of Online Official Campaign Engagement

Based on the preceding review it can be argued that a common element in the instruments developed for the measurement of online campaign engagement is citizens' involvement with social media. The present study aims to (a) measure in a valid and reliable way young voters' negative as well as positive online official campaign involvement and (b) investigate the antecedents and consequences of this engagement.

3   Conceptual Framework

Researchers have tried to identify the impact of citizen's political interest on their internet behavior regarding politics. For instance, the early study of Kaye and Johnson (2002) found that voters were likely to visit sites of politicians or political parties if they were politically interested. Moreover, in the case of Taiwanese citizens, Wang (2007) found that higher levels of political interest resulted in higher use of Internet for obtaining political information and expressing one's political opinion. Gibson et al. (2010b) investigating UK voters behavior during the 2010 elections found that political interest significantly impacted voters' engagement in official online campaigns of politicians. Hence, the following hypotheses could be developed:

H1: Higher levels of political interest will result in higher levels of (a) Twitter Engagement, (b) Facebook Interaction, (c) e-negative content generation, (d) e-deliberation, (e) e-voluntary expression of interest, (f) e-visitation.

Political cynicism reflects the level of mistrust citizens exhibit towards politics and politicians. Hanson et al. (2010) is one study that examined the association of political cynicism with the use of social networking sites and blogs for political purposes. The findings of the study indicate that political cynicism impacts significantly and in a negative manner on online political engagement of voters with blogs and social media. Hence, the following hypotheses could be developed:

H2: Higher levels of political cynicism will result in lower levels of (a) Twitter Engagement, (b) Facebook Interaction, (c) e-negative content generation, (d) e-deliberation, (e) e-voluntary expression of interest, (f) e-visitation.

A number of researchers have focused on the impact of Internet use on voting behavior. Pointing out that exposure of voters to online information about political campaigns affects their level of political participation (Kenski and Stroud, 2006). Gibson et al. (2010a) found a direct relationship between online political campaign engagement (official – unofficial) and voting behavior of UK voters. Investigating the role of Facebook in electoral participation, Feezell et al. (2009) revealed that Facebook membership of voters in political groups had a significant positive effect on voting behavior. Based on the above findings the following hypotheses could be developed:

H3: Higher levels of (a) Twitter Engagement, (b) Facebook Interaction, (c) e-negative content generation, (d) e-deliberation, (e) e-voluntary expression of interest, (f) e-visitation will increase the probability of voting intention.

Figure 2 illustrates the conceptual model that will be tested empirically.

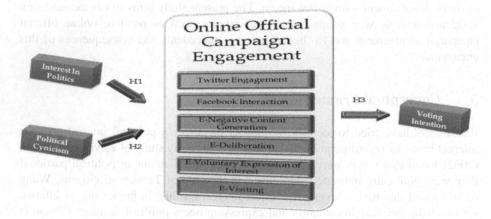

Fig. 2. Conceptual Framework

4   Method and Measures

In order to measure engagement of college students with the official web tools of political parties/politicians and empirically test our conceptual model a survey was conducted among students of a Technological Institute in a Northwestern city of Greece. Respondents were prompted to remember how frequently they had engaged in a 19-item scale of online activities during a six month period preceding the elections of May 2012. To measure the online official campaign engagement of respondents the scale developed by Yannas et al. (2013) was used. Responses to the items were elicited on a five-point scale ranging from "5=very frequently" to "1=never". A number of questionnaires were eliminated due to incomplete responses. The final data set consisted of 491 respondents, 16.9% made up of males and 83.1% females.

4.1   Online Official Campaign Engagement Scale

Table 1 shows the mean values and standard deviations of items that comprise the multi-dimensional scale of online official campaign engagement. Most of the items of the six factors had low mean values indicating that college students in Greece are not involved with the official web tools of political parties/politicians. Moreover, by comparing the mean values across the six factors it can be argued that visiting official YouTube channels, websites and blogs of political parties/politicians is the most preferred e-activity of Greek college students followed by Facebook interaction and negative content generation.

The 19-item model showed good model fit [$\chi^2(134)=413.903$, p=0.000, Comparative Fit Index (CFI): 0.943, Tucker-Lewis Index (TLI): 0.927, Incremental Fit Index (IFI): 0.943, Root Mean Square Error of Approximation (RMSEA): 0.065]. Table 1 shows the validity and reliability measures and the standardized regression weights of the model. The internal reliability of the scale was considered more than adequate as Cronbach's alpha coefficients for the six factors ranged from 0.78 to 0.85, exceeding the 0.70 criterion. All the standardized coefficients of the 19 indicators were significant (critical ratios > 1.96, p value: 0.000) and exceeded the 0.50 threshold (Janssens et al., 2008) (Table 1). The Average Variance Extracted (AVE) for the six factors ranged from 0.56 to 0.70 exceeding Fornell and Larcker's (1981) critical value of 0.50. Furthermore, composite reliabilities of all factors exceeded the 0.70 accepted value criterion (Hair et al., 1998). Hence, it can be argued that the proposed scale showed acceptable levels of convergent validity.

Table 1. Descriptive Statistics, Validity and Reliability Measures and Standardized Regression Weights of Online Official Campaign Engagement Factors

Factors/Items	M	S.D.	S.L.	Cr. R
Twitter Engagement (AVE=0.70, CR= 0.87, a=0.85)				
Subscribed to an official Twitter profile of a political party/politician	1.12	0.54	0.95	
Followed an official Twitter profile of a political party/politician	1.14	0.57	0.86	17.54*
Replied with *positive comments* on a Tweet you viewed on an official Twitter profile of a political party/politician.	1.07	0.36	0.69	17.92*
Facebook Interaction (AVE=0.56, CR=0.83, a=0.85)				
Sent a friend request on the official Facebook profile of a political party/politician	1.40	0.84	0.75	
Accepted a friend request from an official Facebook profile of a political party/politician.	1.56	0.97	0.76	18.47*
Clicked the Like button on the official Facebook profile of a political party/politician.	1.37	0.79	0.76	13.10*
Clicked the Like button on a post you viewed on an official Facebook profile of a political party/politician.	1.38	0.79	0.73	13.67*

Table 1. (*continued*)

	M	S.D.	S.L.	Cr. R.
E-Negative Content Generation (AVE=0.62, CR=0.83, a=0.82)				
Posted *negative comments* on videos you viewed on the official YouTube channel of a political party/politician.	1.41	0.91	0.786	
Posted *negative comments* on a post you viewed on an official Facebook profile of a political party/politician.	1.33	0.79	0.798	16.71*
Posted *negative comments* on a post you viewed on an official blog of a political party/politician.	1.26	0.69	0.784	16.54*
E-Deliberating (AVE=0.59, CR=0.81, a=0.78)				
Participated and discussed in an online forum through the official website of a political party/politician.	1.19	0.61	0.815	
Participated in an online deliberation through the official website of a political party/politician.	1.16	0.51	0.781	15.14*
Expressed your opinion online though a political party's/politician official website.	1.34	0.76	0.708	15.57*
E-Voluntary Expression of Interest (AVE=0.57, CR=0.79, a=0.79)				
Signed up (subscribed) in an official website of a political party/politician.	1.12	0.53	0.757	
Signed up (subscribed) to receive a newsletter from a political party/politician.	1.16	0.56	0.849	14.19*
Signed up for RSS feeds to stay informed about the news of a political party/politician.	1.14	0.49	0.651	13.55*
E-Visiting (AVE=0.58, CR=0.80, a=0.81)				
Visited an official website of a political party/politician.	1.81	0.97	0.746	
Visited an official YouTube channel of a political party/politician.	1.82	1.05	0.771	16.38*
Visited an official blog of a political party/politician.	1.76	1.01	0.780	15.89*

Abbreviations: AVE, average variance extracted; CR, composite reliability; a, Cronbach's alpha; M, Mean; S.D., Standard Deviation; S.L., Standardized Loadings; Cr. R., Critical Ratio
Note: * Significant at the p=0.05 level.

Finally, discriminant validity of the online official campaign engagement scale was established since the AVE of each factor was larger than the square of the correlation between the examined factor and the rest of the factors in the scale.

4.2 Interest in Politics, Political Cynicism an Voting Intention

The 491 respondents were also asked to answer a series of statements regarding their interest in politics, their cynicism towards politicians as well as their voting intention. Responses to the items regarding political interest and cynicism were elicited on five-point scales ranging from "5=strongly agree" to "1=strongly disagree". Intention to vote was measured on a five-point scale ranging from "5=definitely yes" to "1=definitely no".

Table 2 shows the mean and standard deviations of the items used to measure interest in politics and political cynicism as well as the validity and reliability measures. As Table 2 indicates, Greek young voters showed moderate levels of political interest while they scored high on all of the items that comprise the construct of political cynicism. In addition, both constructs showed acceptable levels of internal reliability and convergent validity.

Table 2. Descriptive Statistics, Validity and Reliability Measures and Standardized Regression Weights of Interest in Politics and Political Cynicism

Factors/Items	M	S.D.	S.L.	Cr. R
Interest in Politics (AVE=0.51, CR=0.76, a=0.76)				
I am interested in politics.	2.60	1.14	0.716	
I frequently discuss politics with my friends and relatives.	3.09	1.20	0.692	11.64*
I pay attention to political information.	3.20	1.21	0.751	11.66*
Political Cynicism (AVE=0.52, CR=0.84, a=0.84)				
Politicians are only interested in people's vote, not in their opinion.	4.35	0.96	0.556	
Politicians pay too much attention to the interests of a few powerful groups (i.e. big firms).	3.98	1.11	0.721	11.35*
Politicians do not care about the interests of people because they are corrupt.	3.87	1.17	0.767	11.74*
Once elected, politicians lose track with people quickly.	4.01	1.16	0.823	12.13*
I am frustrated with the politicians of this country.	4.28	1.06	0.737	11.50*

Abbreviations: AVE, average variance extracted; CR, composite reliability; a, cronbach's alpha; M, Mean; S.D., Standard Deviation; S.L., Standardized Loadings; Cr. R., Critical Ratio
Note: * Significant at the p=0.05 level.

5 Hypotheses Testing

A structural equation analysis was conducted for testing the hypothesized relationships of the proposed model shown in Figure 2. The overall chi-square statistic of the model was significant [$\chi2(328)=885.98$, p=0.000] which is accepted for large samples (Byrne,   2010). The values goodness-of-fit indices of the model exceeded the 0.90 criterion [Comparative-Fit Index (CFI) = 0.913, Incremental-Fit Index (IFI) = 0.914, Tucker-Lewis Index (TLI) = 0.900]. Moreover, the Root Mean Square of Approximation (RMSEA) value was smaller than the 0.07 threshold (RMSEA=0.059). Based on the above results it can be suggested that the hypothesized model showed a reasonably good fit to the data. Support of the hypotheses was examined based on the significance of the standardized estimates of the path coefficients as shown in Table 3.

Our hypothesis testing concluded that the interest in politics is an important and strong predictor of online official campaign engagement of young citizens. Specifically, interest in politics is positively and significantly related to Twitter engagement (H1a= standardized estimate: 0.452, p<0.01), Facebook Interaction (H1b= standardized estimate: 0.747, p<0.01), e-negative context generation (H1c= standardized estimate: 0.531, p<0.01), e-deliberation (H1d= standardized estimate: 0.719 p<0.01), e-voluntary expression of interest (H1e: standardized estimate: 0.709, p<0.01) and e-visitation (H1f: standardized estimate= 0.916, p<0.01). These findings support H1a, H1b, H1c, H1d, H1e and H1f. Moreover, based on the values of the standardized path coefficients it can be concluded that the contribution of political interest is greater on the e-visitation factor compared to the other online official campaign engagement factors.

Regarding the impact of political cynicism on the online official campaign engagement of Greek young citizens, results indicate that political cynicism affected significantly but in a negative manner Twitter engagement (H2a: standardized estimate=-0.157, p<0.05), Facebook interaction (H2b: standardized estimate=-0.104, p<0.05), e-deliberation (H2d: standardized estimate=-0.184, p<0.01), and e-voluntary expression of interest (H2e: standardized estimate=-0.141, p<0.01). Hence, hypotheses 2a, 2b, 2d and 2e were supported. It should be noted that the above found significant associations were low. In addition, political cynicism of young citizens does not impact on their e-negative content generation (H2c: standardized estimate=-0.078, p>0.05) and their visits on parties/politicians websites, YouTube channels and blogs (H2f: standardized estimate=-0.094, p>0.05). These findings do not support hypotheses H2c and H2f.

Referring to the third hypothesis, results show that Facebook interaction of young citizens with political parties/politicians impacted significantly and in a positive manner their intention to participate in the Greek Parliamentary elections of May 2012 (H3b: standardized estimate=0.189, p<0.01). Thus, H3b could not be rejected. On the contrary, all the other online official campaign engagement factors were not significantly related to voting intention. Specifically, no significant associations were found between voting intentions and Twitter interaction (H3a: standardized estimate=-0.010, p>0.05), e-negative content generation (H3c: standardized estimate=-0.089, p>0.05), e-deliberation (H3d: standardized estimate=0.057, p>0.05), e-voluntary expression of interest (H3e: standardized estimate=0.051, p>0.05), and e-visitation (H3f: standardized estimate=0.062, p>0.05). Hence, hypotheses 3a, 3c, 3d, 3e, and 3f were rejected.

Table 3. Results of Hypotheses Testing

Path	S.L.	Cr. R.	Results
H1a: Interest in Politics →Twitter Engagement	0.45	6.63*	√
H1b: Interest in Politics →Facebook Interaction	0.75	8.17*	√
H1c: Interest in Politics →E-Negative Content Generation	0.53	7.17*	√
H1d: Interest in Politics →E-Deliberating	0.72	8.09*	√
H1e: Interest in Politics →E-Voluntary Expression of Interest	0.71	7.79*	√
H1f: Interest in Politics →E-Visiting	0.92	8.87*	√
H2a: Political Cynicism → Twitter Engagement	-0.16	-3.15**	√
H2b: Political Cynicism → Facebook Interaction	-0.11	-2.06**	√
H2c: Political Cynicism → E-Negative Content Generation	-0.08	-1.51	X
H2d: Political Cynicism → E-Deliberating	-0.18	-3.57*	√
H2e: Political Cynicism → E-Voluntary Expression of Interest	-0.14	-2.79*	√
H2f: Political Cynicism → E-Visiting	-0.10	-1.96	X
H3a: Twitter Engagement → Voting Intention	-0.01	-0.19	X
H3b: Facebook Interaction → Voting Intention	0.19	2.68*	√
H3c: E-Negative Content Generation → Voting Intention	-0.09	-1.29	X
H3d: E-Deliberating → Voting Intention	0.06	0.68	X
H3e: E-Voluntary Expression of Interest → Voting Intention	0.05	0.76	X
H3f: E-Visiting → Voting Intention	0.062	1.25	X

Abbreviations: S.L., standardized loadings; Cr. R., critical ratio; √, supported; X, not supported.
Note: * Significant at the p=0.05 level.

6   Conclusion

In this study, the online official campaign engagement of Greek college students was measured. Moreover, the relationships among interest in politics, political cynicism, voting intention and online official campaign engagement were examined. To this end, a survey was conducted during the pre-election period of the Greek Parliamentary Election in May 2012.

In general, Greek youth seems to be disinterested in official online campaign activities. Whilst almost ninety percent of young Greeks are active Internet users, findings of the present survey indicate that Greek young students are not digitally mature in using various online platforms for political information and engagement. Greek college students during pre-election period preferred to obtain campaign information by visiting official websites of political parties/politicians, or by interacting with parties and politicians through Facebook. Interestingly, the third preferred online campaign activity of young voters was the generation of negative content through social media.

In times of deep economic recession, respondents evaluated politicians as distrustful. The students of the sample seem to be frustrated with the established political personalities present in the political scene. A possible explanation for this finding is the fact that students might blame politicians for the current state of the Greek economy. There is a marked decrease in the level of engagement as the level of political cynicism increases (i.e. Twitter engagement, Facebook interaction, e-voluntary expression of interest, and e-deliberation). Political cynicism however, does not influence online activities like visits to political parties/politicians' websites, blogs and YouTube profiles as well as generation of negative content via social media. It seems that Greek college students will continue to obtain information from official online campaign tools and criticize negatively politicians regardless of their level of political cynicism. On the contrary, all online official campaign engagement factors were influenced by the political interest of young voters. Thus, political marketers should concentrate in increasing both Greek young students' interest in politics and their trust in politicians respectively.

Last, the majority of online campaign engagement factors do not impact the voting intention of Greek youngsters. This finding is consistent with Gibson et al. (2010b) and Baumgartner and Morris (2010) findings regarding the insignificant influence of digital media use on voting intention. The present study's findings are also consistent with the results of Feezell et al. (2009), making Facebook interaction to be a significant predictor of voting intention. It can therefore be argued, that Facebook plays an important role in the voting behavior of Greek college students. The above findings highlight the importance of carefully choosing the campaign channels for the dissemination of political messages. Political marketers should incorporate Facebook in the online campaigns they develop in order to lure voters.

A basic limitation of the present study concerns the representativeness of the sample. The survey employed a convenience sample as respondents were students of a Technological Institute in a Northwestern city of Greece. Future research should be directed towards the measurement of online campaign engagement of representative samples of voters as well as the investigation of the impact of more antecedents (i.e. personal characteristics of voters) on online campaign engagement.

Acknowledgments. This research has been co-financed by the European Union (European Social Fund – ESF) and Greek national funds through the Operational Program "Education and Lifelong Learning" of the National Strategic Reference Framework (NSRF) - Research Funding Program: ARCHIMEDES III. Investing in knowledge society through the European Social Fund.

References

1. Baumgartner, J., Morris, J.S.: Social Networking Web Sites and Political Engagement of Young Adults. Social Science Computer Review 28(1), 24–44 (2010)
2. Byrne, B.M.: Structural equation modeling with Amos: Basic concepts, applications, and programming, 2nd edn. Taylor and Francis Group, New York (2010)

3. Dimitrova, D., Shehata, A., Strömbäck, J., Nord, L.: The Effects of Digital Media on Political Knowledge and Participation in Election Campaigns: Evidence From Panel Data. Communication Research Article in Press, 1–24 (2011)
4. Feezell, J.T., Conroy, M., Guerrero, M.: Facebook is.. Fostering Political Engagement: A Study of Online Social Networking Groups and Offline Participation. In: Proceedings of the American Political Science Association Meeting in Toronto, Canada (2009)
5. Fornell, C., Larcker, D.F.: Evaluating Structural Equation Models with Unobservable Variables and Measurement Error. Journal of Marketing Research 18, 39–50 (1981)
6. Gibson, R., Cantijoch, M., Ward, S.: Citizen participation in the e-campaign. In: Gibson, R., Williamson, A., Ward, S. (eds.) The Internet and the 2010 Election. Putting the Small 'p' Back in Politics? pp. 5–18. Hansard Society (2010a)
7. Gibson, R., Cantijoch, M., Ward, S.: Another false dawn? New media and citizen participation in the 2010 UK General Election. In: Proceedings of the Elections, Public Opinion and Parties Conference, Essex (2010b)
8. Gil de Zúñiga, H., Puig-i-Abril, E., Rojas, H.: Blogs, Traditional Sources Online & Political Participation: An Assessment of How the Internet is Changing the Political Environment. New Media & Society 11, 553–574 (2009)
9. Hair, J.F., Anderson, R.E., Tatham, R.L., Black, W.C.: Multivariate data analysis. Prentice Hall (1998)
10. Hanson, G., Haridakis, P.M., Cunningham, A.W., Sharma, R., Ponder, J.D.: The 2008 Presidential Campaign: Political Cynicism in the Age of Facebook, MySpace, and YouTube. Mass Communication and Society 13(5), 584–607 (2010)
11. Janssens, W., de Pelshmacker, P., van Kenhove, P., Wijnen, K.: Marketing research with SPSS. Pearson Education (2008)
12. Kaye, B.K., Johnson, T.J.: Online and in the Know: Uses and Gratifications of the Web for Political Information. Journal of Broadcasting & Electronic Media 46(1), 54–71 (2002)
13. Kenski, K., Stroud, N.J.: Connections between Internet Use and Political Efficacy, Knowledge, and Participation. Journal of Broadcasting & Electronic Media 50(2), 173–192 (2006)
14. Kushin, M.J., Yamamoto, M.: Did Social Media Really Matter? College Students' Use of Online Media and Political Decision Making in the 2008 Election. Mass Communication and Society 13(5), 608–630 (2010)
15. Sweeney, J., Soutar, G.: Consumer Perceived Value: The Development of a Multiple Item Scale. Journal of Retailing 77(2), 203–220 (2001)
16. Wang, S.-I.: Political Use of the Internet, Political Attitudes and Political Participation. Asian Journal of Communication 17(4), 381–395 (2007)
17. Yannas, P., Lappas, G., Triantafillidou, A.: Development and validation of a scale to measure online election campaign engagement of Greek young voters using structural equation modeling. In: Proceedings of the 3rd International Conference: Quantitative and Qualitative Methodologies in the Economic and Administrative Sciences, Athens, Greece (2013)

Identity and Presence in Social Media

Emotional Contagion with Artificial Others. Effects of Culture, Physical Appearance, and Nonverbal Behavior on the Perception of Positive/Negative Affect in Avatars

Gary Bente[1], Thomas Dratsch[1], Diana Rieger[1], and Ahmad Al-Issa[2]

[1] University of Cologne, Cologne, Germany
bente@uni-koeln.de
[2] American University of Sharjah, Sharjah, United Arab Emirates
aissa@aus.edu

Abstract. In the present study, we investigated whether cultural stereotypes activated through the physical appearance of avatars would influence the perception of positive and negative affect in in- and out-group members. In a first study, forty-three German and forty Arab participants saw short video clips of a German and an Arab avatar displaying ambiguous nonverbal behavior. In spite of cultural stereotypes, both Arab and German participants attributed more positive emotions to the Arab avatar than to the German avatar. To further investigate these counterintuitive results, we conducted a follow-up study, in which fifty-two German and fifty-two Arab participants rated the valence of both avatars. Both German and Arab participants rated the Arab avatar significantly more positively than the German avatar. Taken together, the results of both studies show that the valence of avatars has the potential to override cultural stereotypes and influence the perception of positive and negative affect.

Keywords: Culture, Stereotypes, Avatars, Nonverbal Behavior.

1 Introduction

Contrary to real-life interactions, online communities allow their members to interact with each other using virtual avatars, giving members control over their physical appearance and helping them to reduce the influence of stereotypes in interactions. In off-line interactions, stereotypes activated by the physical appearance of others can have a strong—and often negative—influence on our perception of nonverbal behavior. For instance, a large body of research has focused on the perception of the nonverbal behavior of African Americans. Because African Americans are stereotypically perceived to be aggressive [1], ambiguous nonverbal behaviors by African Americans are also interpreted as aggressive or negative. In line with this argument, several studies have shown that ambiguous nonverbal behaviors by African Americans are perceived more negatively [2]. For instance, Hugenberg et al. [3] could show that White participants were faster at detecting anger in Black faces as compared to White Faces. Also, Duncan [4] could show that the same nonverbal act was rated to be more violent

G. Meiselwitz (Ed.): SCSM 2014, LNCS 8531, pp. 411–420, 2014.
© Springer International Publishing Switzerland 2014

by White observers if perpetrated by a Black person. Another well-researched cultural group with regard to cultural stereotypes are Arabs/Muslims [5]. For instance, Unkelbach et al. [6] could show a significant bias in participants to shoot men wearing Muslim headgear as opposed to neutral looking men. Taken together, real-life interactions are often influenced by the cultural background and physical appearance of the persons interacting.

On the other hand, online communities, such as Second Life, allow its members to represent themselves with avatars that may or may not correspond to their own culture, giving members control over their physical appearance and helping them to reduce the influence of stereotypes in interactions. One central question is, however, whether results on the influence of cultural stereotypes on the perception of nonverbal behavior also apply to virtual online interactions. In a first study, with regard to general nonverbal social norms, Yee et al. [7] could show that interpersonal distance and eye gaze transfer were comparable between online virtual environments and real-life interactions. Therefore, online virtual environments, with their almost unlimited degrees of freedom, pose a huge potential for research [8]. Consequently, several studies have investigated the effect of avatars on the persons controlling them: For instance, with regard to the effect of the physical appearance of avatars on their players, Yee et al. [9] could show that an avatars height and physical attractiveness affected a player's performance. In another study, Pena et al. [10] found that avatars could prime negative attitudes in their players in group discussions. However, despite their widespread use in psychological research [11], only few studies so far have investigated whether cultural stereotypes also influence the perceptions of avatars. In a first study, Vang et al. [12] investigated the influence of an avatars' culture on its evaluation in a cooperative game. However, contrary to their hypotheses, Vang et al. [12] did not find evidence for the effect of cultural stereotypes, with White participants in their study evaluating Black avatars more positively than White avatars.

It remains, therefore, an open question if the strong effect of cultural stereotypes on the perception of behavior can also be found for avatars in virtual encounters.

In the present study, we investigated whether cultural stereotypes activated through the physical appearance of avatars would influence the perception of positive and negative affect in in- and out-group members. To test this hypothesis, we presented students from Germany and the United Arab Emirates with an avatar of their own culture and an avatar of a foreign culture. These two cultures were chosen because of the high prevalence of negative cultural stereotypes towards Arabs/Muslims [5,6].

Participants saw 40 short video clips of members from both cultures (20 video clips with a European avatar and 20 video clips with an Arab avatar) displaying ambiguous nonverbal behavior. Participants decided for each clip whether the displayed emotion was either anger or happiness. Based on previous studies on the influence of stereotypes on the perception of facial emotions in White and Black faces [3], we hypothesized that positive emotions (happiness) would be attributed faster to in-group members, and that negative emotions (anger) would be attributed faster to out-group members. In addition, we hypothesized that more positive emotions would be attributed to the avatar of the own culture and more negative emotions to the avatar of the foreign culture.

In sum, the goal of the present study was to investigate whether cultural stereo-types activated through the physical appearance of avatars would influence the attri-bution of anger and happiness to in- and out-group members.

2   Experiment 1

2.1   Methods

Participants. Overall, 43 German students from the University of Cologne (21 male, 22 female, M_{age} = 22.37, SD_{age} = 2.98) and 40 Arab students from the American University of Sharjah (20 male, 20 female, M_{age} = 19.70, SD_{age} = 1.54) participated in the study.

Stimulus Materials. In the present study, motion-capture technology was used to record the nonverbal behavior. This approach has the advantage that the same record-ed movements can be displayed by different virtual avatars. We used one Arab and one European avatar (see Figure 1) from a database of commercially available avatars [13].

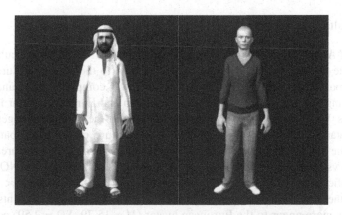

Fig. 1. Arab (left) and European avatar (right) used in Experiment 1

In order not to bias participants towards positive or negative emotions, the avatars showed a neutral facial expression. Five actors were recorded individually performing short emotional scenes displaying either anger or happiness. Out of these recordings, 44 short scenes were selected. In a prestudy, 30 participants (12 male, 18 female; M_{age} = 24.90, SD_{age} = 4.57) watched the emotional scenes with a neutral avatar and decided for each scene whether the displayed emotion was anger or happiness. Ratings of happiness were coded with a 0; ratings of anger were coded with a 1. For each scene, an average score was calculated ranging from 0 (all participants decided the scene was happiness) to 100 (all participants decided the scene was anger). Because the goal of the present study was to investigate whether cultural stereotypes would influence emotion perception, we selected emotional scenes that were ambiguous and could be interpreted as either anger or happiness. Based on the results of the prestudy, 40 emotional scenes were selected. The average score for the 40 scenes was 55.10 %, indicating that participants were equally likely to attribute anger or happiness to the scenes, with a slight bias to perceive the scenes as anger. In the main experiment, cultural stereotypes were activated through the appearance of the avatar—Arab or Euroepan. Thus, each emotion was either displayed by the Arab or European avatar. In the final stimulus set, 20 emotions were displayed by the Arab avatar, and 20 emotions were displayed by the European avatar. Two different stimulus lists were created to balance the emotions displayed by each avatar.

Procedure. At the beginning of the experiment, participants were asked to sit down in front of a computer and told that they would now see avatars display different emotions. Additionally, they were told that their task would be to decide for each emotion whether it was anger or happiness. Also, participants were informed that after each choice they should indicate how certain they were in their decision on a scale ranging from 1 (*very uncertain*) to 7 (*very certain*). After participants had completed four practice trials, they proceeded to the forty experimental trials. At the end of the study, participants were compensated for their participation and debriefed.

2.2   Results

Number of Anger Attributions. At first, we analyzed if participants' culture would influence the number of negative emotions attributed to the Arab and European avatar. It is important to note that because the choice was complementary, analyzing the amount of anger or happiness attributed to the Arab and European avatar leads to the same results. We therefore only present the analysis for the amount of anger attributed to both avatars. To analyze the influence of the culture of the participants and the culture of the avatar on the attribution of anger, we performed a 2 (culture of observer: German vs. Arab) × (culture of avatar: European vs. Arab) mixed ANOVA. There was a significant main effect of culture of avatar, $F(1, 81) = 259.67$, $p < .001$, $\eta^2_p = .762$. All other effects were not significant, $F < 3.45$. German participants attributed significantly more anger to the European avatar ($M = 15.79$, $SD = 2.59$) compared to the Arab Avatar ($M = 10.02$, $SD = 2.36$), $t(42) = 12.71$, $p = .001$, $d = 1.94$. Arab participants also attributed significantly more anger to the European avatar ($M = 15.23$, $SD = 2.87$) compared to the Arab avatar ($M = 10.65$, $SD = 3.87$), $t(39) = 10.11$, $p = .001$, $d = 1.61$.

Reaction Times

Happiness. To analyze the speed with which participants attributed happiness to the two avatars, we performed a 2 (culture of observer: German vs. Arab) × (culture of avatar: European vs. Arab) mixed ANOVA with reaction times as the dependent variable. There was a significant main effect of culture of avatar, $F(1, 77) = 13.17$, $p = .001$, $\eta^2_p = .146$. All other effects were not significant, $F < 1.80$. German participants were significantly faster at attributing happiness to the Arab avatar ($M = 1389$, $SD = $

401) compared to the European avatar ($M = 1681$, $SD = 731$), $t(41) = 2.91$, $p = .006$, $d = 0.45$. Arab participants were also significantly faster at attributing happiness to the Arab avatar ($M = 1244$, $SD = 382$) compared to the European ($M = 1521$, $SD = 817$) avatar, $t(36) = 2.27$, $p = .030$, $d = 0.37$ (see Figure 2).

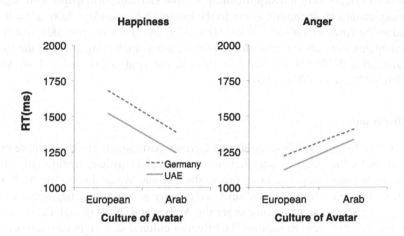

Fig. 2. Mean reaction times for German and Arab participants for attributing happiness and anger to the European and Arab avatar

Anger. To analyze the speed with which participants attributed anger to the two avatars, we performed a 2 (culture of observer: German vs. Arab) × (culture of avatar: European vs. Arab) mixed ANOVA with reaction times as the dependent variable. There was a significant main effect of culture of avatar, $F(1, 81) = 20.25$, $p < .001$, $\eta^2_p = .200$. All other effects were not significant, $F < 1$. German participants were significantly faster at attributing anger to the European avatar ($M = 1209$, $SD = 409$) compared to the Arab avatar ($M = 1398$, $SD = 451$), $t(42) = 3.28$, $p = .002$, $d = 0.50$. Arab participants were also significantly faster at attributing anger to the European avatar ($M = 1126$, $SD = 328$) compared to the Arab avatar ($M = 1328$, $SD = 421$), $t(39) = 3.09$, $p = .004$, $d = 0.49$.

Certainty

Happiness. To analyze the certainty with which participants attributed happiness to the two avatars, we performed a 2 (culture of observer: German vs. Arab) × (culture of avatar: European vs. Arab) mixed ANOVA with certainty as the dependent variable. There was a significant main effect of culture of avatar, $F(1, 78) = 18.97$, $p = .001$, $\eta^2_p = .196$. All other effects were not significant, $F < 1$. German participants were significantly more certain at attributing happiness to the Arab avatar ($M = 4.56$, $SD = 0.82$) compared to the European avatar ($M = 4.13$, $SD = 1.04$), $t(41) = 3.07$, $p = .004$, $d = 0.47$. Arab participants were also significantly more certain at attributing happiness to the Arab avatar ($M = 4.68$, $SD = 1.01$) compared to the European avatar ($M = 4.37$, $SD = 0.99$), $t(37) = 3.44$, $p = .001$, $d = 0.54$.

Anger. To analyze the certainty with which participants attributed anger to the two avatars, we performed a 2 (culture of observer: German vs. Arab) × (culture of avatar: European vs. Arab) mixed ANOVA with certainty as the dependent variable. There was a significant main effect of culture of avatar, $F(1, 81) = 27.99$, $p < .001$, $\eta^2_p = .257$. All other effects were not significant, $F < 2.04$. German participants were significantly more certain at attributing anger to the European avatar ($M = 5.06$, $SD = 0.78$) compared to the Arab avatar ($M = 4.59$, $SD = 0.79$), $t(42) = 4.64$, $p < .001$, $d = 0.70$. Arab participants were also significantly more certain at attributing anger to the European avatar ($M = 5.16$, $SD = 0.96$) compared to the Arab avatar ($M = 4.89$, $SD = 1.00$), $t(39) = 2.82$, $p = .007$, $d = 0.44$.

2.3   Discussion

Contrary to our hypotheses, both Arab and German participants attributed more positive emotions to the Arab avatar than to the European avatar; additionally, both groups attributed more negative emotions to the German avatar than to the Arab avatar. Also, participants from both cultures were faster at attributing happiness to the Arab avatar and slower at attributing anger the Arab avatar. Even though the results of the Arab participants seem to support the effect of cultural stereotypes on the perception of nonverbal behavior, the results of the German participants hint at the fact that some factor other than cultural stereotypes might have influenced participants' perception.

Two explanations are possible: First, the two avatars were not representative of their respective cultures—European and Arab—and did therefore not activate cultural stereotypes. Especially the European avatar, to which more negative emotions were attributed, may not have been perceived to be European by the German participants. It is possible that the German participants perceived the European avatar to be an outgroup member and therefore attributed more negative emotions to it.

Second, both avatars may have differed with regard to valence. Because more happiness was attributed to the Arab avatar, it is possible that the Arab avatar was generally perceived to be more positive by the participants, which might have biased participants to attribute more happiness and less anger to the avatar. Additionally, even though both avatars showed a generally neutral facial expression, it is still possible that participants perceived the Arab avatar to show a more positive facial expression, which might have also influenced the perception of the nonverbal behavior. In sum, based on the results of Experiment 1, it is possible that either the valence or the displayed emotion of the avatars may have overwritten the influence of cultural stereotypes.

To further explore these two possible explanations, we conducted Experiment 2, in which we presented a new group of participants with images of the two avatars in a neutral posture and asked them to rate the valence, displayed emotion, European typicality, and Arab typicality of the avatars.

3   Experiment 2

3.1   Methods

Participants. Overall, 52 German students (21 male, 31 female, M_{age} = 24.21, SD_{age} = 3.94) and 52 Arab students (21 male, 31 female, M_{age} = 19.63, SD_{age} = 1.99) participated in the study. Participants were recruited through email invitations sent via mailing lists of several universities in Germany and the United Arab Emirates.

Stimulus Materials. One image each of the German and the Arab avatar from Experiment 1 was used in this study. Both avatars had the exact same neutral posture.

Procedure. In the study, participants were randomly presented with the image of either the European or Arab avatar. Participants then rated the following attributes: valence, ranging from 1 (*very negative*) to 5 (*very positive*); displayed emotion, ranging from 1 (*very angry*) to 5 (*very happy*); European typicality, ranging from 1 (*very untypical*) to 5 (*very typical*); and Arab typicality, ranging from 1 (*very untypical*) to 5 (*very typical*).

3.2   Results

Valence. To analyze how positive participants perceived the two avatars, we performed a 2 (culture of observer: German vs. Arab) × (culture of avatar: European vs. Arab) ANOVA with valence as the dependent variable. There was a significant main effect of culture of avatar, $F(1, 100)$ = 19.71, p < .001, η^2_p = .165. All other effects were not significant, $F < 2$. German participants rated the Arab avatar ($M = 2.97$, $SD = 0.63$) to be significantly more positive than the European avatar ($M = 2.26$, $SD = 0.62$), $t(50) = 4.05$, $p < .001$, $d = 1.14$. Arab participants were also rated the Arab avatar ($M = 2.83$, $SD = 0.71$) to be significantly more positive than the European avatar ($M = 2.43$, $SD = 0.51$), $t(50) = 2.24$, $p = .030$, $d = 0.65$ (see Figure 3).

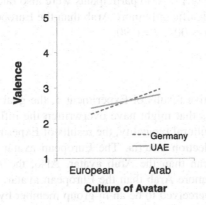

Fig. 3. Mean valence ratings for the European and Arab avatar

Displayed Emotion. To analyze what emotion participants thought the two avatars displayed, we performed a 2 (culture of observer: German vs. Arab) × (culture of avatar: European vs. Arab) ANOVA with displayed emotion as the dependent variable. There was a significant main effect of culture of avatar, $F(1, 100) = 70.47, p <$ .001, $\eta^2_p = .413$. All other effects were not significant, $F < 2.5$. German participants rated the Arab avatar ($M = 3.62, SD = 0.62$) to be significantly more happy than the European avatar ($M = 2.61, SD = 0.58$), $t(50) = 5.99, p < .001, d = 1.68$. Arab participants were also rated the Arab avatar ($M = 3.44, SD = 0.63$) to be significantly more happy than the European avatar ($M = 2.39, SD = 0.66$), $t(50) = 5.89, p < .001, d =$ 1.64.

European Typicality. To analyze to what degree participants perceived the two avatars to be European, we performed a 2 (culture of observer: German vs. Arab) × (culture of avatar: European vs. Arab) ANOVA with European typicality as the dependent variable. There was a significant main effect of culture of avatar, $F(1, 100) = 208.01$, $p < .001, \eta^2_p = .675$. All other effects were not significant, $F < 1$. German participants rated the European avatar ($M = 3.65, SD = 0.78$) to be significantly more European than the Arab avatar ($M = 1.38, SD = 0.56$), $t(50) = 12.26, p < .001, d = 3.34$. Arab participants were also rated the European avatar ($M = 3.57, SD = 1.12$) to be significantly more European than the Arab avatar ($M = 1.34, SD = 0.67$), $t(50) = 8.87, p < .001, d = 2.41$.

Arab Typicality. To analyze to what degree participants perceived the two avatars to be Arab, we performed a 2 (culture of observer: German vs. Arab) × (culture of avatar: European vs. Arab) ANOVA with Arab typicality as the dependent variable. There was a significant main effect of culture of avatar, $F(1, 100) = 113.83, p < .001$, $\eta^2_p = .532$. There was also a significant interaction effect between culture of avatar and culture of observer, $F(1, 100) = 27.22, p < .001, \eta^2_p = .214$. All other effects were not significant, $F < 1$. German participants rated the Arab avatar ($M = 4.38, SD = 0.73$) to be significantly more Arab than the European avatar ($M = 1.48, SD = 0.67$), $t(50) = 14.82, p < .001, d = 4.14$. Arab participants were also rated the Arab avatar ($M = 3.52, SD = 1.07$) to be significantly more Arab than the European avatar ($M = 2.52, SD = 1.16$), $t(50) = 3.23, p < .001, d = 0.90$.

3.3   Discussion

Based on the counterintuitive results of Experiment 1, the goal of Experiment 2 was to explore potential factors that might have overwritten the influence of cultural stereotypes. With regard to cultural typicality, the results of Experiment 2 show that both avatars did match our selection criteria. The European avatar was perceived to be significantly more European than the Arab avatar. Also, the Arab avatar was perceived to be significantly more Arab than the European avatar. Thus, it is likely that the European avatar was perceived to be an in-group member by the European participants and an out-group member by the Arab participants.

With regard to valence, the results of Experiment 2 show that the Arab avatar was rated to be significantly more positive than the European avatar. Also, the displayed emotion of the Arab avatar was rated to be significantly more happy than the European avatar. Combining these findings, the results of Experiment 2 suggest that the generally higher valence of the Arab avatar could explain the results of Experiment 1. Therefore, the valence of an avatar may be a factor with the potential to overwrite cultural stereotypes.

4   General Discussion

The goal of the present study was to investigate whether cultural stereotypes induced by the physical appearance of avatars would influence the perception of two basic emotions: anger and happiness. Based on extensive findings from social psychology [3-5], we hypothesized that positive emotions (happiness) would be attributed faster to in-group members, and that negative emotions (anger) would be attributed faster to out-group members. In addition, we hypothesized that more positive emotions would be attributed to the avatar of the own culture and more negative emotions to the avatar of the foreign culture.

Contrary to our hypotheses and in spite of cultural stereotypes, both Arab and German participants attributed more positive emotions to the Arab avatar than to the German avatar; additionally, both groups attributed more negative emotions to the German avatar than to the Arab avatar. To further clarify this counterintuitive result, Experiment 2 revealed that the Arab avatar was of significantly higher valence than the European avatar. Taken together, the results of both studies show that the valence of avatars has the potential to override cultural stereotypes and influence the perception of positive and negative affect. Thus, nonverbal behavior of an avatar of high valence—even if he does belong to an out-group—can be perceived positively. In sum, avatars have the potential to help overcome cultural stereotypes and can be used in online communities to enable more unbiased interactions.

References

1. Devine, P.G.: Stereotypes and prejudice: their automatic and controlled components. Journal of Personality and Social Psychology 56, 5–18 (1989)
2. Sagar, H.A., Schofield, J.W.: Racial and behavioral cues in black and white children's perceptions of ambiguously aggressive acts. Journal of Personality and Social Psychology 39, 590–598 (1980)
3. Hugenberg, K., Bodenhausen, G.V.: Facing Prejudice Implicit Prejudice and the Perception of Facial Threat. Psychological Science 14, 640–643 (2003)
4. Duncan, B.L.: Differential social perception and attribution of intergroup violence: Testing the lower limits of stereotyping of Blacks. Journal of Personality and Social Psychology 34, 590–598 (1976)
5. Unkelbach, C., Schneider, H., Gode, K., Senft, M.: A Turban Effect, Too: Selection Biases Against Women Wearing Muslim Headscarves. Social Psychological and Personality Science 1, 378–383 (2010)

6. Unkelbach, C., Forgas, J.P., Denson, T.F.: The turban effect: The influence of Muslim headgear and induced affect on aggressive responses in the shooter bias paradigm. Journal of Experimental Social Psychology 44, 1409–1413 (2008)
7. Yee, N., Bailenson, J.N., Urbanek, M., Chang, F., Merget, D.: The unbearable likeness of being digital: the persistence of nonverbal social norms in online virtual environments. Cyber Psychology & Behavior 10, 115–121 (2007)
8. Bainbridge, W.S.: The scientific research potential of virtual worlds. Science 317, 472–476 (2007)
9. Yee, N., Bailenson, N., Ducheneaut, N.: The Proteus Effect: Implications of Transformed Digital Self-Representation on Online and Offline Behavior. Communication Research 36, 285–312 (2009)
10. Pena, J., Hancock, T., Merola, A.: The Priming Effects of Avatars in Virtual Settings. Communication Research 36, 838–856 (2009)
11. Todorov, A.: Evaluating faces on trustworthiness: an extension of systems for recognition of emotions signaling approach/avoidance behaviors. In: Kingstone, A. (ed.) Ann. N. Y. Acad. Sci., pp. 208–224. United States (2008)
12. Vang, M.H., Fox, J.: Race in Virtual Environments: Competitive Versus Cooperative Games with Black or White Avatars. Cyberpsychology, Behavior and Social Networking (2013)
13. axyzDesign: axyzDesign. AxyzDesign (2013)

Connected to My Avatar:

Effects of Avatar Embodiments on User Cognitions, Behaviors, and Self Construal

Frank Biocca

M.I.N.D. Labs, Syracuse University, Syracuse, New York
Sungkyunkwan University, Seoul, South Korea
frank.biocca@gmail.com

Abstract. Mediated experience increasingly involves some representation of ourselves, so-called avatars. Avatars are used to facilitate the interaction with others in social media or are integrated as part of interfaces, used for interacting with 3D spatial environments and objects in games and simulations. These avatars vary in the degree to which they are realistic, representative of our sense of self or social status, or embodied, that is connected via the computer interface to the user's body via sensorimotor interaction. We review some of psychological effects of avatar identification and embodiment including evidence of the effects of avatar identification and embodiment on changes in behavior, arousal, learning, and self-construal. Furthermore, some avatar based changes in perception, cognition, and behavior may carry over and extend into changes into user's real world perception and behavior.

Keywords: avatar, human computer interaction, presence, embodiment.

1   Communication and Interaction Using Virtual Representations of Our Selves

Mediated experience is increasingly a large part of everyday experience as media use extends to more platforms, activities, and parts of day. The average American spends over 250 hours a week interacting with media [1]. Interactive media increasingly require representations of ourselves to mediate the interaction with others and to interface with the virtual environment. Social media, for example, are used by over 73% of internet users. So many of the over than 3.5 billion internet users will have some representation of themselves interacting with the virtual environment. Among American social media users, 64% report using some form of social media every day [1].

These representations and interfaces involve some representation of ourselves that can be static or dynamic, real or imagined. But the representations do play a role in mediating our interactions with others and with spatial interfaces. Often the representations of ourselves are created to have a communication and psychological effect on other users. They are used strategically to represent our bodies, our "look," or some aspect of our identity, personality, or social status. While these representations are the

G. Meiselwitz (Ed.): SCSM 2014, LNCS 8531, pp. 421–429, 2014.

interfaces used for impression management, our avatar representations can in some cases significantly interact with our own psychological states and behaviors.

1.1   Avatar Forms

Digital representations of our selves are commonly referred to as avatars, a word borrowed from Hindu myths regarding embodiment of gods, or divine intelligence, in human form. In the digital realm avatars are virtual entities or representation controlled by a human being or human intelligence. Avatars are contrasted with computer agents. Agents are virtual entities, anthropomorphic or seemingly sentient and intelligent, controlled entirely by a computer program.

Avatars vary in the representational and technological dimensions that connected them to the user. Within the range of avatar presentations there is a wide continuum of forms and interface embodiments. At the extremes avatars can vary from simple illustrations or pictures, such as individual's image use to represent and interact with others in social media to fully articulated, 3D body representations fitted to our actual bodies like those that might be found in high-end simulations or games.

Along the interface dimension of avatar control and interactivity, avatars vary to the degree to which they are passive, non-interactive representations or interactively controlled or embodied. Passive representations include a full host of pictures and images used in variety of social media and some games. These are representations of the self-presented to others.

In dynamic media a 2D or 3D avatar may be controlled directly by our body in some way. This creates a level of sensorimotor connection to the avatar, or to put it another way a level of sensorimotor embodiment [2]. By embodied avatar we mean that some body based action, a motor action of hand, head, or full body, is linked directly to movement of the avatar and experienced in some visual or multisensory feedback or stimulus. In the physical world this direct sensorimotor connection, the link between perception and action, is how we experience our own bodies and the sense of our interaction with physical space [3, 4].

But the link between perception and action can be mediated by some technology. As in the rubber hand illusion even simple perceptual motor coupling (in this case the synchronous stroke of a brush on our real and extended rubber hand) can lead to distortions in the perceived morphology of the body and a projection of the perceived locus of the body and sensation into a technological extension, the rubber hand [5-7].

Low level embodiment might include the control of an avatar via a basic hand interface such as mouse, joystick, or game pad. This form of avatar control is a kind of puppeteering. Higher levels of embodiment might include the three dimensional embodied avatars seen in virtual reality systems and in certain game systems such as those using high level of 3D body sensing and representation provided by devices such as the Kinect.

Avatars regardless of level of embodiment are designed, socially-constructed entities. The selection of images, body types, clothing, or other aspects of representation involve some conscious investment of our identity into the representation. The resulting avatar may vary in its level of resemblance to our physical identity in terms of morphology and appearance. It may also vary in its resemblance to our psychosocial identity such as visual cues of social roles, gender, personality, and behaviors. While any representation of the self is possible, there is tendency in most avatar systems for representations to become more anthropomorphic over time and to resemble in some ways the physical or ideal traits of body morphology and psychosocial identity of the user.

The degree to which the body is embodied and psychologically connected to the avatar has significant implications on the degree and range of psychological responses to virtual environments and stimuli.

2   Psychological Effects of Avatar Embodiment

As in embodied cognition within the physical world [8, 9] even simple avatars can influence cognition and behavior in the virtual environment. As these involve changed in embodiment, they effects persist and extend into cognition and behaviors outside the virtual environment.

2.1   Identification with the Avatar

At the lowest level of psychological effect the simple inclusion of avatar inside a medium or virtual environment can change our perception of the environment. It is widely reported in environments where users construct an avatar such as multiplayer games, that users report high level of identification with their avatars. The simple addition of an avatar representation of the self to a game and virtual environment can increase user enjoyment and motivation [10, 11]. The environment becomes more personally relevant.

A key feature may be identification with the avatar. Neuroimaging studies of interaction with our avatar self-representations support the role of identification. Ganesh and colleagues [12] studied neural activation (fMRI) of gamers and non-gamers in response to personality trait ratings of themselves, their avatar, or familiar others. Neuroimaging results revealed greater activation in the left inferior parietal lobe, a region associated with self-identification from a third person perspective and regions (rostral anterior cingulate gyrus) indicative of emotional self-involvement with the avatar. Memory for avatar traits covaried with the length of time a user was involved in gameplay, suggesting that this identification with the avatar increased with the use and interaction.

The process of identification begins in the vary act of selecting or constructing an avatar in low embodiment interfaces. It is automatically activated when the level of embodiment is higher, stimulated by the sensorimotor coordination between ones perception (sensory feedback) and action (motor movements) linking the user's body to the virtual avatar event [13].

2.2   Avatar Identification and Increasing Arousal and Motivation

Identification with one's avatar may increase the level of arousal and motivation in a virtual environment. This is evidence that users may differ in their levels of arousal depending on their degree of psychosocial connection to an avatar or avatars varying in their level of embodiment.

Bailey and colleagues [10] had children play a simple game that involved an avatar that was either assigned, chosen by the child from a pool of avatars, or designed (customized) by the child. Arousal during game play, as measured via skin conductance, was higher for chosen avatars and higher still for designed avatars. Similarly, Lim and Reeves [14] report that simply having a choice of avatar in a game significantly increased arousal, as measured by heart rate, and this effect was higher for males.

The effect on arousal can increase with level of embodiment. Kim and colleagues [15] report that higher levels of embodiment, that is degree to which the body is connected to an avatar, had significant effect on arousal, heart rate, and behavioral effort in an exercise virtual environment. Users with higher levels of embodiment also reported higher levels of presence, the sense of their body being spatially "there" in the game [15].

As the level of embodiment increases, the level of identification with the virtual body and the perceived threat to this body in virtual environment can increase. In the notorious 'virtual pit' experiment, Meehan and colleagues [16] placed users in full body, highly realistic virtual reality environment with a first person, head centered viewpoint using a head-mounted display. The environment included significant level of sensorimotor embodiment include head-coupled virtual reality system linking head motion to spatial cues from the virtual environment, free body locomotion around the environment, and low level haptic feedback in form of spatially co-located chair and the cue of an floor edge to shoeless feet of the participants. Participants were asked to drop bags on targets over a virtual pit. A gap suggesting a large hole in the floor opened precipitously to a realistic room one floor below.

Participants exhibited high levels of arousal and behaviors suggesting fear. Few participants could walk out over the open space, even though this was the easiest way to carry out the task. Increased levels of embodiment were related to increased arousal, heart rate, and reports of feeling present in the virtual environment. Although not explicitly tested, walking over an "open" virtual space would not be very fear inducing for users playing in the same environment using low level interface embodiment such as mouse and computer screen.

2.3   Changes in Self-construal and Social Behavior

Avatars often do not match the body of the user directly, but may vary in their morphology on dimensions such as attractiveness, height, or size or in social cues such a gender, group, or status symbols. While identification with an avatar is in itself a significant effect of avatar embodiment, there is the question of whether changes in the virtual avatar body can affect the behavior and self-construal of a user. Modification or compliance in the direction of the perceived avatar features would be evidence for particular kind of behavioral and identity plasticity. Bailenson and colleagues have labeled some of these phenomena, the Proteus effect [17], after the Greek god of the sea who seemed like water ever changing and flexible.

Adoption of Social Rules. Changed in body morphology can elicit psychological and behavioral changes. It appears that users may unconsciously adopt attitudes and behaviors associated with the avatar's physical morphology or social role and status. Yee and Bailenson [17] changed the attractiveness and height of avatars in a virtual chat room. They predicted on the basis of social psychology studies that the individuals would behave according to the physical characteristics of the avatar and not necessarily their own physical morphology. Individuals provided with more attractive avatars were more likely to more intimate in self-disclosure and use less interpersonal distance than those with unattractive avatars. Similarly, individuals with a taller avatars exhibited more dominant and negotiating behavior in a negotiation tasks, a behavior consistent with height advantages in the real world. This latter phenomenon is also supported in studies of avatar performance in multiplayer games. Taller avatars consistently outperform shorter avatars in these games.

2.4 Attitudes to Objects and Environments Associated with the Self or Ones Avatar

Self-reference plays a role in constructing attitudes towards objects, positions, or groups in the environment. Avatars interact with objects and items in the environment. These can become associated with the avatar, and indirectly with the identity of the user.

In a study of persuasion, avatars were shown to a user in a picture holding and endorsing a product in a virtual ad. Users were more likely to respond favorable to products that were self (avatar) endorsed.

In the virtual environment objects or others can be entwined with the avatar self in unusual ways. In a manipulation only possible in a virtual environment, the face of the user was morphed into hybrid presentations of the faces of unknown political candidates. Viewers were more likely to be persuaded by candidate whose face looked a little more like their own.

Bailenson and colleagues took this further to show that individuals can be influenced by the bejavioral example of their avatar [18]. An avatar seen as losing weight reinforces one's exercise behavior. In a similar way an avatar engaging in exercise, as opposed to leisure, motivated the user to exercise as well, even outside the virtual environment.

2.5 Changes in Perceived Physical Identity: Changing the Recognition of Ones of Own Face

Embodiment increases perceptual information from sensorimotor links to an avatar. This can lead to different kinds of changes in perceived identity.

A dramatic example of this is the instability of identity is the recognition of one's own face. In an extension the rubber hand illusion Tsakiris [19] altered the user's recognition of their own face in the direction of an avatar. This was accomplished using a simple visual tactile link to an avatar. Participants' faces where stroked with a soft brush while they watched the face of a morphed avatar being synchronously stroked. The sensorimotor coupling of the visual and tactile sensation produced a significant effect in self, face recognition. When presented with a series of morphed images blending their face with that of the avatar's, the manipulation produced a bi-ased shift in self-recognition in the direction of the avatar's face. That is when pre-sented with an array of pictures that included their real picture and a series of pictures morphed with the face of the avatar, participants reported that an image that blended their face with that of the avatar was their actual face.

Multisensory integration of stimuli appears to trigger changed cognitive represen-tations of one's body. Although the face is something we see in the mirror for decades and is a key feature linked to our identity, it can still be shifted slightly by embodied links (sensorimotor coupling) to avatar representations. So if a feature of identity as seemingly anchored as the recognition of one's face can be shifted, this suggests a certain malleability in self construal and identity via embodied avatar identification.

3   Sensorimotor Changes in Embodied Avatars

With higher levels of avatar embodiment or identification, there can be some signifi-cant perceptual illusions created regarding the environment and ones body

3.1   Presence and the Sense of Spatial Displacement towards the Environment of the Avatar

Identification with an avatar representation, especially with interactive and embodied avatars can create the illusion of spatial displace or presence, the sense being there in the virtual environment and feeling less in one's actual physical location in the physi-cal environment [2, 20, 21]. The feeling of spatial presence in a virtual environment is widely reported to increase with more immersive and embodied interfaces.

The ability to feel as one is in a different location, seeing the world from a different spatial perspective, may be part of set of evolutionary cognitive tools for modelling the viewpoint of another or modelling another position in space than the one currently occupied. This is supported in part by research showing that avatars can assist a user in priming the perception of other viewpoints on a scene. When avatars are present in the scene, they help prime an observer's ability to model that viewpoint and pers-pective a viewpoint in a scene [22], even if that is not their current perspective.

3.2   Sensory Suppression of Sensation in One's Body

High levels of presence and avatar identification can reduce the level of sensations in one's own body. In the rubber hand illusion it has been reported that the actual temperature of one's own hand drops as individuals shift their sense of the location of their hand to the rubber hand. Similarly in clinical settings virtual environments and avatar manipulations have been used to reduce self-reported pain during procedures [23-25]. Hansel and colleagues [23] increased visual tactile stroking such that the user experiences significant changes in presence (self-location) and decreases in reported pain.

3.3   Sensorimotor Recalibration

Virtual environments often provide a virtual body and can sometimes recalibrate the coupling between the sensory and motor systems. This kind of sensory recalibration is well known phenomenon which can be triggered by any distortions or changes the relationship between motor output and sensory input [26-28]. Interaction in embodied, highly coupled virtual environments can alter the relationship between motor action (interface inputs) and sensation (interface display outputs). Users can experience a recalibration of sensory and motor systems. For example Biocca and Rolland [29] demonstrated that displays that alter the relationship between the felt location of the user's eyes and their hands can experience some sensorimotor miscalibration such that they under-or-over reach for objects when emerging from an augmented reality system that altered the morphology of the body by shifting the location of the eyes.

4   Conclusions

Representations of oneself in the form of avatars has more than effects on our representations and communication with others. An avatar may do more that signal shifting personal status or affect. Avatar representations appear to connect to individual identity through the identification, the representation of social roles, and though sensorimotor coupling in the cases of more embodied avatars.

The representations of the self in the form of avatars appears to a user can invoke psychological effects on user arousal, attitudes, and behaviors in virtual environments. Some of these behaviors and attitudes may extend beyond the interaction in the virtual environment influencing judgments or behaviors in the physical world.

Inserting the self into the virtual worlds, designed and self-referencing avatars can increase arousal and motivation to engage in these worlds. Avatars can play a role in triggering attitude and behavioral change via identification with avatar characteristics or morphology.

Although highly embodied avatars are still rare, we see evidence that the can significant support unusual perception illusions about body morphology, location, and identity of one's body. These phenomena have implications for the design of virtual environments and the use of avatars and virtual environments in systems design for cybertherapy, persuasion, learning, and behavioral modification.

References

1. Nielsen, Digital consumer. Nielsen Corporation, New York (Febraury 2014)
2. Biocca, F.: The cyborg's dilemma: progressive embodiment in virtual environments. Journal of Computer-Mediated Communication 3(2) (1997), http://www.ascusc.org/jcmc/vol3/issue2/biocca2.html
3. Gibson, J.J.: The senses considered as perceptual systems. Houghton-Mifflin, Boston (1966)
4. Gibson, J.J.: The ecological approach to visual perception. Houghton-Mifflin, Boston (1979)
5. Yuan, Y., Steed, A.: Is the Rubber Hand Illusion Induced by Immersive Virtual Reality? In: IEEE Virtual Reality 2010, Proceedings, pp. 95–102 (2010)
6. Ijsselsteijn, W.A., de Kort, Y.A.W., Haans, A.: Is this my hand I see before me? The rubber hand illusion in reality, virtual reality, and mixed reality. Presence-Teleoperators and Virtual Environments 15(4), 455–464 (2006)
7. Botvinick, M., Cohen, J.: Rubber hands 'feel' touch that eyes see. Nature 391, 756 (1998)
8. Clark, A.: Being there: Putting brain, body, and world together again. MIT Press, Boston (1997)
9. Clark, A.: Natural-born cyborgs: minds, technologies, and the future of human intelligence, vol. viii, p. 229. Oxford University Press, Oxford (2003)
10. Bailey, R., Wise, K., Bolls, P.: How avatar customizability affects children's arousal and subjective presence during junk food-sponsored online video games. Cyberpsychol. Behav. 12(3), 277–283 (2009)
11. Lim, S., Reeves, B.: Computer agents versus avatars: Responses to interactive game characters controlled by a computer or other player. International Journal of Human-Computer Studies 68(1-2), 57–68 (2010)
12. Ganesh, S., et al.: How the Human Brain Goes Virtual: Distinct Cortical Regions of the Person-Processing Network Are Involved in Self-Identification with Virtual Agents. Cerebral Cortex 22(7), 1577–1585 (2012)
13. Smets, G.J.F., et al.: Designing in Virtual Reality: Perception-Action Coupling and Affordances. In: Proceedings VRST 1994: Virtual Reality Software and Technology. Association for Computing Machinery, New York (1994)
14. Lim, S., Reeves, B.: Being in the Game: Effects of Avatar Choice and Point of View on Psychophysiological Responses During Play. Media Psychology 12(4), 348–370 (2009)
15. Kim, S., Searles, R., Biocca, F.: This time, it's personal: The effects of avatar realism on heart rate variability, feelings, thoughts, and behaviors. Computers in Human Behavior (submitted)
16. Meehan, M., et al.: Objective measures of presence in virtual environments. In: Presence 2001, Philadelphia (2001)
17. Yee, N., Bailenson, J.: The Proteus Effect: The effect of transformed self-representation on behavior. Human Communication Research 33(3), 271–290 (2007)
18. Fox, J., Bailenson, J., Binney, J.: Virtual Experiences, Physical Behaviors: The Effect of Presence on Imitation of an Eating Avatar. Presence-Teleoperators and Virtual Environments 18(4), 294–303 (2009)
19. Tsakiris, M.: Looking for Myself: Current Multisensory Input Alters Self-Face Recognition. Plos One 3(12), 6 (2008)
20. Lombard, M.: Presence explication (2000), http://nimbus.temple.edu/~mlombard/Presence/explicat.htm (cited July 15, 2001)

21. Lombard, M., Ditton, T.: At the heart of it all: The concept of presence. Journal of Computer-Mediated Communication 3(2) (1997)
22. Amorim, M.A.: "What is my avatar seeing?": The coordination of "out-of-body" and "embodied" perspectives for scene recognition across views. Visual Cognition 10(2), 157–199 (2003)
23. Hansel, A., et al.: Seeing and identifying with a virtual body decreases pain perception. European Journal of Pain 15(8), 874–879 (2011)
24. Hoffman, H.G., et al.: Virtual reality as an adjunctive non-pharmacologic analgesic for acute burn pain during medical procedures. Ann. Behav. Med. 41(2), 183–191 (2011)
25. Hoffman, H.G., et al.: Modulation of thermal pain-related brain activity with virtual reality: evidence from fMRI. Neuroreport 15(8), 1245–1248 (2004)
26. Welch, R.: Perceptual modification: Adapting to altered sensory environments. Academic Press, New York (1978)
27. Welch, T.B.: Adaptation of space perception. In: Boff, K., Kaufman, L., Thomas, J. (eds.) Handbook of Perception and Human Performancech, John Wiley, New York (1986)
28. Welch, T.B., Warren, D.H.: Intersensory interactions. In: Boff, K.K., Kaufman, L., Thomas, J. (eds.) Handbook of Perception and Human Performance, ch. 24. John Wiley, New York (1986)
29. Biocca, F., Rolland, J.: Virtual eyes can rearrange your body: Adaptation to visual displacement in see-through, head-mounted displays. Presence: Teleoperators and Virtual Environments 7(3), 262–277 (1998)

iCONFESS

Mirroring Digital Self-Disclosure in a Physical Booth

Alma Leora Culén, Sisse Finken, and Andrea Gasparini

University of Oslo, Department of Informatics, Gaustadalléen 23 B
Oslo, Norway
{almira,finken,andreg}@ifi.uio.no

Abstract. In this paper, we describe an installation, iConfess, used to explore the question of disclosure in a physical space, when conditions for remaining anonymous are provided. The iConfess booth, a physical space where one could confess a secret, was tried at a large Student Faire. The paper reports on our findings on its use. The principle was simple: people could confess any secret in the privacy of the booth, on an anonymous site, using a tablet. After a period of time, confessions were handwritten on homemade cardboards and hung in the vicinity of the booth for everyone to see. In order to collect data on how it felt to reveal a secret in this way, we have offered to visitors a possibility to answer a questionnaire after the act of confession. 49 people did, a majority of them students (34), but also some others (15). In addition to the questionnaire, both participant and passive observations were made during the Faire. We have found that people enjoy revealing secrets, and reading those from others, although one participant still wondered just how anonymous the set up was. Attempts to connect people who confessed face-to-face during a social event, using a glow-in-the-dark bracelet, symbolizing that they have confessed, was not a success.

Keywords: anonymity, physical booth, social interaction, confession, design.

1   Introduction

In this paper, we consider the question of self-disclosure in a physical space when conditions for remaining anonymous are provided. The phenomenon of increased self-disclosure through social media may be understood in terms of anonymity and reduced social presence [7], as well as other factors such as reciprocity [5]. Assuring anonymity, as well as reciprocity, in a physical space is generally considered to be more difficult than online.

The idea of the project came about in the context of a human-computer interaction class, where four graduate students decided to make a space for themselves and their fellow students. The students chose to design a room where some weight can be lifted from stressed students' shoulders. Various concepts were explored: a relaxation room, a match making booth, and finally, a confession booth. Confessing something they strongly feel about, e.g., love, classes, friendship, politics, exams etc., [4], should feel

G. Meiselwitz (Ed.): SCSM 2014, LNCS 8531, pp. 430–439, 2014.
© Springer International Publishing Switzerland 2014

good. Taking into use a confession booth as a metaphor, but providing some technology that blurs the boundary between the online forms for self-disclosure and the physical ones, we hoped to increase the willingness of participants to make disclosures. The installation that the students made was seen by the authors as an opportunity to explore how the sense of anonymity and trust can be created in a public, physical space [1]. Furthermore, we were interested in how people perceive the difference in anonymity in the digital world as opposed to a physical space [1,6]. Reciprocity, as an important factor for disclosing, is difficult to achieve in the public context. We attempted to provide a possibility for some reciprocity, by giving to all confessants a glow-in-the-dark bracelet. The bracelet was to be worn at a social event, and used as an icebreaker, enabling people who made confessions, to discuss them.

When it comes to previous research using installations similar to this, there was little to find. There is a lot of literature on confession and its benefits in psychology, e.g. [9,16], where findings show that the act of confession has positive implication on psychological health for a person who confessed. Much is also written on self-disclosure and self-presentation on social media, e.g. [8]. Recently, there is a clear trend within social media, favoring portals for disclosing secrets. A trendy site Whisper.sh [17], states that it is about expressing one's true self within a community of honesty and acceptance. Whisper was launched in the spring of 2012 out of a belief that the way people share and interact with each other is changing. Whisper claims to have over 2.5 billion visits to its pages per month [18]. An older, and smaller scale, artist initiated site, PostSecret [19] has a similar feel as the Whisper online, but it does some of what iConfess does: it combines the physical and the virtual. Here, users create homemade postcards and mail them to an address in Maryland, and the photo of the postcard is then posted on the PostSecret site. PostSecret is now considered to be one of the largest ongoing community art projects, organizing live events, exhibits, etc. Warren, a person behind the project, believes that PostSecret brings relief and hope to the people world over [15]. The art project, by Canadian artist and Ted fellow Chang [20], is similar to that of iConfess in the look and manner of posting confessions. This project, however, came to our attention only recently, long after the iConfess was made, and thus, has not influenced the design of it.

Within the HCI community, there are some examples of design involving confessions. One of our favorites is the Embroidered Confessions: *"A disconnect exists between the perception of the transitory quality of digital data and the truth of its enduring existence. Through the weaving of the stories and secrets of strangers from the Internet into a material artifact, Embroidered Confessions represents the physical manifestation of the duality of digital information"*, [1, p. 1].

Another interesting project, which combines the digital and the physical, enabling social interactions, is Mobile Sawing [11]. In this project, people were invited to embroider SMS by hand, and with an embroidery machine connected to a mobile phone.

The paper is structured as follows: in Section 2, we describe the design of the booth. Section 3 describes the use of the iConfess during a Student Faire. Analysis of collected data, the questionnaire, confession cards and qualitative data obtained is presented in Section 4. Section 5 concludes the paper.

2   Designing the iConfess Booth

One of the authors was a member of the design team working on the iConfess project. The idea to design a space for students came from a fellow student, a very busy lady, working while studying. She envisioned a small relaxation space with interactions around music and nature images. While brainstorming around what relaxation is and what places there are to relax in, we discussed churches, chapels, massage rooms, and other cool places that people have seen world around.

Design thinking, with rapid prototyping, focus on empathy, and abductive reasoning, was used to explore. A wooden box was used as a tangible tool for exploration. Through role-playing and paper prototyping around relaxation, it became obvious that people have vastly different ideas about what relaxes them. The box, though, was well liked. In the next iteration of scenarios, brainstorming and paper prototyping, a 'match-making' box, intended to support social and fun interactions, was conceived. The idea to combine the virtual and the physical came alive: people could fill an online 'profile' with their interests and be matched with others with similar interests. The participants' interests were grouped in six categories, each represented by a different color of a glow-in-the-dark bracelet received after making their profile. Then it was just to smile to another person wearing the bracelet, same color for similar interest, or another color for brave souls wanting to explore differences!

As the project group dug deeper into anonymity and privacy issues around the match-making idea, the final concept with confessions emerged. It retained some aspects of previous iterations, but had a richer content, and was more in tune with the course requirements [3]. The idea of confessing was motivated by well-being effects of confession [9,16], and 'wish for peace' trees by Ono [12]. The size of the wooden box, now called the 'booth', was perfect for the purpose, reminiscent of the church confessional just the right amount. It was mobile, making it easy to move around the institute.

Fig. 1. Making the iConfess booth: painting the box, making curtains, floor cover and cushions, lighting, Fawkes mask symbolizing anonymity. Photos: the project team and faculty.

The interior, several soft cushions and the floor cover, was carefully designed, paying attention to colors and their effect on perception. The green color was used to invoke soothing, nature-like balance and well-being. The color purple was used on the outside, invoking the more spiritual and mystical feeling. The color also coordinated well with the color schema used for the space where the booth was to be used. The inside was painted in light green and azure color, round light spheres gave a soft light. Curtains were made to support the feeling of trust. On the booth, a Guy Fowler's mask, [14], was painted, as a symbol of anonymity, see Fig. 1.

3   iConfess Installation at the Student Faire

The Student Faire at the Institute of Informatics is an annual event, carefully organized by students. The Faire includes a large number of local companies presenting their work, talks, events, exhibits, games and a large party to round up the day. The Faire is always well visited by students, employees and outside guests. The iConfess booth was strategically placed by the stairs between two floors with exhibits, and thus was on the walking path for everyone visiting the Faire. In addition to this exposure, the students went around wearing Guy Fowler's masks, a symbol of anonymity, handing out a little flyer about the installation. The flyer was designed in same color tones, with a mask on it, making the booth easy to spot, even during 'rush' periods, between talks and presentations, Fig. 2, image in the middle.

Fig. 2. A project team member wearing the Fawkes mask, waiting for the confessant with a gift bag, two project members sharing flyers about the booth, students reading confessions. Photos: Culén.

Once someone showed an interest in the booth, they could go in and confess a secret using an iPad. The iPad was chosen because it is mobile, easy to use, and we thought, still a techno-cool, [2]. Indeed, the iPad worked without a glitch. Nobody had problems or questions about its use. Confessants wrote their confessions on a secure digital schema. When the schema was submitted, the confessions were emailed to an administrator, completely anonymously [13]. Every hour, confessions were handwritten by the administrator on a homemade cardboard and displayed at the exhibit space, on long lines of rope, fastened with cloths pins, Fig. 2, image on the right.

When a confessant was done confessing, one of the people behind the project (and the mask) handed them a gift bag, Fig. 2, the first image. The bag contained a muffin and a glow-in-the-dark bracelet. The bracelets were to be used at a social event, a party, concluding the Faire that evening. All participants who wished to fill in a short, five questions questionnaire were offered a possibility to do so.

Fig. 3. A confessant filling out the questionnaire, the installation space with confessions, and a person wearing their glowing bracelet at the party. Photos: Culén and Gasparini.

4   What We Learned from the iConfess

In what follows, we analyze the content of the confession cards first, then the data from the participant and passive observations, next the questionnaire, and finally, we provide a discussion about social interactions at the event and the overall user experience with the iConfess installation. We also consider the relationship between disclosure and privacy, and offline and online confessions.

When developing the iConfess concept, we considered the use of 'likes' with confession cards, which has become customary with Facebook and other social media (SM). 'Likes' provide interaction and excitement, making the interest of others visible. We chose not to use the 'likes' feature, because in the context of the Faire, people could not confess repeatedly. Not receiving likes on their confession could potentially make someone feel bad, and they could not try 'a better confession'.

4.1   Confession Cards Analysis

After the Faire, we collected and worked with 49 confession cards. Some cards were written in Norwegian and some in English, see Fig. 4. For the purposes of this paper, the Norwegian text has been translated into English by the authors. We grouped the cards into four categories by topics of confessant's concern: love, about me, ethics, and trivia. The 'trivia' category contains, in our judgment, confessions without large impact from the confessant, although they may be pieces of non-trivial wisdom such as "It's not what you look at that matters, it's what you see". A sample of ten confessions, picked at random, is shown bellow. After each confession, we show how we categorized it (in italics).

"I kissed a girl and I liked it" (*love*)

"I miss mamma!" (*love*)

"I always think I'm fat :(" (*about me*)

"I'm lonely" (*about me*)

"I was a shoplifter" (*ethics*)

"I have often pretended to be interested in guys I meet when I go out, just to get a free beer" (*ethics*)

"I drink cola every day for breakfast" (*trivia*)

"I only did this to get a free muffin!" (*trivia*)

"I like to dance necked in the flat" *(about me)*

"It's not what you look at that matters, its what you see" (*trivia*)

In summary, 20 of 49 confessions were categorized as *ethics,* 15 as *trivia*, 6 as *love*, and 8 as *about me*. The high number of trivial confessions may, in part, be attributed to the setting and not being certain just how anonymous it was, given that, in spite of having outside visitors, many people know each other.

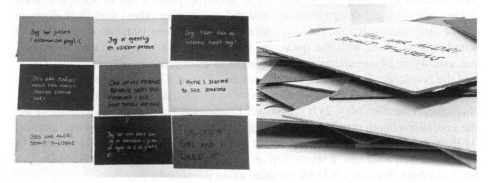

Fig. 4. Confessions. Handwritten on homemade cardboards by the iConfess project team. Photo: Finken.

4.2   Observations

Both participant and passive observation were conducted during the day and passive observation during the party in the evening.

People stopped in front of the confession cards that were displayed on the string to read them, see Fig. 2, last image. Most of the visitors read all the displayed cards, and clearly showed signs of enjoyment, smiling, and frequently laughing. When there were groups of people, confessions were often read aloud and expressions like "check this one out", "cool", "funny" and similar, were used.

While confessing, many confessants sat inside the booth for quite a few minutes before they came out. Some commented that it was hard to come up with a secret, and others that they just enjoyed the coziness of the booth for a little while. Almost everyone who went into the booth came out commenting on how cozy it was to sit inside it. Many Faire visitors who passed by the installation did not confess, but commented on the exhibit. Some of those said that they did not have any secrets: "I am like an open book", or "I do not have any secrets". One visitor explained that he had issues with claustrophobia, but he wanted to confess anyway, which he did outside the booth.

As the number of confession cards increased through the day, the interest in the confession cards, and confessing, also increased. We could observe some people putting the glow-in-the-dark bracelets on, intended for the evening, right away. In the evening however, only four people had bracelets on, in addition to all the students taking our course in advanced interaction design. Since many students were familiar with each other, it was hard for the observer to tell if any had started conversing because of the bracelets. So, at the party, we had neither the critical mass of strangers, nor the bracelet wearers.

4.3   Questionnaire Analysis

The students who designed the confession booth, as pointed out in Section 2, used design practices and design thinking, and did not involve others than themselves in the design process. It was, thus, of interest to evaluate the installation. We made a simple questionnaire with five questions, which would not take much time to answer, but would give us an indication about how the users experienced the act of confession and the booth, see Fig. 3. The questions we asked were: 1) Have you ever disclosed a personal secret on Social Media? Place a cross by all that apply: Facebook, Twitter, Snapchat, Your own blog. 2) If the answer to question 1 was yes, was it easier to use the confession booth than other social media to tell a personal secret? (yes/no answer) 3) How easy was it to tell a secret inside the booth? (Likter scale, 1-8, 1 not easy at all) 4) Are you a student, a researcher, an employee, a visitor (place an X) 5) Do you have anything else you would like to share about iConfess?

Thus, one of the aims with the questionnaire was to gain understanding about relationships between disclosure and privacy and offline and online sharing of secrets, in relation to the exhibit. The answers to question 3) gave indication of participant's emotional response. In their answer to the open question 5), several confessants have addressed other issues, such as aesthetics of the booth. In this way, we could say, the outcome of questionnaire came to stand as an evaluation of the concept as a whole.

We first take a closer look at the answers we got to the open question: *"Do you have anything you would like to share about iConfess?"* The answers to this question contain semi-qualitative data, which give a bit more detailed insights into how the confessants related to the booth *(aesthetics)*, to confessing *(emotions)*, and to anonymity issues *(privacy)*. As with the confessions above, we provide a sample of 10 answers, translated and categorized, category written in italics.

"Nice booth :)" *(aesthetics)*

"The booth was cozy with modern decor – happy lights and all that. Nice idea! :-)" *(aesthetics + emotions)*

"It's very nice to sit in that calming box and think. Confessions rock :-)" *(aesthetics + emotions)*

"I think it is a fun idea." *(emotions)*

"It was cool" *(emotions)*

"I was fun and serious!" *(emotions)*

"Exiting!! And scary!" (*emotions*)

"It was very difficult to write a secret" (*emotions*)

"I have never post a personal secret in social media but I think in Confession booth it's so much easier to tell your secret because you are anonymous" (*privacy*)

"On SM, one still has clear identity. The boot is giving a feeling of privacy. But I do not know exactly if anyone can find out who I am" (*privacy*)

What we can learn from the answers above, is that disclosure is closely connected to emotions such as exiting, scary, fun, serious, and so on. Further, emotions and aesthetics were woven together in some of the answers we received, for example: "It's very nice to sit in that calming box and think. Confessions rock :-)" and "The booth was cozy with modern decor – happy lights and all that. Nice idea! :-)".   Such weavings fall along the line of reasoning, which initially was part of the relaxation box concept, and which may indicate that the well-being effect was supported through the act of confession.

Addressing the first two questions, most of the participants did disclose a secret using the SM before: 15 disclosed on the Facebook, 10 on Snapchat, 4 on Twitter and 6 in their own blog. 25 participants thought that using the booth was easier, 5 opted for other SM, 16 left the question blank and 1 was undecided.

For the Likter scale question 3), the average was 6.02. Some of the lowest scores were given by faculty (out of seven faculty members, three gave scores of 2, 2 and 4, outside visitors gave scores of 5, 5 and 8, and university employees 7, 8 and 8). The evaluation given by 34 students averaged 6.98. Two persons did not answer the question 4).

Taking into consideration the results from the questionnaire and our observations, we can conclude that the majority of the participants at iConfess liked to reveal a secret to the public in this manner. They also liked the installation as a whole.

On the other hand, the use of bracelets at the party did not fulfill its purpose as an icebreaker. As mentioned in Section 3, only four, other than the students in the class, had them on. Since many students are acquainted with each other, it was hard for the observant to tell if any have started conversations because of the bracelets. So, at the party, we had neither the critical mass of strangers, nor the bracelet wearers, Fig. 3.

Being in the physical booth, while revealing secrets through an online channel, the iPad, creates an interesting relationship between the private and the public. The booth itself, is placed in the public, yet the inner space of the booth created a safe environment for confessing. Although the project group, to the best of their knowledge and skills, had secured anonymity, it was not possible to forget the public sphere: "On SM, one still has clear identity. The boot is giving a feeling of privacy. But I do not know exactly if anyone can find out who I am". The issue of having a private thought, released in physical form, so that by passers can engage with it and openly discuss it, creates an interesting area of tension between disclosure and privacy and between offline and online sharing of secrets. This area of tension we could call social interaction 2.0. We choose this term because the handwritten confessions on the cardboards attracted attention, made Faire-goes converse about the secrets and the booth itself, and, motivated others to share their secrets. The latter claim is based on our observations. At the same time, the secrets, we believe, would not have been revealed to the public without the concealing act performed by the secure digital schema, which was anonymously forwarded by email to an administrator. With the mix of offline and online settings, thus, it became possible to bring together disclosure and privacy more intimately, and, support revelations on the same physical location. This aspect distinguishes our work from online sites such as Whisper and PostSecret [17,19], or the artwork by Chang [20].

5   Conclusion

An installation, iConfess, was made and used during a large public event at the institute. Students, faculty, employees and outside visitors alike, could confess a secret in the privacy of the booth, using a secure digital schema. In one-hour time intervals confessions were downloaded by administrating students, handwritten and exhibited for all to see. This interplay between the digital and the physical was interesting, especially because it took place at a work place, where many confessants are acquainted with each other. iConfess also gave an opportunity for people, who confessed, to interact, of course, without knowing what they confessed. The interplay of the private and public spaces as they relate to the act of confession was interesting. Confessants have found the booth to be easy to use and, certainly not more difficult than using social media.

Acknowledgments. First and foremost, we thank the iConfess project team: Lena Risvik, Agnethe Heggelund and Rebekka Castro. Thanks are also due to the rest of the participating students: Henrik Kjersem, Lena Risvik, Paria Tahaee, Anja Simonsen, Sylvia Saxlund, Rita Johnsen and Ingrid Arnesen.

References

1. Benedetti, J.M.: Embroidered confessions: an interactive quilt of the secrets of strangers. In: Proceedings of the 8th ACM Conference on Creativity and Cognition, pp. 313–314. ACM (2011)
2. Culén, A.L., Gasparini, A.: Situated Techno-Cools: factors that contribute to making technology cool and the study case of iPad in education. Psychology Journal 10(2), 117–139 (2012)
3. Culén, A.L., Mainsah, H.N., Finken, S.: Design Practice in Human Computer Interaction Design Education. In: The Seventh International Conference on Advances in Computer-Human Interactions, pp. 300–306. ThinkMind (2014)
4. Gasparini, A., Castro, R., Risvik, L., Heggelund, A.: iConfess at dagen@ifi (2013), http://folk.uio.no/andrega/iConfess/
5. Jiang, L.C., Bazarova, N.N., Hancock, J.T.: From Perception to Behavior Disclosure Reciprocity and the Intensification of Intimacy in Computer-Mediated Communication. Communication Research 40(1), 125–143 (2013)
6. Johnson, D.G., Miller, K.: Anonymity, pseudonymity, or inescapable identity on the net (abstract). SIGCAS Comput. Soc. 28(2), 37–38 (1998)

7. Joinson, A.N., Paine, C.B.: Self-disclosure, privacy and the Internet. The Oxford Handbook of Internet Psychology, 2374252 (2007)
8. Kaplan, A.M., Haenlein, M.: Users of the world, unite! The challenges and opportunities of Social Media. Business Horizons 53(1), 59–68 (2010)
9. Kelly, A.E., McKillop, K.J.: Consequences of revealing personal secrets. Psychological Bulletin 120(3), 450–465 (1996)
10. Leong, T.W., Brynskov, M.: CO_2nfession: engaging with values through urban conversations. In: Proceedings of the 21st Annual Conference of the Australian Computer-Human Interaction Special Interest Group: Design: Open 24/7, pp. 209–216. ACM (2009)
11. Lindström, K., Ståhl, Å.: Threads - a Mobile Sewing Circle: Making Private Matters Public in Temporary Assemblies. In: Proceedings of the 11th Biennial Participatory Design Conference, pp. 121–130. ACM (2010)
12. Ono, Y.: Imagine Peace Tower. Imagine Peace Tower (1996), http://www.IMAGINEPEACETOWER.com/
13. Tanner, A.L., Jefferson, S., Skelton, G.: Revealing the Unseen in Social Networking Sites: Is Your Metadata Protected? International Journal 2(4) (2013)
14. Taylor, A.: How Guy Fawkes Inadvertently Created the Word "Guy". Slate (2013), http://www.slate.com/blogs/business_insider/2013/11/05/guy_fawkes_day_how_the_word_guy_became_popular.html
15. Warren, F.: Postsecret: Confessions On Life Death And God by Frank Warren. William Morrow (October 6, 2009)
16. Emotion, disclosure and health. American Psychological Association, Washington, DC (1995)
17. Whisper - Share Secrets, Express Yourself, Meet New People, http://whisper.sh/
18. Where the truth lives. Where the truth lives, http://blog.whisper.sh/
19. PostSecret. PostSecret, http://postsecret.com
20. 6 art installations by Candy Chang that make the viewer part of the piece | TED Blog, http://blog.ted.com/2012/09/04/6-art-installations-by-candy-chang-that-make-the-viewer-part-of-the-piece/

I'd Rather Die Than Be with You:
The Effects of Mortality Salience and Negative Social Identity on Identification with a Virtual Group

Lena Frischlich, Diana Rieger, and Olivia Rutkowski

University of Cologne, Department of Psychology, Richard-Strauss Str.2, 50931 Cologne
lena.frischlich@uni-koeln.de

Abstract. Research inspired by terror management theory has demonstrated that mortality salience (MS) triggers defense of one's self-esteem and cultural worldview, for instance in terms of in-group identification. A necessary precondition is that this in-group contributes to a positive self-evaluation by being successful in relevant social comparisons. Unsuccessful in-groups pose an identity-threat and trigger dis-identification. Nowadays, virtual worlds and avatars offer new pathways to in-group identification and self-enhancement, raising the question which virtual groups and self-representations serve terror-management needs. The current study examined this question in a life simulation game. Participants either wrote about their death or a control topic before they were confronted with an identity-buffering (successful) versus identity-threatening (unsuccessful) virtual in-group, manipulated via ethnicity. Subsequently, preference for in-group avatars and identification with the virtual group were assessed. The results confirmed an increased identification after MS only when one's identity was buffered. Results are discussed with regard to their implications.

Keywords: terror management theory, Negative Social Identity, Avatar Selection, Virtual Group-identification, Simulation Games.

1 Introduction

"I am not afraid of death, I just don't want to be there when it happens" [1, p. 99]

Over the last decades, this desire to flee from death has been examined by research in the area of terror management theory (TMT, [2]). TMT is based on the assumption that humans are trapped in an existential dilemma between the innate desire for continued existence and the insight that their life is ultimately finite. To defend against the paralyzing terror resulting from the awareness of one's mortality (mortality salience, MS), mankind has developed a symbolic anxiety-buffer encompassing two interwoven components: (a) the *cultural worldview* one commits to; and (b) *self-esteem* if one matches the norms inherent in that worldview. Cultural worldview thereby reflects one's social identities [3]. Identification with them provides the individual with a level of existence that is immune to the limited existence of one's

G. Meiselwitz (Ed.): SCSM 2014, LNCS 8531, pp. 440–451, 2014.
© Springer International Publishing Switzerland 2014

personal identity [4]. Moreover, in-groups also influence one's self-esteem crucially: Besides providing group-norms which the individual can strive for to feel valuable [3], the comparison of one's in-groups to relevant out-groups provides the individual with important status informations [5]. The more positive one's in-group is evaluated, the better oneself can feel too. Evidence is large, that both, one's cultural worldview and self-esteem are defended under conditions of MS [6].

Nowadays, modern technologies and virtual realities enable their users new pathways to flee from life's inevitable end. As Malda [7] wrote in the Washington Post "I'll never write the Great American Novel or direct the Oscar Award Winning Film. But the Internet let's all of us live forever". Virtual realities that offer their users parallel realities 24/7, are especially well-suited to defend one's cultural worldview and self-esteem. Their users can (a) represent themselves as a self-esteem enhancing avatar [8]; and (b) affiliate with desirable in-groups via mouse-click [9]. Yet, the quasi-infinite options for avatar creation and virtual group attachment raise the question which characteristics of a player might be transmitted to virtual realities under conditions of MS. If anything is possible, what will persist?

This question is particularly relevant when it comes to the transmission of real-life characteristics that might trigger aversive experiences, such as ethnic-discrimination. Indeed, it has been found that ethnic diversity is lower in virtual than in real environments [10]; with most created avatars being White. This disappearance of, for example, Black characters in virtual worlds has raised attention and concerns [11]. Albeit, the effect is partly due to fewer options to create ethnically realistic Black avatars [12], Lee [13] found a vicarious circle triggered by low ethnically diverse virtual environments. Black participants who were confronted with a predominantly White second-life community, created more White-looking avatars as compared to Black participants confronted with an ethnically diverse community. Moreover, those in the low ethnic-diversity condition also reported less willingness to reveal their real-life ethnic identity through their avatars.

This is striking because it has been demonstrated that avatars generally display one's personal [8] as well as social identities [14] and identification with virtual groups also follows the principles of social identity theory (SIT [5]). Identification with a virtual group is an integral part of the players' overall identification with a virtual world [15] and also affects one's real-life identities [16]. Due to the relevance of social identities for one's self-esteem [5] in-groups that lose a relevant social-comparison (because they are numerically underrepresented [13], negatively presented [17], or simply not successful [18]) not only lose their death-anxiety buffering potential, they even pose a self-relevant threat themselves and consequently trigger defensive behaviors [19]. Hence, although group-identification has been found to be effective in transcending the own mortality [4], this effectiveness strongly depends on the status one's in-group has compared to relevant out-groups: In case of identity-threatening in-groups, individuals preserve their self-esteem by distancing from them even more after MS [17]. Most plausible, this effect will be even stronger concerning the (dis-) identification with virtual ethnic groups, as it is much easier to distance from them than from a real-life ethnic in-group. The buffering-potential of one's ethnic identity in face of MS thus might contribute to an understanding of the low ethnic-diversity in virtual worlds.

1.1   Terror Management Theory and Negative Social Identities

The basic assumption underlying TMT is that humans are ultimately caught in the existential dilemma between the desire for continuous living and the awareness that life is not endless. Within this dilemma lies the potential for paralyzing terror [2]. In order to cope with this threat-of-death and to ensure continuous functioning [20], humans subconsciously1 strive for symbolic immortality by becoming part of a cultural worldview larger than the own limited existence [3]. Referring to social identity theory (SIT, [5]), cultural worldview is related to one's social identities. Castano [21], [22] has pioneered the idea that the shift towards social identity and the depersonalization from an individual to a group member is particularly well suited to transcend the own physically limited existence [4]. Yet cultural worldviews are fragile social constructions [23] and thus need constant consensual validation by others.

The main hypothesis of TMT therefore predicts that under conditions of MS, individuals prefer those who share their cultural worldview (the in-group) and derogate those who question it (the out-group). Supporting this hypothesis, MS has been demonstrated to increase a variety of in-group biases. For instance, subjects were found to evaluate essays criticizing their nationality more negatively under conditions of MS [24]. They also have been found to prescribe their in-group more positive traits [21], to prefer in-group products [25] and to show pro-social behavior predominantly towards in-group members [26] after MS. These effects have been found for religious [27], national [22] as well as ethnic in-groups [28].

Albeit the ample evidence for increased in-group biases under conditions of MS, the positive effect of a certain in-group for one's self-esteem is a necessary precondition for increased in-group biases. Due to the identity-threatening nature of negative in-groups ([19], [29]) individuals have been found to distance from such in-groups even more after MS. For instance, Arndt, Greenberg, Schimel, Pyszczynski, and Solomon [17] found Hispanic participants after MS to evaluate Hispanic art more negatively if they had read an identity-threatening description of a negative in-group member (here: A drug dealer) than following an identity-buffering positive in-group example (Identity-buffer, here: A missionary). In a related vein, Dechesne, Greenberg, Arndt, and Schimel [18] provided evidence that the identification with a successful sports team (identity-buffer) increased after MS, whereas the identification with an unsuccessful team decreased (identity-threat).

Most plausible, this effect also holds for virtual self-representation and group-identification as both have been found to mirror real-life mechanisms. Moreover, identification with a virtual group can be regarded as more permeable than real-life boundaries. Research has shown that dis-identification in order to protect a positive self-evaluation is particularly effective if group-boundaries are permeable [29].

1.2   Avatars and Virtual Groups as Extensions of the Real-Life Identity

Avatars are computer-generetaed self-representations [30], that usually allow for a large control over one's appearance and soetimes also over one's personality characteristics [31]. Gamers usually refer to their avatar as "I"[15] and avatars form part of one's self-

---

1   For the difference between the conscious and unconscious death-anxiety defenses see Pyszczynski, Greenberg, and Solomon [54].

concept ([32]), expressing actual as well as ideal self-aspects [33]. Bessière, Seay, and Kiesler [8] for instance found smaller differences between World-of-Warcraft avatars and the ideal self of their players, than between these players actual and ideal selves. In line with that, avatars have been demonstrated to have similar effects than real-life behavior in terms of the effects of self-discrepancy [34], for example between actual and ideal physical appearance [35], and the influence of behavior-perception [36] on subsequent self-image [16].

Avatars can also be understood from a social identity perspective, reflecting personal as well as social identity aspects. On the one hand, avatars which are distinct from others can be regarded as the expression of one's personal identity, characteristics that distinguish the individual from others [37]. On the other hand, avatar selection and creation also reflect one's social identities. The adaption to group-norms has been found to be as present in virtual as in real-life contexts [38]. Accordingly, virtual contexts also influence avatar selection and creation. Players tend to (partly) adept their self-representation to a virtual context. For instance, Trepte and Reinecke [39] found game competitiveness to foster creation of avatars dissimilar to their players. In a related vein, Vasalou and Joinson [40] found participants to adapt their avatars for instance for virtual dating purposes. People even breathe life into virtual agents and computers [41]. For example, the nonverbal behavior (such as smiling) of avatars stimulates the same brain regions as real human behavior [42], causing similar effects [43] and nonverbal behavior follows the same rules online as offline [44]. This even exceeds to computers becoming members of one's in-group an fostering increased in-group cooperation, just as found for cooperation in real groups [45]. The identification with virtual groups forms part of one's social-identity [15] wherefore players strive to evaluate their virtual groups as positively as their real ones to preserve their self-esteem [29].

Most of time, avatars mainly display the actual self of their creators, for instance in terms of gender. Gudagno, Muscanell, Okdie, Burk, and Ward, [14] found that only 5.7% of the female and 9.8% of the male second-life users used an avatar of the opposite gender. However, when it comes to the expression of one's ethnic-identity, the willingness to play a non-White avatar seems to be strikingly reduced [46]. Higgin even speaks from "blackless fantasies" [11]. Although, the lack of options to customize ethnically-realistic non-White avatars [12] and a potential "White-avatar norm" ([10], [47]) have been discussed, research so far did not address the role of a loss of a social comparison for the identification with a virtual ethnic group and avatar selection directly. Further, most studies focused on Black players ([13], [47], but see Groom, Bailenson, and Nass for an exception [48]). Yet, if there actually is a "White-avatar norm" in virtual realities ([10]), this does not allow for a direct comparison of the same ethnic-identity as identity-buffer and identity-threat (for instance after one's in-group had won versus lost a relevant game). Moreover, it does not control for pre-existing real-life discrimination experiences [49] that might underlie the decreased willingness to play a Black avatar (see Lee [13] for a discussion).

Thus, the current study was designed to examine the effects of MS on avatar selection and group identification depending on the identity-buffering versus threatening potential of one's ethnic identity. Using the SIMS 3 [50] (a life-simulation) as virtual reality, we examined whether participants in the MS versus a Control-group would prefer an in-group (White) over an out-group (Black) avatar and how much they were eager to identify with a virtual group after having watched a Human chess game that had been either won by their in-group (identity-buffer) or the out-group (identity-threat). Based on the literature, we predicted MS to increase preference for in- as compared to out-group avatars (H1). Furthermore, we expected that MS would increase identification with an identity-buffering virtual group (H2a) but decrease the identification with an identity-threating virtual group (H2b).

2   Methods

To test these hypotheses, we realized a 2(Condition: MS versus Control) × 2(Identity-buffer versus Identity-threat) design whereby ethnicity of participant and avatar served as social identity manipulation.

2.1   Sample

A total of 82 subjects participated in the study. Eleven of them had to be excluded because they reported non-White ethnicity. The remaining $N = 71$ subjects (35 female) were all German and on average 24.59 years old ($SD = 4.13$). Gender, $\chi^2(2) = 2.07$, $n.s.$ and age, $F(3,69) = 1.04$, $n.s.$ were equally distributed among the conditions. The majority of participants ($n = 58$) was studying at the moment of data collection. Nearly all reported pre-experiences with computer games ($n = 68$). Neither educational level, $\chi^2(6) = 6.46$, $n.s$, nor pre-experience, $\chi^2(3) = 2.17$, varied with the experimental condition.

2.2   Procedure and Measurements

Subjects participated via an online-survey. They were informed that the study would be about the relationships between cognitive abilities and computer games by testing a new feature of the SIMS 3 game. After the assessment of the demographic variables (*age, gender, educational level, nationality*) and game-experience, participants completed a set of bogus personality questionnaires, used later on to serve as cover story for the told similarity between player and avatar [51].

Condition. Following the standard manipulation of MS [6], participants then answered two open ended questions about their own death [52] or a control topic (here: dental pain) before they worked on a delay task for five minutes to enable their distal defenses [53].

Identity-Buffer Versus Identity-Threat. Afterwards, ethnicity was made salient via a gameplay video of a SIMS human chess game by EA-games[2] (duration 01:00 minute) with White and Black avatars as chess figures. To compare identity-buffer

---

[2]   The Sims Movie Mashup Tool Example 3, http://www.gamespot.com/articles/
the-sims-3-exclusive-hands-on-making-movies-with-the-sims-3s-
mash-up-tool/1100-6207981/

and identity-threat, participants randomly saw either a video that was manipulated to present the in-group (White) or the out-group (Black) as winner. Moreover, an introductory scene was added showing a White, respectively Black avatar as team-master. Avatars differed only concerning their skin color and few ethnic characteristics (for instance, lip-size, see Figure 1). After the video, a scene was added in which the team-masters expressed happiness or anger, depending on their teams' success. Scenes were produced with the SIMS 3 moviemaker [50]. Each video was accompanied by the same neutral piece of classical music ("Pictures at an exhibition" by Mussorgski [54]). Furthermore, gender of participant and avatar were matched: Female participants always saw a female chess master and vice-versa.

Avatar Choice and Team-Identification. Subsequently, participants were informed that they would play the Human chess game themselves and should choose which team-master (and team) they would prefer to play. To control for the effects of avatar and player similarity ([15], [39]) participants were informed that, based on their answers on the personality-questionnaires filled out before, both avatars were 25% similar to them. After making their choice, identification with the virtual group was measured with the six-item scale by van Looy et al. [15]. Wording of the scale was changed to "team" instead of "guild" to match the experimental situation (for instance *"My team members are important to me"*). Reliability was good (Cronbach's $\alpha = .84$). After the last question, participants were checked for suspicion and released.

Fig. 1. Black and White team-master avatar on the avatar choice slide. Order of avatar presentation was random.

3   Results

3.1   Avatar Choice

H1 predicted an increased selection of the White in-group avatar for participants in the MS condition. However, avatar choice was not associated with Condition,

$\chi^2(1) = 0.41$, the Black avatar was always preferred. Odds ratio to choose the Black avatar was $OR = 1.59$ in the MS and $OR = 1.75$ in the Control group. This pattern did not change, when Identity-threat was included in the analysis, the interaction revealed no significant differences, $\chi^2(1) = 0.29$.

3.2   Identification

A 2(Condition) × 2(Identity threat) ANOVA on the aggregated team identification score revealed no significant main effect for Identity-threat, $F < 1$. The main effect for Condition reached marginal significance, $F(1,65) = 3.12, p < .09, r = .20$. The predicted interaction became significant, $F(1,65) = 6.81, p < .02, r = .30$ (see Figure 2)

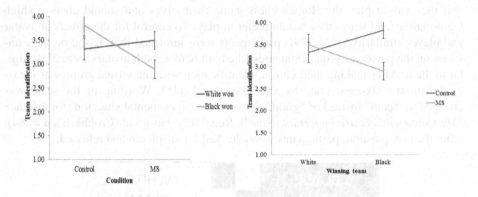

Fig. 2. Effects of Condition and Identity-buffer (White won) versus Identity-threat (Black won). Each item was answered on a 5-point scale ranging from 1(= *totally not*) to 5(= *totally*).

Hypotheses were tested via one-tailed independent t-tests. Results showed the predicted disordinal interaction. Only under conditions of MS, $t(31) = 2.95$, $p < .001, r = .47$, identification was higher when Identity was buffered (Mbuffer = 3.82, SDbuffer = 0.72) than when Identity was threatened (Mthreat = 2.89, SDthreat = 1.00). No differences were found for the Control group (Mbuffer = 3.32,SDbuffer = 0.64, Mthreat= 3.50,SDthreat = 0.94), t < 1. Moreover, in comparison to the Control-group, participants after MS identified more with an Identity-buffering virtual team, $t(26) = -1.93, p < .04, r = .36$ (H2a), and less with an Identity-threatening team, $t(31) = 2.00, p < 03, r=.31$(H2b).

4   Discussion

Overall, our results confirmed the hypotheses derived from TMT and SIT for the identification with virtual groups (H2a,b) but not for avatar selection (H1). White participants increased their identification with a virtual group under conditions of MS if their ethnic in-group was presented as winner in a social comparison (Identity-buffer) but decreased it when their in-group had lost the comparison (Identity-threat).

There with our results partly support the assumption by Blascovich and Bailenson [10] that "existential anxieties are at the heart of humans penchant for psychological travel away from grounded reality to virtual reality" (p.142). Mortality salience did influence the willingness to "travel to virtual reality" only when the virtual reality buffered their worldview and presented their in-group as more successful. Our results are therewith in line with the assumption that the identification with virtual groups follows the same mechanisms that have been described for real groups [15] with identification decreasing for unsuccessful in-groups (([19], [55]). Our results are also compatible with recent research demonstrating in-game success as a key factor for game enjoyment and the effectiveness of games in regulating aversive states ([56], [57]).

In contrast to the expectations, participants did not prefer the White avatar in general or under conditions of MS. Albeit numerous studies have shown a greater number of White as compared to Black avatars in virtual worlds ([12]), participants in our study always preferred the Black avatar. Different explanations for this finding are possible and should be addressed in future studies. On the one hand, it might be that the ethnicity manipulation was too obvious. Although only three participants assumed the study to deal with racism or ethnicity, it might be that social desirability influenced the choices [58]. Although excluding those three participants did not change the pattern of results, future studies should include more ethnic manipulations, for instance by using a football game (such as Fifa 14 [59]). On the other hand, it might be that the reported low-similarity of participant and avatar (always 25%) has contributed to the effect. In line with this assumption, Frischlich, Rieger, Dratsch and Bente [51] could show that in online dating environments, dissimilar ethnic in-group members raise the least dating interest as compared to similar in-group and dis- as well as similar out-group members under conditions of MS. In order to better compare our results to those by Frischlich et al.'s [51] online dating study, next steps should add a high similarity condition as well as a cross-gender setting to further disentangle the important factors for avatar selection under MS and its potential moderators.

Several limitations of the current study have to be noted. First of all, only White participants were examined. It is thus unclear whether Black participants would show the same pattern after MS under conditions of identity-threat. Although research on the response of Black participants towards identity-threats in virtual worlds point towards this assumption [13], future studies should test this more directly by replicating the results with a Black sample. Yet, the high likelihood that Black participants (examined in a pre-dominantly White country) have pre-existing discriminative experiences [49], has to be regarded by selecting an adequate context were Black ethnic-identity can serve as identity-buffer too.

Further, in our study, participants were told that they would play a chess game themselves. However, this explanation was only used to make avatar selection necessary. Nevertheless, mapping the actual virtual behavior of participants after MS would shed light on the real implications of MS and the consequences of the respective avatar selection and team membership. Future studies therefore should aim at investigating real consequences of the awareness of death anxiety. Virtual environment seem especially useful for this purpose.

Summarizing, the current study was the first to directly examine the effects of existential concerns on the identification with threatening and non-threatening virtual groups. We hope that future studies will address the questions that can be pulled out of our results.

References

1. Allen, W.: Without feathers, p. 210. Random House (1975)
2. Greenberg, J., Pyszczynski, T., Solomon, S.: The causes and consequences of a need for self-esteem: A Terror Management Theory. In: Baumeister, R.F. (ed.) Public Self and Private Self, pp. 189–212. Springer, New York (1986)
3. Pyszczynski, T., Greenberg, J., Koole, S., Solomon, S.: Experimental existential psychology: Coping with the facts of life. In: Fiske, S., Gilbert, D.T., Gardner, L. (eds.) Handbook of Social Psychology, pp. 720–825. McGraw-Hill, New York (2009)
4. Castano, E., Yzerbyt, V., Paladino, P.M.: Transcending oneself through social identification. In: Greenberg, J., Koole, S., Pyszczynski, T. (eds.) Experimental Existential Psychology, pp. 305–321. The Guilford Press, London (2004)
5. Tajfel, H., Turner, J.C.: An integrative theory of intergroup conflict. In: Worchel, S., Austin, W.G. (eds.) The Social Psychology of Intergroup Relations, pp. 33–47. Brooks-Cole, Monterey (1979)
6. Burke, B.L., Martens, A., Faucher, E.H.: Two decades of terror management theory: a meta-analysis of mortality salience research. Personal. Soc. Psychol. Rev. 14, 155–195 (2010)
7. "CmdrTaco" Malda, R.: The Internet and the secret to immortality. The Washington Post (May 23, 2012)
8. Bessière, K., Seay, F., Kiesler, S.: The ideal elf: identity exploration in World of Warcraft. Cyberpsychol. Behav. 10, 530–535 (2007)
9. Cole, H., Griffiths, M.: Social interactions in massively multiplayer online role-playing gamers. Cyberpsychology Behav. Behav. 10, 575–583 (2007)
10. Blascovich, J., Bailenson, J.: Infinite Reality: Avatars, Eternal life, new worlds and the dawn of the virtual revolution. Harper Collins, New York (2011)
11. Higgin, T.: Blackless Fantasy: The disappearance of race in massively multiplayer online role-playing games. Games Cult. 4, 3–26 (2008)
12. Dietrich, D.R.: Avatars of Whiteness: Racial expression in video game characters. Sociol. Inq. 83, 82–105 (2013)
13. Lee, R.J.: Does virtual diversity matter?: Effects of avatar-based diversity representation on willingness to express offline racial identity. In: 63rd Annual Meeting of the International Communication Association. International Communication Association, London (2013)
14. Guadagno, R.E., Muscanell, N.L., Okdie, B.M., Burk, N.M., Ward, T.B.: Even in virtual environments women shop and men build: A social role perspective on Second Life. Comput. Human Behav. 27, 304–308 (2011)
15. Van Looy, J., Courtois, C., De Vocht, M., De Marez, L.: Player identification in online games: Validation of a scale for measuring identification in MMOGs. Media Psychol. 15, 197–221 (2012)
16. Yee, N., Bailenson, J.: The Proteus effect: The effect of transformed self-representation on behavior. Hum. Commun. Res. 33, 271–290 (2007)

17. Arndt, J., Greenberg, J., Schimel, J., Pyszczynski, T., Solomon, S.: To belong or not to belong, that is the question: Terror management and identification with gender and ethnicity. J. Pers. Soc. Psychol. 83, 26–43 (2002)
18. Dechesne, M., Greenberg, J., Arndt, J., Schimel, J.: Terror management and the vicissitudes of sports fan affiliation: the effects of mortality salience on optimism and fan identification. Eur. J. Soc. Psychol. 835, 813–836 (2000)
19. Branscombe, N.R., Fernández, S., Gómez, A., Cronin, T.: Moving toward or away from a group identity: Different strategies for coping with pervasive discrimination. In: Jetten, J., Haslam, C., Haslam, A.S. (eds.) The Social Cure: Identity, Health and Well-being, pp. 115–131. Psychology Press, New York (2012)
20. Pyszczynski, T., Greenberg, J., Solomon, S.: Why do we need what we need. Psychol. Inq. 8, 1–20 (1997)
21. Castano, E., Yzerbyt, V., Paladino, M.P., Sacchi, S.: I belong, therefore, I exist: Ingroup identification, ingroup entitativity, and ingroup bias. Personal. Soc. Psychol. Bull. 28, 135–143 (2002)
22. Castano, E.: In case of death, cling to the ingroup. Eur. J. Soc. Psychol. 384, 375–384 (2004)
23. Festinger, L.: A theory of social comparison processes. Hum. Relations 7, 117–140 (1954)
24. Greenberg, J., Simon, L., Harmon-Jones, E., Solomon, S., Pyszczynski, T., Lyon, D.: Testing alternative explanations for mortality salience effects and Terror management, value accessibility, or worrisome thoughts? Eur. J. Soc. Psychol. 25, 417–433 (1995)
25. Friese, M., Hofmann, W.: What would you have as a last supper? Thoughts about death influence evaluation and consumption of food products. J. Exp. Soc. Psychol. 44, 1388–1394 (2008)
26. Jonas, E., Schimel, J., Greenberg, J., Pyszczynski, T.: The scrooge effect: Evidence that mortality salience increases prosocial attitudes and behavior. Personal. Soc. Psychol. Bull. 28, 1342–1353 (2002)
27. Greenberg, J., Pyszczynski, T., Solomon, S., Rosenblatt, A., Veeder, M., Kirkland, S.: Evidence for Terror Management theory II: The effects of mortality salience on reactions to those who threaten or bolster the cultural worldview. J. Pers. Soc. Psychol. 58, 308–318 (1990)
28. Greenberg, J., Schimel, J., Martens, A., Solomon, S.: Sympathy for the devil: Evidence that reminding Whites of their mortality promotes more favorable reactions to white racists. The Journal is Motivation and Emotion 25, 113–133 (2001)
29. Ellemers, N., Spears, R., Doosje, B.: Sticking together of falling apart: In-group identification as a psychological determinant of group commitment versus individual mobility. J. Pers. Soc. Psychol. 72, 617–626 (1997)
30. Schroeder, R.: The Social Life of Avatars: Presence and Interaction in Shared Virtual Environments. Springer, London (2002)
31. Turkay, S., Adinolf, S.: Free to be me: A survey study on customization with World of Warcraft and City of Heroes/Villains players. Procedia - Soc. Behav. Sci. 2, 1840–1845 (2010)
32. Turkle, S.: Constructions and reconstructions of self in virtual reality: Playing in the MUDs. Mind, Cult. Act. 1, 158–167 (1994)
33. Przybylski, A.K., Weinstein, N., Murayama, K., Lynch, M.F., Ryan, R.M.: The ideal self at play: The appeal of video games that let you be all you can be. Psychol. Sci. 23, 69–76 (2012)
34. Higgins, E.T.: Self-discrepancy: A theory relating self and affect. Psychol. Rev. 94, 319–340 (1987)

35. Kim, Y., Sundar, S.S.: Visualizing ideal self vs. actual self through avatars: Impact on preventive health outcomes. Comput. Human Behav. 28, 1356–1364 (2012)
36. Bem, D.J.: Self-Perception Theory. In: Berkowitz, L. (ed.) Advances in Experimental Social Psychology, 6th edn., pp. 2–57. Academic Press Inc., New York (1972)
37. Reynolds, K.J., Turner, J.C., Haslam, S.A., Ryan, M.K.: The role of personality and group Factors in explaining prejudice. J. Exp. Soc. Psychol. 37, 427–434 (2001)
38. Postmes, T., Spears, R., Lea, M.: Breaching or building social boundaries SIDE effects of computer-mediated communication. Communi. 26, 689–715 (1998)
39. Trepte, S., Reinecke, L.: Avatar creation and video game enjoyment and identification with the avatar. Media Psychol. 22, 171–184 (2010)
40. Vasalou, A., Joinson, A.N.: Me, myself and I: The role of interactional context on self-presentation through avatars. Comput. Human Behav. 25, 510–520 (2009)
41. Nass, C., Moon, Y.: Machines and mindlessness: Social responses to computers. J. Soc. Issues 56, 81–103 (2000)
42. Schilbach, L., Wohlschlaeger, A.M., Kraemer, N.C., Newen, A., Shah, N.J., Fink, G.R., Vogeley, K.: Being with virtual others: Neural correlates of social interaction. Neuropsychologia 44, 718–730 (2006)
43. Bente, G., Dratsch, T., Rehbach, S., Reyl, M., Lushaj, B.: Do you trust my avatar? Influence of seller avatars on trust in online transactions. In: 63rd Annual Meeting of the International Communication Association (ICA). International Communication Association, London (2013)
44. Bailenson, J.N., Blascovich, J., Beall, A.C., Loomis, J.M.: Equilibrium theory revisited: Mutual gaze and personal space in virtual environments. Presence Teleoperators Virtual Environ. 10, 583–598 (2001)
45. Nass, C., Fogg, B.J., Moon, Y.: Can computers be teammates? Int. J. Hum. Comput. Stud. 45, 669–678 (1996)
46. Williams, D., Martins, N., Consalvo, M., Ivory, J.D.: The virtual census: representations of gender, race and age in video games. New Media Soc. 11, 815–834 (2009)
47. Kafai, Y.B., Cook, M.S., Fields, D.: Blacks Deserve Bodies Too!": Design and discussion about diversity and race in a tween virtual world. Games Cult. 5, 43–63 (2009)
48. Groom, V., Bailenson, J.N., Nass, C.: he influence of racial embodiment on racial bias in immersive virtual environments. Soc. Influ. 4(3), 231–248 (2009)
49. Rusche, S.E., Brewster, Z.W.: Because they tip for shit!': The social psychology of everyday racism in restaurants- Sociol. Compass 2, 2008–2029 (2008)
50. The Sims Studio: Sims 3. EA games (2009)
51. Frischlich, L., Rieger, D., Dratsch, T., Bente, G.: Meet Joe Black? The effects of mortality salience and similarity on the desire to date in-group versus out-group members online. J. Soc. Pers. Relationships (in press)
52. Rosenblatt, A., Greenberg, J., Solomon, S., Pyszczynski, T., Lyon, D.: Evidence for terror management theory: I. The effects of mortality salience on reactions to those who violate or uphold cultural values. J. Pers. Soc. Psychol. 57, 681–690 (1989)
53. Pyszczynski, T., Greenberg, J., Solomon, S.: A dual-process model of defense against conscious and unconscious death-related thoughts: An extension of Terror Management theory. Psychol. Rev. 106, 835–845 (1999)
54. Mitterschiffthaler, M.T., Fu, C.H.Y., Dalton, J.A., Andrew, C.M., Williams, S.C.R.: A functional MRI study of happy and sad affective states induced by classical music. Hum. Brain Mapp. 28, 1150–1162 (2007)

55. Dechesne, M., Janssen, J., van Knippenberg, A.: Derogation and distancing as terror management strategies: The moderating role of need for closure and permeability of group boundaries. J. Pers. Soc. Psychol. 79, 923–932 (2000)
56. Rieger, D., Frischlich, L., Wulf, T., Bente, G., Kneer, J.: Eating ghosts: The underlying mechanisms of mood repair via interactive and non-interactive media. Psychol. Pop. Media Cult. (2014)
57. Wulf, T., Rieger, D., Bente, G.: The winner takes it all: The effect of in-game success on mood-repair. In: 64th Annual Meeting of the International Communication Association (ICA). International Communication Association, Seattle (2014)
58. King, M.F., Bruner, G.C.: Social desirability bias: A neglected aspect of validity testing. Psychol. Mark. 17, 79–103 (2000)
59. Fifa 14. EA games (2013)

Extended Episodic Experience in Social Mediating Technology: Our Legacy

Haliyana Khalid[1] and Alan Dix[2]

[1] Putra Business School,University Putra Malaysia
[2] Talis and University of Birmingham
haliyana@putrabs.edu.my, alanhcibook.com

Abstract. Drawing from an online survey and a focus group study, we extend the concept of the extended episodic experience to include truly long-term interaction. As our life is still unfolding, we leave many legacies in the flow; both printed and more subtle. Although much effort is being made to preserve digital legacy in online space, we also need to look into the subtle legacy that is equally important in the long-term experience. This subtle legacy is untouchable and often forgotten but it follows us till the very end. Our concern on the consequences of this legacy has led us to suggest the need to design for virtue.

Keywords: extended episodic experience, long-term interaction, digital legacy, virtues.

1 Introduction

The way we use social media is changing. The technology allows new forms of control, encouraging new forms of social interaction, promoting certain values while discouraging other values. Crucially, the technology was often not designed for its current use in the first instance but has been repurposed [1, 2] by its users to satisfy their evolving needs.

To date many researchers are working on imparting human values in their research and design. This is not just about improving usability and effectiveness of interaction design but more on thinking how moral and ethical values are affecting certain parties upon whom the technologies are being implemented [3, 4]

Our concept of extended episodic experience was developed to understand the emotional and human values implicit in long-term interactions, and we hope can also a means to promote positive values. Extended episodic experience or EEE is defined as a long-term experience that combines multiple individual experiences that happen at different times and places. Each individual experience, which we call an episode, involves reflection, perception, awareness and emotions. The concept was defined from our study on user experience in photologging. Although the study has focused on photologs, we believe the knowledge could be applied in other social applications such as Facebook. There are three aspects that allow experience in Facebook to become a long-term experience as mentioned in [5]. Every action in Facebook has its direct and reflective effect, often influenced by our mood; is motivated by our offline communication and interactions in other domains; and lasts until the very end.

G. Meiselwitz (Ed.): SCSM 2014, LNCS 8531, pp. 452–461, 2014.
© Springer International Publishing Switzerland 2014

In a recent development, we are trying to understand user social interactions and their legacy in social mediating technology. For most of us, Facebook has become a place to meet, socialise, share our thoughts and preserve our memories. But as we all rely heavily on the social media for our day-to-day interactions, what will happen if we stop using the application, or it suddenly disappears? And what will happen to people who rely on us for information, for making connections and preserving our personal histories? What will happen to the flow of the long term-experience? How does our interaction today affected our future life including the hereafter? And what happens if a person dies? Will their legacy remain in the sites or shall we delete the data to respect the deceased?

Legacy is something precious that we leave behind. In today's world, our legacy also constitutes the digital print that we leave in the social media. There have been some cases where families dealing with death are using Facebook for handling public rituals and memorialisation. However, due to some restriction and websites rules, this case is never straightforward. Different social media have their own processes, but this is usually unclear or not made apparent to the public. Thus, it is not a surprise to see a lot of people still do not know what will happen to their content after they die and who will keep their digital legacy.

Social media is an important 'place' for many, not merely a 'space', but invested with social meaning [6], for example, Facebook, which is often the locus for extensive interaction and sharing personal content. The application has become a place to some people, because of their ongoing interaction, purpose and meaning. Outside social media, we hire advisers to write our will in order to protect our legacy; money and properties. Information, personal treasures in social media are also our property, but are kept by strangers. Creating awareness about the importance of these treasures and providing means to support them is very crucial as more and more data are being shared online. To date there has been some research in managing post-mortem data [7], [8], [9]. Although having a tool is very important, the awareness of the importance of managing the digital legacy is significance too. Thus, in this research we hope to contribute to the growing literature on managing post mortem data from the Malaysian perspective. Data has been sought from an online questionnaire from 104 respondents from students and staff of a private institution in Malaysia.

However, this initial study, in common with similar studies by others, only considers 'tangible content' such as photographs, notes and also status published in the user account as the digital legacy. In this paper, we also consider another digital legacy that we think is important to be highlighted. We discuss the intangible features that are the accumulation of actions that we perform in our interaction in the space, the feelings and emotions that we had and the thoughts and perception that we had for others in our interaction. In EEE flow, our content might stay in the space, but its implication will stay with us until the very end.

To have a deeper understanding on the second issue presented in this paper, a focus group was used for data collection. In terms of data analysis process, we used online statistical software to analyse data from the survey and network thematic analysis for data from the focus group.

The paper is structured as follows: after this Introduction, we present some related work on the main issues. The research methodology is described in Section 3. In

Section 4, findings on the survey is presented and discussed. We discuss findings on focus group in Section 5. Finally, we offer some conclusions and future work.

2   Related Works

In HCI, the work on digital legacy and its 'life after death' are slowly gaining its momentum. Massimi, Odum et, al [10], discusses research ethics, methods and design consideration for death and dying. Their approach is called thanatosensitive design [11] that also suggests there are 4 stakeholders (bereaved, dead, dying and in living) that need to be considered in research end of life in Lifespan. To date, there are many applications and websites developed to preserve the digital legacy of the dead such as My Wonderful Life [12], Kathryn [13], Legacy Locker [14] and some have repurposed Facebook page for obituaries and memorilization [15].

Maciel and Pereira [7] try to understand how user's religiosity could help in designing digital legacy systems. They study a sample population of youngsters in Brazil who prefers to have some flexibility to configure their account in order to manage their digital legacy. Other work on techno-spiritual [16] also has touched on preserving personal memories.

3   Research Methodology

This research is conducted in two stages. The first stage is to understand users' digital legacy and their plans for post-mortem data management. This was done through an online survey that was sent out randomly to 120 students and employees in a private institution in Malaysia. The questions are 17 open and close questions, which was divided into demographic information, Facebook activity and usage and their planning for post mortem.

In order to have a deeper understanding on user experience interacting in Facebook, a focus group was conducted. The focus group was chosen as the method because it provides different insights from different participants in a discussion. We also can observe their emotional reactions when discussing certain issues. Participants were recruited through email. 20 participants agreed to participate; all of them are Malay and Muslims. The age of the participants ranges from 20 years old to 45 years old. Data from the online survey was analysed using web based statistical software whilst we used network thematic analysis to analyse data from the focus group.

4   Findings from Online Questionnaire

4.1   Demographic Information

A set of online questionnaire was given randomly to 120 respondents. From this figure, only 104 replied to the questionnaire. It contains a total of six variables, which include gender, age, occupation, citizenship, race and marital status. Among the 104 respondents who participated in the survey 36% are male and 64 % are female. The result also indicates that most of the respondents are in the age range of 21 to 29, which represent 77.7% of the total sample. The second highest are respondents between the range of 18 to 20 which represent 29% of the total sample followed by respondents between the range of 30 to 39 which represent 16% of the total sample. Based on the respondents, 94% are Malaysian while 6% are foreigners. From the total number, 62% are single while 38% are married. The respondents are coming from diverse ethnicity, with Malay 48%, Chinese 35%, Indian 8% and other races 10%.

4.2   Facebook Usage

74% of the respondents have subscribed to Facebook for more than 3 years, 19% for between 1-2 years while 2% for less than 5 months. 78% of the respondents access Facebook everyday, 12% in 2-3 times a week and 4% of the respondents access the application once a week.

The respondents also were asked how they access their Facebook account. Based from the total number of respondents, 61% access their Facebook account using mobile phones, 32% using laptop and PC and 7% using other devices.

4.3   Facebook Password

Accessing Facebook through a mobile phone requires people to log in every time they access it. Thus, we are intrigued to know if they still remember their password after some period of time. 95% of our respondents remember their password while 5% did not remember. 88% from the total number of respondents said that they did not share their password with other people, while 9% did share it with their spouse and 1% with their mother, 1% with fiancé, 1% with their children and best friend respectively.

85% of the respondents did not keep their password somewhere else while 15% wrote it in their diary, notes in mobile phone and email. Most of them are protective of their Facebook and do not allow anybody else to have access to their account. This is evidence by the figure that shows 84% did not give any access to anybody, while some married couples share the access with their spouse (11%) and other respondents share the access with their parents (1%), children (1%), mother (1%) and finance (2%).

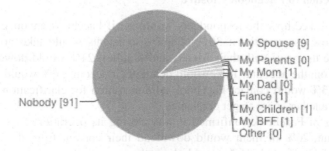

Fig. 1. Who else remembers your password?

4.4   Who Will Managed Their Account When They Die

To date we have seen that many Facebook accounts belong to someone who has already died. The question is who is keeping this account for them? We have asked the respondents about their plans with their Facebook account if they die. 64% of the respondents said they have not considered anyone to look after their account, 25% are not sure and 12% thought that their family members would look after the account.

4.5   Do They Want Their Account to Be Deleted?

61% of the respondents wanted their account to be deleted by if they passed away, 17% wanted the account to be remained and 22% of the respondent said they are not sure.

4.6   Any Idea about Post Mortem Data Management by Facebook Administration

If they passed away, 85% of them did not know what will happened to their Facebook content while 15% think that the content will stay there until someone deleted them.

4.7   Activity in Facebook

They were asked about their three most active activities in Facebook. The three most active activities in Facebook by the 104 respondents are commenting, sharing photographs with others and like other people's upload.

4.8   Consequences of Action

Of those who responded, 98% believe that their Facebook interactions do in fact have consequences. This may stem from their upbringing, cultural experiences or religions- we cannot know with certainty why they believe as they do.

4.9   Reaction to Facebook Closure

The survey asked how the respondents would act if Facebook announced that it had plans to close its operations; 30% of the respondents would take no action, 28% would share the news with their friends and families, 21% would download all their materials from the account, 11% would delete their account, 6% would write a status about this, 3% would contact Facebook administration for clarification and only 2% would find another space to get connected.

However, if Facebook confirmed it was closing its operation, 31% would delete their account, 26% of them would download their content from the account, 19% would not feel affected, 16% would share the news with friends and families, 6% would find a new space immediately and 2% of them would upload a status regarding the matter.

5   Findings from Focus Group

As mentioned earlier in Section 3, the focus group method was chosen because we wanted to have a deeper understanding on user perceptions and their experience interacting in Facebook. Other studies on social interaction in Facebook have used other methods such as in-depth interview and online observation.

The focus group consisted of 20 respondents. The respondents were divided into two groups. Each group was coordinated by one moderator. The focus groups were audio taped and photographed. The study was divided into two sessions. The groups were given a picture (Fig. 2) that illustrates an individual experience and interaction when trying to post a picture on Facebook. In the first session they were asked to discuss about the picture.

In the second session, they were asked to discuss this question:

> *"Sharing our personal legacy in Facebook is a big responsibility.*
> *What are your opinions?"*

The two questions related to each other. Information was recorded, transcribed and analyzed using thematic network analysis (see Section 3 for further info). In the following we explain findings from the focus group.

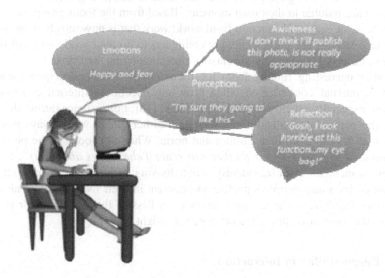

Fig. 2. User interaction in posting photographs

5.1   User Perception and Their Legacy

When publishing content in Facebook, participants are usually conscious and aware of their audiences and their reaction, thus performing accordingly to suit the norm and standard that will be accepted by their audience. For instance, in sharing photographs, their past experience on reflecting on their own photographs in Facebook and viewing others' photographs, contributes to their decision of what kind of photographs are suitable for their personality, lifestyles and also expectations of visitors.

When posting status, respondents are involved in task attention and self-attention. Task attention is giving attention to the task that is choosing the right words to form the sentences. It can take a few minutes before they satisfied with their 'work' and press the button 'publish'. In the case of publishing photographs, participants did some screening before publishing. Browsing and screening their photographs before deciding what to upload involves reflecting on their experience, their culture and norms, and responsibilities towards their friends and families. Some of the participants are afraid that they will get negative feedback from their audiences, whilst others think that they are not concerned about people's criticism because it is their wall. The common view amongst this group is *"this is my wall, it is up to me what I want to share, people can say anything about it"*.

Participants interact with many people. Their personality is not static but a dynamic and relational one. Goffman suggested people construct their identity through a region in which the parties reveal personal information selectively according to their relationship and tacit moral code. He suggests in everyday life, we are 'the performer', 'the pretentious', 'the motivator and the actor'; which have stories to conceal and unhide [17]. Our interaction is fluid and dynamic based on situational and relational factors. The activity of browsing Facebook is usually done alone; giving them a lot of freedom to explore and indulge in their own moment. Based from the focus group, interacting in Facebook is one-way of distraction from work; work that is now mostly done in front of computers. Most of our participants use computers to do their work, and will find interacting in Facebook as one way of relaxing after completing their tasks.

Another interesting finding from the focus group is that participants always involved in internal conversation when browsing Facebook. Internal conversation is common, especially when we are alone or silent [18]. For instance during the session, one of the participants talked about members of her clique who always post photographs that deviate from their culture and norm. When she looks at the photographs, she thinks, *"I wonder how her mother will react if she knows about this"*. Some participants sometimes criticize silently when looking at strangers' photographs. The freedom of browsing people's profile and content in their own time and alone gives them more freedom to express themselves regardless of the fact that their perception or internal conversation about the other people might be wrong.

5.2   Responsibility in Interaction

Some thought interaction in social media such as Facebook is a leisure activity. Other participants thought it is a form of self-exhibitionist. Although this perception might be true, nonetheless, everyone agrees it comes with a big responsibility. Unconsciously, they hold a responsibility to supply their friends, family even strangers with updates; sharing valuable information, sharing photographs or even showing some support through the button 'Like'. In Goffman's Face-Work [19], he describes how one may expect to find an understanding on how to save someone's face and his own in his social circle.

All of our respondents are Muslims. They believe everything that they do in this world including interacting in Facebook have both moral and eternal consequences. Other religions such as Buddhism and Hinduism also believe in these consequences, which they defined as Karma [20. This finding echoed with our survey results that show 98% of the total respondents agree that their interaction in Facebook have its consequences Thus in our focus group, those who believed in Karma agree that they have to foster good relationship with others. They believe that their actions in Facebook will have effect in the hereafter. This also includes their feelings and emotional reaction towards certain issues, their misjudgment about others and things that they said about other people in Facebook and also offline communication. If they do good deeds, then they will be get a good reward and vice versa. Thus, some of them are cautious in their interaction in Facebook and the content that they shared in the application.

6   Discussions

Our relationship with technology is quite different now and expected to be more so in the future. Computers and humanity are inseparable giving new challenges to all designers to think of the best technologies to support our needs. However, as much as we want to create the best and most humane technology, understanding what it means to be human in a digital future must be better understood first.

It is evident from the focus group, that for many, the scope of design must now include virtues, not just values. In HCI, many designers have concentrated in fostering and supporting human values. Designers are not just focusing on improving usability and effectiveness of technology, but also weighing up various moral and social impacts to the affected parties whom the technology is being proposed [3].Thus, rather than focusing on values alone, designing for human today must also includes virtues.

In order to design for virtues, we must understand the meaning of being human [21]. Understanding what it means to be human will help us in designing application that help people better understand the purpose of their existence in this world. For many, both religious and secular, our human intelligence includes a focus on virtue: having a sense for others, reflecting on creation, hope, and wisdom, and for those with religious beliefs this may also include thinking about the Creator in everyday interaction and being spiritual. Some technology today, although not designed for virtue, has been repurposed by some of its user to help them in seeking virtue. Facebook for instance, allows for self-reflection. The application helps people to understand themselves and others through social interaction and things that we shared inside. The application also has been repurposed as techno-spiritual tool [22] by some people to promote religious practice to the public. In this multicultural world, it is acknowledged that our views on virtues can be diverse. Thus future research needs to address this concept first before we can emphasize designing for virtues.

Designing for virtues is very important especially to people who believe that our actions in this world will affect us in the hereafter. Sigmund Freud suggests that *"the aim of life is death"* [23]. It is interesting to note that this Western scholar would consider death to bear such influence upon human behavior in the world. This is also true in Islam that believes the world is the bridge to the hereafter. Discussing about death and life after death can be a bit taboo for some of us, but there is a growing interests about it in HCI as we are accommodating the evolving needs of people, where we need to consider all aspects (physical, psychological, sociological, spiritual etc.).

7   Conclusion

We are extending our ideas on the extended episodic experience concept to include truly long-term interaction. Our life has many episodes; coming and passing; still unfolding. In our long-term experience, we leave many legacies, some in clear digital content and some more subtle ones. In this paper, we highlight virtues in our findings. Interacting in Facebook is seen as a leisure activity but it comes with a big responsibility. This responsibility is not only being cautious about the content that we publish but also the actions and the hidden interactions that we had in our heart. All these accumulate and influence our long term experience, and as the paper reveals, it lasts until the very end.

References

1. Carroll, J., Howard, S., Velere, F., et al.: Just what do the youth of today want? Technology appropriation by young people. In: The Proceedings of the 35th Hawaii International Conference on System Science (2002)
2. Mackay, H., Gillespie, G.: Extending the Social Shaping of Technology Approach: Ideology and Appropriation. Social Studies of Science (1992)
3. Harper, R., Rodden, T., Rogers, Y.: Being Human; Human Computer Interaction in 2020. Microsoft Research (2008)
4. Friedman, B.: Human values and the design of computer technology. Cambridge University Press (1997)
5. Khalid, H., Dix, A.: The experience of photologging: global mechanisms and local interactions. The Personal and Ubiquitous Computing 14(3), 209–226 (2010)
6. Harrison, S., Dourish, P.: Re-place-ing space: the roles of place and space in collaborative systems. In: The Proceeding of CSCW 1996 of the 1996 ACM Conference on Computer Supported Cooperative Work (1996)
7. Maciel, C., Pereira, V.: Digital Legacy and Interaction. Springer (2013)
8. Carrol, E., Romano, J.: Your Digital Afterlife. New Riders, Berkeley (2011)
9. Forever Missed, http://www.forvermissed.com/
10. Massimi, M., Odom, W., et al.: Matter of Life and Death: Locating the End of Life in Lifespan-Oriented HCI Research. In: The Proceedings of CHI 2011, Vancouver, BC, Canada (2011)
11. Massimi, M., Charise, A.: Dying, death and mortality: towards thanatosensitivity in HCI. In: The Proceedings CHI Extended Abstract. ACM (2009)
12. MyWonderfulLife, https://mywonderfulllife.com
13. Kathryn, http://Kathryn.org
14. Legacy Locker, http://legacylocker.com

15. https://www.facebook.com/washpostobits
16. Wyche, S., Hayes, G., et al.: Technology in spiritual formation: an exploratory study of computer mediated religious communications. In: The Proceeding of CSCW 2006, New York, USA (2006)
17. Goffman, E.: The Presentation of Self in Everyday Life, Anchor (1959)
18. Archer
19. Goffman, E.: Interaction Ritual- Face to Face Behaviour. Pantheon (1982)
20. Karma, http://www.buddhanet.net/e-learning/karma.htm
21. Salleh, A., Ahmad, A.: Human Governance, A Paradigm Shift in Governing Corporations. MPH Publication (2008)
22. Ahmad, N.H., Abdul Razak, F.H.: On The Emergence of Techno-Spiritual: The Concept and Current Issues. In: The Computer and Mathematical Sciences Graduate National Colloquium (SISKOM 2013) (2013)
23. Freud, S.: Beyond the pleasure principle. In: Penguin Freud Library, vol. 11, Strache, J.

Reinterpret 3G Emoticons from a Persona Theory

Minseo Kim, Chungkon Shi, and Jeounghoon Kim

Graduate School of Culture Technology, KAIST (Korea Advanced Institute of Science & Technology), 291 Daehak-ro, Yuseong-gu, Daejeon 305-701, Republic of Korea
{artmin,chungkon,miru}@kaist.ac.kr

Abstract. As the use of Instant message service increased, emoticons also have been changed and developed in various forms. Especially, 3rd-generation (3G) emoticons are being spotlighted as new communicative tools because they provide wide selection of choice through vividly personified characters. To reflect this trend, this study formulated and confirmed a hypothesis that the more emoticons are personified and sophisticated, the more people tend to regard emoticons as persona. And to prove it, we follow three steps: 1) we account the definition and characteristics of 3G emoticons; 2) we examine whether 3G emoticons reflect people's social personality by adopting Five-Factor Model; 3) based on a great deal of research that has revealed gender differences during real conversations, we analyzed gender differences in 3G emoticons usage through self-report questionnaire. As a result, we verified that people recognized 3G emoticons as kinds of their' persona rather than just tools to facilitate conversations.

Keywords: Emoticons, Five Factor Model (FFM), Gender difference, Computer-mediated Communication (CMC), Instant Message Service (IMS).

1   Introduction

As instant message service (IMS) like Kakao Talk, Line, and MyPeople released PC version at the end of last year, instant message service finally do away with limited mobile environment and expand their services in the whole online. The rise of instant message service is threatening NATE ON, which has monopolized in the past ten years, and has the biggest influence on computer-mediated communication (CMC). According to the study of Korea Internet Security Agency, the number of subscribers to the instant message service estimated that more than 380 million people (i.e., 89.2% of the total smartphone users) as of October. 2013 [1]. This remarkable growth has fueled a burgeoning market for emoticons, and the emoticons now being used as core tool in computer-mediated communication. In particular, 3rd generation (3G) emoticons have attributes of human and particular characters because 3G emoticons are designed to resemble human, unlike 1st generation (1G) and 2nd generation (2G) emoticons. For this reason, many people can utilize 3G emoticons to suit their preferences as well as trend. Accordingly, we assumed that 3G emoticons could be used as evaluation criteria for people's social personality.

G. Meiselwitz (Ed.): SCSM 2014, LNCS 8531, pp. 462–473, 2014.
© Springer International Publishing Switzerland 2014

In this paper, we will present and verify three questions with regard to 3G emoticons. First, there has been little discussion about 3G emoticons so far, even though 3G emoticons basically differ from 1G and 2G emoticons. This study, therefore, tries to account the definition and characteristics of 3G emoticons. Second, we examined whether 3G emoticons reflect people's social personality by adopting Five-factor model (FFM). Third, based on a great deal of research that has revealed gender differences during real conversations, we analyzed gender differences in 3G emoticons usage through self-questionnaire method. To sum up, if individual personalities and gender differences are obviously observed in usage patterns of 3G emoticons, can we regard that 3G emoticons reflects people's social self? And can we consider that 3G emoticons are working as a persona? This study, therefore, formulated and confirmed that the more emoticons are personified and sophisticated, the more people tend to regard emoticons as persona.

2   Background and Previous works

2.1   Computer-Mediated Communication and Instant Message

Computer-mediated communication is defined as any communication that occurs through the use of two or more electronic devices, and refers to a cluster of interpersonal communication systems used for conveying written text over the Internet. Generally speaking, the two major parameters across which types of computer-mediated communication most significantly differ are first, whether they are synchronous or asynchronous (i.e., whether or not transmission is essentially instantaneous and interlocutors are assumed to be physically present to read messages and respond to them) and second, whether the communication is one-to-one (i.e., between two people) or one-to-many (i.e., one person's message is broadcast to multiple potential interlocutors) [2]. Instant message, especially, come under one-to-one and synchronous forms because instant messenger is based upon a premise that interlocutors already know one another and communicate with their cell phones in real-time. In view of this, IMS is stronger than other computer-mediated communication forms in respect of private matter, and optimized for comfortable conversation through high-connectivity. Hence, we focused on the study of instant message service, which will provide the examination of reported events and experiences in their natural, spontaneous context, providing information complementary to that obtainable by more traditional designs [3].

2.2   Non-Verbal Communication and Emoticon

A central issue in the research about computer-mediated communication is whether and how the social meaning of interactions is affected by the absence of nonverbal cues when communicators substitute text-based electronic messaging for face-to-face encounters [4-7]. And there have been numerous studies showing that computer-mediated communication lacks nonverbal communication cues and prevents the conveyance of emotions and attitudes to receivers. In addition, research from Lee and Wagner (2002) shows that people express more emotions in positive social contexts than in negative social contexts, and use more emoticons in socio-emotional contexts than in task-oriented contexts. To sum these studies, it is clear that emoticons allow receivers to correctly understand the level and direction of emotion, attitude, and expression of attention. However, because previous studies used 1G and 2G emoticons for their experiment, those results cannot reflect 3G emoticons in the present. On that score, this paper will examine whether 3G emoticons perform non-verbal communication functions like previous emoticons.

2.3   Personality and Gender difference through Five-Factor Model

As a core aspect of personality, Five-factor model (FFM) has gained widespread acceptance among personality psychologists [8-11]. Much of what psychologists mean by the term "personality" has summarized by the Five-factor model, and the model has been of great utility to the field by integrating and systematizing diverse conceptions and measures [10]. For decades, researchers also have used various research paradigms to examine the relationship between the five-factor model dimensions and gender differences. According to past studies, female are more likely to thank, appreciate, apologize, and to be upset by violations of politeness: they more often challenge offenders who violate online rules of conduct [13-15]. In contrast, male generally appear to be less concerned with politeness; they issue bald face-threatening acts such as criticisms and insults, violate online rules of conduct, tolerate or even enjoy "flaming," and tend to be more concerned about threats to freedom of expression than with attending to others' social face [16-17]. As well, females more likely to qualify and justify their assertions, express support of others, and in general, manifest an 'aligned' orientation towards their interlocutors [13][18-21]. But males sometimes adopt an adversarial style even in cooperative exchanges while females often appear to be in agreement even when they disagree with one another, suggesting that these behaviors are conventionalized, rather than inherent character traits based on biological sex. Finally, males and females tend to participate more equally in chat environments, both in terms of number of messages and average message length [14]. On average, response rates to males and females are also more balanced [20-21]. In spite of these findings, however, little research has directly addressed that individual personality and gender difference are reflected in the emoticons usage. In consequence, this study will survey whether personality and gender difference appear in the emoticon usage by using Five-factor model.

3   3rd Generation Emoticons

Emoticon, also known as smiley, is derived from the hybrid of "emotion" and "icons", and is either composed of punctuation characters or of graphical symbols [14]. Emoticons are generally described as important tool, which implement nonverbal communication in computer-mediated communication. As online interactions lack the non-verbal behaviors like facial expressions and body gestures vital to expressing opinions and attitudes, emoticons were introduced to fill a void in online communication [22]. Nonverbal behavior in face-to-face communication may serve three basic functions: (a) providing information; (b) regulating interaction; and (c) expressing intimacy. And, emoticons can, at least partially, serve the same functions in computer-mediated communication [23-24]. Since emoticons may serve as nonverbal surrogates, suggestive of facial expression, they may add a paralinguistic component to a message. Emoticons may thus enhance the exchange of social information by providing additional social cues beyond what is found in the text of a message [25]. Computer-mediated communication users often incorporate emoticons as visual cues to augment the meaning of textual electronic messages [26]. That is to say, the fact that emoticons are used, implies that individuals at least feel the need to express some of their emotions with simple symbols rather than text.

Fig. 1. (From left) 1G, 2G, 3G emoticons

Emoticons has been busy changing and evolving. The earliest emoticon, which is called 1st-generation (1G) emoticon, is nothing but a text form, as opposed to 2nd-generation (2G) emoticon has evolved into pictorial form by modeling the various expressions of human faces. But, 3rd-generation (3G) emoticon called flash-con or sticker, enables to express various feelings and depict specific situations because it reflects certain kind of attributes of human behavior and particular characters (Fig. 1). 3G emoticons thus encouraged greater freedom of expression by adding specific gesture and background, because of these aspect, many people can utilize it to suit their preferences as well as trend.

Another special feature is that the 3G emoticon's realistic characters allow people to identify with them. Actually, 3G emoticon's characters have gender, individual personalities, and even relationship because they are designed to be similar to a real person that has one's persona. These make it is easy for people to connect 3G emoticons and real people who are main characters in the popular TV drama or celebrities (Fig. 2). And, as the use of Instant message increased, these kinds of play have become widespread online. In this regard, this study assumes that 3G emoticon can be used as an evaluation criteria to measure people's social personality. Accordingly, we classified 3G emoticons on the basis of Five-factor model, and proved whether personality and gender difference appear in the use of 3G emoticons.

Fig. 2. (a) 3G emoticons featuring popular TV drama character (b) Matching between 3G emoticons and celebrities

4 Five-Factor Model

Five-factor Model (FFM) is a core model to understand personal taste or characteristics, and consists of five dimensions. The five dimensions can be described as follows: Extroversion (outgoing, physical-stimulation-oriented, assertive, energetic, talkative), Agreeableness (affable, friendly, conciliatory, cooperative, good-natured, trusting), Conscientiousness (dutiful, planned, organized, dependable, responsible, orderly), Neuroticism (emotionally reactive, prone to negative emotions, easily upset, maladjusted, not calm), Openness (inventive, curious, open to new ideas and change, imaginative, independent-minded, intellectual). These dimensions are related to a variety of important life outcomes [12]. For example, high conscientiousness predicts good work performance and good health while low agreeableness and high neuroticism are associated with poor health; high agreeableness is related to helping others;

Personality Dimension	High level	Low level
Extroversion		
Agreeableness		
Conscientiousness		
Neuroticism		
Openness		

Fig. 3. Categorized of 3G emoticons based on five-factor model

high extraversion predicts leadership; high neuroticism is associated with depression; and high openness is related to creativity [27-29]. Also, numerous meta-analytic studies using the five-factor model personality traits as an organizing framework have shown that personality traits are valid predictors of job performance for numerous criteria. In particular, conscientiousness, and to a lesser extent emotional stability, is the most consistent predictor across jobs and criteria [30-32].

Therefore, we categorized 3G emoticons according to five-factor dimensions, and each factor was divided into two levels on the authority of previous findings that five-factor model is generally clear to reveal personality (Fig. 3). Based on specialists' opinion investigation, extraversion contained emoticons with activity. Agreeableness covered emoticons that chime in with other, and openness involved many types of the positive reaction of changes. Also, conscientiousness included diligent emoticons, but in contrast, neuroticism included emoticons that showed negative or anger responses.

5   Methodology

We performed self-report questionnaire methodology to verify whether personality and gender differences appear in the usage pattern of 3G emoticons. We chose main instant message channels, which are LINE and Kakao Talk and used 11 emoticon sets (5 sets from Line, 6 sets from Kakao Talk) for experiments because too many emoticons can cause the ambiguity of standard as well as difficulty of the interpretations. First, self-report questionnaire for pilot test was done for three days on and offline, and total number of 42 participants commented on the questions. Second, personality and gender difference experiment were done for seven days online, and total number of 80 participants commented on the questions. Finally, we drew a conclusion through gathering and analyzing questionnaire results based on five-factor model.

5.1   Pilot Study

To keep current with trend in the general awareness about emoticons, we conducted a survey on 42 students   (30 male, 12 female). Questionnaire consists of two categories (personal information and usage pattern of emoticons) and total number of 13 questions. The questions were as follows, for instance. How often do you use instant message in a day? With whom do you usually exchange instant messages? What are the main reasons for using Instant Message? What are the main reasons for using emoticons? When using emoticons, do you feel vividly/friendly with other people? When do you mainly use emoticons? Do you think emoticons effect your image making? Do you have any emoticons that are most often used? What are the main reasons for using particular emoticons? Do you think emoticons reveal your character or personality? etc. There are thus some of the most frequently asked questions about the recognition of emoticons, and a few questions allow respondents to choose more than one choice.

As a result, first, both male and female equally responded that 3G emoticon is an important factor to help people represent their feelings or personality. Also, most of the participants said that 3G emoticons provided them with social presence and friendliness like in face-to-face conversation (average male: 88%, female: 92%). Second, the moment they use 3G emoticons, male and female showed different tendency. While male tend to use emoticons in the following order: Making jokes (24%), expressing joy (23%), and showing appreciation (19%), female used emoticons as follows: expressing joy (31%), Making jokes (18%), and expressing sadness (18%). This result showed that female are more likely to show high-level of neuroticism than male, and this is essentially in agreement with the previous study that showed female score higher on neuroticism than male. Finally, both male and female commented that they much used emoticons that is reflect their images and characters than others (male: 64%, female: 84%). In sum, these results highlight the fact that 3G emoticons provide tools to express self, emotional communication, formation of sympathy, and even social presence, which are generally revealed in face-to-face communication. And these facts suggest a new possibility that 3G emoticons can be interpreted as persona theory.

5.2   Main Study

The purpose of main study is to verify specifically that people recognized 3G emoticons as kinds of their persona. In order to do that, we conducted two surveys, 1) analyzing relationship between personality traits and the usage patterns of 3G emoticons; 2) examining whether gender differences appear in the usage patterns of 3G emoticons. On that account, we analyzed a correlation between five-factor dimension value and a corresponding tendency in 3G emoticons usage.

Procedure. We used data from 80 participants who are students and office workers (40 male, 40 female), and the age range is from 20 to 40 years old. Especially 25 to 35 year olds make up the majority of the participants (88% male, 80% female). To figure out how personality affects the usage of 3G emoticons, we followed three main steps. First, we used personality dimensions from 'A Korea Version of Big Five inventory (BFI-15)' [33]. The BFI-15 inventory consists of 15 items. Each question is associated to a Likert scale including five points ranging from 'strongly disagree' to 'strongly agree' which maps to the interval from one to five [34]. Second, we used self-questionnaire methodology to examine the usage patterns of 3G emoticons. The survey comprises   33 multiple-choice questions and each question has 4 choices, in which five-factor dimension and gender of emoticons were evenly distributed.

"Recently, I had a very strange experience!?"

Fig. 4. Example of survey question with four answer choices

For example, we asked people to respond to ambiguous sentence like "Recently, I had a very strange experience!" Within four choices, there are 1) neutral gender and neuroticism, 2) female and openness, 3) neuter gender, openness, and extroversion (Fig. 4). Finally, we compared BFI-15 results and questionnaire results, and drew the conclusion that 3G emoticons play important roles in computer-mediated communications.

Results

We made observations to test hypotheses that people who are outgoing and open to experience would be more favorable to use emoticons. To do deduction, we analyzed corresponding scores for each participant and categorized into three types, which considered valid range: more than three, roughly all, and degree of distribution (Fig. 5). As a result, we have found notable findings in the analysis as follows. First, female earned high score for matching personality dimension and tendency to use emoticons (60%), but in contrast, male got low score (22.5%). Second, only 5% of male applied than female (37.5%) in case of type 1. Second, female scored 15% unlike male scored 5% in type 2, and then female earned 7.5% similarity than 5% of male. Third, while people who high level of openness and agreeableness more used emoticon, people who are high in level of conscientiousness and neuroticism less used emoticons. Finally, the average distribution between personality dimension value and frequency of 3G emoticons usage also showed almost the same interval, and neuroticism especially more often used precise than others. In view of these facts, it is quite likely that people tend to use 3G emoticons to accommodate individual personality traits.

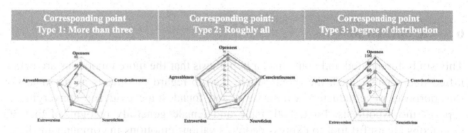

Fig. 5. Three types by corresponding point

Gender difference in emoticons usage also proposed a number of key issues. First, while male use emoticons most often to express teasing/sarcasm (50%), female use emoticons for expressing sympathy (50%) when consolation was required (Fig.6.a-b). Second, male showed the strong tendency not to use feminine emoticons unlike female freely used emoticons regardless of emoticons' gender. Third, female tended to report high neuroticism while talking to people in intimate people, and male were more likely to reveal neuroticism in public situations or to third person (80% male, 52.5% female) (Fig.6.c-d).   Fourth, both male and female did not use emoticons in serious conversations or when they could not precisely capture the feeling of interlocutor (45% male, 32.5% female). Particularly, male tended to respond to ambiguous sentences as negative actions; on the contrary, female did not (50% male, 7.5% female). Finally, male who respond 'not use emoticon' are about twice as many as female in most cases (66.7% male).

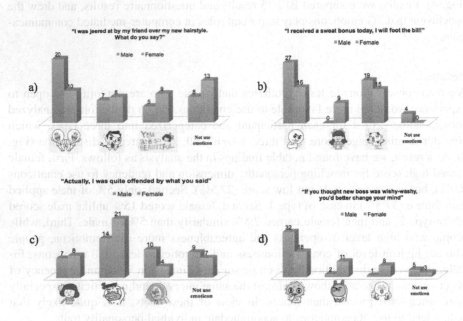

Fig. 6. Examples of gender difference in 3G emoticons usage

6   Conclusion

This study formulated and confirmed a hypothesis that the more emoticons are personified and sophisticated, the more people tend to regard emoticons as persona. For this purpose, we conducted two surveys, and found some evidence converging to support the hypothesis. First, both male and female generally recognized that 3G emoticons are useful tool to express people's various emotions in computer-mediated communication. Also, when using emoticons, many people tend to equate interlocutor with emoticons. Second, female earned high marks for matching personality dimension and tendency to use emoticons than male. And, the average distribution between personality dimension value and frequency of 3G emoticons usage also showed almost the same interval. This result implied that personality traits would influence the pattern of emoticon usage, or in other words, emoticons also would affect user's personality.

At first glance, the results of this study seem to reinforce the stereotype of the emotional female and the inexpressive male. However, there are noticeable distinctions between male and female in usage pattern of 3G emoticons. Mostly female more express feelings of sorrow than male, and male showed the strong tendency not to use feminine emoticons unlike female freely used emoticons regardless of emoticons' gender. This result was considered to be the cause that male were more encouraged to socialize with manly persona because gender difference normally includes gender pride, which often invokes binary gender stereotypes. Second, male tend to use more active and sarcastic emoticons, but in contrast, female tend not to use sarcastic or offensive emoticons. This result verified that female considered emotional stability as an important thing in relationship than female. Third, both male and female did not use emoticons in serious situations, even female used emoticons less often in appreciative situations. And, both male and female did not use emoticons when they could not precisely capture the feeling of interlocutor at the moment. This result implied that female tend to respond in earnest to other's appreciation because of their high-level agreeableness, and people want to use emoticons when they wants to appear approachable to unfamiliar people, or in casual situations.

This study verified that people recognized 3G emoticons as kinds of their persona, and reflection of personality and gender differences also is shown likewise real conversation. Also, this study presented that 3G emoticons are not just tools to facilitate conversations, and as more and more emoticons are personalized, people can assign them specific meanings and use them in specific contexts. Although further research is needed, this study is meaningful in terms of present, making it possible to interpret the 3G emoticons with Persona theory.

7   Discussion

Major difficulty of our study was the classification of 3G emoticons according to five-factor dimensions. Although we categorized 3G emoticons based on specialists' opinion investigation, problem of subjectivity still remains. We think that more consideration needs to be given to alternative methods. Second, this study will be additional survey like 'Participant observation method' because we could not control some variables that may be released in real conversations. Actually, relying on reported data may have an unintended impact on the dependent variable. Next study should include the case study of 3G emoticons usage in real conversation. Finally, future research involving the five-factor model and gender difference might determine the multivariate correlation of five-factor dimensions with 3G emotions, and test the ability of five-factor dimensions to predict people's usage patterns of 3G emoticons.

Acknowledgments. This research was supported by the Converging Research Center Program through the Ministry of Science, ICT and Future planning, Korea (2013K000333).

References

1. Korea Internet Security Agency. A Study of the utilization on the instant messenger by gender and age. Internet & Security Focus 11, 35–51 (2013)
2. Baron, N.S.: See you Online Gender Issues in College Student Use of Instant Messaging. Journal of Language and Social Psychology 23(4), 397–423 (2004)

3. Bolger, N., Davis, A., Rafaeli, E.: Diary methods: Capturing life as it is lived. Annual Review of Psychology 54(1), 579–616 (2003)
4. Walther, J.B., Loh, T., Granka, L.: Let me count the ways the interchange of verbal and nonverbal cues in computer-mediated and face-to-face affinity. Journal of Language and Social Psychology 24(1), 36–65 (2005)
5. Lo, S.K.: The nonverbal communication functions of emoticons in computer-mediated communication. CyberPsychology & Behavior 11(5), 595–597 (2008)
6. Walther, J.B., D'Addario, K.P.: The impacts of emoticons on message interpretation in computer-mediated communication. Social Science Computer Review 19(3), 324–347 (2001)
7. Derks, D., Bos, A.E., Grumbkow, J.V.: Emoticons and social interaction on the Internet: the importance of social context. Computers in Human Behavior 23(1), 842–849 (2007)
8. McCrae, R.R., John, O.P.: An introduction to the five - factor model and its applications. Journal of Personality 60(2), 175–215 (1992)
9. Costa Jr., P.T., McCrae, R.R.: The five-factor model of personality and its relevance to personality disorders. Journal of Personality Disorders 6(4), 343–359 (1992)
10. McCrae, R.R., Costa, P.T.: A five-factor theory of personality. In: Pervin, L.A., John, O.P. (eds.) Handbook of Personality: Theory and Research, pp. 139–153. Guilford, New York (1999)
11. Ozer, D.J., Benet-Martinez, V.: Personality and the prediction of consequential outcomes. Annu. Rev. Psychol. 57, 401–421 (2006)
12. Wolf, A.: Emotional expression online: Gender differences in emoticon use. CyberPsychology & Behavior 3(5), 827–833 (2000)
13. Smith, C.B., McLaughlin, M.L., Osborne, K.K.: Conduct control on Usenet. Journal of Computer - Mediated Communication 2(4) (1997)
14. Hall, K.: Cyberfeminism- Computer-Mediated Communication: Linguistic. Social and Cross-Cultural Perspectives (1996)
15. Herring, S.: Posting in a different voice: Gender and ethics in computer-mediated communication. In: Philosophical Perspectives on Computer-Mediated Communication, pp. 115–145 (1996)
16. Herring, S.: Politeness in computer culture: Why women thank and men flame. In: Cultural performances: Proceedings of the Third Berkeley Women and Language Conference, vol. 278, p. 94. Berkeley Women and Language Group (1994)
17. Herring, S.: Politeness in computer culture: Why women thank and men flame. In: Cultural performances: Proceedings of the third Berkeley Women and Language Conference, vol. 278, p. 94. Berkeley Women and Language Group (1994)
18. Hall, K.: Cyberfeminism. In: Herring, S. (ed.) Computer-Mediated Communication:Linguistic, Social and Cross-Cultural Perspectives, pp. 147–170. John Benjamins, Amsterdam (1996)
19. Erring, S.C.: Virtual gender performances. Talk presented at Texas A&M University (September 25, 1998)
20. Bruckman, A.S.: Gender swapping on the Internet. In: Proceedings of INET 1993. The Internet Society, Reston (1993), Available via anonymous ftp from http://media.mit.edu/pub/MediaMOO/papers.gender-swapping
21. Herring, S., Nix, C.: "Is "serious chat" an oxymoron? Academic vs. social uses of Internet Relay Chat". Paper presented at the American Association of Applied Linguistics, Orlando, FL (March 11, 1997)
22. Crystal, D.: Language and the Internet. Cambridge University Press, Cambridge (2001)

23. Ekman, P., Friesen, W.V.: The repertoire of nonverbal behavior: Categories, origins, usage and codings. Semiotica 1, 49–97 (1969)
24. Harrison, R.P.: Nonverbal communication. In: Pool, I.S., Schramm, W., Maccoby, N., Fry, F., Parker, E., Fern, J.L. (eds.) Handbook of Communication, pp. 93–115. Rand McNally, Chicago (1973)
25. Thompson, P.A., Foulger, D.A.: Effects of pictographs and quoting on flaming in electronic mail. Computers in Human Behavior 12, 225–243 (1996)
26. Rezabek, L.L., Cochenour, J.J.: Visual cues in computer-mediated communication: Supplementing text with emoticons. Journal of Visual Literacy 18, 201–215 (1998)
27. Malouff, J.M., Thorsteinsson, E.B., Rooke, S.E., Schutte, N.S.: Alcohol involvement and the five factor model of personality: A meta-analysis. Journal of Drug Education 37, 277–294 (2007)
28. Malouff, J., Thorsteinsson, E., Schutte, N.: The relationship between the five-factor model of personality and symptoms of clinical disorders: A meta analysis. Journal of Psychopathology and Behavioral Assessment 27, 101–114 (2005)
29. Malouff, J.M., Thorsteinsson, E.B., Schutte, N.S.: Smoking and the five-factor model of personality: A meta-analysis. Journal of Drug Education 36, 47–58 (2006)
30. Barrick, M.R., Mount, M.K.: The Big Five personality dimensions and job performance. Personnel Psychology 44, 1–26 (1991), doi:10.1111/j.1744-6570.1991.tb00688.x
31. Hurtz, G.M., Donovan, J.J.: Personality and job performance: The Big Five revisited. Journal of Applied Psychology 85, 869–879 (2000), doi:10.1037/0021-9010.85.6.869
32. Salgado, J.F.: The five-factor model of personality and job performance in the European community. Journal of Applied Psychology 82, 30–43 (1997), doi:10.1037/0021-9010.82.1.30
33. Kim, J.-H., Kim, B.-H., Ha, M.-S.: Validation of A Korean Version of the Big Five Inventory. Journal of Human Understanding and Counseling 32(1), 47–66 (2011)
34. Liu, C.J., Wu, C.H., Chiu, Y.H.: BFI-based speaker personality perception using acoustic-prosodic features. In: 2013 Asia-Pacific IEEE Signal and Information Processing Association Annual Summit and Conference (APSIPA), pp. 1–6 (2013)

"Presence in Absence": Distributed Family Communication Practices for Familial Bonding via Mobile Communication Technology

Fazillah Mohmad Kamal[1], Nor Laila Md. Noor[2], and Hanif Baharin[2]

[1] Faculty of Quantitative Sciences, Universiti Utara Malaysia, UUM Sintok, Kedah, Malaysia
fazillah@uum.edu.my
[2] Faculty of Computer and Mathematical Sciences, Universiti Teknologi MARA, Shah Alam, Selangor, Malaysia
norlaila@tmsk.uitm.edu.my, ahmadhanif@perlis.uitm.edu.my

Abstract. Technology for bringing family together or coined as *Family Connecting Technology* (FCT) has become a prominent topic in HCI. As familial bonding has significant implication in affecting the design and use of FCTs, research on familial bonding is deemed important, yet challenged by discrepancy on its actual operationalization due to the diversity of current research focus. Therefore, this study aims to discover underlying patterns of mediated familial bonding from family's actual practice of FCT that is social messaging system. From a thematic analysis of interview data, we identified two main issues: 'online shared activity as transitory platform of familial bonding' and 'effects from technology design on familial bonding'. Then, we discuss potential indicators of familial bonding that provide insights to our future work in developing a conceptual model of mediated familial bonding.

Keywords: HCI, family connecting technology, social messaging, mobile technology, familial bonding, extended family, mobile communication, mediated family interaction, online shared activity.

1 Introduction

In the realm of Computer Supported Collaborative Work (CSCW) technologies, research in the organizational setting have highlighted how connection is entrenched in supporting collaboration and coordination of workgroup in improving productivity, efficiency and effectiveness [1]. As of its early invasion to the domestic life has been realized in the late 1980s [2], research in CSCW has been expanded broadly from functional to social aspects of technology where one of the increasing interest and importance is family connection [3]. An abundance of technologies has been designed including readily available applications to connect distributed extended family members – those who are related but do not co-residence [4]. Drawing on the definition of family connection posited by [3], we coin the term "Family Connecting Technologies" (or FCTs) referring to a group of technologies that support families to

G. Meiselwitz (Ed.): SCSM 2014, LNCS 8531, pp. 474–485, 2014.
© Springer International Publishing Switzerland 2014

communicate with each other, to share their lives and routines, to engage in social touch, and to negotiate for being together, or being apart.

Strong familial bond is prevalent across cultures in collectivist countries such as Malaysia, China and Bangladesh [5]. However, demands on career and education advancement have forced people to migrate [6], creating a scenario of contemporary families that lead hectic lifestyles. Since "families are more closely bound together as a group of interacting persons" [7], the adoption of FCT helps bring family members together, anytime and anywhere. In the earlier studies of FCT such as cell phone [8], short messaging system (SMS) [9] and electronic mail (email) [10], familial bonding merely captured insignificant attention despite of its importance. Later, with burgeoning interest from society towards the technology and realization of its capability in engendering affective sense while maintaining interpersonal relationships [11] makes it essential to explore how it is appropriated by family in the pursuit of familial bonding. As in non-mediated environment, familial bonding is manifested through joint activity or mutual interests [12][13], and expression of care or protection [14], which can be evidenced from facial expressions and body gestures displayed during interaction. However, the trace of familial bonding seems to pose more challenges within technology mediated environment as all the bonding cues are embodied in other forms. Even though current research has provided valuable insights on the 'do's and 'don'ts in FCT design, there is a paucity of unified understanding in how mediated familial bonding is perceived, particularly in the context of using social messaging system.

As the first step, this exploratory study sought to capture initial patterns of perceived mediated familial bonding through actual practice of mobile family interaction. We believe that this newly emerged FCT that was predicted as a future trend in 2014 and beyond [15] can be a great advantage in terms of its practicality and mobility to enable extended family members virtually bonded in group. In the broader sense, this study is a fragment of our long-term aim in solving a problem of designing FCT informed by operationalization of mediated familial bonding that is theoretically, methodologically and empirically supported [16].

2   Related Studies

Connectedness or bonding [17] between distributed extended family members has received considerable attention recently and has become a very intuitive design orientation for FCTs. Research shows that familial bonding is facilitated via FCT in various forms. For example, SPARCS [4] was designed to support serendipitous and lightweight sharing of photos through daily sharing suggestions to minimize the effort which is one of the important concerns emerged in distant family communication. Along this line, the Digital Family Portrait [18], the Wayve [19], as well as the Family Window and Family Portal [20], are other variants of FCTs to support familial bonding between distributed family members through the use of messaging feature bundled with multimedia elements such as photos, text, scribbled handwriting, video, audio and drawing. The lightweight feature of technology has often been taken into design consideration in promoting frequent sharing of information. Interestingly, FCT design does not merely employ explicit messaging as means of connecting family. FamilyPlanter [21] for instance, has been designed to support a sense of closeness between remote family members through its unique design concept *tsunagari-kan* or 'closeness' that continuously and interactively provides situational cues such as motion signs. Likewise with shared family calendar [22] that was designed to support coordination between remotely located members through sharing of certain calendar information. From synchronizing routines of different households, shared activity could be organized without having to ask for similar information repetitively such as the whereabouts of adult children during weekend. Essentially, these studies point to the use of FCTs to facilitate familial bonding among extended family members outside of their daily interaction circle, in which qualitative indicators or self-reported psychological experience have been used to indicate the emergence of bonding with exception to [21] that combined both qualitative and quantitative indicators of bonding. Furthermore, all aforementioned studies focus on either dyadic or triadic interaction between members.

Also of interest regarding familial bonding lies on family appropriation of readily available FCTs in the market. As an obvious case in point, the use of social network sites (SNSs), for example Facebook has attracted much global interest. A study on privacy within family communication upon using Facebook has discovered positive use by family that signifies ongoing evolution of SNSs as family communication medium [23]. Besides, social spaces like Blogspot and Flickr serve as platforms for continuous interaction in the form of photo-narrative among remote family members [24], and more recently, explosive growth of smartphones along with the broadband services has witnessed an increasing trend in utilizing mobile social messaging or also known as mobile instant messaging in daily life. People including family use this technology in enacting friendships and groups, however studies involving social messaging is very limited [25] particularly in understanding mediated familial bonding through FCT.

3   Research Method

The virtual family group formed via social messaging system can be categorized into intra-generational family or inter-generational family. The former is restricted to siblings and siblings/spouses, and the later may also include aunts/uncles and nieces/nephews. In this study, a purposive sampling was used to inform an understanding of the research problem [26]. The need to gather thick descriptions were constrained by time and financial limitations, however, makes it unfeasible to have a large number of participants. Due to this, no assertion are made that the results represent general population as a whole. The Malaysian family selected for this study adopts a social messaging system to connect with distributed family members. The family relationship of this family may include both intra-generational and inter-generational family. In-depth interviews were conducted with seven participants from the family members between August and December 2013.

3.1   The Participants

At the beginning, ten members from the family were approached but three of them were disqualified since they did not participate in the family group communication. Although all of the participants installed several types of mobile messaging applications such as WhatsApp, WeChat and LINE in their smartphones, all of them only use WhatsApp or WeChat for their family group interaction. Table 1 shows the demographic detail of the participants, their current residential location, and details of the family group interaction such as the number of virtual family groups they participated, duration of participation and virtual family group structure, whether intragenerational (Intra) or inter-generational (Inter). Two participants are residing in United Kingdom; one is residing in Dubai, while the rest are residing in Malaysia. Pseudonyms are used to protect participants' anonymity.

Table 1. Demographic information and family relationship information of participants

Name	Age	M/F	Residential Location	Employment	# of group	Duration of group participation	Intra / Inter
Sarah	40	F	Kedah, MAL	Teacher	2	< 6 mths	Intra/Inter
Omar	32	M	Manchester, UK	Businessman	2	Nearly 1 year	Intra
Ahmad	39	M	Sabah, MAL	Teacher	3	< 6 mths	Intra/Inter
Jasmin	40	F	Manchester, UK	Fulltime housewife	4	Nearly 2 years	Intra/Inter
Zaki	49	M	Dubai, UAE	Engineer	4	< 6 mths	Intra/Inter
Siti	22	F	N.Sembilan, MAL	Student	1	< 6 mths	Intra
Faizal	27	M	Kelantan, MAL	Clerk	1	< 6 mths	Intra

3.2   The Interviews

Owing to the geographical barriers and the different time zones, five out of seven participants were interviewed over Skype and Facebook Messenger with the account of considerations discussed by [27] such as providing a brief introduction to the aims of the interview, estimated duration, and also a need of building good rapport with virtual participants since common visual cues are absent. With the two remaining participants, both online and face-to-face interview were conducted. The face-to-face interviews were conducted at the participants' choice of venue. Each interview session lasted for approximately 45 minutes for the face-to-face interviews and 90 minutes for the online interviews. All of the interviews were conducted in the Malay language as the conversation generated is inherently bounded by the social context in which it takes place while placing the interviewees at ease [28].

In general, participants enthusiastically drew on their experiences to offer insights about social messaging system in mediating familial bonding. During the interview, the participants may elicit genuine responses throughout the session.

3.3   Data Analysis

For the data analysis, the transcriptions of audio recorded interviews were analyzed along with the text-based online interviews in an iterative manner using thematic analysis [29], involving several rounds of analysis to categorize recurring themes. Qualitative data analysis software ATLAS.ti has assisted in the extraction and categorization of emergent themes. In the needs of supporting arguments, English translation only involved with the whole segment of which excerpts of transcripts was taken, and re-examined by professional translator.

4   Findings

4.1   Online Shared Activity as Transitory Platform of Familial Bonding

Several themes emerged from our data indicate that shared activities during online family interaction are quite similar to activities supported by current FCT design. These findings illuminate how FCT is used as a transitory platform by extended family members to gather virtually before actual meeting is made possible. Online encounters between the members through these activities are not limited to typical conversation or "catch-up" but can be as much as simulating a living space in physical home of which familial bonding can take place.

Surrogate Social Care. [18] defined this activity as "a form of mediated awareness intended to re-establish certain aspects of naturally occurring social support that have been disrupted". As the geographic distance of extended family is seen as the source of disruption, FCT affordance is deemed advantageous to the point that naturally occurring social support system that require physical proximity is not possible as Sarah indicated, *"my sister, a doctor who acts as a kin-keeper create our own virtual sibling group in addition to other family groups as a private and confidential channel to discuss about our ageing mother's well-being. She is almost 80 years old and always sick. Whenever our mother is admitted to the hospital, she will share the results of the diagnosis on the spot. We will discuss on what to do next"*. Indicator of care and support does not restricted to the ailing parents only but could also be shown to this extend: Ahmad, a teacher who was transferred to remote area far flung from others about nine years ago longed to live nearby. Since his application of transferal was kept denied, Ahmad regularly expressed his frustration by giving a call to his mother, and then she will contact others encouraging them to relax him. As of using FCT, he just expressed his feeling in the virtual group and later, other members will provide various kinds of support.

Spiritual Materials Dissemination. The participants feel that it is their responsibility to remind each other about their faith. In performing this responsibility, social messaging has been appropriated for the dissemination of spiritual and religious materials. This was the case with Sara *"I like to share excerpts of hadith and snapshots of Quran citations to remind others. It is one of my efforts to inform my family members,* *especially about the importance of righteous acts in this challenging world"*. We also discovered that Omar, Ahmad and Jasmin have considered this as a convenient and subtle alternative of encouraging others to perform good deeds.

Serendipitous Sharing of Everyday Moments. Sarah who resides in another country often use location sharing as *"a way to inform my family members that I am shopping at certain shopping store especially designer's outlets and if they want me to buy something for them, they can spontaneously make the order"*. This transactional interaction is indeed not business-oriented as she was glad to help others in having something which is unaffordable in her own country. Besides, photo or video sharing while at work, at dinner, during shopping, or even involved in bad incidents such as accident is also reported.

Breaking news. FCT is viewed as an appropriate channel for breaking news instantaneously as mentioned by Omar, *"When my wife got pregnant, I just post a picture of the pregnancy test kit used by my wife without any description signifying the existence of our oncoming baby. Then, others started congratulate me"*. Faizal also mentioned that social messaging adds a dimension of empathy not offered by conventional medium such as phone call, email or SMS since original intent of the message sender could be captured by facial or emotional expressions embodied in emoticons, live images or video clips. Any curiosity and misunderstanding is normally resolved when the sender offers further textual explanation after being requested by others. At first glance, we found the similarity of this activity to the cultural trope of *vaguebooking* which effectively prompts other members to respond immediately due to the nature of message or status that is vague and may attract the curiosity of others.

Event Planning and Coordination. Sara described this activity as provocative and 'infectious', *"Usually I will throw the idea in the first place and ask about the participation, and later propose the tentative of the program. I have a big family so I don't expect that all members will join. At the beginning, there might be only several members will join but as the discussion progress, more and more members are enthusiastically taking part in the preparation and even join the event after seeing the merriness of the discussion. Normally, there is an overlap in the dates of the events with individual programs which created an atmosphere of dissatisfaction and disappointment but humorous statements and emoticons replied by others heal the situation"*. Figure 1 shows a photo of a pamphlet provided by Sarah, signifying their anticipation on this activity. The pamphlet was designed by her family member prior to the "Family Day" and represents a small portion of their online discussion. Interestingly, she conveyed that all the details about the activity were completely organized through social messaging.

Supporting Long Distance Family Relationship. The importance of FCT in familial bonding between distanced family members is further highlighted by Siti, *"Usually, I post my live pictures at college so that my mum who lives with my sister in our hometown will know that I am not going anywhere except in college, so that she would not*

Fig. 1. Snapshot of Sarah's virtual family group in event planning and coordination

worry about me! *Then, whenever possible I chat with my nephews or nieces who already know using their mum or dad's smartphones to share our brief story of that particular day"*. As for Omar, Jasmin and Zaki who reside in another country, FCT is essential to stay in touch with others. Omar indicated *"If I make a phone call, I cannot talk to more than one person at a time but using WhatsApp, I can talk to many members. It's like a black magic, I am not 'there' to be touched but I am there to talk to. I can feel that all family members are at the same place"*.

4.2   Effects From FCT Design to Familial Bonding

The kind of online shared activities being shaped upon using FCT has further characterized how the design of technology could actually give impacts to familial bonding that recurrently drives family interaction. These findings essentially point out the importance of FCT design in bringing family together virtually, which may be considered by designers.

Continuous Presence and Awareness through Shared Context. Desires for the sense of continuous presence and awareness for other family member around them are often mentioned eloquently. As Zaki commented *"I am physically far away from others. Now, it feels like I can reach them anywhere, anytime without limits. I feel they are near me even with the smallest hint, and that's better than nothing. This reminds me a lot of our childhood memories"*. Similarly, Ahmad stated, *"at once I thought that all group members are living next door and sometimes I feel like if I want to talk to them, I just need to enter a special dark room with some lights and say hi as someone is in there to accompany me"*. When probed on the term *'special dark room with some lights'*, Ahmad explained that prior to the interaction, he would not know who will be online with him but status information like 'typing' or 'online' might provide some clues who are available to talk to. On the contrary, Faizal indicated that *"just by knowing what's going on with my family members is enough. It gives me sort of peace of mind just by looking at the pictures and read tons of messages. I don't bother to post anything about me"*.

Privacy. The secrecy of family matter is the utmost concern of most participants when discussing about the content of messages. Zaki expressed his concern of external privacy when indicated *"Family is number one for me and I'd prefer not to share about our family issues with outsiders such as friends or colleagues. When joining family groups, there's like exist unspoken agreement not to share the contents unnecessarily"*. On the contrary, Sarah offered an insight on internal family privacy *"I have two groups currently because in my sibling group, we discuss more serious topics related to making decisions about our ageing mother or perhaps considering a plan for each of us to contribute certain amount of money for her well-being. In another group, more general topics like planning a vacation or surprises are discussed by more members"*.

Immediacy. All participants expressed their appreciation on the promptness of the messages delivered to all group members. For example Zaki commented *"There are times when I restlessly need to know about my mum's condition usually when she's not well. Luckily we have this app, so I know the most up-to-date progress about her no matter if I am at the office or at home"*, whereas Siti who often encountered unintended situation like insufficient water supply at the hostel expressed her relief, *"Luckily I have WhatsApp. I just message them to pick me up as soon as possible and then someone will reply back as I know they are online most of the time"*.

Embodiment of Affective Contents. Jasmin and Siti mentioned that the occurrences of unordinary events or incidents that emotionally involved often invite responses from others, and the messages are diverse depending on scenario as expressed by Faizal, *"one of my sisters told us about her miscarriage. All of them kept posting messages including digital condolence card and emoticons to console her"*.

Reciprocity. [30] defined reciprocity as "actions that are contingent on rewarding reactions from others and that cease when these expected reactions are not forthcoming". In this sense, the Social Exchange Theory [31] suggests that family members assume mutual reciprocity to align with their initiatives in terms of time spent for mediated interaction through FCT. This affects the number of replies posted by participants and their family members during interaction. Significant mutual reciprocity between family members had resulted with many messages being posted during interaction as expressed by Sarah *"when discussing about our family day, about 300++ messages being posted by approximately eight different members if I am not mistaken. The conversation took less than 15 minutes and it was havoc but I feel so close with them!"* In the opposition of the frequent replies within a short timeframe of interaction, Omar has indicated the lack of mutual reciprocity *"I realized there's a few times when somebody post the message or photo, no one replies or if any, perhaps one or* *two members only and the conversation ends there"* and when asked about the reasons, he speculated that others were perhaps busy, getting offline or uninterested. However, we note that family kinship play its role in the norms of reciprocity as Jasmin highlighted, *"I have four groups: siblings only, my siblings with their spouses including my husband, my husband's siblings group with their spouses, and another one is joined by my nieces and nephews. So, the number and frequency of post to each group is different depending on my status. I regularly post to my sibling group and another one but less in the groups which my husband family is there"*.

5   Discussion and Limitation

This study highlights that familial bonding in the online shared activities over family interaction. This study uncovers several new activities in the family interaction such as product or service recommendation and spiritual materials dissemination. The other activities that took place having similarity with current issues of FCT in other studies as in the serendipitous sharing of daily moments in SPARCS [4], surrogate social care was being studied through Digital Family Portraits [18], family coordination through shared family calendar [22], and supporting long distance relationships as common aim in other studies [20][24].

Despite of having specific questions requiring the participants to describe how the sense of bonding is formed and the perceived feeling experienced by other members, all participants vaguely and repetitively mentioned that leaving comments or messages as an indicator of bonding [19], apart from emphasizing the phrase *"I feel close"*. To further illuminate this, we had another round of reading the transcripts and the emergent themes, in relation to the reported indicator to identify possible implicit cues of mediated familial bonding which is bound in an interwoven of virtual shared activities and effects of FCT design. These include: 1) the frequency of mediated interaction through FCT, 2) the degree of reciprocity, 3) embodiment of family emotions through contents, and 4) visualization of the shared context. These propositions are compatible with the results of [32] that found higher level of family emotions or termed as affectual bonding lead to higher frequency and intensity of contacts of which referred as associational bonding. Our findings have shown that FCT or social messaging system in particular, serves as an affordance for frequent family interaction over online shared activity driven by the amount and types of multimedia elements as well as other features used, which embody family emotions. This in turn, permits distributed family members to mutually reciprocate in the shared context provided by FCT design.

Although the findings are encouraging, our study has limitations since each family is characterized by great diversity. We made no claim on the universality of these findings particularly on family online shared activities across cultures, but as the familial bonding is rooted in similar sources [12][13][14], the sense of bonding articulated in our study is apparently manifested through the equivalent ebb and flow of all family life.

6   Conclusion and Future Work

This study has reported a preliminary study of a variant of FCT that has shed some light on how mediated familial bonding is perceived in virtual environment. It has appeared that mediated familial bonding can be maintained and facilitated through online shared activities that serve as transitory platform embedding the expressions of care, protection and mutual interests, interlaced with a myriad of family emotions. However, the findings suggest that the manifestation of mediated bonding does not entirely depend on its transitory platform but the right combination between family interrelated acts and technological design of the 'platform' that indeed warrants the emergence of familial bonding. Moreover, the study also reveals the ambiguity of bonding manifestation perceived by participants, apart from self-reported experience. Therefore, we plan to explicate these issues further with theoretical explanation by developing a conceptual model of mediated familial bonding through FCT as our future work.

Acknowledgement. We would like to thank our participants for their invaluable sharing of experience, and also the anonymous reviewers for their insightful comments.

References

1. Wilson, P.: Computer Supported Cooperative Work: An Introduction. Intellect Books, Oxford (1991)
2. Venkatesh, A.: Computers and Other Interactive Technologies for the Home. Communications of the ACM 39(12), 47–54 (1996)
3. Neustaedter, C., Harrison, S., Sellen, A.: Connecting Families: An Introduction. In: Neustaedter, C., Harrison, S., Sellen, A. (eds.) Connecting Families, pp. 1–12. Springer, London (2013)
4. Brush, A.J.B., Inkpen, K.M., Tee, K.: SPARCS; Exploring Sharing Suggestions to Enhance Family Connectedness. In: CSCW 2008. ACM Press, San Diego (2008)
5. Hofstede, G., Hofstede, G.J., Minkov, M.: Cultures and Organizations: Software of the Minds. McGraw Hill, New York (2010)
6. Abdul Aziz, R., Yusooff, F.: Intergenerational Relationships and Communication Among the Rural Aged in Malaysia. Asian Social Science 8(6), 184–195 (2012)
7. Jansen, L.T.: Measuring Family Solidarity. American Sociological Review 17(6), 727–733 (1952)
8. Leung, L., Wei, R.: More Than Just Talk on the Move: Uses and Gratifications of the Cellular Phone. Journalism & Mass Communication Quarterly 77(2), 308–320 (2000)
9. Ling, R., Yttri, B.: Hyper-coordination via Mobile Phones in Norway. In: Katz, J., Aakhus, M. (eds.) Perpetual Contact: Mobile Communication, Private Talk, Public Performance. Cambridge University Press, Cambridge (2002)
10. Boneva, B., Kraut, R.: Email, Gender, and Personal Relationships. In: Wellman, B., Haythornthwaite, C. (eds.) The Internet in Everyday Life, pp. 370–403. Blackwell Publishers, Cornwall (2002)

11. Licoppe, C.: "Connected" Presence: The Emergence of a New Repertoire for Managing Social Relationships in a Changing Communication Technoscape. Environment and Planning: Society and Space 22, 135–156 (2004)
12. Angell, R.C.: The Family Encounters the Depression. Sribner, New York (1936)
13. Atkinson, M.P., Kivett, V.R., Campbell, R.T.: Intergenerational Solidarity: An Examination of a Theoretical Model. Journal of Gerontology 41(3), 408–416 (1986)
14. Kane, S.W.: The Consolidation of Attachment and Family Systems Theories: Introducing the Family Chores Model. The American Journal of Family Therapy 17(1), 57–65 (1989)
15. Ovum, http://ovum.com/press_releases/ovum-reveals-2014-will-witness-social-messaging-players-challenge-the-status-quo-of-mobile-social-networking/
16. Shilton, K., Koepfler, J.A., Fleischmann, K.R.: How to See Values in Social Computing: Methods for Studying Values Dimensions. In: CSCW 2014. ACM Press, Baltimore (2014)
17. Barber, B.K., Schluterman, J.M.: Connectedness in the Lives of Children and Adolescents: A Call for Greater Conceptual Clarity. The Journal of Adolescent Health: Official Publication of the Society for Adolescent Medicine 43(3), 209–216 (2008)
18. Mynatt, E.D., Rowan, J., Jacobs, A., Craighill, S.: Digital Family Portraits: Supporting Peace of Mind for Extended Family Members. In: Proceedings of the SIGCHI Conference on Human Factors in Computing Systems, pp. 333–340. ACM Press, New York (2001)
19. Lindley, S.E.: Shades of Lightweight: Supporting Cross-Generational Communication through Home Messaging. Journal of Universal Access in the Information Society 11(1), 31–43 (2012)
20. Judge, T.K., Neustaedter, C., Harrison, S.: Inter-Family Messaging with Domestic Media Spaces. In: Neustaedter, C., Harrison, S., Sellen, A. (eds.) Connecting Families, pp. 141–158. Springer, London (2013)
21. Miyajima, A., Itoh, Y., Itoh, M., Watanabe, T.: "Tsunagari-kan" Communication: Design of a New Telecommunication Environment and a Field Test with Family Members Living Apart. International Journal of Human Computer Interaction 19(2), 2530276 (2005)
22. Plaisant, C., Clamage, A., Hutchinson, H.B., Bederson, B.B., Druin, A.: Shared Family Calendars: Promoting Symmetry And Accessibility. ACM Trans. Comput.-Hum. Interact. 13(3), 313–346 (2006)
23. Fife, E.M., Lacava, L., Nelson, C.L.: Family Communication, Privacy, and Facebook. Journal of Social Media in Society 2(1), 106–125 (2013)
24. Jomhari, N., Gonzalez, V.M., Kurniawan, S.H.: See The Apple Of My Eye: Baby Storytelling In Social Space. In: Proceedings of the 23rd British HCI Group Annual Conference on People and Computers: Celebrating People and Technology. British Computer Society, Cambridge (2009)
25. Church, K., Oliveira, R.D.: What's Up with WhatsApp? Comparing Mobile Instant Messaging Behaviors with Traditional SMS. In: Proceedings of the 15th International Conference on Human-Computer Interaction with Mobile Devices and Services, pp. 352–361. ACM Press, New York (2013)
26. Creswell, J.W.: Qualitative Inquiry and Research Design: Choosing Among Five Approaches, 2nd edn. SAGE Publications Ltd., United States of America (2007)
27. Connor, H.O., Madge, C., Shaw, R., Wellens, J.: Internet-based Interviewing. In: Fielding, C.N., Lee, R.M., Blank, G. (eds.) The SAGE Handbook of Online Research Methods, pp. 271–290. SAGE Publications, London (2008)
28. Welch, C., Piekkari, R.: Crossing Language Boundaries: Qualitative Interviewing in International. Management International Review 46(4), 417–437 (2006)

29. Aronson, J.: A Pragmatic View of Thematic Analysis. The Qualitative Report 2(1), 1–3 (1994)
30. Blau, P.M.: Exchange and Power in Social Life. John Wiley & Sons, New York (1964)
31. Thibaut, J.W., Kelly, H.H.: The Social Psychology of Groups. John Wiley & Sons, New York (1959)
32. Roberts, R.E.L., Richards, L.N., Bengston, V.: Intergenerational Solidarity in Families. Marriage & Family Review 16(1-2), 11–46 (2008)

Beyond Facebook Personality Prediction:

A Multidisciplinary Approach
to Predicting Social Media Users' Personality

Carrie Solinger[1], Leanne Hirshfield[1], Stuart Hirshfield[2],
Rachel Friendman[2], and Christopher Lepre[2]

[1] Department of Mass Communications, S.I. Newhouse School of Public Communications,
Syracuse University, Syracuse, NY 13210
{casoling,lmhirshf}@syr.edu
[2] Department of Computer Science, Hamilton College, Clinton, NY
{shirshf,rlfriendm,cleper}@hamilton.edu

Abstract. We investigate creating a predictive model that increases accuracy in personality prediction of social media and social network site users through a multidisciplinary pilot analysis. We present a novel method for increasing personality prediction accuracy of Facebook users. We discuss an experiment that combines natural language processing and machine learning methods, as well as the Big Five Personality and other cognitive psychology metrics and scales. Our machine learning predictive model showed promising results in personality prediction accuracy of three personality traits. However, the results indicate that more research and further data collection will improve prediction accuracies.

Keywords: Big Five, personality traits, propensity to trust, trust propensity, need for cognition, Facebook, social media, social networking sites, SNS.

1   Introduction

Accurately predicting social media users' behaviors and activity on social networking sites (SNS), such as Facebook and Twitter, is a quickly expanding research domain; this is no surprise given the exponential growth of social media and SNS users. Pew Research Center reported that 72% of online adults are active users of social networking sites [1]. This figure is more than double the 35% reported in 2009 [2]. Additionally, of the 72% adults with online profiles, 67% of these individuals use Facebook [1].

Existing social media and SNS personality prediction research is primarily within the context of a single discipline, such as human-computer interaction, social computing, and behavior modeling [3-6]. While each of these prior studies provides valuable insights, we believe there is greater benefit in applying a multifaceted approach to increase prediction accuracy. Specifically, inclusion of additional components from

G. Meiselwitz (Ed.): SCSM 2014, LNCS 8531, pp. 486–493, 2014.

computer science, computational linguistics, cognitive psychology, and information science would be advantageous.

The primary goals of our study were to increase accuracy in social media and SNS user personality prediction, and determine his or her susceptibility to (social) influence by others in social media and SNS environments. As such, our research study implemented a multidisciplinary method for higher personality predication accuracy, and broader-based applicability in understanding how users of social media and SNS act and behave based on the individual user's representation of his or her own social identity and social presence within the social media and SNS domains. In particular, our study differed from prior studies via application of sentiment analysis and machine learning (ML) to conduct contextual analysis though classifiers. Additionally, cognitive psychology metrics and scales were utilized through survey deployment.

2   Background and Relevant Literature

2.1   Personality

As social media and SNS user populations have grown, research studies within these areas have similarly expanded. In particular, the high usage level of the Facebook social network has garnered attention in the personality prediction research domain. Many of these research studies applied the Big Five factors (of personality traits) model to Facebook profile information and usage in assessing personality prediction accuracy. The Big Five, also known as the Five-Factor Model, consists of five broad personality dimensions used to describe the human personality [7]. Often collectively referred to as OCEAN, these factors are: openness, conscientiousness, extraversion, agreeableness, and neuroticism. Table 1 illustrates the five personality traits and values describing HIGH and LOW scorers for each.

Research conducted using the Big Five as the basis for personality prediction, as applied to Facebook, indicated correlations between some of the personality factors and publically available Facebook profile information [6, 8]. Significant findings in these studies included prediction accuracy of each of the five factors within 11% of the user's survey based values [8]. Additionally, these studies reported the highest prediction accuracy for *extraversion*, and the lowest prediction accuracy for *agreeableness* [6, 8].

Table 1. The Big Five (Factor) Model descriptions

Personality Trait	HIGH scorers tend to be:	LOW scorers tend to be:
Openness	Creative, imaginative, unconventional, intellectually curious, open to new experiences.	Conventional, traditional, conservative, prefer familiarity, skeptical.
Conscientiousness	Organized, self-disciplined, efficient, hardworking, reliable, neat, systematic, thorough.	Easy-going, spontaneous, careless.
Extraversion	Energetic, enthusiastic, talkative, assertive, gregarious.	Quiet, low-key, independent, prefer time alone.
Agreeableness	Kind, warm, considerate, cooperative, trustworthy, trusting, friendly, sympathetic.	Competitive, analytical, skeptical, suspicious, unfriendly, detached.
Neuroticism	Sensitive, anxious, moody, self-conscious, perfectionist, more reactive to stress.	Calm, even-tempered, less likely to be affected by stressors.

2.2 Propensity to Trust

Trust is a complex phenomenon and considered by many different research disciplines to be primarily situational within the social context [9]. In relation to personality, trust is often included as a facet of the Big Five agreeableness dimension. However, some scholars dispute the notion of trust as a momentary state. Instead, trust is reinterpreted as a *propensity to trust,* and therefore viewed as an underlying aspect of personality [9, 10]. The Propensity to Trust Scale was created to more accurately measure trust related behavior. This assessment is an 8-item Likert-like scale that estimates an individual's wiliness to trust other people [11].

2.3 Need for Cognition

Need for cognition is the overall tendency for individuals to engage in and enjoy intensive thinking [12]. An 18-item Likert-like scale was created to measure an individual's need for cognition [13]. The assessment indicates characteristics about individuals with HIGH or LOW need for cognition. Individuals with high need for cognition are more likely to receive well a message that emphasizes cognitive information rather than emotion. Conversely, individuals low in need for cognition tend to form opinions based on more simple cues such as the credibility or attractiveness of the message source. Additionally, higher scoring need for cognition individuals tend to have stronger opinions than their lower scoring counterparts [14].

Table 2. 8-item Propensity to Trust Scale statements

Item Statements
Most people can be counted on to do what they say they will do.
I tend to trust people, even those whom I have just met for the first time.
Unless you remain alert, someone will soon take advantage of you.
Most people would tell a lie if they could gain by it.
My typical approach is to be cautious with people until they have demonstrated their trustworthiness.
I usually give acquaintances the benefit of the doubt if they do something that seems selfish.
Most people pretend to be more honest than they really are.
I believe that most people are generally trustworthy.

3 Experiment

3.1 Participants

Our pilot analysis sample population consists of 20 college students. The majority of the participants (90%) are in the 18-24 age group. The remaining two participants are in the 25-34 and 35-54 age groups. Out the 20 participants, 15 are female and 5 are male. Participants were required to have existing Facebook accounts.

3.2 Facebook Application Access

Each participant was required to download a program while logged into his or her own Facebook account. The program was built into the existing Facebook application interface (API), and collected the participants' account data. Data collected via this application included profile bios, status updates, photos, and number of "Friends" (account-to-account connections). Data collection was limited to a two-year timespan, from June 2011 – June 2013.

3.3 Surveys

Participants used an online survey tool to complete three self-report personality-based surveys: Big Five personality inventory, propensity to trust assessment, and need for cognition assessment. The three personality-based surveys measured seven dimensions. The Big Five personality inventory measured *openness*, *conscientiousness*, *extraversion*, *agreeableness*, and *neuroticism*. The *propensity to trust* and *need for cognition* dimensions were measured by its respective assessment. Participants' responses were scored and assigned values of either HIGH or LOW.

Table 3. Need for Cognition Scale Short Form

Item Wording
I would prefer complex to simple problems.
I like to have the responsibility of handling a situation that requires a lot of thinking.
Thinking is not my idea of fun.
I would rather do something that requires little thought than something that is sure to challenge my thinking abilities.
I try to anticipate and avoid situations where there is likely a chance I will have to think in depth about something.
I find satisfaction in deliberating hard and for long hours.
I only think as hard as I have to.
I prefer to think about small, daily projects to long-term ones.
I like tasks that require little thought once I've learned them.
The idea of relying on thought to make my way to the top appeals to me.
I really enjoy a task that involves coming up with new solutions to problems.
Learning new ways to think doesn't excite me very much.
I prefer my life to be filled with puzzles that I must solve.
The notion of thinking abstractly is appealing to me.
I would prefer a task that is intellectual, difficult, and important to one that is somewhat important but does not require much thought.
I feel relief rather than satisfaction after completing a task that required a lot of mental effort.
It's enough for me that something gets the job done; I don't care how or why it works.
I usually end up deliberating about issues even when they do not affect me personally.

3.4   Data Preprocessing and Machine Learning Analysis

Data analysis consisted of three-primary phases. In the first phase, participant responses from each of the three surveys were converted into seven different predictor variables, which represented personality, propensity to trust, and need for cognition, respectively. The participants' predictor variables were ranked as either high or low.

For the second phase, an open-source natural language processing tool, Natural Language Toolkit, was used to create and apply a sentiment analysis classifier. This classifier was applied to the contextual data collected from the participants' Facebook account, which included user-generated status updates and user-generated comments. Statistical data output was converted to percentages for machine learning (ML) preparation. Lastly, an open-source data mining with ML application, WEKA [15], was used to build a neural network classifier. The classifier consisted of 10 hidden layers with a learning rate of .1. A three-fold cross validation was used to test the accuracy of our models.

4   Results and Analysis

4.1   Machine Learning Classifier

The most significant results from the initial application of our ML classifier indicates a personality prediction of 75% accuracy in *need for cognition*, and 65% accuracy in *agreeableness* of Facebook users. The latter result is significant as prior studies indicated a low accuracy prediction of this personality trait [6, 8]. Additionally, we were able to replicate a similar level of *extraversion* prediction accuracy with that of prior studies [6, 8]. While our pilot study consisted of only 20 Facebook users, we anticipate these prediction accuracies to improve with further data collection.

Table 4. Personality prediction accuracy results

Personality Dimensions	Prediction Accuracy
Openness	50%
Conscientiousness	40%
Extraversion	65%
Agreeableness	65%
Neuroticism	55%
Propensity to Trust	55%
Need for Cognition	75%

Table 5. Survey results for the four participants that passed along the Kony video

Sent Kony	Openness	Conscientiousness	Extraversion	Agreeableness	Neuroticism	Propensity to Trust	Need for cognition
YES	HIGH	HIGH	HIGH	HIGH	LOW	HIGH	HIGH
YES	LOW	LOW	LOW	LOW	HIGH	HIGH	LOW
YES	LOW	LOW	LOW	HIGH	LOW	HIGH	LOW
YES	LOW	LOW	LOW	LOW	HIGH	HIGH	HIGH

4.2   Kony 2012

Of the 20 subjects, only four subjects passed along a viral event (the Kony video). These numbers are too small to produce significant findings, but we did look at the personality, propensity to trust, and need for cognition survey results for each of these four participants to see if there were any notable trends. Table 5 shows the survey results for these four participants. It is interesting to note that all of these subjects had a high propensity to trust. And three of the four participants had low levels of openness and conscientiousness.

Although we can not draw any concrete conclusions from such a small sample, the trends seen in the data from these four subjects suggests that further research should explore the ties between propensity to trust, personality type, and whether or not that individual will be likely to send a viral event.

5   Conclusion

In this paper, we discussed and presented relevant Facebook personality prediction studies, and the benefit of including additional cognitive psychology metrics in a multidisciplinary approach to increase Facebook personality prediction accuracies. We demonstrated that the inclusion of additional personality dimensions, specifically the need for cognition and agreeableness, may be predicted with a high degree of accuracy. Although our pilot analysis shows promising results, future work to explore additional factors and a larger participant pool is needed to achieve a more stable machine learning predictive personality model.

References

1. Brenner, J., Smith, A.: 72% of online adults are social networking site users (2013)
2. Lenhart, A.: Adults and social network websites (2009)
3. Amichai-Hamburger, Y., Vinitzky, G.: Social network use and personality. Computers in Human Behavior 26(6), 1289–1295 (2010)
4. Quercia, D., et al.: Our twitter profiles, our selves: Predicting personality with twitter. In: 2011 IEEE Third International Conference on Privacy, Security, Risk and Trust (passat) and 2011 IEEE Third International Conference on Social Computing (socialcom). IEEE (2011)
5. Golbeck, J., et al.: Predicting personality from twitter. In: 2011 IEEE Third International Conference on Privacy, Security, Risk and Trust (passat) and 2011 IEEE Third International Conference on Social Computing (socialcom). IEEE (2011)
6. Bachrach, Y., et al.: Personality and patterns of Facebook usage. In: Proceedings of the 3rd Annual ACM Web Science Conference. ACM (2012)
7. Costa, P.T., McCrae, R.R.: The revised neo personality inventory (neo-pi-r). In: The SAGE Handbook of Personality Theory and Assessment, vol. 2, pp. 179–198 (2008)
8. Golbeck, J., Robles, C., Turner, R.: Predicting personality with social media. In: CHI 2011 Extended Abstracts on Human Factors in Computing Systems 2011, pp. 253–262. ACM, Vancouver (2011)
9. Evans, A.M., Revelle, W.: Survey and behavioral measurements of interpersonal trust. Journal of Research in Personality 42(6), 1585–1593 (2008)
10. Grabner-Kräuter, S., Kaluscha, E.A.: Empirical research in on-line trust: a review and critical assessment. Journal of Human-Computer Studies 58(6), 783–812 (2003)
11. McShane, S., von Glinow, M.: Propensity to trust scale. In: Organizational Behavior: Essentials 2008. McGraw-Hill (2008)
12. Cacioppo, J.T., Petty, R.E.: The need for cognition. Journal of Personality and Social Psychology 42(1), 116 (1982)
13. Cacioppo, J.T., et al.: Dispositional differences in cognitive motivation: The life and times of individuals varying in need for cognition. Psychological Bulletin 119(2), 197 (1996)
14. Petty, R.E., et al.: The need for cognition. In: Handbook of Individual Differences in Social Behavior, pp. 318–329 (2009)
15. Hall, M., et al.: The WEKA Data Mining Software: An Update. SIGKDD Explorations 11(1) (2009)

Social Psychology of the Digital Age: The Interpersonal Neuroscience of Mediated Communication

Michiel Spapé[1] and Niklas Ravaja[1,2]

[1] Helsinki Institute for Information Technology, HIIT, Aalto University
[2] Department of Social Research, University of Helsinki
Michiel.Sovijarvi-Spape@HIIT.FI, niklas.ravaja@helsinki.fi

Abstract. Psychological science has a rich tradition of investigating how interaction with others affects individual affect and cognition. Findings from neuroscience suggest that the reason for this is that we perceive others as fundamentally part of us. However, with the advent of mobile networks and the internet, the physical presence of others has become more and more often mediated by technology. In order to better understand the consequences, we call for the rise of a combined effort between human-computer interaction, psychology and social neuroscience which we term the interpersonal neuroscience of mediated communication. We demonstrate the many faces of this new field by describing five paradigms that provide insight in the question of how the technological medium – from the most sparse, haptic type to rich, computer-gaming scenarios – affects the message and inter-individual interaction. Furthermore, the paradigms show how the mediated interaction field may provide new answers to the perception of others affects individual affect, cognition and decision making.

1 Introduction

Social psychology enables us to understand how the actual or implied presence of others influences perception, cognition, emotion and action. When the presence of others is only implied, by means of communication technology, we speak of the field of mediated social psychology. One of the first studies of this type was carried out by one of the founding fathers of social psychology, Gordon Allport in 1936. He investigated the phenomenon that, during a religious revival, those who were listening in an adjacent hall to the service through a loudspeaker "contributed little to the collection and supplied no converts" [1].

Of course the presence of the speaker is reduced in a way we would now call something like "multimodal richness", or in Allport's words, a "reduction in the stimulus situation". Thus, an exaggerated social effect was observed relative to the fairly minimal physical change. The importance of this observation was shown only two years later by Orson Welles, who caused widespread panic (or at least the suggestion thereof, see [2]) with the radio broadcast of the War of the Worlds. Thus, the seemingly simple difference between mediated and direct communication is considerably more complicated than an explanation in terms of "more or less stimulus" suggests; an observation that remains at the heart of the study of mediated psychology.

G. Meiselwitz (Ed.): SCSM 2014, LNCS 8531, pp. 494–505, 2014.

The present article is an overview of the questions and potentials of modern, mediated communication for human-computer interaction, psychology and neuroscience. In section 2, we will briefly sketch some of the dramatic developments in human interaction since the 30s. In section 2.1, we define some of these questions as they relate to the developments in psychological science. In section 2.2, we focus on the parallel developments in neuroscience that allow new insights in mediated – as well as direct – interaction. The main thrust of the article, sections 3 – 7, is used to present five recent, experimental paradigms developed in our lab to investigate the interpersonal neuroscience of mediated interaction. Finally, we summarize what brings these paradigms together in section 8 and give an overview of what lies ahead.

2   Developments in Society, Psychology and Methodology

Much changed since Allport's radio study and The War of the Worlds. WW2 and the Cold War saw rapid development of communication protocols to convey personal information (along with the rise in cryptography) as well as rich, multimodal messages to the masses (along with the rise of television). In personal communication, the introduction of transistors in 1947 resulted in the unwieldy, manually operated switchboards of the 30s quickly making way for landline telephony as we now know it. Similarly, the first BBC television broadcast coincided with the year of Allport's article, while more the 50% of US households possessed a TV set only 18 years later.

Radio, television and telephony remained the most common forms of mediated communication until, in the 1970s, the internet slowly evolved from early computer networks [3]. Most of its familiar structures (e.g. email, www, and newsgroups) were added in the 1980s, after which it mushroomed exponentially in the 1990s, with an economically violent peak of popular uptake at the turn of the millennium. Soon, the internet became pivotal in providing new experiences of mediated interaction with formats ranging from the most information-sparse (e.g. Twitter) to those that allow near-complete audio-visual communication (e.g. Skype). Mobile telephony and the ubiquitous smart-phone have meant that the reach of the internet is no longer easy to measure and is rapidly becoming part of us, society and perhaps soon, physiology.

Yet, psychological science has struggled to keep up with the phenomenal pace of advancement in communication and all-too-often takes a model of full, direct communication for granted.

2.1   Developments in Psychological Science

A prevailing question in the psychology of communication is "how does one person understand another person". Arguably, the first step is to recognize raw, sensory information as "another person" rather than any other vector of features. Thus, even the earliest models suggested some type of template of oneself, which can then be matched to the other [4]. This can then also explain learning: by linking the observed actions of the other to oneself, new behavioral patterns can be acquired.

Findings from across the diverse science of psychology point, however, to a rather different story: instead of this serial process of modeling, matching and adapting, not acting as another is more difficult than actual imitation. Early findings from developmental psychology showed that at an impressively early age, human infants seem to imitate facial expressions [5]. Social psychologists demonstrated the other, darker side of this seemingly innocent behavior: violence was even without instruction exhibited by children seeing a role-model act aggressively towards a dummy [6]. Finally, experimental psychology shows that even adults find it remarkably hard to act against an impulse to automatically imitate [7].

A recent model that explains this is known as the mirror neuron system (MNS, [8]), which was informed by the finding that neurons in the premotor areas of the brain of macaques were activated both by a monkey performing an action and by the same monkey observing that action in others [9]). Thus, observation pre-activates an imitative act, which explains the apparent primacy of imitation. The MNS further suggests this to provide a neuronal similarity between the self and the other which enables one to understand others as fundamentally similar to one-self.

While the MNS provides a powerful explanatory framework, it comes with an intriguing paradox: if we see others as the same as ourselves, how can we distinguish between the self and the other? Or, put differently, if we always imitate, how can we meaningfully interact with someone without creating an automatic echo-chamber? In the course of the present article, we will return to these questions and argue that mediated interaction paradigms can provide answers where traditional communication studies fall short. However, before continuing, we will discuss an important new tool available for the study of the social psychology of mediated interaction.

2.2   Developments in Neuroscience

Anyone keeping in touch with the news will know that the functional mapping of the brain has become a popular, scientific endeavor. The scientific apparatus of the neuroscientist – particularly magnetic resonance imagery (MRI) and electroencephalography (EEG) – has become increasingly cost-effective and precise while technological and methodological advances have pushed the boundaries of what is possible with the machinery.

The neuroscience of interaction associated various cortical areas with the functions involved in the syndrome of communication. Early studies focused on verbal communication, and showed the left-hemispheric known as Broca's and Wernicke's areas to be involved in respectively language production and comprehension (though the story is somewhat more complex, cf. [10]). Yet, as we already noted, humans communicate long before they use language and it is in this more comprehensive scope that the premotor and "mirror" areas are typically considered. Nevertheless, it has been observed that reading about different actions activates the associated cortical motor areas, suggesting that the motor areas provide a meaningful grounding of language [11]. Finally, social interaction has been found to critically depend on areas involved in emotion and empathy, particularly the insula and prefrontal cortex [12, 13].

Despite the wealth of research on human interaction, few studies have directly investigated ongoing communication. Of course, the expense involved in constructing and maintaining even a single MRI scanner continues to be immense, and the technical difficulty of simultaneously scanning multiple persons remains nontrivial. However, as these problems are addressed, a call has been heard for a new, two-person neuroscience which harnesses the potentials of using multiple scanners to better understand natural, rich interaction [14].

One such potential could be in what is traditionally known as linkage. Physiological linkage refers to the effect that the biological signals of two persons who communicate with each other exhibits a degree of similarity related to the interaction. An early observation of the effect was found in the heart rate and skin conductance of distressed couples. They showed a physiological similarity that was found to account for marital satisfaction [15]. Further evidence was observed during a variety of social situations, particularly those with a strong affective component [16–19].

The neuroscience of communication has recently begun to show that linkage also occurs at a more central level. For instance, an fMRI study showed affective content in movies to elicit a type of inter-individual synchrony [20]. Furthermore, two guitarists who play together show linkage in terms of synchronized EEG activity just prior to their first note [21]. In our first mediated interaction paradigm, we demonstrate linkage during gaming and show how the type of interaction can affect linkage.

3   Paradigm 1: Rich Mediated Interaction in the Hot Seat

In order to replicate an earlier finding that competitive interaction promotes peripheral linkage [19] and extend this to EEG, we designed a study in which pairs of participants (dyads) sat together in a room, sharing a single computer (hence the "hot seat")

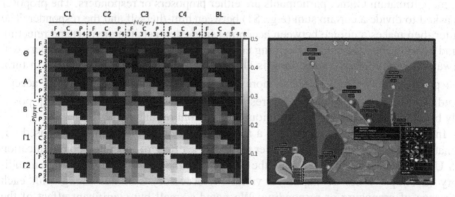

Fig. 1. Linkage and game of Paradigm 1. Left: linkage (cross-correlation, R) in spectral power across five frequency bands (theta Θ to higher gamma Γ2) between two players across 6 electrodes (F3/4, C3/4, P3/4) and four conditions ranging from low (C1) to high competitiveness (C4) and a common baseline (BL). The middle, dotted square shows the maximum linkage to occur in the C4 electrodes at beta (B) frequency during the most competitive condition. Right: the game scenario used in the experiment. (Source: PLOS ONE, [22]).

to play a computer game while both their facial electromyography (fEMG) and their EEG were measured. Crucially, the setup involved a game – an artillery game known as Hedgewars (www.hedgewars.org, see Figure 1) – in which the participants never acted at the same time, since the game was strictly turn-based. Furthermore, the type of mediated interaction was designed to vary along a cooperative-competitive dimension. In the most cooperative condition, the players belonged to the same team, and shared a common goal of winning from the PC-controlled opponent team. In the most competitive scenario, the players each belonged to a different team, and took aim at one another, in order to win directly from the other person.

As shown in Figure 1, EEG linkage was found to be particularly high in most competitive condition, particularly in centrally localized electrodes and the beta frequency band, suggesting a possible role for the motor cortex [22]. Furthermore, fEMG linkage was observed to be strong in the same condition, particularly in the facial muscles related to smiling. This effect was, somewhat counter-intuitively related to negative emotions, which were mainly found in the most competitive condition. Consequently, we speculated that the emotional mirroring demonstrated by linkage could have an adaptive role (knowing the competitor in order to win) or a compensatory role (smiling together in the face of another's adversity).

Although the rich setting of this experiment allows for a great amount of ecological validity, many types of mediated interaction are characterized by a much sparser flow of information and interindividual feedback. Despite innovations such as Skype, telephony by and large involves solely low bandwidth audio. In our next paradigm, we set about to study how a very small amount of mediated information could change a decision game-scenario.

4   Paradigm 2: Mediated Touch in the Ultimatum Game

In the Ultimatum Game, participants are either proposers or responders. The proposer is asked to divide a certain sum (e.g., $1) between him-/herself and the responder. The latter then makes a choice between accepting (and each gets the payout) and rejecting (and nobody gets) the shares. Seeming economic rationality holds that responders will always accept; after all, something is always better than nothing. Therefore, in turn, the proposer only needs to share more than €0, expecting the responder to accept. Studies have repeatedly shown that responders reject very unequal offers [23], possibly because judgments involve emotion, not just cold rationality [24].

In our paradigm [25], we created a mediated version of the simple, turn-based Ultimatum game (see Figure 2). In order to study the effect of mediated communication on Ultimatum bargaining, we gave the participants the single ability to send an auditory (a simple tone) or haptic (a vibration) accessory stimulus along with each message of proposing or responding. We noted a small but significant effect of the message, particularly that of the mediated touch; more offers were accepted, and higher proposals were made following tactile messages. Furthermore, we noticed a consistent effect of touch on late cognitive processing, as found using event related potential analysis of the EEG. These results suggested that the mediated touch might have triggered a type of effect known in the classic social psychology literature as the Midas Touch [26]: a touch positively affects generosity towards strangers.

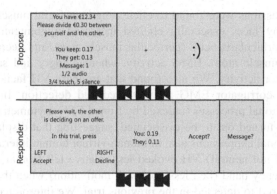

Fig. 2. Proposers in Paradigm 2 were required to divide €0.30 and indicate the type of message (indicated with loudspeaker icons) to send along with the proposal. Responders were shown divisions, received a proposer's message and asked to accept (receiving shares) or reject (receiving 0). They, too, were then allowed to send a message.

Thus, even if hardly any information other than a simple, cold vibration is presented during mediated interaction, people will still affectively attribute the communication, with measurable, economic consequences. It is, of course, also possible to more directly send out expressive messages. In the next paradigm, we turn our attention to what happens in decision making when participants are asked to deal with mediated communication that directly display affective content.

5   Paradigm 3: Mediated Negotiation with Affective Virtual Humans

In Paradigm 3, we examined the effects of the emotional facial expressions of a virtual human (VH) on human emotional-motivational processes (brain activity and facial expressions) and social decision making (cooperation/defection). In a within-subjects design, participants played the Iterated Prisoner's Dilemma game with a male and female VH with different dynamic facial expressions (e.g., angry and neutral; see Figure 3). In each of 192 trials, the participant was presented with a VH, the facial expression of which depended on the condition, followed by a prompt to decide to collaborate with the VH or not. The players (human and VH) received points as follows: (a) if both players chose to collaborate, both received three points, (b) if both players chose to defect, both received one point, and (c) if one player chose to collaborate and the other one chose to defect, the former received zero points and the latter five points.

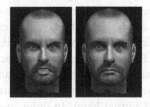

Fig. 3. Angry and neutral facial expressions of a male virtual human used in Paradigm 3

VH facial expressions were found to elicit congruent facial muscle activity in the participants. Happy faces especially elicited increased zygomaticus major (cheek muscle area) and orbicularis oculi (periocular muscle area), and decreased corrugator supercilii (brow muscle area), EMG activity, whereas angry and sad faces elicited increased corrugator activity. We also found that an angry VH facial expression and high pre-decision corrugator EMG activity predicted defection. Importantly, inner emotional-motivational processes (indexed by frontal EEG asymmetry) and emotional facial expressions turned out to be dissociated, suggesting that display rules may affect human emotional expressions also in human-virtual human interaction. We found that an angry (but not neutral) VH evoked less relative left frontal activation in the broad alpha frequency band (i.e., less approach motivation) when the participant has cooperated compared to defected in the previous trial. We interpreted this to indicate that especially an unjustified VH angry emotional expression decreases human approach motivation. However, an angry (but not neutral) VH evoked lower zygomatic, orbicularis oculi, and corrugator activity (i.e., less smiling and frowning) when the participant had defected compared to cooperated in the previous trial. This may relate to a social norm that one should not smile/laugh after refusing to collaborate with another person, especially if the refusal appears to elicit anger in the other person. Moreover, justified anger expression (anger in response to defection) by the VH appears to elicit less human anger expression. This paradigm showed that human approach motivation and facial expressions elicited by VH facial expressions depend on preceding interactional events (e.g., justifiability of VH emotional expressions). Also, the paradigm showed that VH facial expressions influence the human decision to cooperate. These findings may have many implications when designing VHs.

6   Paradigm 4: Mediated Imitation and Collaboration

Psychological studies have consistently shown that we tend to like people who are perceived as similar to us. This similarity has traditionally been defined in terms of perception, e.g., of perceived group memberships [27] or physical attractiveness [28]. However, recent studies showed that a similarity in action also promote a positive view of the other, possibly because of the aforementioned complex interrelationship between imitation, interaction and empathy [29, 30]. The authors provide evidence that seeing someone act similar to oneself results in perceiving interpersonal similarity, which in turn leads to positive emotions.

One can show the involvement of affective areas and provide questionnaires demonstrating self-reported affinity, but the significance of the effect is questionable if there is no consequence. Furthermore, it remains unclear whether imitation causes the effect in itself, or merely the observation thereof. In a classic, intra-individual, psychological scenario, it is difficult to manipulate a similarity in interpersonal action without affecting perception. However, mediated interaction allows easy manipulation over which aspects are shared between participants and which are unique.

Our new design involves dyads of participants in separate rooms who are presented with a left and right presented virtual hand. In order to give the impression that the virtual hands were "part of" the participant, we presented action congruent, photographed motions showing exaggerated key-presses which were expected to result in associations between the observed "virtual" effects and the intended actions [31]. Participants were then asked to use their virtual hand to tap along with a constant beat, cued by a flashing light. After tapping for some time, they were presented with a Prisoner's Dilemma with, like in Paradigm 3, an option to collaborate or defect.

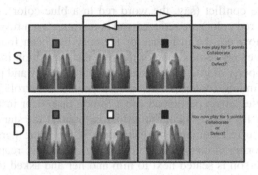

Fig. 4. Paradigm 4: Mediated imitation and Collaboration. The participant is required to press their left index every time the central square turns black, with the left, "virtual" hand showing corresponding movement. The other participant controls the right hand but is shown a different square which blinks either in synchrony (S) or in de-synchrony (D). After ca. 20 s, participants are given an option to collaborate or defect during a Prisoner's Dilemma.

Crucially, the paradigm allowed us to affect the two flashing lights independently, which we predict, based on [29], to cause collaboration. That is, in one condition, the two lights are synchronized to blink at the same time, effectively eliciting imitation. In the other condition, the lights blink at different intervals, causing no perception of imitation. Given the well-known effect in the motor control literature regarding the "bimanual advantage", generally measured as the facilitated stability of tapping in the presence of another [32], we furthermore predicted the reduced standard deviations in the inter-tap intervals as a function of inter-individually synchronized tapping.

The task thus incorporates many aspects of virtual imitation across perception and action, while the effect of "liking" was tested using economic game theory. However, the idea that we should have some sort of affinity with our virtual, mediated partners seems intuitively plausible, to the effect that few expressly test this hypothesis. In our final paradigm, we show how it is possible to empirically probe the very depth of our internalizing of the conflicts of others; even if they are only virtually present.

7   Paradigm 5: Mediated Cognitive Control

It has long been known that perceiving action-relevant information can lead to distractions, which in turn require us to use willful control or attention in order to successfully cope. To make this measurable, psychologists over the years used *conflict* paradigms, including the famous Stroop [33] task – in which we are required to name colors of words and disregard their identity –and the Simon task [34] – in which a directional stimulus is presented at a sometimes response-incompatible location. Such effects have taught us much about the psychological mechanisms by which we can achieve goals in the face of countless distractions. This, in turn, remains critical for HCI, since interface designs with low cognitive distraction should result in high performance.

However, it has become clear that conflict is not necessarily due to design, but is dynamic in nature. The Conflict Adaptation, or "Gratton", Effect [35] shows that, after reacting to one conflict (say, the word red in a blue color), subsequent effects (the word blue in a red color) are reduced and sometimes even reversed [36]. In order for this effect to show up, the influence of memory has been found crucial – if the new presentation does not remind one of the old, the adaptation is erased [37]. Thus, conflict is less a property of interface design than our memory and perception of it.

Another recent finding concerns the social aspects of control. That is, it was observed that if a single person participates in a Simon task – for instance, pressing *left* for circles and *right* for stars – a conflict effect is found if the star is presented to the left. However, this effect completely disappears if the same person would merely attend to stars (ignoring circles). Yet, intriguingly, the effect reappears in the same person if another person is seated next to him and her and asked to attend to the circles [38]. This was taken to suggest that the added person's "response-space" is incorporated within one's own, underlining the social nature of a task representation, although this interpretation remains controversial [39].

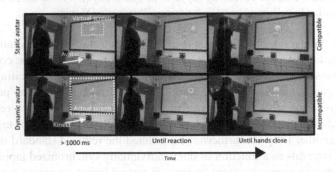

Fig. 5. Paradigm 5: Mediated conflict. The participant is asked to wave right to stars (upper panels) and left to circles (lower panels). In the lower but not the upper panels, the stimulus' location conflicts with the response. In the dynamic conditions, a Microsoft Kinect enabled us to display a self-reflecting VH.

We created a mediated design using Microsoft Kinect to better understand conflict adaptation and social conflict. As shown in Figure 5, participants were invited to engage with an experiment through the eyes of a VH. This makes it possible to see not only whether the similarity in source of conflict affects conflict adaptation, but also the target. That is, changes in conflict adaptation are predicted to depend on which avatar is shown. In effect, it allows us to directly test what happens to our attention if our own subjective self is changed.

The platform also allows many possibilities that are well outside the traditional range of the psychologist. Rather than the single reaction time that has been the core measure in the field, the Kinect records the entire gesture across continuous time, giving us insights on the time-course of conflict. We also recorded the task-irrelevant hand (e.g. left in the upper panels of figure 5), which provides an additional metric of conflict – that is, a person slightly moves their unattended hand due to the distracting stimulus [41]. We are continuing to develop this platform, in order to study, for example, implicit stereotypes in avatar use and the use of dyadic setups.

8   Conclusion

In this article, we argued that the modern, digitally networked age requires a new approach to social psychology: the interpersonal neuroscience of mediated communication. This field investigate how absent others can be psychologically present, enabled by communication technology. We focused on quantifiable, social effects in terms of economic (paradigm 2, 3, 4), cognitive (1, 4, 5) and/or physiologic (1, 2, 3) consequences. Unlike with direct communication, mediated interaction varies across a dimension from complex, multimodal interaction (e.g. video conferencing, compare paradigm 1) to short, unimodal messages (e.g. Twitter, compare paradigm 2).

The five very different paradigms show how the mediated presence of others can be tested and measured. This shows two important benefits for psychological science and HCI related to the freedom gained with the potentials of mediated technology. Firstly, it allows stricter manipulation of the inter-individual dimension and removes confounds that have often plagued the social sciences. Thus, in paradigm 2, rather than relying on confederates, we demonstrate the mediated touch of another, implied person and show this still affects decision making. Secondly, it allows new and exciting possibilities. This is shown in paradigm 5: changing the self in a traditional way is clearly not an easily attainable proposition. The mediated paradigms thus demonstrate both high control and high potential.

Finally, we have argued that society has rapidly steered in a direction of mediated, rather than direct, interaction. We have quickly plotted the historical course of communication media and noticed the increased speed at which new formats of mediated interaction are developed. While with the rise of the internet, the speed and diversity of mediated communication technology rocketed, psychology has steadfastly stuck to its course, concentrating on direct interaction. We believe that, in order for social psychology to remain up to date with contemporary humanity, it should heed our call for the mediated interpersonal neuroscience of mediated interaction, and we hope our specific examples underlining the possibilities of the field will promote this cause.

References

1. Allport, G.W.: The radio as a stimulus situation. Acta Psychol. 1, 1–6 (1936)
2. Pooley, J., Socolow, M.: The Myth of the War of the Worlds Panic (2013), http://www.slate.com/articles/arts/history/2013/10/orson_welles_war_of_the_worlds_panic_myth_the_infamous_radio_broadcast_did.html

3. Leiner, B.M., Cerf, V.G., Clark, D.D., Kahn, R.E., Kleinrock, L., Lynch, D.C., Postel, J., Roberts, L.G., Wolff, S.: A brief history of the Internet. ACM SIGCOMM Comput. Commun. Rev. 39, 22–31 (2009)
4. Piaget, J.: Play, dreams and imitation in childhood. Routledge, London (1951)
5. Meltzoff, A.N., Moore, M.K.: Imitation of facial and manual gestures by human neonates. Science 198, 75–78 (1977)
6. Bandura, A., Ross, D., Ross, S.A.: Imitation of film-mediated aggressive models. J. Abnorm. Soc. Psychol. 66, 3 (1963)
7. Brass, M., Bekkering, H., Wohlschläger, A., Prinz, W.: Compatibility between observed and executed finger movements: comparing symbolic, spatial, and imitative cues. Brain Cogn. 44, 124–143 (2000)
8. Rizzolatti, G., Craighero, L.: The mirror-neuron system. Annu. Rev. Neurosci. 27, 169–192 (2004)
9. Rizzolatti, G., Fadiga, L., Gallese, V., Fogassi, L.: Premotor cortex and the recognition of motor actions. Cogn. Brain Res. 3, 131–141 (1996)
10. Just, M.A., Carpenter, P.A., Keller, T.A., Eddy, W.F., Thulborn, K.R.: Brain Activation Modulated by Sentence Comprehension. Science 274, 114–116 (1996)
11. Hauk, O., Johnsrude, I., Pulvermüller, F.: Somatotopic representation of action words in human motor and premotor cortex. Neuron 41, 301–307 (2004)
12. Decety, J., Jackson, P.L.: A Social-Neuroscience Perspective on Empathy. Curr. Dir. Psychol. Sci. 15, 54–58 (2006)
13. Hennenlotter, A., Schroeder, U., Erhard, P., Castrop, F., Haslinger, B., Stoecker, D., Lange, K.W., Ceballos-Baumann, A.O.: A common neural basis for receptive and expressive communication of pleasant facial affect. NeuroImage 26, 581–591 (2005)
14. Hari, R., Kujala, M.V.: Brain basis of human social interaction: from concepts to brain imaging. Physiol. Rev. 89, 453–479 (2009)
15. Levenson, R.W., Gottman, J.M.: Marital interaction: Physiological linkage and affective exchange. J. Pers. Soc. Psychol. 45, 587–597 (1983)
16. Gottman, J., Levenson, R., Woodin, E.: Facial expressions during marital conflict. J. Fam. Commun. 1, 37–57 (2001)
17. Marci, C.D., Orr, S.P.: The effect of emotional distance on psychophysiologic concordance and perceived empathy between patient and interviewer. Appl. Psychophysiol. Biofeedback 31, 115–128 (2006)
18. Xygalatas, D., Konvalinka, I., Bulbulia, J., Roepstorff, A.: Quantifying collective effervescence: Heart-rate dynamics at a fire-walking ritual. Commun. Integr. Biol. 4, 735–738 (2011)
19. Chanel, G., Kivikangas, J.M., Ravaja, N.: Physiological compliance for social gaming analysis: Cooperative versus competitive play. Interact Comput. 24, 306–316 (2012)
20. Nummenmaa, L., Glerean, E., Viinikainen, M., Jääskeläinen, I.P., Hari, R., Sams, M.: Emotions promote social interaction by synchronizing brain activity across individuals. Proc. Natl. Acad. Sci. 109, 9599–9604 (2012)
21. Lindenberger, U., Li, S.-C., Gruber, W., Müller, V.: Brains swinging in concert: cortical phase synchronization while playing guitar. BMC Neurosci. 10, 22 (2009)
22. Spapé, M.M., Kivikangas, J.M., Järvelä, S., Kosunen, I., Jacucci, G., Ravaja, N.: Keep Your Opponents Close: Social Context Affects EEG and fEMG Linkage in a Turn-Based Computer Game. PloS One 8, e78795 (2013)
23. Güth, W., Schmittberger, R., Schwarze, B.: An experimental analysis of ultimatum bargaining. J. Econ. Behav. Organ. 3, 367–388 (1982)

24. Sanfey, A.G., Rilling, J.K., Aronson, J.A., Nystrom, L.E., Cohen, J.D.: The neural basis of economic decision-making in the ultimatum game. Science 300, 1755–1758 (2003)
25. Spapé, M., Hoggan, E.I., Jacucci, G., Ravaja, N.: The Meaning of the Virtual Midas Touch: An ERP study in economic decision making (in revision)
26. Crusco, A.H., Wetzel, C.G.: The Midas Touch the Effects of Interpersonal touch on Restaurant Tipping. Pers. Soc. Psychol. Bull. 10, 512–517 (1984)
27. Brewer, M.B.: In-group bias in the minimal intergroup situation: A cognitive-motivational analysis. Psychol. Bull. 86, 307–324 (1979)
28. Folkes, V.S.: Forming relationships and the matching hypothesis. Pers. Soc. Psychol. Bull. 8, 631–636 (1982)
29. Kühn, S., Müller, B.C., van Baaren, R.B., Wietzker, A., Dijksterhuis, A., Brass, M.: Why do I like you when you behave like me? Neural mechanisms mediating positive consequences of observing someone being imitated. Soc. Neurosci. 5, 384–392 (2010)
30. Launay, J., Dean, R.T., Bailes, F.: Synchronization can influence trust following virtual interaction. Exp. Psychol. 60, 53 (2013)
31. Hommel, B.: The cognitive representation of action: Automatic integration of perceived action effects. Psychol. Res. 59, 176–186 (1996)
32. Helmuth, L.L., Ivry, R.B.: When two hands are better than one: Reduced timing variability during bimanual movements. J. Exp. Psychol. Hum. Percept. Perform. 22, 278 (1996)
33. Stroop, J.R.: Studies of interference in serial verbal reactions. J. Exp. Psychol. 18, 643 (1935)
34. Simon, J.R., Rudell, A.P.: Auditory SR compatibility: the effect of an irrelevant cue on information processing. J. Appl. Psychol. 51, 300 (1967)
35. Gratton, G., Coles, M.G., Donchin, E.: Optimizing the use of information: strategic control of activation of responses. J. Exp. Psychol. Gen. 121, 480 (1992)
36. Hommel, B., Proctor, R.W., Vu, K.-P.L.: A feature-integration account of sequential effects in the Simon task. Psychol. Res. 68, 1–17 (2004)
37. Spapé, M.M., Hommel, B.: He said, she said: Episodic retrieval induces conflict adaptation in an auditory Stroop task. Psychon. Bull. Rev. 15, 1117–1121 (2008)
38. Knoblich, G., Sebanz, N.: The social nature of perception and action. Curr. Dir. Psychol. Sci. 15, 99–104 (2006)
39. Dolk, T., Hommel, B., Colzato, L.S., Schutz-Bosbach, S., Prinz, W., Liepelt, R.: How "Social" is the social Simon effect? Front. Psychol. 2 (2011)
40. Spapé, M.M., Ravaja, N.: Actors and agency in the mediated sequential Simon task. In: 54th Annual Meeting of the Psychonomic Society, Toronto, Canada (2013)

What Does Your Profile Picture Say About You?
The Accuracy of Thin-Slice Personality Judgments
from Social Networking Sites Made at Zero-Acquaintance

Mark Turner and Natalie Hunt

Department of Psychology, University of Portsmouth, Portsmouth, United Kingdom
Mark.Turner@port.ac.uk, Natalie.Hunt@myport.ac.uk

Abstract. The study investigates impressions formed through social networking sites, specifically the initial judgments we make of others when first momentarily exposed to their photograph. The personality characteristics of 52 Female Facebook profile owners were evaluated by a group of raters who briefly viewed the current profile picture of each person. Analysis revealed consensus between raters when judging personality attributes, although self-other agreement was low: raters' judgments correlated with profile owners' judgments of their own personality for only 2 out of the 10 attributes examined. Profile owners perceived as more physically attractive were rated more positively on other personality attributes. Smiling, and being alone or with others in a profile picture was also demonstrated to have a significant impact on personality assessments. It was concluded that whilst profile pictures can strongly influence how we judge others, such initial judgments are not highly likely to be accurate.

Keywords: First Impressions, Personality, Facebook, Thin-slice judgments.

1 Introduction

The popularity of Social Networking Sites (SNSs) has seen a change in the way people meet and interact with one another. In some cases, impressions of new acquaintances may now be formed initially online rather than face-to-face. However, current academic research has provided contradictory evidence concerning the accuracy of judgments based on SNS profiles and it is unclear how much influence personal images posted by users have on impressions formed.

It is known that first impressions can be formed rapidly from facial images and that this tendency is both spontaneous and continuous [1, 2]. Nevertheless, some authors [3] have suggested that online social networks contain a different set of implied norms that guide self-presentation. For example, Facebook users are known to use images to create desired impressions that promote the self as being highly social [4]. Since SNS users have the ability to selectively control personal details and images displayed online, this may lead to the creation of viewers' perceptions that are inconsistent with a target's true offline self. This is evidenced by research examining the concordance between impressions formed from online personal profiles with those offline which

G. Meiselwitz (Ed.): SCSM 2014, LNCS 8531, pp. 506–516, 2014.

suggests only a weak correlation to exist between the likeability of target individuals judged from their Facebook profiles compared to evaluations of the same individuals following face-to-face conversations [5].

When several observers are asked to judge the personality traits of people with whom they are not acquainted, it has been demonstrated that high levels of consensus between raters can be achieved whether based on visual cues [6] or auditory cues only [7], and when judgments are made from very brief periods of exposure ('thin slices') to the target individual [8].

It is also known that observers' impressions of a target individual's personality can be consistent with the target person's view of their own personality [9]. Levels of self-other agreement between targets and observers are known to improve when more overt, highly-visible traits such as extraversion are evaluated; or more desirable traits (e.g. intelligence, conscientiousness) as opposed to neutral or pejorative traits (e.g. unreliable, arrogant) are considered [10]. Whilst agreement between self-ratings and observer impressions are sometimes assumed to provide a proxy measure for the accuracy of first impression judgments, e.g., [11] other authors have argued that self-other agreement cannot be used as a criterion for accuracy since self-reports may provide an unreliable indicator of true personality [2].

When considering impressions formed from Facebook profiles, previous studies [11, 12] report good convergence for personality ratings made by close acquaintances from Facebook profile pages when browsing is restricted to key information, although the accuracy of judgments made at zero-acquaintance by strangers varies considerably between different personality traits. Stecher and Counts [13] found personality judgments for online profiles to be equally as accurate from condensed profiles showing limited information, as the impressions formed from seeing a user's full profile. This would suggest that SNS users neither seek nor normally require much information in order to make initial judgments of others.

Ivcevic and Ambady [14] compared raters' personality judgments of target individuals either based on full Facebook profile pages or based on other single sources of online information, such as profile pictures, interests or personal preferences. Consensus between raters when making personality judgments was found to be greatest when based on profile pictures alone compared to all other sources of user information available through Facebook, whilst personality ratings judged from full profile pages were most highly correlated with ratings of profile pictures. This suggests profile pictures to be a decisive factor when first forming impressions of others online.

However, Steele et al [15] demonstrated that the level of impression agreement between observer ratings of profile owners' personalities may also be dependent on the style of photograph used on a profile page, with agreement being greater for profile images that depicted the owner smiling or outdoors. Similarly, Naumann et al [16] showed that judgment accuracy can be manipulated by requiring participants to pose with neutral facial expressions compared to posing with spontaneous expressions. This suggests freedom to choose one's appearance may more readily convey cues to true personality on one hand, but that such cues are also subject to misinterpretation.

Haferkamp et al [17] observed that males and females use social networking sites for different reasons. They suggest that men are more inclined to look for friends or start new acquaintances, whereas females are more likely to use social networking sites to compare themselves to other people and to seek out information. Such differences in motivations for use may also consequently lead to differences in the forms of information which men and women rely on when making judgments through SNSs.

A further factor when forming impressions of others is physical appearance. Previous research has identified that more attractive people are generally assumed by observers to have better social skills and are typically rated as more likeable and thought to possess other positive personality traits than less attractive people [18, 19]. When a person is smiling they are also seen to be more beautiful and are rated more generously on other personality traits and general virtuousness [20], whilst both male and female Facebook users have been shown to be more willing to initiate friendships with opposite-sex profile owners with more attractive profile pictures [21].

The current study therefore investigates both consensus and agreement for first impressions formed from profile pictures by male and female observers when judging the personality characteristics of individuals with whom they are not acquainted. The influence of picture content and other owner characteristics such as perceived level of attractiveness on personality judgments are also explored.

2   Method

2.1   Participants

Female Facebook profile owners (N=52; mean age, 19.4 yrs; SD, 1.6) who consented to their current profile picture being viewed by others, completed a questionnaire regarding their general use and behavior on SNSs, questions regarding their choice of profile picture and a 10-item self-evaluation of personality.

A group of 10 observers (5 males and 5 females) of similar age and background to the female participants then viewed all 52 profile pictures and were asked to complete the same questionnaire evaluation of personality for each profile owner.

All profile owners were experienced users of Facebook with 71% of the sample reporting checking the site on average, 4 or more times per day, and 67% reporting having 400 or more friends on the site. The mean number of pictures participants reported currently having in their 'Profile Pictures' album was 64.4 (SE, 7.0).

Observers were also selected to be experienced Facebook users with 100% of raters reporting checking the site at least 4 or more times per day and having an average of 561 friends (range, 200 to 833). None of the 10 observers were previously acquainted with any of the 52 profile owners, prior to the study.

2.2   Measures

Participants were asked to write a brief open-text explanation for choosing their current profile picture and to rate on a 7-point scale (where a score of 1 represented 'extremely unlikely' and a score of 7 represented 'extremely likely') the extent to which they might select different types of images as their main profile pictures (e.g. "Full body picture of yourself alone"). Questions concerning the types of profile picture participants were likely to use were derived from the categorization of picture types identified by Steele et al [15].

The personality characteristics of each profile owner were assessed using an adapted version of Bond's dimensions used in perceiving peers [22]. This involved the rating of 10 bipolar objectives (e.g., Nervous – Calm) on a 7-point scale where a higher score was associated with the more positive attribute.

2.3   Procedure

Consistent with the minimum display durations used in other thin-slice judgment studies e.g., [1], [8], pictures were serially presented on separate slides for a set time of 10 seconds. Pictures were shown abstracted from any other Facebook information about the profile owner, with a blank slide being shown between pictures during which personality judgments were made. Where pictures contained more than one person, the position of the target individual was stated below the picture. The presentation duration of each picture was controlled by a computer with a researcher present to ensure the task was completed correctly. No discussion of the photographic content of pictures was permitted between the researcher and observers. Observers were allowed as much time as they required to complete the personality evaluation for each picture, before moving on to the next picture. This procedure resulted in a total of 5,200 thin-slice personality evaluations being made across 10 different personality attributes and 10 different observers.

3   Results

3.1   Choice of Profile Picture

Four common response types were identified in participants' explanations for choosing their current profile picture, with most common reason given by participants being: 44% (n=23) because of who was in the photograph (e.g. friends or family); 29% (n=15) because it reminded them of a good memory; 21% (n=11) because they felt they looked good in the picture; and, 15% (n=8) because they had wished to update their picture.

In order to statistically compare whether participants were more likely to consider using some types of profile pictures more than others, a one-way repeated measures ANOVA was performed on the likelihood ratings for choosing different photograph types (F(10, 510)= 55.83, p<.001, η^2_p = .52). These data showed the likelihood of choosing some profile pictures to be higher than others: participants were most likely to use a picture of themselves with others as their profile picture, a picture of themselves smiling, or a picture of themselves making eye contact with the camera; and least likely to use pictures that did not include themselves such as drawings, pictures of landscapes, animals, other objects (Table 1).

Table 1. Mean likelihood rating of selecting 11 different image types as a profile picture. Possible score range, 1-7; higher scores indicate greater likelihood of selection.

Profile Picture Content	Mean	SD
Picture of yourself with others	6.38	0.93
Picture of yourself smiling	5.56	1.58
Picture of yourself making eye contact with the camera	5.46	1.26
Picture of yourself doing an activity	5.06	1.73
Portrait (face only) picture of yourself alone	4.38	2.16
Picture of yourself with face covered (e.g. wearing sunglasses)	3.81	1.92
Full body picture of yourself alone	3.69	2.06
Picture of a pet or other animal	3.08	1.94
Picture of a landscape	2.17	1.77
Picture of another object	1.96	1.47
Drawing or pattern	1.63	1.33

3.2   Observer Agreement and Self-observer Agreement when Judging 10 Personality Characteristics from Current Profile Pictures

Observer agreement (consensus) was calculated for each type of personality judgment using intraclass correlations (ICC) with a two-way random effects model. Both single measures, ICC(2,1) and average measures, ICC(2,k) of observer consensus were calculated (Table 2). These data suggest a good level of consensus between raters in their evaluation of profile pictures based on 10-second exposures (Cronbach's Alpha values > 0.70). Observer agreement was greatest for attractiveness and other overt attributes typically associated with extraversion (e.g., friendly, outgoing, confident). Observer agreement was lowest when judging calmness and reliability.

Self-other agreement was examined by correlating each profile owners' self-evaluation with aggregated observer ratings for each of the 10 personality attributes. Correlations were calculated using personality judgments averaged across all 10 raters, and separately for the 5 male and 5 female raters.

Significant relationships were found for only 2 of the 10 personality attributes: self and observer ratings were positively correlated for sensitivity (r= .58) and loudness (r= .32) suggesting observers' ratings were more likely to co-vary with profile owners' own judgments of these attributes. Self-other agreement estimates were largely consistent across genders with the exception of the intelligence attribute; male raters' evaluations of intelligence correlated positively with female profile owners' ratings of their own intelligence (r= .28) but a corresponding relationship was not found in the case of female raters.

For the remaining personality attributes no significant relationships were found such that raters' judgments did not agree with the profile owners' own evaluations of their personality; this suggests impression ratings for these attributes can be assumed to be inaccurate.

Table 2. Intraclass correlations for single (ICC 2,1) and averaged (ICC 2,k) measures of observer agreement (consensus) and Pearson (r) correlation coefficients between self-ratings and averaged observer ratings for 10 personality attributes (* p< .05 ** p< .01; *** p< .001)

Attribute	Consensus		Self-Other Agreement (r)		
	ICC(2,1)	ICC(2,k)	All Raters	Female Raters	Male Raters
Nervous-Calm	.23***	.75***	.20	.12	.26
Insecure-Confident	.42***	.88***	-.11	-.08	-.12
Shy-Outgoing	.43***	.88***	.16	.20	.11
Unattractive-Attractive	.54***	.92***	-.01	-.01	-.00
Unfriendly-Friendly	.42***	.88***	.24	.22	.23
Insensitive-Sensitive	.28***	.80***	.58**	.56**	.50**
Careless-Perfectionist	.33***	.83***	-.03	-.03	-.02
Quiet-Loud	.37***	.85***	.32*	.31*	.29*
Unreliable-Reliable	.20***	.72***	.15	.13	.14
Unintelligent-Intelligent	.28***	.80***	.24	.17	.28*

3.3   Observers' Judgments of Attractiveness with Other Personality Attributes

To examine the relationships between the 10 raters' judgments of the attractiveness of each female profile owner and their judgment of other traits of each female, Pearson correlation coefficients were calculated separately for both male and female raters (Table 3).

For female raters, judgments of attractiveness were positively correlated with calmness (r = .49), confidence (r = .53), outgoingness (r = .36), friendliness (r = .56) and perfectionism (r = .51). Furthermore, significant correlations were found for attractiveness with reliability (r = .38) and intelligence (r = .45) whereby profile owners who were rated as more attractive were thought to be more reliable and intelligent.

For male raters, a similar pattern of significant relationships was found. Perceived attractiveness was positively correlated with calmness (r = .59), confidence (r = .65), outgoingness (r = .57), friendliness (r = .43) and perfectionism (r = .60).

Taken together, these findings suggest that both male and female raters who thought the target person was more attractive assumed them to have more positive attributes. However, only female raters showed judgments which associated attractiveness with reliability and intelligence.

Table 3. Correlations between perceived attractiveness and other positive traits in male and female raters. ** p< .01;   * p< .05 (2-tailed).

Attribute	Male	Female
Calm	.59**	.49**
Confident	.65**	.53**
Outgoing	.57**	.36**
Friendly	.43*	.56**
Sensitive	.21	.27
Perfectionist	.61**	.51**
Loud	-.15	-.08
Reliable	.07	.38**
Intelligent	.25	.45**

3.4   Effect of Smiling and Non-smiling Pictures on Observers' Judgments

Differences in observers' ratings of participants who smiled and did not smile in their profile picture were analyzed for each of the 10 personality attributes using one-way independent groups MANOVA. The multivariate effect of picture type was found to be significant, $F(10, 41) = 2.86$, $p = .009$, Wilks' $\lambda = .589$.

Significant univariate effects were found for the ratings of friendliness, sensitivity and reliability, whereby profile owners were judged to be friendlier, more sensitive and more reliable if they were smiling in their profile picture compared to non-smiling pictures. No significant differences were found for the remaining 7 personality characteristics (Table 4).

Table 4. Univariate F test comparions for effect of smiling (n=35) and not smiling (n=17) in a profile picture on personality attribute judgments made by observers. Possible score range, 1-7; higher scores tend towards right attribute pole.

Attribute	Smiling		Not Smiling		F value	Sig.
	M	SD	M	SD		
Nervous-Calm	4.48	0.71	4.15	0.67	2.40	.13 ns
Insecure-Confident	4.70	0.89	4.59	1.10	0.16	.69 ns
Shy-Outgoing	4.52	1.06	4.31	1.04	0.43	.51 ns
Unattractive-Attractive	4.03	0.99	3.85	1.40	0.30	.59 ns
Unfriendly-Friendly	5.14	0.59	4.14	0.91	22.17	< .001
Insensitive-Sensitive	4.77	0.70	4.21	0.59	7.82	.007
Careless-Perfectionist	4.45	0.81	4.47	0.89	0.01	.93 ns
Quiet-Loud	3.97	0.98	3.94	0.86	0.01	.91 ns
Unreliable-Reliable	4.86	0.59	4.29	0.49	11.31	.001
Unintelligent-Intelligent	4.73	0.75	4.34	0.74	3.01	.09 ns

3.5   Effect of Individual or Group Pictures on Observers' Judgments

A further independent groups MANOVA was conducted to analyze differences in judgments of the 10 personality attributes when profile owners either posed individually ('alone' condition) or as a part of a group ('with others' condition) in their profile picture. The multivariate effect of picture type was found to be significant, $F(10, 41) = 3.55$, $p = .002$, Wilks' $\lambda = .536$.

Significant univariate effects were found for observers' ratings of calmness, outgoingness, friendliness and loudness, whereby participants were judged to be significantly calmer, more outgoing, friendlier and less quiet when other people were present in their profile picture. No differences were found for the remaining 6 personality attributes.

Table 5. Univariate F tests of being alone (n=19) or with others (n=33) in a profile picture on personality attribute judgments made by observers. Possible score range, 1-7; higher scores tend towards right attribute pole.

Attribute	Alone		With Others		F value	Sig.
	M	SD	M	SD		
Nervous-Calm	4.05	0.82	4.56	0.57	6.87	.01
Insecure-Confident	4.35	1.20	4.86	0.74	3.59	.06 ns
Shy-Outgoing	3.90	1.04	4.77	0.92	9.84	.003
Unattractive-Attractive	3.71	1.31	4.13	1.01	1.65	.20 ns
Unfriendly-Friendly	4.32	0.97	5.10	0.63	12.10	.001
Insensitive-Sensitive	4.43	0.73	4.67	0.69	1.39	.24 ns
Careless-Perfectionist	4.61	0.73	4.37	0.69	0.96	.33 ns
Quiet-Loud	3.59	0.94	4.17	0.87	4.97	.03
Unreliable-Reliable	4.50	0.52	4.77	0.66	2.24	.14 ns
Unintelligent-Intelligent	4.57	0.63	4.62	0.84	0.07	.79 ns

4   Discussion

A key finding of the current study was that individuals who were seen as more attractive were rated more generously on other personality attributes. This finding is consistent with previous research on attractiveness [18, 19] suggesting that attractive individuals are seen to possess more desirable personality traits in the context of Facebook profile photographs, and that physical appearance is also an important criterion when forming impressions of a new person through social networking sites.

Good agreement was found between observers when evaluating the traits of profile owners in the present study, suggesting strangers can readily form a consensus opinion when encountering new individuals, even at very brief exposure durations.

It is important to note however, that although the evaluation of two attributes; sensitivity and loudness showed some similarity between observer and self-ratings, overall personality traits were not judged with great accuracy. Additionally, neither male nor female observers were found to be more accurate when judging aspects of unknown females' character. This implies that, from brief exposure to a profile picture alone, it may not be possible to gain sufficient information about a person to make accurate assumptions of their personality and intelligence. This finding is inconsistent with some previous research of first impersonation formation on Facebook [11, 12] which used more involved browsing tasks, suggesting that when viewing an online profile, people may need more time to consider other aspects of a person's profile, or require additional information to make a better judgment of them.

In relation to the influence of attractiveness on personality judgements, the only two traits found not to be influenced by attractiveness were loudness and sensitivity, which were also the only two traits that were found to be assessed with a significant degree of self-observer agreement. A potential explanation for these findings could be that the influence of attractiveness on personality judgements would lead to inaccuracy in personality judgements. It could be suggested that too much weight is placed on attractiveness during impression formation leading individuals to make less accurate judgments, although this does not preclude other explanations of these data.

Pictures of profile owners who were smiling were seen to be more reliable, sensitive and friendly than if they were not smiling. Similarly, where pictures contained more than one person, profile owners were rated as less quiet, more friendly, calm and outgoing. This would suggest that smiling and the presence of others in a profile picture, in addition to the profile owner's level of attractiveness, positively influences a viewer's perception of the individual.

Given that Facebook users are not naïve to the public nature of the site, an implication of the current findings is that individuals are likely to choose a profile picture based on the knowledge that their selection will have an influence on the way others judge them. For example, it was found in the current study that some profile owners feel it is important to choose an attractive profile picture, in order to give a more positive impression of themselves. This in turn may lead to a further potential source of inaccuracy when evaluating personality attributes since individuals seek to present their best rather than true self [3, 4].

Previous research exploring exposure time and the accuracy of first impressions formed face-to-face suggests an optimum level of accuracy can be achieved between 20 to 60 seconds when judging personality [1], [8]. In the current study, sub-optimum exposure times to each picture of 10 seconds were used. Whilst this was partly done for practical reasons to limit observer fatigue, this also served to address the theoretical issue of whether impression accuracy *can be* achieved more rapidly through the structure and implicit conventions that determine the format and suitability of profile pictures within the Facebook community. Self-evidently, increasing exposure time to each picture could, in turn, have led to different accuracy predictions. It remains to be established what a true representation of the time to form accurate opinions from Facebook profile pictures might be.

It can be concluded from the current study that the content of profile pictures can impact on the judgments others make of profile owners featured within the photographs. Specifically, personal attractiveness, smiling, and being in the presence of others leads to more positive evaluations of a profile owner from their main profile picture, which may not necessarily lead to accurate representations of the individual's true character. This effect held regardless of whether same sex or different sex evaluations were used in the assessment of the profile owner.

References

1. Ambaby, N., Rosenthal, R.: Half a minute: Predicting teacher evaluations form thin slices of nonverbal behaviour and physical attractiveness. Journal of Personality and Social Psychology 64(3), 431–441 (1993)
2. Rule, N., Ambady, N.: First impressions of the face: predicting success. Social and Personality Psychology Compass 4(8), 506–516 (2010)
3. Hum, N.J., Chamberlin, P.E., Hambright, B.L., Portwood, A.C., Schat, A.C., Bevan, J.L.: A picture is worth a thousand words: A content analysis of Facebook profile photographs. Computers in Human Behavior 27(5), 1828–1833 (2011)
4. Zhao, S., Grasmuck, S., Martin, J.: Identity construction on Facebook: Digital empowerment in anchored relationships. Computers in Human Behavior 24(5), 1816–1836 (2008)
5. Weisbuch, M., Ivcevic, Z., Ambady, N.: On being liked on the web and in the "real world": Consistency in first impressions across personal webpages and spontaneous behavior. Journal of Experimental Social Psychology 45(3), 573–576 (2009)
6. Kenny, D.A., Horner, C., Kashy, D.A., Chu, L.C.: Consensus at zero acquaintance: replication, behavioral cues, and stability. Journal of Personality & Social Psychology 62(1), 88–97 (1992)
7. Holleran, S.E., Mehl, M.R., Levitt, S.: Eavesdropping on social life: The accuracy of stranger ratings of daily behavior from thin slices of natural conversations. Journal of Research in Personality 43, 660–672 (2009)
8. Carney, D.R., Colvin, C.R., Hall, J.A.: A thin slice perspective on the accuracy of first impressions. Journal of Research in Personality 41(5), 1054–1072 (2007)
9. Penton-Voak, I.S., Pound, N., Little, A.C., Perrett, D.I.: Personality judgments from natural and composite facial images: More evidence for a "kernel of truth" in social perception. Social Cognition 24(5), 607–640 (2006)
10. Kenny, D.A., West, T.V.: Similarity and agreement in self-and other perception: a meta-analysis. Personality and Social Psychology Review 14(2), 196–213 (2010)
11. Back, M.D., Stopfer, J.M., Vazire, S., Gaddis, S., Schmukle, S.C., Egloff, B., Gosling, S.D.: Facebook profiles reflect actual personality, not self-idealization. Psychological Science 21(3), 372–374 (2010)
12. Gosling, S.D., Gaddis, S., Vazire, S.: Personality impressions based on Facebook profiles. In: Proceedings of the International Conference on Weblogs and Social Media, Boulder, Colorado, U.S.A., March 26-28 (2007)
13. Stecher, K., Counts, S.: Thin slices of online profile attributes. In: Proceedings of the Second International ICWSM Conference, Seattle, Washington, U.S.A., March 30-April 2 (2008)
14. Ivcevic, Z., Ambady, N.: Personality impressions from identity claims on Facebook. Psychology of Popular Media Culture 1(1), 38–45 (2012)

15. Steele, F., Evans, D.C., Green, R.K.: Is your profile picture worth 1000 words? Photo characteristics associated with personality impression agreement. In: Proceedings of the Third International ICWSM Conference, San Jose, California, U.S.A., May 17-20 (2009)
16. Naumann, L.P., Vazire, S., Rentfrow, P.J., Gosling, S.D.: Personality judgments based on physical appearance. Personality and Social Psychology Bulletin 35(12), 1661–1671 (2009)
17. Haferkamp, N., Eimler, S.C., Papadakis, A., Kruck, J.V.: Men are from Mars, women are from Venus? Examining gender differences in self-presentation on social networking sites. Cyberpsychology, Behavior and Social Networking 15(2), 91–98 (2012)
18. Dion, K., Berscheid, E., Walster, E.: What is beautiful is good. Journal of Personality and Social Psychology 24(3), 285–290 (1972)
19. Goldman, W., Lewis, P.: Beautiful is good: Evidence that the physically attractive are more socially skilful. Journal of Experimental Social Psychology 13(2), 125–130 (1977)
20. Reis, H.T., Wilson, I.M., Monestere, C., Bernstein, S., Clark, K., Seidl, E., Franco, M., Gioioso, E., Freeman, L., Radoane, K.: What is smiling is beautiful and good. European Journal of Social Psychology 20(3), 259–267 (1990)
21. Wang, S.S., Moon, S.I., Kwon, K.H., Evans, C.A., Stefanone, M.A.: Face off: Implications of visual cues on initiating friendship on Facebook. Computers in Human Behavior 26(2), 226–234 (2010)
22. Bond, M.H.: Dimensions used in perceiving peers: Cross-cultural comparisons of Hong Kong, Japanese, American and Filipino university students. International Journal of Psychology 14(1), 47–56 (1978)

Inventing Partners in Computer-Mediated Communication: How CMC Sustains Self-fulfilling Prophecies and Relational Attributions

Joseph B. Walther[1] and Stephanie Tom Tong[2]

[1] Dept. of Communication/Dept. of Telecommunication, Information Studies & Media,
Michigan State University, USA
jwalther@msu.edu
[2] Dept. of Communication, Wayne State University, USA
stephanie.tong@wayne.edu

Abstract. Research on computer-mediated communication (CMC) vacillates between arguments that the medium of text is too barren to experience partners' personalities, to claims that we "fill in the blanks" when encountering others online. This metaphor of filling in the blanks can be substantiated scientifically by examining data from several studies that demonstrate when and how CMC users form idealized false impressions, and what false attributions they bestow when they anticipate or interact with online partners. These instances take place when users are provided insufficient descriptions of chat partners, or with avatars that are knowingly random with respect to their operators. Going beyond mere impressions, CMC users create their own versions of their partners' attractiveness and sociability. They do so outside their own awareness, creating demonstrable self-fulfilling prophecies in ways that traditional research eschews in the CMC context. Research examining behavioral disconfirmation online, the behaviors that actuate it, and the erroneous relational attributions CMC users apply to partners, depict how these self-fulfilling prophecies are realized.

1 Introduction

The dominant view of computer-mediated communication (CMC) and its social impacts have shifted dramatically, from models depicting how CMC is devoid of social cues and social influence, to models explaining how online communication can foster hyperbolic levels of mutual influence leading to exaggerated perceptions of others. The most applicable theoretical approach to how the restrictions and affordances of online social interaction has suggested an interconnected set of influences involving how one individual perceives one's partner, selectively communicated with a partner, and through such exchanges, reciprocally influences and transforms partners' interaction style [1].

In exploring how CMC users form impressions, and how they perceive and affect their conversation partners' emotional behavior, recent research has focused on the influence of both expectancies and attributions as important cognitive factors that

G. Meiselwitz (Ed.): SCSM 2014, LNCS 8531, pp. 517–527, 2014.
© Springer International Publishing Switzerland 2014

impact interpersonal perceptions and behaviors, and whether these factors catalyze self-fulfilling prophecies in terms of altering partners' demeanor and reciprocal behavior. The results of several studies, in aggregate, appear to suggest that an individual's own expectations and attributions have an extraordinarily great impact on that individual's experience of his or her partner. Although there is some evidence for reciprocal behavioral influence in CMC, it appears as though intra-individual processes and one's own behaviors toward a partner disproportionately affect one's interpretations of partners' behavior. That is, one's own cognition and behavior, and one's own self-perceptions about that behavior, may more greatly influence an individual's social judgments about the partner than the partner's behavior warrants.

These conclusions tell us in greater detail than we have previously understood just how individuals fill in the gaps for missing information about their partners in online interaction. Looking across these studies leads to the metaphoric conclusion that CMC facilitates the cognitive creation of one's online partner. That is to say, interpersonal interaction transpires online in ways by which pre-interaction expectancies exert a particularly profound influence on individuals' initial interpersonal perceptions, and although these expectancies appear to influence partners' social behaviors to some extent, the perceivers' own perceptions and behaviors may be those that most strongly affect their perceptions of partners over and above the role that their partners' actual behavior conveys. Because most of the cognitive and behavioral work leading to transformed interpersonal judgments appears to take place at intrapersonal level rather than interpersonally, we may suggest that individuals invent their partners: Although they indeed cause their partners to behave in certain ways, they do not perceive that they themselves are the cause of their partners' responses. Instead, in CMC to a greater extent than in other media, individuals believe that their partners' reactions are spontaneous and that their partners manifest their own physical, social, and affective inclinations toward the individual instigator, despite the strong role that the instigator's own perceptions and behaviors play in this inferential process.

The following essay reviews a number of original studies that support and illuminate the treatise that individuals unwittingly create their online partners out of the naïve participants with whom they interact.

2   Background: Idealization and Feedback in Hyperpersonal CMC

To appreciate fully the extraordinary shift that research has revealed in terms of our understanding of how individuals affect and perceive online partners, we review perspectives on CMC about perception and mutual influence online. The hyperpersonal model of CMC [1] suggested that CMC users may develop exaggerated positive or negative relations with online partners, relative to offline interaction settings, through four concurrent cognitive and communicative processes. First, as receivers of text-based CMC messages, CMC users form exaggerated impressions of others based on overattributions of whatever meager information about partners may be conveyed in mediated messages. Contextual cues suggesting a partner's social category